OUTRAGEOUS

FORTUNE

Outrageous Fortune

by

Terence Frisby

First Thing Publications

First published in 1998 by
First Thing Publications, 72 Bishops Mansions, Bishops Park Road,
London SW6 6DZ

Distributed by Gazelle Book Services Limited
Falcon House Queen Square
Lancaster England LA1 1RN

A CIP catalogue record for this book is available from the British Library

ISBN 0-9532208-0-X

Typeset by Amolibros, Watchet, Somerset

Printed and bound by Professional Book Supplies, Oxford, England

ACKNOWLEDGEMENTS

Ted Whitehead's article 'Let's Do It' on page 364 is reproduced by kind permission of *The Spectator.*

Avenging Angel in Suburbia by John Russell Taylor reprinted on page 23 was first published in *The Times* on twenty-seventh March 1962, and is © Times Newspapers Ltd, 1962.

The photographs of Sir Donald Sinden, Barbara Ferris and Jon Pertwee in *There's A Girl In My Soup* are reproduced by kind permission of Lewis Morley; the two photographs of the First Night Party at Sardi's by kind permission of Harvey Unna; photograph of Christine & Terence Frisby along with son Dominic courtesy of Hulton Getty; photograph of Peter Sellers and Goldie Hawn in the film of *There's A Girl In My Soup* by kind permission of Columbia Pictures (© 1970 Ascot Productions Inc, all rights reserved); Christine outside law courts, May 1970, courtesy of Hulton Getty; Christine outside law courts, July 1971, courtesy of Solo Syndication Ltd; Christine and Rutter courtesy of Hulton Getty; *It's All Right If I Do It* by kind permission of Alec Riddett, ARPS; the five judges pictured facing page 281 courtesy of Universal Pictorial Press & Agency Ltd.

Note: All other photographs are either copyright of the author or cannot be traced for copyright purposes; any information leading to the establishment of the copyright therein would be gratefully received by the publisher.

INTRODUCTION

I first started writing this story twenty-odd years ago, as it was happening, for my son Dominic, now an adult. My purpose was to show him where he came from, what shaped his early life and the life of his parents at that time. But the story continued to unfold and grow (it had already changed my life), with serious resonances that concern us all.

So what started as a paternal letter - being part rags-to-riches-love-story and part cautionary-tale - became part detective-story, part lid-off-our-divorce- and legal-system, part exorcism, part David-versus-Goliath and, finally, J'Accuse. For that is now my additional purpose in publishing this, though years late: to point the finger at an adversarial and vindictive legal system which disastrously let down my family and thousands like us.

Why is it so long? The legal profession doesn't even enter till about halfway through. Well, the first part is the dream (if that is not too sentimental a word) that gave birth to the second part. I am asking you to read about the dream first so that you fully appreciate the nightmare of the second half.

The book covers twenty-two years: the six-and-a-half years of our marriage; the month or two of the painful and unnecessary conclusion of it; and the fifteen years of the crazy litigation it caused. I would never have disclosed certain details if they had not already been disclosed in countless legal hearings and documents already in the public domain, and if I were not serving an important public interest by doing so.

I believe there are great issues at stake here. The events in this book make a powerful argument against the legal profession being allowed anywhere near the break-up of marriage, especially marriages with children. But the charges that I make do not merely apply to the divorce section of our legal system, they cover all of it. The trouble is, this is written by a man who can be accused of complaining about losing his money and his wife when, possibly, he deserved to lose both. And anyway, who cares if some rich git gets turned over by a few judges and lawyers? I wasn't wrongly incarcerated for bitter years like others. I was always free, never cold or hungry. But unnecessary pain can be inflicted in many ways. This is the well-heeled version of the malfunction of British Justice.

Such was my situation after the first year of the nightmare that I dispensed with my own lawyers altogether and represented myself. I became a litigant-in-person to sort out the mess the law had thrust me into. I won the majority of my numerous hearings, which were before masters, registrars, High Court judges, the Court of Appeal and eventually, the House of Lords. But I lost a few, too, and it took, off and on, another thirteen years, involving many members of the legal profession all of whom are all listed at the back of this book.

Being a litigant-in-person for years gave me an unparalleled viewpoint from which to observe our legal system and those who run it. I arrived at some cheerless conclusions.

CHAPTER I

Spring 1963

I was playing chess with Ivor when the telephone rang.

'Do you want to do a day's extra-ing with me tomorrow?' he said, covering the mouthpiece.

'No.'

'Come on. It's a TV commercial. Mrs. Whatsit says they want another actor to stand around as a party guest.'

'I'm busy writing a play.'

'You're always writing a play. It'll wait. We get four quid, we can play chess all day, and...' he seemed to know something, 'there's bound to be some crumpet in a party scene.'

I was disbelieving. 'Yeah? Who?'

His voice became confidential. 'There's this nice dark-haired girl coming tomorrow; wears glasses, but smashing. I'll introduce you.'

Ivor need not have taken so much trouble; I didn't need much persuading to leave my pen down for the day in favour of the welcome four pounds.

'OK, Mrs Phlawhum.' He remembered few names, even then. 'We'll both be there. Eight o'clock, Barnes studio. Yeah fine. Alka-Seltzer. Wonderful.'

'You only want me for one thing,' I said, falsetto.

'What's that?'

'A lift in my car.'

'It's not yours.'

'Well.'

I was renting a room from Ivor and Henrietta. They had a maisonette in Finchley, part of a Victorian semi. It was cold, haphazard and echoing. Vague attempts had been made by Henri between repertory jobs and tours to make a home of it, but it seems to me now that it was cold even in summer. The kitchen was painted blue, which didn't help. Ivor had sloshed some sealer over the damp patch on the plaster where the fireplace had been. It was damp purely for lack of a ventilator brick, but nobody could contemplate the effort and disturbance needed to put one in, so Ivor continued to slop on sealer after rainy days. At the other end of the flat was the bathroom. I can see the bright fishes on the semi-attached plastic curtain now. You had to throw one corner of it over a piece of wire as you lay there soaking - if one can think of such a luxurious occupation in connection with that flat - or your eyes met the startled stares of the passengers on the top deck of the buses that stopped directly outside. To the left of the bathroom was the living-room, not a bad place when the divan bed wasn't occupied by some transient actor. Beside the living-room was Ivor's and Henri's bedroom. It seemed permanently to consist of an unmade bed, two overflowing theatrical skips and some cats.

The lavatory was quite different, the sole room that completely succeeded. A stream of passing actors had stuck rejection letters all over it. The walls, the pipes, the cistern, the ceiling were a mass of reasons why we were none of us required by anybody. One morning Ivor came out of the loo after his mid-morning evacuation and hurled the *News Chronicle* across the kitchen. 'I can't stand it any more. Just as you've got relaxed and comfortable you see that *Emergency Ward 10* is fully cast for the next year. It's giving me constipation.'

So we looked out our rave reviews from Guernsey, Penzance, York, Scunthorpe, High Wycombe, Salford, Tunbridge Wells, Newcastle; the names read like a cavalcade of tat provincial theatre. Between us we had knocked them cold in every theatrical dump in the UK. We found old provincial bills with our names writ large. We found terrible, wooden photos of rep productions of Agatha Christie. We invented captions for them - the actual dialogue was generally funny enough. We found mementoes of our moments of glory for pride of place and stuck the lot up: Henri half-way down the bill of a West End production, Ivor starring in the tour of *Fings Ain't Wot They Used T'be* and my first play on at Guildford with a rave notice in no less than *The Times*.

The loo became heaven. No matter how cold the seat, one finished with a warm heart and a sense that one did exist after all. Visitors to the flat would disappear for half-an-hour at a time and come out with cricks in their necks. 'Did you play Scarborough?' 'You worked with so-and-so? She was with me at...' People not in the business (infrequent visitors) stared, bemused and impressed. That loo should have been taken to the V and A theatrical history section. It gave us all endless pleasure and reassurance; we were recorded somewhere therefore we *were*, or at least had been.

Up some steep curving stairs were a pair of freezing attic rooms where Dennis, another actor/would-be writer, and I lived and worked and whenever possible - which wasn't that often - fornicated. So that was our home and our way of life as, unsuspecting, London started to swing into the middle of the sixties.

The winter of 1962-63 had been furious. The cold had seeped in everywhere while Ivor had toured, giving his Tosher in 'Fings', and Henri was in Panto at Bexhill. Lindsey, their five-year-old daughter, my god-daughter, was left in my care, as she often had been since she was six months old. And there was Dennis who used to share my room as we worked. We did it to save on paraffin fuel and for company. Neither of us could bear to be alone with our bits of paper and scribble. Finally my incessant giggles, sighs, fidgets, growls, mutters and occasional loud exclamations over my work drove Dennis out, and he went away and wrote a very successful rep comedy. That winter, together we saw that Lin got to school, got fed, had stories read to her, was played with and kept as warm as any of us were in the whistling draughts of 220 Ballards Lane.

The ripples of interest created by the notices for my first stage play had led to my first commission for a teleplay from the BBC, so I spent womb-like days in the Put-U-Up while I wrote it. An actress friend called Sarah who had rich parents had turned up with a Mini which she couldn't drive and so left behind. So, now it was spring, the world was burgeoning, I was hoping to get the post at Bromley rep of resident director, and I seemed to have a car.

Ivor and I piled into the Mini and went to the studio at Barnes. It was a boring affair, the commercial. Some pea-brained male model, picked for the look of faint suffering on his face, needed endless takes to down a glass of Alka-Seltzer that was given to him by an increasingly irritated blonde. I found Danny Blanchflower's *The Double and Before* on the set bookshelf and Ivor chatted up the dark-haired girl in glasses: Christine.

She was pretty enough, as I remember. Without being an actress she had excellent diction, although her voice was a shade too light in tone. She must have attracted me, because I took her telephone number and muttered something about a part in my first production at Bromley rep. I needed two pretty girls for WRACS in *Reluctant Heroes*. They had about two lines apiece and their prettiness was more important than their ability. I remember thinking, 'OK, let's take one attractive, passably intelligent-looking girl who knows what to do in front of a camera and stick her on stage and see if she can do it.' I have tried to remember how else she impressed me that day. Staring raptly at me through her glasses she had that rather owlish look of concentration that women use when they are not listening to what you are saying but have decided to look as though they are. When we had lunch in the cafe opposite the studio she somehow made the other two pretty girls in the crowd of extras look grubby. That was all.

Anyway, a week or two later, after half-heartedly trying a few proper actresses for the part ('Two lines? No, thank you, darling'), I rang her. The offer was four-pounds-ten a week for two rehearsal weeks, ten pounds a

3

week for the two playing weeks and how would she like to come out on Sunday evening.

We went to a pub by the river in Richmond for a drink. She wore an immaculate, lemon duster-coat in linen over something pretty good. She had light streaks in her hair and the sun danced about in her thoroughly Knightsbridge flick-ups. A column of gnats wavered above her head and the dry air was dusty round her kemptness. She looked genuinely interested as I explained how it was all a ghastly mistake that I wasn't starring in the West End in one of my own stunning plays directed by me, but that a benevolent (though non-existent) God and a lot of work from me would remedy all that. It was a glorious, golden evening. The Edwardians aren't the only ones who imagine their pre-First-World-War youth was all strawberries and sun; the river at Richmond was just as magical then, in May sixty-three, when I was thirty and she was twenty-one and the two halves of bitter were less than a shilling each. And she laughed her thoroughly lady-like laugh at the unquenchable torrent that flowed from my lips then (then?), and managed to get in her own, upper-middle, well-articulated, if light-toned, answers to my actorish, tidied-up, former-South-London bawl. She enchanted me.

We went back to Robert's place. When Ivor's place drove me round the bend, or I drove it, I used to go and stay at Robert's. Robert was Resident Director at Richmond theatre and had money. He owned a flat in Ebury Street with spare rooms, decently furnished. He was singularly good-natured and suffered the more limpet-like friends who arrived on his doorstep. I used to stay for odd days or weeks and then quickly go, full of guilt that I had taken advantage of him. I adored him; for Robert I had played Jimmy Porter in *Look Back in Anger* in Penzance, *The Seven Year Itch* in Aldershot, *Love in a Mist* at Richmond and about twenty other parts ranging from Aldwych farce to whatever is the opposite.

Anyway, it was Sunday and all the smarter inmates of 99 Ebury Street were in the country (where else?), so Christine and I switched from cheap bitter in the sunset in Richmond to free coffee in the lamplight in Ebury Street. And when I started to kiss her round her mouth and ears and flick-ups she took off her glasses, untied my tie and we clambered into bed.

We lay there afterwards listening to our bodies slowing down, I on my back with one arm round her, she on her side looking at me. I became more aware of her. The way her neck was set into her shoulder and the curves of flesh over the hollow of her collarbone were exquisite - and cool when I touched her there. Her breasts were perfect. Yes, just perfect. Easy to say, but they were. Full without being ostentatious, nothing was ostentatious about Christine. Her skin seemed translucent. I noticed her eyes properly for the first time. They were enormous and at that moment the expression was unreadable. I think she was uncertain, waiting. Being made aware of her eyes made me examine her face. The Knightsbridge prettiness was merely superficial; she was beautiful; the mouth was full and sensual; there was a small cleft in her chin; her nose was precisely straight; the hairline was soft and heartbreaking. I kissed it. We regarded each other opaquely for a while.

'Didn't you like that?' she asked.

'Yes.'

Throughout 1960 and the early part of 1961 I had been what we called juv (to rhyme with love) lead at Bromley weekly rep and had played over forty parts with a week's rehearsal for each. Now, in 1963, Bromley had gone fortnightly and I was being tried out to become resident director, with *Reluctant Heroes* as my debut. David Poulson, the Director of Productions, joined me in the bar in the second interval of the first night.

'Where d'you find that one?' he asked, referring without warmth to Christine.

'On a commercial. She looked good on camera. I thought I'd give her a whirl on stage; only two lines.'

He grunted and got us drinks. 'The play doesn't wear too well, does it?'

Patrons kept coming up to us in the bar enquiring if I was back to act again.

'Maybe I should stick to that.' I said. Nobody should mess up *Reluctant Heroes*; the play was idiot-proof. I was most depressed.

Christine and I left after the opening night and fell into my bed at Robert's.

'Slowly,' she said.

'What?'

'Don't leap about so.'

'Don't you like it?'

'Yes, but...'

'That was lovely,' she said afterwards.

'You're funny aren't you,' I said. 'I know everything and you don't really know nuffink but you make me feel about eight.'

'You're just a man.'

I pulled a face.

'Come on, she said. 'Take me home.'

We drove - I still had Sarah's unclaimed Mini - across the railway from Belgravia to Pimlico, figuratively, in those days, as well as literally, on the other side of the tracks. She lived with her parents. They were waiting up, excited at their daughter's theatrical debut.

'She was super,' I said in answer to their repeated queries. Dad was an Italian waiter called Vic. He looked like the poor man's Vittorio de Sica; a sweet, down-trodden little man with only a few sparks left. Mum was English, arthritic and hell. An elderly neighbour from the flat downstairs cluttered

5

up the room. The flat was rent-controlled, with loo on the landing below and shared with the neighbour. Christine, nevertheless, had what American lyric-writers used to call style, then revised to class. She certainly had not got it from nice little Dad and I saw in the occasional steel of Mum's eyes and heard in her clear upper-middle-class diction where the roots could be. I wondered what had brought that particular pair together.

I called for Christine the following lunch-time.

'Where shall we go?' she asked.

'Robert's.'

'What for?'

'What d'you think? I can't bear it at night, having to get up after to take you home.'

'OK. Let's get some shopping.'

'What for?'

'I'll do us lunch first.'

She had asparagus boiling and two pieces of veal in the pan when the doorbell rang. It was two pretty teenage girls who had some connection with Robert's flat that escapes me now. They were both single and one of them was very pregnant. She behaved with attractive unconcern and I wondered at her courage in the situation we all feared in those times, before the pill. They came in, giggling, and carried on the sort of conversation that referred to our mutual friends and events, but excluded Christine.

'Would you like some lunch?' she asked them.

'Oh, well. Thank you.'

The two already-minute pieces of veal miraculously became four, and four plates of steaming asparagus were before us with hot butter sauce in a silver sauceboat of Robert's that Christine had discovered and cleaned. I stared at mine and half-toyed with my knife and fork, wondering how to cope. The two girls were just as lost. Christine poured herself some sauce, took one piece of asparagus in fingers and thumb, dipped it in the sauce and popped the end in her mouth. Her teeth primly nipped through it. After sucking the core with relish, she laid the stump on the side of her plate and wiped her fingers. We followed her example. It was only in retrospect that I appreciated how unobtrusively the lesson was given. I would have shown off; most people would have let you feel their superiority somehow. It was a tiny, awkward moment, not in the least important, but Christine just passed something to us free of any sort of price-tag, as though she were unaware she had done it. She sloshed her last piece of asparagus about in the sauce and slid the end significantly into her mouth. She gave me the tiniest of private smiles and bit it with extra force. She took about three hours to pull the stump from her reluctant lips. I nearly broke out in a multicoloured rash. I have never associated asparagus with anything else since. Hot asparagus with butter sauce, prince of hors d'oeuvres, you put the Cadbury Flake commercials in the shade. I pointedly moved the table

6

up and down on my knees. The two girls were watching the private dialogue, fascinated, and Christine frowned prudishly at her plate. The rest of the lunch was delicious, but what amazed me was the ease. Nothing was any bother. The sort of production I made out of buying a tin of baked beans, some sausages, potatoes, a tin of rhubarb and rendering the whole thing inedible wasn't even thought of. We got rid of the girls. As we closed the door behind them we dashed simultaneously for the bedroom. 'Last one in bed's a ninny,' she yelled as we wrestled on the stairs and pulled each other's clothes back on so as to win the race. 'Have you had those two?

'No, but I wanted to, once.'

'I knew it. I was furious. So jealous.'

'Eh?'

'I thought that baby she was carrying was yours.'

I stopped undressing and stared; she had offered a meal when she needn't have, performed the Gracious Hostess definitively and had apparently enjoyed herself. Such self-control was beyond me.

'Why'd you ask 'em to stay to lunch then?'

'I was curious. You lose. I'm in.'

I grinned foolishly at her sitting on the bed with just her glasses on. A foolish grin was becoming a commonplace expression on my face. We made love, this time slowly, as she wanted. She had to wrap her legs round mine and hold me tight in her arms to let herself really go. I was used by her and loved it.

Christine, unlike me, had no shyness about nakedness and as she went from bedroom to bathroom and back it was a covert delight to admire her. I had always thought of myself as white and weedy. 'But you're lovely,' she said prodding me as though I were something on a butcher's counter. 'A bit skinny, but lovely. Not like Harry.

'Harry?'

'The chap I lived with in New York. He had a body like a wasp, same measurement all the way up and down, chest, waist and bum,' she giggled.

I wondered how she could be so careless of her beauty as to couple it with such dimensions. 'Why did you come back?'

She pulled a face, 'Mummy,' then kissed me all over. 'Hm, yes, I'm glad I did. You're much nicer.' I tried kissing her all over. She made me want to explore. After a decade of thinking myself a helluva-feller I realised I hadn't a clue. My adolescent gropings behind the youth club and up the woods, followed by my athletic explorations of all the positions were so much semi-liberated, Protestant fumblings compared to the sensual freedom that Christine brought to bed with her and introduced me to.

———————

The auditorium at the New Theatre, Bromley was the worst I have ever worked in, bar none. It was narrow and too long, with a low circle, a bitch to project into. There were dead acoustic patches in the most unlikely places

7

as well as the obvious ones. The stage was just as awful, too shallow and narrow, so there was no chance to get any depth into anything. The theatre had been a swimming bath then a cinema. During the lush days of films some interior designer had put in a row of huge urns down either side of the auditorium in a long recess with back-lighting. They capped the dreary decor with a funereal flourish.

Christine's mother, father and decrepit neighbour were smiling nervously in the shabby foyer. The play was poorly attended. Spring and Christine had made me feel generally light-hearted, but the theatre, the thin crowd and the sight of the Italian waiter and his semi-crippled wife were depressing.

Reluctant Heroes is, in my view, superb. The lunacy of conscription into the army in peacetime is a perfect farce framework just as the lunacy of marital double-standards at the turn of the century made a perfect framework for Feydeau. Colin Morris had seized his frame in sure hands and filled it with glowing theatrical colours. Ruefully I watched my production sputtering along on three cylinders, then drifted up to the office.

'Shame,' said David, peering through his peephole. 'Needs a house. Perhaps they don't go for it now there's no conscription.'

'The army's out, all right.'

'Well, d'you want the job?'

'I'm on? ' I felt quite short of breath I was so excited.

'If you want.'

'Even after this?'

'Not your fault.'

'I do.'

'OK. Fortnightly rehearsal, year's contract, month's notice either side, eighteen pounds a week, plus two a week expenses and...' he stopped and grinned at me, '...was there something else?'

'I get three weeks rehearsal for my play and a free hand.'

'You're on.'

'When can I do it?'

'Well, not in the first list, eh? Give things a go first.'

'Fine'

'Oh, you'll tread the boards occasionally, eh? Can't think why, but Bromley seems to like you.'

I walked out of that office on air. Part of the deal had been that if David took me on I was to be given a free hand to direct my first play, *The Subtopians*, with my own cast and three weeks - yes, three whole weeks - rehearsal. After its premiere the previous year at Guildford it had had a blighted life and now I could do something to remedy that. I had a job, a job I wanted, and for a year. I had my first teleplay scheduled for rehearsal; my own production of my own baby to crown my reign as director; and I was having a lovely affair. There are times when life dissembles and it seems good and solid and sure with Purpose and Future.

Chapter II

Background

'Exposition is B-O-R-I-N-G,' said a TV producer to me once, mouthing each letter for fear of corrupting the children. I don't agree, it can be fascinating and is usually essential. I shall try to make it palatable.

Brought up in Welling, a nowhere between Bexleyheath and Eltham, I left Dartford Grammar School in 1949, aged sixteen, full of idealism. Politics and Christianity were all that interested me. I looked for a job as a cub reporter; political journalist then Labour MP was the aim. While I searched and waited for a newspaper vacancy, I had to get a job, it didn't matter much what, two years military conscription loomed at eighteen.

'Would you like to work with people?' said the Youth Employment Officer.

'Yes, please.' His phraseology was seductive.

'Then go along to Selfridges. They want a junior in the Staff Office.'

Selfridges didn't want a junior in the Staff Office but they did in tailoring, so I waited behind the counter in Men's Tailoring, waiting for a vacancy in the Staff Office, while waiting for a vacancy on a paper, while waiting to be called up.

Two years later an army medical board rejected me because of asthma. I was glad to escape the embarrassment of having to claim to be a pacifist, mortified not to be deemed adequate for something as mundane as the army. After a further two years I was still behind the counter at Selfridges wondering what to do with my freedom.

The particular form of Christianity that infected my adolescence was merely Church of England, not famed for being the most injurious of viruses, but my fervent view of the world gave me a severe dose: from about sixteen to nineteen I cycled the twenty-odd mile journey to Selfridges and back to give the commuter train fare to God, along with most of the rest of my wages; I attended early morning communion three times a week, trying, on my knees, to squeeze spirituality out of my all-too-corporeal heart, to no avail; I left my first, pretty girlfriend's sixteen-year-old lips unkissed in case it led us on to sin (she soon chucked me for someone more enterprising and I still have regretful dreams of her). Religious fervour even prevented me from masturbating. Yes, I know the old one about ninety-nine per cent of boys do it and the other one per cent are liars; I was the hundred and first. Eventually, aged nineteen, I suddenly spewed Christian zeal out overnight. Pent-up to the point of explosion, I grabbed a willing girl from the church youth club and on a Wednesday evening in Holy Week, the evening my parents were out at the dogs, took her to our house and attempted to initiate myself with her on the sitting room floor. 'Not on the first date,' she said, primly, but when I pushed her hand down to my trousers she obligingly undid the buttons, pulled out my bursting member and gave it a couple of amicable tugs. Some sort of earthquake engulfed me, an ejaculation like a volcano swiftly followed and after my spinning head slowed down we spent ages cleaning ourselves up.

The following Friday, on a damp April evening, we went up into Oxleas Woods on our second - and therefore in her view, permissive - date. I was lying on her, fumbling and thrusting fruitlessly, fully clad in both clothes and contraceptive. 'Take your jacket off,' she ordered. She folded it, shoved it under her behind and in I surged. It was Good Friday, a fitting curtain to God in my life.

At twenty I was walking out with the junior in Ladies' Furs every Wednesday and Saturday. She lived in Wembley, precisely at the opposite pole of Greater London from Welling. Courting was a tiring business, full of last tubes and trains. At least they were better than the bike. On Sundays and Tuesdays I went to St Mary's Youth Club and continued the liaison with my initiator. She lived a few streets from me so the mileage was minimal, but so were convenient locations. Horizontal sex was the exception, bed a rare event.

The drain on my energy was considerable: shop hours; four evenings of pleasure; three of night school for economics, shorthand and politics; football on Saturday and Sunday; homework (whenever did I do that?); and the constant journeys had rendered what I had liked to think of as a pale, interesting, blond young man into a gaunt ghost with lank hair hanging into red-rimmed eyes. I thought, to hell with all of it, and went to the emigration offices. Nobody would have me. The asthma that had kept me out of the Army, now kept me in England.

I was twenty-two when Ivor appeared in my life; he was the turning point. I suppose if this book demonstrates anything it is the random way fate blows us. My route out of the doldrums into which I had drifted seemed clear: a Co-operate Society scholarship to Oxford, well within my grasp, followed by a career in journalism and Labour politics. But Ivor, the same age as I, the new assistant in Hector Powe's Gents Natty Ready-to-Wear (I had moved on from Selfridges) had starred in a film. Son of an actor, he'd been a child actor unable to bridge the puberty gap. His girl friend was at drama school and he regaled me day after day with stories of the theatre. I, who had never even indulged in school or amateur dramatics, found myself bewitched. He had worked the previous summer in the Isle of Wight at a hotel/holiday camp; I made up my mind; Ivor fixed me up with a summer job there and I worked out that I could save enough to pay my way to

Canada in the autumn. I had vague, private ideas about hitch-hiking to Hollywood and bursting upon an eagerly expectant film world.

However, even this new plan was due for instant modification. Ivor came to work one day looking even paler than I. 'She's chucked me,' he said, hollowly. 'It's all over.'

For three days, as he mooned about, I watched anxiously, convinced that this romantic figure, who looked a bit like Dirk Bogarde for good measure, was about to end it all. Finally I had an idea to save him.

'Why don't you come to the Isle of Wight? We'll save some money and both go to drama school.' I had timidly voiced for the first time what I now knew I most wanted. 'You want to act again and - if I had training - I mean, I've always wanted - well, perhaps even I could earn a living at it.'

We got entrance forms that lunch-time and paid our one pound fees. The next day Ivor and his girlfriend, Henrietta, were reunited, but it was done; I was on a new road. I was going into the Theatre, and by God, did it have a capital T.

That summer of 1955 was a scorcher. The joy we took in it was enhanced by anticipation. We sold tea and ice creams from a refreshment hut on the cliff top at Whitecliff Bay. The hut was run by us and a chap called Dave. Every Saturday morning, while Ivor wrote to Henrietta and read lyric poetry, fingers pressed lightly to his forehead, Dave and I each played a tender farewell scene behind the hut with some tanned young female. Every Saturday afternoon we sat on the counter like vultures, examining the new batch, white and willing, as they came tripping along the cliff path.

'He's an actor,' Dave used to inform them for purely lecherous reasons, but I used to burst with pleasure at the thought of it. Behind me was Men's Tailoring, boredom, greyness; ahead of me was the Theatre, life itself. What a glorious, carefree summer. It never occurred to Ivor or me that we would fail the entrance auditions and we didn't. The school gave two scholarships. Ivor got one and I shared the other. We ran from the audition held in Kensington, and danced to Piccadilly, then stood among commuters on the train from Waterloo to Portsmouth with our arms round one another in rapture.

September came and we set out for London. Yes, set out. We should have had little sticks and our belongings bound in spotted kerchiefs on the end of them. Peter Shaffer has Clive, the protagonist in *Five Finger Exercise*, say of going up to Cambridge, and I misquote, 'It was like going to a foreign land and hearing a new foreign language spoken. Only it was *my* language and I heard it for the first time...Birds flew with one wing...' The Central School of Speech Training and Dramatic Art was my Cambridge; my life changed from black and white to colour as quickly and simply as television changed in 1968. Only my grass turned green in 1955 and it was on my side of the fence. Doors opened, trees sang, birds swam, fishes walked and I flew.

Central was situated in the perimeter rooms of the Albert Hall, so we had concert rehearsals, festivals, meetings and other unexpected events that were fermenting down in the main hall, tossed casually into our curriculum between classes. Any school is as good or as bad as its teachers. Central contained Oliver Reynolds and Cicely Berry. Cis, now Voice Director at the Royal Shakespeare Company and author of standard works on her subject, is generally regarded as the best voice teacher in the country; as far as I'm concerned she always was. She looked like an unmade bed, but not just any old unmade bed. The unmade bed that was Cis was still warm from its occupants, who had assuredly made delicious love in it. She was the personification of loving femininity and was herself loved by everybody. She was always laughing, or to be more exact, giggling. Her ear was too sharp to allow any sustained period of gravity in the ludicrous world of drama students. The first hint of portentousness or self-importance in front of Cis was doomed, her face muscles would start to lose control, the mouth would twitch and the moment her unevenly made-up, upward-slanting eyes caught those of one of the other students, off she would go. And we would follow her. Classes with Cis were sometimes a continuous, audible roar. She would be delivering some judgement on someone's work and would suddenly stop and laugh till the tears ran.

'Can you hear me?' She'd ask us. 'I mean really, have you ever heard such rubbish? What do I know about it? Nothing. How dare I pontificate?'

However in the face of one of those indefinable moments of what I can only imperfectly call honest self-revelation, when the student was defenceless and open, no matter how bad the technical execution, she would turn relentlessly on any person who didn't recognise the real McCoy.

'That's *it*.' She would hiss. 'That's *it*. Don't you see? That's what you're all here for. The rest is shit.'

Oliver, or Ollie as he was known at school, was as Puritan as Cis wasn't. A severe, neat, gnome-like figure amid the theatrical exuberance, he could strike terror. Like Cis he had a lethal sense of humour. He was feared by many, disliked by some, admired by most and worshipped by me. He quickly became the intellectual and cultural father-figure I had unknowingly lacked. No actor or writer had ever longed for good reviews in the press as I yearned for good crits from Ollie,

He was always available for private chats with us in his mews house and I took him up quite soon. As soon as you walked through the door Ollie the demon tutor became Oliver the charming host. The acid came out of the humour, the drinks and cigarettes appeared. All was grace, except for one thing: he would leave alarming pauses; endless acres of time that he left for you to fill. Before long, students found themselves burbling out their hopes and fears. He got inside all of us. Any budding actor who passed through

Oliver's hands and didn't learn how to hold a pause deserved to sell socks in Harrods. After the drink, you were taken to a restaurant you couldn't afford and bought dinner. As with Cis you were special.

After our first meal we were walking down Kensington Church Street. I stopped on a corner. I had failed to grasp the Ollie/Oliver technique.

'Excuse me asking. It's none of my business I suppose, but are you queer?'

His eyebrows shot up and he stared off down the road, squinting over the smoke that rose from the cigarette that always hung from his mouth. 'Yes.'

I was amazed to hear anyone admit it. Queerness, as far as I was concerned then, was confined to erring curates and the chap from Travel Goods who had touched me up by the freight lift at Selfridges. I stared at Oliver, a very different specimen of homo-something-or-other.

'I'd like to talk to you again like this evening. It's been wonderful,' I blurted.

'Good.'

'Only...' I again didn't know how to put it, '...you know, there's nothing doing.'

His eyebrows rose further. He removed the cigarette from his mouth and looked at me. 'So what?'

We smoked in class, we called teachers by their Christian names ('Forward, Mr. Frisby. Suits, please,' gone forever), we slept with each other; virgins were actually urged by one female teacher to get screwed and get it over with. I didn't believe such places existed and in spite of the severe picture I've drawn of Oliver, there he was, under his deliberate anti-camp exterior, the guiding spirit behind our drama training, adoring his students and, like Cis - or Cis like him - scathing about rubbish or laziness and passionate about good work.

However, the thing Ivor and I did most in that first year was work to earn our keep. The scholarship and a half had been awarded to us not for our brilliance but our poverty. We could manage on about a fiver a week each. The problem was to find work that paid at least five shillings an hour, or else the time involved became disproportionate. We became experts, and worked everywhere, day or night, and rode about on a tandem to save bus fares. I became a chucker-out at the Hammersmith Palais (qualification, one dinner suit) and nearly had my face pushed in before my career had started. I don't think there is a menial or unskilled job that exists in a modern society that we haven't done.

And of course, I fell in love. Oh boy, was I in love. Wiekie was unlikely and foreign; a big person, mature beyond me, though two years younger. On top of the other turmoil in my life she took me up by the heels and shook me inside out. If someone as extraordinary as Wiekie loved me, I couldn't be an entire washout.

And what about the Art and Craft of Acting: the purpose of the exercise? Well, I was in deep trouble at once. I read everything I could find about the subject and in the discussions and analyses that formed a large part of our timetable I was prominent. I could dissect, criticise, judge, offer imaginative ideas, but I couldn't do it.

'Perhaps Mr. Frisby is destined to become one of our prominent critics,' said Ollie in mime class one day after I had demolished another student's efforts in discussion, then produced a dud myself. After the more humiliating sessions I would sit on the floor of the loo back against the wall, my head between my knees, trying to force sobs of anguish from myself to prove I could 'feel it.' Even they wouldn't come. In *Twelfth Night* I was awful as Feste. My brief appearance as Valentine, a courtier in the opening scene, was a blemish out of all proportion to the importance of the role. The embarrassment of speaking the words of the bard in my semi-cockney, slovenly speech produced a noise of the volume and clarity of something nosing its way up the Thames on a foggy November afternoon. All my joy at my new life, all my passion for Wiekie, was blighted, as the awareness was steadily forced on me that I wasn't up to it. At the end-of-year showing of *The Country Wife* I managed to play the sex-obsessed Horner as a space in the air, quite a notable achievement really, and a step forward for me.

'I'm no good,' I told Ivor, head in my hands.

'You've got a good practical mind. You'll make a good stage manager,' said Ivor, helpfully.

After one year at Central they had a weeding out of untalented, unlikely or unsuitable students and I was given the chop, sentenced to death. Selfridges yawned under me, eager to swallow me up. In pieces I wandered from the Albert Hall. Wiekie was thrown out too, and Ivor. It was unbelievable. Wiekie was out because they regarded her as already formed theatrically; so she was, basically using the school to perfect her English, which Central wasn't having. Ivor, too, was heaved out because of his earlier professional experience. They were out for exactly the opposite reason to me. Wiekie, coming up Kensington Gore, saw me and reacted in a way that would have made Eleanora Duse sick with envy, then ran at me with her arms out and her waist-length hair streaming behind. I spread my feet and took the shock.

'What'll you do?' I asked after we had disentangled ourselves.

'Go home to my country and act. Central, huh. Ollie, pah. What do they know?' My misery increased. Everything was going to be taken from me. Wiekie didn't ask me what I was going to do, she knew my fears intimately. Ivor was coming up the road. 'I've been chucked out,' he shouted gleefully. The world was going mad. 'I told Henri I'd got the boot. She said, "Why wait?" so we're going to get married, then get a job together in rep.'

'Just like that?'

'Yeah. Rotten about you. Come on, let's go for a drink, celebrate; I'm a married man, practically.'

We drank a glum half of bitter each. Ivor's high spirits were out of keeping with my blackness and Wiekie's compassion. He did his best to look grave but gleeful expressions kept sliding into his face from unexpected angles. His and Henri's faith in each other was a rebuke. Why didn't I ask Wiekie to marry me and gambol happily up Kensington Gore. We looked at each other and understood. We were not in the least ready to take each other on at that moment.

I found Cis Berry and drew her into an empty room. 'Why have I been given the boot, Cis? I thought I was showing signs at last?'

'There was quite an argument about you. I didn't think you should be - I mean, I - ' She stopped, embarrassed. She had certainly been on my side.

'Well?'

'It was a question of attitude to work.'

'What's wrong with my attitude? I thought I was a public example.'

'You were - are, in some ways, but well, you and Ivor, you're so light-hearted.'

'Eh?'

'I mean about all your jobs. It all seems a bit of a game to you. You slide out of classes sometimes and fall asleep, you never seem to worry about it or *care*.'

It all came pouring out of me in a rush. 'Care? This place and Wiekie is all I care about. Do you remember when we arrived, we all got a talking-to. "You're in the theatre now. We don't want to be bothered in school time with your private problems. Do your work. No bellyaching. If you don't behave like pros you'll never work. The theatre is hard. The profession is overcrowded." All that was drummed into us by everyone. If I fell asleep it was because I hadn't been to bed for the weekend. If I cut half a class it was for a job that paid to keep me here at all. We looked light-hearted because we were happy. Happy? I never knew what happiness was. I wasn't even alive before I - I was - ' I was choking on the stream of pain that poured from me. I was 'feeling it' all right. Cis burst into tears. It seemed to be the day for it. I put my arms round her. 'You should be doing this for me,' I said.

'Oh Terry. You'd better go and see Oliver.' I left her with my last Selfridges handkerchief covered in mascara.

That evening at Oliver's the pauses would have driven Macready mad. Eventually: 'You're in your own way. We might take you back, but...' He waited for what seemed like fifty minutes while I tried not to scream. I felt sure that I would never have been chopped against his vote. '...there would have to be evidence.'

'What evidence?'

'If you were to do some work with someone in the summer holidays, me

15

for instance (who else, for instance?), and the results of that work were positive...'

'What an offer. There's nothing I'd like better.'

'There's a condition.'

I struggled to stay silent while I waited.

'No outside job.'

'Not possible. I couldn't live.'

'Family?'

'They've no money. You know that.'

'How much does it cost you?'

'About a fiver a week.'

'That must be tight.'

'It is.'

'I'll give you a hundred quid, you do no jobs, you work with me as directed and after a while we'll know whether you can act or not.'

This day was piling one incredibility on another.

'I'll pay you back one day.'

'No need.'

I have never really known what was in the depths of that Machiavellian mind. He has never let on. I am sure he contributed to my being sacked, but why? Just to get me alone for a few weeks, I mean alone artistically, and work on me? I wasn't worth it. He wasn't buying my affection, he knew he already had it. Perhaps he diagnosed accurately what I needed and was simply fond enough of me to do what he did.

Wiekie caught the boat-train. We had an emotional farewell on the platform, then, unable to leave her, I jumped into the guard's van as it passed me, walked down the corridor and grinned through the compartment window at her surprised, smeared face. We held each other, soaking in emotion, for the seventy-odd miles to Harwich. I hitch-hiked back to London and worked as hard as I could on Oliver's course, living on the wealth of eight pounds a week and writing love-letters of inordinate length and sentimentality to Wiekie. By the end of that summer, to stand up and act was no longer an ordeal but a joy that I couldn't wait to begin. Oliver took me often to the theatre, analysing constantly, giving me insights I would have missed; everything began to gel. In the privacy of my solo acting course, Oliver was able to do what could never have been done in class: to get my rusted-in imagination free and show me how to get it working productively at a part. It is not important how good or bad an actor I subsequently became, the process itself was priceless. Wiekie had got to the roots of me as a man and given me a pride in myself that was utterly new and exciting. Now Oliver had worked every creative fibre that existed in me. I suppose if I were less inclined to think and write in extremes I would call it all simple growing-up. But it was my life and, by God, was it not extreme to me. So Central took me back for my second year.

The first day was heaven. What a re-union, even without Wiekie and Ivor. Students milled about in the common room, we fell on each other's necks. At our first verse class with Cis, I got up and said some D H Lawrence. I hadn't seen her since chucking-out day. She made the customary invitation for comments from the others. 'What about *that*?'

First day of term, we weren't yet into tearing each other to shreds with our usual callousness. There were one or two peripheral comments while Cis's slant eyes searched the class; one eye was made up, she seemed to have forgotten the other. Somebody started to say, 'Well, I don't think he quite got the rhythm of the verse in the - '

'He *communicated*.' She spat.

There was silence.

'He *communicated*. That's what it's all about. *Communication*. Jesus, that's all.' After the class Cis asked me to wait. When the room was empty she came up to me, put her arms round me and gave me such a hug that I was breathless. Did ever a lucky, lucky student get two such teachers as Oliver and Cis?

———————

In my final week at Central I went to the Royal Court to see a play that was creating quite a stir. Even Ollie had, curate-like, commended it in parts. I was quite unprepared for what I saw. I sat, or rather jumped up and down in my seat, hugging myself with glee while the humour, rhetoric and invective exploded into my head. Everything I, and indeed the whole young generation of the lower orders, seemed to want to say, if only we had known now to say it, was hurled from the stage without apology or restraint. The entire Establishment seemed to totter before the power and wit of it. The play was, of course, John Osborne's *Look Back in Anger*. I was young and optimistic enough to believe that I had heard the Messiah, and into my longing simply to be in the theatre was directed my other, earlier moralistic fervour of the humanistic reformer. It would all work through the theatre. Life, work, had even more purpose.

However, the immediate problem for a young actor was not the fulfilment of a crusade but to earn a living. Oliver claimed to have perceived literary talent lurking in letters I had written to him, so I wrote my own audition pieces; gaudy, excessively emotional extracts that I believed displayed my histrionic strong points. One director who gave me a job said afterwards, 'I like the Shakespeare you did, but couldn't stand that other rubbish, whatever was it?' But, headily fuelled by John Osborne, the idea of my writing a play took root.

I got my first job and hitch-hiked between Gloucester Road and High Wycombe weekly rep theatre (my first converted swimming baths) for four weeks at £7.10.0 a week which was fun, then for the head-reeling offer of £10 a week to York rep, which wasn't. The director and I were at loggerheads at once. After two months my letter of resignation and his of dismissal crossed. On the Tuesday morning of *The Scarlet Pimpernel*, my last play at York, I realised I had five rehearsal-free days and started my first play, planning to take the completed script back to London with me that Saturday night.

I finished my play three jobs and fourteen months later. Nobody wanted it.

During the four years following Central I became a thoroughly experienced actor. There was little difficulty getting work, often tatty, but with enough of those moments of magic that make theatre what it is, and acting an enchanted profession. I played many of the best roles in modern theatre and loved the life, but never made serious efforts to Get On. Instead of hustling for the right jobs or a smart agent, I descended on friends, shared the rent and scribbled till I was broke again.

I have had a few love affairs in my life, but one of the best - if not the best - was the love affair that was my four years in rep. And, if the concluding marriage was Bromley, the exuberant spring of it was the summer in Penzance under Robert's guidance. My route to Robert and Penzance was as fortuitous as the rest of my life. After just a dozen roles in weekly rep, I was offered a leading part in a new musical at the Players Theatre, although I had never sung or danced publicly except in Tunbridge Wells rep panto. This musical was meant to be the follow-up to their previous enormous hit, *The Boy Friend*. It wasn't. *Gentlemen's Pastime* flopped without trace under those arches at Charing Cross. It showed me that I knew far too little about my chosen profession, and as a penance, I went for an interview with some idealistic idiot who was going to re-open the near-derelict Pavilion Theatre, Penzance, for the summer. It was symbolic; I could scarcely go further from the theatrical centre to start my trek back.

Robert Peake, the idealistic idiot, greeted me at the interview with the news that my first role, if I got the job, would be Jimmy Porter in *Look Back In Anger*. I was galvanised, here was the part that I wanted to play more than any other. But, glories, to follow this was a list of plays to make any actor's mouth water, including *A Streetcar Named Desire* and *Waltz of the Toreadors*. Penzance had had no theatre for some years and so we were not obliged to play the usual summer-season diet of the latest flimsy comedy or unexciting thriller from the West End. There was a backlog of meaty, well-made stuff to present in Penzance for the first time, and Robert found a young company as besotted with his aims as he was. That summer, 1958, the rain poured down, the holiday-makers poured in and we poured out every ounce of talent and effort we could muster. It was bewitching for me, for all of us I think, and most of us from that company remain friends to this day. Robert and his partner even made a profit - which they later lost trying to do the same elsewhere.

I played several rep seasons between Penzance in 1958 and my final, fifteen, non-stop months at Bromley in 1960-61, but Penzance was fourteen weeks of formative heaven, tucked away down there on the big toe of the country. Then, and in the years that followed that summer, I learned to love the craft of theatre; the way you could actually do it; the way a playwright could turn a scene or suddenly reveal a character; the way experienced actors could create their effects. I communicated on the most intimate terms possible, namely on stage, with the minds of most modern playwrights (especially the writers of comedy) and often played in the work of England's two most-performed stand-bys of the rep season: William Shakespeare and Agatha Christie. But, even with a play which I despised - and hers were high among them - it was riveting, while appearing in it, to dissect it from inside and peer into the author's mind. To learn what not to do is as important as the opposite. When you know the clichés, you've no excuse for using them.

By 1962 I regarded *Look Back in Anger* as a play due for future oblivion, with possibly the occasional exhumation for curiosity value. On the other hand, if there is a National Theatre in the year 2050, I'll bet *Sailor Beware* is playing there as a perfect example of twentieth century domestic comedy, loved and worked on by craftsmen until shining with humanity and humour. Yet, it is insupportable to argue that *Sailor Beware* is worth a tenth of *Look Back in Anger*. Craft is, after all, only the means; artistic achievement is the goal.

But by 1962 I was still an unproduced writer. The theatrical social realism of the late fifties that followed Osborne and Anger had given way to Satire; *Beyond the Fringe* had arrived. England was already convulsed by that decade-long yell of laughter at all her sacred cows. The Zeitgeist had sailed and left me on the dock with *The Subtopians*. Yes, that was the red-hot-box-office title I had chosen. I wrote several things after I finished that, but that was the one that mattered: my first full-length stage play. To say that the rejection slips poured in would be painting a rosy picture. Most of the time you don't even get your play back or any acknowledgement that you exist. After more than four years of scribbling and rejection even the firmest refusal to look the facts in the face couldn't keep out the aridity of the idea that I was no good. Then it happened: lift off.

CHAPTER III

Background

The Subtopians was at last presented - as a rehearsed reading at The Mercury Theatre, Notting Hill Gate, one Sunday night. Perhaps a dozen people turned up. It was Autumn 1961, four years after I had started it. A group of actors I had joined, called 'The 24', put it on; such groups still abound, actors who work on new plays for love only. The Director of Guildford Rep, Eric Longworth, attended the reading and said he would put the play on for a week if he could get an Arts Council grant. This would depend on the reports of four of their readers. The reports appeared, teeming with such words as 'squalid,' 'sordid,' 'boring,' 'kitchen-sink' (the play took place in a sink-free living-room) 'dull,' 'repetitious,' etc., but one of them finished with the words, 'but the play has a sort of honesty that makes it worthy of production.' That sentence did the trick, £400 was coughed up; production was scheduled for a week in March 1962.

Meanwhile, I had a job as understudy and chorus boy in a new musical on its way to the Adelphi Theatre. This musical had been adapted by Hugh Hastings from his own long-running play, *Seagulls Over Sorrento*. It was called *Scapa*. The all-male cast consisted of actors and dancers impersonating sailors. Hugh, one of the sweetest men imaginable, had hit the jackpot once with *Seagulls* and had since been having a very rough time in many ways. He had every hope pinned on this expensive venture. It starred Pete Murray, Edward Woodward and David Hughes. As *Scapa* opened to critical assassination, *The Subtopians* went into rehearsal. On the Friday before my play opened I had to go on in *Scapa* for Pete Murray. Everybody was extremely nice, which always happens when an understudy actually finishes the piece without fainting or screwing-up the other principals, and Hugh wangled me the following Monday night off to go to my opening. That act has him canonised as far as I'm concerned.

I watched the dress rehearsal on the Monday afternoon and reeled out, shattered. The play was jerry-built. An ASM. asked me if I would like a cup of tea and was subjected to a stream of self-criticism and recrimination. 'Oh, I rather like the play,' she said, shovelling tea leaves.

'No, no, no, everyone was right.' I moaned. 'It's broken-backed. It's supposed to build to Tom stealing Dad's joke in Act II and humiliating him, then everything flows from that. That's the hinge and it's no bloody good.

You can't build a play round one unfunny joke.'

'The party scene's funny,' she said.

'But after that Act II falls apart and Act III will just be a rattle of seats as they go.' I pallidly went to wish the cast well while she spread my despondency among the stage management.

By seven o'clock the Guildford clientele had filled the theatre, four hundred seats, top price six shillings, two for the price of one on Mondays; I was being supported in the bar by the equally sick-looking Eric Longworth. I wished I was anywhere else, especially hoofing away in the chorus at the Adelphi.

The Subtopians has a cast of six: Mum and Dad, Older Brother and Wife, Younger Brother and New Girl Friend. Mum and Dad are buried in the trivia of suburbia; Older Brother and Wife are up to their waists, still faintly struggling; Younger Brother has escaped to Art, a New Life and Love. There are no prizes for guessing whose story it was. The theme was the petty, and eventually huge, cruelties we inflict on our nearest and dearest. Dad is painted as a cracking bore, pathetic but lethal, and Mum as the long-suffering, armour-plated one who copes. The dialogue asked for laughs, but the underlying strength of the pain should, if played properly, make the laughs die in the audience's throats. 'No, don't laugh, these aren't your neighbours to titter at, they're you and me,' I wanted to say. 'What can we do about it?' It was all very young, uncompromising and idealistic. I don't think it is claiming too much to say that Guildford had never seen anything so immediate. Act One ended with the re-entrance of Dad, boring the pants off everyone and horrifying Girl Friend. The act curtain, if the play was working only on the surface level, could have come down to laughter. The only sound from the audience that night was a sort of corporate groan that rippled across the house. There was no applause. The atmosphere was too electric. Elated but fearful of the collapse to come, I turned from my seat and hurried up the aisle to find myself looking into the ashen faces of my mother and father. They were sitting near the back, holding hands. I shouldn't think they had held hands for decades. My mother smiled wanly and my father looked stonily through me. My stomach seemed to drop out of my body.

It's funny about writing a play, or, I suppose, creating anything; you set out to make a thing and don't know till you have finished what you've made. No matter how predictable the story and theme, no matter how pre-planned the project, it is a jump in the dark. I had set out to write meaty parts for Wiekie and myself; I had a Grand Theme; I had constructed according to the best Ibsenite methods. Admittedly I had drawn on my own life and

21

experience for the background, but I had invented all the action of the play; every detail. It was only when I read the finished article that it began to dawn that it resembled my own family. Or perhaps previously I hadn't wanted to admit it to myself. After the rehearsed reading at the Mercury, and then during rehearsals, the awareness of the similarities grew to the certainty that I had created an exact, photographic reproduction of my own family. Besotted with my play, I had stood on my head to keep my parents away, kidding myself that a bit of running it down and pretending the whole thing was a non-event would stop them from making the thirty-mile drive from Welling to Guildford. To imagine that was the act of an ostrich; they had already traipsed over most of the country watching me perform. When I had acted at Bromley for over a year, a mere stone's throw from Welling, they had graced the theatre, every Wednesday, like the Duke and Duchess of Bromley, while their blue-eyed boy had laid the audience in every available aisle week after week. For the ones they specially liked they had returned on Saturdays. Any idiot should have guessed that my mumbled evasions and excuses on the phone would have no effect. Now the apple of their eyes had turned round and delivered a most accurate, thought-out, cold-blooded kick in their teeth.

I watched the curtain rise on Act II with an unbearable load of guilt heaped on to my apprehensions about the structure. Not only had I publicly humiliated my parents, but it was all in the cause of my own imminent mortification. The party scene got the sought-after laughter; the moment I feared, the climax or anti-climax whichever it was to be, arrived. It was sublime, like a silent explosion that surged from the stage, up the auditorium and back again, leaving devastation in its wake.

Anyone as much in love with theatre as I, must have experienced some of those moments when to have moved a muscle or breathed would have been sacrilegious. Well, at Guildford that night there was one of them. The hinge was sound, efficient and beautiful. Afterwards, the family on-stage sank their claws into each other as only families can, and the remainder of Act II and the whole of Act III were received in pin-dropping silence. The final curtain came in, then out, the cast bowed and the curtain was coming in again before anyone started to applaud, then there was a storm. They took ten calls with a curtain that was slow and hand-operated. As I shuffled out with the crowd I heard a teenage girl say, 'I'll never be horrible to my parents again,' and I was left to face Mum and Dad.

'It seemed to go very well, ' said my mother with her face attempting and failing at a smile. I mumbled something.

'Well, everyone seemed to like it,' she added, focusing over my shoulder. 'Yes.'

'We'd better be off. We've got a long way to drive. Goodnight dear. Give us a ring soon.'

As she moved away my father shrugged his coat up and pulled his hat

down, a familiar gesture. 'So that's what you think of us, is it, old son?'
Then quite brightly, 'Well, pip, pip. Be in touch soon.'

I stood, wrapped in shame and exultation. Eric Longworth came up to
me. '*The Times* and *The Telegraph* were in.'

'Oh?'

'*The Times* said, "That was a surprise."'

'What d'you think that meant?'

'Dunno.'

I went for a drink with the director, George Little, and cast. They looked
to me like a composite of Garrick and Irving. I got plastered and woke up
in a friend's room in Pimlico about noon the next day feeling awful, I
staggered into the street, found a newsagent's and bought *The Times* and
The Telegraph. I eased my way round to Robert's, let myself in, made some
coffee and opened The Times.

Well, there are moments in life which are beyond one's cherished
fantasies. Or, perhaps they precisely fulfil them. The notice is below:

AVENGING ANGEL IN SUBURBIA
PLAY OF FAMILY TENSIONS

Mr T P M Frisby's play looked at first like a passionate
denunciation of suburbia and suburban values, and so among
other things it is, but before long it acquires a dramatic complexity
which leaves any such simple doctrinaire formula far behind.

The Manns live an unremarkable life in an ordinary suburb; the
house is called Mon Repos and inside they're all tearing each
other to pieces, as the wandering son remarks to his fiancee when
nearing the front door. The reasons for the family arguments
are of the sort which seem petty to outsiders but can make all the
difference between happiness and misery.

At the beginning of the play they are 'a happy family' in the
sense that they do not actually scream and kick and come to
blows. But beneath the surface there are tensions. Dad and Mum
get on each other's nerves, in a quiet sort of way. The elder son
and his wife are expecting a child, and he feels he cannot take a
more exciting but less lucrative job; with that between them all
the good intentions on both sides will not put things quite right.

Into this situation comes an avenging angel with a flaming sword
- the younger son's fiancee. She senses that the family is held
together only by self deception, compromise and fear. With the
selfishness of someone in love she determines to extricate at least
Tom from this web of deceit, and precipitates the family row to
end all family rows. Unforgivable things are said and then those

23

involved are left to piece their lives together as best they can. 'We can't all live out in the open,' says the elder brother; 'We should,' snaps back the other, without thinking, and there is the dilemma in a nutshell...The centre of the play is strong, disturbing and true - if not as a generalisation, at least of these particular, wholly believable characters. There is one short scene (between Tom and his fiancee at the station) which should be removed, as making feebly explicit something which is powerfully implicit throughout, but otherwise Mr. Frisby's writing is direct, assured and devastatingly accurate. The cast, admirable individually, play together as though possessed and the net result is as satisfying an evening in the theatre as one could hope for, in or out of the West End . As for Mr. Frisby, if he can go on writing as powerfully as this, he may turn out to be the major realistic dramatist we have all been waiting for ever since Mr. Osborne discovered Brecht.

Simultaneous peace and triumph filled me. It is irrelevant that the anonymous second-string reviewer of *The Times* might not have been infallible, that man performed me a tremendous service: from the moment I had read him I knew who I was. For the first time. It wasn't that I had previously feared failure, I doubted my right even to be trying. Self-delusion was the spectre; the twin dreads that I didn't belong and that Men's Tailoring beckoned. The ghosts were laid. *The Telegraph* was another rave, not so well-written, but most acceptable, thank you. The local papers and *The Stage* later in the week went potty. Between the lot of them I was compared to Chekhov, Ibsen, Osborne, Miller, and I thought reviewers the most sagacious of people.

I tried to telephone Finchley. The line was engaged for an hour. Finally I got Henrietta, she was hysterical. 'Where have you been? What's going on? I've had everyone on the phone all morning. Phone Eric Longworth at Guildford. He's got to speak to you. Very urgent. What's happening?'

I got Eric. Satisfaction oozed from the telephone into my ready ear. 'The seating plan for the week looks like *Who's Who in the Theatre.* We're going to sell out for every performance.'

I floated about for the afternoon, then got to the Adelphi to hoof and sing my way through the evening in naval uniform and dancing pumps. The producer and company manager were waiting for me at the stage door.

'What about the rights of this play? Has anyone got 'em for the West End?'

I could have set that to music. Beethoven's Ninth.

Everyone was crowding into the chorus dressing room. Hugh entered, delightful Hugh, recently smashed by his reviews. He clasped me emotionally. 'Oh, Terry, Terry, I remember what it was like.'

Two carloads of us from *Scapa* made up a party to see the Thursday matinee at Guildford. Longworth, tall and gaunt, seemed to have grown sleek in three days. 'We've got four offers for the play from West-End managers, one offer from Oscar Lewenstein to take this production to Stratford East, and Peter Bridge is seeing it this afternoon.'

Peter Bridge was at that time one of the younger, brighter producers, on the crest of a wave; very commercial, rather square. After the performance he tried to draw me out of the theatre for a word. It started to rain, Longworth called me in to the telephone leaving Bridge standing damply on the pavement.

Edward Woodward started a jig on the other side of the road, water running off him. 'I want to see that again. I want to see that again,' he kept chanting. 'A West End producer waiting in the rain for a chorus boy to come off the telephone.' He repeated variations all the way back to the Adelphi and snatches of *Singing In The Rain* every time he passed near me on stage that evening.

Of all the West End producers, I wanted one of two to have my play: Oscar Lewenstein or Michael Codron. They were the two in sympathy with the post-Osborne generation, indeed Lewenstein produced nothing else. However, he only offered to take this production to Stratford East and Michael Codron wasn't interested.

The decision was inevitable. Peter Bridge made a handsome donation to start the fund to build the new Yvonne Arnaud Theatre in the town and acquired his year's option to produce my play in the West End.

He never did so.

It was a perfect example of left is left and right is right and never the twain, etc. Bridge, who believed in publicity and packaging, went to star after star and was turned down flat because there were no starring parts, the play required integrated group work. Bridge began to wonder what was wrong with his lovely new property stamped with *The Times* seal of Good Cultural Value and in exasperation persuaded the Alexandra Theatre, Birmingham, to put it on for three weeks so that he could have another look at it. In a dismal production without balls or passion, temporarily retitled *Family Joke*, the play brought the gales of laughter so properly throttled at Guildford. It looked like a domestic comedy or sitcom with Serious Bits. How I longed for the commitment of George Little and his cast.

Birmingham put the tin lid on Bridge's failing faith and our uneasy affair was over. For four years of writing and after all the excitement, I had earned a couple of hundred pounds in royalties, less ten per cent agent's commission, typist's charges and £17 legal fees for drawing up the West End contract. My intoxicating high slid, during the discontented winter of Bridge's option, into the low I was in at the start of this story.

CHAPTER IV

1963 - continued

So entered Christine. Ah, Christine. Shiny, new Christine. We would meet and hurry to Robert's flat where we snuggled into sweet, cocooned lovemaking. One day, I stretched with pleasure and said, 'How many have you had, anyway?'

'What?'

'How many? Men?'

Her eyes widened. Saucers weren't in it. 'My God, you slipped that one in quick.'

'You're so expert. Sometimes I feel like a great clod-hopping oaf.'

'That's because you are.'

'Well, how many?'

She stared a moment. 'Does it matter?'

'Course not. I just wondered. You look so...' I couldn't think of a word to finish the sentence that didn't sound syrupy.

So...what?' She asked

'Untouched.' The saucers clouded over as I rambled happily on. 'You're new-minted. You're so composed and organised. You're so fresh. Sweet's an awful word but that's what you are. Sweet. You even taste it.'

'That's more than you do.' She jabbed me, but the saucers clouded more. 'Untouched?'

'That's right.'

'I'm not a virgin.'

'Don't be daft.'

She went on in a phoney French accent, giggling at her own wit. 'I muzz be perfectly frank wiz you m'sieur. Zere was zhust the man I lived with in New York before I met you and ze man who took my 'onour when I was drunk one night.'

'Two?'

'M'sieur is a genius wiz figures.'

'Only two?'

'Hm.'

'That's perfect. A twenty-one-year-old female who's stunning and only had two fellers.'

She giggled. 'And the other hundred-and-fifty-three in between, of course.'

'If you looked like the back of a bus I could understand, but - you. It's unbelievable.'

I considered this paragon; she contrived to be simultaneously experienced and innocent; to have her life organised brilliantly, without effort; she must have dealt with years of male approaches yet she had given herself to me at once. The implicit flattery was enormous. I laughed and regarded her with admiration. 'Only two. Blimey.'

'What about you?'

'Oh, loads. Like to hear about them?'

'No, thank you.'

She was light. She was fragrant. She was undemanding, except about some of my more uncouth habits, which she coolly censured and I willingly abandoned. The only snag in this delicious, uncomplicated fun was getting up at two or three a.m. to take her home from Robert's. It was only half a mile or so, but a director draped over two rows of stalls and gently snoozing after lunch next day wasn't conducive to productive rehearsals.

One evening we sat in the bath facing each other. She looked beautiful and ridiculous wearing only her glasses and a towel knotted round her head. Her perfect body glistened at me and her mouth was faintly puckered in a smile that seemed always to be there. Actually, she wasn't perfect: it was a source of permanent anguish to her that she didn't have long slim legs nor the height to be an *haute couture* model. Solid Italian hips and thighs, inherited from her father presumably, had made sure that her modelling work would always be primarily photographic. She had a good, round, well-developed bum and that was it. However, she wasn't reconciled, even though she was sitting happily on it at this moment.

I grinned back at her little smile. 'Would you marry me?'

She regarded me for some while, while I wondered what had made me do that. 'You'll have to ask me properly.'

'You mean you want me to go down on one knee or something?'

'You can't say, "would you marry me?" That's conditional. That means, "Would I, if you were to ask me?"'

We went back to bed. 'All right, then. Will you marry me?'

'Yes, please. What will Mummy say?'

———

Mummy sniffed and said 'I should have thought you could have done better than that,' then didn't speak to Christine for weeks. Father and I later shuffled and smiled stiffly at each other across the living room. Italian fathers are not casually told of the impending matrimony of their daughters like most Anglo-Saxons, so when Christine asked me to for his sake, I put myself and Vic through the motions. His name was Luigi Vecchione but he was known to the restaurant world as Vic. When I say the restaurant world, I mean of course, the other side of the kitchen doors.

'Please may I marry your daughter, Christine, sir,' I said dutifully and with punctilious accuracy.

'Yes, yes, would you like a cup of tea. Oh, no, we'd better have a drink hadn't we?' He called to his wife. 'Fancy a nice drink, dear? Celebration.'

———————

I sat in the kitchen of my parents' house as my mother ironed.

'I've got something to tell you, Mum.'

'You're going to get married.'

'How did you know?'

'I just did. What's she like?'

'Lovely.'

'I'm sure she is if you chose her.'

'I've got a feeling she chose me.'

'I hope you'll be very happy.'

'We will. We are.'

'Good. You know, when you were little I always felt like a hen who'd hatched out a duck's egg and now…well, I always knew you'd do something with yourself, but I never thought of you writing plays. I suppose we must make allowances.'

It was one of the longest speeches I ever heard her make.

My father was considerably more loquacious. He ended a lot of rambling reminiscences with 'That play of yours, you know, it brought your mother and me very close together.' I squirmed with guilt as he overplayed the scene. Affectionate though he certainly was, he had no idea how to cope with his emotions nor, as far as I could see, with any aspect of his life. Reality and he were virtual strangers. He grew heavily confidential. 'Closer than we've been for years.' He engineered one of those sudden, unnatural switches of mood that seemed necessary to him. It carried heavy overtones of deeply-felt but unspecified emotions that he wanted you to see he was struggling with. 'Well,' bright smile, 'when are we going to meet her, eh, old son? You bringing her down to meet the old folks? Not too ashamed of us?'

Oh, Mum and Dad, Dad and Mum. Dad in a brown trilby, walking across the cow field from Falconwood station when I was eleven, pushing my first, big, straight-handlebar bike, with a huge grin on his face, sharing my joy as I detached myself from a football game and ran, shrieking at the treasure in his hand; Mum holding me aged four when I stood on my bed terrified, unable to breathe from whooping cough; both of them squabbling about something, almost anything, but especially about my brother, Jack, and me. Mum defending us from Dad's rages, not that he was dangerous, just lost. Our semi-detached in Welling, named Jackter after their sons. Dad breathing stertorously over some repair in the loft as I went mad with boredom holding his tools, then blaming me for the hole he banged in the bathroom ceiling;

throwing himself across us in the living-room shelter when a German bomb exploded (that shelter, a monstrous affair built of stolen railway sleepers and our piano, must have made us the best-protected people outside the underground, war-cabinet room. When bombs landed nearby the piano-strings hummed in harmony). Mum walking down the road, loaded with two shopping baskets, and I, pausing in the inevitable game of street football to note with merciless, juvenile eyes that she no longer walked like a young woman. Mum tying labels onto Jack, aged eleven, and me, aged seven, on evacuation day, giving no sign of her fears. She handed us a stamped, addressed card with the message, 'Dear Mum and Dad, arrived safe and well, love Jack and Terry,' already written on it.

'Put the address where they send you on this,' she told us, 'and then put one kiss if it's nasty and I'll come and take you away. Put two kisses if it's all right and three if it's nice. That'll be our code. We'll have a code like the secret service.'

We were thrilled to pieces.

She walked us under a canopy of barrage balloons to the bus. 'You'll go on a steam train, much more fun than boring old electric,' she said, still making it all fun, and, as seven hundred yelling, excited children were puffed out of the station to adventure, stood smiling and waving in a crowd of smiling, waving mums. I don't remember seeing a single tear, but Mum told us later she went home and sobbed.

'You'll go over my works. Lean out on the left side and wave and I'll wave back,' said railway-employee Dad. 'I know where you're going. Don't worry, you'll love it there,' and he winked heavily.

He could never have guessed how right he was. Jack and I landed up in a Welsh platelayer's cottage in Cornwall, with a cat by the hearth, a canary in a cage, hens outside and a pig in the linney. Express trains roared by the garden and Uncle Jack and Auntie Rose became our second parents for three years while their own grown-up children fought in the war. Three days after our departure the postcard landed on Mum and Dad's mat. Jack and I had ringed it with kisses. Mum still turned up unannounced in Cornwall a week later, just to make sure.

Mum and Dad: the Amateur Boxing Association, South of England, Welterweight Champion and female drummer in a jazz band who met in the nineteen twenties, got it wrong, and stuck together for their two sons and perhaps for more that I didn't understand. I wrote that play from love, but, yes, I was ashamed of you at some point, as I searched for my own identity.

———————

Christine and I were married in Caxton Hall on twenty-eighth August 1963, while a quarter of a million people marched in Washington behind Martin Luther King and civil rights. 'I have a dream,' he cried. Well, so did we. It was, as they say, a smashing day.

29

The night before, Robert took me out for what he called 'your farewell dinner,' in an Italian restaurant called Pompeii. Two attractive girls dressed in what looked like tennis togas had ministered to us invitingly.

'Look what you're giving up, you madman.' Robert was staring hungrily at the one who had just delivered two plates of spaghetti by forehand.

'Ah, but look what I'm getting.' My mood was serene.

'Good God, man, don't think like that. You're not just gaining a wife, you're losing the whole sex.'

Not the faintest tremor of pre-marital doubt crossed my mind. Everything was right. I hadn't fallen desperately for Christine as for Wiekie and been Racked with Love. Christine quietly, but quickly, took me over and that was that, like a car's cooling system silently filled with water. I could peer into the radiator cap and see the gentle trickle out of the overflow showing that every remote bend of piping was flush. I thought contentedly of the last four months.

We had met in May, I had proposed - properly - in June. Then, quite suddenly, she left me for two weeks. 'It's one of those modelling jobs that come up out of the blue, thank God,' she had said. In Majorca this time. To say I was lonely and distraught for a fortnight would be nonsense but it was a shock to realise how grey were the days that loomed. Even my attempt to take her to the airport, to put off our farewell, was foiled. She told me she was obliged to go on the unit transport that would pick her up from her parents'. Her absence was palpable; deliciously agonising to savour my brief loneliness. Whatever had I done with myself, I wondered, before she came into my life? Then, suddenly, the mini-ordeal was over. She was back, tanned and fresh, and we booked the registrar and looked for a place to live.

The flat just off Baker Street was a snip: £7.10.0 a week plus £2.10.0 for rates and we had to buy some useless lino and curtains for about £100, which broke us. Presents rolled in including a munificent cheque from Oliver for £50; the accompanying note said 'Returnable on divorce.' It bought a Knole sofa. Suddenly I was a property owner. I owned half a fitted, Cyril Lord, rubber-backed carpet; half a double bed; half a table; two of four ten shilling kitchen chairs; half of Robert's ancient fridge that didn't work; and half a set of ornate cutlery that had little scraped, bare patches in the plate where Vic had filed off the words 'Dorchester Hotel;' except that I no more thought of owning half of those things than I thought of owning half of Park Lane. They were ours. Those reassuring words, 'ours' and 'we', had become part of my life. We examined our new, empty flat a week before the wedding.

'It's a mess. Where do we start?'

'Easy. Sling out the rubbish and paint it all white.'

'But I can't paint.'

'You dip the brush in that and slosh it on that. Come on.'

30

The bare flat was transformed into a glistening white cave as actor friends who couldn't afford wedding presents were coerced by Christine into taking a wall each. Light-voiced, light-natured, choosy Christine showed a practical turn that left me stumbling, admiring and happy, in her wake. Vic laid fresh kitchen lino with a skill that I had thought confined to craftsmen. Even Babs, Christine's mother, got caught up in the enthusiasm and, when not standing in the middle of the place directing work that was progressing of its own volition, heaved her arthritic frame to the sewing machine and lined curtains.

'I'm not living with unlined curtains,' Christine had said firmly.

My mother produced sheets and utensils, junk shops were raided for thirty-shilling bits and pieces that immediately disappeared under two coats of white eggshell. Our flat, furnished with junk and the Knole stood glowing and stylish on the eve of our wedding. It wasn't that Christine had more energy than anyone I'd ever met, she just made everything simple.

She found for the wedding a white dress in which she had modelled and a white picture hat. She look pure and ravishing. 'Hypocrite,' I whispered and she giggled at the Registrar, a man who had assumed episcopal reverence to compensate for his laity. Outside Caxton Hall was an army of photographers. I stared at them, confused. 'I didn't realise the Director of Bromley Rep. was so newsworthy,' I muttered, flicking confetti from my Hector Powe best blue barathea, final relic of the years of men's tailoring. It had already been up the aisle on Ivor's back.

'It's not for you, soppy.' She was still giggling. 'I'm international fashion mudhole, Christine Vecchione, didn't you know? They always like a picture of some crumpet.'

International fashion model, Mrs. Frisby, and I went back to the less-than-jet-set, rent-controlled flat of her parents into the arms of her horde of Italian aunts and uncles. I would never have thought a wedding could be such fun. My father's verbal diarrhoea seemed like constipation in the cascade of Italian dysentery, and my mother cried, full of gin and emotion. Christine's Auntie Nancy from Tottenham hugged the world and, fixing me with a glare that would have left the Ancient Mariner comatose, told me earnestly, repeatedly and superfluously how lovely Christine was. She moved on to my mother, who simultaneously and no less fervently told Nancy how lovely I was. They reached agreement on the main points and I remember them, arms round each other, crying with joy at what lovely spouses their favourites had found. As a finale, each assured the other what a lovely person the other was, and if anyone had produced a razor they would have become blood sisters on the spot. Good old Auntie Nancy, she went through Mum's reserve, acquired over thirty-five years of marriage, like a laser.

Christine and I drove off in my parents' car with all sorts of rubbish tied to the back and the windows open.

In the queue of rush-hour traffic going out of West London it started to rain and we wound up the windows to discover various witticisms lipsticked onto them. Grinning drivers gave way with a toot, and the petrol pump attendant where I stopped to wipe the windows clean gave us a free gallon. The whole world was a smile.

We had four days. Over breakfast next morning at the Montague Arms, Beaulieu, we stared, impressed, at our pictures in all the popular papers (we propped them up on the table but nobody recognised us) sharing the front pages with shots of that awe-inspiring march in Washington. Then we went to Bournemouth for the rest of what the papers called our 'secret destination honeymoon.' Bournemouth? Well, John Slater was appearing there in summer season; I wanted to persuade him to play Bert Mann in my production of *The Subtopians*. He seemed to me ideal.

'You've brought me to bloody Bournemouth for my bloody honeymoon just so that you can see a bloody actor?' protested Christine amiably.

'He's not a bloody actor. I could build a strong cast with him as the centre-pin.'

'Bloody hell.'

Every hotel in Bournemouth was full. We searched Branksome, Poole, Corfe and Wareham and found ourselves entering Swanage; I dived out of the car for the ninety-second time. 'Have you got a double room with a double bed?' I asked the proprietor of the Melton Lodge Guest House.

'We've got a double room with two single beds,' I was primly told.

'Fine, we can shove 'em together.'

Under the disapproving eye of a formidable Scottish landlady we carted-in our luggage.

'Supper is from 6 to 6.45,' she informed us in a medley of pure, Edinburgh vowels and crisply articulated consonants. 'We have mostly married couples,' a disbelieving glance at our bright new rings, 'with young children. They like to eat early.'

'Fine, we have to go out.'

We appeared at 6.45 to find her tapping her foot in the empty dining room; a sulky waitress lurked.

'The kitchen's waiting to go.'

I refrained from asking where. 'But you said 6 to 6.45. It's not quite 6.45.'

'Aye, but that's the finishing time, not the off.'

After the meal I approached her in the hall. 'We're going to the theatre in Bournemouth. We'll be late back. Do we need a key?'

'Och, no. Lots of our guests go to the theatre and are late back. We'll be up.'

'And we'd like morning tea in our room, please.'

'Fine.'

After a promising meeting with Slater we returned at 11.30 to find the place locked and dark. We rang and knocked until the landlady appeared, fearsome in night attire.

'What time d'you call this?'

'I said we'd be late.'

'Aye, but I didnae think you'd be *this* late.'

We were woken by a knock the next morning.

'Come in.'

The sulky waitress from the previous evening sidled in, averting her eyes from the sinful mess before her. She put down the tea and shot out. We made it down to breakfast just in time to get our cold toast and congealed eggs, sullenly served.

Back in our room Christine said, 'Sod this for a game of soldiers,' took a handful of confetti that had been stuffed into a suitcase and threw it round the room. She propped up our newspaper photos, strategically. 'Come on, let's go out. It's lovely.'

That evening small boys had placed the fire bucket outside our door and chalked, 'Danger man at work' on it. Fresh flowers graced our room. As the children giggled, couples smiled indulgently at us in the dining-room and husbands who had been eyeing Christine with covert lechery now felt able to meet her eyes with open approbation. On our table was a half-bottle of claret with flowers and a card, "With the Compliments of the Management." The sullen waitress had metamorphasised into a rosy-cheeked, country girl, still silent, but now with obvious goodwill. Her silence finally exploded the following morning when she brought our tea in giggling, blushing confusion, peeping goggle-eyed at the pushed-together single beds, clearly a talking-point below stairs. The certainty that the figures before her had been at it with legal sanction seemed to be a great comfort.

As soon as supper was over Christine ran upstairs to get something as I backed out of the barrage of benevolence. We were off for another meeting with John Slater, who'd been re-reading the play. I was waylaid in the hall by the landlady. She approached me sideways, like an assassin edging through a crowd. I hoped Christine would be quick.

'You'll be going to the theatre in Bournemouth again?'

'Yes.'

'Here's your key.'

'Oh, thank you.' I was backed-up between a clothes stand and a table bearing postcards with views of Swanage.

'If you'd told me you were newly-weds I'd 've made allowances.' The one-woman pincer movement continued; she nudged me in the ribs with a force that made me blink and brought her lips close to my ear. 'If you'd tipped me the wink you could have had breakfast in bed.' Then she dissolved, if I may use the word about such a substantial being, into repressed mirth.

Later that evening John Slater made up his mind. He said no.

Ever since we had met, Christine had paved my life with pleasantness, but earlier that day I was given a very different glimpse of her, one that perhaps should have set warning bells ringing but did not. We were driving along the coast road. 'Let's go to Shell Bay and make love,' I said. 'It's baking. It'll be lovely in the dunes.'

She stared ahead, lips suddenly set. 'You've been there before.'

'Of course. How d'you think I know about it? '

'I mean with a girl. You had her there.'

'Yes. I discovered the place when I was touring two years ago. She was nice.' I added insensitively.

'I don't want to go there.'

'Why ever not?'

'You'll be thinking of her.'

I laughed. 'Why on earth should I think of her?'

'You're thinking of her now.'

'That's because you brought her up.'

'That's right, it's my fault. It was me who screwed her in the sand.'

This was getting beyond me. 'Why does "where" matter? If you're going to worry about my past, it's not "where" it's "who." And I don't mean the female, I mean *me*: the only constant factor. Wherever I did it, or who with come to that, it was *my* body, my choice, *my*self.'

'Don't. I can't bear it.' She started to cry, then shook with sobs. 'It's insupportable.'

I was lost in this torrent of emotion. 'Well, you've done it, too.'

'That's got nothing to do with it.' She was crying too much for me to take that up.

'Anyway, they've all gone now, all my exes and both yours.'

We went up onto the downs instead of the beach, on soft turf among gorse and ragwort with soft, chalky outcrops reminding me of the white walls of our new home. She said in a broken voice, 'I love you, I love you, I love you so much.'

'Well, that's no tragedy, is it?'

'I don't like feeling like this. Out of control. I like being in charge.'

I laughed. 'In charge? I've never seen anyone so in charge of everything and everyone round them.'

'D'you think so?' She looked instantly pleased, her change of tone so total that had I asked an actress to do that in rehearsal she would have objected to it being glib.

'I should think I do. Look at what you've done to our flat.'

'You, too.'

'Unskilled labour. It's your creation.'

'D'you like it?'

'I just love it.'

'So do I. But I hate where we're staying.'

'Oh, they're sweet now, thanks to you.'

'No, not them. The place; plaster ducks and Swanage. When I saw it I thought, "My God, is this what I've condemned myself to; plaster ducks for life?" '

I stared. 'We don't know each other at all, do we? You're a blinking snob.'

'That's right.'

'OK. I'll take care of the culture, you see to the decor, and we'll have white walls and elegance for life.'

'I didn't think you'd noticed.'

'I notice everything.'

'Arf-arf.'

My 'I notice everything' became an affectionate, binding catchphrase between us that highlighted my blindness to all things, material or emotional, outside the private world of my imagination. It emphasised my utter trust in her and reliance on anything she did on our behalf, as I floated along with her. Her snobbery was easy, I understood that at once, probably shared it in my own way. But her earlier, sudden, passionate jealousy was alien to me; it was unreal and utterly unreasonable, I thought. And the ease with which she apparently threw it off camouflaged it. I soon learned that Christine was one of nature's chameleons, taking on the colours of those round her the moment she thought her own feelings inappropriate or inadequate.

Chapter V

1963-4

Christine suggested a wedding party for those we hadn't invited to the wedding.

'What for?' I was worried. 'We can't afford it.'

'Wedding presents,' she muttered, poring over her address book. 'If we lash out on a few bottles of plonk, we'll make a terrific profit. Who do you know who can afford a present?'

About a hundred guests surged up the stairs and couldn't get into our flat because of the crush. Drinks were passed out. Good wishes and gaily wrapped presents were passed in. Christine made her profit and I was mildly surprised at the people who turned up from her list. No sign of warm Italian relations here. These people were smarter than the working actors I knew, but without their breadth; hairdressers, models, photographers; they were infinitely more worldly but, to me, lacking. I didn't care for them, their views and values were not mine; inadequate, I then thought, and materialistic. It did not occur to me that the differences between her friends and mine could have expressed differences between us that were, as yet, concealed. I was still naive and unworldly, even at thirty. Literature, poetry and drama were no substitutes for living; years of tailoring and rep had left gaping holes in my education. Cavities overdue for a course of painful fillings.

My first teleplay, *Guilty*, was scheduled to go out one Sunday evening as BBC Play of the Month, it was an anti-hanging play. My parents bought a TV set especially to see it, but it must have got the worst audience figures ever; it was transmitted against ITV's *Sunday Night At The Palladium* which featured a new pop-group called the Beatles. Christine and I watched the Beatles, we had seen my play in studio. The next day I was asked to go into BBC TV Centre where I saw Vincent Tildesley, the script editor who had commissioned my first play.

'Sydney's crazy about your play. He's sent a memo round telling everyone that this is what powerful, contemporary, relevant TV drama should be.' He grinned. 'Sydney gets these sudden enthusiasms.'

I wondered whether Sydney Newman's enthusiasm was real or the action of a Head of Drama covering up for the hiding ITV must have given him in the ratings the night before.

'He wants to commission you to do a full-length one this time.' Full-length meant seventy-five or ninety minutes as opposed to the fifty minutes of *Guilty*. 'You can write what you like. He said so.'

This flummoxed me. Like the schoolboy faced with writing an essay on any subject he liked, for me the choice was too wide. I found my ideas melting away. We examined and rejected a few Grand Themes that were powerful, contemporary, etc.

'What about a comedy?' Vincent suggested.

I was nervous. 'I've never done that.'

'*The Subtopians* is a comedy, isn't it?'

'Yes, but it's not supposed to be funny.'

'Do us a nice romantic comedy with a bit of gloss and glamour instead of all this significant gumph.' He kicked a large pile of scripts with a bored foot. This was heresy in the BBC Drama Department at that time.

'I couldn't do a romantic comedy, but I'll do an anti-romantic one. How's that?' Heresy appealed to me for its own sake, and I had an idea already germinating.

'Fine.'

'About a guy who's got everything; education, money, looks, super job, is terrific with the birds, but is just going over the top. And a little bird who's got nothing and gives him his come-uppance. A real anti-male play.'

'Excellent. What'll we call it? Just a working title.'

'Oh, anything.' I thought of Ivor. '*Mr. Danvers' Downfall.* How's that?'

'I hope the play is better than that title.'

A BBC contract for £250 arrived from my agent. I phoned him. 'I got this for my last play.'

'Ah, did you - er - where's your file...?'

'I told you Newman was mad about it; that this was to be at least one-and-a-half times as long and you've accepted £250 on my behalf without even contacting me.'

'Er, yes, well it seemed like a fair offer. I'll look into it, though, if you feel—'

'Forget it. Goodbye.'

So I had no agent. After weeks of negotiation and an eyeball-to-eyeball confrontation with their Assistant Head of Copyright, I got a good deal more out of the BBC. I was in no hurry, I was busy directing at Bromley. Getting him to raise the price was like nudging an elephant with vertigo towards the edge of a cliff. He unbelted at a fiver a time once we had got past £700. At £725 I gave up, exhausted but satisfied.

The days followed sweetly on. Christine got a reasonable string of modelling bookings and I was a commuter from Baker Street to Bromley, travelling against the rush-hour tide, which beat working at Selfridges and doing it the other way round.

If I was home first the place seemed unbearably empty till the bell went to announce that Christine had started the four-floor climb. On Sundays we lay in bed, devouring the *Observer, The Sunday Times*, each other and the lunches that Christine seemed to will to appear. One Sunday we leaned from the bedroom window, eating fruit and choking as firemen fought a fire in a flat below us. Blazing furniture came hurtling out of the windows to smash onto the pavement.

'You'd better come out of there,' yelled a fireman.

'Not bloody likely. You're not messing up our place,' we yelled back and, delighted at our panache, threw grapes to the crowd.

It was all a delight; heaven to write in night-time peace, then get into bed beside my wife, turn her over and feel her snuggle sleepily into the crook of my arm as I went to sleep in a warm tangle of arms and legs; pleasure to sit, as she cooked or made things, bathed or rubbed cream into her skin; to talk endlessly about my future work.

––––––––––

We had been married a few months when Christine knocked me sideways. The blow was as surprising as it was painful. She lay in bed as I sat on it burbling on about Why I Write and The Important Of Truth In Relationships and similar Issues that concerned me. I think it was my moral ardour that started her off.

'I lied to you, you know. Twice.' she said.

'What?'

'The first lie was about my two affairs. There were more!'

'You mean before you met me? More than two?'

'Yes.'

'But you said there were only two.'

'Yes, I lied.'

'You mean, you lied?'

'I've just said that.'

'You lied?'

'Oh, come on, catch up. Does it matter?'

I was utterly confused. She spoke so casually that the fact that something important was being revealed hadn't percolated. People don't lie to their loved ones; that is to say, liberal, grown-up people don't. That wasn't a belief, it was a certainty. 'Why lie?'

'I thought you wouldn't love me.'

'What a daft idea.'

'No, it's not. Men are funny.'

'I'm not men, I'm me.

'Ha.'

'How many was it, anyway?' I suppose I expected her to say three.

She giggled, 'Seventeen.'

'Seventeen?'

'Seventeen.'

'How many?'

'Seventeen.' She giggled again.

'What's funny?' The chill that had touched my innards at the first 'seventeen' had developed into ice.'

'Sorry, I'm nervous.'

'Bloody Hell, Christine. Seventeen. You told me two.'

'Yes, I thought you'd laugh.'

'What's funny about two?'

'It's trad. Every tart in history. "How many men have you had, my dear?" "Two, m'sieur. Zere wuz just ze man who took away my 'onour when I wuz drunk, zen ze one I loved." Don't you ever go to French films? I thought you were a fanatic.'

'Of course.' Light was filtering into the remoter recesses of my understanding.

'And then you got such a look on your face. You were so surprised and pleased; you hadn't expected that. A virgin would have been too much, almost offensive. But only two: chastity without avarice, I was perfect. And you looked so silly, but lovely. I couldn't spoil it for you so I kept quiet. Then it became important to you; I couldn't bring it up again.' Her eager explanation of how she got trapped fell on deaf ears and she saw it.

'Till now.'

'Till now.' All the colour was gone from her voice.

'Why now?'

'Well, you're always going on about truth in love and being totally honest with each other, and trust and - well, I thought I'd better tell you. It's not my style, but—' she regarded me carefully, then looked wearily down. 'God, I'm such a fool. I shouldn't have told. Not ever. Ever. Ever.' She started hitting a pillow with her fist.

Her external rise in temperature allowed me to let go a little. 'Never mind about you shouldn't have *told* me. You shouldn't have lied in the first place.'

'I should have bitten my tongue off first. Why did I let you persuade me? I've spoiled it all.'

'So you married me under False Pretences.' I must have said it with capital letters then, as I write it now.

'Oh, big words. What does it matter how many I've had?'

'It didn't, to me, but clearly did to you because you *lied*. And your lying matters.'

'I've told you, I lied because I love you.' She was nearly inaudible, her face in a pillow which became smeared with removing cream.

'Rubbish. When you lie to someone it's because you've decided either that you're too scared to tell them the truth or they're not fit to know it. It's cowardice or arrogance. In this case it seems to have been both.'

'You'd have never fallen for me like you did if I'd said seventeen.'

'It would have made no odds.'

'Rubbish. Look at you now.' Her voice rose. 'The man who doesn't feel jealousy. Much. You're shaking. You're riddled with it.'

'No, no, no. It's because you *lied*.' I could feel the resentment rising in my throat; I nearly choked on it. 'You could have kept quiet, said it was none of my business, told me, refused to tell me, anything, but you *lied*.' Even though I've never hit a word harder my voice was still low.

'What about you and all your women?'

'I offered to tell you anything you wanted to know.'

'Did you imagine we'd snuggle down and have cosy chats about your previous girl friends?'

'Why not?' I asked her the question seriously and was surprised at her surprise. I tried to explain myself. 'I'd share anything with you.'

'Like in the pub with the boys? "Good performer that one: nice tits, bit broad in the beam, goes down like the Titanic. Fancy the other half"'

My stomach constricted further. 'Did you?'

'What?'

'Go down? Often?'

She paused only momentarily. 'No. Never.'

I leaped onto her pause. 'Of course you did. You must have. You were expert when we - when you - ' I couldn't get my breath to go on and we just sat. She was immobile, I was panting as though I had just run up the stairs. When she spoke at last her voice was carefully hopeful.

'I told you I lost my virginity when I was sixteen, didn't I.'

'Well?'

'And I was twenty-one when we met.'

'Well?'

'That's not bad. I mean, five years, seventeen fellers.'

She was counting on her fingers, 'I mean, that's only three and two-fifths fellers a year.'

'Three and two fifths...? I don't believe it.'

'Have I got it wrong?' She started counting again.

'I mean, I don't believe this whole conversation.'

She finished her sum triumphantly. 'Yes, less than one every three months.'

My head was stretched forward, tortoise-like with intensity, though my voice was strangled and quiet. 'How the Hell do you get screwed by two-fifths of a feller?'

Christine giggled involuntarily. 'I don't know. Very badly, I should think.'

I ignored my absurdity. 'OK. You said there were two lies. What was the other one?'

'Oh, yes. Well, you know just after you asked me to marry you I had to go straight off to Majorca, modelling.'

'Well?'

'Well, it wasn't a modelling job. I went with a feller.'

I can remember just groaning and rolling round on the bed so that I faced away from her. She went on quickly, 'But I didn't sleep with him.' Silence. 'I didn't really.' I wanted to believe her but heard this as a last-minute withdrawal from a full confession because my reaction of a moment earlier had alarmed her too much. There was nothing I wanted to say. I just stared down into my own blackness. 'Honest, I didn't. But I knew there'd be no trips like that after we got married; not on our money, so I went. He's quite rich and I've known him ages. I've never slept with him. I went to make up the party.' She must have looked at my back for some while then she added, 'I thought you wouldn't like it.' With that unwitting understatement she fell silent.

It is odd, but my memory has my new-found seventeen predecessors as giving me the more pain, when surely the trip to Majorca should have. Perhaps the first image-smashing confession had rendered the second irrelevant. But her last fling - if that is what is was - in Majorca surely must have involved some sort of offering on her part. Air flights and luxury hotels with a man rarely come with no price tag for a beautiful girl. I tried to imagine such an undemanding escort. He was possible if I preferred to think so.

I don't know how long we sat in silence then I said. 'OK, these seventeen fellers.'

'What about 'em?'

'Tell me.'

'Tell you what?'

'Everything.'

It was her turn not to credit her senses. 'You are mad.'

'That's right.'

There followed four quietly murderous days while I dragged every conceivable detail out of her, then went over them, round them, into them, regurgitated them, discussed every aspect of Us, and, and in short, drove us both barmy.

Those few days were quiet only because I didn't trust myself to raise my voice. Me? Jealous? Rubbish. As I sit and read my retrospective description of that event and remember how I felt, it seems almost pathological self-delusion to argue that it was not her actions but only her lies about them that bothered me, yet I believe that to be so in essence. She had presented an image of herself to me. I had accepted it and now she had calmly smashed it. Was my pain about jealousy or illusions? I think the latter. What is it the Bible says? Something like, 'Lay not up treasures on earth for moth and rust doth corrupt.' I had laid up my emotional treasures in sublime security; they were as safe as the Bank of England with Christine. My emotional life-insurance had long been worked out and I had cocooned myself cleverly in the strong-room of my own personal morality; a liberal code that had been worked out to play to my virtues and ignore my vices. Through Christianity, Socialism and Art I had arrived at the shrine of Truth. Tell the truth and all good will follow.

Well, Christine had time-bombed my little moral world into pieces. I felt about lying to one's partner (see how theoretical it all was, it's "one's" not 'my') like Judge Brack did about Hedda Gabler's suicide: 'People simply don't do that.' It didn't occur to me that any survey would show that 99% of the population: lie without inhibition when necessary (and the other 1% are liars); lie about absolutely anything; lie to their loved ones only marginally less than they lie to themselves. And, oh, the blazing banality of it all. What did they matter, those seventeen secret sharers of my Christine? No, of course, fifteen. Two had their credentials already. Who cares what we all did before Mr/Miss Right came along? Me? Jealous? Rubbish. But the lie had to be rooted out and as I learned who, where, how often, I found, under my liberal, free-thinking philosophy an older model buried: prejudiced, male-chauvinist, possessive, suburban, hypocritical, a wholly detestable being. She was supposed to have stylishly managed - well, everything, but especially the men in her single sex life. And if she wasn't the collected person she pretended and who I had married, who was she? I tried to see into her, and withdrew quickly, frightened. Her seventeen had some bruising inclusions; she had given herself to men who fitted every prejudice I had about exploiters of women: some were married, that upset me the most; some rich, who through her were now exploiting socialist me; most, of course, older than she, but a couple far so; one MP (I nearly muttered, 'Thank God,' when she said, 'Labour'); some had been invited to our wedding party and one to our wedding - I had wondered why she had asked me so meekly if I minded that particular person coming.

And to cap it all, as I tried to accustom myself to the idea of her screwing these strangers, so the idea of the other, even more personal, intimacies made my set teeth chatter uncontrollably and my imagination play voyeur to my wife through time and space while I wriggled on this hook she had caused me to swallow. And why had she lied? Because she had thought I wouldn't love her; I was deemed unfit to choose - one of the neatest castration jobs in surgical history. I remember trying to make love to her during those four days; it was an anguished, wild, business in which no amount of effort could root out the sin. I felt fifteen faces in the room with us, watching.

There was an air crash. By some obscene coincidence one of the fifteen was in the list of the dead and I felt a surge of joy, one less; a little more room in our overcrowded, pure, white, pure-white, moral slum. Oh, thank you, thank you damned quaking insecurity that taught me to rejoice in the death of a total stranger.

On the fourth night Christine, who was going to bed, suddenly started re-dressing.

'What are you doing?'

'Going home to Mummy.'

'Oh, really.'

'Nothing I can do, I've told you everything. I can't do any more. It's up to you now.' She started putting on something.

I took it from her. 'That's lovely isn't it. You create the crisis then you deliver the ultimatum.'

'Tough. No good arguing any more. We've covered everything. I've had it. Are you going to let me pass?'

'You sleep there, I'll sleep in the other room, on the sofa.' I managed a brief grin, 'My God, I must have been ghastly if I've driven you back to Mummy.

'You have been.'

'Sorry.'

The next morning we sat at breakfast; brief nervous grins had been exchanged but that was all. She looked at me over her cup, cool and impeccable for a job. The unrepentant effect was shattered by her dismal attempt at a smile. The muscles just wouldn't work properly, and her eyes filled with tears behind her glasses. 'How was the Knole?'

'Too short.'

She tried to arrange her face again. 'Would you sleep with me tonight, please?'

'Ask me properly. Would is conditional.'

The smile spread a bit. '*Will* you sleep with me tonight, please?'

'Yes, please.'

———————

Our reconciliation, as after her outburst of insecurity on our honeymoon, made welcome peace but ignored some new differences that were now visible between us. Nothing was tackled, let alone settled.

The event, for all its sentimental conclusion, sobered and confused me. My ideal of Utter Frankness With Your Loved One was, if not scuttled, at least holed. But the richness and pleasure we were getting from our marriage were worth more than my former sterile ideals. Not that I had properly accepted the episode; it felt unconcluded. Idols and feet of clay spring to mind. Perhaps I was just growing up - rather late.

Anyway, more to the immediate point, I also learned that if I could display so much feeling about Christine's undisclosed affairs (she never accepted that it was only the deceit that upset me) then she, too, could join in the act. She developed a sudden, new-found antipathy to any ex-girlfriend of mine. Surely this was some sort of a defence mechanism, but was it simulated or couldn't she stop herself? I never asked. The Christine who only months before blithely divided the veal cutlets and shared the asparagus with someone she had thought pregnant by me belonged to another era. If we met any female I had known of old, she would whisper, 'Did you?' This became shortened to 'Well?' and finally to a mere raised eyebrow. Anyone about whom I answered, yes, was immediately rejected, thus a friend was lost. I quickly learned to say, no, nearly every time. Hey-ho, lying is easy, really. What had I said to her? Lying is cowardice or arrogance? Either you were afraid to tell me or you have decided I was not fit to know? Well, I decided her reaction was not worthy of her, so I lied. I made her decision for her. Arrogance? Or just learning to live with someone? I don't know. There is a closed symmetry about such self-examination which renders it the pointless exercise that it is.

I discovered another characteristic of hers: she carried a grudge. Christine, the chameleon in all other matters, found it hard to forgive, to shed her resentment about quite minor incidents. I put it down to her being half Italian and used to chide her, 'Ah, come on, darling. We're luckier than them. Let it go, it doesn't matter.' Sometimes she would throw it off in one of her sudden volte-faces but sometimes she just turned half away and growled or stared stonily past me and I knew that particular grievance lay festering. When all the dust has settled there are only two things that bring happiness: to work at something you love and to live with someone you love. The rest is chaff or, at best, decoration on the cake. I had both and was vibrant. At the beginning of my marriage and with my own production of my first play before me, what more could anybody ask?

I became a lunch-time haunter of the Marks and Spencer's in Bromley, opposite the theatre, glancing covertly at bras, knickers and other female apparel, till the shop-assistants began to suspect me. The reason was simple: Marks was covered in photographs of Christine looking primly over spectacles while dressed in thoroughly antiseptic underwear, or pouting in Angora woolly sweaters and boring tweed skirts. There was a 1950s revue number in which a chap carried an advertisement and sang of his love for the girl on it, The Girl In The Maidenform Bra. His love was hopeless, poor sap. Mine wasn't, I was the lucky sap who had married her.

There were further astounding discoveries: Groucho Marx was presenting a new TV quiz programme; Christine was a contestant, asked so that Groucho could bounce some of the famous ad-libs off an attractive female. Groucho did his stuff, she disposed of two antagonists with help from him (he wasn't going to let such a rich source of laughter go), then she was asked the meaning of the word deciduous. Silence. Groucho nearly stood on his head to give it to her, singing *Falling Leaves* and miming feverishly. I sat, amazed. I had married a girl who didn't know the meaning of deciduous. Natural selection is an extraordinary mechanism.

But she wiped the floor with me in other areas: shrewdness, organisation, practicalities. I regarded myself as creative, her creation was our life together. She was an imaginative materialist, tiny events were made a delight. If I shopped it was something done, unremarked. When she did, she produced an Aladdin's cave of shared treats from perfectly ordinary articles. It was an extraordinary talent. Intellectually she was a non-starter, any attempt by her at philosophical inquiry merely made a pattern on the surface of the subject without probing it, and if the shape of the subject didn't fit the pattern the protuberances were ignored or, if possible, removed. Who cared? She filled my life with sweetness. That excruciating sentence is exact. I just laughed and ambled happily along with her. We formed something I would never have thought I could have been half of: a thoroughly conventional, rather-role-playing marriage. We both loathed squabbles, perhaps because of our parents, so gave way simultaneously and instantly on all minor matters; major rows, apart from the one just described, didn't exist. Just being married was a palpably civilised pleasure to both of us. Natural selection wasn't so daft after all; proximity had bred affection. We both had the same rather childish sense of fun. One night she commented that I never brought her flowers; it wasn't said as a complaint and it was correct. I shot out of bed and ran to Regent's Park, climbed the railings at considerable risk to the future generation and returned with a municipal tulip. We kept it in bloom for weeks with care and, eventually, glue.

Chapter VI

1964

Early in 1964 I started rehearsals on *The Subtopians*. Bill Fraser was the name actor who had finally agreed to play Bert Mann. We met, at his request, at the Café Royal for tea. He seemed about to run rather than take this part of a boring man, in a first play, directed by the unknown author, in an outer-London rep company, for peanuts. I don't know which of us was the jumpier. He reared his head like a startled stallion when I said that I wanted an unknown actress, Edna Landor, from the earlier rep production to play his wife. His head went back, his teeth were bared by anxious lips; I expected to see him cantering away down the Café Royal, leaving me, if I wasn't careful, with - yet again - no production of my play. It was no contest; I quickly gave in and Bill accepted Arthur White from the Guildford production. One out of the two that I most wanted wasn't bad. So, at Bill's request, I asked Betty Baskcomb to play his wife, a splendid actress with a sound reputation. Helen Cotterill was to be Arthur's wife, Dot; Mark Kingston and Margo Jenkins the two youngsters, Helen and Tom, originally written for Wiekie and me. We had three whole weeks in which to rehearse. They were a joy.

We opened in March. Two years previously at Guildford I had found my parents white-faced in the back stalls at the first interval. This time, in Bromley, my father turned the event into a state visit. Proprietorially ushering a group of friends, solid-looking railwaymen and their wives, to their seats, my father waved regally to me, then strolled across with agonising slowness, nodding to imagined acquaintances as he passed, to give Christine a casual, lecherous hug and my hand a condescending squeeze. During the intervals he explained to his bemused but impressed guests how the whole play had been built around him. My mother gave us both a hug, and me one of her hopeful smiles with raised eyebrows which indicated that things were all out of control as far as she was concerned; she was just a dinghy, bobbing along in the wake. Only on issues that she regarded as crucial did she put her foot down, and to her, her own feelings were never that.

As soon as the final curtain came down we were back to superlativeland again. Everybody clambered over everybody else to say how wonderful it all was. A local headline with an appealing surfeit of adjectives said, 'A Brilliant, Perceptive, Funny, Moving Play.' What was more relevant was that the

Financial Times gave it a rave and urged someone to take it to the West End. We waited expectantly. Nobody showed the slightest interest.

My opinion of my own production was that although it was thoroughly competent it lacked the fire of George Little's at Guildford. I think, in retrospect, that was due to the absence of Edna Landor. At Guildford she gave Maggie an exterior of armour plate; then, as the play progressed, peeled off layers of it with a reluctance that had you rigid in your seat with pity for the soft-bodied, naked creature she had exposed. It was one of those achievements of character revelation that would have made Cis and Oliver at Central hiss, 'That's it. Don't you see? That's what you're here for. She communicates. The rest is shit.' In fact Oliver had seen her at Guildford and said something similar. When Edna broke down in Act III it was never an actress playing her big scene, it was simply a poor creature who fell apart under the pressures of her life. I longed to see how Bill's comic wreck of a character would have reacted to her steel. He might have been even better than she was. She came in one night to see the Bromley production and I happened to be in too. We sat on opposite sides of the auditorium, watched the stage and both realised what (or rather, who) was missing. Our mutually sad hug at the end was no recompense to her; although there were no recriminations we both knew what the score was. She never got another chance anything like that and left the business early, an unsung, unfamous, but talented, actress.

Sheila Hancock was working at Bromley at that time as guest director, having just finished a long successful London run in a Michael Codron production. She liked *The Subtopians*, was indignant at the indifference of London managements and hauled the unwilling Codron to Bromley. Afterwards he said, 'Sorry, it's too late. It belongs to the fifties,' and left, our last hope. I still believed the play could bridge the decade gap. A few days later, there was a phone call. 'Michael Codron here. I don't know whether you know, but besides my own business, I run the Arts Theatre.' He loved to play himself down to the point of parody. Everybody in the business knew.

'Yes, I had heard whispers.'

'You're very well-informed.' I could almost see a little smirk down the phone. 'We have four weeks free in April, if you'd care to bring your play here.'

'You mean, you'll take it in to town?' I tried to keep calm.

'No, I won't. But you can.'

'I - er - I - don't quite follow - '

'I've told you. The theatre is yours, free for four weeks.' He spoke with ironic distinctness as though I were not too bright.

'Oh. I - er - can I call you back?'

'I'd like an answer soon.'

47

'Yes. OK. Yes.'

'What?'

'The answer is yes. I'll take it.'

The Arts Theatre wasn't the West End, technically, but it was everything else that I had been aiming for, namely to get my work where it mattered, into London, the middle; to get it reviewed and evaluated by the business. My vague dreams of a long commercial run and riches, always fragile, burst and were no loss. I worked out that £1,000 would cover all possible losses for the four weeks. Bromley couldn't and wouldn't risk anything. Codron wouldn't. I became a producer. Robert invested £200. I went to each of the six producers who had originally wanted to buy the play at Guildford. Tiny Oscar Lewenstein, almost hidden by the vast desk over which he peered like a benevolent Mr. Chad, gave me £150.

'I'll send you an investment contract,' I said.

He smiled. 'Never mind that. Just give me my £150 back if you make any money.'

John Gale, Jack Minster and one who I have ungratefully forgotten gave me £100 each. Peter Bridge managed £50. £300 short. The only person I knew who had so much was my mother, savings from twenty years of cashiering at Dickins and Jones. She handed it over without hesitation.

So into London we came on April 14th 1964. The date is relevant. My 1950s-social-realist piece was listed at the Arts between *The Formation Dancers* by Frank Marcus and *Entertaining Mr. Sloane*, Joe Orton's first bobbydazzler. The first night went well enough, back at the flat we were on a high and there was enough to drink, so when somebody suggested we wait up for the papers (obtainable at 4 a.m., Leicester Square) it seemed like a good idea. I was used to rave notices, indeed, was coming to expect them. The papers were eventually produced and read and it was all over. The general critical condemnation wasn't vicious, merely patronising or dismissive. The marks were about six or seven out of ten. 'Has tried hard,' ' can write dialogue,' 'will probably do better next time,' ' should write out 100 times, "I must not crib from other boys in the class like Wesker, Shaffer, Bolt."' *The Times* and *Financial Times* remained loyal to their earlier compliments and the actors all came out of it well, especially Bill. Christine suddenly ushered everybody out and sent me to bed. She said after, that my face went grey, like old, badly-cooked beef. The London public stayed away in their millions and when the final tally was added up, or should I say subtracted down, I had lost more than the £1,000 I had raised.

I was in the Arts Theatre adding up the bills when Michael Codron asked me to have coffee with him. It was my first chance to have a good look at this rather awe-inspiring figure who was only a year or two older than I. The Royal Court, Joan Littlewood and others had changed the face of British

Theatre, but it was Michael who had brought the exciting new work actually into the middle-class, middle-aged, middle-brow West End. Without big budgets, big stars and ballyhoo he had given chances to a string of actors, directors and playwrights who became sleek-headed and successful. He and Lewenstein were the only producers whose taste and courage I had any respect for, but it was Michael who was of my generation. I was excited just to be connected with him, however tenuously.

I sat at his desk and studied him. He was immaculate, with thick, black, shiny hair and well-fed hamster cheeks. Everything he did was smooth and tasteful; he loved the pause technique I had been first subjected to by Oliver; he was very feline and even charmed you like a cat, picking you up and dropping you during a meeting with a cat's apparent indifference. He would try an idea or unexpected comment on you as he looked out of the window, then would turn, looking quite vulnerable, amused at his own wit, to catch your exposed reaction. He practically never sat, but moved about restlessly, making notes and phone calls on his feet; often staring out of the window. He always claimed to be insecure, but if he was, the word has no meaning; we all are, that much.

Early on he did something that was utterly captivating. We were talking about an actor he had cast in something whose ability was something of a joke in the profession. Michael at first tried to defend his choice on artistic grounds, but saw my expression. He let a smile of supreme charm and lechery slide over his face before looking slyly sideways and down, under his lashes. 'He is *very* pretty though, isn't he.'

I loved Michael from that moment on. 'I wouldn't know,' I said.

'Well, I'm telling you.' He gave me a brief sparkle then went and looked out of the window, pleased with himself, at his candour with a hetero near-stranger; self-mockery was one of his better assets. He once translated, "Je suis un peu fatigue" as, "I am a little stout poof."

Michael turned back from the window, the fun and games over. 'How much have you lost?' He did a nice line in restrained concern, the face and tone of a man who took money seriously.

'All I had, and some.'

'Hm. Pity. It was a good play. It was too late, though.'

'So you said.'

'It was already too late, two years ago at Guildford.'

'So you said then, I gather.'

He pursed his lips, faintly enjoying my ruefulness, like a parent with a child who has hurt itself, but not enough to give concern. 'You must allow me the pleasure of saying I told you so.'

'Must I?'

'It must have been good to have survived all that it has.' He smiled a little more warmly, but I wasn't in the mood for salves. He went on staring at me for some while then he stuck his chin out in a mini-gesture of decisiveness. The self-parody was unintentional. 'Send me your next play and I'll do it.' And he abruptly dismissed me.

———————

Back in Bromley I stared moodily at the posters of a new thriller by Philip Levene. He had created, among other things, *The Avengers*, and was one of the highest-paid television writers in the country. He came up to me and started pumping my hand, waxing enthusiastic about *The Subtopians*. He said he wished he had written it and I offered to swop it for his income. He was astonished that I hadn't made anything from writing. 'Who's your agent?'

'Haven't got one.'

'Come on. Let's see mine.'

———————

Harvey Unna ran the best TV and radio literary agency in the country, though his theatrical clients were less aggressively successful than those in the electronic field. After he had seen 'Subbers' he said 'I'll handle all your new work but none of that stuff you've been pushing round already. Shop-soiled.'

'OK. Fine.'

'What about teleplays?'

'I've had one done and I'm writing another for the BBC when I get some time.'

'Now's the time.'

'I'm busy. I've got this job: resident director at Bromley.'

'What do you want to be, a director or a writer?'

There wasn't too much doubt about that. 'I'll have to give a couple of months' notice.'

'I'll make you some appointments with script editors. You must make some money.'

Chapter VII

1964-5

Being a full-time writer was torture. It isn't facing that much maligned blank sheet of paper at nine a.m. that is The Writer's Rack, but peering into the void between your own ears. You are brought face to face with the poverty of your imagination all day, every day; and it is not a pretty sight. I no longer had the escape hatches of a rep job, a few days filming, a play to direct. I had sentenced myself. I walked Christine daily to work at the wholesale house whose new range she was modelling (it briefly delayed the ghastly moment), came back to the flat, stared blankly at the current piece of work, then gave a guilty start as I realised I had wasted half the morning. As I shaded my eyes to stare across the Sahara of my imagination, or peered into the corners and angles of the sterile white walls that surrounded me, I would start working out how much rent it was costing us just for me to sit working out how much rent it was costing us.

'I can't go on,' I said sepulchrally. 'It's the insecurity of living in a flat. We must buy a house.'

'Lovely,' said Christine. 'I'll live in W1, SW1, SW3 or SW7.'

A Victorian terraced house in SW15 turned up for £3,750 and Wandsworth Borough Council gave 100 per cent mortgages, which was just as well because we had no money and building societies did not advance loans to freelance writers and models. We took possession on the same day in October 1964 that Harold Wilson first moved into 10 Downing Street.

16 Bective Road, Putney (just), had real charm: the front looked north past a steam laundry that thumped all day. The interior heaved with dry rot; the cellar smelled as though something unspeakable would rush out from between the brick piles, but the back trumped all that. Roses climbed up the south-facing kitchen wall and framed the door. The window of the back bedroom that became my study looked over our garden on to an oasis: trees, grass, flowers, an area of some two or three verdant acres between the London stock bricks. We had our own apple tree. Children played, people weeded, all was suburban peace except for the distant thump of the steam laundry and, when the wind was in the west - which was most of the time - the scream of the jets that went over every ninety seconds. I used to dream of installing a machine-gun nest in the loft to bring them flaming down into Putney High Street like JU 88s.

We loved that house and each other in it. Although we were still broke, gone was the neurotic counting of the time I wasted at my new desk. Instead, I wasted it staring happily out of my study window, watching the plants grow and listening to the caressing sounds of Christine moving about below. But the work started to flow. Her diaphragm failed to do its job, this was still pre-pill time, and she got pregnant. But neither of us wanted a child yet, so she had an abortion. It was, though still theoretically illegal, easy to arrange. Oh, we intended to have children all right, but we would choose when and how many. That was our (arrogant?) attitude when we were young and confident of our continuing fecundity.

I got a job for two-and-a-half days a month as presenter on a new-style children's programme called *Playschool*. It paid for the installation of central heating and got me away from the desk to recharge the imagination. TV commissions and some money started to appear in our lives. We acquired a rattling box-on-wheels, an old Ford Popular, and a white poodle from a couple who had separated. Minnie was sybaritic and timid; she attached herself firmly to whichever one of us looked like staying indoors. Golf became my principal pastime; the Sunday-morning dawn patrol was the week's high spot, with Minnie as an unwilling companion. Striking off into melting mist or frost at Wentworth, making the first footprints in sparkling dew across an unswept green, or watching the, as yet, unscarred ball soar in low-angled sunlight and drop against a background of sky and trees banished the pain of writing.

I had gone full circle from Subtopia to Subtopia. The flame of Art burned on, but comfort and happiness meant that it warmed rather than scorched. So it was for a year. Only a recurring fantasy about a little man in bowler hat and raincoat disturbed my peace. It demonstrated the insecurity I felt about writing for a living, in spite of the solid appearance that life was taking on. The fantasy always started with a knock on the door one day while I was working. As Minnie barked her way timorously down the hall I would answer it. There was The Man in the Bowler Hat. He had the sort of accent that belongs only to petty officialdom, full of nasal, repetitive inflections. 'Good morning, Mr. Frisby, do you own this house?'

'Yes, we do, subject to the mortgage.'

'And how do you pay that?'

I smirked. 'I write; plays, you know. Telly, things like that.'

Unlike the remainder of the population, this man was unimpressed. 'Could I see, please?'

'Certainly,' and I would show him the red and blue children's exercise books into which everything went in my scrawled longhand. I write on every other line, then cross out and write on the lines in between, then vertically down the margins, sometimes in pencil with ink corrections, the effect is as though a mortally wounded spider, dipped in various dyes was searching for a final resting place.

With pursed lips, the man would flick disparagingly through these squalid objects. 'Who pays you for these?'

'Well, you know, the BBC, ITV.'

'And you've bought this house, a car, you feed and clothe yourselves, you even have a dog and play golf...' His voice would have a rising inflection. '...from *these*?' And between forefinger and thumb he would dangle an offending exercise book before me like a livid schoolmaster presented with inadequate homework.

'Well - er - yes,' hands behind back, feet shuffling, the fourth-form re-born. 'My wife earns a bit, too.' He would give a mirthless snigger and shake his head.

'You must realise, Mr. Frisby, there's been some mistake.'

'Well, yes, I do see...'

'You've got to give it back.' His voice held the empty regret of a man who gets full job satisfaction. 'And I've come to take it.'

'Oh. Yes. OK. I'm sorry if I've caused any trouble. No dishonesty was intended.'

'And none taken. You'll be out today, won't you?'

'Yes, of course.'

'Leave the car keys. Good morning.' And I, humiliated, would be out on the pavement with Minnie and our belongings, to explain to Christine that my ability had been a sham all along. I was not aware that this fantasy, along with others that I much preferred, was capable of becoming real.

I dreamed many variations both waking and sleeping, but the contents of the exercise books went well. Gwen Watford became TV Actress of the Year for being in one of my telescripts and then the script was nominated for Best TV play. The award was rightly won by something else. Bread-and-cheese work, even if well-carpentered, shouldn't get into award lists.

And what of my progress as '...the major realistic dramatist we have all been waiting for...' (*The Times* 28.3.62)? As I went from one TV script-editor to another, trying to earn a living, flogging my wares like any other respectable salesman, I occasionally threw in ideas that I thought might make stage plays. If I could get TV to pay me for writing what might be a draft for a stage play, that seemed a sound policy. And that is what accidentally happened with *Mr Danvers' Downfall*, the anti-romantic comedy I have already mentioned. When I had finished the TV script I realised it smelled of theatre and, particularly, Shaftesbury Avenue.

'Would you come in and see, me please,' said a stranger's voice on the phone.

I presented myself at BBC TV centre to Roger Smith, who had taken over as script editor on Theatre 625 from Vincent Tildesley. 'You see, the fact is, we want powerful, searching stories that have relevance to the lives of our viewers *today*.' He obviously hated my piece.

'Vincent asked me to do a comedy.' I said, remembering Sydney Newman's memo about me.

'So I gather.'

'Can't comedies be searching and relevant?' I was only arguing for the sake of forcing him to say he thought my play was a stinker. There is a polite, rather formal game that is played throughout the business and is ignored less often than you would think. The basic rule is, if you think a play, performance or production is rotten, you may say so to anyone except the perpetrator. Life would quickly become intolerable without this rule. It is a bit like infidelity; the spouse is always last to know. My income depended on this meeting. I continued, 'In fact I thought it was a function of comedy.'

'Well, yes, but this is so glossy.'

'The gloss is only superficial.' I hurried on as I realised how daft that was. 'I mean, the veneer is split by the girl. She tears him to pieces.'

'Yes, but do you think our viewers are going to be even faintly interested in what happens to a man like that?'

'Yes.'

'Ah.' He left a gap for me to fill but I decided that it was his go. Finally he had to say something. 'I mean, all that stuff she talks about seduction. Who would care in, say, Sheffield?

'Don't they do it up there?'

'What I am saying is that we want powerful, contemporary…'

I picked up his inflection '…Searching, relevant dramas for today.'

'Yes. Like these.' He slapped a pile of clean-looking scripts on the floor beside his desk. I could have sworn it was the dusty pile that Vincent Tildesley had kicked some months earlier.

'Well, Vincent asked me to write a comedy, a romantic one in fact. We compromised with an anti-romantic. I've fulfilled the contract.'

'Oh, we'll pay you, of course.'

That was the sentence I was waiting for. I took my script and was gone.

A month or two later I finished the first stage draft and took it into Harvey Unna's office. 'It's just a draft, Harvey. See what you think. Don't show it to anyone, eh?

That was Wednesday. On Friday he phoned me. 'I liked your play. I've sent it round to Michael Codron.'

I let out a squawk. 'I told you it was only a draft. Not to show it to anyone.'

On Monday the phone rang. 'Hallo, Terry, Michael Codron here. I've just read your play.' I knew what was coming next from the tone of his voice. The pause that he left had no tension whatsoever. I held back the rush of delight till he spoke. 'I'm going to do it.' He then left one of his long specials, but I was in no condition to speak. My first play had taken six years from my finishing it to getting it to the Arts Theatre. Now, sixteen months later this one had taken just five days to be in business. 'I told you I would,' said Michael.

'It's only a draft,' I said.

'Splendid. We can discuss re-writes when you come in to discuss casting. Who would you like to direct?'

It was one of those moments that make you want to tie your feet together and hop round the block yelling, or just stand and scream inarticulate noises.

Chapter VIII

1965-6

Mr Danvers' Downfall was a triple conflict: the battle of the sexes, the generations and the classes. It was, I know, just a light comedy, but I couldn't write even the lightest of work without a theme. I felt strongly about the unfairness of the sexual set-up outside marriage, being sufficiently guilty about my advantages as a male (I wasn't for continence, merely equity). In the play I reversed the situation by taking a man who had everything, but was just over the top in years, say, the late forties (then considered well over the top for a woman, part of the injustice). Against him I set a teenage girl, apparently his natural prey; but the prey ate the predator, a device not unknown, I know. She had to be down-market with only one advantage over him other than her youth: to be more intelligent. I invented the character of the man, thinking that if he comes out a bit phoney (which he did) that would help. The girl, however, I didn't so much invent as piece together from two or three people; her views were mine.

I made him a lawyer, I wanted my cold-blooded philanderer to be eminently establishment, but decided that was not right, so Ivor and I had a couple of days chess together dreaming up a better occupation for him. We hit on TV gourmet. Males connected with food, who looked as though they could perform in the bedroom as well as the kitchen were just emerging in this country as a new phenomenon and nobody had written about them, although continental culture must be littered with examples. Making Robert a gourmet had another bonus: it added to his sensuality.

I took a final precaution: remembering how stars had turned down Subbers because it was a team play, I made the man and the girl two socking-great leads to attract two big names - well, one, the likelihood of anyone who could play a teenage girl being a box-office name was slim; the play would have to make its own star, to shine with her established consort.

Harvey phoned me. 'I have sent Michael my standard contract for stage plays.'

I was impressed. 'I've got right of veto on casting and choice of director, haven't I?'

'Yes, yes, of course.' Harvey sounded rather cross at being interrupted in his pleasing task. 'Michael wants to pay royalties on a sliding scale; not, as is usual, on the weekly take but on the play's profitability. That will cost

56

you if the play doesn't make much, but benefit you considerably if it is very successful. He's offering this to cut his early overheads but it's riskier for you. Well?'

'Take the risk, what the hell. My whole life's a risk.' Control over my work was the only point that really interested me.

———————

Michael duly arrived for dinner with David Sutton, his production manager and boyfriend. They were elegant, besuited, bearing the statutory bottle of quality claret with bunch of flowers. They politely admired our white walls, junk furniture and Christine's cooking. She adored them. It was the beginning of an enjoyable four-way friendship, although just occasionally the sheer preciousness of the three of them together, always groomed, always modulated, the picture of sophistication, used to make me want to fart or perform some other public gaffe to let in some fresh air, so to speak.

David I warmed to as much as I had to Michael. He reminded me of Terry, in *Terry and the Pirates*, an American comic-strip of the forties, with his fair crinkly hair, freckles, snub nose and eager, open expression. David played bright-eyed ingenuousness to Michael's Machiavelli; they combined and contrasted perfectly, two super-smoothies of whom I grew most fond, though I never got behind the facade of either of them.

I knew who I wanted to direct: Robert Chetwyn. He was relatively unknown then, an actor turned director who had run Ipswich Rep and the Belgrade Theatre, Coventry. Michael wanted someone established but neither of us wanted to touch a 'comedy director'. The division between The West End Comedy and plays that had characters resembling human beings was sharp. I had tried to put real people into a glossy West End setting. If they weren't played for real the play was dead. Michael called the play a 'bridge play,' between the Old Wave and the New, a description that I found very pleasing (actually, the play owed little to the Old Wave's style or values, more to American comedies I had performed in and admired). So Michael asked one or two of the serious directors of the day. When they turned us down flat, he was forced to ask Chetwyn; the most important issue was successfully resolved.

The second step turned out to be a stinker: male lead. We were rejected by every star in the business who was likely - and one or two who weren't. The more serious actors clearly regarded the play as too insubstantial for their services, but the reasons offered by the others were pathetic: they simply would not be depicted as being over the hill. We got answers from agents like, 'My client will do it if you'll cut out the references about his greying hair/thickening waistline/failing powers/etc.' The vanity of our notable stage stars left me breathless, as did their talent in missing the point. Michael would have none of that nonsense. It was new and reassuring to feel the support of the producer. Another mainstream objection was that the girl would steal the play; one or two even objected to not getting the girl in the end.

However, this wasn't as bad as it looks. One of the first we had gone to was Donald Sinden (now Sir Donald, of course). He had said yes but was not available till the following spring. Here was a man whose career had nicely spanned the very gap my play allegedly bridged. He had gone from rep to fame in *The Cruel Sea*, to Hooray Henrys in British film comedies, to West End business plays, to the Royal Shakespeare company. Donald's record of work was satisfyingly broad. His agent agreed we could try elsewhere while we waited. Sinden would not take another offer without contacting us; he became a sort of half-committed reserve. More tantalising from my point of view was that each refusal gave a better chance to two men, either of whom I was mad for. I mentioned earlier that *The Subtopians* had gone into the Arts Theatre following Frank Marcus's *The Formation Dancers*. In this, the part of a pompous, hilariously randy, middle-aged art dealer had been brilliantly played by Robin Bailey, but Michael wouldn't hear of him.

'No s.a.,' he said, when I first brought up Bailey's name.

'No what?'

'Sex appeal.'

'I think he has.'

Michael buzzed David in the next office to come in, then asked him what he thought of Robin Bailey.

'No s.a.,' said David promptly.

'You've been ganging up,' I said.

'Look what happened to *The Formation Dancers*. Funny play, not unlike yours in certain respects, excellent notices, nobody came. No s.a.'

I said the name of the other actor I wanted. Michael and David exchanged knowing looks. 'Don't be silly,' said David with a big , open smile and left. After that, every time I went into the office I used to mutter, 'Robin Bailey.'

We had been looking for four months when Michael suddenly said, with Chetwyn's approval, 'OK. Let's ask Bailey.' A script was sent round and we were told we would be answered next day. I went home, grabbed Christine and danced her round the kitchen. 'It's all working out. We've got Chetwyn and now we'll get Bailey.'

In Michael's office the next morning he stood, as usual, behind his desk looking out of the window into Regent Street. 'There's something rotten in the state of Denmark.'

'What?' I didn't like the tone of his voice.

'Bailey's said no.'

The blow was not merely a surprise; for an actor of Bailey's status (then) to reject out-of-hand a leading part for which he was ideal implied a condemnation of the play that was crushing. The fate of Subbers loomed in my memory, I saw this production of Codron's disappearing too. 'Let's sign Sinden before we lose him,' I urged.

Michael flew into a rage. 'How dare he?' he asked the window, the walls, the telephone, finally me. 'Who does he think he is? How often does Bailey get offered leads in the West End that he can turn *me* down?' There was a considerable amount of this and I saw with relief that this was the anger of someone who felt the snub as personally as I, so hadn't given up on the project. One of Michael's admirable characteristics was his commitment. 'OK. We'll go with Sinden if that's what you and Bob want. I can wait if you can.'

Our next task was to find the right girl, but in the meantime another running problem got brilliantly solved by Bob. *Mr. Danver's Downfall* was a perfectly frightful title but I couldn't think of another. Every time Bob, Michael and I met in the office we produced crumpled bits of paper with titles scribbled on them and, of course, after you've looked at fifty alternatives you can't tell any more. A title that I had used for a teleplay was *You Should Hear Me Eat Soup*, and I had mentioned it.

One day Bob came in with his development of that.

'It's a bit jokey,' he said in his diffident way.

'Well, what is it?'

'I mean—huh—you know, it might be a bit light for this piece, thinking of the direction you want to push it on the re-writes.'

'Well, what is it?'

'I mean, I hope you won't think it's too—'

'Come on, you tease, tell us,' said Michael.

'Well—uh—I—er—what do you think of *There's A Girl In My Soup?*'

Michael pursed his lips. 'It'll diminish the play, I mean, we want to be taken seriously, don't we? Don't you?'

'Well, it's only a suggestion,' said Bob. Contrary to his words, he looked quite assertive. He obviously liked his own idea.

To stop further discussion on the subject I said, 'Let's call it *There's A Girl In My Soup* until someone thinks of something better.' We left the matter there. No-one would. I didn't even try. I thought it perfect in every way. It is a wonderful title. As it is Bob Chetwyn's, I can say so.

Now to cast the girl. The list of actresses subsequently claiming to have turned down the part is long, but the truth of the matter is that the first person we asked said yes. I wanted a nice, common girl; a girl who would comment on Robert Danvers' affluence, his bachelor pad and, indeed, his whole life with that envy and proper derision that only the lower orders have. Barbara Ferris had been a dancer and moved on stage with marvellous abandon; she had worked with Joan Littlewood in several productions and was excellent in the film of *Sparrers Can't Sing*. Bob and I went to a matinee at the Royal Court to see her in *Saved* by Edward Bond, which, contrary to all the nonsense talked at the time, was a truthful, well-made and unshocking play. In one scene she had to squeeze her boy-friend's blackheads, something she did, as she did everything else in the play, with no silly, so-called-feminine frills. She was beautifully direct in her work, funny and as pretty as paint; an appealing and very sexy combination. Afterwards, Bob, she and I had a perfectly awful, monosyllabic tea together which nearly put us off her (God knows what she thought of us). Michael later did a lot of heavy breathing about the salary her agent insisted on. 'I'm being screwed over her,' he said from time to time.

Jay Hutchinson Scott, the definitive designer of West End glossies, was engaged to do the set and finally we caved in to an agent who had been worrying Michael for months to let a client of his play Andrew, the second male lead. We had been turned down by all our earlier choices so Jon Pertwee got the part by default. We held auditions for the remainder of the cast and got Anthony Sagar, Clive Francis and Zeynip Tarimer. That left one part to fill: Clare. Clare is a bloody-awful part, one of the worst I have ever written. It requires a glamorous actress with long legs; a skilful, beautiful comedienne to play a leading-lady part that opens the play and then peters out after one more scene. Michael had been trying to get Jill Melford, who would have been perfect. She had firmly and repeatedly turned him down. We took, instead an excellent actress who certainly had the looks, talent and legs, but not the height and sheer glamour of Jill.

I recount these details of casting, not to diminish those actors I have mentioned, I regard them all with affection and respect, but because the story is typical. The constant factor of nearly all productions is the chaos of casting: the lists; the rejections; the second, third and fourth choices. Such balls is talked about the subject. I want to roll on my back with all four limbs in the air, shaking with laughter, when reviewers say, 'So -and-so was clearly cast for the quality of...' or, 'It is beyond me why that heavyweight was chosen to play a sensitive, slim...' nearly every actor playing every part in every teleplay or West End production is not first choice. They are cast - for a variety of reasons, yes - but almost always because they were available when someone else was not.

All preparations seemed complete for rehearsals to begin in April 1966 when a further complication arose, a very nasty one: Michael appeared to have insufficient money for the production.

The first I had known of his predicament (and therefore mine, too, of course) was when he finally asked Robin Bailey to play Robert. 'I'll never get backing behind him,' he had muttered, in a semi-grumbling, semi-ruminant way. Then he had made an oblique remark about Donald's lack of power to attract capital. Now, with the production about to start, he asked me in a very diffident manner if I would mind doing a matching deal with Nat Cohen of Anglo-Amalgamated films over the screen rights of the play. I had, till then, always ascribed Michael's diffidence when talking about money to natural discretion. Suddenly the penny dropped, he was in trouble. Nobody would invest in this production. The Michael Codron who I, and my generation of professionals, had admired for presenting Pinter, Orton, Saunders et al, was, to his backers, a Michael Codron who hadn't made much money and had frequently lost some. I couldn't quite believe it. I still don't know how much Michael needed me to say yes, but I think he was in bigger trouble than he would admit. I jotted down the package we were offering a backer.

Producer: Not yet made any real money.
Author: Unknown
Director: Unknown
Male Star: Not a box office banker; recent stage, supporting roles at the Royal Shakespeare Company; recent TV, a vicar in a series; films, former devil-with-the-ladies.
Female Star: Unknown outside the business.
Second Male : Lead: Funny voices on the radio.

It was not impressive.

'What precisely is a matching offer?' I had already decided to agree unless it turned out to be an absolute swindle.

'Oh, it's nothing much really.' Michael sounded casual. 'You can't sell the film rights to anyone else without first asking Nat if he wants to offer you the same terms. If he doesn't want to match them, you go ahead with your own business. If he does, you must sell to him. That's all. It doesn't cost you a penny.' He paused for a moment before giving the end of his next sentence the merest extra emphasis, 'We get backing to go ahead with the stage production...if you agree.'

'How much will the production cost?' I thought I would find out what mess of pottage I was selling my matching-right for.

'Six thousand pounds,' said Michael, 'but it is capitalised at a higher sum than that for safety's sake.'

'How much higher?'

'Well, a thousand or two.'

'Or three or four?'

'Hm.' Michael was looking at me with absolutely unfocused eyes, reflecting his tone. I thought if he gets any more vague, he'll vanish.

I guessed ten thousand to be the total capitalisation cost and left that subject for the next. 'And how much is Nat Cohen offering?'

'A lot.' Michael's mouth closed rather firmly.

I had a last go. 'All?'

'Well.'

I don't know how much Nat put in, but I have always understood it was about six thousand and that Michael had to put some money of his own in to make up the total, or at least guarantee the end-money.

So, that is how one West-End production got set up. I had, during all that, lovingly finished the re-writes that were going to make the play the most significant sex comedy of all time. The new copies were pushed round to the company a day or two before rehearsals were due to begin, a last minute mouth-watering surprise for the lucky actors about to perform my deathless prose.

We were due to have a read-through at Michael's flat on a Sunday evening. I was all of a delightful twitter in anticipation of the ravishment of my virginal re-write. I arrived, bathed and sparkling, carrying a pristine exercise book, two sharpened pencils and a vast Havana. All was grace and amiability as I settled in a cloud of costly, blue smoke, pencil at the go position: the picture of A Successful Playwright. Two hours later I was a chain-smoking, twitching, wild-eyed wreck. The read-through was an unmitigated disaster.

Chapter IX

1966

The blame lay in my desire to bring out the underlying polemic. I had written the play into a forest of arguments, side issues and would-be pungent aphorisms about Life and Sex that made my flesh creep with embarrassment. I had written for posterity or someone. Through self-indulgence I had forgotten every craft rule from Stanislavsky's super-objective to Mack Sennett's, 'When does the villain kick the dog?'

The reading started with those chuckles of good-will that a cast will always give. These had died before the end of the first scene. There had been a brief renaissance in response to Barbara's entrance, then gloom had descended and eventually enveloped us all. Jon, in an effort to raise spirits, had tried a funny voice on his re-entrance in Act III which had only pointed to the awfulness of it all. As soon as the cast were on their depressed way out Bob and I got our heads together.

'We know how awful that was, so we needn't even discuss it,' I said, to stave-off euphemisms. 'It's not even viable as it stands.'

'No, I don't think it is,' he agreed with wounding candour. 'What are we going to do?'

David poured drinks as Michael returned from seeing the cast out. He promptly hit the ceiling. 'That was a disgrace. I shall phone Sinden's agent first thing in the morning and complain. I've never heard such a bad reading.'

I was, as they say, flabbergasted. I didn't know whether to be grateful to Michael for his attempt to save my feelings or to giggle at the irrelevance of it.

Bob stepped in. 'I think Donald was lost, poor chap.'

'I should think so; bloody blindfolded,' I joined in. 'It's me. I've screwed it up, I've got to put it right.'

'Just go back to the draft I optioned,' said Michael.

I didn't believe my original stage draft was good enough so that was out. Bob and I decided that I would quickly write a sufficiently entertaining version of the play for us to put before the public on tour. We could use that as a basis from which to work. We would have six touring weeks to re-write and re-shape what we had, then polish it for London. What it amounted to was two complete re-writes of the play, with the first, or tour, version of Act I, Scene I, to be ready the following morning to rehearse. I left them,

Bob looking composed, David grinning encouragement, and Michael putting a pretty good face on what must have looked, to him, like a certain failure. As I drove down the Kings Road, I picked up a hitch-hiker who had missed his last bus. About a mile further on, at Parsons Green, a black cat shot across the road under the car. There was a sickening double thump. We got out. The cat was a dead, twitching mess. Omens and superstition spun in my head.

'Oh, no,' said the hitch-hiker, 'I wish I'd walked home, this wouldn't have happened.' He acted on his word and strode off.

I put the cat, which had no name-tag, into a dustbin on the pavement. With spirits at rock bottom I arrived home.

'The read-through was awful, I've ruined the play and killed a black cat.' I nearly burst into tears.

Christine stared at me with a sort of surprised detachment, then made sympathetic noises and coffee. My typist was telephoned and asked if she would mind working from 6.30 a.m. the following morning and every morning for the rest of the week. She agreed and I got to work.

The three weeks of rehearsal and the six weeks of the tour that followed were a sort of wrought-up, weird dream, the most testing two months of my professional life. The fourteen-hour day and weekly opening-night nerves of my years of rep proved their worth as training, as was the knowledge I had gained of what would work for an audience. This is written from my point of view so the word 'I' appears frequently, but most of the time it should be 'Bob Chetwyn and I'. Bob'n'I became a new pronoun in my vocabulary. 'Bob'n'I said', 'Bob'n'I did', 'Bob'n'I thought'. I would have lost my head in the ensuing chaos but Bob never wavered. No play ever owed more to its director (title apart) than *Soup* did to Bob.

He called in on his way to rehearsal the next morning, read through the new scene and pronounced himself temporarily satisfied, not that he had much choice. I went off to BBC TV to do the first of five days of *Playschool* that was booked, came home and got stuck into the second scene that night, round to Joan, my typist, to put it through her door, back to collect it in the morning, give it to Bob, back to *Playschool* and so on all week until the first version was done. By Friday morning I was stupid with fatigue. There wasn't enough adrenaline left for *Playschool*. I sat in front of the cameras and had a blackout over a nursery rhyme I was trying to sing. Large idiot boards held up by studio hands failed to get me to completion and after nine takes the director gave up. I sat there, paralysed, one of those performers who is never going to get it out; we have all had the misfortune to work with at least one of them. I got home from the studio on Friday to meet a phone call from the script editor of the Adam Adamant series on BBC.

'Where's our script?' he asked. 'It's due today.'

I gave a better performance than I had in the studio. 'Good God, haven't you had it? My bloody typist promised. She'll have to go. I'll see you get it on Monday.'

Adam Adamant was one of our less-distinguished TV series, about a Victorian detective who had been brought back to life from a giant ice-cube. Quite. Well, the script they got from me that I wrote that weekend must have depressed even those hardened readers of rubbish.

Early in the third week of rehearsals we had the producer's run-through in a theatre. Michael and David left afterwards, apparently satisfied. Chunks of the play were on the floor, they hadn't got out of the rehearsal room, but little passages were getting the right look and feel about them. However, the overall effect was of confusion and at the heart of it was Donald. He wasn't showing any sign at all of understanding or playing the character. Bob was at a loss how to get through to him and after a long discussion we decided to do nothing until we had opened in Wimbledon. I went round to Michael's office.

'Oh, Terry, we've just heard from the Lord Chamberlain's Office. Here is a copy of the script, stamped and authorised - and their cuts.' He handed me the officially-stamped script and a letter. It was all an irrelevance as the cast were already rehearsing something different, and that was only temporary. I glanced at the letter. The cuts insisted on by the Lord Chamberlain were the usual piffling, humiliating idiocies. I had never realised I was so dirty-minded. There was one beauty which arose out of the fact that the play hadn't been read accurately. John, the porter, had to say of Clare's legs. 'Lovely legs on her...very leggy legs, if you see what I mean. And long, phaw, right up to her bum.' This had been misread as...'right up her bum' and was therefore cut. I was mystified.

Michael pursed his lips and gave one of his prim smiles. 'Anally speaking, nothing must go up or come down. Our Lord Chamberlain doesn't care for that sort of thing.'

'How the Hell can her legs go up her bum?' I demanded. 'And if she were deformed, why should that get the porter going?'

'They're deeply suspicious of us in the theatre. God knows what they think we get up to. Let's start a little flippant correspondence.'

After the Lord Chamberlain's office had seen their error we had the line allowed on the understanding that '...it is two heterosexual men talking about a normal woman and no accompanying gestures are indulged in by the actors concerned.' The rest of the Lord Chamberlain's cuts I threw away. I didn't risk sending in the final, revised text in case they found something else to object to, so all performances of the play were illegal.

We opened at the Wimbledon theatre in April, praying for the current version to be a reasonable evening's entertainment while we got down to serious matters. It was just about that. At least Jay's complicated set looked lovely. However the disadvantage of opening so near to London is that every wife, husband, lover, agent, second cousin Mabel and self-appointed play-doctor connected with anyone in the cast turns up and produces a definitive and different answer to every problem. And they did. I wrote the final version of Act One that week but Bob and I made only one change in the production: to put in the cooking of an omelette on-stage by Donald which involved some flashy, one-handed egg-breaking, dead right for the character and fun to watch. Donald did it beautifully which enabled me to write a nice sequence round the business.

On Saturday, unknown to me, Michael had invited Jill Melford to come and see the play, she who had turned down the part of Clare originally. In the interval he, David, Bob, Christine and I were gathered in the circle bar. The atmosphere was awful. Contractually I couldn't stop our current Clare being sacked but I could veto any replacement.

'What's Jill Melford here for?' I demanded. 'We've got a Clare and she's bloody good.'

'I think we could do better,' said Michael, chin up.

'That applies to any part. We might do worse.'

David and Christine edged away and had a drink in relative peace. Michael's voice and mine were raised enough to get the interest of the Wimbledon playgoers. Bob, who was trying to pour oil, gave up and went outside for a breath of air. Jill Melford said no.

We opened the second week of the tour at Wolverhampton to the Mayor and various other dignitaries. The performance was greeted in silence, except for Anthony Sagar's appearance. He had played rep in Wolverhampton for years; his entrance drew loud applause. The audience laughed at everything he said for the three minutes he was on, then relapsed into silence when he left.

'I told you they'd be good in Wolverhampton,' said Anthony. In the first interval the Mayor, disgusted by the dirt being presented on the stage, got up and noisily left. His wife, obviously of a different turn of filth, stayed on, enjoying herself. The rest of the play was performed to a few scattered chuckles. On Tuesday morning Bob started rehearsing the final version of Act One to go in later in the week. On Saturday night, for no apparent reason, the whole play was received with good solid laughter and warm applause. Act One, at least, was nearly how we wanted it. We went on to Nottingham and the work on Act Two. Nottingham received the play with no more enthusiasm than Wolverhampton. The new Act Two went in on the Wednesday when Michael came to see the play. He and David had had a row and weren't speaking. The performance that night was a mess. Donald lost his place and cut backwards and forwards making nonsense of the play. He was so mortified he locked himself in his dressing room afterwards and would speak to nobody. The Act Two curtain came down to a baffled audience and Michael went barmy. 'You've wrecked it. I've got John Perry of Tennent's coming up on Friday. They have the Globe. They'll just laugh at us.'

'Look, d'you want it ready for London in four weeks or for Friday?' said Bob. 'You can't have it both ways.'

'What's the good of having it ready in four weeks if we've got no theatre?' snapped Michael. 'You must go back to the original draft version.'

'That's ridiculous. It'll be just as hard to do that as to get this lot straight.'

'And what about Donald?' He's all over the shop,' was Michael's next one.

'He got muddled, poor sod,' said Bob. 'He's got a lot on his plate.' This was putting it mildly. Donald, more than anyone, was bearing the brunt of our work.

We all dispersed to our hotel rooms breathing rather heavily. In the morning I got a note from Michael who had left for London. It was to the effect that he could no longer get any sense from Bob and could only talk coherently to, and through, me. Later that morning he telephoned with a new female name to take over the part of Clare.

'Good God, no.' I squawked down the phone. 'I've worked with her, it's a three-act tragedy every rehearsal. She's bananas. Anyway, we've got a Clare. She's very good. Spend some money on her clothes.' The matter was left.

On Friday John Perry came. Act One passed without mishap (or laughter). The moment arrived in Act Two when Donald was hit in the eye by a door. The blow he received was the spring for the remainder of the action. Because of confusion caused by the rewritten script, Donald was on the other side of the stage. The door missed him by feet. Someone panicked and cut to Act Three, back to Act One, got back into Act Two and they went on as though Donald had been struck. The audience was mystified; the rest of that act and Act Three were torture. John Perry returned to London and after another sputtering performance on Saturday I got into the box-on-wheels and followed him back. I remember that the motorway looked like a little yellow pool in my headlights with an awful lot of blackness surrounding it.

I got home in the small hours and climbed into bed with Christine. The telephone went. I answered it. It was a man calling her from Switzerland. Falling asleep I heard her being brief and formal. Then she hung up and explained while I tried to stay awake. She had been doing extra work on a film being made at Shepperton, *Casino Royale*. Every model and attractive small-part actress in London had been appearing in it as dressing. Christine had been on and off this for a few weeks and there were innumerable stories she, and everybody in the film world, told of the uninhibited amount of screwing that had gone on. The idea that Christine could have been involved was not even a passing thought in my head. Nor would I have dreamed of asking her. The man on the phone, Bert Mortimer, was Peter Sellers' chauffeur/man Friday. He had been having a bit between takes with one of

Christine's friends who was married to a large, potentially violent man. Out of prudence Bert and she were using Christine as an unwilling go-between.

'You frightened the life of out him,' she giggled. 'He thought he'd dialled the wrong number and got her husband or something. Did you notice how nervous he was?'

'I notice everything.' I invoked our catchphrase as I dropped off, uninterested in the intrigues of her friends. Bert called again the following week, still at an outlandish hour but bolder, knowing he was safe.

Our next stop, Cardiff, was worse than the previous dates. The new Act Three went in and the major re-writes were finished. To Bob and me the play looked about right. Cardiff received it with indifference. One performance was like some awful, eerie nightmare; the only sounds that disturbed the tomb-like peace that reigned in the auditorium were a few female giggles at Donald's underwear. As we had altered the play, so the audience's reaction had got cooler. We kept muttering to the cast that things would get better the nearer we got to London. These mutters had the hollow sound of whistles in the dark. We would soon know, our next stop was Brighton.

Simultaneously with the re-write campaign ran the other important problem: the performances. Barbara was on course from the word go. She got it right in one, stayed right and bore the changes and messing about she received with excellent humour. She was a dream to work with, she could understand and execute what you wanted even before you could finish your sentence. Barbara, in conduct and in performance, was like an extract from some manual on *How To Be A Star*. I was crazy about her. Our Clare was fine in spite of the battles raging round her unknowing head. Zeynip Tarimer, the au pair girl, looked and sounded good, which was all she could do in a tiny part and Anthony Sagar was brilliant as the porter; the clashing of the upper and lower orders was vital and he brought a whole world of below-stairs with him on every entrance. He was full of suggestions and enthusiastically cut his already small part if he felt that what was left would benefit from the pruning. Clive Francis, in the very showy part of the drummer with the hangover, was well on course. I had written this part for myself in the TV version of the play so Clive had to endure being subjected to a doubly jaundiced eye from me: critical author and deprived actor is a lethal combination.

Jon Pertwee's state still makes me smile when I think of it. He was terrified. He knew his business as a funny man with funny voices, now he was in the tricky position of playing a character in a straightish play. He would sometimes subdue his performance to the point of effacing himself completely then would pop up and go over the top. As Robert's married friend and commentator on the action he had most of the one-liners. The problem was, in my view, that he had too many, and removing a possible laugh from Jon - as with most comedians - was a bit like removing the proverbial cub from the tigress. However, as things began to work for him, he joined in the general cut-and-changes game with vigour, but he always treated with disdain the idea that, because he was a married man with hordes of children, he should look less than immaculate. In contrast to Robert, leading the fantasy-life of a rich, randy bachelor, we wanted Andrew to look like the bloke mowing the lawn next door. Jon just said, 'Yes, yes,' to all our arguments and went impeccably on-stage each night. We gave up on that. His built-in timing and his smell for what would be entertaining rivalled that of anyone I have ever worked with. Just to see him pull on a cigarette or take off an apron in anger was a lesson in clean, clear, comic statement.

But Donald was the big problem. He had started uncertainly and was soon all over the place. I was still learning about the character of Robert Danvers as I was re-writing, so could scarcely have expected Donald to see him clearly. I wanted him to be, not only sexy, charming, funny and all those attributes so coveted by leading men, but also a vain, pompous, ruthless, self-centred shit; the term male chauvinist pig was not then coined but Robert was to be archetypal. When he closed in on a woman I wanted him to look as though it would end juicily for both of them, not with the usual feeble excuse for chastity to triumph as the curtain fell. Our Anglo-Saxon, non-conformist, guilt-ridden culture had always demanded that portrayals of philanderers had to be distorted to fit some false morality, or castrated so that they couldn't be taken seriously. Nobody in popular entertainment was natural about sex (in public that is).

After we opened at Wimbledon, Bob and I decided that we would take shifts in keeping the pressure on Donald. Donald must have got sick of the sight of me, as rehearsals finished, trying to drink with him, eat with him, cadge lifts off him, anything I could think of to keep hammering away at what we wanted. I bored him with intimate details of my life in an effort to get him to do the same (which he didn't). During that tour Donald had to endure, besides a mountain of re-learning and rehearsing, a constant, probing barrage. I don't know how he stood it. In rehearsal his suggestions were always to the point, he was quick to discard and change as we worked. Chief among many ideas he had was to take the line he said to every woman, 'My God, but you're lovely,' and say it to himself for the final curtain. It was perfect. I grabbed it gratefully. I had been going to bring the curtain down in a minor key, but that flipped it back into major. However, during all that he never began to play the character.

He floored me one day over a steakhouse lunch. 'You see, Frizzers, I don't see him.'

'But we've talked about him till we're all black in the face, Donald.'

'Oh, yes, but that's not what I mean. It's all very well *talking* about him. That's easy. But I have to *act* him. And I don't know what I'm acting when you keep changing the text every day.'

Well, I had to admit it. He had a point.

I removed my insensitive self from his presence and chewed over with Bob how to help Donald without holding up the re-writes. We were both actors, surely we could solve the practical problem of helping another actor to see the character through the mountains of verbiage. We decided to concentrate on one single line, a key line which Donald was saying in precisely the wrong way. He had to say it to Marion and Clare, who were squabbling about him. 'Please. You mustn't fight over me like this. I'm not worth it.' Donald played this line, and, indeed the whole scene like one of those farces where the husband has been caught by his wife trying to have a bit on the side (not that he ever got it in those plays, poor sod). We kept insisting that Robert didn't give a damn about being found out, on the contrary, two women fighting over him was a delightful massage to his ego. The line should be the hollow, delighted protestation of a vain man having a ball, not an abject entreaty. We hammered at this line with enough insistence to have driven anyone with less reserves than Donald mad. But he couldn't or wouldn't play it our way.

We arrived in Brighton and, after a dire opening night to a lot of shocked old ladies (Brighton was famous for its reactionary opening nights), the whole production, except Donald, started to swing. We were back in the land where professionals were in the audience, only now, instead of a list of prescriptions for a sick production, praise started to ring round the dressing rooms after the show. Incipient complacency is as dangerous as panic. We still had problems.

Michael called Bob and me into his office 'I can do a deal for one of the best theatres in town,' he told us, but looked set.

'Which one?'

'I'm not finalising anything until we have a new Clare.' He fixed me with a very glittering eye.

'We've got a Clare,' I said. 'And she's very good. She'll be even better when you spend some money on her. Which theatre?'

Michael produced a list of possible new Clares and the old argument dragged on. Bob and I left for rehearsal. After a long silence on the journey, Bob said, 'I think you should give way. It's poisoning everything. We can't sink the whole thing over one actress. She'll go down, too.'

'Michael's only using it as a threat,' I replied. 'He won't throw everything away because of her.'

'Nevertheless, you should.'

Perhaps I only needed an excuse to end the row. I gave way. In retrospect, I think Michael's meanness over her clothes sprang from the fact that he never really saw her in the part and would only spend the money on someone he did.

On Friday, Michael and David arrived in Brighton to announce to the company which theatre we were going to, and to do the sacking. I was mooching about, simmering with resentment because I had let a member of my cast down.

70

'We've got the Globe,' said Michael. 'But John Perry is screwing me over the deal.'

'You should print tickets for that. It'd be a sell-out.'

Michael, David and I stood uneasily with nothing further to say to each other. It should have been a terrific moment; the Globe (now the Gielgud) was easily the best theatre in London for us.

'You telling her tonight?' I asked.

Michael's chin went up. 'After the performance. Our new Clare goes in tomorrow in the matinee.' The new Clare had been rehearsing that day secretly with Bob, would have another rehearsal tomorrow with the cast, then straight in. It was best to get it done quickly.

'Do me a favour would you, please?' I made the request as warmly as I could. 'Pay Clare over the odds to show our appreciation. It's not much help, but it's something.'

'Of course,' said Michael.

I'll contribute,' I added. 'Conscience money.'

'That won't be necessary,' Michael's chin went up further.

After the show, David came up to me backstage. 'Now look, Terry. You must be nice to Michael. He's got a terrible job. He's doing it now and he feels awful.'

'Ah, dear. She, of course, will be fucking ecstatic.'

We avoided each other for the rest of the evening and I found her in the actors' bar with some of the cast. For a company that had just got the Globe I've never seen such a set of glum faces. I tried to buy her a drink but was well down a long queue of offers.

'I'm sorry,' I said. I wanted to add that I had done my damnedest, but I patently hadn't.

'I know,' she said. 'I understand. I really do.'

There were no tears, no tantrums and no reproaches from her. She left and that was that. I've been involved in several sackings; if I thought someone wasn't doing their work, or couldn't adequately, I've never hesitated. Things are hard enough in the theatre without carrying passengers. There is always the sock counter at Harrods if you don't like it. But that was unjust and left a rotten taste.

Michael, David, Bob and I, took our seats next matinee to see the replacement Clare. Ten minutes later, with the opening scene over, I got up and clambered urgently over the others to get to the aisle. 'I told you so' was written into every overstated move I made. The change had been a ghastly error. The new Clare is an excellent actress, with a considerable, justified reputation; she was simply wrong for that part. The scene is the hardest in the play to get right. It parodies the phoney atmosphere of the West-End sex-comedy of that period; the very atmosphere the rest of the play was in reaction to. It was on the floor and the play took some while to recover.

71

Michael, David, Bob and I spent the interval in silence drinking moody cups of tea. Not to say, 'I told you so,' was a major effort of will. The scene that involved Clare in Act Two was as flat as the first, and in the next interval I could keep quiet no longer. 'Perhaps if you ask our first choice back very, very nicely, she won't spit in your eye.' Michael and David left for London, tight-lipped.

Our final touring week was at the Golders Green Hippodrome, a dump that is mercifully no longer a theatre. I say mercifully as far as straight plays are concerned. No doubt it was excellent for musicals. Playing that vast auditorium made the play spread alarmingly. We put minutes on and it looked doughy. We kept polishing and chipping away at little bits, but basically the thing now was to let the actors settle. I caught Oliver slipping into the theatre one evening. After the performance we met briefly in a crowd, unable to talk. He pulled a face as though he had just inadvertantly sucked a lemon, which did me no good.

Bob decided on the big showdown with Donald. He must get That Line right. A rehearsal was called with just Bob and Donald in that vast, empty theatre. I paced the pavement. The Line was the sole subject of the afternoon. They argued for ages. I don't know what was said, but that night Donald cautiously removed the guilt from the scene, playing it neutrally. The scene was going well, with lots of laughter. Barbara said her preceding line and got her usual solid laugh. Donald drew a deep breath and dived in 'Plee-ase,' he pleaded, dripping with false humility, 'You mustn't fight over me...' He never got out '...like this. I'm not worth it.' All three actors on the stage stopped dead, shocked by the shout of laughter that rolled back from the audience - a tidal wave of joy. Bob and I nearly did a war-dance in the back of the stalls. Every night, from then on, it was one of the biggest laughs in the show. The effect on Donald was magical: pomposity, vanity, phoniness, started to break out all over his performance like galloping chicken pox. He had been frighteningly late in getting there, but now he had it he came roaring through on the rails showing his class as a leading comic actor prepared to take a play by the scruff of its neck and make it his.

On Friday Michael phoned me. 'I've got Jill Melford.' He left one of his pauses for me to congratulate him. I let it run. He continued in a very different tone of voice. 'But, my God, did her agent screw me.'

We had a spare week to rehearse Jill in, then into the Globe. Michael told us of the terrific row he had had with the replacement Clare over her dismissal. She was in the production for one week and two performances only, after two or three days rehearsal. Not surprisingly, she was furious and told him what she thought. He was smarting badly; I wished I could have heard the conversation. She and I met some years later at the BBC and she gave me a piece of her mind about her treatment. After she had got it off her chest she laughed as she recalled the episode. I said that I hoped she had at least got well paid-off for her pains and that brought her quickly to the boil again.

We previewed on the Monday and Tuesday. Jill had a lovely silver-fox fur that was perfect in the scene, as indeed, was she. Jill's agent demanded extra payment for the fur.

'He screwed me over that fur,' muttered Michael.

'You must be getting used to it on this production,' I said unsympathetically. Bob chivvied up the cast to get on with it on the two previews, and we saw to it that only half the seats in the house were sold to get the thing taut and to cut out easy laughs. Only one other incident occurred before we opened and that, too, concerned Jill. It was welcome light relief.

Following The Line I have mentioned earlier of Robert's, Clare had a reply, then her exit. Ideally, we wanted to get her off to a big laugh, but it was now impossible to cap Donald's 'Please. You mustn't fight over me like this. I'm not worth it.' We had settled for a reply that was only adequate. As a problem I had never solved, it maddened me.

On Tuesday I arrived for rehearsals excited; I had got it. Instead of giving her a direct reply to Donald I came up with an oblique jab at him that I swore would get first a beat while the audience took it in, then a belter. Neither Jill nor Bob could see it.

'It's perfect,' I urged them. 'Haven't I been right all along about these things?'

'No,' said Bob.

'Trust me. You'll see. It's the magic three-in-a-row.'

They agreed. That night the moment came. Jill stopped at the door in reaction to Barbara's jibe which got its usual laugh, listened to Donald's line, reacted beautifully during his laugh, then delivered her own new telling thrust. There was utter, uncomprehending silence from the entire house. This was eventually broken by the hysterical scream of mirth that came from the author at the back of the stalls. Jill staggered off apoplectically and Donald and Barbara were too convulsed to go on with the scene. Jill and Bob gave me some terrific stick and we reverted to the previous version.

We opened on Wednesday, fifteenth June, 1966, the hottest day of the year. Christine and I spent it trying to get rid of opening-night tickets to anyone we knew. It was hard to give them away. Our advance bookings weren't enough to have kept us on for one night, about £145.

The curtain, as they say, rose. There was no doubt whatsoever that Jill's imperious presence (to say nothing of the silver fox) helped us through the tricky opening. Anthony Sagar was bang on form. Jon was having a subdued evening. Donald was a bit tense. Then in the second scene Barbara came on and got a terrific response almost at once. Donald settled down beautifully. His late run had meant that his performance had matured at exactly the right moment. Their long duologue is the best scene in the play, in my view, and was played impeccably. Bob and I looked down the row at each other, white but satisfied. Michael and David couldn't be seen. An agent who had found me a lot of work in my rep days sat across the aisle from me sighing and shaking his head impatiently, visibly loathing every moment. Mum and Dad and Christine's parents were smiling, glad to be overwhelmed by the occasion.

The second-weakest scene, Act Two, Scene One, slipped by easily, helped by the cooking business we had invented. I started to relax. I had every faith in the rest of the play, it was solid. Clive Francis did his stuff well and we were just a few minutes off the Act Two curtain when the performance suddenly went dead on its feet. The heat was so great in the auditorium that the audience had simply laughed themselves out, the good feeling created was slipping away. The audience was gasping for breath as the curtain came down; the skids were under us.

I grabbed the front of house manager in the interval and we shot round opening every door but it was just as hot outside. In Berwick Street, beside the theatre, I saw four reviewers in a group, talking animatedly: Milton Shulman, Herbert Kretzmer, David Nathan and B A Young. I sidled up to them, my nose in my programme. One of them was saying 'Well, you see, if you've got black spot on your roses, you've got to get the secateurs in under the shoots and...' I went and had an ice-cream with Christine.

The short scene at the opening of Act Three played to the sort of silence we had experienced at Cardiff. The only sound was of nearly a thousand programmes fanning back and forth. It looked very ominous. The final scene opened with the meeting of Marion and Andrew. Barbara opened the door to him and Jon stared at her in a wonderful mixture of lust and surprise. Her speech finished with '...Can I help you?' Jon said his line, 'I think it's too late,' with a world of middle-aged regret and there was a spontaneous shout of laughter from the whole house. It was such a simple little moment, but his playing of it was perfect. It turned everything round. From then on we were home and dry. I unwound like an elastic band as Act Three cruised in. I wanted to throw myself, blubbing with gratitude, at Jon's feet.

Christine and I sat slumped in our seats at the end, watching the audience pushing its way out into the air. Two amply-proportioned men in dinner jackets were jostled against me. They had well-brushed hair, grey at the temples, and an air of considerable affluence. One was preparing a cigar to smoke.

'What d'you think?' said the first, casually.

The second fiddled with his cigar. 'It'll do.'

I aimed a kick at his ankle, but was past accuracy.

Chapter X

1966

The telephone went at 8.30 next morning 'Have you read your press?' My agent's voice was honeyed.

'No.' I had already learned my lesson.

'Oh, Terry, Terry, Terry,' said Harvey with joyful reproach. 'Go out and buy the papers. They're wonderful.' He read me some. They didn't sound very wonderful to me but I regarded anything less than abject adulation as an affront.

Michael was next, sharp on nine a.m. He was in no mood to carp that I hadn't been hailed as Coward, Wilde and Congreve combined. 'It's a good selling press.'

They were both right, of course. For all practical purposes, never mind playwright's whingeing, the notices were excellent for everybody connected with the production - except for one thing: the title. *There's a Girl in My Soup* was panned; 'The worst title of the year,' 'awful,' 'belittling.'

'I told you it was too flip,' said Michael sanctimoniously, then could contain himself no longer. 'Who cares?' he chortled. 'Let 'em vent their spleen on that, what an escape valve. Look at these other quotes we've got.'

The reviewers couldn't have been more wrong. Bob's diffidently offered little joke had what Michael would have called s.a.; it is unforgettable; it translated attractively into even the most obscure of languages; its impact and memorability still make a significant difference to the play wherever it goes.

The day passed in a pleasant daze and in the evening Christine and I drifted to the Globe; the house had just gone in. Michael, David and Bob were in the foyer; we all looked at each other sheepishly, I had never seen a trio I liked more.

I didn't know what else to do with myself,' said Bob.

'You going in to watch?' asked Michael. Bob and I groaned. Of the fifty-one performances of the play to date we had seen about fifty. David popped into the auditorium and out again.

'There's a chap in the circle, alone in a sea of empty seats, laughing like a drain,' he said. 'Go and look.'

It was Harvey, exuding the enjoyment of a man who is on ten per cent of a Good Thing. He was slapping his thigh and rocking with uninhibited glee as though every moment was as fresh as an April shower.

The take that evening was over £350, more than double our entire advance in one night. We went off for a meal. During it Michael kept looking at me and laughing. 'I feel like one of those characters in a cartoon film,' he said. 'Every time I see you I hear the ching of a cash register and my eyes change into little dollar signs.'

The bandwagon began to roll. A fortune made its entrance into our lives, as palpable as any being. The break-even or chuck-out figure for each week at the Globe was £3,000. In the first part-week we took over that and then steadily climbed.

Two days after we opened we had our first offer for the film rights - £20,000. We turned it down and Christine hauled me off to Ibiza for a holiday. When rehearsals had started I weighed over eleven and a half stone and was not overweight. When we opened I was just over ten and a quarter. We lay on the beach for a month and turned sleek and brown while weekly telegrams arrived from Harvey with the box-office figures, £3,500, £4,000, £4,800, £4,600. What? A fall? No, £5,000 the next week. Just a hiccough. When we got back things started to accelerate. After ten weeks the production moved into profit and my off-hand gamble on the method of royalty payments paid off, spectacularly: my royalty rate doubled.

The Boulting brothers offered us £50,000 for the film rights, we turned it down. The weekly take went to £5,500 and broke the record for the Globe theatre. The next week we broke our own new record by a small margin, the following week smashed it by a further thousand pounds. We stayed at about £6,500 for a long time. The theatre was packed every night. The reviews had got us off the ground very nicely, thank you, but it was word-of-mouth that shot us into orbit. We learned how lucky we were to be at the Globe. When John Perry of H M Tennent Ltd had come to see us on that ghastly night in Nottingham, he had the theatre earmarked for Neil Simon's *The Odd Couple.* Perry had reported back that we would stagger along for just a few weeks. Now they had to gnash their teeth while a Michael Codron production occupied their theatre. *The Odd Couple,* a Ustinov play, a Coward season, came and went next door at the Queen's while we roared on. Finally, it got through even my cautious reactions that we would run for at least a year, probably two. Options were taken up for the play across the world.

There was silence, though, from the direction in which we were hopefully looking: America. That was, as they say, the big one, but neither Broadway nor Hollywood showed interest. After the two initial offers, the film world went silent.

I suggested that we form our own film company and put in an enormous bid to ourselves. Then Nat Cohen could exercise his matching offer if he wanted and we could clean up, or better still, he would back out and we would have the rights free to make the film ourselves. Harvey was horrified at such tactics and Michael didn't want to get involved in making films. In retrospect, if I had really wanted to make the film myself I should have formed a film company and offered myself 100 per cent of the profits. That would have cut out Nat's matching offer. But although I had incipient ambitions in the film world, the theatre was my home and I lacked the will.

The American tourists were flocking to *Soup*, among them was a woman who booked agencies and theatre-going clubs right across America. The story goes that she came out of the Globe and said loudly, within earshot of an American journalist, 'That is the funniest play I've ever seen. When it comes to Broadway I'll book it right across the States.' The journalist published this remark.

Michael and I were nearly bowled over in the rush of New York producers, cheque-books in hand. They were closely followed by the dinosaurs from Hollywood. It should happen to everybody at least once in their life.

Of the film producers, two are most memorable: Ray Stark and Harry Saltzman. Stark had recently had two huge box-office successes, *The Magnificent Seven* and *Funny Girl*, which he also produced on Broadway. He wanted to do a combined deal for the film of *Soup* and the Broadway production. He had the reputation of being a shy, retiring man. This shrinking violet had arrived in London, taken the top floor of the Dorchester, known as the Chinese suite, and seen Soup. I was invited to talk to him at four p.m. the next day. I asked for him at the desk of the Dorchester and was taken to the lift and escorted by a uniformed flunkey. At the top I was handed over to a white-jacketed flunkey who took me a few yards to a door and handed me over to an alpaca-suited flunkey. He showed me into The Presence. In an outer room of the suite was a rail of suits. An obsequious tailor was just being dismissed. It could have been me, I thought.

Stark was small and pleasant, not a bit loud, but continuous, the verbal flow was unquenchable. 'Come in, come in. Excuse me, I was just getting fitted up. I always buy my suits when I come to London. Order 'em on one trip, fittings and alterations on the next.' I rang my fingers along the suits, my professional touch assured me that the quality left nothing to be desired.

'What would you like to drink?' went on Stark affably as he led me into the main room. 'Something strong? I've got this stuff here I've just had flown in from Yugoslavia, or somewhere. Can't pronounce it, it's made from buffalo shit or something.'

I asked for tea. He laughed. 'Don't drink during negotiations, eh? Very wise. I'll have some tea as well.'

The main room was covered in papers. Every conceivable form of written matter was strewn about the place, especially over the two matching sofas and vast coffee table at which we sat facing each other. The park looked lovely out of the window. The compliments about my play flowed; the casual references to the cinema-box-office bonanza he had been enjoying and was about to create for me were thrown in; the picture of film and stage success was rosy indeed as the white-coated flunkey trekked round the coffee table dispensing tea and biscuits. However, there was one huge flaw: Stark was determined to Americanise the play, he saw it that way and was convinced. Several times I tried to interrupt him to tell him that wasn't on, but it was useless. Eventually, he paused to drink some tea.

'Mr. Stark,' I said. 'That's all very wonderful, but there's just one thing I must say—'

He rose to the surface of his tea and held out his hand like a policeman. 'Just a minute. Just a minute. Let's get one thing straight right now.' His expression was avuncular. 'You call me Ray...' he gave the merest pause to accent his goodwill '... and I'll call you Clarence.'

Well, of course, the anecdote really ends there. In an old-fashioned film comedy it would have been a cut to surfers in Hawaii, or anything to get out of that scene at the top, but I couldn't resist pushing it into untidy naturalism.

'Over my dead body, you will.'

Ray turned red. 'Oh, oh, I'm sorry. Don't you approve of Christian names?'

'Yes,' I said, 'when it's my own. My name is Terence.'

'It's Clarence.'

'Terence.'

'Clarence.'

'I assure you it's Terence. My parents would have told me if I'd been getting it wrong all this time.'

'It's Clarence,' came through clenched teeth.

'I'm sorry.'

'It's Clarence in the programme.'

'No.'

'It is. I remember.' He started searching the papers near him for the programme. He couldn't find it. I joined in, saying I hoped he would call me Terry if we were going to be chums, but I wasn't mad about Clarry. The alpaca-suited flunkey and the white-coated flunkey were called in to assist. As Ray's agitation increased, the air seemed to be full of papers. Finally the evidence was produced. He stared at it in disbelief. 'I could have sworn it was Clarence,' he repeated as he turned the pages, searching the small print for a loophole.

The next day Stark offered, for the film rights, an escalation deal of £100,000 plus five per cent of the producer's profits, on condition he had the Broadway production which would be Americanised. We turned it down.

———————

Meeting such men introduced me to new meanings of old words and phrases: the jargon of their world. Let me explain: the first is 'property.' Anything or anybody who has been contracted is a 'property.' It is a sobering word that leaves you with few illusions. At first I used to get pointlessly upset. 'It's not a bloody property, it's a play, a work of art,' I would mutter. I once heard an American film star say, 'Of course, I'm a wonderful property...' When the film rights of a play are sold the spoils are divided. The proportions vary, but in this case, which was the best possible deal for an author, I got fifty-four per cent, my agent ten per cent and eighteen per cent each for the West End and Broadway producers. A play has no value until it is produced, nor a book until it is published, so there is fairness in the arrangements; the risk-takers get the profits. Of course, there are many sad cautionary tales on the subject. An 'escalation offer' is one that escalates with the run of the play up to a specified limit. This particular offer of £100,000 was divided into two parts: £50,000 for the London run of the play and the same for Broadway.

'Producer's profits' is my favourite: a euphemism for legalised robbery. A producer and a distributor do a deal over a film for, say, a fifty-fifty division of profits. Therefore five per cent of the film's whole profits is the same as ten per cent of the 'producer's profits.' But here is the catch: as long as the producer's and distributor's accountants are each watching the other party, the books have to be straight or there could be no film industry. However, once the producer has his share of the profits, you are in his hands. If he has any sense he is assiduously trying to hide his profits if only to save his tax bill. By the time his accountants have got to work on the books, you will find that 'producer's profits' have been swallowed somewhere or other. You don't accept 'producer's profits,' you get your cut earlier. I don't think Ray Stark seriously thought we would accept 'producer's profits.' He was probably just trying it on to test Harvey's calibre.

Harry Saltzman, co-producer of the early James Bond films was, if possible, hotter than Ray Stark, the hottest thing in the film world. I was invited to join his party at the Trattoria Terrazza one evening after he had seen the play and was placed at his right hand at the circular table; the current court favourite. There followed the ritual blast of adulation about my talent. It was my first glimpse into the yes-man hierarchy that accompanies a tycoon. P G Wodehouse wrote of a meek little man who could never hope to reach yes-man status and aspired merely to becoming a second nodder. Something like this went on at Saltzman's table, only his nice-looking, stylish, French-Canadian wife stood aside. Any coherent sentence I uttered was greeted by a wave of laughter, I had never realised I was such a wit. Passing personalities from the film world joined in as they paused to pay homage at The Court of King Harry. However, under the bonhomie was one of the toughest-looking personas I have ever been near. Saltzman was built like the Michelin man and the similarity was emphasised by the waves of energy that radiated from him. I felt he would bounce across the room rather than walk. On top of his globe-shaped body, was a round head with close-cut hair. The overall effect suggested that you would sprain your wrist if you punched him; not that anyone would have dared.

After the meal we went back to his mews house in Mayfair. He and his wife went in the chauffeur-driven Rolls, I followed in our nearly-new Triumph Herald Estate. The Saltzmans were en route to their country house. 'We're going in half an hour, Harry,' said Mrs. Saltzman and left us. Mrs. Saltzman's influence was also visible in the impressive room in which I found myself. After going through a perfectly ordinary front door in a mews, we were in an Aladdin's cave. It was superbly furnished with antiques and I admired the lovely reproductions of Impressionists and other famous artists' work that covered the walls. With a jolt I realised that they couldn't possibly be reproductions. There was more money hanging on the walls than I had ever seen: art properties. Saltzman flicked a switch and an ornamental garden was lit up. As I grappled with a brandy balloon the size of a fruit bowl, he painted glowing pictures of what he would do with the film; these too, seemed quite impressionistic. Sharp on thirty minutes later Mrs Saltzman appeared. 'We're going now, Harry.' And they did.

Harvey and I met Saltzman in his office a day or two later to learn his final offer. We would then take it to Nat Cohen to see if he would match it and I would know to which of these two I had sold out. The £100,000 figure offered by Stark seemed to be the ceiling. Saltzman offered the same, so the pith of the meeting would be what percentage of the film's profits I could get on top of the fee. Although inflation makes these figures now seem unremarkable I believe £100,000 was then a record for an English play.

My control over my own material ended here. The writer in films has no status. Even his title is a diminishment: dramatist to scriptwriter. So the sale of a play to a film company is literally a sell-out. Since the income from a film can be anything, there is no sum you can sensibly sell for; the deal must include a percentage of profits.

Harvey was edgy, as was I. We sat on a beautiful, squashy, leather sofa in Saltzman's office. We had a similar one on the set of *Soup* in Robert's swinging bachelor pad. It was le dernier cri and had excited much admiration; there were two of them in this office.

Saltzman started off politely, but the excessive bonhomie had disappeared now that we were down to hard figures. 'No one else has an interest in this property?' He asked suspiciously.

'My play, you mean,' I said.

'That's what I said.'

'No,' we both lied in open-faced unison.

'That's not what I hear.'

'Really?' We both looked blank.

Saltzman let that go. The £100,000 figure was agreed for the rights on the same escalation deal I have already described, plus a further £7,500 for my labour in adapting the play for the screen. At this point Saltzman told us a story of the making of *The Ipcress File*. 'The script was useless. We had to fire the writer. That scene where they're walking along the Mall with the Horse Guards riding by in the background; there was no script; we made it up on the spot; it was the best scene in the film. I fired seven scriptwriters off *The Ipcress File*.' I pondered the workings of the mind of a man who could tell that story to a writer with whom he was negotiating.

We got to the question of percentage of profits. He offered five per cent of producer's profits. 'I always get a fifty-fifty deal with the distributor so that's equivalent to two-and-half percent of the film's profits,' he told us.

Harvey, mindful of the pitfall of 'producer's profits,' moved in. 'In that case I wonder if we could take our percentage that way, Harry?' He said. 'From film's profits.'

Saltzman flew into a rage. I thought he was going to bounce over the desk and barge Harvey off the sofa and out of the window. The implications of Harvey's remark were insulting. Didn't we trust him? Who did we think we were? The spectacle was amazing. I got to my feet and ushered Harvey out. Saltzman was as surprised as he had been angry.

'I don't have to listen to my agent being insulted, I like him and I don't like this.' We got down two-and-a-half flights of stairs before Saltzman, his fury gone, stopped us, the personification of good humour. Arms round us, he ushered us back up to his office. Getting us up those two-and-a-half flights cost him a further two-and-a-half percent of 'producer's profits.' At seven-and-a-half percent we were back in the office. That became three-and-three-quarter percent of the whole film's profits as we were re-seated on the squashy leather. Harvey and I, used to the subtle persuasiveness of Michael Codron and the gentlemen of the BBC Copyright Department, had never seen anything like this.

We rushed round to Nat Cohen's office to see if he would exercise his option to match Saltzman's offer. 'Too rich for my blood,' he told us and smiled contentedly through the cloud of cigar smoke that shrouded him. I can never see Nat in my imagination without the omnipresent Havana. He didn't seem in the least concerned that the price was supposedly beyond his means. There was a bit of easy chat before he said he would like to make a call to Hollywood. 'Let's see what I can do.'

He got Mike Frankovitch, who had a deal as an independent to make four films through Columbia, 'Mike, I know you're looking for properties. I've got that hit comedy over here, *Girl In My Soup*, that's coming to Broadway. I can have it for an escalation up to £100,000 sterling, plus three and three-quarters percent of the film's profits, the author to write the screenplay.' The screenwriting fee obviously wasn't even worth mentioning. 'It's too rich for my blood. D'you want to come in?' He hung up. 'We're in business.'

All of which only leads one to ask, if Mike Frankovitch and Columbia were looking for properties, why hadn't they bid on their own account? Could there have been a previous private arrangement with Nat over his 'secret' matching option? Perish the thought, but there wasn't exactly a protracted negotiation over their deal.

I have only seen Harry Saltzman once since then. The following spring, during the film festival at Cannes, I was standing outside the Carlton Hotel, about to go and play golf with Eric Sykes. Harry Saltzman approached us, 'Hi, Eric, just caught your film, *The Plank*. Great. Very funny. I laughed a lot.' I was trying to get my car between me and Saltzman.

'Thanks,' said Eric, 'Oh, d'you know Terry Frisby? He wrote *There's a Girl in my Soup*. Terry, Harry Saltzman.'

Saltzman turned, an affable hand outstretched. As he heard the title of the play, he congealed and two cold slabs stared straight through me. I felt chilled in spite of the Mediterranean sun. 'Ya. We met.' His voice had no tone. I was still quivering when Eric and I reached the golf course. I heard there was also a lengthy argument with Nat during a transatlantic flight (all eight hours of it? I wondered) in which he kept shaking his head and repeating, 'You screwed me over that one, Nat. You screwed me over that one.'

Christine found an eight-bedroomed, detached, Victorian house on Putney Hill which we decided to fill with children.

Number One, Genoa Avenue had everything she wanted. After turning it down at £17,500 in August, we got it in September for £12,750. The prices don't seem possible now, but it was the nadir of Harold Wilson's first freeze and squeeze.

We started having the interior bashed about: three rooms became one marvellous kitchen; two more rooms became a forty-seven-foot-long drawing room; small bedrooms became bathrooms, after all we didn't need eight bedrooms, not even including the nanny's; I had a sunny study right at the top. It was fantasy-fulfilment time.

Frank Young, my accountant, was a stocky, melancholic man who regarded anything to do with income as a trial to be borne. With the film deal about to be concluded, I told him that unless I was assassinated on the way to signing it, nothing would stop me earning less than £70,000 that year. He drew in his breath through pursed lips and shook his head. 'My God, you've got problems,' he said. 'I might be able to hold your tax bill at £40,000, but a more sensible figure for you to set aside would be £50,000 or you could find yourself in trouble.' Frank was doing sums as he talked, income tax, surtax, gains tax, taxes I hadn't heard of. 'You need legal advice. We must get Bill Fournier to go to a tax counsel and see what he has to say. In the meantime, get as big a mortgage as you can or you'll be short next

82

year when the Revenue comes at you.' He had voiced my fears, exactly; this blizzard of pound notes might stop without warning.

It was light relief to apply for a mortgage. 'The house has cost £12,750, we are spending a further £8,000 on improvements. What is the most you will advance us?' The Building Society manager raised his eyebrows at such profligacy in that economic climate. 'What was your income for the last three financial years?'

'About seven hundred; just over a thousand; and nearly fifteen hundred pounds.'

Disapproval deepened. 'And what do you expect to clear this year?'

I smiled with relish. 'Well I can't be quite precise. You know, I'm in an uncertain profession.'

'Well, to within, say £500?'

'Oh, I think perhaps seventy-five.'

He was getting impatient. 'Seventy-five what?'

'Thousand.' Saying it out loud was like tipping ball-bearings into a brass bell or shouting in a canyon. The word 'thousand' seemed to echo and re-echo into infinite distances and sums. The reverberations hung in the air. Oh, to be rich, no matter how temporarily, is deeply satisfying. I was given a £7,000 mortgage, the maximum allowed. Whoever was being freezed and squeezed, it certainly wasn't Christine and me. Fortune, not in the least outrageous as far as we were concerned, was regarding us with a smile of glowing benevolence.

Chapter XI

1966

New York held a glamorous place in my imagination in those days, with Broadway at its heart. Each stage of our journey there was increasingly exciting. The thrill of sitting with Christine and Michael Codron, both seasoned transatlantic travellers, for over eight hours in a pre-jumbo yet was almost too much for me. By the time we were on the long approach to New York, gliding snail-like over the Canadian tundra, I was convinced that nothing could stay up that long. From the excitement of the plane we transferred to the intoxication of the helicopter bus. This flirted with skyscrapers, then, unbelievably, landed on top of one of them (no longer allowed). A stomach-turning sixty-storey plunge in an elevator to street level preceded the lurching finale of a ride in a yellow cab, with my head thrown back, staring straight up out of the rear window at the pinnacle where we had just landed, one of many which disappeared behind vast man-made cliffs, while we wriggled through noisy canyons to the Algonquin, the mandatory English-theatrical hotel. As we alighted, armed police were surrounding the building down the road which was being robbed. It was a journey that lived up to every cinematic expectation, right to its thrilling climax.

To discover, after the initial zing, that New York, of all cities, was not only dated but positively parochial, took me by surprise. The feeling shared by most English theatricals who crossed the Atlantic then, that London was the centre of the world, was reinforced by everything we saw; only the big musicals impressed. The theatrical conventions of Broadway and Off-Broadway looked dog-eared; English theatre was overwhelming theirs; entry of English actors was very severely restricted.

We were there to interview several producers, candidates to put *Soup* on Broadway. What relish to contemplate such a queue. One had such a plausible line in quiet sincerity he managed to convince Christine (neither gullible nor a stranger to the place) that the fountain in The Four Seasons restaurant was of champagne. Another, eminently successful, stared at us on introduction then roared, 'My God, but you're children,' and took us out to a meal that was a demonstration in rudimentary methods of eating. When his plate was removed it left a clean patch on the tablecloth. He was eager for Bob to direct and Barbara Ferris to play but at my mention of

Donald a muffled roar seeped through his mouthful of salad with Roquefort dressing, 'I wouldn't have that faggot on my stage.'

Had this been the first time I had heard this sentiment, even without the escorting airborne edibles, I might have been more surprised, but I wasn't. Anyone less queer than Donald would be difficult to imagine, but New York producers had been unable to accept his performance as straight. Donald's characterisation of that temple of vanity, Robert, was splendidly full of posturing and self-love. This said only one thing to a 1966 New York producer: queen. If an actor played it camp, as Donald did, he must be gay. Theatrically speaking, ambiguity hadn't arrived (Orton's bi-sexual *Entertaining Mr Sloane* had been blasted by the New York reviewers), and in spite of each producer sitting in the Globe and hearing the gales of American-tourist laughter that Donald created, none of them would touch him. Evidence is no antidote for prejudice.

Donald, from being under on tour, had, after we opened, taken off almost into another dimension. Bob and I had asked for a period, let's say Restoration, feel from his performance and we were getting it in spades after only a month or two. He was about to go on to the Royal Shakespeare Company to play a succession of fops and ensure his reputation for years to come. One evening I had gone backstage, full of wonder at the lengths to which he had taken his performance in *Soup*.

'Hallo, Frizzers, old chap, how are you?' said the well-known, rich-baritone voice.

'Wonderful, Donald. I hope you are.'

'You know I'm going next to the RSC to play Lord Foppington in *The Relapse.*'

'Yes. Congratulations.'

'Well, Trevor Nunn was in last night. "Donald," he said, "that's perfect for Foppington. I want a caricature of this performance." '

My jaw dropped. 'Donald, that's not possible.'

He gave me an old-fashioned look for a moment, then let out a peel of fruity laughter. 'Same old Frizzers.'

We saved till last Arnold Saint Subber, known as Saint; I must say, he was a most unlikely Arnold. He was then on the crest of a wave with Neil Simon's comedies; Neil's money, I later discovered, would be behind this venture. Saint Subber was Michael's first choice as Broadway producer.

'I love him,' Michael had said. 'He came into my office and sidled along the wall. He's shy, introspective, minute, quiet. You'd never know he was American.' He grinned, 'What's more he has—er—taste.' He knew my opinion of the concepts of 'good taste' and 'bad taste.'

I grinned thinly back. 'I see. We don't know the quality of this sensory achievement, merely of its existence.'

'My God, he's American. What more do you want?'

Christine and I turned up at Saint Subber's terraced house in the smart East-sixties. A young Japanese manservant showed us in (Oh, the pretty black one's gone, has he? said Michael later.) We were kept waiting for a while in a room of mysterious decor that involved a lot of black, then were shown into a tiny lift for a journey of just one floor. He was reclining on cushions; we were offered low, chair-like objects. He was even smaller than I expected, very quiet and impossibly thin, like an expensively-clad, bald stick-insect. He had on some sort of Japanese dressing gown. Every time it was his turn to speak he would screw up his face, stiffen, then gently squirt the sentence from himself. The whole process was like a low-keyed birth spasm and the semi-audible remarks it produced were given an aura that exceeded the worth of their content.

He screwed up, stiffened, gripped a cushion for support and convulsed gently towards Christine. 'You're beautiful,' he got out. That never did any harm to relations with Christine, she smiled graciously. 'She's beautiful,' he jerked at me.'

'I know.' I was sitting very still, trying not to break something and smelling joss-sticks for the first time in my life.

He pointed himself at me again. 'Mr Frisby, I'm...'

'Oh, Terry, please.'

Grimace, shudder. 'Terry doesn't suit you.'

'Oh.'

'May I call you Terence?'

'Please do. It beats Clarence.'

He came to a complete halt for a moment, apparently unable to speak. Then, 'What?'

'Nothing. sorry.' I was going to have to cut out the asides if we were ever to finish a conversation.

'I'll get dressed. We'll go and eat.'

Somehow he got to his feet unaided and disappeared. I heard distant but quite clear sounds of dissent between him and the Japanese manservant. I didn't realise Saint could make so much vocal noise. Christine crept about the room, examining everything. 'He's incredible, isn't he?' she whispered gleefully. 'I'm mad about him.'

He reappeared in a suit that was clearly expensive yet was cut too tight for him. He looked frailer than ever and I wondered at a mind that chose to accent his physical oddity so. I was also burning to get a tailor's tape on him to find out just what was the girth of that tiny chest: thirty two inches? Thirty? In the twenties?

Over dinner he told us again with what was, for him, a light-hearted smile, but would have frightened sensitive children, that Christine was beautiful. Then he suggested that she play Clare in the play. Before the polite smile of refusal or acceptance could form on our faces he groaned abjectly. 'Oh, but she'd never get an Equity card or working permit. But wouldn't she have been great!'

Over coffee he waxed lyrical. 'I've just come back from Japan. I've been watching their Noh theatre. It's fantastic.' His little face was alight with fervour. 'Their plays go on for nine hours. You can go out for a meal and come back and it doesn't matter. Nothing's happened; the actors are still holding the same poses. Then suddenly, someone'll do something and it's fantastic; like an eruption, a supreme theatrical experience.'

'It must be.'

'All I really want to do is put on Noh plays in New York. They'll be a sensation.' He shook his head and signed at the beauty of his vision.

'What's stopping you?' I asked.

'I'd lose my shirt.'

Michael did a deal with Saint Subber which I approved and the Broadway production was settled.

A cheque for the first part of the film sale landed on our doormat. It read 'Thirty-four thousand, six hundred and fifty pounds only.' Ivor had come round for coffee and we all sat at the kitchen table and admired it , chortling. It was the 'only' that got us. It seemed a pity to pay it in. I walked round to the Putney Hill branch of the Westminster Bank with that and some other cheques. As I arrived home Christine was on the telephone.

'It's the bank manager. He's very agitated.'

His agitation was covered under a new-found respect. 'Did you know that you had just paid over thirty-five thousand pounds into your current account?'

I said that I recollected the event.

'Yes, no, yes. of course. I didn't mean that,' he said, clearly feeling silly. 'I mean it's gone into your current account, not on deposit. It should be earning interest. Do you need any help? We can send an adviser round.'

Money, the sheer excitement of it. Our lives changed, sometimes subtly, sometimes obviously, but they changed. Friends' faces changed. They didn't mean to, but they did. People who dealt with us dealt differently, even when they tried not to: a tenth of a second more respect; a little more attention; the gravity of one's utterances was weighed differently; smiles wherever we went; a cushion quickly and unobtrusively forming between us and anything not quite - well, not quite. Christine was twenty-four, I was thirty-three. We were attractive, presentable, a 'lovely couple,' above all, rich. I would like to know how you beat it.

However the 'rich' idea didn't fit reality. We had serious financial problems to deal with. If we weren't careful we could be back to square one.

Even though I was going to earn over £70,000 that year, £50,000 would go to the tax-man. The top rate of income tax in those days was 19/6 in the £

(ninety-seven-and-a-half per cent). When we had bought our new house we would have nothing left. What would happen the following year? A prolonged cold spell in winter and the play could be off; perhaps it wouldn't take abroad; New York might hate it. Write another hit play was, of course, the answer, then another and another, but until *Soup* I had earned in my seventeen years of adult life, sweet damn-all. Those days could easily return. I regarded myself as responsible for several people: we wanted to start a family and I was going to make sure Christine did it in comfort; Christine's father was dying of cancer, a year or two was all he had; her mother was semi-crippled from arthritis; my father was about to retire, after forty years on the railway, to a railwayman's pension; my mother, after twenty-five years in Dickins and Jones, was about to retire to no pension at all. I was a writer, I could work anywhere. Not to conserve what we had just got and what could come over the next year or two was mad.

Bill Fournier, our lawyer consulted an eminent tax counsel: if we became foreign residents for the following year, the £70,000-odd I was currently earning would become ours tax-free; while abroad we could set up an offshore trust to take my foreign royalties; if we then returned to the UK and I went on earning big money we left the trust funds to grow in their foreign tax haven; when we, our parents, or anyone else we named as beneficiaries, needed money in future years, we or they would draw it from the trust and pay tax at current, less swingeing rates. It was simple: spread the windfall and make it last a lifetime. We chose the Cayman Islands to be the home for the trust money, Cannes for ourselves.

Christine's parents were installed in 16 Bective Road. Vic set about the garden he had wanted all his life with amazing new-found energy, even without four-fifths of his stomach. We gave Minnie the poodle to Babs, whose immobility matched the dog's laziness. Even the set lines of discontent on Babs' face softened.

My parents found a house for themselves in Kent, a mile or two from my brother and his wife, one of a pleasing circle of houses that backed onto a communal paddock with fruit trees. I went to their old house in Welling to talk to them about things. A neighbour popped his head over the privet hedge as I passed.

'I hear you're very successful now, Terry. You got three plays running in the West End.'

'Eh? Who told you that?'

'Your dad.'

I tackled my father. 'Did you tell Mr Fletcher I've got three plays running in the West End?'

He didn't even look shifty. 'Well, you have, haven't you?'

'Eh? What are they?'

'*There's A Girl in my Soup.*'

'Yeah.'

'*The Subtopians.*'

'That was years ago for one month; at the Arts, not the West End.'

'Same thing.'

'No, it's not, you know that. Anyway, what's the third one?'

'Well, you're writing another one, aren't you.'

'Oh, Dad.'

'Well, huh blimey, if I can't enjoy meself a bit now you're a celebrity, when can I?'

My mother was misty-eyed. 'It's no good talking to him. And don't you waste all this money on us. You take care of yourself.'

'We are, Ma. Don't worry.'

'Hm. I know you. Anyway a house is a good investment and you'll have it back after we've gone, so I suppose it's all right.'

We took a few other steps so that everyone close to us was housed and cared for; if the play went on earning, all our futures were safe. I felt clever and smug and couldn't wait to get away from the endless desk work that the money had created and start my new play.

I listened unmoved to the jibes about my skin-deep socialism, about running from a tax system for which I had voted all my life. Political philosophy came later, the figures were irrefutable, 'we' were my first priority. My glib parry to all probes became, 'Yes. I shall still vote Labour. And with a clear conscience. People need protecting from the likes of me.'

Chapter XII

1966-7

Life with Christine was a picnic without the wasps. We had been married just under three years, *Soup* had just opened, when she produced a new goodie from her brimming hamper: the gift of sexual liberty. Only this gift had strings.

'Do what you like but don't bring it home to me' she said one evening as we were going to bed.

'What?' I said, looking up from the latest Margaret Drabble.

'You can sleep with whoever you like but don't tell me,' she repeated, liberally slapping on the removing cream. I put Ms. Drabble aside and leaned up in bed on one elbow, carefully watching Christine. Married friends had been to dinner and one of those discussions had sputtered on about infidelity. Secure in my wedded wholeness I used to feel most ambivalent during these conversations. Husbands, who had banged anything available whenever possible, professed views that could not be reconciled with their behaviour. Wives, who had discreetly lowered the relevant garments, primly assumed their own chastity and, with theirs, their husbands'. 'I know John could never be unfaithful because he has told me so.' And John would take her hand and look equally fond. 'And of course, *I* don't want to, so that's that,' she would conclude. My feelings were ambivalent because the pleasure of watching hypocrisy and self-delusion rampant was marred by compassion. How could they lie to their partners so? For those who do it openly, or by arrangement, it is another matter, but dishonest infidelity is so discourteous, apart from anything else; everyone (except the relevant spouse) always knows. I wanted no part of it, the whole business was out of court as far as I was concerned.

However, over dinner Christine had, to my surprise, thrown into the discussion the commonplace that it was all acceptable if everyone kept quiet. Now it appeared that her generalisation had a particular point. I was riveted and cautious. 'Erm. Three things: a) I don't want to, b) if I did, I'd want to tell you about it, and c) you'd find out anyway.' I watched her beavering away with a tissue.

'Well, a) you will, b) don't and c) I won't,' she answered.

I said, 'Remember The Seventeen? Two men, you said, before we got married then seventeen. Remember the pain that cover-up caused? And you want to start a new one?'

90

'That cover-up hurt no one. The lie, as you call it, gave you pleasure. It was telling the truth that caused the pain.'

Such logic is argument-proof, but I couldn't help re-treading old ground. 'I didn't give a sod how many. Only about the lie.' A dismissive snort was all she thought that was worth. There was a permanent gulf between us on that issue. I changed tack. 'What about always sharing, no secrets, all that?'

'Oh, lovely,' She was quite worked up now. 'Darling, I've met this super bird, lovely long legs, terrific figure, beautiful boobs, I'm wild to screw her. I knew you'd want to share in the news.' A piece of tissue zipped accurately into the waste bin.

I laughed. 'Seems unlikely, I must say.'

'It's impossible. You're successful now, you'll have loads of chances. When it happens just keep quiet.' She seemed to change tack. 'You know why I married you? You made me feel safe.'

I was amazed. 'Safe?'

'Yes I was going to marry money, but it had to be you. Now I'm safe *and* I've got money, so keep me safe, keep quiet.' She giggled and jumped into bed but there was a strong undercurrent, almost of hysteria. The matter was clearly important to her.

I found the conversation disturbing. Why had she brought up the subject when it was superfluous? Had she seen something, some straw in the wind that I hadn't? She saw most things sooner than I; it never occurred to me was that this code might be designed to apply to her own activities so I never raised that issue; indeed I would not have offered her similar licence. I tried to imagine myself trampling across her feelings with an admission of intended - or merely desired - infidelity and couldn't. And since I had no wish to be unfaithful I let the matter go. She seemed right, but something that I couldn't pinpoint was terribly wrong with her creed, which was repeated a few times during the following years. 'Do as you like but don't tell me.'

But the desire to enjoy some different female body didn't take years to appear, it took about three more months. The clinical phraseology is intentional, I am not writing about a love affair, or even what plays used to call infatuation, but about extra-marital sex: basic adultery.

Jane was one of those females who causes locked bumpers in the Kings Road. Proximity to her made my pulse race and we were thrown together frequently. She indicated with the merest look that she was game - Christine was right that my sexual attractiveness seemed to be rising in direct proportion to material success - and I was pitched into a protracted struggle with myself. Which of the three possible courses should I follow? Do nothing; tell Christine how I felt and see how we go from there; don't tell and get on with it. Boorish or enlightened - I think, in fact, naive - I believe I would have followed the second. Open marriage was being talked about all round us in the middle of that decade of sexual liberation. But Christine's instruction pushed us back into the old hypocrisy. It led me to the moment of ambiguity, the chicken and egg question: was obedience to her instruction my reason or my excuse for following the third course? The first course was never really likely, certainly not for an entire lifetime. It was really only a choice between the second and third, and that key question of my moral, ethical and emotional core was begged; I still do not really know what the answer would have been. It is maddening. And in avoiding the issue I allowed a significant gap to open between us. We went happily on without noticing but I, who till then had believed in and practised utter frankness with my wife, was going to travel my own road.

Into all this heart searching was thrown another event that complicated matters further, it set a time-bomb that ticked for years: Christine gave me a surprise birthday party. Friends leaped out of the woodwork bawling 'Happy Birthday,' and bearing champagne and presents. I, who had to strain to remember Christmas, had forgotten this day. Gratitude crawled through me as food, drink and goodies abounded. A large pot of some sort of stew was dished out by Christine. It had been bubbling on the stove for days. 'What's that?' I had asked idly. 'I'm boiling down some bones,' or something, was her unlikely answer, accepted in full by me, as I accepted everything from her. Experience is no teacher.

'You didn't even notice,' crowed Christine, full of delight at the success of her subterfuge. 'I knew you wouldn't. Enough here to feed us for a month and if you'd fallen into it you wouldn't have seen it.'

'I notice everything,' I told everybody, our old shorthand for my inability to remark any domestic change short of demolition.

The surprise birthday party prolonged my internal struggle about Jane. It sputtered fitfully on for about nine months and it might have continued indefinitely (I felt no particular urgency) but precisely the right opportunity offered itself. Her green light had continued to wink and the date of my departure into tax-exile was imminent. There was the solution: a roll in the hay; no chance of repetition and therefore gossip; away to foreign parts (no pun intended).

After the theoretical heart-searching, the practical steps were suitably lugubrious. A few days before our departure date I turned up at Jane's flat by arrangement, with a bunch of flowers, a bottle of whisky and one of champagne. We sat drinking while I wondered whether I should fall on her straight away like a detonated chimney stack or whether she preferred a decent interval of verbal foreplay. The doorbell rang. It was a well-known actor, an old acquaintance, who entered proprietorially and stopped dead on seeing me. We viewed each other with mutual loathing before I disappeared into the middle distance at an untidy gallop, leaving the field and the booze to him. I was still breathing heavily when I drove Christine onto the air ferry at Southend a few days later, still technically faithful. There is always some bugger who will find out.

———

The bed-of-roses condition into which my life had changed seemed to be stretching ahead indefinitely. Cannes was all it was cracked up to be. Our villa, one of six in a cosy *domaine*, was set on the side of a hill behind Cannes with a view that brought a lump to your throat; both human-scaled and spectacular. Immediately before us in the garden, then dropping away, were flowers, bright primary colours, faded yellows and browns . In the distance were La Croisette, le vieux port, the Mediterranean and the mountains of Estoril over which we watched summer storms rage from our afternoon bed. Behind us were the snow-capped Alps: everything hazy and shimmering in summer; cool, hard and clear in winter. In autumn, sunsets that I couldn't believe; in spring, wisteria and mimosa everywhere. One winter morning everything was covered in snow which vanished as we looked at it.

It was bliss to jump into the open Triumph first thing, wind down the chemin to the boulangerie, back with the croissants and baguettes, the air rushing past; to breakfast on the terrace all the year round and spend the morning working at my desk with the windows open and the blue and green of sea and pines pouring in; to lunch on the terrace or on the beach, listening to the French talking to each other as though an instant's pause will bring execution; to spend hours skiing round the bay watching flying-fish skip away and to slalom over the wakes of the liners and ferries, mouth open in a continuous yell. One day, when Michael Codron and David Sutton were staying nearby, I took them out into the middle of the bay and broke down in the path of a vast ship while they sat bolt upright in their seats, scarves neatly tucked into their shirts, stifling squeaks of terror as I tried to start the outboard.

Outside our *domaine* the overriding impression was one of richness; I mean of the sort that money can and does buy. Having collared one of the best bits of the world for itself, the money spoke loudly and clearly. The boats, the houses, the restaurants, the clothes, the comfort, the women (yes, yet another commodity), the cars, the barriers against unpleasantness; money can and does buy something very like happiness. My income of £1,000 a week rising to about £2,500 a week during our stay there made us poor relations to many we met. It was an eye-opener I had not really expected. One knows about the super-rich but, like anything else, you have actually to be confronted with them for the penny to drop. There were many so rich that to accuse them of selfish materialism would be an irrelevance. They understood no other condition.

One day our boat broke down when we were well out to sea. A fifty-foot cabin cruiser pulled up beside us, a mechanic and glasses of champagne were offered for our benefit while the owner, an elegant-looking cad, chatted up Christine in an indescribable accent. Extraordinary accents of unplaceable origin were commonplace in that cosmopolitan melting pot, phonetic mutations of English that would have given the staff of The Central School of Speech Training joy to investigate. The cad towed us into Antibes harbour and said, 'Wirrs yur yaat?' He didn't believe us when we told him we were sitting in it.

We made vague efforts to speak French properly. After eighteen months Christine could produce for, 'I'm going down to the shops in a minute,' 'Me went shops later on today for sixty seconds,' which gave everyone, including her, a lot of pleasure.

I started on a new play but it wouldn't come. In *Soup* I had got the singles scene off my chest, now I wanted to write about jealousy and infidelity in marriage, the subject of double standards that had plagued my creative areas (wherever they are) since The Seventeen. And even as I struggled with it I knew why it was impossible. It would have been bad enough to have betrayed my inner obsessions to Christine, but to have betrayed her and The Seventeen to the world... I remembered my parents' grey faces five years earlier on the first night of *The Subtopians*. I could no more do that to Christine than fly, yet there I sat morning after morning in the soft, clear air of my working-room at Cannes trying to write the unwritable. 'Do as you like, but don't tell me,' rang in my ears on both a personal and a professional level. It became 'don't tell anyone,' a separate, silent road that was creatively a blind alley.

So, under the twin strain of my artistic constipation and her ignorance of the cause, we had only our second bloody-good row in four years - well, first really, The Seventeen couldn't really be classed as a row. We were both miserable. The solution was easy, I gave way, I shelved work and took three months holiday; ostrich behaviour but lovely.

In May the sleepy little seaside town bursts into maniacal life when the film world and every sort of hanger-on arrives. A memorable moment worthy of a dentist's probe was provided by a dishy, young, French, so-called film producer whom we called Ace-Puller-Jean-Yves, always in full, because that is what he was. He appeared to be devoted to fucking his way through the entire array before us on the beach and, unlike the other devotees, looked like succeeding. Propped up on one elbow he would regard the fresco of passing crumpet. 'I 'ad 'air yesterday. She 'as 'ad tew lerveurs.' Then at another, 'I'm going to 'ave 'air ce soir and she will 'ave 'ad tew lerveurs.'

'How do you know?'

'They 'ave all 'ad tew lerveurs.'

'Why?'

'We-ell,' long, lazy gesture, 'it sounds better than 'undred and tew, two-hundred and tew. Don't you agree?'

Christine and I didn't exchange glances. I was frozen.

'But why do you ask 'em, if you know they're lying?'

'I 'ave a sense of comfort to see zat nozzing changes. Ze 'ole world is in ferment, but women will keep us straight.'

In the middle of the Festival fun and games was Nat Cohen, head of Anglo-Amalgamated films, one of the most powerful men in the British film industry, never without his Havana, circle of friends and decorative female. His passions were gin rummy and racing, there were two Grand National trophies on his mantelpiece. He was the most easy-going, generous and Philistine of men. His wit was well-known: 'If you make it with her, I'll have the pick of the litter,' was his most-repeated sally. Any breakdown in what he saw as reasonable behaviour was judged by his all-embracing 'You know his problem? TMM.'

'What's that Nat?'

'Too much money.'

'No, I'm not going to the cinema,' in answer to our invitation. 'I've been coming here fifteen years and I've never seen a film yet.' One day we lay at Eden Roc sunbathing and I got him between gin-rummy sessions and asked him what were his favourite films. He gave a list of figures about takings, profits and losses for answers, but I persisted over a period of days.

'But what did you *think* of that film, Nat?

'It took a lot of money.'

'Yes, but did you *like* it?

'I've told you. It made a good profit.'

'Well, what about so-and-so?'

'Lost.'

'Yes, but did you *like* it?'

'How can you like a film that loses money?'

'Yes, but Nat, setting aside profit and loss for a moment -'

'How can you set aside—?'

'Yes, yes, I know, but when you saw the previews, before the film was released, was there ever a film you liked then, before you knew the figures?'

He paused, distant love being recalled. '*The Grand National*, with Basil Radford. that was good. I liked that. It was about racing. Lost money though. Bloody public. It was too good for them.'

And what of my adultery? Any person who spends a summer in Cannes without feeling at least a passing twinge in the loins needs a libidinist or whatever, but the matter was shelved. I was to go to New York in August to set up the Broadway production of *Soup*. I would have eleven weeks alone there full of the intoxicating excitement of preparation. In the anonymity of that place, with an assumed name if necessary (we didn't want any scalp-hunters, did we?), anything could happen before Christine arrived to join me for artistic and commercial triumph on Broadway.

There was an incident, though, to remind me of the danger of my project. It was a Thursday, two days before I was due to go. A telegram arrived: I wasn't required for a few more days. I took it down to Eden Roc where Christine was sunbathing with a group of people we knew, one of whom was Nat Cohen with accompanying sex-object. She was one of those you had to force yourself not to stare at for longer than you did other women; it was quite difficult. I watched several men drag their gaze away with reluctance only to twitch as though slapped on meeting the eyes of their spouses. One of the wives once made a remark about the pattern on the sex-object's bikini bottom as she walked away from the group. All the men shot smartly up on one elbow, nodding at what the wife said and staring with studious zeai at the pattern, grateful for the brief opportunity to drink her in without retribution.

'I don't have to be there till Tuesday,' I said to Christine.

'Well, stay here, then.'

'But you're going to London this Saturday. And we've arranged flights and everything.'

'Well, change 'em. Stay here. New York's horrible at this time of year.'

A chorus of voices told me how foul New York was in August. I dived into the sea and swam to the other side of the raft that was about thirty yards offshore. With my body trailing in the water, I rested my forearms on the raft and my chin on my forearms, staring back at the land. Suddenly I was aware that Nat's companion had joined me. I tried to feel casual about her proximity, resisting the urge to grab her and, limbs entwined, sink bubbling to an orgasmic, watery death.

'Are you leaving when your wife does on Saturday or staying till Tuesday?' she asked.

'Dunno,' I stared hard at the land.

She, too, stared back at the land, placed a hand on my chest, slid it underwater, down over my stomach, under my trunks and grasped my astonished tool. She squeezed firmly. 'Stay.'

No salmon ever erupted from a Highland stream, tail threshing, more abruptly than I did from the Mediterranean that day. For the second time in six months I boarded a plane still breathing heavily. To have accepted that invitation would have been like making an announcement in *Variety* or the *Jewish Chronicle*.

In New York I set about - to express it their way - getting laid. I found one, two, three attractive would-be layers and once, twice, thrice couldn't manage it. Guilt sustained limpness. I came to a rueful conclusion: I was sentenced to lifelong fidelity by my uncontrollable conscience. God (or someone) had brought back my days of willing teenage continence and put paid to mature would-be sin.

Chapter XIII

1967

Soup was going to the Music Box theatre. Our advance was nearly half a million dollars, just short of the record held for a straight play by *The Odd Couple*. We would easily beat it. Barbara Ferris was to play Marion; Jon Pertwee, Andrew. They were, with Bob Chetwyn to direct, all that American Equity would allow to come from London where Barbara had won the Variety Club award for Most Promising Artist. Awards were fewer and further between then. We had the good fortune to find Gawn Grainger in New York with a work-permit. Gawn had been giving his Romeo to Jane Asher's Juliet; we grabbed him gratefully.

I haven't mentioned our Robert. Since Donald Sinden had been denied us, we had asked every suitable English leading man of international status that we could think of to play Robert. As with the original production, we had refusal after refusal, the same fears of being seen publicly to be ageing, of Barbara stealing the play, of goodness knows what, put them all off. Only an American showed half-hearted interest: Gig Young. Setting aside my reservations about making Robert American, thus weakening the play, Gig looked a good thing. He had, besides his film work, a good stage background, which was difficult to find in film stars, and precisely those devastating good-looks-going-over-the-hill that we wanted.

Rita Gam, George Hall and a spectacular girl, Erica Fitz, completed the cast. Her audition caused a scene which eloquently demonstrated Gig's massive Hollywood personality. It is extraordinary how starry some stars can be and Gig was by no means one of the biggest.

Bob, Gig and I were sprawled, yawning, in the stalls as a string of stunning girls auditioned with Whizz, the stage manager. Whizz had to say the line 'My God, but you're lovely,' to each girl; I have never heard so many different readings of one line, each a wonderful barometer of lust. Erica appeared and we in the stalls sat up smartly. Whizz, who was nearer than us and so got the full impact, just gawped. She read well and gave the cue. Whizz's hand holding the script fell to his side and he gazed at her. A world of unfulfilled anguish came into his voice, 'My God,' came wailing from Hades, 'but...you...are...love...lee.' He was nearly knocked over as Bob and I arrived on-stage.

'How do you do, Miss Fitz, I am the author of the play. My name is—'
I was interrupted.

'Hello, I'm Robert Chetwyn, the director. I—'

We were both brushed aside. She looked past us, eyes shining.

'Hi, I'm Gig Young,' a little pause then a slow, big, reassuring smile. 'I'm your star.'

I don't know what effect he had on Erica, but I felt quite weak at the knees myself.

But Gig never got to first base with Robert. It can happen to any actor with any part. Since *Soup* he has won an Oscar in *They Shoot Horses, Don't They?* and his reputation is secure, based on a long, honourable record of work. Some years later he married for the sixth time and shot his new young wife and himself in their New York apartment, so these observations can't harm him, nor would I wish them to, he was already dreadfully wounded by something. The neuroses that must finally have killed him and his wife were well in evidence when we started work. In view of the reluctance of all those other leading actors to admit their greying hairs, sagging muscles, failing powers and irrelevance to a new generation, it is puzzling that Gig, hooked on those very fears, took the part. Perhaps that is the answer. I went to his apartment for a meeting to go through his lines for changes of idiom. Some three hours later I staggered out. I had tried to keep my alcoholic intake down to a minimum but I was plastered on my share, about a third of a bottle, of the two bottles of vodka Gig opened and consumed while we talked. We need not have bothered with the script alterations, Gig couldn't learn them accurately anyway. Such was the state of things that, following the final rehearsal run-through, I learned the part before we opened in New Haven for our pre-Broadway tour. Bob told me later he had done the same.

Christine arrived, four weeks early. At the airport, as I stood in a gallery watching the passengers go through customs, she repeated her old trick of making everyone near her look grubby. She wore something green, spring never looked fresher.

'What are you doing here?' I asked, the smile stretching nearly round my head.

'I remember your stories of tours.' She tapped me on the chest. 'I thought I'd better be here.'

My laugh was maniacal. Projected adultery was a forgotten irrelevance in the crisis.

Back in my apartment she looked round and said, 'You've had someone, haven't you? In here. I can tell.' As I was able to look her straight in the eye and deny it, I didn't think of asking her how she had behaved in London. There was no need.

On the opening night in New Haven, Gig somehow got through it but the production was nowhere right. The evening was saved by Gawn Grainger's entrance in Act II. Jimmy is a good part but Gawn was breathtaking. He gave one of those performances playwrights pray for. We needed one that night. For his opening hangover scene he walked, or rather groped his way, zombie-like, onto the stage, picked the production up off the floor and shook it till the audience roared their approval. There was nothing Barbara could do, she had to play nearly everything with Gig. Gawn virtually did a solo turn. During that tour I wrote extra lines for him to quieten the audience for a moment so that he could get on, but he just got more laughs with them. One night after his hangover scene I heard someone say, 'Jesus, when that guy went off, everybody in the theatre had a headache.' It about summed up his powers of communication. However, word travels fast in the American theatre and the torrent of our advance bookings abruptly dwindled to a dribble. We never broke the record of *The Odd Couple*.

Gig improved, but there was a quality he was never going to be able to supply, and that was the impregnable self-satisfaction and vanity that Donald had so massively radiated. The idea of playing a character, as we understood it, was foreign to Gig. He was just nice, good-old himself (who was, may I sadly repeat, extremely nice indeed), but this turned Marion into a shrew, and try as we did, we and Barbara couldn't adjust her to Gig because it wasn't possible. The production got slick and professional during the tour but the heart of the play was gone.

One evening in Boston Christine, Gig and I were in a crowded lift in our hotel. He had been under pressure from Bob and me for some while. Suddenly he started shouting. For weeks he had been listening and trying, and trying and listening, now, after some late night drinks he let us have it. 'You mother-fucking, smart-assed Englishman and your smart-assed, mother-fucking wife, and your smart-assed, English, mother-fucking director and your smart-assed, English, fucking play…' he kept going for several floors while the doors opened and closed and people got on and off or stood reading the advertisements on the walls and feigning deafness. We piled out into a corridor. I encouraged him to go on, perhaps this breakdown would lead to a breakthrough.

'But I thought you liked the part and wanted to do it,' I said during a break in Gig's transmission.

'Yeah, that was before I said "Yes." You were the mother-fucking supplicants, I was in the driving-fucking-seat. Now it's the other fucking way.'

'Surely we're working together to get it right for all of us.' I tried.

Gig gave a wild, derisive laugh and fell into his room. The next day he smiled the Gig Young smile, apologised, and we stayed at square one. Barbara had the only weep I ever saw her give way to and when I tried to comfort her delivered a wonderful, sad aphorism, not just about Gig, but about life. It is unprintable.

We opened in New York to a reasonable press and ran for nearly a year, thanks to the advance. I tried to convince my parents, just off the QE2, that the slightly hysterical partisan tinge to the opening-night laughter was how the Americans did it, but oh, I missed that full-bodied, gut response that a good comedy should get.

The New York production was summed up by William Goldman in his book, *The Season*, which covered all the productions of the year. Goldman is a well-known screenwriter (*Butch Cassidy and the Sundance Kid, The Sting*, and many others) whose critical prose is refreshingly free of the uptight analisms of English theatre reviewers. He understood what made something popular without being inferior (adjectives that seem to be synonymous over here) and got to the heart of the attitudes of my play. As I was basking in his praise I came to his painfully accurate final words: "I think if *Girl In My Soup* had also been funny it would have run for years."

Donald, Sir Donald, how we missed you.

A week or so after the opening, my New York agent shuffled through all the reviews, the box-office takings and advance bookings on his desk. He pursed his lips judicially. 'I think we can say we're a hit, Terry, but not a smash.'

Never mind to which pigeon-hole I or my work was consigned, America, with my play on Broadway, was not half bad. We saw my father and be-minked mother off to Canada and relatives, my mother blinking happily. I wondered what exaggerations of my achievements my father would impress the Canadian branch of the family with when they met. Christine and I decided to go to Hollywood. Hitchcock wanted to talk to me about a film script. Excitement reigned. I wanted, more than anything, to drive across America. 'Don't do it,' pleaded our New York friends. 'Take a plane. There's nothing in the middle. It's empty.' A telephone call from Christine's mother postponed all that. Through the sobs and chokes we learned that Vic was dying.

Chapter XIV

1967-8

Vic's final slide was so quick that he wasn't aware of it. The doctors had said, 'Anything over three years,' precisely three years earlier. He had been eaten from inside during his years of devotion to his semi-crippled wife. At least he had a few months in his own house before the end. He made the garden, like himself, immaculate.

While Christine in London coped with her father's death and her mother's grief, not to mention her own, I wandered aimlessly round the villa and the town of Cannes with a bad attack of writer's block. The words 'tax exile' were suddenly real. For me to have entered the UK before April 6th would have destroyed our financial scheme. It was the depths of the close season, Procol Harum's *Whiter Shade of Pale* was being played everywhere, its melancholy accented the dying fall all round. Aimlessly? Not true. Since my earlier half-hearted attempts at adultery had failed, it was becoming an imperative, just to prove something to myself, it seemed, I am really not sure. But my anonymous wanderings could only be brief. Christine would be back. I soon found myself in bed beside a girl who spread her legs proudly and said, 'Il est petit, non?' The shock of her action, the use of the masculine pronoun for something so essentially female and the sight of her petit-ness ensured that I remained in a similar condition. She shrugged and went to sleep, I dressed and went home. Then one of the those competent French women took me in charge and demonstrated that I was capable of satisfying both of us, guilt or no. The rush of relief that I felt drowned any shame over the timing of my debut.

Christine arrived with her mother, who sat doped and sobbing in the corner of the living room. 'What'll become of me? What'll become of me?' was her refrain and our concern. To uproot her and keep her with us in Cannes was clearly no answer and she refused to let us arrange for anyone to live with her in London as companion. 'I don't want some bloody old maid, some old has-been or never-was living with me; two old hags together. Can you imagine it?' I liked Babs for that speech but it didn't reflect her real state. She returned to London to be met by some of Vic's brothers and sisters who rallied in the best Italian tradition. At least there she had Minnie the poodle, now devoted to her, friends nearby, relations, the telly.

As Bab's wheelchair disappeared from our sight into the Air France Caravelle, Christine sighed with relief. She had, in introspective moments, said to me 'If ever you see me behaving like mother, stop me. Do anything, but don't let me grow like her.' There was little in their relationship to stand strain, certainly not that sort of strain.

The telephone in the villa had one of those penetrating, shrill bells that the French specialise in. From time to time it would clang, generally late at night. We would shoot bolt upright in bed. Babs would be talking, hysterical. She refused to stay long with any of Vic's relatives and would manage for a short while on her own at Bective Road, then came the cry for help to Christine.

As winter crept over Europe, but not apparently over Cannes, we lived unremarkable, comfortable French lives. I dropped the play about double standards in marriage that I had found unwritable earlier in the year. Instead, I adapted for the stage *And Some Have Greatness Thrust upon Them*. This was the telescript of mine that I had written two years earlier with adaptation always in mind; I changed the title to *The Bandwagon*. It was going back to London with me for Michael Codron to read on April 7th, 1968, one day after the financial year ended. Life was languidly full. I only dimly realised what a profound relief it was to be re-writing something. It dispels the awful, hollow fear of facing original work. Creating something new, from nothing, from just yourself, is one of the great joys of life. But when it won't come, or won't flow, is unsatisfactory, or just isn't there - as is the case for any writer on many mornings - to wake up is misery. For years I didn't recognise what caused my a.m. depressions.

We lived modestly. The future was all. Every investment we made with UK royalties grew healthily. Foreign royalties flowed into the nascent Trust from Broadway and all over the world. A lifetime free of financial worries was the prize and it was speeding towards us, a lifetime to do just whatever we wanted. The only flaw was that Christine didn't get pregnant. We had tests. I was pronounced normal and we feared that Christine's abortion might have affected her. She had to go and have a D and C, or scrape, as women offhandedly call it. A scrape. I hear a knife screeching against metal or a navvy's shovel clanging on ballast. She discovered, the hard way, that she had an allergy to penicillin by being pumped full of it and taking a day to come round. This minor operation was turned into a nightmare, I sat beside her for hours while I was told unconvincingly that she would sleep it off. She look inappropriately lovely; all colour had drained from her and I seemed to be able to look into her flesh as she slept, only the merest breathing movement disturbing the unreal picture. I was scared to touch her beyond holding her hand to make sure the pulse was good, and sat there not daring to contemplate the horror of horrors if this waxy object in front of me should really become a corpse. Sometimes the urge to shake her into life or make love to her, to somehow pump life back, was like a wave, but I didn't even touch her face in the end in case I left a mark.

Christine came round and I met Lucienne. Lucienne didn't live in Cannes, she knew nobody in our circle and I got to know her quite by chance. We bumped into each other a few times and when, one day, at a drinks party, I planted a farewell kiss pointedly on her mouth instead of her cheek, she held me at arms length, looking at me hard. 'Tu es serieux?' My stomach gave a lurch of anticipation, 'Oui.' She led me off to bed. She lived alone and made no demands. She not only accepted that I loved Christine, she expected it, almost insisted on it. She had seen us together and approved. She was terrific. She took to country walks that coincided with my afternoon golf at Valbonne, where Christine never went, so that we could spend some time together outside bed, then would drift away into the pines. I had become a poor sleeper, often spending half the night pacing the villa, reading or working. Sometimes I would drive to the top of the Chemin de Vallauris and watch the sun rise over the Alps. After I met Lucienne I occasionally extended my drives, made love to her, drove home, showered and climbed into bed to embrace the waking Christine. It was delightful, I no longer felt guilt, it gave me exquisite pleasure which was passed on to Christine with interest. 'Do as you like but don't tell me' was proving to be an admirable creed.

When Christine and I had to time our sex to get her pregnant, Lucienne insisted on continence. She allowed herself only those bits of me that didn't disturb my marriage. The massage to my ego was formidable. Trust a French woman to get all that right.

The end of the financial year came and I gleefully set foot on soil under the jurisdiction of the UK Inland Revenue. My parents showed off their new house to me. As he had now retired, Dad was busy on some terrace and gardening project which seemed to involve an unnecessary quantity of hard work.

'Jesus, Dad, does it matter?' I asked, feeling weary just looking at it. 'You're sixty-five now. It is supposed to be have-a-rest time.'

He looked crestfallen. 'It'll put up the value of the property for you when we've gone.' He hastily went on 'Oh, yes, I know you're rich now, but property's property and I'm good at this.'

'Yes, Dad. It's lovely. Just take it easy though.'

'Incidentally, old son, the expenses have been a bit heavy, you know, moving and that. You couldn't…?' He watched my laughter and joined in. 'That's it. I'd do the same for you only you're the one who's got it, aren't you?'

He was right. It was such a pleasure to be able to. My mother got me alone. 'You be careful. You'll have lots of people asking you for—'

'We are careful, Ma. Very. Don't worry.'

'Has he been asking you for—?'

'Why don't you pack it in now at Dickins and Jones? You don't have to any more.' She still commuted daily to her cash desk in Regent Street for her part-time pittance.

'Oh, well, I'll see.' She looked away from me and into herself in that vague way she used when she wanted to shut out something. 'I'll think about it. I don't think I'm quite ready to...I'm not sure that I...' She trailed off, leaving a blinking smile of affection to cover her fear of retirement.

As for my new play, *The Bandwagon*, I had spread myself; it had several sets and a huge cast. With *Soup* making all that money, I thought, 'If I can't indulge in a little expensive writing now, when can I?' Michael was horrified. The cost of producing it, he claimed, was prohibitive. Bob and I discussed it and Bob thought some condensation of the play would lose it nothing, so I took it back to France to re-write it.

The film festival hit the sleepy town and once more lunacy arrived, only this time it was compounded by the 1968 near-general strike and the student riots in Paris. The contingent from the French Cinema stood on the steps of the Palais des Festivals, solemnly proclaimed solidarity with the workers, and the film festival came to an abrupt halt. The town emptied. Shouting Americans ordered taxis to Geneva and Milan. French taxi-drivers showed no solidarity whatsoever and fares rocketed. The panic was something to be seen. In fact it was about as dangerous in Cannes during the left-bank riots in Paris as it would have been walking the dog in Torquay during a demonstration in Grosvenor Square.

Christine and I sat drinking pastis in the Carlton and watched Americans fight for transport before the Red Menace struck them down. One rushed up to us. 'Get out, you two. Get out while you can.'

'But we live here.'

He pumped our hands, stared as though taking his last look and hurried away. Nat Cohen, Mike Frankovitch and Sam Spiegel barely glanced up from the gin rummy. Spiegel, so rumour had it, merely took the precaution of re-stocking his yacht with starlets before the shelves were empty.

There was a phone call from my brother's wife. My father was ill.

'But what's up?' I asked in answer to some vaguenesses.

'I think you should prepare yourself,' said Joan, to my dismay. This was right out of the blue.

'Should I come back?'

'No, we don't want to frighten him. If you turn up suddenly he'll think something's very wrong.'

'Well, it is, isn't it?'

'Not that wrong. He's done something inside him, heaving paving stones about for the terrace.'

I cursed the terrace. 'What shall I do?'

'We'll phone again. Don't worry.'

We watched the French riot police and the students on our neighbour's TV. They might as well have been on Mars. We couldn't get through to England by telephone. Three days later Joan managed from her end. 'We've been trying for ages,' she said. 'Nothing's working.'

Right: **28th August 1963 - Wedding Day**

Below: **Spring 1964 - *The Subtopians*, New Theatre Bromley; then New Arts Theatre, London**. Bill Fraser and Betty Baskcomb as Bert and Maggie Mann failing to communicate with each other

Above: **June 1966 - *There's A Girl In My Soup*, Globe Theatre, London (now the Gielgud)**. (Sir) Donald Sinden and Barbara Ferris doing themselves, and me, proud; Donald, Barbara and Jon Pertwee, from the poster

Opposite, above: **October 1967 - First Night party, Sardi's, NY**. Michael Codron and Christine.

Opposite, below: **October 1967 - First Night party, Sardi's, NY**. Mum and Dad next to Bill Fournier, lawyer, seated; Robert Chetwyn, the director, standing.

Left: **May 1968 - Cannes Film Festival.**
Christine (with me) making an
entrance to an enthusiastic cheer from
the French crowd.

Below: **October 1967 - *There's A Girl In
My Soup*, Music Box Theatre, NY.**
Barbara Ferris and the doomed Gig
Young.

'How's Dad?'

'They are not hopeful. Can you get back?'

'Christ Almighty. Of course. At once.

The flight to London, normally ninety minutes, couldn't overfly French airspace so took all day as we hopped round Europe. It was June 6th, the twenty-fourth anniversary of D-day. All I could think of was being eleven years old and banging my spoon on the cereal bowl at breakfast as the BBC announcer said '...allied troops have this morning landed on the mainland of Europe...' and Dad in his ARP tin hat.

We arrived at West Hill Hospital, Dartford, and hurried to the ward. My father was in a room at one end of it. As I rounded a corner Jack, my brother was leading Mum from the room. She was quietly crying and fell on me. 'He's gone,' she said. 'He was looking forward to seeing you.' I went into the room. He had died moments before. He was half propped up, eyes closed, but mouth yawed open. His teeth weren't in. His face, normally square and pugnacious, looked long and stupid because of his open, toothless jaw; and very old; an aged simpleton. I stood looking at him for some while. It was so undignified. This thing didn't look like him. Sixty-five years of hard-fucking-work and only six months of the prized retirement. All my money was useless. A paving stone had got him because he didn't know how not to work. I said, 'Goodbye Dad,' again and again, very quietly so that only he would hear. Then, the schoolboy excusing himself, 'I'm sorry I was late. I tried to get here, Dad. I did, honest,' and the choking rush came up my throat. That was quickly gone, it wasn't even tears. I had to do something to say goodbye properly: kiss him. As with Christine months earlier I couldn't bring myself to touch him. He had loved Jack and me so much, and especially since I had been in the theatre he had burst with pride, from being the Duke of Bromley Theatre on Wednesday nights to my supposed three plays in the West End, but it didn't alter the fact that I had frequently avoided his company. Even early adolescent mannerisms I had adopted were to dissociate myself from his; my adult passion for accuracy, for truth was a derivative of earlier reactions to his fantasies. Nearly always difficult, often impossible, with his stories and posturings, that fault sprang from the same well that made him give himself totally to us. Perhaps he added those ludicrous frills because he felt he wasn't enough, that he needed dressing up. I couldn't say I often liked him but I loved him terribly: a frustrated, unconsummated passion.

Joan came in. 'Are you all right?'

'Yes.'

'You've been a long time, Mum wants you.'

After some minutes with Mum a nurse drew me aside. 'Do you want his wedding ring left on or taken off?'

'I'll let you know.'

'No,' she said. 'Unless I do it now we'll have to cut it off.'

'What?'

'Yes. Rigor mortis.'

'Take it off.'

I went to see Dad for the last time. 'We've got to go now, Dad. There's no—' I was going to say, 'point in staying any longer,' but didn't. 'Goodbye, Dad.' I stood staring at his open mouth. I had to kiss him goodbye or it wouldn't be fair to him. I compromised by kissing his hand, a trimmer to his end.

———————

I felt then, and still feel, bitter that the actual presence of a person, difficult, untidy, has to be removed before you can see what he is and how you feel about him. And even worse, that Dad couldn't have guessed how I loved him, although his feelings for me were so paraded, too often in vain.

Dad's funeral was actually a pleasant affair, bearable even for my mother. Corpulent, retired railwaymen appeared from nowhere; men like old photos, dressed in black and white, solid and stuffy. They were dependable-looking, with watch chains across generous waistcoats. They told me affectionately that my Dad was 'a character' and a good railwayman, a good union man, a good friend. They reminded me of my dodging vast 4-6-2 locomotives, Pacifics, Atlantics, racy 4-4-0 Schools class, when I was a boy, collecting nearly every engine number on the whole Southern Railway. They were all anachronisms, but the loss is ours.

Dad had disliked the church all his life. 'Bloody bigots. Think they own heaven,' not that he believed in its existence. 'I don't want the church to have me.' He willed his body to science of which he approved, then for cremation. But Mum wanted him buried and Jack had worked as a hospital porter. 'You want to see what they did to bodies up the War Memorial Hospital.'

'You mean cutting 'em up and so on?' I asked.

'No, maltreatment, no respect. We can't let Dad be—'

I, too, couldn't bear the thought of Dad being hacked about, then burnt. We buried him in the pretty churchyard of St. Mary's Platt, C of E ground that he detested, but I was glad of somewhere to focus my thoughts of him and went back to his grave and told him that it didn't made any difference to him, and Mum wanted it.

Christine and I took Mum back to Cannes for a while, as we had taken Babs. It was first prize in life's lottery to be in our family: lose your husband and you got a two-week holiday on the Riviera.

———————

We decided to return to England at the end of that summer. Nearly £100,000 had built up in the Cayman Trust in a year and a half and money was still coming in, though slower. I went to Zurich to discuss investment. Yes, I had my own personal gnomes. After the money reached Cayman it was to be sent to the Swiss Bank Corporation who would deal with investment. I was given lunch and regaled with hair-raising stories about Swiss bank secrecy. 'Yes, Mr Frisby,' said a reassuringly competent-looking Mr Orsinger in a heavy accent. 'We know when there is trouble in a country; when pressure is put on people to remit their money. Where eyes cannot pry, movements of money illuminate. In the nineteen-thirties, the Jews suddenly wanted everything sent to Germany. Of course, they were being tortured. When we have sent money to closed countries and people there are relieved of it then released, they sue us. We have now made our national laws of secrecy and stick by them.'

'But perhaps some people would rather lose their money than their lives.'

'We think our way is safest for both. Some people must die, we can't control the world. After the war it was when the Russians took over East Europe, now it is Greece; those colonels. There is obviously much torture.'

'If you get as much as a faint wave from me, send everything at once,' I said.

Money was too serious for banter. Mr Orsinger was not only not amused, he treated the remark in deadly earnest. 'We couldn't. You own nothing. It is in trust. Only your trustees, or whoever they give a mandatory signature to, can claim or have information. No one else.'

'You mean I can't even know what's going on?'

'Only if your trustees, the account holders, instruct us. Anyway, what do you want information for?' He smiled as he found something that amused him. 'If you don't know anything you can't tell the UK Inland Revenue, can you?'

'But I only have to ask the trustees.'

He was again serious, weighed down with the financial world's legitimate fiddles. 'Ah. That is another matter.'

'It is like playing tag really, isn't it. The Revenue is It and it's fainlights when you get to Zurich.'

'We are not playing anything, Mr Frisby.'

I made a mental note to make sure I knew what the financial state of the Trust was at all times.

Christine left Cannes a month before me. I completed the film script of *Soup* and the re-write of *The Bandwagon*, loaded the Triumph, said goodbye to Lucienne and drove back to London. That week the London Stock Exchange, Zurich, Frankfurt and Wall Street were at their highest point for the next decade.

CHAPTER XV

1968-9

We set about our twin goals of getting my play and our firstborn into production. Bob was not immediately available to direct *The Bandwagon*, and Michael still voiced doubts about its cost. I dearly wanted the old firm of Bob, Michael and me to be in business again so I once more re-wrote the play while I waited. This re-write was particularly onerous. The view from my study in 1 Genoa Avenue, SW15, was nothing like that from my room in Cannes: the limp willow in the garden next door, the swirling leaves and events in the kitchens of St Simons Avenue behind us were no substitute for the former glorious panorama. I quickly grew to detest the enclosed feeling, the dormer window with the oppressive sloping ceiling, and didn't realise that my feelings were merely part of a normal attack of writer's block. Evelyn Waugh summed it up best: 'It's the thinking that's so unpleasant.'

There was a repeat performance of the fertility test, this time at University College Hospital. I was deemed healthy, Christine was deemed healthy, the trouble appeared to be purely mechanical, a kink in a tube inside Christine. She must lie on her side with the lower leg straight and the upper bent, I must enter from behind, she must lie still for twenty minutes afterwards (assuming she wasn't quivering too much from the excitement of this revelry) and, presto, she was pregnant for Christmas.

We transformed the interior of our house with antiques and other good things. Ivor rubbed his hands together stickily. 'A veritable Aladdin's cave,' he said. 'And what an investment.' Next came a Blue Persian kitten of great beauty and impeccable antecedents followed by a puppy of equal descent. Our pets outranked their owners by a wide margin.

Daisy was, allegedly, a poodle, but looked, when fully grown, like a miniature light-brown sheepdog. I trained her carefully and, as with Minnie, took her to golf at Wentworth where I was still known as 'The poof with the pink poodle.' Daisy, unlike Minnie, loved these outings; we became very attached.

Christine had made of us a Disney family: a charming, solid, expensive setting; beautiful, young mum-to-be; dependable, fun-loving dad; adorable pets; an environment into which the story-book villains could enter, but only to create an adventure of utter reassurance. Fate was benevolent, no Brothers Grimm could cast their Gothic shadows across our fairy-tale. All we needed to complete the idyll was our firstborn, and she was on her way.

But Christine being pregnant made me feel sick. I mean nauseated. The bulge and the change in her walk. That bulge, revealed at bedtime as a distended stomach with enlarged blue veins. The distortion increasing until it was a grotesque pear, made of her. The very word fruitful made me shudder. Michael and David came to dinner one evening. 'She looks magnificent,' whispered David, and she did. She wore a long thing that swept the floor in a thoroughly regal manner, but I knew what was under that gown and felt worse that two gays could admire what made me shudder. Useless to tell myself there was a precious new life in there; feel, she's kicking, she is moving. Personalise it though I tried, the fact of pregnancy revolted me. Perhaps it frightened me, too, and because I felt like that I felt guilty about feeling like that, wave after wave. I had done it after all, I was responsible Who was I to reject my handiwork? Years later I learned from a doctor that I had a common condition among fathers-to-be, made far worse by my concealment of it. A simple talk to let some light and air into dark corners and it would have disappeared, or been diminished to insignificance, but I didn't dream of seeing a doctor, nor did I talk to Christine. The gap we had allowed to form between us on one subject was widening into the next area. Instead, I rolled away from her in bed. An invitation to feel the kicking was like being asked to plunge my hand into something unspeakable, I had to fight not to retch, fight again not to show it, to look pleased, anticipatory.

I talked to male friends, fathers. 'Did you like it? Your wife bulging, giving birth?' 'Yes, old boy.' 'All right.' 'Quite fun.' 'Not bad.' 'Smashing.' 'I was present at the birth. It was wonderful. Messy (fight the nausea at the picture that work implied), but wonderful.' Enthusiastic descriptions of pregnant sex, 'Putting a cap on his head, old chap,' of new babies, their sweet, sickly smell, of breast-feeding, all made me convinced I was a uniquely despicable ingrate. Here was the centre of all the fuss about sex and I couldn't face it. Surely, women's bodies were for pleasure, something to go 'cor' and 'wow' over; to long for; to lust after; to be graded according to desirability, not bulging, sweating organisms that produce babies. Such ignorance and such inhibition seems incredible now as we calmly sit with trays of food on our laps and watch television documentaries of women giving birth by every possible method; fat peas popping from their pods; standing up, lying down, in water, in hospital, at home, head first, breech births, natural births, unnatural births, an electronic torrent of fertility before our eyes. But just those few years ago in the sixties the windows were only just being opened. The contraceptive pill had just made fear-free sex available to all, the Penguin *Lady Chatterley* case (the issue was not about publication, but about paperback publication for the masses. 'Would you want your servants to read this?') was just over, theatre and film censorship was newly removed and if the camera had stared up a woman's vagina to watch the end product - a new citizen, arriving in a mess of placenta and pain - the Grundys' outcry would have echoed across the land. Rot, in all meanings of the word, flourishes in dark corners, and my head was one such place. What a blessing the light is.

Before Christine my sex life had been relatively clinical. I had never looked, felt, smelled, tasted with the full relish sex deserves, which is why I was so full of wonder at her and had followed her lead. Now it was she who needed a leader, so we were both lost. To look back now makes me marvel. And there must still be an army of men like me who don't begin to understand their own conflicting feelings. Shoddy attitudes. 'As common as the cold,' the doctor said. 'It isn't necessarily callous not to want to rub your nose in the before-and-after-birth, just a matter of taste. Cheer up. Your turn will come as a father.' But that advice didn't come till far too late.

We sat at the kitchen table one morning in a scatter of literature on maternity. 'Do you want to be present at the birth, darling?'

I kept my coffee cup to my mouth as I quelled the heave with which my stomach answered the question. She continued 'George was, Gilly said he loved it. Lots of fathers are now. If you are queasy or anything they just sling you out. They don't want fathers fainting across the delivery table.'

I made sure I sounded sincere. 'Yes, darling, I should love to. If I faint, I'll be sure to fall backwards.'

How do you tell your pregnant wife she revolts you, no matter how temporarily? I tried. I don't know whether I deserve an award for stupidity, callousness or both; it was in a restaurant one evening, an upstairs room in a smart Italian trattoria. I seemed to have a weight in my head that affected my eyesight, everything was seen as though through a dim tunnel with blurred edges.

She answered my opening, whatever that was, with, 'If you want to sleep with someone else, I quite understand.'

'The idea of going with some other female while you're pregnant is disgusting.'

'I should have thought now was the obvious time.'

'No, no, never. That's not fair. It's out of court. It was never in.'

I can't remember anything that followed. Having got the red herring of infidelity out of the way, the conversation is a blank. I still wonder that such an important moment has just disappeared, leaving only that feeling that I was looking at her through a tunnel. Pain has wiped the tape. I think I tried to cuddle her in bed afterwards and had one of my rare feels of the movement inside her, so it seems as though I was trying to make up for something. The Gothic shadows of the brothers Grimm did exist after all.

The baby was late, nearly a month. Each successive day was more anxious. Christine went into hospital one afternoon and I went with her. Contractions started or were induced. I held her hand and watched her stomach writhe. This went on for most of the following night. By six o'clock the next morning they decided something must be done as the baby showed no sign of appearing. I was utterly shagged, so you can guess at Christine's state. They took her into the delivery room.

'No, Mr Frisby, you can't come in. Everything is quite all right but it will be a forceps delivery. We don't allow fathers in then (thank God, I thought). It might be a bit messy.' That euphemism again.

After about fifteen minutes a sister came out. 'They are both fine. He's a boy. He was facing round the wrong way. That's why we had to help him out.' Impossible, Christine was going to have a girl. I didn't mind him being a boy, I was just staggered, it hadn't occurred to me and seemed inappropriate. Everybody round me was female. Who was this to break the magic circle? Christine went to sleep, exhausted, and I had a look at our son. New-born babies are supposed to look knocked about when delivered by forceps, but he didn't, he looked extremely attractive: clear skin and pretty, regular features, while bearing a strong resemblance to my father, which was clever of him. I went into the telephone booth and phoned Christine's mother, then mine, then sat on the floor of the booth and sobbed.

The day after next Christine greeted me with, 'I think four, that's the right number.'

'Fine, darling. Yes, just right.'

'Boy, girl, boy, girl, in that order.'

'Perfect.'

'Now he's a he, we can't call him one of those double-barrelled French names, can we?' We had planned on Marie-Claude or something.

'No. Imagine lumbering the poor little sod with Jean-Yves Frisby.'

'That leaves Piers or Dominic."

'Piers is pissy; Dominic. It's French and its got a good rhythm, Dominic Frisby.'

'OK.' We looked at him. 'He's very nice, isn't he?'

'Very.'

I love the way his eyes go, in the corners.'

'Yes, a Disney baby.'

'Yes, isn't he. Aren't you proud of me?'

'Extremely.'

'There's only one thing wrong.'

'What?'

'He's got no fur. How are Daisy and Poubelle?'

Everything was back to normal, the Gothic shadows had rolled back, the tunnel widened into a proper picture and Christine brought our Disney son back to our Homes-and-Garden house where the cartoon nanny was waiting to deal with smells and sick and all those other irritants we now paid others to bear. But the fairy story didn't last; the picture wouldn't hold.

It is sometimes difficult to decide precisely when your life has taken a step in a different direction. Life, is after all, a continuous flow. Changes are not often as clear as, say, getting married or jumping out of men's tailoring into the theatre. But roughly, until this point, an extremely benevolent speciemen of the many forces of outrageous fortune seems to have been watching over the joint life of Christine and me, culminating in the birth of Dominic. However, in the course of our triumphant progress - I can call it that without fear of being accused of complacency because you know it that it is not going to last - I had become a sort of displaced person, wandering in the labyrinths of administration, tax schemes, profound changes in our lives. I was not, still am not, acquisitive, have never wanted property, don't like it. Oh, yes, I love money as an abstract concept, that is freedom. But, beyond the enjoyable basis of home and car, I equate property with chores, distractions, not pleasure. My work was my pleasure, my life was quite intense enough for me, without owning things. Things, and especially the chores associated with things, had attached themselves to me like sweet-papers, always obtruding into my consciousness, always coming between me and the private world of my imagination. They were getting me down. But I was the luckiest man on earth, wasn't I? How dare I complain? I was only dimly aware of my state myself and I certainly gave no hint of it, that was not my way.

It is from somewhere about now that a different face of fortune becomes obvious. Like a good craftsman I have tried to trail the events and the traits in our characters that were leading us to this change in which events began to happen fast, faster and more furious. Even to recall them now, twenty-nine years later, still upsets me and if this were a work of fiction I would condense the following few months, especially for my own sake. But I am reporting, not inventing. What follows is essential exposition.

So, to the first step in this different direction: my new play.

CHAPTER XVI

1969

The Bandwagon went into rehearsal in October 1969, a month after Dominic was born. Like *The Subtopians*, it was built round one line; there the resemblance ends. It is the story of a poverty-stricken family in which all the women are pregnant, the youngest with quins. A fortune in advertising fees has been negotiated, but she reveals, live on TV, that her quins-to-be are illegitimate. 'My friend, Sylve, told me it was safe standing up,' she calamitously explains to the nation, and the baby-food manufacturers are left to explain away the fact that their five expensive little sacks of advertising gold are the result of a knee-trembler down a back alley between participants who cannot even remember each other's name. The Line, in the TV version of the play, had already been the centre of a legal battle two years earlier. Fearful of possible bowdlerism, I received the agreement of Executive A at the BBC that The Line was essential to the structure, had this confirmed by Executive B and re-confirmed by Executive C. Six months later, with the play about to go into rehearsal, Executive D said The Line was 'offensive and must be cut.' As a result of this besuited inconstancy the BBC and I ended up in a High Court action over copyright which I won and which, via the press, TV and radio, entertained the country for a few days and caused the Judge at one point to cry with laughter. Nevertheless, the issue was serious. I had my play returned unperformed so that I could adapt it for the stage. The absurdity of censorship was highlighted when, with the play banned, every TV personality cracked jokes for the next few months about 'it (whatever) being safe standing up.' It was the first time that car-stickers appeared saying 'windsurfers do it standing up' and other variations of the line. Among the considerable mail I received, most from cranks, my favourite was from a vicar who supported my attempt to 'dispel this popular misconception.'

In writing the play my aim was a low comedy that could be taken seriously. Low comedy is a huge, flourishing part of our culture, especially working-class culture, but nobody is ever asked to actually believe in the characters or situation. I wanted to use my ballooning, pregnant, Donald McGill women and the illegitimate, vertically-conceived quins to tell a story that spoke the truth, or at least a truth, while it entertained. An early rehearsal run-through of the first half of the play showed that, in the first half, the six members of

113

the Botterill Family were a single, six-headed creature that rolled all before it: a comic steamroller. The second half changed direction but looked in equally good shape, only the very end needed work; none of the horrors of the *Soup* tour lay before us. The Botterill Family, the six-headed giant, was played by Peggy Mount, Denise Coffey, Toni Palmer, Ronald Radd, Ron Pember and Ron Wellings. In addition, Marigold Sharman, as a slush-peddling journalist, was brilliant. All through the cast there was solid strength. What more could an author ask? To sit inside your play, as it were, during rehearsals, which are so public, is a wonderfully private experience. It is like hiding in the lining of a jacket: everyone else sees the cut and style and colour of it, but you have this special creator's view of seams, stitching, linings and canvassing; of knowing which scenes flowed into being in a morning, which were laboriously mortared together because that was the only way they would come.

The Bandwagon was the antithesis of *Soup* even to the economics. This led to a disastrous decision, made before we went into production. Michael had hummed and hawed and looked out of his window across Regent Street. 'We won't be able to take this out on the road like *Soup* while you work on it; it's too expensive.' I had got the cast down to seventeen with only one main set, still a costly enterprise, but no longer punitive.

'I only need a week or two near London. I don't think there's much to do to this one.'

'Hum. What about the Mermaid?'

'What about it?'

'I think that would suit the play very well. You'll have ten days of previews to make adjustments.'

The Mermaid, which was then a converted warehouse at Blackfriars bridge, had been in existence a few years and had presented various plays, some of which had transferred to the West End. A play had a limited run there, say three months; if it transferred subsequently, fine; if not, that was that. It was not the place for my rollicking, vulgar, low comedy but I told myself that all the best plays there transferred and let Michael go ahead. When we were in rehearsal I learned from the Mermaid that although the playbills said, 'Presented by the Mermaid Theatre Trust in association with Michael Codron Ltd,' the entire cost of the production was borne by the Mermaid. Michael had contributed not a penny. The actors were working on Mermaid, not West End salaries, £40 per week each. Bob Chetwyn was on a cheap Mermaid deal. I was most upset.

'Oh, yes,' Bob said when I asked him. 'I thought you knew.'

'Bloody Hell, so we could have come here without Michael!'

'Yes. Or gone to another producer to put it on direct in the West End.'

I went to Harvey. Why had he let this situation develop? What were agents for?

'Now calm down, Terry. You have a very good relationship with Michael.

He's the best producer to arrange a transfer and get the right theatre. You are all right. Just see that the play is in good shape.'

I did some sums. *Soup* was an investor's bonanza, possibly the biggest-ever for a straight play; it eventually earned something like sixty times its capital outlay; it had made Michael and me rich. Yet Michael couldn't find backers to risk £20,000 on a play by the same author? I didn't believe it. I could have picked up the telephone myself and been bowled over in the rush, but here we were on this back-door route. I was angry and sad and thought with longing of the commitment Michael had given to *Soup*.

I went to see Michael with a proposition which seemed to me to be fair. 'At no cost you have the right to transfer my play. The actors, Bob, the Mermaid and I have taken the whole risk on this venture; if it dives we cop it, not you. The actors are working for the next four months on a maximum of £40 per week. They will then transfer on salaries which are not princely, as you know. If the play makes any money, sixty per cent of that profit will go to your backers and forty per cent to you. I think it only fair that you should take half of any profits you personally make and divide it up among the cast. They deserve it. What do you say?'

It was the end of a beautiful friendship.

On the opening night, Peggy, Denise, Toni, Ronald, Ron, Ron, Marigold et al were irresistible. By the interval the audience was rocking and reviewers were sighted like rare birds, falling from seats, wiping tears from eyes, guffawing helplessly and blocking the aisles they had rolled down.

Even Bob allowed himself a moment of counting our chickens as he gripped my arm. 'If four hundred-odd people make this much noise, what'll happen when we get to a bigger theatre?'

The second half generated a different response, as it was meant to, and the play closed to an extremely enthusiastic reception. The reviews were eighty-per-cent raves, not just good, but raves, correct reviewer-position, forehead bumping and all. The superlatives tumbled like confetti 'the funniest play of the year,' 'a riot,' 'stunning,' 'hilarious,' 'this play is a masterpiece.' The quantity and quality of quotable material was enormous, and the praise for the cast and director was universal, as they deserved.

I would like to mention the quality of the work in the production. The mere fact of so many hard-edged, funny, moving performances together says all that need to be said about Bob's contribution; the layer of humanity the cast achieved when they could merely have got laughs was exemplary. The point, if not the trouble, was: they were so funny one needed to watch them two or three times to appreciate the other qualities and subtleties that were there. Denise Coffey, who looked like the head of a lank mop attached to an oversized medicine ball, made Aurora, the quins' mum-to-be, a creature of the most moving inadequacy while still being hilarious. Every line she uttered was like a flute gone flat against Peggy Mount's bassoon. Having wrecked all their futures with her admission on TV, Aurora suddenly had An Idea to save the situation by identifying her co-parent. She gripped the interviewer's arm and peered anxiously into his face. 'He's a soldier,' she offered. Denise was wonderful. Later, as the situation closes in, she asks her mother whether she should marry the man she scarcely knows and clinch the money or go it alone in continuing poverty. 'Marry him,' rumbled Peggy, knitting massively. 'You marry him. It's the best chance you'll get in this life, my girl. Make no mistake.' It was so simple, yet Peggy made the ordinary words well up from some subterranean source that seemed to be the root of all underprivileged, working-class common-sense. When I was writing the play I had imagined the line as tinged with bitterness. Peggy's breadth left bitterness far behind, dwarfing it. I had not seen how good both those moments, and many others, could be. The actors showed the author; that is the real McCoy: art.

Denise won the Clarence Derwent Award that year, an award given (by actors to actors and therefore prized) for the Best Supporting Actress. 'That's funny,' she said. 'I thought I was playing the lead' I must say, so did I.

However, there was one drawback with the notices. Because the subject of the play was vulgarity of various sorts, the reviews made the play sound vulgar, which, in that sense, it was not. For good business at the Mermaid you needed Cultural Status, not laughs. *Soup* would have died there. We should already have been in a West End theatre after a short tour, with none of these problems.

Michael couldn't get a theatre. We had nowhere to transfer to.

'Could you and Bob do some work on it?' he said.

'What work' exploded Bob. 'It doesn't need any work. You've got a hit on your hands. Read your press.'

'The Strand say they'll take us if you can make Peggy louder, like she was in *Sailor Beware.*

'Oh, really, Michael.'

'Perhaps you could give her more in the play.'

'How can I mess up the play just to give her more lines. She'd be the last one to stand for it.

'Well, he's very old, the owner of the Strand. He's quite difficult.'

None of these vague offerings was the Michael I knew. 'What about the other theatres?' I asked.

'There's nothing much available. And the notices don't really help. All that stuff about vulgarity and poverty and so on. It's not a selling press you know.' He had a point there and I said so to Bob.

Bob exploded again. 'Well, that's what a bloody producer's for, isn't it? To sell the thing. There's a huge audience for it if he tries.' He contacted Michael directly. 'Spend some money, Michael. Money. Remember? On advertising. *Soup* never had a press like this. There isn't a play running in London with better notices.'

Michael, did no more and spent nothing. I tried to get another producer involved, but people who a few months previously would have jumped were no longer interested. 'That's Michael's isn't it? Why doesn't he...?' Soiled goods. Our only chance was that if the Mermaid was packed to the gunwales every night, box office evidence might save it. Without the cultural status I mentioned earlier, and without advertising, the box office at the Mermaid was dull. Passing trade was nil. After six o'clock at night the north end of Blackfriars Bridge is a concrete desert. I longed for the crowds and life of the West End, people out to enjoy themselves, where the word of mouth and passing trade had kept *Soup* on for nearly four years. For the last few nights of the run of Bandwagon, the Mermaid gave complimentary tickets to fill the house. The production died in January to roars of free laughter and applause. One of the cast, who didn't know that the packed, enthusiastic house to which he had just played was non-paying, said as he came off for the last time, 'Well, if it's like this to be in a flop, I can't wait to be in a hit.'

I cannot claim bad luck for *The Bandwagon*. The real wound was self-inflicted; if one works in a risky business one must get the basic decisions right or take the consequences. The play had the potential for a solid, successful run; I should have ensured that it got a proper chance to create its own watermark when I was in the enviable position of being able to do just that. I didn't.

As for Michael and me, my suggestion that he give some of his profits to actors because they, not he, had taken the risk was, indeed, the beginning of the end between us. I was very sorry. I loved Michael and David and all they brought into our lives. If I hadn't been so fond of him I would never have let him do *The Bandwagon* in the first place under those conditions. To discover - not for the last time - that money is so important to people who have plenty of it was a surprise and disappointment. Some years later a friend suggested me for a part in a Codron production. Michael pursed his lips. 'I think not. We want someone loyal, a good company man.' I was saddened that he felt the need to knock me.

Abroad, *The Bandwagon* went on to success in country after country, often bigger than *Soup*. But London was all that counted to me and, justly or not, I felt dismayed and betrayed that my healthy, thriving infant was throttled at birth. Worse than that, I was frightened; for the first time in my life I was utterly idea-less, my creative imagination seemed to have gone missing. My old a.m. writer's blues became a twenty-four-hour state of panic. I had no clue what to write next.

And so to my next step in the wrong direction. Perhaps, by now, slither would be a more appropriate word.

Chapter XVII

1969-70

For the first time in my life I was completely lost. I am a person who gives the appearance of being singularly unlost so there were no evident signs. Everything suddenly seemed to go into what pilots call a hammerhead: that terminal-looking, falling-leaf dive that can be achieved by stalling a biplane. Unlike an experienced pilot, I couldn't pull out of it. The fate of *The Bandwagon*, ever-growing fiscal complexities, a small army of dependants, artistic infertility, the death of my father, the birth of Dominic and Christine's pain in that event; all had disturbed me deeply (why should she have the pain and me the reaction?).

I suppose what it all boiled down to was responsibility. I have always been a person who readily takes on responsibilities, perhaps often the wrong ones, and then get cross that I have. While I had been accumulating, along with success, a cartload of inessentials, my focus should always have been on that blank sheet of paper at my desk (perhaps I sometimes took on the inessentials as part of avoiding that disturbing rendezvous). And there, I am sure, lay the heart of the conflict that was undermining me: writing versus the rest. Precisely the wrong struggle to be in. This was an area where Christine was of no help to me. That is not a criticism, merely an observation. I wonder if a person existed who could have solved for me my then-problem. Anyway, she had her own responsibility: Dominic. And his new presence in our house that autumn was, in a strange way, the penultimate straw for me. Not that I felt anything but paternal towards him, but I had to adjust and it took time. I thought that if I didn't get away from the house, away from everything, but mostly the new resident, who seemed to wake to feed the moment any idea, or the mirage of one, drifted across the perimeter of my imagine, I would go barmy. I suppose a working office out of the house could have been the simple answer.

I called the blameless Dominic the penultimate straw. There was, of course, the last one to come. Taking *The Bandwagon* to the Mermaid had consequences that were not all artistic: I met Sian there. Sian was what I have to call My Fantasy Woman; tall and slender, red-haired, green-eyed, pale-skinned, with that pre-Raphaelite, romantic look that often goes with such colouring. She seemed to live at an absent-minded saunter, and the amused detachment with which she viewed the male havoc she caused reinforced her desirability. I watched her covertly during rehearsals and, after the play opened, made a beeline. She put up a firm resistance which one day ceased abruptly. At just thirty-seven I had achieved the brilliant and original stroke of getting entangled with a nineteen-year-old.

Do not misunderstand, at no point did I ever see Sian as The Younger Replacement; apart from the fact that I have always regarded that particular betrayal with contempt, there was no temptation to indulge in it. Christine and I were reality; Sian was a dream, to be enjoyed and suspended before the inevitable, but not unwelcome, morning; her attitude towards me was of a similarly temporary nature. She also seemed to be an escape from my personal tangle, which was nonsense, of course. Making a successful pass at her just increased my confusion. These things were as clear to me then as now. What was not clear to either Sian or me, having let ourselves in, was how to handle the situation.

I had fallen for her all right. This was at a different level than the uncomplicated affair with competent, mature Lucienne. And, of course, I felt responsible for Sian because she was so much younger (another complication, you fool). So, with me in crisis, enjoyment played little part in this affair except, I have to be honest, in bed.

A few weeks before Christmas Christine and I talked about everything (except Sian). I would go away for a while (from Sian too) to stay with a friend in Spain and play golf. But I couldn't leave London while I was trying to get a transfer to the West End for *The Bandwagon*, so the half-cocked action of my taking a working flat for a while in Dolphin Square was agreed.

Merely to write glibly '...I had to leave home...we talked...it was agreed... a flat in town...' is to skirt events that must have been traumatic. What pain there must have been in the events surrounding those words, especially for Christine. But I remember none. That can't be true; memory must be lying by omission. Every action I took then looks suspect (even to me now), with my new, young mistress available. But if my motives still look ambiguous, the facts are easy to recall: at no point did I ask or want Sian to move in, and she didn't, I just had to get out of my own house for a while. I even wanted (yes, longed) to talk to Christine about Sian and the problem I had given myself with her. Christine made so many problems easy, I believed she could even handle that. But, of course, 'Do as you like but don't tell me' was an eternal barrier to frankness. In at least two vital areas, my work and this affair, Christine and I were shut off from each other.

We had dinner together at home a few evenings later. I thought she was calm. To my amazement she suddenly broke down, attacked me and threw my belongings in a suitcase out of the house with me. Then she telephoned me, sobbing, in the middle of the night. I abandoned the Dolphin Square flat and went straight home. I had seriously misread her feelings about my departure, or her stability three months after the birth of Dominic. What mountains of thoughts and feelings we must have been hiding from each other. And for how long? She went away to a health farm: a retort, it seemed, for my departure, and I was back home with Dominic, his nanny and Christine's mother who had temporarily moved in. This grisly domesticity was over when Christine returned a week later. I ruefully complained to myself that it was Christine who had got away, not I. I was, if anything, in a worse state.

Dominic's nanny, unobtrusively at first, then like a force-fed cuckoo chick started to play an important part in our lives. I have already mentioned our 'cartoon nanny'. She was precisely that: from Norland's (where else?); a reliable spinster in her late fifties; tall, gaunt and Lancashire; full of saws and folk wisdom. She asked to be called Mimi, a ridiculously inappropriate name for her. To say she was an old maid, was, I would guess, a literal truth. Christine and I enjoyed this figure about the house and were relieved that Dominic was in such competent hands while we, or rather I, agonised and waffled. But Mimi's astringency suddenly developed into rudeness. She had been surly to Christine for a couple of days and upset our cleaning woman, a practically unupsettable person. At Christine's request I told Mimi to pack her bags, I would take her to the station. She cried and apologised. I forget what the explanations were but we relented and she was kept on, a calamitous decision.

While Christine was at the health farm she wrote to me saying, 'Do go away if you like, for anything up to six months. I shall be waiting.' I resolved to take her up on that after Christmas.

The Seventies entered our lives on the pettiest of notes: we were dancing at a party; New Year 1970 struck; we embraced, 'I'm sorry you're so miserable, darling,' she said. 'I hope I make you happier in 1970.'

'So do I.' I answered without thinking. She looked as though I had punched her. It is a remark I am still ashamed of having made.

Immediately after the New Year I again arranged to make the trip to Spain to stay with the friend on a golf course there. What could be better? Put some miles between me and my problems, beat hell out of a few Dunlop 65s and, as they say, rediscover myself. Not least among the situations to be escaped from and reconsidered was that between Sian and myself. This would obviously never be the cosy man/wife/mistress triangle that had evolved without effort in France. It was Lucienne who had handled the former affair so well, just as Christine managed our marriage. I was the lucky male passenger in each case. Now, without female guidance, I was lost and Sian hadn't a clue. Lessons in adultery should be mandatory in all Anglo-Saxon sixth forms. It is mainly a question of territory, there must be no spillage. In France I had sped home, contained and wound up tight with happiness, ready to tick all day. Now, slopping emotions, I walked Daisy round the block at night to spend five furtive minutes in a telephone box, making the dog whine and Sian and me miserable.

I was doing something in this crisis of mine that was typical of me but was extremely short-sighted, not to say dotty. I was packaging my problems. I had three: my own state, Sian, my marriage. But I only saw two: Getting out of my emotional hole, then concluding my affair with Sian. My marriage meanwhile was on hold, in that third package, over there in Christine's safe hands while I indulged in introspection. It seems astonishing to me now that I could be so blinkered but I was. It was childish, literally; like that child who walks carefully round a puddle, off the pavement and under a passing bus because Mummy said to keep clean shoes. Such children are called inconsequential, I believe. Well, that was me then: inconsequential. One's problems, when left unattended, do not remain inert like packages, they change shape and size. Our marriage was doing that. My eye was fixed firmly on the wrong ball.

It was at this point that a succession of events happened that took everything out of my hands; not that it was ever in them. The drift we were in was suddenly caught by a current that hurried us swiftly along and I never heard the whisper of the distant waterfall. I believed I was, up to a point, in charge, despite my poor condition; after all, I had transformed our lives and, despite the current crisis they were going to get even better, it was just a question of 'sorting myself out.' I think I thought that, ultimately, I was fireproof. Well, of course, fate has collared far bigger fry than me, and we all know about hubris.

So, in that first week of the new decade (how tidy for the astrologers), the day before I was off to Spain to get-away-from-it-all, the first event was an unexpected telephone call that seemed at first to be a blessing. 'Hallo, Roy Boulting here. John and I are making the film of *Girl in my Soup*. John is producing, I'm directing. We would like to use your draft screenplay. Could you spare a few weeks to work on it with me?' Could I? The Spanish trip was cancelled at once.

I heard from Roy the story of the moves behind the scenes since I had handed my draft to Nat Cohen eighteen months previously. Dissatisfied with it, Frankovich had engaged four American writers for four successive screenplays. I understood the cost had been $400,000, more than the screen rights had cost in the first place. 'I've read them,' said Roy. 'See what you think. I'll send 'em round.'

I ploughed through. There wasn't a usable line or situation in all four.

'Yes, we thought so, too,' said Roy. 'Yours has all we want. We must get to work on that. Do you remember that John and I made an offer to you for the film rights?' He looked at me reprovingly, forgetting that they had offered less than half what I had finally got.

'I do, indeed,' I answered.

'Well, to get the film now we've been screwed by those Americans.' A great feeling of rightness crept over me. To hear that the gentlemanly, cricketing, all-English Boultings considered themselves to be in the long line of those screwed helped me to orientate myself. 'We've got a hell of a budget round our necks. It'll cost well over a million pounds to make. John and I could have made it much cheaper.

'What about casting?' I asked and held my breath wondering what horrors the film world would come up with.

'Well, Peter wants to make another film with us,' said one of them diffidently. I worked out who he meant and was delighted; Peter Sellers was just the star to *act* Robert Danvers without falling into the trap of tying to promote his own image as an object desired by woman.

'Super. And the girl?' More breath was held.

'Goldie Hawn.'

'Oh, no.'

'What's the matter with her?'

'She's American. It doesn't work half-American. It didn't on Broadway.'

'Goldie is doing it. It's settled. We go into production in a few weeks. We need the shooting script at once.'

Goldie does not need me to confirm her status or her ability, indeed I admire her greatly, but I thought her wrong because, besides being American, she was essentially a rich-man's woman, not a teenager off the street. Marion should belong to Jimmy, failed drummer and lino-layer, and then develop; Goldie already belonged with Robert Danvers, successful celebrity. I have already said that the comedy in *Soup* was built on three legs: the battle of the sexes, the generations and the classes. By having an American play the male lead on Broadway we had thrown away one of the three legs on which the comedy stood; this time two were amputated before we started. Thus are films set up.

My escape route to Spain was blocked: I had to be in London. Christine and I talked it over once more (those flat little words again). I was to start work in two days; she agreed that I take the Dolphin Square flatlet again. Again I cannot remember the conversation, but recall the following perfectly miserable evening with horrid clarity. As I packed some things I was unable to stop myself sobbing. It was uncontrollable and weird to undergo. I watched myself with the same surprised detachment as Christine did and wondered whether I was cracking up. The inevitable question must be: was I leaving her and unable to admit it even to myself? I am absolutely sure that was not so. But I cannot explain further what was in my mind; nothing clear, that is obvious. I wanted to cry, 'Help me, help me' especially to Christine. Perhaps I did, I am not sure. The radio was playing *Bridge over Troubled Water* by Simon and Garfunkel. Subsequently, it seemed that, every time I turned a switch, that dirge filled the air. The first few months of the Seventies were spent, in memory, in my car, peering down dull winter streets with that playing. It still makes me shudder.

———

The next morning Roy Boulting and I started work on the shooting script in his office. As we got down to it, the second of the series of unlikely events was developing; offstage, fortune was arranging a hideous crash between Christine and me. There was a telephone call from a shrink, a Dr Wilfred Lester, with an address near Regents Park. He left a message to say that my wife was in his office in a state of collapse. Roy looked suitably concerned and I was released. I arrived to discover that the call had been arranged between the psychiatrist and Christine so that I would go and talk to someone. I had been steadfastly refusing her suggestions that I saw a shrink. I don't, as they say, believe in them. There was some fencing.

'Your wife is worried sick about you, you know,' Dr. Lester tried at one point. He was sixtyish and mild.

'I'm worried sick about myself,' I answered. 'This really isn't me.'

'She's coming later to see how we've got on.'

'She must never know anything. What's churning round in here is too awful.'

'Shouldn't you be sharing it with her?'

'That's all tripe. You deal with these things alone.'

It was a shock to realise that in a short while I had gone from 'no secrets, share all,' to this statement; a further shock to realise that the 'short while' was over three years since 'Do as you like but don't tell me.'

'Well, here you are now,' said Dr Lester. 'I am on oath never to reveal what passes between us, so why not talk?'

'No notes?'

'None.'

'Have you got a tape recorder in here?'

'There's one over there. As you can see, it is not in use at the moment.'

I began. After a while his doorbell rang. He answered it and showed Christine to another room which had two sets of double doors between it and the consulting room where we were; there was a four-foot space between the sets of doors. He returned, closing both sets of doors. By now I had got going. All the welter of black, bottled-up introspection came pouring out: the loathing of her pregnancy, possible fear and resentment of the new boy-child I had thought would be a girl, feelings I didn't begin to understand about him; fear of impotency, of ageing, of death, of artistic aridity; longings to be anywhere but where I was at any moment, things so insubstantial I couldn't identify them then, let alone remember them now. Indeed, none of those questions still trouble me except the omnipresent fear of facing new writing, so that it is the only one that still seems real, but who knows which seemed to matter the most then? Bad feelings, once past, are the first to be obliterated by memory and thus it distorts. I went on for about forty minutes and it must have sounded awful, not to say unbalanced; it included, of course, the fact that I was having an affair.

Christine entered. She had heard everything. Dr Wilfred Lester had failed to close the first set of double doors properly and, as he closed the

123

second, the compression of the air in the four-foot space between them had puffed both sets slightly open. My voice, never the quietest of instruments, had been carrying clearly through for nearly three quarters of an hour. The three-year-wide gap of silence between Christine and me had been closed with an avalanche.

———————

Christine and I sat and stared at each other while Dr Wilfred Lester made tea. She looked white and set. God knows what I looked like; devastated was the word for how both of us felt. 'I never trusted bloody psychiatrists, now I know why,' I said.

'Who is it?' she asked.

Further silence seemed pointless. 'Sian.'

'I knew it.'

'Well, if you knew, how come—?'

She cut me off quickly. 'Anyone else?'

My denial was plum on cue. No chink there.

'There now,' said Dr Lester, pouring tea. 'It's better now it's all out, isn't it?'

'No,' I said. 'It's a bloody sight worse.'

'Sugar? We all have these crises. My wife and I have been together now for ages but it hasn't all been a bed of roses.' He fetched his wife to prove their continued co-existence.

Eventually Christine and I left. I should think Dr Lester's, by then, irrelevant oath of silence was shattered the moment the front door closed behind us. His wife was clearly burning to hear the details. For months he kept sending me a bill for that calamitous, negligent consultation until I wrote the rudest of letters and shut him up.

Christine refused my less-than-heartfelt offer to go home with her so I returned to Dolphin Square. She or Lester had given me a strong sleeping pill. Sleeping pills sit somewhere near psychiatrists in my list of undesirables but I chalked up my second first of the day, took it and went to bed. The telephone woke me. It was Sian. Then the telephone went again. It was Christine. Memory tells me that the switchboard operator put them both on together in the second monumental cock-up of the day, but that must be my confusion because I am sure that Christine accused me of being with Sian at that moment. The ice-pack that had been Christine in Lester's consulting room had now broken up; she was furious. I remember only a general outline and kept finding myself asleep on the floor with Christine's voice streaming from the telephone beside my head.

The next day, my second day on the film script with Roy, various friends contacted me in his office to say that Christine had telephoned; she had the same message for all of them. 'Terry's left me with a four-month-old baby and run off with a nineteen-year-old girl.' I felt very tired. What Roy thought of my private life he never told me.

124

I spent that evening with Christine in our bedroom. Her mother and Mimi were downstairs. Christine went through an emotional pattern I had only seen twice before but remember sharply. It had four distinct stages. The first was a sort of cold, social politeness. That was too brittle to last and was abruptly, though predictably, shattered by rage. In this state, as I had seen on the previous two occasions, Christine revealed a turn of invective vivid enough to be amusing while it bit. But the most surprising revelation to me was the insecurity she showed when feeling threatened, not by someone I might love or care for far more than her, or who might outwit her, but simply by nineteen-year-old long, slender legs. To confirm the impression that I am the blindest of men, I was amazed at this. The sheer ferocity of this outburst, born of fear, upset me on her behalf and I tried to stop her, but this was interpreted as a defence of Sian and merely fanned the fire. She grabbed my hair and removed a couple of tufts before I got free. With her attack frustrated, her rage broke into the third stage of tears, and as they were exhausted and the defensive veneers dropped away there was the fourth stage, a re-assertion of the person I knew.

I was told not to go downstairs with her while she went to the kitchen to make us tea and toast so I went to the nursery and peered at Dominic. He was asleep in apparent contentment. I went back to our bedroom and stroked Daisy and Poubelle.

'I shouldn't be doing this,' Christine giggled, as she tiptoed back with the tray. 'Mummy and Mimi would be livid. They think you're a monster.'

'I'm not surprised if you've been treating them to what everyone else has been getting today. What's all this "run off with a nineteen-year-old and left me with a four-month-old baby"?'

'It's true.'

'Oh, Christine.'

'Well, I wanted some sympathy. Precious little from you.'

'Who did you call today?'

'Ivor and Henri, Mark and Mari, Tony and Jacky, Harvey and Judy, Michael and David, Kitty and Leslie, your mother, mine and Nat.'

I was horrified. 'Nat? What d'you call him for?'

I like him. He's nice and kind.'

'Jesus. What did he say?'

'TMM.'

I sighed. 'Too much money. Trust Nat to get right to the heart of things.'

'I think he might well be right.'

'Maybe, but what do you suggest? That we give it all away?'

'Not likely.'

'Exactly. Anyway, I thought you thought the cause of it all was Sian, not money.'

'D'you think she'd be interested in someone of your age if you were a bus conductor? Little bitch.'

'Calling her names helps nothing.'

'It helps me. Cow. Sleeping with someone else's husband.'

'You did it when you were single. Does that make you a cow and a bitch?'

'I didn't steal anyone's.'

'Just borrowed, eh? It was all right when you did it, was it?' This question was ignored.

'What do you talk about? "My wife doesn't understand me"?'

'No. We don't talk that much. It's amazing how much I don't have in common with a nineteen-year-old.'

'Just screw like crazy, do you?'

'Ah, come on, Christine.'

'What's it like with her?' This was the sixty-four thousand dollar question. The answer that tingled through every nerve in me was 'magical.' The surge that swept through me just to think of being in contact with Sian was one thing I was going to make sure was not even glimpsed by Christine, or we would be in even deeper water, possibly permanently out of our depth.

I half shrugged. 'Just like anyone else.'

'All cats are grey in the dark, eh? Or do you leave the light on to look at her while you have her?'

The inevitable cross-examination on details passed the tricky point and just went back and forth. I remember my own feelings of insatiable jealous curiosity when Christine had told me of The Seventeen. How I reached the indigestible lump, bit it, turned away, then kept returning to worry it uselessly till my jaws ached and there was no mind left. To stare at the shambles immediately after a bad accident must be like that. 'Oh, if only - if only. Please God, take me back a few moments and I'll look in the mirror and signal first.' And you beat your brains out on an impenetrable barrier only seconds thick.

I tried to move us on to something that had been gnawing away at me, 'As a matter of fact, my having little to say to her has a bearing because there was one thing I wanted more than anything and I couldn't have it.'

'What do you mean?'

'You know you said "Do as you like but don't tell me"?'

'Well?'

'The one thing I wanted more than anything was to talk about Sian to you. I don't mean just to tell you. I mean to talk about her.'

'You are mad,' she stressed the 'are' as though I had merely confirmed something.

'I think I'm quite sane. You know the fun we have just making stories out of whatever happened during the day. Telling each other and laughing and - well, just enjoying things. I've wanted to come home and talk about Sian like that to you. Share her with you.'

'I don't believe you're real sometimes.'

Christine quite forgot all other emotions in her astonishment.

126

'You see, although you're pulling faces, I don't think it would be so difficult, not if you felt secure. Look at that fellow you lived with before we were married, Harry, with a body like a wasp, you said. Same measurements for chest, waist and bum. Look at the mileage we've got out of him. If we can share incidents of the day and funny things from past affairs why not share a current one?'

'You see us lying in bed, laughing about Sian's measurements, do you?' The temperature was rising fast.

'You know very well what I mean.'

'Yes, I do. All too clearly. And tell me, are these cosy exchanges to include you slipping her the juicy little details about me along with your throbbing dick?'

'Of course not.'

'Why "of course"?'

You're my wife.'

Christine's jaw dropped again. Then she recovered. 'Oh, yes, so I am. I'd almost forgotten.'

'No, you hadn't, not for one second. That's the trouble.'

'What's that supposed to mean?'

'What it says. If you'd forget your precious status for one minute and think about the subject, we'd do better. I love you; I thought you did me. I want to share everything with you.' I wanted to say that I wished to share Sian because she was something good in my life, so why not ours, but had the sense not to. Instead, 'Your rules are different, we have to play roles that aren't real.'

'I never asked you to be unfaithful.'

'No, but you excluded discussion of the issue from our lives and that's not possible.'

'Oh, it's all my fault now.' I had to bite back laughter. Christine saw and went with it. 'My husband was unfaithful because I wouldn't let the poor little chatterbox rattle on.' She was laughing, too. The tone wasn't too good, but getting better. When Christine behaved like that, what I thought of as normally, I felt a rush of love for her. This was the woman I knew, my wife. When she was different, as she just had been, instead of wondering what was wrong, I simply thought she was being unreasonable. After all, she had played Sian's part in her own life, why could she not deal with this. I really couldn't see.

'You see,' I sobered up a bit. 'Once boring bloody sex gets into the issue everything else gets blotted out. There was supposed to be a crisis in our lives, or mine anyway, before Sian. Now all we can talk about is her.'

'She is the crisis.'

'No, I hadn't even met her four months ago. Remember?'

'She's the crisis now.'

'Ah, it all makes me so tired.' As though in a bad production of a play, I flopped out across the bed and buried my face in my hands to illustrate my

127

tiredness. Daisy started licking my ears. 'Oh, get off, Daisy.' I shoved her onto the floor.

'That's right, take it out on the dog now,' said Christine, laughing better now.

'Yeah, then I'll kick the cat. Then I'll go and get drunk.'

'Perhaps I should've married someone like that,' said Christine. 'At least I'd know how to react.'

'You'd hate it.'

'Yes.' She attempted a casual tone. 'Do you want a divorce?'

It was another of those questions I was dreading. My stomach buckled at the word, perhaps because it might be partly true. There is no doubt that I wanted to shake something off, I just didn't know what, and dared not look inside me in case I discovered it was her. It took me a few more weeks to be sure it certainly was not and never had been. I cursed her need always to define everything. 'Good God, no. What a question.' By being dismissive I drove the subject underground and there was a silence. Daisy returned to licking me.

'You see I don't think it's sex that blots out everything with you,' Christine said after a while. 'It's guilt. I watch you turn in on yourself and you don't know what to do. Guilt seems to motivate you more than anything, more than love or anything; you do everything out of guilt. You're especially guilty about your parents. All your generosity is really just you buying your way out of everything you can. And now you have the money, well, it's all easy isn't it. Bountiful St. Terence of the cheque book.'

I thought then and do now that there was some truth in this but I couldn't grapple with the subject. 'I just wish most people would leave me alone to work.'

'And now you feel guilty towards me. That's terrible because now I'm another liability in your life instead of someone useful. And you feel guilty about Dominic. But you mustn't feel guilty about us. That's the dregs.'

'Yes.'

'I don't know what to do about Dominic, but I can relieve you of your guilt towards me.'

'How?'

'I was unfaithful to you.'

'When?' The question was automatic. No penny had dropped.

'Ages ago. Before *Soup.* '

'But that's nearly four years ago.'

'Yes.'

I sat up and stared incredulously. 'Who with?'

'His name was Bert.'

'Bert what?'

'Does it matter?'

'I suppose not. But—*Bert.* You can't mean it.'

'I do.'

'How often?'

'Three times.'

'Where?'

'At the Dorchester.'

'*Bert.* At the Dorchester hotel. What was he, the doorman?'

'No, we went there, you fool.'

'You're just saying this to make me feel better.'

She laughed at that. 'Yes. And the awful thing is that you do. Look how you've perked up. It's a miracle. I've never seen such a change in anyone in a few minutes. You look almost human.' She was enjoying herself after the initial step in the dark.

'Have you done it since?'

'No.'

'Why not?'

'I value all this too much.'

'Ha. When it was just you and me, you could do it. Now you value all this too much. Puts me in my place, doesn't it.'

'No. You, me, Dominic, our house, our lives: *that's* all this.'

'There's all this hair-pulling and screaming and "My husband's left me for a nineteen-year old" and you did it first.'

'Yes.' She looked quite pleased with herself.

'And you allow me to flagellate myself while you just sail through it.'

'Yes. You always make life unnecessarily difficult.'

'Wait a minute. Wasn't this the guy who was phoning you from Switzerland at night, while I was on tour with *Soup,* supposed to be screwing your friend?'

'That's right.'

'And it was you who was at it, not her.'

'Yes.'

Pennies were dropping in cascades. '*That's* why you said, "Do as you like but don't tell me." You weren't giving me carte blanche, you were excusing yourself.' No sense of betrayal gripped me, I just laughed 'You little cheat.'

'Oh, I was freeing you, too. I realised it was inevitable.' She looked introspective for a moment. 'Then there was your surprise birthday party. Do you remember?'

'Of course I do. What about it? That was months later.'

'I did that out of guilt. You were being so good to everyone. I wanted to pay you back.' She giggled. 'Your catch-phrase, "I notice everything." Ha. You didn't even notice all that food and drink round the place for days before. You live in a world of your own. How would you ever have noticed Bert?'

I laughed too. 'I was so grateful. I was contemplating a bit of extra-mural activity then for the first time; that party made me postpone it.'

129

'But I can't stand it.' Suddenly she was deadly serious, and the unsteady growl returned to her voice. 'I can't. I just can't take it, that's all.'

'But you can still dish it out. And keep quiet about it for four years.'

'I was afraid you'd divorce me.'

'I see. As when we were married and you lied about The Seventeen, I wasn't given the option. You made up your mind for both of us.' I tried to think my way back to my pre-adultery frame of mind. 'Hm. I think you're right. I would have divorced you, then.'

She sighed. 'All that righteous, truth, truth, truth.'

'I believed in it.'

'Believed? Past tense?'

'Dunno,' I thought for a moment. 'Sian wasn't the first one.'

'I know.'

'There was France.'

'I know. Don't go on. During that last month after I left. It must have been then.' She looked tense again. I thought it best to leave it at that, or more likely lacked the courage to go on. However Christine did. 'And New York. When I arrived I knew it.'

'Wrong. I didn't then. I tried but I couldn't. Three times. Too guilty.'

'Fool.'

'If you knew or suspected all this you must have suspected someone when I took that flat in Dolphin Square.'

'I thought that wasn't why you took it,' she said accusingly.

'It wasn't, but it doesn't half *look* bad, doesn't it,' I answered.

'I didn't want to look. I was too frightened.'

I thought my confessions were full enough. The brief tussle with the French woman while Christine was burying her father and my zooming back happily over the mountain from Lucienne would keep for another day, or never. At this moment they might, I thought, cloud what was now a positively sunny atmosphere. 'OK, then, Bert. Tell me all.' I leaned back, feeling better than I had for months. Perhaps that fool of a doctor was right. Better out than in. Christine's confession had done wonders for me. Was it guilt that weighed me down so?

If you remember, it was Bert to whom I had spoken on the telephone late one night when I had come down from Nottingham during the tour of *Soup*. Bert had been calling Christine from Switzerland; she was not, as she had told me, an answering service for her girl friend with the tough husband. Bert had been working on the film, *Casino Royale*, and was, in Christine's words, 'nice and kind.' I didn't like the *Casino Royale* connection; the stories of joyful fornication, in all conceivable ways and numbers, with the droves of girls on that film had resounded round the business for years. Her being a part of that seemed to taint an otherwise perfectly straightforward action. I thought her reason pretty feeble, too, but it fitted Christine. Anyway, who was I to judge reasons? She hadn't done it out of irresistible attraction or romantic fervour but, having just moved into suburban Putney, married to an unevenly earning actor/writer, it was fear of being condemned to the supermarket and the kitchen and missing everything glam and lovely that had motivated her. It had been, so she said, her last fling (that is what her pre-nuptial trip to Majorca was supposed to have been). Bert, who mystifyingly represented all this high life, was the chauffeur and general dogsbody of one of the stars on *Casino Royale*: Peter Sellers.

'I don't believe it,' I said wearily.

'Sorry. I didn't know you'd be so successful, did I?'

'That's a pissy thing to say. Anyway, you might have had some faith.' Poubelle rolled on her back with all four legs in the air, purring, so I tickled her stomach. Daisy, scared she was missing something, came nosing in. I gave them a hand each. 'If he was so "nice and kind" why did you pack it in with him?'

Christine shrugged, an action she generally made when covering up. '*Soup* opened, I stayed with you because I knew where the money was.' She gazed at me with a deliberately direct stare. I couldn't work out whether the effort was designed to convince me she was telling the truth or to retaliate by wounding. I decided to believe it was the latter. While I was grappling with that she delivered another shock. 'I am going to New York to stay with Julie.' Julie was her closest friend who had moved from London some while ago and married again.

'Why?' I asked.

'I have always said to myself I would go and spend time with Julie if I was in trouble. She'll help.'

'But you're not in trouble. Anyway, I thought it was, "You go away. For six months if necessary. I'll be waiting."'

'You're working on the script, you can't go anywhere, can you? I can.'

'Are you taking Dominic?'

'He's better off at home with Mimi and you.' And that was that.

We crept down to the kitchen and made bacon and eggs.

'Don't let Mummy or Mimi hear or I'll be in trouble,' whispered Christine.

'OK' After the food I said, 'Why don't I stay the night? Be nice. I'd like to.'

Christine looked at me in mock shock. 'What would they say?'

I left, drove towards Dolphin Square, then changed direction to Sian's. I felt that nothing that mattered had even been touched on by Christine and myself. Mutual adultery had obliterated the rest.

———————

Clearly something massive had happened but I didn't properly register it. I merely felt grateful to Christine for confessing to make me feel better. What the content of that confession would lead to would come quite soon. Something else I should have noticed, but didn't, was that it was demonstrated once more that she could lie freely about anything that suited her. Here was the big difference between us. I could, and did, tell myself that I had been playing the game honestly by the rules laid down by her: 'Do as you like but don't tell me.' I could, and did, tell myself that I was therefore playing fair. But I agonised as to whether I was deluding myself. Christine appeared to have no such problems, she just lied. I am not sure that there was much difference between us. Perhaps we both lied - to me.

CHAPTER XVIII

January - February 1970

Christine promptly went to New York and I again returned home in the wrong frame of mind: feeling cheated that, for the second time, it was Christine who had got away, not I.

There was a brief incident on the evening that Christine left that seemed insignificant but, I believe, was a vital link in the chain that fortune seemed to be forging for us.

Two of the newer friends we had acquired, Kitty and Leslie Massey, were among the people that Christine had phoned with her, 'Terry has run off with a nineteen-year-old and left me with a four-month-old baby.' Leslie was one of those grey businessmen, a director in his family's clothing business, who seemed to have little other function in life than to provide a luxurious lifestyle for his wife and two daughters. Kitty, pretty Kitty as she was known in her circle, was health-farm-honed, a dynamo of nervous energy with too little to discharge it on. She saw herself in the current situation as a benevolent fixer. Christine was impressed by these two, I could take them or leave them alone.

In answer to a summons from Kitty, I sat limply on a pouffe in the middle of a vast Chinese carpet in the sitting room of their house in Avenue Road while Kitty gave me a not unkind lecture on the values of wife, child and family. As she only knew the corner of the story that Christine had chosen to tell her, everything she was saying was irrelevant or offensive. I had come only with the idea of diffusing her vigorous interventionism and had not the slightest intention of revealing one syllable of Bert, or our other private difficulties. I was sick at the way Christine had gone public, the people she had chosen and the inaccuracy with which she had done it.

Kitty, Leslie and I had a fruitless hour or two while I thought glumly about Christine wheeling away westwards from London Airport and stonewalled their comments. I must have looked quite intractable to them both - certainly to Kitty. However, under-used, overactive Kitty still felt she had a part to play in our lives.

What about Dominic in these comings and goings? The answer from a child psychiatrist, a nice sensible woman at Great Ormond Street Hospital, was clear: Dominic was temporarily fine as long as the continuity of Mimi was maintained. 'But the sooner you sort out your differences the better, before he becomes a pawn or weapon in some battle (unspecified) between you.' I wrote to Christine of this and other matters. My letters, now in front of me and barely legible with age, are eloquent in their dreariness.

Mimi, in the evening of her career, had walked into a drama which fulfilled her lifelong prejudices; she saw herself as holding the fort. 'Don't worry. He'll have to get a policeman to get me out,' she had said to Christine, preparing for a non-existent siege. Mistakenly, I allowed the child psychiatrist's opinion to secure Mimi's status and she soon realised that she could take more or less what liberties she liked with me. Her insolence overflowed; I took to avoiding her; whenever she entered the nursery I would leave. In her absence, getting to know my son became a new and secret delight; he was extremely nice, although I had a tendency to handle him as though he might break, Mimi came into the nursery one evening as I was putting him to bed. He said something that sounded suspiciously like 'Dada.' She took him from the cot, held him up and said, 'Don't say Dada, say Mama.' She was earmarked for dismissal on Christine's return.

Julie telephoned me from New York. 'Honestly, Terry. I don't understand you. It's not like you.'

'What's not like me?' I asked, wearily wondering what Christine had been saying.

'Running off with this girl.'

'Oh, blimey, Julie. How did you get me on this number if I'd run off?'

'Don't pick nits, Terry. You know what I mean.'

'No, I don't. Look Julie, you're sensible. Can't you remove those distorting lenses from Christine's eyes? It's all this bloody girl to her; there's more to life than an affair.'

'She says it wasn't the first one.'

'No, and I'll bet it's not the last, but what's it got to do with anything?' That remark was certainly an error, Julie was a person who would both give and expect fidelity; what would she say to Christine in their girlish chats? I continued quickly. 'What about her affair, eh? What does she say about that?'

'Nothing really. I can't answer that.'

'No-one's asking you to answer anything, Julie. It's not a competition. Christine and I are not you and your feller. Remember that, will you? You know me, Julie. Christine'd be lost without me, even if she doesn't know it. Use your loaf and talk some sense to her.'

Pointing out Christine's needs was probably another mistake, like throwing down a gauntlet to feminist Julie, but I was tired of explaining myself and my life to all and sundry.

<hr>

Christine was in New York for six weeks, longer than it took Roy Boulting and I to complete the shooting script for *Soup*. I liked both the Boulting brothers but we would never be artistic soul-mates. I had written the play from the viewpoint of teenage Marion looking askance at forty-something philanderer, Robert Danvers. Roy, a whole generation older than Robert, always referred to him as 'that young man.' There wasn't anywhere very much for us to meet. An American writer was closeted with us; his alleged function was to see that Goldie's dialogue was in the right American idiom. His actual contribution was to say, 'Charming, I think it's just charming,' to every idea suggested. At one point we were looking for a device to stop Robert from screwing Marion when they were practically at it.

'I know,' I said. 'Just as he's about to climb on, she could say that the last guy she slept with had the clap. 'That should stop anyone, even in mid-mount.'

Roy puffed out cigar smoke as though to dispel a nasty smell.

I turned to the American. 'What do you think?'

'Charming, it's just charming.'

So, with Christine still in New York, the Boulting brothers and I marched into the next - perhaps the most unlikely - coincidence of this story. We presented ourselves at a characterless, rented, luxurious flat in Clarges Street to discuss the completed draft shooting script with the resident, Peter Sellers, boss of Bert the late-night telephoner, lurker at the Dorchester, four-year-ago ravisher of my willing Christine. My face and manner were rigidly in neutral as the bell was rung. I braced myself. The door was opened by an Oriental. No, surely not, Christine would have mentioned. Sellers was the only other person in evidence and Bert was quickly forgotten in the presence of Sellers' wonderful, overflowing inventiveness; I was besotted with him in no time. At first he was a little tense, presenting his offerings over-eagerly, quickly dashed if the response was not effusive; however his comic fertility was like the tide coming in, it soon surrounded you. We sat on a sofa and ad-libbed the dialogue of a sequence we had jointly invented. It became a scene in the finished film. I longed to work more with him. I was, figuratively, about a foot off the cushions; the laughter of the impeccable twins, at first dutiful then genuine, was subsiding; there was a lull.

'Black or white, sir,' said a voice in my ear. It was a nondescript man with a potato nose. He was late forties, about ten years my senior.

'Ah, coffee. Lovely, Bert, thank you,' said Sellers.

Bert did the rounds and the conversation washed past me. His movements were awkward and he was slightly clumsy. Nervous? He got back to me. I hadn't taken my eyes off him, he hadn't lifted his from the tray. I found myself staring straight up two hairy nostrils. It was a curiously intrusive experience. I wanted to whisper, 'Pull down your nose, they're showing.'

He must have looked even less alluring from the point of view of a female in the common-or-garden copulatory position, as, no doubt, practised at the Dorchester. Not for the first time I speculated in wonder about what motivated the woman I had married.

'Sugar, sir?' There was a silence. His eyes flicked up to mine for the briefest of instants; if he had any doubts of my knowledge they must have been dispelled in that moment; his eyes slid off mine. 'Sugar?'

I knew precisely what I should do. I should stand up, smack him straight on his potato, and as he crashed through the rented furniture say calmly to the others, 'Sorry, but you see he screwed my wife four years ago and he had that coming. I'll pay for the damage, Peter. Yes, two lumps, please and avoid me in future would you, old chap.' This course seemed to me satisfying, civilised and therapeutic. The scenario stopped short before he picked himself up and came flailing back. I think I pictured him dabbing at the now dribbling nostrils and muttering broken thanks at my magnanimity. One thing prevented all this. Nobody else in the room (did Sellers?) knew of Christine's brush with this unattractive space-in-the air, to broadcast it would be to place another brick on the wall that seemed to be rising between us. Her action in telling so many friends of my affair, was, I thought, utterly misguided; it fixed things. 'Terry's having an affair,' brick in place; 'With Sian,' mortared in; 'He's left me,' new brick in place; 'Twice,' more mortar. And that wall would have to be torn down, sooner or later, causing bleeding fingers and piles of rubble. No, socking Bert was out, blast it. I retreated and did nothing. Then in the eye of the storm created in me by the combination of adrenaline and inaction, I realised that all my urges for some time had been to do nothing, just to go with the tide: I was waiting for something. But what? Christine had tried to clarify and classify in a precisely opposite manner: 'adultery,' 'affair,' 'nervous breakdown,' 'crisis'. For me, labels prevented thought (or was I trying not to identify something?); but for her to slap on a label was to cope with the problem. If the label was wrong, change it; but things labelled became bricks mortared into place.

'Would you like a biscuit?' The space where 'sir' had been in the previous question hung between us. The whole question was gruffer, even surly.

I found him more bearable without the sir. Christine had been, in the spring of 1966, just twenty-four; my lovely, shiny, new-minted, fresh-as-eggshell-white-paint wife of two and a half years. Why had she needed to? Why had she bothered? And she had gone back for more. At least twice. I wondered if I would have felt better or worse if Bert had been Adonis. I wanted to scrub him, then Christine, then me. The room was becoming unbearable. The meeting was breaking up anyway. Roy, John and Sellers swam back into my consciousness. I arranged to meet John and Roy after lunch and went off to have it with Bill Fournier, who was by now more than just our lawyer, he was a trusted, older friend. I did not tell him of Bert. Christine, for sympathy I am sure, had told her version of events to our world. I couldn't even whisper the raw humiliation I felt at that moment about Bert.

'Find out what it is you want, then tell Christine. Find out soon,' was his theme over the sole and Meursault. I used to think that fish was lighter for a working lunch; in fact, sole goes down like lead. No wonder they live on the sea bottom.

'But I don't know, Bill.' I had never spoken a truer word.

'Go away if that's what you want. Go off round the world. My God, now's the time. You can afford it.' He was getting quite passionate; the skeleton of his own longings was grinning clearly through . 'Get away from us lawyers and trusts and accountants. You're supposed to be a creator, nor a sort of super-clerk; you should be producing the goods that make the money that pays us to do all that for you. Do it.'

I had a moment of clarity. 'I'm waiting for something, Bill. I've just realised. I wonder what it is.'

'Well I should find out quick or it might be horrid.' His warning was pointless. I was paralysed about everything, a hateful condition.

Back in Roy's office his face was long, his voice hushed. 'No work this afternoon, Terry; crisis. It's Peter, we might lose him. It's touch and go.' It sounded, for a mad moment, as though Peter were in the throes of terminal illness.

'What's up?' I asked appalled.

'He thinks you hate him. Peter must feel wanted.'

'Hate him? I'm crazy about him. What's he mean?'

'Well, I must say you did start,' Roy paused in his discreet way, 'er, behaving peculiarly. He's very sensitive.'

I let out a sigh of laughter and sagged into a chair. 'I don't believe it.'

'It's not funny.'

'Oh, it is, Roy. It's sublime. More shapely than Bach.'

Roy sounded aggrieved. 'Things are very dicey, you know: Peter shouting down the phone, "Bloody writers, don't like anyone's ideas but their own. Coming round here with black looks. If he can't stand me, get someone else."'

I sobered up. 'Look I love him. Tell him so. In spades. It's the truth, so you can lay it on. Or I'll come and grovel. Is that what he wants?' I smiled again and thought of Bert waiting there. 'Why don't we go round together and go down on him in a queue?'

Roy appeared to consider this seriously. Then, 'I think you'd better keep away. It's tricky enough. We don't want to compound it.'

'Tell him I've got trouble at home. That's why the black looks. He knows what trouble at home is, I'm sure.' Roy seemed relieved to have an instantly comprehensible condition to use as a scapegoat.

The events of the morning had at least one important effect. I went home and made a proper start on the play I had been picking at for two years. Christine had demonstrated that my scruples about invading our privacy were no longer relevant. One log in the jam in my head was released. It was the start the stripping process which I was about to undergo and has been more or less total. It has resulted, years later, in my being able to write so much in this story that would otherwise be too personal to set down.

A day or so later there was another movement in the jam, causing it to grumble loudly as the logs readjusted. I was giving Ivor a lift to Putney from the West End. From somewhere in me a tidal wave of rage and resentment came boiling up that I hadn't even known was there. It was a shock to me, my own version of the anger Christine had shown the day after the disastrous consultation with Dr Lester. It seemed the first time I had felt anything positive for ages, except depression and desire.

'The trouble is she's a liar,' I began as we shot away from the kerb.

'Aren't we all?' Ivor said largely.

'She lied her way into our marriage. She lied her way into all the success and goodies. Every time there's anything important her response is not to deal with it, but to *lie* about it.' I was lathering up nicely.

'You've been doing your share too,' he said, putting out a hypocritically casual hand to fend off the dashboard; the Triumph Vitesse was left-hand drive, bought for tax exile. Ivor was in the wrong seat.

'That's because I was daft enough to play it her way. Ha, "Do as you like, but don't tell me" that was just her excusing herself with Bert.' I changed down to overtake.

'Yes, yes, I see.' His foot stabbed at a non-existent brake.

'I'm the mug of all time. The three biggest things in our lives: our marriage, *Soup* and Dominic and she *lied* about two of 'em. While I was sweating my guts out in Wolverhampton and Nottingham making our fucking fortune she was screwing that half-a-pound of margarine at the Dorchester. And then kept quiet about it for four years. And my surprise birthday party; what about that?' I waved my hands in anger at the recollection.

'What about it?' he gasped. 'Fun, wasn't it?'

'That was my recompense.' There was no trace left of the laughter with which I had greeted Christine's admission. I glared indignantly at Ivor for a concurring sentiment. ' "I notice everything," that was our private joke. *On me.*'

He shouted back with some spirit, 'Well, notice the sodding road, can't you. Make a start.'

I glowered at the tarmac for a few hundred yards before the inevitable thought hit me.

'If she's lied about two out of three, what about Dominic?'

'What about him?'

'D'you think she could've lied about him? My foot stamped on the accelerator.

'He'll be an orphan if you don't watch out.'

'Oh, shut up. You always were a terrible passenger.'

'And so will my kids. Anyway, what are you going on about? Anyone'd think you were chaste or something.'

'It's not screwing I'm on about, it's *lying;* fucking *lying* about every fucking thing.' I was red-faced and shouting. 'Now she's nearly screwed up the film of *Soup* and it's *her* who's pissed off abroad. Always her. And I'm left to cope with that bloody nanny.'

To give himself some relief from the intimate details of my grievances, Ivor turned on the car radio. The inevitable *Bridge over Troubled Water* was playing.

'If I hear that again, I'll scream. *Bridge over Troubled Water,* huh. Straddling the Atlantic? She runs off, I stay here. She bleats to everyone about my infidelity while I'm supposed to keep quiet out of chivalry. I'm the fucking villain, she's the victim. I'm bloody up to here with all of it.' We had arrived at Ivor's front door and I sat behind the wheel breathing heavily and staring down the narrowing funnel of my vision. It was like the wintry suburban street we were in.

'Well, thanks for the lift,' said Ivor heavily. 'If you want to talk about your problems again I'd be happy to pay for the taxi.'

As I bustled in through the front door of Genoa, Mimi appeared. 'Ssh. He's asleep.' Dominic would have needed a bat's senses to hear me from his nursery.

I went upstairs to look at him, I had never seen a child look less like his father. Again I went over the dates of our departure from France: she had been alone in London for a month; not possible, that was over eleven months before his birth; but he was late. She could have met someone then and kept it going after I got back; no, not possible, all that business with the fertility clinic. Ah, perhaps that was it; I was infertile. No, the tests had showed otherwise, but then, we had been together constantly, I would have noticed if...'I notice everything.' Like Hell, anything was possible. And if Bert, what about her trip to Majorca just before our marriage? That couldn't have been innocent, as she claimed. Dominic gurgled at me, unconcerned, while speculation swirled. Whatever his paternity I was getting to know him a great deal better than Christine during her absence. It was a binding and rewarding experience.

Mimi entered. 'What are you doing?' Her voice was rudely proprietorial.

I left the nursery and got Bill Fournier on the telephone. 'Bill, I want to talk to a divorce lawyer.'

'Oh, Terry, surely you don't want—?'

'No, no, no. Don't worry. I want information, that's all.' I knew just what I wanted and it was not a divorce. I wanted to establish that I had the power

139

to take everything material from Christine. I wanted to have the choice myself to offer it back freely, when I, and only I, wished. My resentment at her entering our marriage under false colours, buried under years of happiness, now joined with the humiliation of again having my free choice removed at the very moment when *Soup* changed our lives, to create in me that furious feeling that being married to sweet, compliant Christine was to be on permanent call for castration, a treatment she administered whenever convenient. I wanted a fresh start.

'Divorce lawyers are the dregs of our profession,' said Bill. 'They trade in people's unhappiness. Even the technical aspects of divorce law are uninteresting.' Bill had a whole list of what was wrong with lawyers who specialised in divorce; eventually he came up with one he seemed to respect, Leslie Taylor of Nabarro, Nathanson and Co. I made an appointment then discreetly tried to find out from medical acquaintances how you established paternity. Discreetly? To have had the father of a five-month-old son on the telephone obliquely enquiring about such things must have seemed as discreet from the other end as watching someone creep home late at night with a brass band on tow. Finally, I telephoned Sian.

We went off for the weekend and behaved as though we were in a French film of that period. We walked along February beaches and got soaked; steaming, we made love in front of a log (of course) fire, ate, did it all again and slept the sleep of the sated. Sian, lovely, thoroughbred Sian; feeling the hook of middle age down my throat, I was pretty certain she was my last squirming thresh. The lack of clarity with which I have drawn her is deliberate. One way or another she got it in the neck for being involved and I ached to compensate her. I now felt guilty about her feelings for me. My guilt was ubiquitous.

By the time I saw Leslie Taylor of Nabarro, Nathanson I had lost interest in what he would have to say. My rage had blown itself out. Material factors had nothing to do with relations between Christine and me. That was for us to deal with. I remember little of the meeting beyond thinking how obscure lawyers were when you asked simple questions. The only subject Leslie Taylor was clear on was the way to establish paternity, not that I followed that up. I suppose it is all right for a lawyer to divulge the secrets of the medical profession. Perhaps one should consult a doctor to learn the law.

There was another meeting at Sellers' flat. It went beautifully. Everyone, except me, seemed delighted with the draft shooting script. I thought the best new stuff lay in the wastepaper basket. 'No, no, old chap; bad taste,' Roy had said with wrinkled nostrils to idea after idea. 'That's what everyone originally said to the whole play,' I had argued. 'They were wrong, weren't they,' answered Roy blandly.

Bert was nowhere to be seen at this meeting. Coincidence? Had there been discussions? 'Oh, Peter, I'd better keep out of his way. I gave his missus a few during *Casino Royale*.' 'Did you, you devil. What's she like?' Or had Bert exercised his own discretion and found an errand for the morning? The mill of my anger ground on into the grist of such imagined scenes.

Mimi greeted me when I got home. 'Your wife telephoned while you were out.' I gave her full marks for managing to make 'your wife' and 'you were out' two distinct rebukes in one sentence. 'She's coming back in two days. And about time too. Six weeks she'll have been gone. That child won't know his own mother.' Each of these sentences was a further admonition - to me, not to Christine.

I nodded earnest agreement. 'You're absolutely right. I was only saying so last week.'

I didn't even think about what to do, my moves were automatic: I found a couple of rooms in Chelsea and moved out again; I objected to being at home waiting for Christine to decide when to return. I was still attempting what I had tried three and a half months earlier, to get away for a while, and actually felt some sort of relief as I shut the door behind me. I left a short note for her. She telephoned me, upset at no welcome so I went straight home to talk. Now I had a grievance too. We were on slightly more level terms.

I wonder, in retrospect, what Christine thought she was coming home to. Flowers? Mutual forgiveness, absolution and reconciliation? Certainly not a cold little note. I still do not know how much of a slap my absence was to her but I was in no mood to offer bouquets.

She looked tired and pale, but good, probably because she had lost quite a lot of weight. This was intentional, she had been trying to, off and on, since the birth of Dominic. I liked that and told her so. I told her of the Bert episode and couldn't resist telling it well enough to make us both enjoy it, briefly, before I went on to my wild reaction in the car with Ivor and after.

'Have you been seeing Sian while I've been away?' her face and voice tightened only a little.

'She's an irrelevance,' I said, carefully.

'Well you've just spent twenty minutes on Bert.'

'No, Christine, I have spent twenty minutes on your lying about Bert. That's different.' I seemed to be watching her through binoculars across a chasm.

'Ah, isn't it always.' She seemed as detached as I.

'Yes, it is. We played this scene in the first year of our marriage and you said you understood then. I don't believe you did and I don't believe that you do now. I don't think the words trust, truth, frankness mean anything to you. That is not a complaint, merely an observation.' The prissy phrasing went with my careful approach.

'Have you seen Sian, is what I asked.'

'Of course. What do you expect?'

She seemed to grow a little smaller. I waited for the next question. 'Are you still going to see her?' or, 'Will you give her up?' It didn't come. Indeed, it never came. I was surprised and very grateful. I never asked myself what stopped Christine: pride, fear of the answer, or even consideration. I knew that the moment she asked me to stop the affair, I would, without hesitation; I would have to. But I did not want to give Sian up under that sort of duress; more than anything I wanted to want to. If I did it out of duty then the next woman would have been ten minutes away in our lives. Clearly that wouldn't do any more.

Christine went on, 'I see. You're a philanderer and I'm a hypocrite...'

'And apart from that we're perfect,' I concluded and smiled, but she didn't.

'I have just had six dreadful weeks in New York and I come back to this.'

'I have just had six dreadful weeks in London,' I answered, consciously like a child playing tit for tat. 'No-one asked you to go. You seem to have passed some of the time adequately,' I nodded at the mink coat I had sent two thousand dollars for her to buy.

'It was cold there.'

'It was cold here. If you remember Christine, I was going to go away for a while and you would be waiting for up to six months. I'm still trying. While we talk about Bert and Sian we're not even beginning with what matters.'

'Oh, yes, let's ignore the realities and talk some air-fairy nonsense about Life and Truth,' Christine said. She suddenly burst out, 'The truth is simple, Terry-bloody-Frisby: you're a bastard who wants to have his cake and eat it. I'm supposed to sit and wait while you make up your mind whether you want me or not.'

'That is not so.' I remained unnaturally flat in the face of her outburst; at that time I was always so in front of her. I believed I was trying to remain reasonable, to avoid a slanging squabble, but what I imagine was an appearance of coolness might well have looked icy, spineless or merely indifferent. 'You told me to do as I liked but don't tell you. Then you break your own rules by listening at that door. In any case you only made that rule in the first place because you couldn't keep your knickers on, so what is all this wronged wife bit?' Scoring debating points didn't dispel my feelings or change hers.

'So you want a divorce?'

'Oh, Jesus, Christine, no, no, no. Believe it or not, I love you. I want to be left alone for a bit, that's all.'

'Yes, and she's the bit.'

––––––––––

Let me just clarify, for a moment, a few coolish facts from the broth of emotions that was bubbling. Although, like any narrator, I have concentrated on the high and low spots of our lives, the important, the overall fact that gets lost in recounting extremes is that we had lived together for six extremely happy years. Those six, excellent years were followed by a short period of difficulty which had, in turn, burst - via Dr Lester's ill-fitting doors - into flaring crisis. Without that crisis, aggravated by the subsequent ill-timed revelations and confessions, that period of difficulty would, I am sure, have dissolved into the past and been forgotten, like the vague mists in my head that comprised it. And, even though a crisis had been precipitated, it was by no means terminal; fraught, yes, but final, no. As for our mutual infidelity - setting aside the fact that the majority of people who indulge remain blessedly undetected - most marriages, happy ones I mean, survive it, indeed, may well be fortified by it when the dust has settled. Certainly Christine and I were both equipped to cope. The point is that our dust was still thick in the air.

There was also the question: how on earth could she have left her four-month-old Dominic behind and then stayed away from him for six weeks? There was nothing to stop her taking Dominic with her. Her friend, Julie, already with two or three children, would have welcomed him, she was like that. And if Julie couldn't have taken Dominic too, was her support more important to Christine than to be with him? If she felt it necessary to get away from home she could have taken him anywhere. This was nearly thirty years ago, official ideas of mother/child bonding have developed enormously since, so perhaps Christine could have reasoned in the then-jargon that Dominic was better off at home. But what were her own feelings for him and what had happened to those feelings during her absence? I didn't ask then and have no answers now.

Into this precariously poised situation a new ingredient was introduced. Christine had returned on the last day of February; three days later I received a letter from Sydney Rutter, divorce lawyer. This letter rang only the faintest of warning bells; indeed, I am giving it more attention now than I did then; it seemed irrelevant, almost comic. It told me in a stilted, unctuous style, that I had 'a baby son' and a wife who had 'a deep affection for you,' although I had 'left her three times since December.' I wondered why it didn't mention her longer absences from home and I was offended by the inaccuracy and presumption of 'We are pleased to hear that notwithstanding what has happened in the past, you have expressed the thought of making a fresh start and return to live with your wife at some time in the future,' but that is all. What both Christine and I didn't see was that her meeting with Rutter was the watershed in her life, mine and Dominic's.

143

CHAPTER XIX

March 1970

I took Rutter's letter home to Christine that evening.

'What's all this, darling?'

'I was talking to Kitty Massey two days ago. She said, "what you need is a good lawyer," and sent me to see Mr Rutter.' Christine continued with some self-righteousness in her tone, 'Kitty said, "He'll never enter my house again."'

'Why, what have I done to her? Of course, you told her of Bert and The Seventeen, didn't you?'

Christine was silent.

'Precisely.'

Kitty with whom I had spent the fruitless, stonewalling hour or two at her home on the day Christine went to New York, must have had her speculation fermenting for six weeks, I had not been in touch with her since. Now, with no real knowledge of what was going on she had seen the need to intervene again. I reflected on an expression I hated: with friends like her, who needs enemies.

I crumpled Rutter's letter, then smoothed it again. 'Now you've got a sharp little divorce lawyer. Oh, Christine, it's too awful to contemplate. You should hear Bill on the subject.'

Christine's chin went up a bit. 'I thought Mr Rutter was just nice and rather old-fashioned.'

Friday, the sixth of March, was Christine's birthday. We went out with two friends and had a perfectly frightful evening. Back at home Christine told me that someone else had told her that I 'wanted out' and that yet another friend had been telling her a story of some other fictional affair of mine. 'Why do you talk to these people in the first place?' I asked. 'Let alone listen to 'em.' We went to bed together and made love in a frenzied, unloving way. The last time we had made love it had been all rather sad and beautiful.

At about two a.m. Mimi walked in. She let out a squawk when I rose out of the bedclothes.

'It's all right Mimi, it's only Terry. What is it?' asked Christine.

Mimi recovered a bit. 'A friend telephoned you from New York.'

144

'Thank you, Mimi, goodnight,' said Christine.

Before Mimi could move I spoke. 'What was the message?'

'No message.'

'Who was it, then?'

'They didn't say.'

I wondered who this sexless plural was who had chanted in unison down the telephone from New York and I admired Mimi's sangfroid in covering. 'Then why did you come into our bedroom at two a.m. with no message?'

Mimi said, 'I didn't know *you* would be here,' then left. I lay for a while between sleep and wakefulness in an emotional limbo. Christine says that I then sat up and said, 'What the hell am I doing here?' But I think it was, 'What the hell am I doing?' a rather different remark. Anyway, I got up and left.

On Sunday, two days later, Christine and I were walking Daisy on Putney Heath. The weather was bitter but we wanted to be alone together and, as her mother was staying, had abandoned home for the biting air. The mood between us was, in contrast, warm.

'My God, we've got four hundred and fifty-seven centrally heated rooms down there and we're freezing up here,' I said. Even Daisy viewed the terrain of the outing without enthusiasm.

'We can go down and have tea with Mummy if you like,' Christine said.

'Gee, thanks.'

We walked on for a bit. I threw a stick which Daisy ignored.

'If we get divorced, Terry, I want it to be civilised.' This had been an oft-repeated remark. So had my answer.

'Do you want a divorce, darling?'

'No.'

'Of course you don't. Neither do I. Why bring it up, then?'

'Because it keeps coming into my mind.'

'Just play with Dominic and don't talk to so-called friends who knock me. Please. Everything'll be all right. Soon. You've got friends and fellers in queues to take you out; everything is taken care of for you; relax a bit, just relax, life's better than you think.'

We returned to our cars.

'What are you doing tonight?' she said.

'Work.'

'Tomorrow?'

'I'm going to see *Butch Cassidy and the Sundance Kid.*' Sian had seen it and wanted to take me. Stopping the affair with Sian and mending our marriage were two separate issues to me; I still couldn't see that they weren't to Christine. I was boneheadedly, as concerned and guilty about Sian as I was about Christine. Adultery was proving to be a wearisome business.

'Who are you going to see it with?' said Christine taking out her car keys.

I was toying with the thought of saying Robert, then I thought to hell with those lies. 'Sian.'

Christine's reaction was instantaneous. She flared up and dived into her car. 'Oh, yes, I stay at home and play with Dominic while you gad about with your nineteen-year-old girlfriend.' The car crashed into gear and shot out into the middle of the road nearly hitting a passing learner-driver while I stood, regretting my loose tongue.

Sian and I went to *Butch Cassidy and the Sundance Kid*. Its glib forays into danger and death irritated me beyond reason; a good dose of Dostoevsky might have been doomy enough for me, but I doubt it. Sian and I slept together that night at Smith Street. At about eight-thirty the next morning the doorbell rang. I answered it. Two men were there.

'May we see Miss Sian, please?' said one of them, giving me a card. 'We're from the Acme Detective Agency.'

'No you may not.' I closed the door and telephoned Christine. 'There are two detectives at my door asking for Sian. Did you send 'em?'

'No.' She sounded mystified.

'Well, who the hell's done that?'

'I don't know.'

'Your mother? Mimi?'

'I don't know.'

'That lawyer?'

'No. Why should he?'

'Exactly. Try and find out who, will you.'

'OK' We hung up.

I went outside. The two men were sitting in a car, waiting. I went inside again, further perplexed. 'They're out there, waiting.'

'Look,' said Sian 'the wall's not too bad here.' She was pointing out at the back garden. 'We could get over that into the next street.' The row of houses behind were in a terrace. We would have to knock on someone's door or window to ask for a passage through.

I went back into the street. 'Who sent you?' I asked the two men sitting patiently in their car.

'S Rutter and Co.' One of them answered. I went back in and telephoned Christine. 'They say they're from Rutter's.'

'Well, I don't know anything about it,' she said.

'What's he playing at? Find out will you.'

'His office won't be open yet.'

'Well, find out later.' We hung up again.

'Come on, let's get over the wall,' said Sian. I thought of the excruciating moment of knocking on someone's back door. 'We're dodging detectives, do you mind if we just...oh, this is Miss... and I'm...I found myself saying, 'Not likely. I'm not running away from those two gits.'

146

And, after breakfast, we went through the front door, I with my golf clubs over my shoulder. I did not possess even a rudimentary sense of self-preservation.

After golf I went home. 'What was all that about this morning?' I asked Christine. 'Was it your mother got those men?'

'No.'

'Well who?'

'Me.'

'What?'

'I was ashamed to tell you.'

I sat down and stared at her across the kitchen. I couldn't believe my ears. She was making something and concentrated on that, mixer whirring, fork clacking against dish. 'Oh, Christine.'

'I was taken by surprise. I didn't think he'd move so quickly. I was going to tell you.'

'Oh, Christine, how could you?' I was sickened. For once a rebuke from me brought no answer from her. She kept her head down and worked on. 'Christine, that's the bottom.'

'I wanted evidence.'

'Whatever d'you want evidence for?'

'Just in case.'

'But if it came to that, don't you think I'd give you some, if necessary?'

'Mr Rutter says he won't be a party to collusion.'

'Isn't that wonderful of him. Nobody asked him.'

'You're scared of him.'

Once again I was dumbfounded. 'Why should I be scared of him?'

'Of what he can do to you.'

'What do you mean?'

'I've got someone who'll stand up to you now.'

'What does that mean?'

'You do as you like and I'm supposed to take it.'

'Is that how you see things, darling?' I waited for an answer. None came, so I went on, 'My problem is that I'm trying to reconcile myself to you always doing precisely what *you* like when the chips are down. You can't use that evidence so why waste the money?' She was silent again.

'Christine, she has a mother and father: a family.'

'That's their funeral.'

'Supposing some wife had done that to you before we met? Or, say, Bert's wife when your father was dying? How would he have felt?'

'You're always defending her.'

'Jesus, Christine, it's you and us I'm defending. You couldn't do it. That's beyond everything.'

'Mr Rutter wants £250.'

'What for?'

'To cover expenses.'

'Wonderful. You hire detectives, you lie about it, then you want me to pay for it.' I laughed. It was actually quite good, I thought, in its awful way.

'He said I should ask you for it.'

'I'll bet he did.'

I telephoned Leslie Taylor, the lawyer I had seen, and asked him to send £250 to Rutter. Leslie Taylor said 'If I'm going to act for you, Mr Frisby, I shall require £500 on account.' I paid that, too. £750 seemed cheap to get rid of these irrelevancies, for that is how I still regarded those lawyers.

On the Friday of that week Christine was cooking us dinner at home. We had put Dominic to bed, seen that Mimi wouldn't disturb us, and were in the sitting room.

'I've got a surprise,' said Christine and she showed me.

I peered at it. 'What is it?'

'Pot.'

I practically reared up and cantered out of the house neighing. I had a horror of all drugs and imagined that one sniff, drag, jab, pull, swallow, or whatever, of any of them meant you were hooked for life. 'Where did you get it?' I asked in mixed fascination and admiration.

'Never mind,' she said. I was sure that nobody I knew had the stuff. 'Everyone in New York uses it. It's like the pre-dinner drink. This is grass. Come on, have some. It'll make you feel better; you could use something, you've been awful lately.'

'What d'you mean?'

'Well, not like you; just awful; miserable and mushy.' She wrinkled her nose.

I liked her sounding like that, sensible and ordinary, telling me off and pushing the nightmares back where they belonged. I smiled. 'That's what I've been trying to tell you.'

'Well come on. Anyway this is very light stuff. You get the giggles, then you get hungry. I've got something lovely for us to eat when we do. Julie said she could always tell when I was stoned 'cos I'd dive for the larder,' she giggled. 'Terrible if you're on a diet like I was. Colour telly looks lovely.'

· I got smashed out of my brains. Christine smoked little, urging me on. I lay on the sofa chortling contentedly, then ate some wonderful gateau; colour TV was brilliant. I blearily told Christine I was scared of her, that she was the strong and I the weak member of our marriage. I repeated this under cross-examination from her. I told her, and believed it, that I loved her and always would and what about a bit of the other here and now. She wasn't having any of that. She had sat or stood watching me carefully for some of the time at least, asking me a series of questions. After enough time for me to recover enough to be safe to drive I was shoved off back to the two rooms in Smith Street.

The next morning I woke like a feather; it was like magic. On the infrequent occasions when I have smoked since, I have always found refreshing sleep and an alert awakening to be an after-effect, so whatever marijuana does to you can't be all bad. But that morning was miraculous; for only the second time since early in Christine's pregnancy the shadows were dispelled, my tunnel view of the world widened and life was again a matter of pleasant certainties. My crisis, whatever it was, was over. I had a will of my own again and knew what mattered; Christine and Dominic, Dominic and Christine.

It was just two weeks since she had returned from New York.

Chapter XX

March - May 1970

That day, the fourteenth March, was the day I thought of as the day of my rehabilitation, a red-letter day. It was the first time I had felt whole for nearly a year. I was ready to put everything to rights; indeed, I was eager. So it seems like the right moment to get the timescale of what was happening in proportion.

The surprising thing that you may not have noticed in the swamp of emotions that I have been describing is that, since the disastrous consultation with the incompetent Dr Lester which had turned my crisis into our crisis, only two weeks had passed when Christine and I had actually been with each other. And, of those two weeks there had been only a day or two together before Christine was guided by Kitty Massey to Rutter. We had had, literally, only a few hours to sort out major problems.

The sequence was as follows: Dr Lester in early January; the next day Christine told me of her affair with Bert, then off she went for six weeks to New York, leaving me at home to meet - by the most astonishing of coincidences - Bert; Christine was back for one or two days only before she went to Rutter on first or second of March; we went out on her birthday on sixth of March and she invited me to spend the night with her, which I did; about ninth or tenth of March she got her evidence; finally the cannabis-smoking evening of thirteenth and my rehabilitation. These dates within those two weeks are crucial. They come up again and again. It was such an agonisingly short time.

However, irrespective of the magical restorative properties of marijuana, there was another problem on my plate: I had to go to Paris where I was producing *Soup* at the Theatre de la Madeleine. There always seemed to be something happening at that time which made me defer decisive action regarding Christine. One thing I did do: I saw Sian before I left and we ended matters. Under the expressions of mutual regret we were both relieved. From Paris I wrote an exuberant letter to Christine making much of the virtues of smoking grass and the vices of lawyers. For a week in Paris, I had daily amicable telephone conversations with Christine. Feeling utterly confident about her, I went to Cannes and I booked our old villa for the three of us to recover and knit ourselves properly as a family. Madame Paqui, our former femme de menage, was beside herself at the thought of our return with new baby. I telephoned Christine to surprise her and got Mimi who was insufferable; Christine wouldn't come to the telephone. I returned at once to London and went straight home; the door was locked and some of my belongings had been put in the porch. Dismayed at this overtly aggressive action, another pointless retrograde step in relations between us, I believed that Mimi must have suggested it to Christine. It did not occur to me that Rutter had played a part, he was still too shadowy for me to take into account. Or, rather, was I too naive? I imagined him taking instructions, as they call it, not holding the reins.

Unwilling to make a public issue of the matter on our doorstep, I took my things and went back to my two rooms in Chelsea. Some friends told me later that about half an hour before my telephone call from Cannes some thoughtful person had shown Christine a photograph in the *Daily Express*, a paper we didn't take, of Sian. It was a standard Express picture of young actress/model and bore a reference to 'an influential friend' helping her in her career. This was not me, but of course conclusions had been jumped to.

The lawyers were in the middle of a squabble about the £250 I had asked Leslie Taylor of Nabarro, Nathanson to pay Rutter. Rutter wouldn't accept it for some reason obscure to me. The cheque had been going back and forth with increasingly acrimonious letters. To stop that nonsense I told Taylor to do whatever Rutter asked. There was a female junior solicitor in Taylor's office called Gudrun Collis; she was rather Joan Hunter-Dunn with a whiff of wintergreen. I thought her no-nonsense, sympathetic manner just right and when Taylor suggested she dealt with Rutter I was relieved; a woman, or this particular one, would keep the temperature down.

Suddenly Rutter was pressing to get the divorce petition served. This action, like his others, made me exasperated with him for being such a hindrance, but I still didn't take him and his evidence and bits of paper and pompous little letters as seriously as a wiser man might have. We were not getting divorced so he didn't matter, was my overall view. I told Miss Collis to go slow and to advise Rutter to do the same because Christine and I would surely get together. A meeting was arranged between Rutter and Taylor to put Rutter in the picture financially (had to have the top man to deal with money. Minor matters like your life can be dealt with by juniors). Even this meeting seemed nearly impossible to arrange, the lawyers squabbled so. I assumed that Christine had told Rutter of our complicated finances but wanted him to understand fully that rocking the financial boat could be disastrous for all of us. I was not allowed to be present.

For the next month I was going backwards and forward to Paris for the production of *Soup* there. They were just overnight stays of one or two nights each. Christine and I met at home about three times a week between my journeys to Paris. She was tight and withdrawn, very much in phase one of her emotional pattern. I waited confidently, there was no question of my forcing myself on her, I wanted her to throw open our door and invite me home with good heart. The salient points of our meetings I have compressed into one conversation.

———————

'Fancy not answering the phone to me, just because of a blinking picture in the paper.'

'How are you helping her in her career?'

'I'm not. I don't even know what she's up to. I'll tell you what, darling, I'll make a bargain, it's over now with Sian; if you don't bring her up, I won't bring Bert up, even if I meet him again on the film with Peter.' I laughed as though the encounter would be fun.

'I met her in the street while you were away.'

'Ah, well, now we're even. Let's call it a draw and abandon the match. Better still, let's sack the legal zombies, put Dominic in his pram and take him for a walk.'

'Then she won't be named as co-respondent. You're just defending her. Mr Rutter told me on the phone that the detectives' report said that you held her hand when you crossed the road and kissed her at the street corner.' The pitch of her voice went up half an octave although the inflection stayed cool.

I damped down my anger. 'Look, darling, I know that Mr Rutter is marvellous and kind and trustworthy and all the rest of it, but he must know that such details hurt you. Why tell them to you? You hurt me, I hurt you, that's part of marriage because the other parts are so super - or have been for us.' This got through her guard and allowed me to go on a rare offensive. 'But I didn't marry Sydney-fucking Rutter or Kitty-bloody-Massey. Do you hear any of our real friends putting in the spoke like that?'

'Your friends defend you, naturally,'

'Now they're your friends and mine. I thought they were ours. Look, on March 6th, your birthday, you went to bed with me, you wanted us together. After March 13th when you gave me that joint, so did I. Only one week separated us. What happened in that week that's so important?'

'I got my evidence.'

Always we came back to that damned evidence. How could I have been so stupid as not to have dived over that wall with Sian like scrumping children? 'OK darling, Miss Collis tells me that there is a three-month period allowed in law in which we can get together for a trial reconciliation. If it doesn't work you can still keep your evidence. There. Does that prove that I am not doing all this for Sian?' This seemed to get through.

The next day her answer was, 'Mr Rutter says the reconciliation period rarely works in his experience.'

I had to struggle control myself. This man, 'Mr Rutter says,' 'Mr Rutter told me,' was becoming worse than an irritant, he was a potent negative force. 'To hell with his experience, let's get two new lawyers whose experience is different. I don't know why I don't just come home anyway.'

'You do, and I'll have you thrown out.' This was said with enough confidence to stop me in my tracks.

'But it's my home, too, darling.'

She was silent. 'Isn't it?' I said. But Mr Rutter appeared to have offered no views on this subject, or if he had, Christine kept them to herself. Still no alarm bells rang in my head.

She changed tack. 'If we stayed together would you always be faithful from now on?'

This one took me totally by surprise. There was only one sensible answer, 'Yes, yes, yes, forever and a day.' I should have repeated all the declarations of fidelity ever made, I, however, was not sensible, I was reasonable, I considered it. 'Who knows, darling. I'll try. And what about you? You were unfaithful first.'

'I didn't know how much you would matter to me then.' While I was still blinking at this, she continued, 'In other words 'no'.'

I began, 'Then there's Dominic—'

'Don't start using him as a weapon—'

'Not a weapon, a white flag,'

We were moving closer than the dialogue implies. Or, at least, I felt that we were.

During the month of that conversation we were getting into financial trouble. It wasn't serious, but *Soup* had a thin winter and apart from royalties being lower at the Comedy Theatre where it had transferred, I had, during bad weeks, waived them to keep the play running; this is common practice. The fortune I had earned from *Soup* was locked up in trust, tax reserve, houses; there was no spare cash, so I had run up a considerable overdraft. Indulgence of emotions was proving expensive. I drew $4500 from the account in Zurich to cover my expenses in Paris. This withdrawal was significant.

On one of my visits home my key wouldn't fit the lock, Christine had changed it on Rutter's advice. I sighed. Now I had to ask permission to get into my own home. Another backward step that will have to be retraced, was how I saw it. The idea of re-entering to safeguard my property never even entered my mind. Christine was there, it was safe.

Taylor's meeting with Rutter was fruitless; he advised me to give Christine no more financial information in case Rutter tried to use it to cause damage. 'But any damage he did me would harm Christine,' I said and wondered at this creature I had never met who seemed to be my enemy.

Michael and David met me over some matter. David grinned his 'Terry and the Pirates' grin. 'Why don't you just go home and clump her round the side of the head? Tell her to make some supper and not be a soppy cow,' he said. Such common sense sounded quite heady in the atmosphere in which I was then living.

Apart from what I think was considerable patience on my part, there was a practical factor that made me reluctant to follow David's metaphorical advice during that month. The threats, originating from Rutter, that Christine had made about having me removed, had their effect. After not objecting to the change of locks, my view of things shifted. I was afraid that if I returned home while shuttling back and forth to Paris, something else (I wasn't sure what) might happen behind my back. I maintained my supplicant posture while resolving to go home after *Soup* had opened. What I didn't know was that Christine was coming round as a result of our meetings. I got nothing but brittle ice, but she told friends we were going to 'give it a whirl.'

On Sunday evening, twentieth of April, I went to Paris for the technical and dress rehearsals of *Soup* and called in to see Christine and Dominic on the way to the airport. Mimi had taken a holiday at short notice so Christine was very tense, she and Dominic alone in the house. I offered to stay, spare bedroom and all. She said no, so after a couple more futile attempts, I went on to Paris. The venture was additionally nail-biting because, as producer, I had £13,000 of Trust money risked.

I couldn't get through to Christine on the telephone until the following evening about six o'clock. She was hysterical. Amongst the emotional imprecations, two precise nuggets of fact gleamed; that I wasn't to go near Dominic except for two hours a fortnight until he was sixteen (such accurate statistics amazed me in the middle of her outburst); and, when I said I would come straight home, 'Don't you dare, I'll have you removed.' She rang off. I telephoned straight back. She rang off again. Worried stiff, I telephoned two friends to contact her at once, but not to say I had spoken to them. One, Marian, telephoned back within twenty minutes. She had had a pleasant, friendly chat with Christine who sounded perfectly happy and had invited her to a meal the following day with Robert. Christine had greeted Marian's suggestion that she was lonely or upset with amazement. I left my hotel and went to the theatre, concern fast changing to anger. I had enough on my plate without staged histrionics. At the theatre was a telephone call from Sian; I didn't know that she even knew where to get me.

Sian was not hysterical, merely resigned. The photograph of her that had been in the *Daily Express* had been sent to her father with full information and obscenities scrawled over it. I exploded, sure that Christine must have sent it. 'Oh, to hell with it all. I'm going to Morocco for a few days after the opening. Come with me and let the rest of 'em get on with it.' Sian agreed. I was past caring. For my month of contrition I felt I had been eating humble pie, had been cursed and threatened. I was by no means the sole guilty party in this matter but had been putting up with this

154

treatment for the sake of peace while earning the money to keep it all going. This last action was too much. I thought Sian and I could get away with it for a few days and I would deal with all the pother when I got back. I would go home, sit down with Christine and have all the cards on the table once and for all.

If this were a work of fiction the next words I should write would be 'Sian came over to Paris and off we went.' That would be logical, set up emotionally, and would push the story nicely along, but there were a few more events, quite unangry and unexplosive, to come before Sian and I got on that plane. They deny easy excuses for my actions but do serve to show the strange, almost casual, everyday atmosphere that, in general, existed on the surface between Christine and me in contrast to what must have been boiling underneath.

I had to be in London the day before the opening and went straight home. Christine was preparing the dinner for Marian and Robert. Dominic was sleeping 'What was all that about on the telephone, yesterday?' I asked, sitting at the kitchen table.

'I just felt like it. You deserved it,' she answered, busy.

I said, 'Let's for God's sake stop all this nonsense and talk some sense.'

'Not now,' she answered, the double meaning unintentional. 'I've got some people coming to dinner. They're due any minute.'

'Some people?'

'Yes.' She was not going to tell me that two of my dearest friends were about to ring the doorbell.

'Not gorillas, people?'

'Yes.'

I sat on patiently. We both had an ear cocked for the bell. She gave up. 'If you must know it's Robert and Marian.'

'Ah. Wonderful. They'll be delighted to see me.'

'No. I want you to go.'

'Why? You've got enough grub there for another one.' I had no intention of gate-crashing. The doorbell rang. Daisy ran barking into the hall.

'Please go,' said Christine. She looked suddenly distraught.

'OK, but how?'

'You can go out the back door and dodge round the side of the house,' she said. 'If you're careful they won't see you.'

'On one condition. That we meet and talk when I get back. No calling lawyers and fitting new locks or any of that rubbish. We just meet and talk quietly and sensibly for a while. Be a change.'

'All right. Only go.'

'I'll write to you while I'm away.' Christine knew that I was, at last, going to get away for the long-planned break. What she didn't know was that Sian was a last-minute addition.

155

'OK. Oh, could you come by tomorrow on the way to the airport and leave your car. I need it. Mine's got to go in.'

I slid out of the back door as she went to the front. Daisy was by now beside herself. I crept round the side of the house. Our neighbour was polishing his car in his driveway. He said, 'Evening,' and started to talk about the weather or something. I put my finger urgently to my lips. He stared, then returned to his car. The back he presented to me quivered with curiosity as he started to work his way quickly round the bonnet to be facing me. I got to the front bay window of the sitting room and could hear everyone inside. It would be easy to crawl under it unseen but my retreating bum on the garden path was going to be like a beacon. I got down on all fours and set off, sliding my weekend bag along with me. The neighbour had now given up any pretence of polishing his car and gawped. I grinned and fluttered my fingers at him. Then I saw Daisy peering down at me through the window, paws on the back of a sofa and tail wagging. I heard someone coming inside and flattened myself. I looked up, Christine was closing the curtains. She smothered a laugh, then quickly pulled them closed. I rose to my feet, nodded again to my neighbour and sauntered away.

The next afternoon, Wednesday, I stopped on my way to the airport with a taxi in tow and left my car for Christine to use, as arranged. I was very pushed for time and arrived at the front door at a gallop. I was greeted by a different Christine: gone was the set expression, the icy, phoney composure, she was relaxed and warm. I gave her my car keys and her first-night present. She waved Dominic's hand, 'Say goodbye to Daddy, Dominic,' like any doting wife and mum. I jumped into the taxi, waving fondly.

The play opened that night and two mornings later Sian arrived. We went to Morocco for six days, returned and, for the second time, parted for good. I telephoned Christine.

'You took Sian with you on that trip, didn't you,' she said before I could begin the comprehensive lying I had planned. 'Don't trouble to deny it. I've got proof. I've checked up on her.'

'Why on earth did you do that?' I asked, my heart sinking. 'Did you get detectives again?'

'No. A friend.'

'Some friend. What's her name?'

I telephoned Sian and learned that a man had telephoned her flat while we were away asking for her. That surprised me. Detective, lawyer or 'friend?' A girl in the flat had blown it completely. I cursed the inadequacies of middle-class, teenage girls at lying on the telephone, forgetting my own supreme incompetence in similar circumstances.

When I went home to get my car from Christine I discovered all my draft work and the scripts and papers from my study spread over it, soaking from at least one night in the rain. I left the stuff with nearby friends.

The next day, Sunday, Christine went to my brother's house for a day or two. I followed. Under the pressure of pleading with her I offered several inadequate excuses for taking Sian to Morocco, then with surprise I hit upon something that made a neat argument but, convenience apart, had much truth in it. I still believe it was at the root of why I did it.

'Morocco equals Majorca.'

She made a contemptuous noise.

'It's true. You wanted a final fling or something before you committed yourself to marriage, so you went off to Majorca without telling me, and I think that, underneath all the rest of it, I wanted to do much the same. Morocco was my Majorca. Now we're quits. Let's start again.' And yet again I stared inward in curiosity at what made me tick. In the middle of this feverish climax I still talked of rules; my taking Sian to Morocco boiled down to 'Yah-boo, sucks to you. We're even now.' Was I really so childish? Or had her original betrayal at the start of our marriage cut so deep? Or was this merely rationalisation? I hadn't wanted to go with Sian that much, but after the outburst in which I had asked her was over, I had not for an instant considered withdrawing the invitation, I was determined to go through with it. 'Determined to go through with it.' What a phrase to use about running off for a few days with a beautiful girl. Yet it is the right one. My principal sensation during that trip was that I was the protagonist in a Victorian morality entitled, *Pleasure Is Not Happiness,* or *The Heart Remains at Home.* I kept thinking, 'What am I doing here with this girl?' Yet, although I was awfully sorry to have got caught, if I hadn't, I would have looked back on the trip with secret delight and part of that delight would have been that I had put the ledger straight with Christine. Indeed, I feel real shame over only one action towards her in all our marriage, that was the moment when the clock at the party struck the beginning of the seventies and she said, 'I hope I make you happier next year,' and I said, 'So do I.' She offered love at that moment and got selfishness in return.

It is obvious that Christine didn't mind about adultery. Her own behaviour both before and since I had met her confirmed that. But the way mine was discovered, in Dr Lester's surgery, had caused her to take up a public posture, an entirely unsuitable action for her. Her talent was infinite adaptability; to roll, ride, slip, duck, dodge, lie when convenient, impeccably dressed and with unsmudged make-up. The combination of her adaptability and my preoccupation with what went on in my head explained much of our cool, polite, charming life together, each of us giving way with the alacrity of snails' horns at the hint of abrasion; not for us the commonplace squabbles of domesticity. Thus we had no training for the crisis when it came. That precise affair, me with a tall, slender girl, struck at the sickly plant of Christine's emotional security, but in general terms marital infidelity was a situation for which she was perfectly primed by sophistication, culture, gossip and her own inclination. What she was not equipped to deal with was the idea that her husband was leaving her for a younger body and longer legs. Christine, who was only twenty-seven then, had (inaccurately) grasped at this cliché from the word go. Her affair with Bert was four years old, a dimly remembered thing for which she had, no doubt, forgiven herself. But Bert's potato nose was in my face on a daily basis, giving me fresh justification to be hurt and hang on to Sian - who, in turn, was in Christine's face. This delicate balance of wounds and resentments needed arbiters, friends. It had got Kitty Massey and Rutter. And, in seeing Sian as a threat, Christine had missed the real de-stabiliser in our marriage; my contorted, inadequate affair with writing plays. My work was a closed book to Christine and any shoots of interest she had, or understanding, had long been crushed under the ton of irrelevant rubbish that discovered infidelity had sluiced down on us.

Christine and I argued for much of that day at my brother's house. Joan, my sister-in-law, told me what other friends subsequently confirmed; that Christine, who had presented a steely front to me, only wanted to make peace.

'Why doesn't she tell *me* that?' I asked, 'Instead of perpetuating this fight?'

A day or so later on the telephone Christine told me that I couldn't see Dominic. The same day Gudrun Collis got a letter from Rutter which told me that I must not enter my own house again or telephone Christine. 'If he does an Application will be made to the Court for an Injunction.' The letter continued, 'Our Client has no objection to your Client calling at the house to see the child...once a fortnight at 2.00 p.m. for a period of two hours either on Wednesday or Thursday.'

Legal war had been declared. But, although I was dismayed and dumbfounded, none of this was real to me. People don't do things like that except in America or in stories, do they? Certainly not Christine. I did not believe that she could be committed to such squalor and blamed everything on the malignant Rutter.

Chapter XXI

May Eleventh, 1970

I sat in Miss Collis's office and stared at Rutter's letter. 'What's an injunction?'

'Oh, that's just bluster,' she said. 'Those injunctions are to protect wives and children who are being beaten up and so on. Doesn't apply here.'

'And what's all this about only seeing Dominic once a fortnight?'

'I must say, I know old man Rutter likes to pile it on, but that's going it a bit, even for him.' And she shook her head, chuckling again at his nerve.

I felt very differently about his nerve. 'Does he have the power to decide when I can see my son?'

'Of course not.'

'Well, he seems to think he does. Christine's come up with this once-a-fortnight business before.' It all smelled wrong to me. 'I'm going home.'

'Splendid,' said Miss Collis. 'Best thing you can do.'

'What's to stop me,' I asked.

'Nothing. You're not going to beat her up, are you?' She saw my look at her levity and arranged her features accordingly. 'Of course not. Well, then, don't molest her, I mean don't try and force yourself on her, I mean—you know.'

'I'll sleep in another room. What does molest mean legally?'

'Well, it's broad. Use your loaf.'

'OK Anything else?'

'Nothing really. You could take someone with you if you like, as a witness that it's all peaceful. Er, some friend perhaps...?' She looked at me doubtfully.

'Oh, really.' I tossed the letter aside. 'Do you think I'm going to take some bloke home to witness that I'm not assaulting Christine?'

'Quite, quite, ' she said quickly. 'Very silly, I agree.'

'What about the nanny?'

'Hm, tricky. Leave her alone. Might be misconstrued.'

'Can't I sack her? She's a perfect pest, the sooner she's out the better.'

'Better not. Leave her there. See to all that later, eh?'

'OK What else?'

'Nothing, really. You might take notes of what's said at the actual time. That's always prudent. Stops any nonsense later.'

'OK I'll phone you from home if there's anything I need to know. Now, you can do something: the first thing Christine will do is to phone Rutter, so will you phone him now and tell him to keep out; keep a low profile; do as little as possible, just for a day or so. It will take a little time for Christine to unbend, then it'll be all over; no more trouble. We'll be able to sack both of you.'

'Splendid. Delighted to hear it. I'm sure Rutter will be too. He's all right, really,' said Miss Collis heartily.

'One last thing; suppose I can't get in, the locks have been changed. Can I get in through a window; break one or something?'

'Why not?' she said. 'They're your windows. Make sure nobody gets cut.'

I tried once more by telephone to talk to Christine or to see Dominic. Mimi tried to make an appointment for a week hence like an irritable dental receptionist. I hung up, packed my cases and got home in the afternoon just as our cleaning lady was leaving.

'Hallo, Chris, how are you?' I said as she closed the door and came down the path.

'Hallo, stranger.' She grinned at her cheek.

'Would you like to give me your keys,' I said, smiling too. 'If Christine asks, I'll say I forced you to give 'em to me.'

'Oh, you don't have to say that.' She handed them over eagerly. 'Here you are.' She nodded her head at the house. 'It's all right, *she's* not in.' This clearly meant Mimi. 'Taking him for a walk in his pram, she is.'

'Don't you like her, Chris?' I asked innocently.

She was indignant. 'I've only had two of me own. I don't know how to touch a baby, do I? I might drop him.' She tipped her head sideways. 'Go on, get in there quick.' This didn't refer to entering the house, but getting in with Christine. 'Before she gets back. She's no friend of yours. You watch out for her,' and she set off up the road leaving me full of warmth.

I went into the house and straight upstairs. Christine was on the landing. 'What do you want?' she asked, startled.

'I've come back,' I said and walked straight on up to a second floor spare bedroom to give her a chance to digest this.

I came down a little later. Christine met me on the landing. 'Would you please go,' she tried to say it politely but it came out wrongly.

'No.'

'I don't want you here.'

'Well, I'm staying, darling. Separation has been a disaster.'

'Well, you wanted it.'

'And now I don't.'

'If you stay, I'll go.'

I didn't believe this for one moment. 'All right, darling, go, and take Dominic if you must. But I want you to stay. Please, please, stay.' My pleading disarmed her temporarily so I added, 'Why don't we go down and have a cup of tea.' While I made tea and toast Christine sat tense, holding in her anger. I tried to be merely casual. We must have looked extraordinary. 'I promise I won't molest you or interfere with you at all,' dutifully repeating my lesson. 'I'll sleep upstairs. We'll just be near each other for a while. I don't quite know what molest means but I'll give it the widest possible interpretation. Do tell him.' I nodded towards the telephone.

'Who d'you mean?' she asked.

'You know perfectly well. But don't phone him, darling. What good can he do? They're all pests.' Christine said nothing so I continued. 'Now, Mimi. In order to make things bearable between us in the house I'll behave to her as she does to me. I'll be polite as long as she is. She must knock when she enters any room where I am. She must call me Mr Frisby, not Terry as before, and I'll call her Miss Day, not Mimi. She must refer to you as Mrs Frisby, not Christine and she must speak first as I am fed up with speaking to her and getting no reply for my pains. I had six weeks of that while you were in New York. If she is pleasant, so will I be. If she is rude, so will I be.' I thought about that for a moment. 'No, even if she is rude and surly I'll be polite and pleasant for a day or two to give her a chance to adjust. If she doesn't, then I'll sack her.'

'Tell her all that yourself.'

'With pleasure. Now I'm going to play with Daisy in the garden. You're not going to try and bolt the door on me or anything silly like that, are you, darling?'

'No.'

I went out leaving the back door, the kitchen windows and the French windows open, in case. I heard Mimi come in with the pram. I gave them a few minutes then went in to see Dominic. He was in the pram in the hall. I heard Mimi's voice from the landing. It was raised and emotional, her thin Lancashire accent cutting the air in unlovely, sharp tones. 'Well, get the police. Have him kicked out. Phone your lawyer.'

I turned and ran up the stairs. Those stairs are wide and spacious, rising from the hall in three flights to a large first-floor landing. There is a tall window lighting both the hall and landing. Mimi heard me coming when I was on the second flight. She moved away from Christine. I spoke coolly at, rather than to, Mimi. 'You will confine yourself to looking after Dominic.' She hurried down past me as I reached the landing. Without looking at her I continued, 'You will keep out of our affairs and you will leave my wife alone.'

Mimi was already red with emotion. She kept going, but turned to shout up at me, 'Your wife? Your wife? You should have thought of that sooner.' The result of this was that she missed a step and nearly dived down the remainder.

I waited for her to get her balance. 'Pull yourself together, shut up and look after Dominic.'

She went to Dominic and I went with Christine into the bedroom, immediately dropping the master-of-the-house pose.

'Darling, this can't go on. If you won't tell her what's what, I will, but it'll be easier if you do.'

'All right,' said Christine wearily.

'There's nothing to be tired about, darling,' I said. 'Everything's done for you. Just ignore that woman and don't phone Rutter. Stop and think for a bit. You're leaning on him, you're leaning on her; lean on me for a change like you used to.'

'Some hopes.'

'It's easier than you think,' I went into the nursery and played with Dominic. Mimi came into the room.

'Put him down,' she said. I looked at her with the most neutral expression I could manage. 'Because he's tired,' she added rudely. I counted a few numbers then turned my back on her. She left the room. A little later I heard her go into the main bedroom with a cup of tea for Christine. I put Dominic in his cot, went, knocked and followed her in.

'Nurse Day I have something to say to you that should be said in front of Mrs. Frisby.'

'What could *you* have to say to me? ' she made 'you' a dirty word.

I repeated to her what I had said earlier to Christine about her future status. Mimi came towards me saying something I didn't hear and tried to push past me. I closed the door, barring her way and went on with my rehearsed speech. She said, 'Get out of my way. I'll have the law on you.'

Christine broke down and started to sob, repeating, 'Don't fight over me, please don't fight over me.' Then she asked Mimi to leave, but I don't think Mimi heard her.

I ploughed steadily on as Mimi cried out melodramatically, 'You shan't hurt her any more.'

When I finished the speech I opened the door and stood aside. Now Mimi refused to go. I grabbed her arm and shoved her out of the room, closing the door. Christine calmed down. I waited, then said quietly and evenly, 'You see what you're relying on, Christine? She's a silly old maid who understands nothing of our life. Neither does that lawyer. He's never met me but he must be passing judgements based on what you have told him and we know how accurate that is, don't we? Give 'em both a holiday.'

Christine blew her nose and mopped up a bit, 'Will you leave me alone for a bit, please.'

I promptly left.

A little later Christine asked me down to the kitchen. We were talking and having our umpteenth cup of tea when Mimi entered.

'Nurse Day,' I began, levelly, 'Perhaps you didn't quite hear what I said to you this afternoon. I'll repeat it. You are to knock before you come into any room where I am. In any case we are now having a private conversation, so leave.'

Mimi stood her ground, 'I don't take orders from you.'

I turned to Christine and said gently, contrary to the phrasing, 'Get that bloody woman out of here.'

Christine was starting to cry again. She tried to say something but Mimi overrode her. 'Anyway, I need the kitchen to prepare Dominic's feed.'

'That's fine Mimi,' said Christine. 'We'll go into the sitting room.' I went with her. We sat down and listened to Mimi lurking about in the hall behind the sitting-room doors while Christine calmed down again. 'I've got to go and visit Mummy. I promised. I'm late,' said Christine. Her mother was in hospital.

'Fine,' I said. 'I suppose there's no chance of my getting fed is there? No, I thought not. I'm going out for a meal later. I would like you to promise two things, please.'

'What?' She looked quite interested.

'Please don't try to lock me out every time I leave the house. I'm going to come back in, darling, and it just means that windows will be broken and there'll be unnecessary fuss and damage.'

'What if I don't promise?'

'It's charming really, isn't it, darling? This is our house. We both live here and you're going to see your mother. You don't have to ask me to promise not to lock you out, why should I have to ask you?'

She sensibly ignored that. 'What if I don't promise?'

'I could take the doors off their hinges before I go out.' I tried to picture myself wrestling with our considerable front door.

'All right, I promise. What's the other?'

'Thank you. All the accounts are still running; Harrods, Peter Jones, John Lewis and so on. You must promise not to run up bills on them. I'm, very overdrawn.'

'But you can afford to take Sian to Morocco.'

I wasn't going to be side-tracked with that one. 'Six days in Morocco for two is cheaper than six weeks in New York and a fur coat for one, so don't give me the hard luck story, darling. I give you £100 a week and pay all bills. You've already put me in an impossible position financially. Don't do anything else.'

This remark referred to £15,000 I had laid aside for unpaid tax on my UK earnings. Nothing to do with the Trust. I had put half in her name because our house was in my name (the mortgage was in my name so we had no choice). Our personal finances were getting unstable; the purse was deep, but not bottomless. We had four years of back tax to deal with and until that was done (with Trust moneys too) we had no real idea of what we would be left with. But Rutter, true to form, had advised Christine to grab what she could. In spite (or probably because) of my asking her not to rock the financial boat there had been a letter from Rutter demanding that the shares be sent to her by return or he would take legal action. Once again, bewildered by apparent wanton destructiveness that was against her own interests, I had given way. I no longer had sufficient reserve to pay my back tax.

She promised not to misuse the accounts then went to her bedroom and telephoned, I assumed, Rutter. Mimi, unnecessarily, hovered on the landing to see I didn't listen. I felt sick. The call was brief, then Christine left. I went out later, opening one or two windows and returned at about 9.30 p.m. The house was in darkness, all the windows were closed, the curtains drawn and Christine's car was missing. The holdall I had brought home with me was on the front path with my belongings in or round it. I was disappointed but not surprised and walked round the side of the house to see if there was any way in without breaking a window. To my surprise the front doorbell rang so I walked back to the front of the house and saw Christine taking Daisy and Minnie from Pat-The-Poodle-Lady, as she was known.

What casting for the subsequent scene: Mimi, Daisy, Minnie, Pat-the-Poodle-Lady, Christine and me. Why do we writers of fiction bother? Minnie and Daisy had been for their regular cut and shampoo and Pat-The-Poodle-Lady had chosen this moment to return them. I walked past the group into the porch. Christine was taken by surprise but tried to bar my way.

'I don't want you in here. Get out.' She said, pushing me. Her purse fell from her hand and money scattered. I took hold of her gently by the shoulders and removed her from my way. 'I'm staying, darling. Get used to the idea.'

Mimi was in the main hall scuttling backwards and forwards, saying, 'Get the police. Get the police.'

I said to Christine, who was torn between stopping me and dealing with Pat, 'Don't be silly, darling.'

Christine said, 'You can't come in. I've spoken to my solicitor and you can't come in.'

I said, 'It's not his house, darling. It's ours.'

Mimi chimed in, 'You can't come in.'

The calmness that I was maintaining for all this did not apply to Mimi. I snarled at her, 'It's nothing to do with you. Keep out.'

She retired for the moment, then came back and said to Pat, 'Go on, go, can't you? Be off.'

Pat-The-Poodle-Lady stood in the doorway looking hideously embarrassed. She was owed thirty-five shillings. I tried to pay her while Christine and I hunted for coins on the ground. I apologised for the scene. Christine wouldn't let me pay. She apologised too, and both of us stood there offering Pat the money and apologising while the dogs jumped up and down, barking excitedly. Mimi squawked in the hall.

My holdall was only two steps away and I moved to pick it up as Pat started up the path. It was an unsound move. Mimi shouted, 'He's out. Quick, close the door,' and banged the main inner door closed. This locked Christine out. I turned and threw myself at the outer, double doors as Christine tried to close them and get the chain on. They didn't give. At the

164

third go they burst open, glass showering. Only the chain held them. Christine called out, 'All right, stop it. I'll open it,' and took the chain off.

Pat-The-Poodle-Lady stood there with tears welling up. 'Oh, dear,' she said.

Christine, Daisy and I were now in the porch. Pat was on the path and Mimi was inside with Minnie. Mimi was running up and down the hall yelling something about the police, Minnie was barking her head off. Daisy joined in.

Christine shouted through the door, 'Oh, calm down, Mimi. It's all right. Calm down and open the door.'

Mimi did so and all of us except Pat-The-Poodle-Lady trooped in.

'Goodnight, Pat,' I said. 'Thank you for bringing the dogs. Sorry about all this.'

'Oh, yes,' chimed in Christine with exquisite politeness. 'Thank you, Pat. Sorry. Goodnight.'

'It's a pleasure,' said Pat and left.

Christine and Mimi disappeared and, shaking in reaction, I got a dustpan and brush to sweep up the glass. Dominic was crying so I went upstairs to see why. Christine was wheeling his cot across the landing into his nursery which was over the front door. She had wakened him.

'What's all this operatic melodrama about? I asked.

'I was afraid you'd smash the nursery windows and frighten him so I put him in our room,' she answered. I helped her with the cot. 'No, I don't want your help, thank you,' she said.

'Oh, shut up and grab your end and don't be a silly cow,' I said. 'Why would I smash his nursery windows?'

'Trying to get in.'

'If you didn't lock doors in my face I wouldn't need to smash any windows. And hasn't it occurred to you that if I thought Dominic was asleep in the front of the house the very thing I would do would be to break in round the back? You were putting him precisely where there'd be most fuss.'

We went downstairs and got a drink each. Then Mimi appeared again, frightful in night attire.

'Oh, God, I thought you'd gone to bed once,' I said.

'I came to see if Mrs. Frisby was all right, *Mr* Frisby,' she answered.

Christine said, 'Yes, I'm fine thank you, Mimi. Go to bed.'

Mimi left the room. We heard her hanging about in the hall or on the stairs for some time but ignored her.

Christine was in a bad way. I wasn't too brilliant myself. We quarrelled, then argued, then talked for nearly two hours. She had telephoned Rutter all right. He had told her to lock me out thus forcing me to make an apparently violent entry. He told her that if I succeeded in getting in she was to leave the house for the night, leaving Dominic and the nanny behind. The point to be made here being that she was too frightened to remain.

After two hours of it she said, 'I'm going now,' but she didn't move.

I summoned up my last reserves of contempt. 'All right, then, go, if your lawyer told you to. But don't go alone. Take Dominic and be a little dignified about it. Leave me. Show you don't want me. Don't indulge in these legal manoeuvres. You're not the Christine I know. You've become some legal-bloody-zombie yourself; Rutter's puppet.' I ran out of steam and said quietly, 'What a wife. To throw away six happy years and the future of the three of us and those unborn because of a few bad months. Huh.'

Christine just sat. I knelt in front of her and started, yet again, pleading. Suddenly her tears started to flow, a quite different quality from earlier. There was a long pause while I sat at her feet and she stared at me, past me and into herself. Then she spoke so quietly I could scarcely hear. There were long pauses. I could hear Mimi shuffling about in the hall like some rodent behind the skirting board. She had been up and down the stairs for nearly two hours. Christine said in a voice from another world, quiet and drained. 'I don't know what to do...I don't trust you. I can't...I don't trust anyone...I can't make any decisions any more...I just feel like a vegetable...I don't know anything about anything.' Her sheer bleakness, the undefended misery, was moving beyond anything. I had been staring at a series of masks instead of a face and was unready for this sudden revelation. So, for the first time possibly, I was properly involved in her pain. Till then I had felt merely guilty. Perhaps that is what guilt is, the pain of not feeling for another when you think you should.

There was a long silence. 'Let's just get up in the morning and take Dominic for a walk together in his pram.' I said. There was another pause while Christine seemed to be returning to the room and the moment, but Mimi came in. Christine and I left, I had my arm round her. I closed the double doors on Mimi to get rid of her and again put my arm round Christine to help her upstairs. Mimi followed.

I took Christine into our bedroom and she lay on the bed. I didn't dare undress her and put her into bed then stay with her, which would have been the natural thing. I said, 'Sleep well, darling,' or something and went downstairs to get a drink. I heard Mimi go into Christine's room.

A few minutes later Christine came down with her coat on followed by Mimi and said she was going. She looked terrible and refused to tell me where; I presumed to her mother's, our old house in Bective road, only five minutes away. It was empty as her mother was in hospital. Christine had a key.

After Christine had left, Mimi went to bed and I considered going to look for Christine but I didn't think that someone who was dutifully following legal advice was in danger from herself. Then there was the question of my getting back in if I did go out. I could just see Mimi saying, 'I thought you were in bed. I was asleep,' while I beat my brains out on the bolted door below. Instead, I went to bed and dutifully acted on legal advice myself; I wrote up my notes of what had passed. The above is taken from them.

Chapter XXII

May Twelfth, Thirteenth, 1970

Mimi was on the landing as I took Dominic downstairs to give him breakfast. She said, about as rudely as she could manage, 'Do you mind. I feed him up here.' As I gave Dominic to her she added, 'Unless *you* want to feed him downstairs.'

I said, ' No, thank you,' and removed myself swiftly from her presence.

At nine a.m. sharp I telephoned all the shops where we had accounts and told them I would no longer be responsible for any bills incurred by my wife. I told our bank manager the same thing about her overdraft. I didn't intend to face a possible nod from Rutter to her to charge and be damned.

Christine arrived. She was presenting the cool, brittle facade but it looked pretty tarnished.

'You look terrible, darling, have some tea,' I said. 'Lucky-old Dominic's having his with her upstairs. Have you done anything to start having me removed?'

'No. I'm going to see Mr Rutter this afternoon.'

'Ah.'

'I haven't slept at all.'

'Hm. Where did you go?'

'What do you care? You couldn't even be bothered to follow me and find out last night.'

I thought of the various responses to that and decided on, 'I didn't think we could afford the glass that would be broken when I had to smash my way in again.'

This must have been about right because Christine said, 'I'm sorry about being silly and locking you out.'

I liked that, thought it better not to say so and telephoned a glazier to have the front door repaired. Then I said, 'Why don't we just put Dominic in his pram and take him for a walk up the road?'

'No.'

'Well, go and have lie down if you're tired, anything; let's just relax. Go and see Rutter another day.'

'No, I must go today.'

'No, you mustn't. It's only if you want to.' No response. The atmosphere was that of slack water, between tides. 'Well, if you're going to have your fun and see Rutter, I might as well enjoy myself, too. I'll play golf with Tony.' I telephoned and made the arrangement. Work was out of the question. It seemed like a good idea to get out of the house and keep cool while she was out.

When I hung up Christine was speaking in that low distant voice again. It was the emotional movement that I wanted. I listened, dead still.

'I was so miserable I would have killed myself last night but for Dominic,' she said and leaned against the sink staring down. I took that with a pinch of salt, people don't kill themselves while acting under their lawyer's instructions.

The telephone rang. It was my mother. She was distraught. 'Oh, Terry, Clare's had a stroke. She's dying. I've got to go down there. Jack's at work, he can't come and Joan's got the children. I don't know what to do about Milly. I'm sure you're busy, but could you come with me and...'

What timing. Lethal to the second. This was the last in the series of outside events arranged by fortune that seemed to take over our lives at that time. Clare and Milly were ninety-four and ninety-six respectively. They were my mother's aunts, her surrogate mothers really, the surviving two of three sisters who had brought her up in the absence of her mother. They had lived in a basement in Hove for over thirty-odd years and were virtually gaga. My mother visited them regularly.

I tried to be firm, 'Look, I can't at the moment, Ma.'

'Oh, dear, I don't know what to do.'

Christine chimed in. 'Of course, you've got to go, darling.'

'I will if you'll come,'

'I've got to visit Mummy again. I promised. I'll see you when you come back,' said Christine.

'Promise.'

'Yes.'

It seemed reasonably safe. I couldn't do anything at home if she went to see Rutter, except wait for her. 'OK.' I spoke into the telephone, 'How long will it take you to get from Borough Green to Victoria, Ma?' I asked.

She knew the times of the trains by heart. We were a railway family. I turned away from the telephone. 'Oh, come on darling. Come with me. You can see your mother later.'

Suddenly Christine fell to pieces. She was still leaning against the sink, only now facing it so that I didn't realise until I saw and, I think, even heard the tears splashing onto the metal. I went over to her and very gently, not merely out of consideration but out of care not to be shoved away or accused of molestation, I put my hands on her shoulders and turned her round. Christine clung to me. Sobs shook her. I thought they were as much sobs of relief, at letting go of it all, as anything.

'I want to try again but I'm frightened,' she said in a voice that sounded pretty normal, all things considered. The tonal balance was right at last. I leaned back against the sink and kept kissing her head and held her tight. There was a tremendous wave of relief. After a while she said, as though I hadn't heard the first time, 'I want to try again but I'm frightened.'

I said something like, 'There's nothing to be frightened of now, darling. It's all OK,' and I kept kissing her and repeating that. There we stood till the sobs calmed down. I was caught out by her emotional pattern being traversed so quickly. She seemed completely herself. Now, when I should stay here, I was committed elsewhere.

'My mother will be waiting at Victoria,' I said at last.

'You'd better go.' She was mopping up with a piece of kitchen paper.

'Come with me.'

'I can't.' she looked round at imagined responsibilities.

'Yes, you can. Let's stay together. It's safer.'

'I'm all right now, anyway.' And she looked it.

'OK. I'll be back this evening and I'll phone you from Hove.'

'Yes.'

I hesitated only briefly, then, 'Why not put off seeing your lawyer till tomorrow. That'll do just as well.'

'I'll see. Come on, I'll see you off.' We stood in the hall with our arms round each other. It was all right, I was sure of it. I went out onto the path and turned to say a final goodbye. She stood in the doorway looking quite strange. I described her look at the time as like an illustration of a tragic heroine in a Victorian melodrama, it was so unreal. I started to return, thinking, to hell with it all, but she said, 'Go on. Your mother is waiting.' So, torn, I left.

I raced round to my typist's house, a few streets away. From there I telephoned Miss Collis. 'Listen, now listen carefully. It's all going well. Even quicker than I hoped. If we're just left alone everything'll be OK.'

'Splendid. I'm delighted,' came her jolly tones.

'Now, listen, listen. Phone Rutter and tell him so. Ask him as nice as you like just to leave things alone.'

'All right.'

'Grovel if you must. Just tell him to let us all calm down and everything'll be fine.'

'OK.' She was getting impatient with my repetition.

'Ask him to just stay out of things.'

'Yes, yes, all right. I've got all that. Don't worry.'

I took my mother to Hove. It was all predictably awful. Clare lay in hospital barely alive, attached to drips and things. She looked frail beyond possibility. There lay these shrunken remnants of a delightful person, mouth open under beaky nose, breath rasping, just on the brink. Milly was wandering about their smelly basement flat emitting a sort of dotty, detached concern. She looked even more wispy. She kept forgetting what had happened and asking where Clare was in impeccable Edwardian diction as she poured tea into grimy cups. We found someone to take care of her for the time being. I telephoned Christine. I got Mimi.

'I don't know where she is or when she'll be in,' she said. 'Do you mind?'

I drove my mother back to Borough Green and telephoned again. 'I can't speak to you. I'm busy feeding Dominic. Do you mind?'

I arrived home. There was no trouble about getting in, but no Christine either, so I went looking. Her car was nowhere to be seen.

The next morning I had to go to the Comedy Theatre for auditions for the take-over cast of *Soup*. On my way, I took another look for her car and this time found it outside her mother's house. I knocked and knocked. No answer. I went next door. The neighbour, a woman called Ann Reeves, recently divorced, said she hadn't seen Christine. I went on to the theatre.

After the auditions I settled back in a taxi with the evening paper. On the first page inside were photographs of Christine and me. Underneath was:-

PLAYWRIGHT TERRORISES WIFE

Playwright Terence Frisby 37 - he wrote the West End comedy hit *There's a Girl in My Soup* - was ordered by a Divorce judge today to leave his home in Genoa Avenue, Putney.

The order was made on an application by his wife, Christine, a former model.

Judge Potter also granted an injunction restraining Mr Frisby from molesting or interfering with his wife, their eight-month-old son and the nanny who looks after the child at their Putney home.

Mr H S Law, for Mrs. Frisby, said she alleged her husband left home in February, but later broke into the house and 'terrorised her.' He had another address in Smith Street, Chelsea, and there appeared to be no reason why he should not move there.

The judge directed that Mr Frisby, who did not appear at today's hearing, must leave the house within an hour of being served with the court Order which will operate until a further hearing next Monday. He will then have an opportunity to be heard.

Mrs. Frisby is bringing divorce proceedings against her husband.

A group of reporters and photographers were on the pavement of Genoa Avenue. They fired questions at me as I brushed past them. A little man in a hat and raincoat was standing in the middle of our living room. He shuffled a bit and said 'Mr Frisby?'

'Yes,' I answered, although we were both certain who I was.

'I am empowered by the Court to give you this,' he said, or something like it, I wasn't really listening. I took a legal-looking piece of paper.

'What's it say?' I asked without looking at it.

He cleared his throat. 'Er—well you must be out of the house in one hour.' He perked up a bit. 'But you have time to pack your things and—er—any—um.' He gave up.

'Where's my wife?'

'Er—I—understand she's upstairs—er—lying down. She has someone with her. A neighbour, I think.' He looked as though he was going to say something else but changed his mind. I wondered who was with Christine.

'I'd like to speak to her.'

'Er—well, the terms of the injunction are that you may not molest her...' he looked apologetic again.

'I don't want to molest her, I just want to talk—oh—yeah, I see. That includes talking does it?'

'Well, um...' he found another ray of hope. 'Unless she wants to talk to you. Um—yes—quite. You could pass a message.'

I wandered round aimlessly wondering what to take. I didn't want to touch anything in the sitting-room, it all looked too nice where it was. I made a cup of tea instead. I went and looked into the sitting-room again. He shuffled and cleared his throat when I entered. I stared at him standing there. It was an almost precise enactment of the scene I had imagined for years, the little man in the hat and raincoat who knocked on my door and said '...and you've got all this from scribbling in those children's exercise books, Mr Frisby? Er—ha—sorry, there's been some mistake. You've got to give it back...'

I put a few clothes in a bag, trying to think of what message I could pass to Christine that would do any good. I looked round for Dominic. He was nowhere to be seen. I returned to the little man.

'Where's Dominic?'

'Ah—that's the baby isn't it? Your son.'

'Yes.'

'Erm, he's with his mother and his nanny.'

'Ah, good. Safe,' I said.

'Yes.' He smiled in reassurance. Irony was clearly not one of his strong suits, or not when on duty.

The divorced neighbour from Bective Road, Ann, came into the room. That was a surprise. She was playing neutral messenger and overdoing it like mad. That's an interesting acting problem, I thought. How do you overact neutrality?

'This gentleman said you have a message for Christine.'

'I'll come up and see her,' I said, and moved quickly past her and up the stairs to Mimi's room where Christine was. Ann hurried with me, but didn't try to stop me. I hoped Mimi wouldn't be there and she wasn't but Christine looked frightful. She must have been drugged. She was very glazed. I gave her the front door keys and couldn't think of anything to say.

As I was leaving, I found Ann beside me in the hall. I said to her, 'Tell Christine beating me is no good. It'll never work again with a man if she beats him.'

I have little idea what this meant, or what it even referred to. Anyway, it was a singularly puerile remark for one of the bigger moments of life.

Ann emphasised its inadequacy by repeating it like some minor priest learning a message by heart for the Pope. When I got outside the reporters had gone.

It was, indeed, one of the bigger moments of my life but I still didn't realise how big. The ease and swiftness with which I was removed from my home left me flattened. An interlocutory restraining injunction, as had been used here, was not even relevant to our situation. Such injunctions are emergency measures, essentially temporary, to protect women and children who are being beaten up (I knew none of this then, of course). And, even when battered women and abused children were in real trouble, the number of times that judges have refused to eject men even temporarily, from their homes is notorious. Yet it had been successfully and quite improperly used here by Rutter behind my back.

Christine and I were two people who loved each other, had got into trouble of our own making and allowed lawyers into our lives. I do not believe for one second that she wanted a divorce when she came back from New York, but within forty-eight hours she had been directed to Rutter who told her God-knows-what. I believe that she never knew how, rather than didn't want, to get off the runaway vehicle which she had unwittingly started and he now drove. Perhaps it was even I who had started the juggernaut when I told her I had seen a lawyer. No matter that I told her in the same breath that I had subsequently dismissed him from my mind, we were different animals. I knew I didn't want a divorce and especially didn't want a divorce lawyer to lean on; Christine was always looking for a prop. She found first Kitty, then Rutter.

We were both devastated by what was going on, self-inflicted or not. Without intervention we would already have been back together weeks before, in March. As I keep saying, I never really believed what was happening even as it happened. You could sum up our pre-lawyer situation in a sentence: we were a cautionary - almost classically so - tale of the dangers of permissiveness. The banality of that judgement makes me blush as I write it, but it has force, I am sorry to say.

So, please dismiss partiality between us from your mind, take no sides and watch the legal profession at work. If it were not for them I would never have written this story. They are precisely the wrong people to be involved in marital crisis or divorce and are only there by historical accident. I don't just mean the Rutters of the legal profession, who are used to having their noses in the gutter. Keep an eye on the respectable ones, the judges, the solid worthy professionals. They all function in a way that is exactly contrary to the best interests of the principals concerned. Their efforts even encourage you to revise your former feelings about your partner. Indeed, as you may have noticed, that process had already begun with us.

Chapter XXIII

May - June 1970

I was sure that our only hope of a future was for me to get the injunction lifted. If we were just together for a while, healing would quickly start.

I went to see Miss Collis the next day, she showed me the three affidavits used to get the injunction. They were signed respectively by Rutter, Mimi and Christine; all were written by Rutter, his style was unmistakable. These documents, which had such potency, alleged that I had not been home since February, except to see Dominic occasionally and Christine once, when I had slept with her on her birthday two months earlier. None of the documents referred to my constant visits since. I just seem to have appeared from nowhere a day or so ago and forced my way in. In contrast to the statement that I had 'left the matrimonial home', Christine's six-week absence in New York from both her home and her five-month-old baby was called 'a holiday.'

Nowhere did any of the affidavits allege that I was violent or a danger to anyone, the nearest they got to that was that I had been (in some unspecified way) 'threatening.' When I considered all the ghastly things that women and children suffer at the hands of some men I was puzzled that such relatively mild accusations warranted my ejection. The distortion that hurt the most was that Christine said she was 'frightened' of me. I thought of her clinging to me in the kitchen, saying in that low, desperate voice, 'I want to try again, but I'm frightened,' an intimate, defenceless moment between us. How dare he twist it so? That was her voice that I had heard and believed, that guided my next actions, not the dross she had signed in Rutter's office. I had to get back home.

The one-word comic flourish that highlighted how small was Christine's part in the authorship of her affidavit was when it referred to the 'lounge'. Not even stark terror would have induced her to call it that.

Anger might have seemed the natural reaction to all this, but I was merely ashamed. Ashamed of what was happening and what she had put her name to. I dropped the affidavits back on Miss Collis's desk. 'An Englishman's home is his castle…until his wife's solicitor says it isn't.' I muttered. 'I must contest this and get back in again. Fast.'

Miss Collis agreed with much optimism. 'They've found some old buffer of a County Court judge and told him the hard luck story,' she said, cheerfully. 'We'll get this lifted. It's purely temporary.'

I couldn't share her bounce. Embarrassment had a firm hold on me. Every time I thought of what was written in that evening paper and the following dailies my skin crawled and I wanted to hide. Embarrassment, in the quantities that engulfed me, is a potent force. It was difficult, too, to make any decision without being able to talk to Christine. Surely she must feel the same. I half-expected a telephone call from her: 'Darling, I've got to appear in court against you next week. What should I say to win?' I imagined the activity on her telephone, repetition and embellishment, till people would cross the street in fear when they saw me coming. My own telephone had been far from silent. Thank Heaven for one sensible chum who opened with an exasperated, 'Have you been beating her up again?"

'But "terrorised,"' I said to Miss Collis. 'How could they? How could she let them?'

'Oh, that's not uncommon,' she said. 'You should hear some things that are said in these cases.'

So I was one of these cases, was I? 'Who's this Mr Law, this barrister?' I asked. Yes, that was his name, Mr Law the barrister, in this nightmare version of *Happy Families*.

'Oh, good old Harry Law. He's all right,' said Miss Collis. Another one of her professional brothers who was 'all right.'

Only one solid-looking piece of evidence had been put before his Honour Judge Potter when he had barred me from my house: a medical certificate from our GP. It spoke, not very surprisingly perhaps, of Christine being in an extremely anxious state and having lost a lot of weight because of the situation between us. It was being used to demonstrate that I should be kept away from her for the sake of her precarious health. Christine was obviously prepared to have the details of it read out in open court, should I contest the injunction.

———————

I sat in the waiting room of our doctor's surgery in the Upper Richmond Road, an impostor among the ailing. Did any of them recognise the terrorist in their midst? I smiled weakly if anyone's eyes met mine, a gesture of non-aggression.

'I didn't know it was going to be used in this way,' our GP said unhappily, looking at the certificate she had written. 'I wouldn't have signed it if I had known that this was what it was for.'

'Did you weigh her?'

'What?'

Your certificate said she had lost a lot of weight.'

'Well, that's what she told me.' Our doctor shuffled papers on her desk then recovered and spoke crisply. 'Obviously, that is not precise, I don't weigh my patients on every visit. But she had lost weight.'

'So you just took her word for it?'

175

She was silent.

'You know she went to a health farm, don't you, to do just that? And then she spent six weeks dieting in New York.'

Our doctor's crispness disappeared. 'Oh.'

'Well, there it is. And now I can't see her.'

'It was your absence, not your presence, that created the anxiety state I mentioned.'

I grabbed at that eagerly. 'Will you come and say that in court?'

'Er, well, I'm very busy.' She looked harassed.

'Hell, your certificate is the one thing that could dish us.'

'Erm. I don't want to take sides.'

'Is it taking sides to help keep us together?' In imagination I heard impatient shuffling from her waiting room while she considered the problems of the spoiled nouveaux riches. 'If you would just write out something to counteract that in court,' I said, compromising with myself, 'that would do.'

'But then I might be called. I'd have to go up there and wait around.' She obviously regarded that as a calamity.

'You might be called anyway,' I said.

'Hm. Yes.' She gave me a written, guarded version of the dismay she had shown to me at the use of her certificate, and I left her to treat other, more conventional troubles.

Pat-The-Poodle-Lady was terrific. The demands of uncut canines were less pressing than those of the sick. She was eager to talk and did. I pushed the fur clippings back, sat at a bench in the back of the Putney Poodle Parlour, and wrote down what she said, excluding the background yap. She confirmed every detail of my account of the proceedings at the front door and then added this helpful remark:

> Mr Frisby addressed his wife as 'Darling,' and his attitude towards her was quite calm. After the door was slammed he was annoyed and in a bad temper. He used some language to the housekeeper but in my hearing not at all to his wife. The attitude between Mr Frisby and the housekeeper was mutually antagonistic. It seemed the conflict was between him and her, not him and his wife.
>
> Patricia Stoneham

Pat said she would sign her statement. Now I had my account, the doctor's new medical comments, possibly the most telling evidence as they directly conflicted with the ones used without her knowledge, and Pat's statement. I had my written notes of what had happened when I went home. Together with my own appearance in court I was confident we could convince the judge of my fitness to return. I also saw myself in court, converting him to what I believed, namely that if he would allow me to re-enter my own house, far from my being a danger to anyone, peace would be restored and an unnecessary divorce averted. That was precisely how I saw everything that was going on: this was the divorce that neither of us wanted, that shouldn't be happening. But it was. I still did not believe the scenario that was unfolding before me at every step.

On Friday afternoon Miss Collis and I met to go to counsel's chambers for a conference on the hearing to take place the following Monday. I brought the evidence I had gathered and my written account. Pat-The-Poodle-Lady had backed out. She had spoken to her solicitor. He had told her to sign nothing and stay out of matters until served with a subpoena.

'She stands by the truth of this though, doesn't she?' said Miss Collis, waving the statement.

'Oh, yes.'

'We'll subpoena her then if necessary.' And briskly into the folder it went.

'You did telephone Rutter as I asked you the other morning and told him that we would get together if he would just stay out of things?' I asked.

'Oh, yes. He said "Get together? Huh. Not those two." '

Again I experienced that sinking inside me that seemed to greet all Rutter's actions.

'Well, surely, then, my call to you and yours to him are marvellous evidence' I said.

'Oh, no. What solicitors say isn't evidence,' she said. She gave a sort of detached rub of her chin. 'I'm not sure it isn't without prejudice anyway. And you can't use that.'

'But what about my call to you - scarcely the act of a terrorist?'

'Ah, solicitor-client conversations are definitely privileged. We can't use that.' She saw my face. 'Never mind, perhaps we'll get it in somehow.'

There was one other point in Christine's affidavit that bothered me. 'I can see why they'd say I haven't been home since February twenty-sixth except to see Dominic, but why add that we went to bed together on the night of March 6th, her birthday? That doesn't make sense.'

'Oh, yes, it does. You see, she told you on January thirteenth or whenever, that she'd been unfaithful, then went straight to New York. Then she came home, talked to Rutter then slept with you. That was the first time since her confession about Bert Thingy. In sleeping with her you condoned her infidelity. When the nanny came into your bedroom and saw you in bed with Christine that made her a witness.'

'I've never heard such tripe,' I said. 'Who cares about condoning or not condoning?'

Miss Collis shrugged expansively. 'Well, no-one, I agree. But the law is the law. After that date the detectives got evidence of your adultery with

Sian. A few days later, when Christine gave you the pot, she wouldn't sleep with you. If she had, that would have condoned your infidelity. The detectives' evidence would have been useless.'

I felt sick. 'If what you're saying is so, she slept with me, or refused to, on legal advice.' As I said them, my words also offered an unthinkable explanation of why Mimi had burst into our bedroom at two a.m. with a supposed telephone message: the witness. I felt sicker.

Miss Collis saw the look on my face, and without altering a particle of her tone or inflection, changed direction by a hundred and eighty degrees. 'Quite. It's a ridiculous idea. I agree.'

But now unthinkable constructions of Christine's actions were beginning to form in my head.

We arrived at Paul Beard's chambers. This consultation must have been a definitive example of non-communication between two people who allegedly spoke the same language. His legal mind - if that is what it was - seemed to have no understanding of life as I, and everyone I knew, lived it. All I can remember was that he was tall and worried, but only half of that may have been true of him when we arrived. I told him why I wanted to regain entrance: to save our marriage. He asked me questions about the last few months, about my past attempted infidelities and about her. He started to look unhappy. The Seventeen came into it somewhere and my protestations about the importance of Truth and Sharing. His gloom deepened. 'But all these stories about your differences,' he said gesturing feebly. 'And your adultery and—'

'What's adultery got to do with loving your wife?' I burst out. He seemed to glance furtively over his shoulder in case such a thought should be overheard. 'If you have a second child you don't love the first less, do you? Why does everyone seem to think you can love your children, your family, your friends, but only one woman at a time? My God, literature and art are full of examples.'

'I don't think I should mention that idea in court,' he said, anxiously. 'And—um—literature and art won't get us very far either.'

'Well, history, then.' I tried to get through to him by direct means. 'Look, *you* love your wife or partner or whatever you have and you must have been unfaithful. I won't embarrass you by asking, I'll just assume. When you were being unfaithful did you love your wife less? Of course not. It doesn't enter into it. But we're taught we can only love one at a time. Haven't you noticed it doesn't fit reality?'

Paul Beard looked at me in considerable shock. 'Yes, well, quite. But your wife with all these men, I mean—er—'

'Yes, but they were before she met me.'

'Oh, yes.' I had muddled him. Sin on the scale I seemed to be talking about was beyond his grasp. 'But one man wasn't.'

'Yeah, but that was ages ago. I'm only angry about that because she's going on about me. Don't you see? They're all weapons in this game she's got us into. If things had happened differently she wouldn't give a damn either.'

'Yes, but how am I going to argue that to a judge?' he said. 'He'll go berserk at all those stories. I'll be thrown out of court.'

'Well don't, then. Just concentrate on the fact that I am not dangerous, that we have a baby, that we love each other and—'

'But she'll say she doesn't.'

'Of course she does. What do you think all this agony is about?'

'But will she say that?'

I was getting so passionate in my efforts to convince him he must have been forming doubts about his own safety. I calmed down. 'It's that bloody lawyer. And the others. They just seem to believe the surface of what she says. They don't understand her. When she calls me names it doesn't mean she wants to get rid of me. She wants me to make it better.' I paused to gather my thoughts as I clearly wasn't getting through. 'You see, it's like this. She has this emotional pattern...'

Paul Beard and I could never have had much in common but on that afternoon we had nothing. I described Christine's nature as I saw it and saw incomprehension radiate from him like a positive force. I heard conviction dying from my voice. I trailed off somewhere. He looked at me seriously and there seemed to be a considerable silence.

'I really think you two are better apart, you know,' he said with sympathy. 'I really do.'

If Rutter's actions made my heart sink, my own counsel scuttled it completely. If I couldn't convince someone who was supposed to be on my side, what chance was there going to be with a judge?

'If we did succeed in getting you back into your house,' said Beard. 'You'd be hedged in by all sorts of restrictions.'

'What?'

'Oh, yes,' said Miss Collis with her usual cheeriness as though I had known all along. 'You won't be free to do as you like. You probably won't be able to talk to her.'

'Not if we meet in the kitchen making a cup of tea?'

There was a lot of head-shaking. I had lost without a decent struggle. At last the reality that my marriage was slipping/had slipped away was getting through to me. 'If I don't fight this thing, what about seeing Dominic?' I said.

'Oh, that'll be all right. We'll arrange that,' said one of them quite brightly. 'There's no complaint about your conduct towards him.'

An Englishman's home is his castle. Until his own legal advisers say it isn't.

Because my consultation with Paul Beard had so undermined my will to contest the injunction I now had to accept it in full. I would, on his advice, give an undertaking not to molest my wife, or son, or his nanny (good

179

God) and not go near the matrimonial home. Every instinct in me told me not to do this but there was no juice in me. If only it had been an enemy I was to fight in that court, nothing would have persuaded me to give way, but it was Christine. That was the decisive factor. I had no will to fight her especially in public and call her a liar (that should help relations between us), even though I believed it to be the only way. But who was she now, anyway? This person who slept with me just the once, on legal instructions; who set detectives on me and pretended she knew nothing of it; who misused her doctor's report; who gave me dope and made promise after promise which she broke the moment I walked out of the room. As I said: people don't behave like that, do they? I was shattered.

At the Royal Courts of Justice at the wrong end of the Strand, the following Monday morning, Miss Collis was going to give my undertaking for me. I wanted to be there, to see, but I had no part to play in this irrevocable step I had agreed to. Irrevocable? Well, some part of me still said that if I let Christine have her way in this she may feel more secure and good relations be re-established. Pigs might fly.

I sidled into court to see His Honour Judge Potter and some counsels muttering down at the front about another matter. The first person I saw on a bench at the back was Christine. I have never seen Christine appear in public, before or since, looking such a mess. She wore no make-up (a rare event), no lipstick and no false eyelashes, de rigeur for her at that time. Her hair was scraped straight back. She was wearing her glasses, a public sight nearly as rare as the lack of make-up, and an old skirt of semi-mini, by then unfashionable, length. She wore clumpy shoes and wisps of hair were escaping. I was shocked, then upset, by her appearance. I was as uinsuspecting as ever as far as she was concerned. The tactical reasons were revealed to me later when I saw the many newspaper photos of her outside the law courts: still 'terrorised', although I had been gone for ten days by then.

I slid in beside her. 'Hallo, darling, are you all right?' My voice, indeed all of me, was full of concern.

She whispered something I didn't hear.

'What?' I said. 'Are you all right? You look as though—'

'Get away from me.'

'What?'

She hissed louder, 'Get away from me.' She started to slide along the bench towards the middle. I thought for one confused moment that she was frightened of me. I had been reading too many affidavits.

'What for?'

'You're not supposed to sit next to me.'

'Why ever not?'

At this moment Miss Collis and Rutter appeared and a terrific amount of *sotto voce* rhubarbing went on to get us apart. In the end I went out of the court and came in the door on the opposite side. Christine, who had by now slid nearly along the bench to that side found herself beside me again. She went zooming back. This episode depressed me further.

I had my first look at Rutter, though mostly in profile. For someone I was very curious about he left surprisingly little impression on me that day. Perhaps I had other things on my mind. He looked exactly as you might expect a short, stout, lawyer of about sixty to look, and that was all. He did a lot of studying his papers, whispering to his counsel and staring intently at the judge. He never looked at me and only afterwards spoke to Christine. I thought the apparent concentration unnatural, it looked like acted concentration. Miss Collis gave my undertaking and His Honour Judge Potter beamed down benevolently. 'I'm glad it has all reached a happy conclusion.'

Miss Collis said later, 'I'm sure you've done the right thing. When things are a bit calmer you two can start getting together. Pretty little thing, isn't she. Two or three of us outside the court were saying so.' Her years of trying to be one of the boys in the legal profession had made her sound exactly that.

I waited nearly three weeks for the calming down process then wrote to Christine on the tenth of June. The effort was considerable. It was a long, emotional, repetitious letter, scarcely the product of a professional writer. The extracts below give the flavour.

...I know that receiving a letter from me is going to make your stomach churn over, just as trying to write one makes mine...as long as we're apart there is the chance that one or other of us will accidentally, or in a rage, strike another terrible blow and widen the gulf that is already there between us. That is what will happen after the lawyers wrangle their way through the next stages. Humanity will be dead and I can see us meeting in the not too distance future and eyeing each other with indifference. That is the real horror that I fear. We grow apart, we learn to do without each other, and learn to live with others and our feelings for each other are just a distant memory. It's horrible for us and disastrous for Dominic.

'I want to try again but I'm frightened,' you said. I cannot ignore a remark like that. That nullifies the rest and wanting to try again corresponds with what I want. That is why we have to meet. If I see from you, yourself, that you didn't mean that, I'll go my own way...I have constant news of you and I know you're miserable and lonely - whether we like it or not we have a bond between us for the rest of our lives - Dominic...

When I read back what I've written it seems that it doesn't begin to plumb the depths of feeling of what I want to say. Everything in me screams out that I love you and want you. I have to force myself to put these things on paper and send them to you, so strong is the desire in some ways to push you aside, out of the way, and to stop the pain. I know you feel the same, only more so. I believe that is why you take such urgent steps to push me out of your sight...

I'm sorry, sorry, sorry for the pain you've had or are in but it has been vile, too, for me. I don't see any point in the anguish continuing. I want us together again, or if that <u>really</u> isn't on, then apart and friendly and wholesome...

All right, you're frightened; all right, I'm a bastard; all right, it hurts, but there's still Dominic.

I love you

T

PS Unless Ivor tells me to the contrary, I'll write again.

Rutter answered, not Christine. He said that any further attempts by me at molestation would meet with an application by them to have me committed to prison for being in breach of my undertaking to the court. So much for Paul Beard's and Miss Collis's advice to me to give way in the interests of reconciliation. My legal advisers had assisted me in wrapping myself up in a legal flypaper.

Chapter XXIV

Summer 1970

Rutter's activity now centred on getting a hand on the booty. In fact this campaign had been progressing well for some time but I didn't realise. My undertaking to refrain from molesting Christine, Dominic and Mimi had also, in passing, obliged me to refrain from harassing our house and the thousands of pounds' worth of antiques and other goodies we had bought for it. Even my writing desk, desk chair, chess table and chessmen were mercifully spared a beating up. No doubt in consideration of their feelings, my request to have them was refused. Leslie Taylor, Paul Beard and Gudrun Collis, experienced divorce lawyers all, had failed to point out to me these implications of my undertaking or to build in any safeguards when I gave it.

Just what was the booty? I realise that extinct details of my then-finances are of no interest in themselves (anyway, inflation has rendered them archaic), but a few round figures are necessary to follow the legal manoeuvring.

Soup had earned in author's royalties and film rights, from 1966 to 1970, nearly a third of a million pounds (somewhere between three and six million at 1998 prices, depending on how you count inflation). We had invested well and lived sensibly during the bonanza so had saved more than two-thirds of that, well over £200,000. Roughly half of that was ours in the UK and half was in the Cayman Trust, mostly invested by the Swiss Bank Corporation in Zurich. I will call it the Trust, with a capital T, from now on.

But - and this was at the core of everything - because of becoming a foreign resident I had paid no UK tax for the four big years and now that I had returned to the UK I had to face some sort of music. But what? The answer was that my advisers didn't yet know, nor could know for some while, possibly years. Those were the days of 19/6d in the pound (97.5 per cent) surtax on high earners, so I was advised I could owe any sum up to £105,000 on the Trust and £65,000 on my own earnings. Over three-quarters of all we had. Our own (non-Trust) UK assets were all tied up; our house (subject to mortgage), my mother's house, Christine's mother's house and income, our tax-reserve fund (half of which Christine had already taken), our furniture and so on. There were other people benefiting on a regular basis, every penny was working for someone. There was no spare cash.

The big question mark was the status of the Trust in the eyes of the Inland Revenue. If that was sound, so were we. Furthermore, until we knew of the Trust's status none of the assets must be touched or brought into the UK or we could still further weaken its position.

Thus, none of the capital of our considerable fortune could be touched without serious consequences. Indeed, I might already be in the position of having to sell even our house if the worst of the above figures came to reality. However, the true position was that my advisers expected, by advancing behind a cautious series of probes through the tedious but lethal minefield of tax law, to ensure that I had only a reasonable liability. Even if I never wrote another profitable word there should be a secure future for us all from the future income of the Trust. Provided we were prudent now. The last thing we all required was that anyone should rock the boat. That was the capital situation and long term outlook for our income.

But what of our immediate income? I was getting into deep water. In London the box-office on *Soup* suddenly dipped. The play looked as though it was about to come off. Bandwagon, the replacement, had earned virtually nothing. I was giving Christine weekly more than I earned and we had let our spending go unchecked during the months of the emotional crisis. I was carrying a big overdraft. I was told the divorce would cost £5,000. In my new, straitened situation, living in my two rooms, I had to get a grip on things. I told Harvey Unna to tell Christine that from then on she must pay her own bills except for the mortgage on our house, and that he would divide my income as he received it. Half was to be saved for tax and the remainder split equally between us. Rutter responded at once with two letters, one open and one without prejudice. What they amounted to was, pay at the former rate or I will make maximum trouble and run up maximum costs.

Legal activity centred on my affidavit of means. It was going to take months to compile and would even then be incomplete because of the imponderables of tax. Everybody in the divorce knew this, but that merely seemed to encourage Rutter's demands for it to be produced at once. These rose to a scream of acrimony, whipping up the temperature of the already overheated situation. I was 'evasive,' 'dishonest,' 'irresponsible,' the insults were endless. The simple fact was that Christine had our house and far more available cash than I had to live on while fiscal affairs were being settled. No amount of explanation or conciliation from Miss Collis would stop this unlovely correspondence and it proliferated like costly confetti.

All this, on behalf of Christine, upset me dreadfully. What I didn't appreciate was the comic side of it. The letters were written in impenetrable English with superfluous capitals to give weight. I have extracted one section of one letter from the pile of bumf to illustrate. A skim-through will give an idea.

We know that we shall eventually get an Affidavit of your Client's assets and income, but the question is, when! You have known full well for months that we require particulars of your Client's assets and income, and likewise you have known for weeks since you were served with notice under the Rules, that we require an Affidavit of your Client's assets and income, and neither have been forthcoming. We are not as you have stated 'too quick to draw the wrong conclusions.' Your Client's delaying tactics and statement which he made that he intends to drag his feet and delay the hearing of the Suit, unless our Client would come to financial arrangements with him, justifies our view that your Client is deliberately avoiding swearing his Affidavit of assets and income. We propose to apply for an appointment before the Registrar to hear our Client's Application for Alimony and child maintenance in view of your Client's failure to swear an Affidavit of assets and income, pursuant to the notice which we served on you, and we shall ask the Registrar to make an Order for your Client to swear and file an Affidavit of means and for discovery of documents, and for your Client to attend before the Registrar for cross-examination.

As to the last paragraph of your letter, we do not accept the explanation which you have given for the delay in regard to the Answer, because our Client confessed her adultery to your Client which had occurred some years ago and she told your Client who the man concerned was, and she gave him the reason for her having committed adultery when she did. We are informed that the man is in fact known to your Client and that subsequent to our Client informing your Client of her past adultery, your Client told our Client that he had telephoned to the man in question and had spoke to him and he told our Client what he said to the man and what the man said to him. Therefore, the suggestion in your letter that the man was unknown, is untrue. You are no doubt aware that we wrote to your Client before you were instructed on the 2nd March 1970 referring to our Client's confession to your Client of her past adultery. If as you say, you were instructed at the very outset of this matter, that you would in due course have to file an Answer, it is amazing that you did not do so. However, the matter was determined by the Registrar on the 2nd instant, who refused your Client's Application, that he felt that the Application was not being made for the purpose for which it should be made, and that he did not feel that he should allow an Answer to be filed, for side issues which were not in the least likely to succeed.

It is a masterpiece, isn't it? But at the time, my God, those letters hurt. And they came swirling in through the letter-box like leaves in autumn.

Meanwhile litigation had continued in other directions. There appeared to be only one way to delay the decree and give Christine a chance to reconsider: by a cross-petition. To cross-petition I had to name Bert as co-respondent, an action from which I shrank. However, that was the system.

Early one morning in May I telephoned him. It was eerie. 'Hallo, Bert Mortimer, please.'

'Speaking.'

'Terence Frisby here. Can you speak privately at the moment?'

There was a beat, then, 'Yes.'

'Good. I'm very sorry to bother you, but you had an affair with my wife some years ago.'

The pause was predictable. I let him stew for a bit before getting on with serious matters. 'I'm very sorry to say that she is divorcing me and I want to try and stop that.'

'I see.'

'All I can do is slow it up for now and to do that I have to cross-petition and if I cross-petition I have to name someone and that would appear to be you.'

'I see.'

'And you're married, I believe.'

'Yes.'

'So I thought I should warn you. If an official-looking envelope comes through your door, you don't want to open it over the breakfast table, do you?'

'No.'

'Could be a nasty shock for your wife with the toast and marmalade.'

'Yes.'

'I am very sorry to drag you both in, but I can't help this.'

'That's all right.' The guarded neutrality was going from his voice. He sounded surprised.

'Well, forewarned is forearmed. Goodbye.'

'Goodbye,' then quickly, 'and thank you.'

'Well, I won't say it was a pleasure.'

Because of illness, Nabarro Nathanson had failed to cross-petition promptly, so we had to apply to a registrar to do so out of time. This application failed, so Paul Beard was brought out and dusted off to appeal to a judge to overturn the registrar's decision.

'What's all this?' I asked. 'I've acted correctly.'

'Don't worry. My firm will take the blame if necessary,' said Miss Collis.

Into court we went. There was some faffing from Beard but no mention of fault in Nabarro Nathanson, Miss Collis's firm. Then 'good old' Harry Law got up with Rutter prompting from the bench behind. Law was a ponderous, junior barrister who seemed to be used by Rutter, principally because he did everything he was told. He was big, overweight, with careful but appalling diction: a good brown voice, marred by nasal, self-conscious delivery. I remember his face chiefly for the size and quantity of visible pores on it. He wore a dark-grey suit of heavy, worsted bird's-eye that reminded me of old Smudger, the senior salesman in Selfridges Gentlemen's Ready-To-Wear Suits department. Smudger had been old-fashioned when I joined in 1949. While British art and life had exploded in the fifties, causing the swing of the sixties - long hair, miniskirts, hipsters, man-made fibres, the pill, permissiveness and all of it - Gentlemen's Ready-to-Wear, dark-grey, worsted, birds-eye suits had lived on in The Royal Courts of Justice. Every time I went there, the sheer prehistoric appearance of them all used to get me. But Good-Old-Harry was the walking personification of the underside of the legal profession; not the facade, the 'Hello, old boy' brigade, the gentlemen, the public school network, the confident, faultless accents, the starry QCs. No, Good-Old Harry was an ageing junior who often stumbled when speaking in court and would never grab a headline. He was hanging in there in the divorce division, doing as Rutter said and getting his daily tube to N or NW something, or perhaps even to Essex. If you are wondering why I noticed his suit and not his wig and gown, let me explain: most divorce litigation is carried out in chambers (in camera) which simply means in private. Judges, clerks and barristers don't wear the regalia. Keeping people's financial affairs secret has much to commend it, but without that healthy glare of the press and TV there are some pretty funny goings-on in the gloom. The woodwork down there is crawling.

Good-Old-Harry argued that I was only trying to cross-petition out of time because I wanted a reconciliation. Wait a minute. Did I say he would never grab a headline? I wronged him. This was the man who had recently called me a 'terrorist' and made all the newspapers. I listened with more care. He was saying that I had told Christine that I would 'drag my feet' because I wanted a reconciliation. This puzzled me. To paint me as a man who wanted a reconciliation seemed an unexpectedly friendly gesture. As evidence that I was dragging my feet, Law read out Rutter's letters that accused me of dragging my feet. While I was still wondering how Law could argue before one judge that I wanted a reconciliation and before another that I was a 'terrorist,' I heard this one refuse my application. Then I was in the corridor wondering why my man hadn't blamed my lawyers as Miss Collis had promised.

'It wouldn't have made any difference,' she said.

'Why ever not?' I asked.

There was no answer. It was, of course, a straightforward cock-up, or worse. a sacrifice of the client so that the lawyer doesn't look incompetent in court.

I was still confused. 'And Law argued that I was late because I wanted a reconciliation. I should have thought that would help me, wouldn't it?'

'Oh, no,' said Miss Collis as though I should have known. 'Wanting a reconciliation is not grounds in law for holding up court processes.'

I telephoned Bert again.

'It's all right. You can relax. You won't be named after all.'

He was less friendly this time. Perhaps he thought I was playing silly buggers with him.

Miss Collis said I should appeal. I was sure to succeed. I told her to go ahead. Then I remembered that I would have to telephone Bert again. He would be sure I was playing silly-buggers this time. I decided to skip Bert.

That appeal meant that Miss Collis had to ask for an adjournment of the decree *nisi* because it came up first. She was successful.

Outside the court afterwards Miss Collis and Rutter had words. She reported to me that Rutter said to her, 'Silly boy, she would have had him back, but not now.'

That remark caused, of course, the pain it was meant to on the might-have-been front, besides making me squirm at its patronising impertinence. But it revealed the heart of our problem. To see what I mean we have to go back a month when Christine clung to me in the kitchen and said, 'I want to try again but I'm frightened.' I immediately telephoned Miss Collis to phone Rutter and tell him to keep a low profile, Christine and I were going to get together. Then I went with my mother to deal with Clare's death in Hove. His response had been to Miss Collis, 'Get together? Huh. Not those two.' And I had returned not to the reconciliation I expected, but to renewed hostility boosted by him.

And now we had, 'Silly boy, she would have had him back, but not now.' Christine obviously didn't know - hadn't known for months - which way to turn. There had been moment after moment since March when we had both wanted reconciliation but she saw Rutter as her protector. From what? From me? There was no need. I was no threat to her. But, yes, I was, in the sense that I had hurt her. She needed protection from her hurt. But we all need that, that is part of being a couple. The last thing you need at such moments is a lawyer. You love each other and sometimes you hurt each other. And not until the pain is too much do you split up. Christine in her confusion with his fatal reassurances had lost sight of her real feelings and our interests within days of meeting him. That, I am sure, was at the root of everything, of how all those words and actions could get so twisted and misused, as with that word 'frightened.' She was able to tell herself almost anything to justify this course she was on. And he was there to smooth and guide. He looked safe. Safer than floundering out into the deep end of an attempted reconciliation. But what did he get out of this destructive role he was playing? I couldn't see. Not yet.

And then there was Dominic. I hadn't been allowed to see him for over a month. Miss Collis wrote the politest of letters to Rutter. She asked that I see Dominic at least twice a week, preferably alone, but I would agree to any reasonable arrangements.

Below is the relevant part of his answer.

> As you are of course aware, the child is only nine months of age and it would be impracticable for your Client to have the child as suggested. Under no circumstances, will our Client consent to your Client entering the former matrimonial home. The child is much too young to be taken out without supervision and in view of your Client's past conduct, we cannot advise our Client to accept any undertaking by him...

'But you said my undertaking wouldn't affect my seeing Dominic,' I protested to Miss Collis.

'I didn't think it would,' she answered. Once more my legal team had not protected my (and Dominic's) legal interests when they had advised me to sign the non-molestation undertaking. She entered an application for access.

And so we had opened up a new front in this hateful business: access. I learned that if your wife so wishes, or is so advised, you must apply to the court for 'access' to your children. The judge then decides how much is 'in the interests' of each child. A month passed. I dropped the appeal to cross-petition out of time. It seemed pointless. Bert was left in peace. The application for access was due to be heard on July thirtieth. On July thirty-first, the last day of term, the decree *nisi*, that would half-part us officially, would be granted. It would name Sian as Official Adulteress, the cause of our divorce. Then the Royal Courts of Justice would go on holiday.

I hadn't seen or heard from Sian for some while when she telephoned me. Some of the photographers and agencies for which she had worked, modelling, had had a man round asking for photographs of her for the newspapers, 'preferably in the nude.' Did I know anything about it? I didn't, nor could I find out who he was.

On the evening of twenty-ninth of July I arrived home and played back my messages. On the machine a little bell went 'ding' between each message. There were four, all from Christine. Her disembodied voice, 'Leave me alone,' ding. Then in exactly the same distant tone she said, 'Leave me alone,' ding. She sounded mad. The third was in a hissed near-whisper, 'I hate you,' ding. The fourth was in bright, deliberate clarity on two cuckoo-like notes, each word neatly separate, 'Fuck...off.' I played them and played them, searching for clues and hidden meanings between the 'dings.' I telephoned anyone I could think of who would know about Christine's state. She was reported to be fine.

Law, Miss Collis, myself and Rutter junior gathered the next day for the access hearing in one of those appalling corridors where you have to wait for a judge to come free. In the main body of the Royal Courts of Justice the corridors are dim and sunless, heavy with the anxieties of a century of litigants, but in the brand new Divorce and Admiralty Division (why divorce and *admiralty?*), which has now been renamed The Family Division by some comic, the windows are large and the corridors are light and functional. The anxieties are fresh, not in the atmosphere but on the faces of wives with sagging bodies, worried about their houses and future, and husbands with thinning hair wondering how they are going to pay the mortgage and maintenance, besides finding a new place for themselves. The children are absent.

Miss Collis, on my prompting, started to plead with Law that we arrange some access without having to do it through the court. When Rutter junior was some paces away Law glanced over his shoulder to make sure he wasn't heard and said, 'If I had my way he could have the kid for the afternoon now and we could all go home.'

We concentrated on Rutter junior. He was slightly younger than I, I guessed, taller than his father but with the same unathletic shape. He favoured grey, pinhead, worsted suiting, quite modern compared to Law. He had very sloping shoulders, what we called in tailoring 'SRB'. (slightly round back), and a sway figure. That is the sort of shape which if lengthened and accentuated would be a question mark. However, Rutter Junior could never make a question mark, that suggests emaciation. His forward-thrusting hips offered towards you an already too-ample waistline. His hair was black and curly, his skin moist, a thin cigar hung permanently from his lips. His name was Geoffrey, but I got it muddled and thought for ages it was Maurice. I have never been able to think of him as anything but 'my boy, Maurie.'

While Miss Collis started to plead with Rutter junior, I managed to slip in, 'How is Christine? Is she all right?' I was thinking of the telephone messages from the previous day. Rutter junior looked at me as though the questions were an impertinence. 'She's fine, thank you.' His voice was thin and nasal.

'But when did you speak to her?'

'My father did this morning, if it's any concern of yours.'

'No. None. Thank you.'

Miss Collis was following her own line. 'Well, surely, you can phone her and see what she says.'

'I have my instructions.' I took this to mean from his father. I didn't think of a solicitor's interpretation of the sentence. Believe it or not, I still had not accepted that Christine could be knowingly behind these blocks to my seeing Dominic. A few words with her would put it all straight.

'But just phone her,' I chipped in.

'I've told you. I have my instructions.'

'Look,' I was getting angry. 'Here's sixpence. Just phone her and ask.'

'She's not to be disturbed.' And he turned and walked off down the corridor flicking ash from his thin little cigar.

I turned to Miss Collis resignedly 'Oh, well. I suppose we'll have to go through with this charade.'

In court (in chambers) Law argued the letter of the law, that it was improper for an application for access to be heard before the application for the decree *nisi* which was set for the next day: this application for access should be adjourned. Miss Collis argued the human case that I hadn't seen Dominic since May 14th, and that if this hearing was adjourned the vacation would intervene and I wouldn't be able to get access to Dominic before the autumn. The judge adjourned the hearing. The letter of the law came first. Once more my advisers showed themselves to be wrong in predicting both Rutter's actions and the judge's unconcern.

The next day Christine's application was heard for her decree *nisi* This is the halfway stage of the divorce and must be heard in open court. It is a formality, the hearing in which the cause of divorce is publicly stated and so all the juicy details are there for the press, who photograph, on the steps of the law courts, anyone worth snapping who turns up. And those who don't turn up have old photos of them pulled out of the files, dusted off and printed. Christine turned up and her picture duly appeared in the next day's papers, not as she had appeared at the injunction hearing, unkempt bespectacled and browbeaten-looking, the sort of person who would leave crazed messages on your answering machine, but head thrown back, new dress of fashionable length, pearls, false eyelashes and without glasses. Someone had seen that Sian's picture was there too, but not in the nude.

One week after the decree *nisi* Miss Collis had a meeting with Rutter to deal with financial matters. She tried to raise the question of access. This was brushed aside. She often referred to Rutter's attitude to her conciliatory efforts as 'harsh,' 'amused,' 'contemptuous,' in total, 'uniquely shocking' in her experience, but she reported an exchange during this meeting that gave a new, even less attractive view of him. I quote from what she wrote to me later.

> He also asked for an immediate and substantial cash payment for your wife. I cannot remember the sum he mentioned, although he was specific, but I do remember asking what it was for, and when he said, 'a holiday and a few clothes,' I remember thinking that it would have to be a quite staggering holiday and also a quite staggering wardrobe to justify the sum. I also remember saying to him that his client, except on one occasion, always looked well and expensively dressed in any case, to which he replied, 'Oh, well, you know these little pussies, they always have to arrive each time in a different outfit.'

191

The word 'pussies' was so unlikely in the context that I have never forgotten it.

The Bandwagon, meanwhile had started a successful run in Australia. Temporarily, my income bounced up. Christine got her share, as promised. Rutter asked for more.

I had a long think about everything. I was fond of Miss Collis but I sacked her and Nabarro Nathanson, giving her my best wishes as I did so. I had asked her to tread gently and warily and she had, but her advice and actions had repeatedly left me defenceless in the face of Rutter's aggression, worsening my situation. Someone tough had to be found to stop the rot.

And so ended my association with my first firm of divorce lawyers, Nabarro Nathanson, wrong on every forecast of what Rutter would do or the courts would allow him to.

And Rutter? There is much more of him, but my first point, that but for his intervention I do not believe our divorce would ever have happened at all, must be clear to you. However Rutter was not just a rogue among worthies, a maverick who, for personal or exceptional reasons, turned our marital crisis into its protracted death throes. He was part of a whole rotten system which still affects far too many of us.

Which brings me to my second point, a point more important that any personal complaint from me, a matter of general public interest. It is that lawyers and judges - of whom we have seen only one so far, the ineffectual Judge Potter - experts and practitioners in our adversarial system of law, are precisely the worst of people to be involved in the human crisis of divorce. Furthermore, as my story unfolds, it is not merely their destructive unsuitability that will emerge. What follows is a tale of solicitorial, barristerial and judicial ineptitude, complacency, incompetence (even in those non-caring, technical areas in which they are supposedly expert) and eventually something worse.

Chapter XXV

Summer 1970

The offices of Theodore Goddard and Co were situated on the third floor of a large block in St. Martin's-le-Grand. I was shown by a uniformed commissionaire to a waiting-room with current editions of *Country Life* and *Punch*, to say nothing of *Private Eye* for the trendier client-to-be. I was given just long enough to check that the dates on the magazines were indeed up to the minute before I was ushered into the presence of John Calderan.

I disliked him on sight but I wasn't looking for a chum. He rose to greet me from behind a modern desk. His suit was expensive contemporary. There was quite a lot of chrome and steel in evidence about the room. The window was behind him, a reasonable place if you have to sit and work at the desk all day, but trying on the eyes of the visitor. It was hard to see his expression, or perhaps that was because there wasn't much. He was average height, build and posture and had a roundish face with a Roman nose down the middle of it. Where else would his nose be, you may well ask, but his was very in the middle. I had the sensation, not a very accurate one, that I could draw his face with four straight lines for eyes, nose and mouth, on an egg with the big end down. The big end needed to be down, not to denote any peculiarity of the top of his head, but because his cheeks looked full and complacent. But it was his voice that was his most distinctive quality. Although not high, it was thin, cutting, nasal and had an air of accustomed authority. His speech sounded like acquired standard English rather than inherited, correct except that he couldn't pronounce his 'r's properly. They were soft, not so bad that he said 'w', but just wrong and very thin. Try and say something halfway between an 'r' and a 'w' and you have it. I think that this mannerism contributed to the overall quality of his voice. Occasionally he would half roll an initial 'r', to get it out, I suppose. It reminded me of the whirr before a clock chimed. A junior solicitor in the firm, Paddy Grafton Green, later said to me, in a confidential moment, that he loved Calderan's voice and especially his 'r's. 'They have a deadly quality,' he said with devotion, but I could never admire speech defects.

I described the whole mess to him and particularly that I must avoid the time trap of paying: a) Christine, as though there was no £170,000 possible tax liability, b) the divorce legal fees, c) the Revenue, having been already shorn by a) and b). It would mean bankruptcy. Put like that it was quite straightforward.

He listened to the full account, heard how much I was worth and agreed to take the case on.

Calderan wrote to Rutter telling him that he was now handling the case and got back a Rutter special listing all my principal failings except my inability to do the mile in four minutes. Calderan answered this neutrally while he examined the papers then wrote to me calling Rutter's letter, ' a standard form of letter,' which gave me a rancid smile. He told me that Taylor of Nabarro, Nathanson wanted another £1,000 in costs before he would hand over the papers and could he, Calderan, have £500 on account. I paid up. Rutter wrote complaining about delays, and Calderan wrote telling him to keep a civil tongue in his head or shut up. For the first time since these besuited strangers had taken over our lives I found a faint cheer on my lips, then I realised that I was cheering because the man who represented me was telling the man who represented Christine to get stuffed. There was a deep well of love to be emptied before I could unreservedly enjoy even Rutter being snubbed as long as he was connected with Christine.

Calderan pointed out to Rutter and me that because I wasn't deducting tax from what I gave Christine, I was giving her the equivalent of about £20,000 a year. As well as this she was enjoying the advantages of the matrimonial home, so she should consider herself lucky. He suggested that I stop the payments to Christine until the hearing on seventeenth of September as I had paid her enough. I refused.

'Fine,' said Calderan. 'That'll look good in court.'

Something, that wasn't itself of any great moment, but had serious repercussions on what follows came to light next. It emerged in August, from Bank of England correspondence about my former French bank account, that the mandatory signature on the Trust bank account in Zurich, granted to me early in 1969, was illegal for a UK resident. I was horrified. For a year and a half I had been breaking the law on Bill's advice. I told him to have the signature cancelled at once. We had done the unforgivable: broken some, to me, obscure regulation by accident and possibly put everybody's material future in jeopardy. I wanted to kick myself, and Bill a bit, too. This incident caused a series of events to slot precisely into place in my mind. One of Christine's remarks in an outburst during March/April when I had been pleading with her to think again, had been, 'You are terrified of what I can do to you.' Variations on this had recurred in her more emotional moments and made me curse the presence in the background that encouraged them. At last they made sense. She must have told Rutter of the signature, he realised it was illegal and saw himself as having some sort of power over me. 'What should I do about it?' I asked

Bill. 'Nothing,' he replied. 'You've cancelled it now, just forget about it. I shan't tell anyone.'

But all this was nothing compared to the dreary fact that I was miserable. Life looked like rain on a slate roof. And, in contrast to the early winter months, when I hadn't understood my own feelings, this unhappiness was sharpened by my being precisely aware of what was now wrong, I missed Christine constantly. I found myself talking to her at night and when I was alone. To work was impossible because any contemplative moment was immediately filled with Christine and Dominic. Tears would run down my face and nose in surprising quantities and I would watch them drip onto the paper. It had been a source of anguish when I was a drama student that I never seemed to have an accessible reserve of tears to call on when needed. Now they formed a soggy beige puddle on the children's exercise books before me. Sometimes there were sobs and I would give way to them in the hope that one more spasm would expel the pain for good. I was cut off from the only two people I wanted to be with, one of whom seemed to have gone mad. I was convinced she felt the same but had got stuck somewhere up a blind alley of revenge, navigated there by Rutter. Robert saw her once or twice and felt the same. 'You're the one person she wants. Instead, she is running round looking for help from all these strangers.' Frisby versus Frisby the letters and documents said and my whole body would clench.

Soup entered the fifth year of its run. I was congratulated by many who looked with envy on my new freedom combined with such apparent affluence. Sian and I had resumed our affair, there was no point in not. But, although I felt strongly and warmly about her, we had neither of us wanted this unsought extension. We continued together for some while before drifting naturally apart. But my much-publicised divorced looked like the prototype 'off with the old, on with the new,' a course of action I found as unattractive as it was bone-headed. So I imagined that any right-thinkers I met were regarding me with just the astringency I would have felt. 'I see. Success. Ditched the little woman. Got the dolly bird. Huh.' And when I met new people, especially married women, I silently dared them to let such thoughts show in their eyes. The situation had a crooked beauty. There I was, in the eyes of many, the personification of my hero in *Soup*: rich, successful, single playboy, while the bottom line of my feelings was regret, loss and shame.

One day Calderan said 'I want you to meet our trust expert, Patrick Grafton Green. He will be doing the spadework in compiling your affidavit of means.'

I think it was the first divorce that 'our trust expert', who was a very junior solicitor, had handled. I found him most intelligent and likeable. He was thin and untidy. His suit, generally worn without waistcoat, was middle quality, grey, worsted, chalk stripe. Like him it was nondescript. It was overworked and starting to bag at the knees. His shirt would rumple a lot round his middle although he had no fat. His hair was thinning prematurely though he had unusually thick eyebrows. We got on well at once. As when Leslie Taylor passed me down to Miss Collis for day-to-day matters I was content that Calderan should pass me down to Paddy.

The big moment arrived. My affidavit of means was ready, eight foolscap pages with ten exhibits, accounts, valuations, settlements and other bumf. Every penny was in there. Rutter wasn't going to get the chance to say 'Ah-ha. See? He's hiding something. I told you so.' Frank Young my accountant, his assistant, Miss Collis, Bill Fournier and Harvey Unna had done the work. Yes, it is wonderful is it not? This expensive team of experts to produce one document, entirely useless except to aid division of my indivisible assets. It was like driving at top speed into the desert in a vehicle powered by your water supply.

In his office, Calderan was at his most Senior Partner in front of Paddy Grafton Green and me. His chin was raised like Codron's in more authoritarian moments. 'That's a good document, Paddy. Well done.' Paddy muttered and looked down, reddening slightly with pleasure. 'Don't you think it's good, Mr Frisby.' It was not a question. The word Frisby with liquid consonant on either side of his soft 'r' was always an intriguing sound in his mouth. The 'r' became nearly silent giving me the alias of Fooisby.

'It's the first one I've ever seen, so I can't...'

'Take it from me, it's first class. I've been thinking about this case, Mr Fooisby,' I was a case again, but relieved to hear I was worthy of his consideration. 'The battle is going to centre round this trust. I don't want some registrar or County Court judge making a hash of it. I'm having the case set down in the High Court. With your approval of course.' This formality was given. It was difficult not to feel a glow of pride at my new-found status. I was High Court material, too complex for the creatures who dispensed justice in our lesser courts. What I did not know was that the fees lawyers charge can be double in the High Court. 'Now we've still got this wretched hearing before the registrar on the seventeenth September,' Rutter had applied for an interim rise in Christine's payment because of hardship - yes, hardship, 'and I've got Neil Taylor as our junior. He's very experienced and reliable. We use him a lot.' He paused. 'As your leader I've got Joe Jackson to represent you.' He paused again while Paddy looked frightfully keen. As I gave no reaction he went on, 'Joe Jackson is the top Queen's Counsel in divorce.' He allowed another little pause for me to be impressed, then smiled, 'I think he'll deal satisfactorily with Rutter.' He paused again, enjoying his coup of understatement. 'Deal satisfactooily with Ooutter' was a most satisfactory phrase.

I went to meet my brand-new junior counsel, Neil Taylor, who was very tall, and my QC, who wasn't. Yes, a real legal biggy was orbiting into my affairs, and not just any old star but Joe Jackson QC, the top man in divorce, the man who had compiled and edited the text book from which they all worked, the doyen, the man who had told a country court judge, in his own court in Cardiff, he was a cunt, and got away with it: the Superstar. Calderan, Paddy, Neil Taylor, Frank Young (my accountant) and assistant, a legal pupil and I, all filed reverently into The Presence. He was beyond a large desk which, like Calderan's, had its back to the window. I think the window looked over the Thames, but memories of the background are hazy when the foreground was so eventful. I expected Jackson to rise from behind his desk to greet us and experienced a moment's surprise when he didn't. Were we expected to bow, or even genuflect, before he moved? I looked at the others. They wore respectful expressions but no-one showed any sign of obeisance. Then Jackson came round his desk, hand held out, and I realised with a suppressed giggle that he was already standing. However, what this bantam lacked in inches he had learned to compensate for in fire. As we sat round the walls of his room he took the floor and paced between us, laying down the law. His movement was a strut as he explored his territory flexing his neck, legs and wings, I mean arms. He didn't actually peck at any specks of grit or grain in passing but I did glance involuntarily at the carpet for marks. His suit was Savile Row. It was reassuring to see that the sartorial expression of legal rank was properly exhibited.

Calderan, feeling his position as senior solicitor, tried a line of easy familiarity but it was clearly an effort. Jackson barely gave it lip service. Neil Taylor, junior to Jackson in rank, not years, only occasionally ventured an opinion and then in a very low voice addressed to a bookcase on his left. He was more concerned with knowing his place than airing the issues. Not that Jackson was a man anybody would have chosen to disagree with. I tried to have Taylor's mutters brought into the centre of the discussion, but although he was, I guess, over a foot taller he remained coiled submissively on his chair when exposed to the standing, full-frontal Jackson.

'Now this offshore trust,' said Jackson. 'They will try to allege that you control the money in it and grab a large capital settlement on that basis.'

As I realised that Jackson had left a gap for me I said 'Don't I control it?'

'What do you think?'

'I think I do.'

Jackson pounced. 'That is not the law. The law says the trustees control it.'

Neil Taylor started one of his mumbles to the bookcase.

'I don't think Mr Taylor quite agrees,' I said.

Taylor's voice rose briefly above sea-level. The bookcase was being informed that '...a divorce court judge will ignore all those tax-law technicalities. He'll look at the practical issues...'

Jackson brushed this aside. 'That is not the law. The law is quite clear.' Having disposed of Taylor, he allowed reason to modify his argument 'Or it would be if it were an English trust. Plenty of precedent there. But these offshore things, hm, I don't know.'

'Anyway' I said, 'The whole thing is academic. She mustn't have a chunk of it because anything up to ninety per cent of it may be owed to the Revenue now I'm a UK resident.'

Joe Jackson leapt on me. 'Where's your evidence? Tax demands? Assessments?'

'The Revenue doesn't even know it exists yet.' I said. 'We're not asking for trouble.'

'Well, if you don't have any assessments why should a judge believe you have a liability?' said Jackson.

'We all know,' I said weakly. 'She knows, I know, Rutter knows.'

'Huh,' barked Jackson. 'The documents, the deeds, the settlement are all bona fide, aren't they? Just because you *may* owe money is no concern of the judge's. He's dealing with realities, not possibilities.'

Taylor started nodding vigorously at the bookcase.

'I see,' I said heavily. 'So if the judge thinks an offshore trust is just a tax device, which it is, he will take note of the reality that I control all that money but he will not take note of the reality that I already owe it to the Revenue.'

'That's not a reality, that's a possibility,' corrected Jackson.'

'Well, it's bloody real to me,' I answered loudly as the enormity of the situation sank in. Rutter's threats via Christine were real. It had taken me months to get there. I could be forced to give her what I didn't own, then pay the lawyers' fees, only to be left with too little to meet the Revenue's demands. There was only one response to such a threat: I told the assembly that they must preserve me from that situation or else I would collapse the Trust and give it all to the Revenue before any divorce settlement could be made. Scuttle the ship. Our fortune would be thrown away, but at least I could save myself from bankruptcy.

'However,' said Joe Jackson cheerfully, 'that's all in the future. Trusts later. We've got to deal with this hearing for interim ancillary relief before the registrar. You've been very generous, my boy, and now she's trying to screw you for more.'

'It's not her. It's that fucking lawyer,' I said vehemently.

Jackson stood and regarded me seriously for a moment. It was nearly eyeball to eyeball; I was sitting. Then he chuckled and twinkled. 'Yes, well, it always helps to think that. Better for the future of your son, don't you think?' I was grappling with the implications of this when he went on putting the boot in. 'Nothing like having a Rutter to do your dirty work, is there?'

Chapter XXVI

Autumn 1970

The afternoon of seventeenth September was amazing. Hearings before registrars took place in Somerset House in those days. You entered a beautiful courtyard and were insulated from the confusion of modern London, but only briefly. After entering the building you went up narrow stairs to a dim, institutional corridor where a different form of twentieth century confusion engulfed you and probably still does wherever these events take place now. As in the misnamed Royal Courts of Justice over the road, solicitors and their clients jostled each other while waiting higgledy-piggledy for their registrar. I passed a group of three that seemed to personify the whole place. A pompous-looking, overweight ass with too much self-conscious brown in his voice was lecturing an opponent solicitor who was ignoring him and making notes. 'I can't have that,' he was saying very slowly. 'Oh, no, no, no, no. Dear me, no. You don't think I'm going to allow your client *that* do you?' Watching this was a greying, pleasant, middle-class woman. Her eyes were brimming and she was following the words, anxiously searching for meaning as to her fate in some matter connected with income, house or children. I couldn't tell which of the two was representing her but it was she who drew your attention. She was somewhere close to snapping. It was in very line of her face and each angle of her head as her wounded stare swung from one to the other. Neither of them seemed to notice her.

I met Paddy Grafton Green, Neil Taylor and Frank Young with assistant. In the absence of a superior, Taylor said with authority, 'He'll make an interim order for £5,000 a year for wife and child.' This would be considerably less than I had been willingly giving.

Frank Young, like the diligent accountant he was, said, 'Don't forget to get the order back-dated. Both Mr Frisby and his wife will gain from the tax saving.'

I turned and saw Joe Jackson and Calderan strolling along the narrow corridor abreast. They looked like officers taking a turn on deck, deep in conversation of vital significance, oblivious to the lesser creatures who scattered before them or pressed respectfully back against the walls. Even the pompous ass faltered for a moment at the sight of Joe Jackson QC in these shallows.

Calderan pulled me aside. 'Mr Fooisby, if you don't mind, I think it better if I don't come in. I mean,' his gaze went over my army and then down the corridor to the lone figure of Rutter studying his papers, 'there are quite a lot of us. It might look like, well…' he couldn't bring himself to say it.

'Bullying?' I supplied.

'Pooecisely. You have Paddy and Neil and your accountant. Er—I, well, there are costs to consider.'

'You carry on,' I said. I'll manage with these,' and he hurried gratefully away. He was right. The coming battle looked very unfair. As we all filed in I heard the woman's voice from down the corridor. It was raised, hysteria seeping, controls slipping. I wondered how those two bastards would deal with her if she went completely.

The room into which we filed was lovely. High windows overlooked the Thames. The ceiling and proportions were all you would expect. A long table stretched down the room. At the left end as you entered, behind a sort of low partition on the table, against which law books rested, sat Registrar Bayne-Powell. He was half-hidden by this little barricade and seemed, when things got fresh, to duck and lurk behind it. At a separate table sat his clerk, a good-looking, greying man, the NCO type, like all those clerks. The registrar was bald, high forehead gleaming. He wore half-glasses and did a lot of benevolent beaming. My team sat down facing the Thames with Joe Jackson nearest the registrar. Rutter sat opposite. I wondered if we changed sides at half-time. Joe Jackson sat facing towards me and away from the registrar. He put the elbow of his left arm, the one nearest to the registrar on the table, which meant that the registrar saw even more of his back. He only turned full on to the registrar when he was really stressing something. This seemed to have got the rank sorted out all right. Joe Jackson was at the centre and able to see me and his underlings, address Rutter and throw the odd crumb over his shoulder to the registrar. Registrar Bayne-Powell seemed as overwhelmed as everybody at Joe Jackson's presence.

The one person not impressed, or not showing it, was Rutter. Although I had seen him before, this was the first time I took him in. I had watched him briefly in the corridor outside. He was short and portly, as I had said. He, like his son, stood sway-backed, feet at ten to two, stomach thrust forward. He had plenty of grey curly hair trendily over his collar and ample sideboards. He walked like Wodehouse's butlers, slowly with splayed feet, but had not the height to capture their dignity. I had a good look at his face. Not once did he meet my eyes. His own were under quite generous eyebrows and, to use the cliché, darted rather a lot. There was a line of hairs on his cheek, missed by his razor, and another line round his neck and Adam's apple. I guessed he was very hairy on his body. His mouth was broad and lips very thick. I had found him, on first viewing unattractive; by the end of the afternoon I thought he was one of the must repulsive human beings I had ever seen, and with good reason.

He opened with complaints about my evasiveness in delaying my affidavit of means. He read his own letters on this (and every other) subject as though they were evidence. I began to see why the torrent of abuse was created. Jackson let this go for some while. When he judged the registrar to be getting bored he said with studied patience to the ceiling, 'Anyone would think he hadn't got my client's affidavit of means in front of him now.'

Bayne-Powell gratefully took his cue. 'Have you an affidavit of means now, Mr Rutter?'

'Well, this purports to be—' Rutter began in a disparaging tone but Bayne-Powell had found his own copy, filed with the court.

'Ah, yes. Here we are. Shall we get on?' he said, ducking behind his barrier and burying his nose in the affidavit.

Rutter, apparently to impress the registrar, recounted the hearings that had taken place so far and the rout he had achieved. He loved to roll the legal words round and out. There was an almost religious fervour in his manner. It was as though, in intoning them, they gave weight to the proceedings. They rolled sonorously round the room like ten-pin bowls in their chutes. His verbal style explained some of the curious grammar in his letters: a hearing was a Hearing, access was Access, even adjectives like ancillary became Ancillary; part of the mutual massaging of the whole profession's ego. Give us capital letters and raise our status.

It seemed to me that by recounting his successes Rutter would damn his case. In answer to his account of how he had successfully stopped me seeing Dominic wouldn't any sane man say, 'You bastard, what did you do that for?' But the registrar seemed unmoved. Rutter dwelled on the injunction proceedings at great length. The implication was that our house had been a battlefield. The registrar flicked a cautious glance at me, measuring the distance between us, no doubt. In the paper that I had opened months before in that taxi, Law was quoted as saying I had 'virtually terrorised' Christine. Now the 'virtually' was dropped. 'And Mr Law told His Honour Judge Potter how the Respondent had terrorised my Client, sir.' It sounded as though Mr Law in telling His Honour, had witnessed the whole thing with movie camera turning. But all this was merely to bring him to his first climax. 'And so, sir, he was prevented from returning to the Matrimonial Home.' Pause, then on. 'And so out of revenge and spite he immediately started keeping his wife short of money.' He started waving a note of a part-payment of one week to Christine of £20-odd, pretending this was the weekly sum. He had the full figures from us in front of him that day. The week following the £20-odd, Christine had received over £400. He ignored this. I shoved the schedule of payments in front of Joe Jackson who glanced at it uninterestedly then shoved it under the registrar's nose.

'She seems to get more than that, Mr Rutter,' said the registrar mildly.

'That was all she got on that week' said Rutter.

'Are you alleging that this schedule is false, Mr Rutter?' asked the registrar mildly.

'He's cut her money,' said Rutter.

201

'But are you alleging…'

'She has all sorts of expenses: the nanny to pay, the cleaning woman, the gardener…'

Joe Jackson said chattily to a tug passing on the river, 'She seems to be a young woman of no very remarkable amount of energy,' and I smothered a laugh in relief at this antidote to Rutter's venom.

'Am I to be subjected to this while I'm presenting my case?' said Rutter, huffing to the maximum.

'Really, Mr Jackson. If your client can't keep quiet I'll have to ask him to go outside,' said the registrar, his reproof cravenly directed at me instead of Jackson, the culprit.

'It's all very well him laughing,' said Rutter nastily. 'But I'll show him where his responsibilities are.'

Jackson put a finger to his lips and wore an expression in parody of reproof. I blew my nose. For the remainder of Rutter's presentation Jackson went on throwing in asides with the timing of an accomplished comedian. Rutter tried an indignant riposte once but he wasn't in the same class. The registrar pretended to hear none of this, head down, reading hard. Suddenly, while Rutter was trying to do some mathematics to prove I hadn't paid what I had, Registrar Bayne-Powell's domed head rose over the barricade followed by a happy little smile He had just found the settlement deed relating to my parents' house.

'20 Paddock Orchard,' he said as though no-one else were talking. Rutter stopped in mid-subtraction wondering how the number twenty came into his sums. The registrar continued, 'St Mary's Platt. I know that. I live near there. Very nice.' And he was gone again.

Rutter seized on this. 'Yes. He can afford to give his mother a house but he won't keep his wife and child properly. He gives my client's mother a house, and pays her an income but he now abnegates his responsibilities to my client and his child. He has even contributed substantially towards a friend's house but not now to his wife.' While I was reeling from the implications of these arguments he brought this speech to a little climax. 'She has every right to be kept in the style to which he has accustomed her.'

This combination of arguments, that amount to, 'He has been generous in the past, even over-generous, and should therefore be forced to continue so,' is an argument that is often forwarded in divorce. Because it succeeds, the message of the divorce courts to husbands is clear, don't be generous to your wife in marriage or you can be forced into it for life after divorce. Rutter then went on to claim that I owned the two mothers' houses and should therefore pay more because of my considerable property holdings.

'Do I own them or have I given them away?' I whispered to Jackson. 'He can't have it both ways.'

'Shut up,' he hissed.

Rutter went on to claim that I was earning so much that I gave thousands away to charity rather than give it to my wife and child. He waved a deed of settlement that I had made of the South African rights of *Soup* to prove his point. It was a point of conscience that I would take no royalties from the apartheid regime then in power there; I gave the money to various black organisations. Registrar Bayne-Powell studied this document.

'But this is four years old. What has this to do with now?'

'About the same as the rest of his case,' said Joe Jackson to a painting on the wall. Then he turned fully on the registrar. It was a menacing and beautifully timed movement. 'You have there an affidavit of means with details of my client's assets and income. That is the only evidence before this court. The rest is offensive waffle. Shall we ever get on or not?'

Registrar Bayne-Powell was shaken but he wasn't prepared to stop Rutter yet.

'Do you accept these figures, Mr Rutter?' he asked.

'Indeed I do not. He has a secret bank account in Switzerland containing £50,000.'

I nearly went through the ceiling. The registrar glanced at me apprehensively. I was confirming Rutter's report of my violent tendencies. Jackson caught my arm. Rutter and the registrar were shown in my affidavit the information that the Trust contained even more than the alleged hidden £50,000. He blinked at it in surprise. His head was bent, but I could see enough of his face. He was, at that time, nearly sixty, I would guess. During those moments as he stared, caught out, he seemed a much older man. He looked as though this voluntary disclosure had dealt him a painful blow. That look, in that moment, made something that had been floating unformed in my head for months begin to gel: what was Rutter getting out of all this? My theory ran thus:-

He was playing a role to an audience of two: himself and Christine. He was even, possibly, fulfilling a long-nurtured fantasy. I knew Christine. She must have walked into his office and sat down in real distress, but not enough distress to have stopped her arriving in a cloud of scent, fur and shining hair. The long, false eyelashes over the large pain-filled eyes, must have flapped considerably. When Christine removed her glasses and bestowed the full wattage of the unencumbered stare it used to shake me, even after six years of marriage. I have seen strangers lose their way in mid-sentence. I could see Rutter in his office, hooked like many others, thinking it was simultaneously his birthday and Christmas (or Passover or whatever). And this lovely creature needed him. I guessed that, when a young man, he couldn't have been much of a wow with the women and here he was, in the fullness of time, presented with a looker from the Premier division. And she was married to a pig who ran off with a teenager and was an international tax and trust swindler. Of course I would cheat on the divorce. Such men always did. He would arrange his attack accordingly, to trap me. He was going to be the knight in shining armour. By his brilliance, he would winkle me out from the burrows and drainpipes of financial complexity in which I was hiding from my obligations. She would be grateful, impressed. There would be warm glances from those enormous, myopic orbs and who knows what further delights - at least, in his, by now, overheated imagination. At long last the short, podgy, legal tortoise had got one over on the hares. Brain power, application, diligence wins in the end.

He had fallen for her.

But reality will intrude. Here, under his nose, were the figures. His fantasy was exploded. A semi in North London and approaching death were back with him. He had had the affidavit and supporting evidence for only six days, after a wait of months. I guessed that he had flicked through the pages of figures, settlements, documents and missed the Trust, possibly because he wanted to. It would have been easy enough anyway. Now the unthinkable was true. I was honest. Something dreadful was in his face as he stared at para sixteen, page six of my affidavit.

I suppose this pause went on for less than five seconds. He pulled himself away from the affidavit and glared. He said suddenly, 'I don't mean this bank account. He has another one.'

Jackson's grip on my arm tightened as he felt me rising from my seat. He said quietly, 'Are you alleging that my client has another bank account, undisclosed, containing £50,000?'

'Yes, I certainly am,' said Rutter. When you are caught out, attack. But Jackson was the wrong adversary for that tactic.

Jackson leant forward in studied, phoney anger. 'If you are going to make slanderous allegations of perjury would you please step outside and make them beyond the privilege of this court so that my client may take appropriate action.'

Rutter declined and Jackson exploded back into his chair with a 'well so much for that' gesture, giving the registrar a marginally more offensive view of his back. The registrar pegged gamely on.

'Where did Mr Frisby get this money from Mr Rutter?'

'The film rights of *There's a Girl in my Soup*, came the answer. A sort of muffled roar escaped from me. Rutter had had it explained to him directly by Miss Collis, with bank statements and accounts, how the film payment had bought our house, my parents' house, Christine's parents' house and the remainder was kept in reserve for tax, half of which Christine had grabbed.

The registrar looked at Jackson severely. 'I shall really have to ask your client to leave unless he can contain his feelings, Mr Jackson.'

Joe Jackson had his turn. By now the room was seething. The registrar's clerk had done a fair amount of handkerchief-to-mouth work, to hide his amusement. Joe Jackson was wonderfully brief. He opened my affidavit. His finger stabbed it on each word except the definite article. 'There are the figures.' He was giving the registrar the full-frontal treatment again. His finger started again. 'These are the only figures before this court. You must,' stab, 'decide,' stab, 'on the basis of these,' stab, 'figures.' Stab. He changed his tone. 'If Mr Rutter wishes to make accusations or challenge these figures he should do so properly with evidence and examination. Your duty is clear. My case rests on the figures.'

The law (then) stated that a maintenance award for the wife could be up to one third of the couple's joint income and up to one sixth for each child, at the discretion of the judge. Any capital (house, property, etc.) was given a 'notional income' according to its value and circumstances (but this wouldn't apply for this hearing as it was interim, pending the full High Court ballyhoo). Decisions about what the joint income of the couple really was were customarily based on the figures for the past three years.

My net taxable income for those three years was about £15,000, £10,000, £8,000. But: a) These didn't include Trust earnings. b) My business expenses were very generous and could have been questioned because my gross income was far higher. Rutter in his eagerness to sling mud, hadn't attacked this most vulnerable and legitimate target. c) The ominous downturn in my income was already clear even though *Soup* was still running.

Registrar Bayne-Powell allowed about two-thirds of his face to surface for his pronouncement. He reminded me of Mr Chad, who used to be drawn peering over walls. I half-expected him to say, 'Wot, No Money?' Instead he said 'I award the wife £3,000 a year, the child £500 and the husband is to be asked to pay no more bills except the rates and mortgage on the matrimonial home.'

This meant Christine got £39.50 a week after I had deducted tax at source, about a third net or a quarter gross of what I had been giving her. The registrar had indeed decided 'on the figures'. Rutter looked shattered (his white horse shot from under him?). After a moment, speech came. He stammered slightly, 'But—but—she won't be able to live on that amount,' he said. The registrar ducked behind a book and wrote vigorously.

Jackson joined in. 'Then let her sell some of those thousands of shares my client so generously gave her.' Rutter's face turned towards him, but he wasn't really focused. Jackson went on, 'Or work?' He hastily pulled himself together as though he had made an improper suggestion. 'Oh, no, no. Of course. Sorry.'

There was no doubting Rutter's commitment to his cause. I had a moment's fellow-feeling for him. He had expressed in his last sentence exactly the same anxiety about Christine that I felt. But he continued, 'I should like to claim the solicitor's special feel of £40 for appearing against leading counsel, to be incorporated in the order for costs.'

'Agreed. Costs in the cause,' said the registrar and the rest of us half-rose to our feet but the argument wasn't over.

Rutter wanted the order backdated ten days because I had been, according to him, deliberately delaying payments.

Jackson looked at me with affected weariness 'Do you mind what the date of the order is? It might cost you ten days extra.' I shook my head. 'My client would be delighted if the order were backdated by ten days.' It was the only polite thing he had said all afternoon. 'Now may we go?'

In the corridor, all was excitement, in my team. The legal brethren wagged their heads in wonder at Rutter's performance. Apparently the unsubstantiated allegations, insults and general personal venom was special, even to their hardened ears. It increased my belief that Rutter had somehow got himself involved in our divorce in a way that was more than professional. Frank Young, who was as new to it all as I, was aghast. He walked about in a corner, shaking his head, sucking his breathing, tutting, then blowing it out audibly.

Jackson grabbed me and backed me up against a wall. 'Have you got another £50,000 in Switzerland? He asked.

'No.'

'Are you sure?'

'Positive. That's all tripe.'

'Right. If I stick my neck out for a client, I don't want to look a fool.'

'My God, you treated him like dirt. What happens if you were to work for him on another case?'

Joe Jackson contrived to look down his nose at me, which was an achievement from his height. 'I don't take briefs from Rutter. See you in the High Court.' And he strutted away.

Frank Young came to. 'Hey, he didn't get the order backdated. We lose the tax concession.' It was worth the best part of £1,000.

Neil Taylor was too jubilant to care. 'Oh, don't worry about that,' he chuckled. '£3,500. What a one in the eye.'

'But I do worry,' I said. 'We both lose. I'd rather she had it than the Revenue.'

Neil Taylor loomed over me, again authoritative in Jackson's absence. 'Listen, young man. Don't worry about that. You did very well today.'

What dull stuff, to save money from the Revenue, compared to the excitement of vanquishing your wife. I got into the car and drove along the Embankment. Glee filled me at last that Rutter had been routed. I started to laugh, then yelled with released tension. I drove the car into the back of a Morris 1100. A mild-looking, elderly man and his wife got out and stared at the dents then at the chortling idiot who had caused them.

'All right. Don't worry. I'll pay.' I laughed out loud again. 'Have this one on my wife.'

When I calmed down I found that the hearing had given me a little self-respect following the previous humiliations. Then I was concerned. I wondered what version of events Christine would hear. I just hoped the shock might be therapeutic.

It certainly was.

My first visit to Dominic since May had been arranged by the lawyers to be at Christine's mother's house two days after the hearing. When I arrived there was nobody at home.

I went to Calderan and asked him to report Rutter to the Law Society for his behaviour at the hearing. Calderan said there was no point. With disgust he showed me a begging letter he had received from Rutter, dated thirtieth September. In it Rutter asked me for extra money, 'as a voluntary payment, distinct from any question of alimony or maintenance…in the interests of the child.' Here is an extract from the begging letter. His style was at its most Gordian. I defy you to decipher it.

> At the Hearing before the Registrar on the 17th instant, our Mr Sydney Rutter stated that although a payment had been made by your client since the 6th September, it was made specifically to cover maintenance for the week ending 5th September, 1970 and the Registrar was asked to direct that even though payment was received subsequent to 6th September, but related to a period ending on 5th September, such payment should not be deemed to be a payment of interim alimony or child maintenance for the period commencing 6th September.

> The Registrar made it clear that only if the payment made since the 6th September related to a period subsequent to the 6th September, should credit be given, and that if a payment was made subsequent to the 6th September, which related to a period prior to the 6th September, your client would not be entitled to credit. Your client's cheque for £34.13.0 enclosed with your letter of 29th instant, is accepted as the balance of interim alimony and child maintenance the three weeks period ended 27th September.

The complete letter covered three pages.

Till now these letters had been written at the rate of about two a week. Following the hearing the tempo increased. We were just getting under way.

Chapter XXVII

Autumn 1970

Running concurrently and woven in with the fiscal events of the last two chapters was the continuing story of my attempts to see Dominic. The time overlap comes because I have unravelled the simultaneous threads of access and alimony for the sake of clarity.

Mimi was sacked. I don't know why, but heard it was sudden. Out one morning and that was that. Dominic's first birthday came and went. Two days after it, the eleventh of September, Paddy delivered my affidavit of means, for the hearing of the seventeenth of September I have just described. He followed up on the question of access. He was answered by a letter dated 14th September.

> Our client is prepared to agree that your client shall have access to the child at the home of our Client's mother, once a fortnight for two hours on Saturday from 2 p.m. to 4 p.m. provided that your Client must leave the home of our Client's mother sharp at 4 p.m. The first access to take place on Saturday next, the 19th instant...We must also have an undertaking on the part of your Client that he will not arrive at the home of our Client's mother before 2 p.m. so as to avoid encountering our Client there, and that should he by accident see our Client, he will refrain from speaking to her...

Paddy read it to me on the telephone. The familiar sinking feeling overcame me.

'Paddy, I've forgotten more about babies than she knew when Dominic was born.' I thought of the far-off days with Ivor and Henri in Ballards Lane, Finchley, when I had taken my turn with them, changing, feeding, walking and watering Lindsey, my god-daughter. Christine knew all that.

'Neil Taylor says the court will take the view that you're a man. Mum knows best.'

'Has it got to be at her mother's home?'

'Neil Taylor says the court will agree to her venue. It's Granny's, remember.'

'It's 1970, Paddy, haven't they heard? Men can change nappies.'

'Yes, well, there you are.'

'What about this once a fortnight business?'

'Neil Taylor says that's a liberty. You'll get once a week.'

'Right, we'll accept all the other conditions and apply for once a week.'

'Very sensible.'

I turned up at Christine's mother's house on 'the 19th instant' to see Dominic for the first time since May. I stood on the doorstep and listened to the bell ringing through the empty house. It was one of those moments that hang in the memory like an old oil painting, but with full sensory effects. The Victorian terrace in that cul-de-sac seemed to have gone quiet, listening. It was warm and still and everything that was happening was from outside. Distant shouts from the football games in Wandsworth Park, 'Here, Jim, Jim, pass. Here. Down the wing. Down the wing. No, cross it.' Jim obviously wouldn't release the ball. Somebody's radio was playing pop. The inevitable jet whined overhead. Saturday afternoon drifted peacefully round me as I stood stiffly, stomach surging, telling myself not to show anything in case our former neighbour, Ann, was watching from next door or this door finally opened. It didn't. Rutter told Paddy subsequently that I would have to wait another month. This, remember, was exactly two days after Rutter had, by his misguided application, got the maintenance I was freely paying Christine savagely cut. Revenge? Of course not. The law says access and finances must not be connected.

Suddenly I could see Dominic on seventh October. The excuse for the cancellation of the September access was amended from 'a previous social engagement' for Babs to the fact that she had fallen and hurt her leg. The arrangement - that Christine would leave Dominic at her mother's house and then go away before I arrived - was of course, made to avoid seeing me. When I left, Dominic was left in the care of Christine's mother until Christine came back. Dominic was thus left for two periods of unspecified length with Babs. Babs was semi-crippled with arthritis; she could not hold Dominic, nor pick him up if he fell over, nor care for him in any way at all physically. He was half-walking and half-crawling at this time. And all this was allegedly in his interest.

I arrived at 16 Bective Road, rang the doorbell and then quickly sat on the step so that I would be at Dominic's height and not hers. I was glad to sit because I had the shakes again. The first sound I heard was Daisy's deep bark, then Minnie's higher one. There was the heavy shuffling of Babs heaving herself to the door and a lighter, quicker shuffle that was surely Dominic. I heard Babs doing her level best in a situation that must have been giving her at least as many butterflies as I had.

'Yes,' she was saying in baby-talk tone. 'Yes, that's your Daddy come to see you. Yes.' Quick tonal change, 'Oh, get down, Daisy. Shut up.' Back again, 'Yes, he's outside now.'

The door opened. I had carefully framed my vision to below waist height. To the left by the open door were Bab's legs, slippered feet and stick. One of her legs was covered in bandages under the stocking. In the foreground was Daisy on three legs, paw upraised, now silent, head forward sniffing. Behind Daisy was Dominic on all fours. He had just paused in his efforts to get to the door and his Disney-baby, perfect face, with those little folds of skin in the corners of his eyes, was raised staring at this stranger before him. Minnie was in the background. The wallpaper and carpet were the same matching orange that had been fashionable when Christine had chosen it six years earlier, now scarred and grubby. Suddenly Daisy's nose told her who I was and she went mad. An almost human wail escaped her and she put her paws on my shoulders, sniffing my face, licking me and whimpering. She didn't just wag her tail, her whole body convulsed. I had been preparing for many possibilities on that doorstep and I thought I had my defences up, but it was Daisy who tore them apart. It wasn't Dominic who was greeted first. He sat, watching, while I buried my face in Daisy's fur and tried not to cry in front of Babs.

Babs tried heartiness. 'There, she's glad to see you, isn't she. I'll say she is. How are you?

'Fine, Babs, fine. You?'

'Oh, fine, except for this stupid arthritis. You know.'

'Yes.'

She looked at Dominic. 'Yes, there he is. There's your Daddy.' She looked at me. 'He's looking fine isn't he.'

I got up, picked up Dominic carefully, in case a virtual stranger should frighten him, and took him quickly through the house to the bottom of the garden where Babs couldn't follow.

Later Babs and I were sitting having tea. I didn't need to prompt her. She wanted desperately to talk.

'I'm sorry about that business of your visit being cancelled the other Saturday,' she said.

'Never mind.' I concentrated on Dominic.

'Only I fell and hurt my leg so badly on Friday night, I couldn't move.' She was utterly unaware of the implications of her speech. She went on about the pain, the injury, the treatment.

'You fell on Friday, didn't you? Friday evening? You must have had trouble getting treatment.'

'Oh, yes, I know it was Friday because...' there followed an anecdote as to why her memory was accurate.

'Babs,' I said. 'Babs, listen to me carefully.' She heard the note in my voice and I had her attention. 'Babs, Rutter wrote on Thursday evening immediately after he got Christine's money cut, then again on Friday, cancelling the visit because you were unavailable. Now you say the accident didn't happen till Friday evening. Do you see what you're saying?'

The message dawned and tears started to run down her cheeks. Her dumpy old body fell back into the sofa and she let it all go. Usually Babs tried to present her emotions to the world and the result was self-pity or bitterness because she wasn't skilful enough. 'Please don't let me get like her.' Christine used to say. Now Babs was beyond all that. The misery of years of illness and inadequacy followed by the lonely, fearful epilogue of her life without Vic came pouring out. Minnie knew something was up and crept beside her. 'Oh, Terry, she's changed. She's changed, Terry, she's changed. I'm sorry, I had to do it. It was the money. She was upset about the money. I don't know her. Oh, why did you cut her money? She was terribly hurt, you know. By you. She came round here that night she found out about you and that girl. She just fell through that door. Stretched out on the floor of my hall she was. Prostrate. "Oh, Mummy, he's left me," she said. "He's left me for some girl," she said. Now she listens to this lawyer. She's made herself hard. Oh, Terry, I have to do as I'm told, or she'll never speak to me again. I don't know her. And these people she has round there. They're not like you were. Oh, God, what'll happen to me? Let me die please, God. Let me. Oh, Vic where are you? He would have been ashamed, Terry. Ashamed. Let me go. There's nothing for me here.'

So ended my first access.

Neil Taylor was going to plead my application to have weekly access to Dominic. Christine had filed an affidavit opposing this because it was in Dominic's 'best interests' that I should only see him once a fortnight. Dominic's interests should be 'paramount.' the last paragraph was a beauty:-

> Because Dominic is very active and readily grasps hold of things which can be injurious to him if given an opportunity to do so I respectfully ask this Honourable Court to order that access shall only take place at the home and in the presence of my mother as has so far already been arranged so that she can watch him and see that he does not come to harm. The Respondent has no experience whatever with babies.

'We'll subpoena her,' said Neil Taylor. 'If she's as bad as you say, she'll only have to totter into Court and we'll win.'

He compiled a brief affidavit for me that asked for four weekly accesses with Dominic under their conditions while he got used to me, followed by all subsequent access to be on my own so that I could take Dominic to Tony and Jacky Verner's house where he could play with their child, Katy, who was his age. Neil Taylor's wording of the affidavit was grovelling, but I signed.

The flurry of letters and affidavits became a blizzard over the issue of whether I could have two hours a fortnight with my son in the presence of my mother-in-law at her house, or two hours a week elsewhere with another child.

Christine swore an affidavit that made me sadder than ever. I wasn't fit to be left alone with Dominic. I had taken Dominic out and left him unattended in his pram while I had gone into a pub. I couldn't take Dominic to the Verners' because it was too far (it was nearer than her mother's). He would 'undoubtedly cry' if taken away from Christine or her mother (he had managed for six weeks when she had gone to New York). But one inaccuracy at last exposed the Rutter technique of facing one way in front of one judge and in the opposite way in front of another (inaccuracy is legal jargon for lie).

Christine had sworn in her affidavit of twelth of May, when they were trying to get me out of the house, that:-

> The Respondent has not been to the Matrimonial Home since he left on 26th February 1970 save to see the child of the marriage Dominic...

Now, when they were trying to limit my access to Dominic, she swore that:-

> ...he frequently came to 1 Genoa Avenue...and he did not show any real interest in the child.

It is a bit of a mystery as to why I went there at all, really, isn't it?

I was worried about Babs. In view of the state she was in, I thought, if the traditional little man in bowler hat knocked on her door and slapped a subpoena in her hand she would suffer all sorts of horrors. So I told her that she would have to go to court but that she needn't worry. She would merely be asked to say whether Dominic and I got on well or not and it would all be very polite, gentle and in private. I told her the time that the bowler-hatted gent would arrive, the day before the hearing, and joked about it to lessen the impact.

I could have saved myself the trouble. When the server arrived, the house was empty. Christine's mother disappeared until after the hearing. When I next had access Babs broke down again, sobbing uncontrollably for nearly the whole afternoon. She constantly begged my forgiveness. Her principal terror, repeated over and over, was of Christine never speaking to her again. I played with Dominic in the garden or kitchen, and every time I returned to the sitting room to see how she was I heard the terrible litany of fear. I made us tea, then tried to give her something positive to think about by suggesting that she try to use her influence to arrange a meeting between Christine and myself. I was later accused by Christine of using access periods to bully her mother.

We congregated for the access hearing in the familiar corridors in the Family Division of the Royal Courts of Justice at the end of the Strand. Paddy Grafton Green, Neil Taylor and I on one side, Rutter and Law on the other. Christine, was once more, kept away from this.

Neil Taylor was quite confident. We found ourselves in front of a County Court judge, His Honour Judge Trevor Reeve. His Honour had a squarish face with rather a lot of hard-looking jowl. His suit was good, but dated and tight. His dark hair was cut unfashionably very short. The clippers had been up the sides and back of his head. I think he wore a little toothbrush moustache. Why anyone of his generation (he must surely have been in the war) should wear the badge of Hitler struck me as most odd. He read Christine's two affidavits and my one. The barristers said virtually nothing. The whole thing hadn't taken ten minutes before he looked up and delivered his judgement. 'It may well be that this father is being too possessive. I think once a fortnight is appropriate.'

It was all over.

Law got to his feet like a well-fed courtier congratulating the king on a brilliant decision. He asked in his lumbering, servile way for the costs, which he got.

I found myself on my feet saying, 'Excuse me, but how can you say that, when you haven't even...'

Paddy pulled me down and everybody including Trevor Reeve affected not to have noticed me. I tried again. 'I'm sorry, but I don't see how you can possibly know...'

'Shut up. It won't do any good.'

———————

As I stood with Taylor and Paddy in the corridor outside I discovered I was gasping for breath. Our divorce system was triumphant; Rutter had achieved the Cup and League double: Christine was deprived of money that previously had been freely given; Dominic and I were deprived of each other.

Chapter XXVIII

Winter 1970

The insane war resumed, now on three separate fronts.

The first was the most lunatic. It centred in my own camp round the question of the status of the Cayman Trust and who controlled it: me or the trustees?

The second front was the one I shall call Theodore Goddard versus Rutter. This artillery battle of correspondence and affidavits, wrongly labelled 'Frisby versus Frisby' and rumbling constantly in the background, seemed to become increasingly less connected with Christine and me, except that it was used to prevent me from seeing Dominic.

The third was my private one to settle the first two. Yes, to try and get those lawyers talking round a table was indeed a battle.

Although I separate them now for the purpose of narration, the three fronts and their battles were an overlapping, adhesive, pain-filled chaos; a madman's jigsaw with pieces made of soft, malignant tar.

———

It was in the first of these three war-fronts - the one about control of the Cayman Trust - that Paddy Grafton Green ('our trust expert') and John Calderan of Theodore Goddard got all of us into a hopeless and illogical tangle. They later escaped from the mess they had created by leaving me in it, holding the baby. They committed the oldest trick of the bureaucrat when in trouble: after the cock-up, the cover-up. But I will come to that in due course; I found all that out some years later. This whole battle-front became the subject of written and verbal evidence I later gave (and was fiercely cross-examined about) in numerous High Court and Court of Appeal hearings. And my evidence stood those tests. So I recount the essence of it to you now.

I have just called this first battle-front 'lunatic,' and so it was to me, as lunatic as the advice my legal team gave me. It was a battle I urged them not to engage in at all, but I was overruled by their alleged superior legal expertise. Eventually, it became, in the whole war, the crucial, terminal battle.

Of course, they didn't set out to do their client down, that came later as they saved themselves. Anyone can make a cock-up. But the rules say you must then own up. They didn't. The cover-up is far more serious and is some way ahead, so first the cock-up.

The case I had brought to Calderan and Theodore Goddard was, to me, simple and fundamental (forgive me for repeating a few necessary facts):

> Our capital (if we had much after tax) was divided into two roughly equal parts: what we had in the UK; what we had in the Trust, abroad. I had paid no tax at all for four years - my four rich years - because of my foreign residency. So I was due a big - probably a swingeing - bill. My tax assessments would come in two parts:
>
> 1) on my UK earnings. This assessment would certainly be for many thousands of pounds (the top rates then were still at 19/6d in the £).
>
> 2) on my foreign earnings, all of which had been channelled into the Trust. This assessment could be over ninety per cent of the total as it would *all* be at the top 19/6d rate. Or ...the assessment could be for *nothing at all*... if the Revenue accepted the status of the Trust and did not challenge or attack it.

Everything, since we had returned to the UK, had been delicately poised. We had been living very comfortably, but also carefully within our means, not touching capital or tax-reserve money until we would learn what those tax assessments would amount to.

Sooner or later the assessments would be agreed by my accountants and the Revenue, but it was in our interests to let this take as long as possible, because while we held the money it was growing for us. So, while it was the best policy to go slowly, for everyone's sake, Rutter was making a loud, clanging fuss to make us go fast.

My total assets, including the Trust, were perhaps £250,000 and growing, but I could owe up to £170,000 to the Revenue. The only sensible arrangement was to do what I had been doing before Rutter's application screwed it up: namely, divide our continuing UK income fairly, leaving the Trust to grow, until settlement with the Revenue, then see what capital we actually had left. *Only then should we divide it.*

So, my situation was: I had to avoid the time-trap of: a) giving Christine a capital settlement as though there was no tax liability; b) having to pay these pointless legal fees (which were already eating up our considerable income); then c) facing the Revenue with nothing, having been shorn by a) and b).

Rutter was clearly advising Christine to grab all she could, while she could, and to hell with everything and everybody else. But, amid all this wealth, there was no spare cash. Everything was in houses, or tax reserve, or in trust for all our futures.

At the heart of the status of the Trust lay the question of who controlled it, said my lawyers, it was on this ground that we must fight (but it was the wrong ground, a bog). And here was their beautiful, legalistic nit-picking paradox that created this first battle-front of the war:

1) If I controlled the Trust, Christine was due a share. But, if I controlled it, it was open to Revenue attack at 19/6d in the £, so there would be little to share out.

2) If I didn't control the Trust, and it was worth its full tax free value, she wasn't due anything from it, (only from our UK capital).

And sometimes my advisers, especially Neil Taylor, told me, in contradiction of 1) and 2) above, that : 'a divorce court judge will look through all that tax-avoidance flummery and award your wife a share of the Trust as though it was all yours. *But* he won't include your tax liability because you have got no official assessments as evidence. So according to Taylor, a judge would see half the reality, the wrong half for me, but not the whole of it.

This was all part of the absurdest quagmire and was argued exhaustively by all the lawyers concerned (but not by me) and, to this day, has not been settled in law. There is a question of *de jure* (legal) control and *de facto* (actual) control. Never mind that it has never been settled, I had only one view - the *de facto* one that the Revenue controlled it at 19/6d in the £ until all assessments for those years were agreed. Then I (*de facto*) controlled whatever was left. Then Christine and I could share everything fairly, including the Trust. Never mind about *de jure*.

It was in everybody's interest not to rock the Trust boat with regard to the Revenue because there would be more left for us all. However, Rutter seemed hell-bent on doing just that. This I found incomprehensible. Why was he so intent on bringing about a financial collapse that would harm his client (and the long-term future of her son) along with everybody else? It was a tax-avoidance trust, purely a device, a legal technicality to keep my earnings out of the country and out of the reach of the Revenue until the day when we needed income. Then we would pay tax like anybody else as we drew on it. Thus would my big-earning years be spread, and the benefits be enjoyed by Christine, me, Dominic, our family and certain close friends.

216

If you have not made full, proper sense of the above, do not worry, neither did those legal wizards, Paddy Grafton Green, John Calderan, Neil Taylor, Joe Jackson et al. They turned the situation into a dog's breakfast. The cock-up that they all made (but it was only Theodore Goddard who indulged in the cover-up) was in not fighting the case their client brought them: namely, the wait-for-the-tax-assessments-then-share-out case. They knew better (even though their advice pointed in different directions between themselves). They told me that my case, as I stated it, was untenable and I must do it their way (whatever that was). My trouble was that I listened to them.

Into their discord I threw a grenade. A few weeks after the ancillary relief hearing which Rutter so screwed up, I used Trust money, in autumn 1970, to buy myself somewhere to live, as it was now clear that I was not able to go home. I was the only one of the several beneficiaries of the Trust who had nowhere decent to live; I was in two furnished rooms, and was pretty sore about that as you can imagine. On Bill Fournier's specific advice I requested the trustees to send the money to the UK. They would be the owners of the flat, not me. When I say 'requested,' that was how I had to frame it. As far as I was concerned it was an instruction. Nor did I think anyone else, including a divorce court judge, would see it any other way.

'Oh, yes,' said Neil Taylor, in his chambers. He was in long, lean and authoritative mood without Jackson there to inhibit him. 'We all know you control your Trust. Of course you do. It's a tax-avoidance trust.'

Paddy said snappily. 'But the trustees control the Trust. Here are the documents.' He has vested power over the assets in the trustees. It is irrevocable.'

'My dear boy, that may be tax law or trust law or whatever, that's your department. But the divorce court is the Court of Good Sense.'

'Joe Jackson says— ' began Paddy.

'I don't care what Joe Jackson says,' Neil Taylor said, in his leader's absence. 'I'm telling you.'

'All this is irrelevant,' I was impatient with his lofty detachment. 'The taxman controls it and that's that. Until the status of the Trust is settled, no-one must spend anything or I'm bankrupt. I have said it till I'm black in the face. Your job is to stop me being fleeced in the wrong order.'

'You say you can't spend Trust money,' said Taylor.

'That's right.'

'Yet you tell us the Trust is buying a flat for you to live in.'

'Yes, I've asked Bill Fournier and he says it's OK I have nowhere to live and I've no money to buy somewhere.'

'What about a mortgage?'

217

'I already have a mortgage on the matrimonial-fucking-home. I can't get two.'

'And you don't think you're spending Trust money?'

'No. The Trust'll own the flat. I won't.'

Taylor threw himself back in his chair. 'Oh, my God.'

'What do you mean, "Oh, my God."? My wife has our house and I want somewhere decent to live. That's not breaking up the Trust capital. It's a good investment. If the tax-man falls on me then the Trust'll sell it at a profit to pay him and I'll find somewhere else. What could be more sensible?'

'What will it cost?' asked Taylor.

'£26,000.'

He whistled, 'Will you be paying rent?'

'I shouldn't think so. I can't afford any at the moment. Here I am with a play breaking records in London and I can't even afford rent, let alone begin to keep up with these daft costs.'

'If you don't pay rent you're enjoying the capital. If you can enjoy it, why can't your wife? That'll be the argument.'

'No reason at all,' I said. 'That's what the Trust is for. For us all to enjoy. But not to break up before I'm assessed. All we have to do is tell the judge that. The Court of Good Sense you call it.'

'Where are your tax assessments?' Taylor leaned forward in parody of a triumphant cross-examiner. 'Show me the evidence.'

So we completed once more the circuit we had been round and round. The next step of Taylor's logic was in complete reverse. Paddy and he, or one, or the other, had drafted a follow-up affidavit dealing with financial matters. In it were words to the effect that I did not control the Trust or the trustees or the assets.

'I can't sign this' I said. 'We all know I do.'

'No, no, no, said Taylor. 'That's *de facto*. Now we're talking about *de jure*.'

'Eh?'

'You may control it in practice but you don't control it in law. The trustees do,' said Paddy. 'Here are the documents. You have vested power over the assets to the trustees. It is irrevocable.'

'Anyway, I wouldn't want a signed affidavit of yours going to the Revenue saying you controlled £100,000 outside the UK,' said Taylor, and he pursed his lips and sucked in his breath.

'I see. So Rutter can shop me. I am in his power.'

'Don't get paranoid over Rutter,' said Taylor dismissively. 'He's only doing his job.'

'Oh, is that all he's doing?'

Taylor waved me aside. 'Don't be childish. You're safe there. Sydney Rutter always litigates like this.'

'Jesus Christ.' As I took in this thought, sagging in my chair, Neil Taylor chuckled indulgently at my naiveté.

'Then why don't the rest of you people just squash him or something?' I asked. 'These are supposed to be the Royal Courts of Justice.' I hit the word 'justice'.

Taylor chuckled some more. 'I like you,' he said. 'You're refreshing.'

I gave up on that one. 'I see. So I lie in this affidavit.'

'It's not a lie. You don't control it. We've told you...'

We all said the next bit together '...the trustees control it.'

'Wonderful' I went on, 'and when I sit in the witness box and say, "Of course I control it, *de facto*," what then?'

'The judge knows that already. Anyway the documents prove you don't, *de jure*. Your layman's beliefs about trusts are not evidence.'

'I've got it,' I said with the sham triumph of a comedian unravelling his feed's impenetrable logic. 'I forgot, we're in the Court of Good Sense. I don't control the Trust as far as the Revenue is concerned and I don't as far as the documents are concerned, but I do as far as the judge is concerned. When I say in court I do, *de facto*, it won't matter because the documents will prove I'm wrong. Anyway the judge knows what the score really is, because he's probably got an offshore trust himself, so he'll have the good sense to ignore the documents. Unfortunately he'll also have the good sense to ignore my potential tax liability because there's no evidence. And Rutter won't report me because, like Eichmann, he is merely doing his duty, and underneath he loves me, and the judge won't report me because he knows you wouldn't like it if the compromising documents got to the Revenue. And everything is lovely.'

Taylor chose to ignore the form; he dealt with the content of my summing up.

'Precisely' he said.

I went to the only sane lawyer I knew. 'Bill, do I control this fucking trust or don't I?'

'Of course not,' said Bill Fournier. 'The trustees control it.'

'Oh, no, not again. What about the mandatory signature?'

'We discovered that was illegal and cancelled it. You can't do it again.'

'I think we'd better tell someone about that.'

'Who?'

'I don't know; the Revenue, someone. You know better than me.'

'What for? It's cancelled now.'

'Well, then, I must have controlled the money for a while.'

'Not legally.'

'Oh, Bill, this is all so much quibbling.'

Bill came on strongly, 'No, it is not. Listen.' He used an image that impressed me. 'I'm a trustee, right? This is my money in my pocket, not yours. Even if I let you put your hand in my pocket it is still my money. Even

219

if you spend some it is still mine. Even if I let you do that for twenty years it is still mine and I can order you to take your hand out when I like. That money is mine, not yours.'

Well, it made better sense than Taylor's Court of Good Sense. I remember with clarity Paddy's draft affidavit. It said 'I do not have, and have never had, control (or power) over...etc.' I crossed out 'and have never had,' just to be sure.

Front number two, the postal battle of Theodore Goddard versus Rutter, with Christine and me as seconds, started with Christine's affidavit of means. It was the most distressing legal document I had, or have since, ever read.

Even as I look through it now I am reminded of simply how exhausting it was to read, day after day, in post after post, inaccuracy after inaccuracy. It wasn't just the deluge of insults but the inability of the lawyers to agree about anything at all, including, at times, the dates on their letters, 'Your letter, although dated so-and-so, was not received by us until so-and-so.' These quarrels made the simplest of actions a slog.

Near the beginning of my affidavit of means was one contentious sentence. 'The marriage was a very happy one indeed until the autumn of last year.' Yes, I said contentious. When I dictated that sentence it seemed to me an innocuous enough thing to say, even rather sad. The response was astounding. My sentence was called an 'allegation' and spawned paragraph sixteen, nearly four pages long in response. The triviality alone is shattering. May it be a monument to all divorce lawyers.

16) With regard to the allegation by the Respondent in Paragraph 2 of his said Affidavit that the marriage was a very happy one indeed until about the autumn of last year (which I deny) I say as follows:-

Almost from the commencement of my marriage to the Respondent he flirted with attractive women and particularly with coloured women. In or about the year 1964/65 when I was at a party with the Respondent an attractive coloured woman was present and although I had on previous occasions begged the Respondent not to flirt with other women and not to spend his time whilst I was present with coloured women and disregard me he insisted at the said party on spending the whole evening with a coloured woman and dancing with her and he ignored my request and caused me to spend a very unhappy evening in consequence. There were other occasions when I went with the Respondent to a party when the same coloured woman was present and each time the Respondent insisted on spending the evening with her and dancing with her and ignored me which always upset me considerably.

For some time prior to June 1965 the Respondent taunted me and upset me by saying that I had a fat bottom and thighs. In June 1965 when the Respondent learned that I was pregnant he said that he did not want me to have a child and insisted that I should have an abortion to which I agreed reluctantly. The Respondent visited me in a Nursing Home following the abortion but he refused to call for me to take me home in spite of my plea to him to do this. His refusal to call for me and take me home upset me and caused me to cry in his presence but he paid no regard to this. When I arrived home from the Nursing Home in a weak condition which continued for a few days the Respondent paid practically no attention to me and on one day he went to play golf rather than sit at home with me. From the early part of 1966 the Respondent's attitude towards me was one of indifference; he frequently criticised my appearance and often remarked that I had fat thighs and thereby upset me. It was because of this conduct on the part of the Respondent that resulted in my committing adultery with a man on three occasions in the months of March and April 1966. This man had been very kind and attentive to me when I was distressed by my husband's attitude towards me and I grew to like him because of his kindness and consideration to me...

And so on for two more pages. Disgust again sweeps through me as I re-read it. I tried to picture Christine in Rutter's office, guided by him as he took notes, the pair of them searching for something to refute my naive '...the marriage was a very happy one indeed...' I tried to see Rutter, dictaphone in hand, transposing his notes; later, a secretary in another office with telephones and filing cabinets, all the paraphernalia of the daily grind round her, typing these scourings onto legal sheets to make up the affidavit to be presented to the court, to augment the majesty of the law. And then Rutter has the completed documents, the summit of his achievement; he reads it through and is satisfied. Christine leaves what was our home and makes another journey back to the cess-pit, she solemnly signs the affidavit and swears an oath that it is all true. The picture made me bleed. To even begin to answer that affidavit was to add to the humiliation of being involved with such dross, yet pain made me foolish enough to try with one item.

To allege that I could insist that anyone, let alone a reluctant Christine who I loved, to have an abortion, seemed to me the lowest of unnecessary low blows. I have already described what happened between us at that time,

221

but did not tell all the story. Far from being someone who was pushed into it, Christine didn't want a child then any more than I did. She arranged it all. She knew which doctor to go to and how much it cost, because she had had an abortion before we met. Her mother had found a compliant doctor that first time and Christine told me about it all when she made The Seventeen confession. She returned to this doctor, reluctantly of course, as who wouldn't, but in the knowledge it was what she wanted. Now, 'he insisted' was yet another Rutter-inspired accusation which drew from me the wounded denial on affidavit, with the full story; which in turn sparked off another denial on affidavit from Christine; and so drearily on and on. And all in the name of the law.

What was not at first clear to me, though, was the broader, infamous reason for the creation of paragraph 16). It was simply about hard cash. A wife's first-out-of-the-gate infidelity had to be excused. She could scarcely go into court and say, 'I did it for fun.' Some righteous judge could reduce her settlement. So a scapegoat had to be found. But the scapegoat in our case was actually away on tour creating the play that made all the money while she popped off to the Dorchester with Bert. That, combined with the shock of my unwitting 'allegation' that 'the marriage was a very happy one', led inexorably to Rutter and Christine trawling back through our life together, searching for excuses. And there were none. Our adversarial divorce system, which nurtures the Rutters, was bound to produce the numbing nastiness of paragraph 16) somewhere, somehow. It is the system that should be swept away, the scum will float down the drain with it.

But, you might hear argued, the system has been changed. There is no longer the question of guilt in divorce. Well, yes, but it is only the area of lawyer-incited conflict that has changed, not the fact of it. The nineteen-nineties equivalents of paragraph 16) are being written daily. Conflict, hideous conflict, remains a feature of divorce over money, children, possessions; partly because potential conflict is inherent in split-up. But why exacerbate it? Remove lawyers, replace them with conciliators, with independent accountants and assessors, not representing one side or the other, but there to get at the financial truth. Make sharing of parental responsibility after divorce a priority. Use child experts where necessary. There are the beginnings of a system that could reduce the pain and decimate the cost, not increase it. The system should be inquisitorial - in other words truth-seeking - not one that invites battle-lines to be drawn up and manned, or womanned.

The third of the three fronts was the only one that mattered to me: my own private front to get the whole war stopped.

I went to Calderan. 'I want you to have a meeting with Rutter. We now have the two affidavits of means. All the figures are in front of you both.

Frank Young tells me the Revenue could take up to two years even if we hurry them (which was the worst thing to do for both Christine and me). Tell Rutter that if they will wait two years I will then make a generous capital division. Who knows, if you lot will leave me alone for a bit I might even write a play and increase our money. These are my income figures for the last three years. What will a court award her if we fight it out?'

Calderan did his sums. 'Hm. Well, four thousand, perhaps as much as four-and-a-half thousand for her and the child.'

'Right. Offer her the following:-

1) £5,000 per annum for her and Dominic.

2) I'll put Genoa Avenue in our joint names but I must have back the £7,000 worth of shares to pay my tax. I'll continue to pay the rates and mortgages for two years then we review the situation.

3) I visit the house and make a list of what I want of the contents. I guarantee not to take more than a quarter. When we agree this list she has the rest.

4) Christine's mother to stay in 16 Bective Road at £1 a year rent and I would pay her £10 a week.

'How's that?' I asked him.
'Very generous.'
'Good.'
'But he won't accept it.'
'Why not? If it's more than the court will give? No court'll make me keep her mother.'
'I know he won't agree.'
'Why?'

There was no comprehensible answer to this. It just seemed that Calderan thought that Rutter would be bloody-minded. This made me more than eager to pursue the goal of settlement. I would win at least something either way. If we settled, excellent. If we didn't, and Calderan's figures were right, Rutter would get another humiliation in court. That could be the end of him. With Rutter banished, friendly relations could be re-established in the post-war wreckage. Yes, I still hoped for that.

The unwilling Calderan went to the meeting with Rutter. It must have been a convivial affair. The offer was rejected.

So I tried to get a meeting arranged between Christine and me without lawyers but with somebody else there as honest broker. Rutter complained that my efforts to contact her constituted molestation. Any repetition would lead to proceedings.

I hit on a way of contacting Christine that would circumvent that nonsense. And here we come to a revelation about Christine's actions of months previously that at first made me very sad and then contributed to the re-writing of my view of her that I have mentioned earlier when I said that lawyers not only turn the protagonists against each other but lead them to revise earlier-felt emotions. What destroyers they are. Rutter had waved at Registrar Bayne-Powell two letters, then had hidden them before anyone could read the contents. He had alleged these proved that I had the fictional second Swiss bank account. We had got copies of these after the hearing and, of course, they proved no such thing.

But as I read them the pit of my stomach gave another sickening lurch. They were letters from the Swiss Bank Corporation to me, dated March 1970, one of them just a day or so after Christine's first visit to Rutter's office. (I have said that those dates would re-surface). She had, after one visit to Rutter, steamed them open, photocopied the contents for him, re-sealed the envelopes and given them to me. On her very first visit he must have advised her so before writing me his initial crocodilian-tears communication. And she had agreed. From a day or two after she had got back from New York she had been playing a double game. A day or two later she had slept with me after her birthday outing with me. Any lingering doubt that she had not acted under Rutter's explicit instructions was dispelled. It was too painful to assimilate, but there was the irrefutable evidence. And it fitted her covert nature. I remember my old complaint to Ivor during that dangerous, angry ride in my car: whenever there was anything important, whenever there was a crisis, she lied rather than have it out. I thought about all the conversations, scenes, that had taken place between us since the 1st March and - yet again - couldn't swallow the comprehensiveness of the deception.

So, I wrote two letters, one jokey, the other serious about the financially suicidal path we were on. I had them posted in Switzerland in Swiss Bank Corporation envelopes and addressed to me at Genoa Avenue. There was a fierce satisfaction in imagining Rutter in court, crouched behind Good-Old-Harry, digging him in the back and prompting him while Harry stumbled on. 'Your Honour, of course it constitutes molestation. He knew she'd open his mail and read it...' I was getting more pleasure out of outwitting Rutter than in progressing in the main aim.

This ploy got no response, so I telephoned just about the last person who had managed to keep in touch with both of us. Christine trusted Nat Cohen. He had just that quality of successful worldliness that most impressed her. 'Nat, I'm trying to move heaven and earth to see Christine and talk some sense to her. It is impossible to get to her through all these lawyers.'

'Bloody lawyers. Nothing but trouble.' This was another of Nat's catch-phrases along with 'TMM' and, 'Can I have the pick of the litter?' 'Get rid of the bastards,' he said.

'If you could arrange a meeting between Christine and me, would you be there as a sort of chairman to see fair play and to make sure I don't assault her.'

'What d'you want to assault her for?' There are people with whom it is inadvisable to banter, it just confuses the issue. I have always been slow to distinguish.

'No, I mean, I must talk to her.'

'I'll do what I can.'

'Thank you very much. Would you do something else, please.'

'What?' His delivery of the word won him a gold medal in my esteem. I thought him Philistine, a disaster for the film industry, probably as bent as anyone in his dealings, everything foreign to me in outlook, but the streak of generous decency down the centre of him was very wide. He didn't know me well enough for me to be using him as I was, but there was no reserve or hedging in that, 'What?' It wasn't a guard against my next possible incursion. It was open, simply an enquiry. It sounded like, 'Certainly, I will' and probably would have been phrased like that if he hadn't spent a lifetime negotiating on the telephone.

'You'll have to talk to her lawyer.'

'Oh, blimey. Well?'

'Quite. He's called Sydney Rutter. I think he'll make difficulties about this meeting.'

'OK I'll deal with him.'

'Thank you. Also, Christine seems to have got mixed up about my income from the film of *Soup*. She's got him muddled too about my percentage of profits and what it's worth. If we're going to talk sense at a meeting they must know the truth. Would you put them straight, please?'

'Certainly. What is your percentage? I forget off-hand.'

'Well, hadn't you better look it up. If you take my word for it, and it's not precisely—' I got no further. Impatient snorts and grumbles were coming down the line. I could nearly smell the cigar smoke.

'Bloody lawyers...do everything the hard way...Can't he read a contract?' emerged from the background noises.

'He seems to have misunderstood it.'

'Oh, yeah? I can be dense, too, when it suits me.'

'Yes, well, she has sworn on oath that I'm going to get a quarter of a million.'

There was a moment's hesitation. 'You? A quarter of a million? From the film?'

'That's right.'

'That means I'd get...' mumble, mumble. There was a full-bodied laugh, no joke was as good to Nat as one about the serious subject of money. 'You'll be bloody lucky.'

'Yes, well, put them straight, will you? It's difficult settling with someone who thinks you've got a quarter of a million tucked up your sleeve.'

'I'll bet it is. Don't worry. I'll tell 'em what the score is.'

'The lawyer, too.'

'Especially him.'

'Thank you, Nat. Very much.'

Nat could only get a meeting arranged with Rutter present. ('He's a charmer, isn't he,' he said when he called me back.) I was disappointed, but Nat said he had a job to get even that. He said he had disabused both Rutter and Christine about the quarter of a million I was supposed to earn from the film. The film was due to open that month.

I composed with Paddy the letters that Theodore Goddard sent on the subject of the meeting, I didn't want some pointless row sparked off because of misunderstanding. They were most conciliatory in tone. Rutter's response was breathtaking. Flack was fired at everything. When I read about international peace conferences foundering over the shape of the table it all comes back to me. As I look at some of the missiles now it is impossible not to laugh. God knows, I should, I found them unfunny enough at the time. Below is an extract from one of Rutter's incomprehensibles.

> Our objection to having put in correspondence what is said in without prejudice discussions is that it frequently leads to dispute as to what was or was not said without prejudice, and we want to avoid this because it only lends to a lot of argumentative correspondence which cannot be used anyhow as it is without prejudice. We have known cases where dozens of letters have passed between Solicitors (albeit that the letters were written without prejudice) because of dispute as to what was or was not said in discussion. One has a classical example in the present case, because you have disputed in one of your letters of the 1st instant, what we said was agreed in our letter of the 27th ultimo.

Nevertheless the meeting was confirmed for second December. We wrote asking about Christine's possible future intentions so that some imaginative use of the Trust funds could be devised. After all, if it could buy me a flat it could do many other beneficial things without prejudicing the tax position or breaking up the capital.

There was, for instance, one project that Christine and I had already previously discussed. This would give her a new career, one admirably suited to her talents. Her modelling had obviously dried up since we have been abroad and she had been pregnant, not that she had been passionate about chasing modelling work anyway. The new idea was for us to buy properties, do them up and either sell or rent them. With Trust money, her eye and taste and an excellent firm of builders we had found, this looked exactly the right enterprise.

Rutter answered:-

> With regard to the matters referred to in one of your without
> prejudice letters of the 1st instant, we do not propose that these
> points should be discussed at any meeting. Will you kindly refrain
> from dictating to us as you have done more than once, what we
> should do in relation to informing our Client of letters which
> you write to us. We act as we think proper and in the best interests
> of our Client.
>
> In the light of what we have said above, if you still refuse to confirm
> in a without prejudice letter what we requested in the third paragraph
> of our without prejudice letter of the 27th ultimo, we cannot advise
> our Client to attend a meeting with your Client and it will be your
> fault for adopting the attitude which you appear to be doing if your
> Client is deprived of the opportunity of meeting our Client...

So yah-boo sucks to you. Then Rutter postponed the meeting. I had to
pause and count to ten, but, at last, Paddy and I waited in the conference
room of Theodore Goddard with the dry sherry at the ready and the
cigarettes decanted into the onyx box. I was so wrought up that I stammered
occasionally, an extreme state for an actor.

Christine had decided to play it gaily. She entered on Rutter's arm and
greeted me like a well-remembered friend spotted at a smart party. She
uncoupled herself from Rutter and first one cheek then the other was
offered. She was wearing her New York mink (thrown over the shoulders),
pearls, and a lot of those trad. rich-girl things that smell, shine or rustle. I
knew her to be as nervous as me but wondered if it showed to anyone else.
It was stage one of the emotional pattern with a vengeance, some film star
doing a chat show. Her high spirits depressed me. 'This is Patrick Grafton
Green of Theodore Goddard.'

Christine gave Paddy a greeting that was commensurate with his status
and then said, 'And this is Sydney Rutter, my solicitor,' clearly putting him
on a different level.

It was an effort but I put my hand into his. It was grasped firmly. 'I am
very pleased to meet you at last,' he said looking deep into my eyes and
pumping rhythmically. 'I must tell you what a marvellous play I thought
Girl in my Soup was when I saw it.' Two hands had now enveloped my one,
and I had to fight to leave it limply where it was. Rutter continued in a
manner redolent with sincerity. 'We had such an enjoyable evening. Very,
very enjoyable. Your dialogue is scintillating. Brilliant. I mean...' he allowed
words to fail him. 'How do you do it?'

I smiled sickly thanks, reclaimed my hand and said, 'I suppose you know
Patrick Grafton Green.'

'Ah, yes Mr Calderan's junior solicitor. I haven't had the pleasure, no,' said Rutter and Paddy's hand got a briefer massage, without oil. Paddy looked ghastly.

Christine settled herself into a chair that was wielded by Rutter and the mink dropped back over it from her shoulders. A slight shake of her head allowed her hair to bounce into suitable position. Rutter seated himself beside her. The table was between us. At this point they were about two sets to love up.

'What about a drink?' I said, then sent over a deliberate dolly-drop. 'There's some dry sherry.'

Christine smiled and smacked her lips in a little fast rhythm, an old mannerism of hers when anticipating a treat. 'Hm. Have you any ice?' This created a little sub-text. She always put ice in her sherry. Fifteen years before TV commercials suggested the same thing she had thought it most chic, I enjoyed her pose as I was meant to.

'Yes,' said Paddy and turned to get it; leaving me to smile back at her; something private to share for a moment. Christine looked at Paddy's nondescript back as he poured. She pulled a disparaging face and mouthed 'Where did you find that?' It was quite out of key, even for this grotesque meeting, and helped me to get myself straight for the serious business.

There is an item, apparently from the trivia drawer, that remained lodged in my memory and always will. Christine was being the dense little woman about some figures. 'I'm sorry, I can't follow that,' she said to me with a tinkling laugh. 'I leave such things to Mr Rutter.' She turned to him, 'Don't I, Sydney?' and she smiled as she leaned suppliantly in towards him and laid a familiar hand on his forearm. The gesture, combined with the switch from 'Mr Rutter' to 'Sydney' shocked me so that I stammered and shuffled papers before I could coherently continue. 'Sydney' recurred during the meeting, each time making my skin crawl.

I tried to raise the subject of my supposed quarter of a million earnings from the film. Rutter ruled that out of order. 'I'm not going to discuss what my client has sworn on affidavit.' I asked if she had checked on the value of the house with a good agent and was ruled out of order again by Rutter. 'She values it at £20,000' he said and then went on to explain in some detail to Paddy and me why it was only worth that amount, (with the alterations, it had cost us more, four years previously). 'Yes, but have you checked?' was met with a dissertation on the traffic congestion in Putney High Street keeping the value of property down. 'I know where the house is,' through gritted teeth from me, merely meant that Paddy became the focus of the explanation of the deplorable siting of 1 Genoa Avenue, SW15.

'Anyway,' Rutter concluded, 'it makes no difference. I have promised her the house and that is that.' I had to keep my head down to hide my shock as I recovered from the effect of hearing our house so disposed of by this stranger.

As failure emerged as the only possible outcome I simply made sure that Christine should understand what would happen when we failed and why. My attempts to enquire what she might do with her future were ruled out of order by Rutter.

I brought up the house-buying and improvement scheme.

'That's all very well,' said Rutter. 'It sounds very attractive. But, of course, if Mrs Frisby earns money by using Trust capital for this scheme you are the one who benefits, are you not? She becomes less of a liability to you.'

I waxed enthusiastic on the subject, pointed out the advantages and benefits. Christine started to look interested, so I concentrated on her until Rutter cut across all that with the reminder that, for a young mother like Christine, Dominic alone was a big enough responsibility.

I swallowed all the obvious answers to that and enquired as to whether he had ever heard of the concept of increasing the size of the cake for everybody, rather than wastefully squabbling over the division of the existing one, I was told it was me who was being wasteful and squabbling.

On the 'if only' front, if anyone but an adversarial divorce lawyer had been there advising Christine that evening we would have made our fortunes and rendered all future litigation redundant. Within a year of that meeting, house prices all round us doubled and trebled. And throughout the seventies, rent of up-market properties near us rocketed. Such is the destructive power of a Rutter in your life.

When I said for the umpteenth time that I could not give away capital I didn't possess I was again met with, 'I have promised her the house and that is that.'

'How can I give her the house when I can't pay off the mortgage?' was met with, 'Use your Swiss bank account.' We parted agreeing to meet a few days later after considering everything.

That meeting felt like being on the other side of sound-proof glass from Christine. I could see her, thought I knew what was going on inside her, mouth messages, but couldn't be heard. That glass, stage one of her emotional pattern as I saw it, must be so fragile, surely I could give one good...but even a direct rap on it, though noticed, seemed inaudible. I was mad with frustration.

She wasn't even listening. She was only there because I had outflanked Rutter by my use of Nat Cohen - someone I knew she would feel she could not ignore for whatever reasons of her own - to set up the meeting. She knew what the financial score was as well as I did, but was choosing to ignore it.

The second meeting was worse. It soon degenerated. About halfway through Christine rose to her feet and said heatedly, 'I am going on and on until I get what I want,' and walked out. When she had gone Rutter said, 'I don't like to destroy a man, but I'm going to destroy you.' And he said it with that same patronising drawl, voice down in his throat, that he had used when saying that my dialogue was brilliant. He also said he was going to report me to the Revenue and the Bank of England. God knows what for, but that is what he said. Once again I went to Calderan and wanted Rutter reported to the Law Society. Calderan stated that as it had all taken place at without prejudice meetings, his hands were tied.

Still on the subject of the third front (my efforts to bring the whole war to an end) there came an incident that at first looked unconnected.

One evening in December, between the two meetings, I was invited to a party in Putney at s friend's house. Afterwards, I did what I had got into a habit of doing whenever there was an excuse, I drove down Genoa Avenue. It was a silly habit but I often made the detour. The time was after two a.m. I noted it. An old, white Rolls Royce was parked outside. I could see no lights on in the house.

'Hallo, who's Christine having?' I thought. I apologised to my companion, stopped the car round the corner and walked back. I went round the side of the house via the little alley. There were no lights on in any of the downstairs rooms or front bedrooms upstairs. I couldn't see the windows of the main bedroom. I took the number of the old, white Rolls Royce and asked the person with me to note that I had got it right. I drove back past the house to do this. The number was NPA 909. I sent it off to find out who the owner of the car was. A few days later I received the name and address. The slip read: Sydney Rutter, 42 Highfield Gardens, NW11.

Neil Taylor simply refused to believe it.

'What? Do you think I made it up?' I yelped. 'The bloody car was there. I saw it. So did my friend. It was two a.m. There were no lights on downstairs.'

Taylor pursed his lips and shook his head. 'It's not possible. Your wife and—no, not Sydney Rutter.' He laughed as he thought about it. 'No. I just don't believe it.' Then more seriously 'You should have got proper witnesses: detectives, the police, someone irrefutable.'

'My God, if I'd known, I would have had the place surrounded. I'd have had a bloody battalion there with lights, cameras and a brass band.'

'Who's going to believe you?'

I left his office kicking myself. If only I could have proved something, disgraced Rutter and stopped the juggernaut. Why hadn't I got a policeman anyway just to write down the number in case? I would never let such a chance slip twice, I swore to myself. But you don't get two. I haunted Genoa Avenue late at night for weeks after. I rarely went to bed without a drive past. I, too, didn't then believe that Christine was having an affair with Rutter, but wouldn't it have been lovely to have got him discredited for an affair he wasn't having, totally in keeping with all the other ironies and idiocies in this story.

However, time has allowed me to reflect on their relationship. Intimacy of some very special sort there was; certainly based on sex - or more likely on Rutter's sexual fantasy. As I have said, Christine always needed a father-figure, an establishment older male, an authoritative reassurer. And in her big crisis of need, here he was: Rutter, full of certainties in the middle of chaos. But why was she on display like that? Not just in the ordinary sense but ostentatiously so. Why? To demonstrate something to me? If so, what? Independence of me? New-found strength? Perhaps. Power? Yes, a bit, certainly. Given by Rutter. Revenge? Yes, of course. That could account for that deliberate, almost flaunted physical intimacy. But was that part of their private game or just done for my benefit? And Rutter. He had immediately struck me as a vain man, vain and pompous. What a puff she must have been to his *amour propre*, a commodity always in question with such men. This was why he was so heavy about every last ludicrous detail: power, influence, he had to make good those certainties he offered. Christine would have told him early on that I had just dismissed him (and all divorce lawyers) as not being relevant. Oh, yes, he was. I was being taught a lesson.

Just before Christmas Calderan suggested that we make another offer, this to be Without Prejudice and then to be shown to the judge before he awarded costs in the hearing. This is a common tactic adopted in litigation to get at least the costs of the hearing awarded against the other side. I approved of the tactic but disapproved strongly when Calderan said we should increase the sums involved.

'But you said that the last offer was more than a judge would award,' I objected.

'Let's increase it to be sure,' he said.

I believed then as I do now that to make elastic offers to settle is to invite more trouble. My peace efforts were already clearly being regarded as weakness, this would look like appeasement. However, under Calderan's insistence I gave way.

The offer was refused and met with counter-demands that were ridiculous and open-ended. My method, that current income be divided and capital left until the Revenue was dealt with was never proposed officially by my lawyers although I frequently asked them to. Calderan said it was 'silly' and 'impractical.' To me it was the only solution that could be just to both parties.

Below is an extract from an attendance note of Paddy's dated twelfth January, 1971. It refers to the moments after Christine had left the second of the meetings.

Mr Rutter then made the following comments:

1. This was the last approach that he would make to settle the matter, and, indeed this approach was made without the knowledge of his Client who was now determined to

fight the case on *all* points. There will be no further opportunity to settle.

2. Mr Rutter then stated that he thought that it would be necessary for the Bank of England to be made aware of the position and likewise the Revenue Authorities.

3. At the last Without Prejudice Meeting, Mr Frisby had suggested that Mr Rutter had been uttering threats. Mr Rutter said that 'I don't utter threats against persons; I do them.'

4. I pointed out to Mr Rutter that he seemed hell-bent on ruining Mr Frisby and that, if he succeeded, it would hardly be in the interests of his Client. To that Mr Rutter replied: 'Never mind.'

Regarding the threats in (2) above, I had long before told Bill Fournier to report me to whoever was necessary over the illegal mandatory signature in case there was any danger in that action. I learned that he hadn't.

'But I told you months ago to do that,' I said, rather annoyed.

'But we've cancelled it now, Terry,' said Bill, an edge to his voice. It was the only time he ever made me feel uneasy. He seemed too reluctant.

'If someone holds a gun to my head, I'm going to be the one to pull the trigger,' I said. 'To see if it's empty.'

'Quite right.'

'Write to the Revenue and the Bank of England, will you. And anyone else you should.'

'Right.' In the event he only wrote to the Bank of England. It was exchange control regulations I had broken, he said later, nothing to do with the Revenue. The fact that he had again ignored my instructions made me uneasy once more, but I let it go.

Back came the Bank of England's reply. 'Naughty boy. Don't do it again.' The gun was empty.

As a follow-up to the without prejudice meetings, we received an affidavit sworn by Christine and compiled by Rutter that broke the 'sanctity' and 'secrecy' of the talks. After all the hoo-ha about not putting anything on paper and observing this and that condition, it was Rutter who broke the solicitors' oath, the basis of all attempts to negotiate settlements in litigation. He had now done it twice, a matter, so the Law Society have since told me, that would be regarded with grave seriousness were it reported. I quote from Alan Davies of the Law Society: 'Once may not be important, it would depend on the matters revealed and the context, but twice is brazen and should be investigated as 'conduct unbecoming to a solicitor' or 'conduct likely to bring the profession into disrepute.' Calderan again refused to report Rutter.

A week or two later there was one final flicker on the third front, my attempt to settle everything. The film of *Soup* and *The Railway Children* were jointly opening EMI's new ABC 1 and 2 cinemas in Shaftesbury Avenue. It was one of showbiz's big nights out. I decided to go with Sian. Almost the first person I saw in the gaudy crush was Christine. I was taken, to put it mildly, aback. She was putting her life and limb at risk going the same place as me just to see a film. What courage. She alighted from Nat's Rolls Royce (new and red, not old and white) looking singularly unterrorised, took his arm and made an entrance of just the right off-handedness through the admiring polloi.

As Nat's Rolls moved away, the space at the kerb was filled by Peter Sellers' car (same brand) driven by Bert. The coincidences of this story are too banal to have been invented, are they not?

I went up to Christine in the foyer. 'Look, darling, why won't you ask me round for a cup of tea and let's, for God's sake, try and make some sense out of this. If we go on there'll be nothing for anybody, especially Dominic, don't you see that?'

'Go away from me.'

'Don't you care?'

'You're molesting me. Go away.' And she moved off into the well-heeled throng.

And so ended my attempt to bring the madness to an end. I had done my duty to all the beneficiaries of the Trust and knew what my next step would be. Christine, I heard later, said to someone, 'How could I talk to him, that girl was there.' She did not remark on Bert's presence, either at the cinema or in the film, where he appears a few times driving Peter Sellers' car. Although my final peace attempt was predictably fruitless some good did come out of the encounter. Christine's attitude gave me the title of the play I was working on, the one about marital infidelity: *It's All Right If I Do It*, with the 'I' underlined.

Rutter and Christine were clearly on some sort of suicidal course that I could not understand. They could run the costs up astronomically - my lawyers told me that husbands in divorce proceedings normally get the costs awarded against them, no matter what the outcome - but I was sure they could not grab more money for her than I had been willing to give. So ruining me seemed self-destructive. The one financial hearing had already been a disaster for them. On the other hand he could and did use Dominic how he liked. And judges supported him.

My own team, though I thought little of them, had been persistently wrong about Dominic and access, but had routed Rutter at the one financial hearing we had so far had. So they were, sort of, doing their job, in spite of the fact that their continuing financial advice to me seemed considerably less than sound.

The whole situation, quite apart from the fact that these events continually turned a knife in the raw wound of separation, just didn't have any sense. Nobody seemed to be pointing out Christine's better interests - and the interests of Dominic - to her. Divorce litigation seemed to be mad. I was baffled as well as damaged.

I loathed the film of *Soup*. During a shot in which Bert figured, I wanted to stand up and shout, 'That's Bert, the man that screwed my wife, Christine, sitting down there with Nat.' But I lacked the bottle.

Chapter XXIX

Winter - Spring 1971

I was most depressed that my attempt to get the whole war stopped, had so totally collapsed; disappointed that Christine was so far out of reach of good sense; in a resentful rage with Rutter for his obstructiveness and power over her. But not over me, I resolved.

It is another defect of the adversarial system of divorce that I couldn't admit to myself that I was wounded; badly so. This whole disaster had continued from my own internal crisis of over a year ago. What glorious therapy this was. But most divorces arise from crises, so the unnecessary, additional pain inflicted by the system was not peculiar to me. I was/am one of many. To have admitted my wounds, even to myself, to lick them, would have been to admit the power over me of Rutter. And that was unacceptable, so I clammed up and hid my feelings until I heard that Christine had gone into the Harley Street Clinic. My anger changed at once to anxiety. Was this the awful crack-up I had been half-expecting for some while? Having no other means of contacting her I went along to find out how she was. She was well, I was told at reception and sent away.

This act started a volley of letters.

In our view your client's attitude in acting as he did was intended to cause annoyance to our client, otherwise, what explanation has our client to offer for having gone to the clinic to make the enquiry which he did?...

But this little flurry was nothing compared to what was happening simultaneously over Dominic. It started, Dickens-like, on Christmas Eve. 16 Bective Road, the former matrimonial home plus one, was as bleak and cold as any Dickensian setting when I turned up for my Christmas access to Dominic, two to four p.m. Remember, according to law, all of what follows was 'in the best interests of the child.'

Dominic had a new nanny, Iranian and called Rohanna. She was the first of a succession of overweight girls of unlikely nationalities to care for Dominic. They seemed interchangeable and all had few words of English. I once spent an access with two of them together and they weren't exactly chatty to each other in Persian either. They must have brought to Dominic's life all the stimulation of jellyfish. Perhaps I wrong them and they had merely been warned about me, spending access periods in dread.

Rohanna was waiting in the sub-zero temperature for me in 16 Bective Road with Dominic. Christine's mother was ill or spending Christmas with her daughter. The house had been empty for at least twenty-four hours. There were no decorations, so Babs' absence looked planned. Rohanna was quivering gently in the cold and had failed in her efforts to turn on the central heating. This wasn't surprising as the system was operated by a fiendishly difficult mechanical contraption called a switch. I managed to get things going by turning it on and she went, leaving me with Dominic and a spare set of trainer pants. Dominic didn't have nappies then because he had a rash. The trainers and tights he was wearing were soaking and freezing. I took them off and put them on a radiator which was gurgling into life. Dominic and I sat on the floor with our outdoor clothes on and I gave him the presents I had brought. He peed again rendering the spare trainers uninhabitable. The first pair and his tights were still sopping on the not-yet-warm radiator. I couldn't take Dominic out of the house because it was too cold to walk with him in wet things. There was no child's strap-in seat in my car. I telephoned Ivor and Henri who lived less than a mile away. They weren't in. I took Dominic's spare trainers off, found a towel, dried him and wrapped this round him. At 4.20 p.m. Rohanna telephoned (she had coped with that piece of technology) to say the taxi which had been ordered to take her from Genoa Avenue to Bective Road hadn't arrived. At 5.05 p.m., when Rohanna arrived in a taxi, the house was just getting warm. Dominic was bawling for his tea (there was none for him there). His first set of garments was just about dry and I wished him and Rohanna a Happy Christmas, switched off the heating and left.

The fifth of January was my next access. It was again bitter (I mean the weather). Christine's mother and Rohanna arrived with Dominic just before I did. The house had been empty since the last access. It seemed colder inside than out. I had taken the precaution of asking Henrietta to be in that afternoon.

'Come on, Babs,' I said. 'You put Dominic on your knee in the car and I'll drive us slowly round the corner to Ivor and Henri's. Dominic can play with Tommy in the warm.'

Poor Babs was trapped. She wanted to but didn't dare agree. I saw her face start to crack up and dropped the matter. Dominic, Babs and I sat in our overcoats for two hours till Rohanna returned to take Dominic and Babs back to Genoa Avenue. At least he had some tea this time. When I left at 4.20 the interior temperature on the heating thermometer had just got to six degrees Celsius.

On the nineteenth of January (Christine was now in the Harley Street Clinic, but I didn't know), I arrived and the house was still uninhabited. Rohanna had arrived just before me and the central heating had been on for a few minutes. Away went Rohanna and I promptly telephoned Ivor who came and picked me up. No friend's house has ever seemed more welcoming. Just to be with Dominic and my oldest friends in sympathetic, decent surroundings obliged me to fight the tears all afternoon. Dominic played with Tommy, their son, and another child. At four I took him back. The nanny was waiting. She had been watching from Ann Reeve's house next door to see what I did. She was clearly under instructions to do this because of my suggestion to Babs on the previous access.

The solicitors' correspondence as a result of the above sequence of events covers eighteen typewritten pages. It started with a three-page letter from Rutter which concluded with the demand that I confirm in writing that I wouldn't remove Dominic again. If I did remove him they would take proceedings to have me put in prison for being in contempt of court. I gave precise instructions. Paddy was to write and tell them to go and fuck themselves and if the house was cold again I would certainly remove Dominic. Before Paddy could write anything, a follow-up letter arrived from Rutter to say that Dominic had, through my actions, developed a severe cold.

Paddy didn't answer as I instructed, but his answer covered four pages. This got a six page overkill from Rutter. One sentence was one of his goodies, '…although the central heating had been turned on it was not very warm in the house.' My failure to feed Dominic was 'wanton neglect.' In the six pages of my inadequacies he blanketed all the possibilities from brutality to possessiveness via neglect. There was no possible character deficiency that could slip through his net. Let this sum them all up. 'Your client held Dominic and slung Dominic upside down and shook him and said 'let's see what you had for lunch today' and your client made a wretching (sic) noise and almost immediately after your client left on that occasion Dominic was sick twice. We would have thought that your client would have more sense than to do this to a baby who had shortly before had his tea. Please inform your client that he should not treat the child in such a manner again.' A further two pages from each side whistled across before they both got tired of it.

It was, and is, contrary to the law to use the child, or access to the children, as a weapon in divorce. But, as I witnessed, judges and lawyers don't give a toss for such niceties. I never heard of one case of anyone even being reprimanded for such actions, let alone actually punished. The game that is played in our adversarial system, because the woman generally has the children and the husband has the income, is (when the father cares) to bargain access for money. This was the improper game that Rutter was playing because that is how he had learned, or been trained to play it. And it is why my side accepted it. The fact that this particular husband and father had been coughing up freely had escaped their notice. Their eyes were on the main event, further down the road, when there would be a full hearing in the High Court to decide all matters, especially the important capital and income settlement. Meanwhile to hell with anyone's feelings, access arrangements were all 'in Dominic's best interests.'

The above, on top of everything else, convinced me it all had to be stopped. I set about my solution to the war with much bitterness. The only way out was to scuttle the prize. I told Bill Fournier to break up the Trust - the financial umbrella I had created to take care of Christine, me, Dominic, our mothers, other close relatives and friends - pay the Revenue whatever they asked, then let Rutter fight for the scraps, because that is all there would be. At least then Christine and Dominic, my mother and hers would all have houses and I would be able to walk away and start my life again. If I didn't do that I faced the possibility of total bankruptcy and years of debts.

Back came the devastating answer from Bill Fournier: he couldn't.

I went to Frank Young. He could do nothing. 'I'm an accountant, not a lawyer,' was his answer.

I trotted along to Paddy Grafton-Green; 'our trust expert' didn't know how to do it, either. What was more, Bill and Paddy both said there was no method of collapsing it. It had been created. There it was. And there it must stay. 'Right,' I said, 'Then declare all the Trust income to have been mine and get my tax liability quantified on that basis.' Nobody could do that either.

I trotted back to Frank Young. 'OK, I'll just pay the maximum amount possible. What is it? I'll get the Trustees to write out a cheque and send it to the Inland Revenue.'

'They won't accept it,' was Frank's answer. 'If they haven't assessed you, why should they take your money?'

'How do I get an assessment?' I asked.

'You'll have to wait.'

'How long?'

'Perhaps years. We've been through this one.'

'But I'll be bust by then.'

No helpful suggestions were forthcoming on that line.

I trotted back to Bill. 'And you can't send Trust money direct to the Revenue,' he said.

'Why not?'

'That could be construed as stealing.' He continued with the sticky logic of the laws in which I had wrapped myself. 'The trustees can't pay your tax or divorce bills. They're not liable. You are.'

Neil Taylor added his two penn'orth. 'If you send off all your money to the Revenue, that will be construed by the judge as an attempt to deny your wife her legal rights.'

It was beautiful, really. I was bound and gagged in a combination of laws that didn't make sense, while the very financial structure that I had created became the rock to which I was roped. Then my wife (I almost wrote that emotive tautology 'my own wife') was to push the assembled object into the river. I decided to take no further part in the divorce proceedings until I was ordered to. If I couldn't stop them, let them career along without me. And they did. The demands for details, figures, papers, proliferated. The letters crossed and re-crossed and the applications for directions, for discovery, the interminable accusations, polluted the post. As I now flick through the dog-eared folders, one item catches my eye, one sentence of the many that were sworn by the Petitioner.

"...The Respondent only periodically contributed towards the housekeeping sums of £5 or £6 a time..."

In my faded handwriting in the margin of the affidavit is written, 'Oh! oh! Christine.'

I tried to turn back to my work, that forgotten matter. One weekend I stumbled across a cottage in the New Forest with a 'For Sale' board. It was tiny and cheap, a gatekeeper's cottage on a disused railway line. I bought it with some of my UK tax reserve money and tried to write something new in it to make some fast money. I wrote a screenplay of *The Bandwagon* for the Boulting brothers. The project fell through. The film of *Soup* was a massive success in this country, the queues were round the block for weeks, but only lukewarm in the USA so there was little income from that. I was approached by Richard Lester to write a screenplay with him for a continental company. As he was Richard Lester, and as his idea for the film was mad and delightful, I got down to work without advance or contract, although he guaranteed payment. Of course the film never got made, of course the continentals disappeared, and of course Lester didn't pay up.

'Shall we sue Lester?' Harvey asked me. I shuddered.

The Bandwagon played in Australia. It was a wild success, but the production company which put it on went bust on another play and improperly used *The Bandwagon* receipts to try and save themselves. Peggy Mount, Bob Chetwyn and I never received thousands of pounds owed to us.

'Shall we sue?' asked Harvey. Litigation in Australia could have been a new dimension in my life.

In March, Paddy Grafton Green telephoned me. 'There's an application for discovery by Rutter to be heard this week.'

239

'I thought he'd had everything three times over,' I said. 'What are you holding back?'

'Nothing,' said Paddy, 'But he's making a meal of it as usual. He wants orders for everything. God, he's a bastard that man. Taylor says he's never seen anything like it.'

'Well, while there are orders for discovery floating about, I want you to recover all the letters I wrote to Christine last year. OK?'

'What for?'

'They've produced the ones that suit them as evidence, so I have a right for the lot to be discovered, haven't I?'

'Yes,' said Paddy, he clearly thought it a trivial matter.

'I want them, Paddy. I'm not joking. I want all of them.'

I particularly wanted the letter I wrote from Paris after the night of March 13th, the pot-smoking night. It might help blow some fresh air into the phoney near-Victorian atmosphere of their affidavits.

Once more Rutter showed himself to be more persistent, devious and diligent than my team. He was not having that letter read by a judge. He got the discovery order worded so that the vital one slipped through the net. I was disgusted with Paddy and Neil Taylor and told them so. Neil Taylor pursed his lips as he leafed through the letters they had got. A tinge of admiration crept into his tone. 'I say, you can certainly turn it on, can't you.'

I looked at my letters. One year and numerous lawyers later it tore me open to read them. The ones to New York were as dreary as they had always been, but all were full of Christine and Terry, Terry and Christine, a creature as dead as the Dodo. I looked at long, bloodless Neil Taylor. No wonder he was impressed.

'Pity about this one though,' said Taylor. It was from Morocco and very warm. 'You were with the girl when you wrote that weren't you?'

'What the hell has infidelity got to do with loving your wife?' I said.

Neil Taylor jumped like a poor actor in a farce and made a shushing gesture. 'Don't say that in court, will you?' It was an almost exact repetition of the reaction of my earlier counsel, Paul Beard, when I had made a similar remark. The whole lot of them seemed to be afraid that the reality of human failings and feelings might enter the courtroom to disturb the judge's deliberations.

———————

There was a brief, splendid break in legalities. The Writers' Guild of Great Britain deemed the script of *Soup* the Best British Comedy Screenplay of 1970. Two of those three qualifying adjectives had reduced the opposition to *Carry on Something* and *On The Buses*. It was rather like winning an award for the best tan in Antarctica. In black tie I presided at a table of friends at the Dorchester (I wondered, oh God, which room above had contained

Christine and the lovely Bert, coitally entwined while I was on tour with *Soup*) and, when my name was called, rose to receive my plaque. I have a poor head for drink, the post-dinner brandy combined with the rush of adrenaline and a highly polished floor fixed me. I didn't actually fall over, but skidded to the foot of the little dais and, borne by my own impetus, stumbled up a step or two into the arms of Richard Attenborough, not then ennobled. He conducted himself admirably and pumped my hand with a persistency and intimacy that led me to believe we must already be close friends.

'Well done, well done,' he said. 'I'm so glad it was you, so glad. Congratulations. You have deserved it, my word. Well done,' pierced the fog of my inebriation.

'Thag, you, thang you. Thag you ver' mu',' I managed.

'No thank *you*. Really. It was, well, splendid. Well done.'

'Oh, well, thag you.'

'No, really. I'm delighted it was you. I really am. Delighted.'

I tried to remember where we had met before. 'Thag you, you're very—'

'Splendid, absolutely splendid. Well done.'

We continued in this succinct manner for some while before, clutching my award, I skated back to my seat and merciful anonymity. So that is what those people mutter to each other, hands clasped, eyes locked, on those public occasions that are flashed by satellite to the breathless world.

Then the shit hit the fan with a resounding thwack and the air was full of lawyers diving for cover. The cock-up was exposed; the cover-up got under way. Actually, the real, the fatal cover-up had already taken place but I was not aware of it. It was early 1971.

Paddy was sepulchral on the telephone. 'Neil Taylor would like to see you.'

When I saw Taylor in his chambers with Paddy, his vocal delivery, though amply audible, contrived to have even more hushed notes in it than Paddy's. It was an immaculate demonstration of how to project in an appalled undertone. Actors have prayed for such skill. 'Why didn't you tell us about this?' 'This' was handed across in ritual sorrow. 'This' was a copy of the form granting me the mandatory signature that I had held on the Swiss Bank Account from January 1969 to September 1970. I stared at 'this' in some dismay.

'Where did you get it?' I asked.

'Fournier was obliged to disclose everything pertaining to the Swiss Bank Account on the latest discovery order. He sent this down among a lot of other stuff.'

As I said some while back, Bill had told me that I had no need to disclose this particular document ('I'll never tell anyone,' he had said of the illegal piece of paper he had advised me to sign) and now had done just that, without first telling me. What was worse, he had done so only when obliged to by a court order.

'I didn't know it was relevant,' I said. Taylor didn't even try to look as though he believed me. His eyebrows were in his hairline, his lips were pursed like a pantomime dame's. 'Anyway, Rutter's known about it all along.' They both stared at me.

'Rutter knew of it?' said Taylor, '

'He must have done. Christine's always known about it. She's bound to have told him.'

Taylor stared gooseberry-eyed at Paddy and grunted as if I were half-witted.

'You know that you were supposed to tell us everything about your finances, don't you?'

'I have told you everything. Every penny. Fifty times over.'

'Taylor blew out his cheeks in dismissal. 'Oh, don't be naive. You can't just have happened to forget to disclose this one item.'

'But I didn't know it was obligatory to disclose it. So I kept quiet.'

'Ah. So you admit that it was deliberate.' Taylor's court technique was showing through. The impression that the legal profession modelled themselves on dated thrillers once more crossed my mind.

'Of course it was deliberate. I kept quiet about it when I found out it was illegal.'

The word 'illegal' got a different quality of reaction from Taylor. Up till now he had looked like a man who had rehearsed the meeting in advance, but at the word 'illegal' he went guardedly quiet. 'Illegal? Is this signature illegal, as well?'

For the first time I thought I had both his and Paddy's proper attention. I told them the story of the discovered illegality, of the threats from Rutter, of my subsequent confession to the Bank of England and of their indifference to the whole matter.

Taylor came on strongly. 'Never mind the Bank of England. That signature gives you control of the Trust moneys.'

'Eh? But it was cancelled months ago.'

'But if you've had a signature once you can have one again. When the divorce is over, for instance.'

'No, I can't,' I said, surprised at his insistence. 'It's illegal.'

'Huh!' Taylor again leaned back, glancing at Paddy. Apparently, they didn't think much of illegality as an inhibition.

'Anyway, I've always told you I had control of the Trust moneys.'

'But you've sworn on affidavit that you haven't.'

'Yes, *de jure*. You've told me that even if I had control *de facto* I don't have control *de jure*.'

'But I didn't know that this was in existence then.' He poked at the paper on his desk with a ruler as though it might rear up and bite him.

'What difference does this make?' I asked.

The answer that hung heavy in the air but was never spoken was that Taylor didn't know there would be documentary evidence to undermine the legalistic nit-picking of the '*de facto*' and '*de jure*' line. There is nothing like a solid piece of incriminating paper to bring lawyers to their senses. Instead of fighting the case I had brought them (about making everything wait to settle my tax liabilities, as I have described in detail earlier) they had fought their illogical battle, had played the discovery game with Rutter and had lost on my behalf. And it was Fournier who had stabbed them in the back, or rather, stabbed me in the back. Their signatures were on nothing.

'You've committed perjury. You've sworn by the card.' He had to explain that one to me. It was the first time I had ever heard the expression, but it is one with which I grew drearily familiar. To swear by the card, or by the book (the card, I suppose, being the card handed to you in court to swear from, and the book being *The Bible*) means to swear to the literal truth of something while knowing the whole truth to be very different.

'Well, yes, I said. 'If you substitute "*de jure*" for literal truth and "*de facto*" for whole truth that's precisely what I've been doing.'

Taylor achieved the impossible. He looked even more shocked than he had a moment earlier. 'My dear fellow, this is very serious.'

'But we all know it's what I've been doing.' I was beginning to falter. His flesh looked quite grey. He sucked in his breath shaking his head. It wasn't clear whether the head-shaking was a denial of his knowledge or just general disapproval of the world. Paddy's face had nearly disappeared altogether into his jacket. 'Anyway, I don't control anything. The tax situation controls it. Until the tax is settled—'

'No, no, no. Never mind about irrelevancies,' Taylor waved his hand impatiently. 'I'm talking about real control.'

I was indignant. 'The tax is the only reality in all this gibberish.' But the loudness of my protest was only an indication that it was a near-terminal spasm. The true centre of the whole problem, my unpaid, unquantifiable tax on foreign earnings, had been shunted to the periphery. The new occupant of the centre spot in the minds of the lawyers was this, to me, irrelevant piece of paper. It was insane. But what had sanity to do with the law? Especially divorce law in the Court of Good Sense.

Taylor's final comment was nearly *sotto voce*, thrown in, 'Fournier's behind this balls-up, I'll be bound.' I sat in dumb loyalty to Bill. When he got no response, Taylor went on 'He should never have let us get into this position and then blown the gaff. Bloody ridiculous. I've never seen anything...' as he faded into inaudibility there was considerable vigorous nodding from Paddy.

I sat wriggling in my chair, guilty accomplice of Bill in our illegal act, perjurer in the cause of swindling my wife and child. I stared shifty-eyed at the two innocent pillars of the Family Division who shuffled papers, cleared their throats and glanced at me in mutual dissociation. I was the one caught with the apple in my hand and I knew the next line in that scenario. 'I was alone in the orchard, sir. No-one was with me.' I spoke up like any decent fifth-former should. 'If I've done anything wrong I'll take my medicine. I don't think I have but in any case I'm not blaming you two.'

Taylor's eyebrows shot up. 'Huh,' he said very, very quietly. 'I should hope not.'

If only I had known then the truth of their position, well, Theodore Goddard's, if not Taylor's. It was quite simple and utterly damning for them. They, too, had a give-away document about control of the Trust. It was a cable. In the previous October, under an order to discover details about the Trust and control of it, Theodore Goddard had written to the trustees in the Cayman Islands asking for disclosure. Some genius at the bank there had cabled back:

RE FRISBY YOURLET 20TH OCTOBER WE CANNOT DIVULGE INFORMATION WITHOUT FULL WRITTEN AUTHORITY FROM FRISBY STOP CAN YOU OBTAIN STOP

SIGNED
ROYTRUST

If Theodore Goddard had disclosed this document, as they should have, it would have shown, some months earlier, that the advice they and Neil Taylor had been offering was deeply flawed. But it had disappeared.

Paddy Grafton Greene or Calderan, or both of them, must have been horrified at the indiscretion of the sender of the cable. I wonder what passed between them. Or did one of them hide it from the other? Calderan was so lax in his overall control of my affairs, leaving everything to the inexperienced Paddy, that I think that was the most likely scenario. Paddy would have written the letter of twentieth October, the cable would have been sent to him, he must have panicked and hid it. You see, although the cable does not say I control the money, it does say that I control the information, which is a big step down the same road. The inference that a lawyer should draw from that is that I could be in control or probably was. It puts a solicitor 'under notice', a well-known legal phrase with serious implications. 'Under notice' means that they should be aware that all is not as it seems. In the hysterical atmosphere (whenever I was there) of Theodore Goddard's offices and Neil Taylor's chamber, that cable would have arrived like a lightning strike, impossible to ignore. It should have been placed centre stage and the implications thrashed out, just as this document that Bill had disclosed was now being (apparently) treated. Then they would have had to face my case squarely and reverse all their previous advice. Bear in mind, I have always said that I was frank with them all along. But now, some months after they received the cable, they started saying, for the first time, that they didn't know anything about my control, that I had misled them until the document disclosed by Bill arrived and blew my story. Now they could reverse their advice and blame me for the necessity to do so. The cable they had hidden gave the lie to that by several months. The trustees had followed up the cable with a confirming letter and Paddy had answered. Those letters, along with the cable, went missing somewhere among the thousands of papers of my divorce. They did not surface for years.

All the above became part of my evidence in later hearings.

Calderan behaved like the headmaster called in for a particularly intransigent case. 'Why ever didn't you tell us about this mandatory signature form? This proves that you control the Trust.'

I was pretty intimidated by now. 'Bill Fournier said months ago that it proved no such thing.'

'Oh, did he? Perhaps he would like to fight your divorce. Just look at the date of cancellation, about a week before you signed your affidavit of means. It is most incriminating.'

'But that's because there was a time-lag for forms to be sent abroad and returned. Anyway, how could I have known in advance what you would put in those affidavits? I'm not psychic.'

Calderan smiled thinly at Paddy.

'Anyway, it's my tax situation that really controls everything,' I concluded weakly. Calderan just blinked in silence. The tax situation, the vital core of everything, now seemed like a red herring that I towed about to cover the scent of my perjury. 'You all knew I controlled it *de facto*,' I tried for the last time.

'I certainly didn't' said Calderan, crisply, ignoring everything I had told him of the situation when we first met. There was some mumbled head-shaking from Paddy. The implications of all this were unbearable. The second-rate courtroom drama was cast. Rutter was the Hero, white horse prancing through the sheaves of papers. I was the Villain, concealing the true state of my wealth from my Unfortunate Wife. My lawyers were the Dupes, deceived by me. The accusations of molestation, of irresponsibility towards Dominic, of indifference, of unreliability, of intimidation, of lechery and even of their subdivision of that one, of racial partiality in lechery, everything acquired credence. Would not a man who did this, do anything?

I went to see Bill Fournier.

'I've never heard such tripe,' he said mildly. 'They're like hysterical girls.' From his window in Jermyn Street I could see a sign in Lower Regent Street directing the public round the corner to the Comedy Theatre, where we had transferred after three years. There had just been considerable publicity at the latest annual cast takeovers. Gay Singleton had sacrificed '£3.50 per week as a part-time barmaid to earn £40 per week starring in the West End,' boasted the copy. And *Soup* was entering its 'Sixth Hilarious Year.' Ah, well, my divorce wasn't the only long-running comedy in town. It had started out as Rutter versus Nabarro Nathanson: Aggression versus Appeasement. Now it was Rutter versus Theodore Goddard: Malignancy versus Incompetence.

CHAPTER XXX

Summer 1971

The grand finale was to be in the High Court in July. This was the final hearing that would decide how to divide our indivisible capital assets and to decide what rate of maintenance I should pay a) for Christine b) for Dominic. It was what all the blizzard of letters for the past sixteen months, all the interim (or interlocutory) hearings, all the rows about discovery had been about. Although each event so far may have looked self-contained, especially the nonsense about Dominic, it was all, I had learned, part of the build-up to this event. I was not contesting custody (legal guardianship) because I was told by my advisers it would be fruitless (although why joint custody of all children in divorce should not be the automatic system, is beyond me; much the healthiest for the children to keep both parents involved. Then, any parent who wishes to vary that should have to apply and show why). In the absence of joint custody I had something called 'a father's natural rights' which means damn-all. I was also not contesting 'care and control' (who actually had Dominic). That, too, would be fruitless, I was told, as the court would always award a very young child to the mother. Rightly so, I thought. All that I could hope for from the law was proper access to him. But that, officially, would be no part of this hearing: access and money in divorce are not connected. The law says so.

The meetings and paper had proliferated at an ever-increasing rate, one thousand four hundred and fifty-five pages of documents were ready for Theodore Goddard to give to my QC, a further two thousand-odd were sent to him in a large box, but being marked as of little or no importance he was never even going to look at them. As I discovered years later, the vital cable and surrounding correspondence were buried deep down in that two thousand. The staggering statistic was that the lawyers had produced between them ten pages a day, including Sundays, for over a year. One letter alone from Rutter had six closely typed pages of demands for old correspondence, forgotten figures, who-knows-what. Taylor estimated that the legal costs would exceed £20,000 for which I would be liable. Calderan agreed. I remember his words well. 'Even if you contest liability for some of these costs, you must see that the main body, the costs of Discovery, will be laid at your door. They are entirely your ooesponsibility.' Not his, not Paddy's, not Neil Taylor's, but mine.

Calderan pursed his lips and went on casually, 'You might have a case against Fournier.'

He reaffirmed that I did not have a hope in hell of proving that Rutter had behaved improperly although every solicitor and barrister concerned with the case at one time or other agreed that he had. Such words as 'vicious,' 'vendetta,' 'malicious,' 'butcher,' 'no ornament to our profession,' 'bastard,' 'shit' and many other epithets were applied to him. That is the tone in which the legal profession conducts the desperate and painful business of divorce.

I had developed the habit, when Babs opened her door, of calling a cheery greeting while scooping Dominic up off the hall floor and carrying him swiftly to the bottom of the garden so that neither Babs nor the current au pair could follow. There, under the apple tree with the white fungus on the branches, I would hug him and whisper fiercely that I loved him, contrary to anything else he might hear. On one occasion I swept him up and as I hurried through the kitchen found myself face to face with Christine. I stopped dead, stared, then after a quick, 'Hallo,' dived on to the bottom of the garden, this time to pull myself together.

It was an eerie afternoon. Christine, Dominic and I had tea together in the kitchen. She told me anecdotes of his behaviour as though I were a fond uncle home from a long voyage. The pleasure of being with a healthy, burbling, eighteen-month-old child even wrung from us smiles and spontaneous goodwill. The fact that we were together with our child in what had been our kitchen hung with tangibility in the air. I watched her take him on her lap and feed him, shoving a spoon in his mouth and saying, 'Come on, a bit more,' in her sweet, uncommitted way. Then she said 'Why don't you?' and handed him to me so that I could do the same. And so we sat, cool and polite while my innards surged. I tried to use the opportunity before we parted. I said I hoped she would bring Dominic next time. She did. And the time after that. Each time was a pleasure. Then she appeared no more. The High Court hearing was approaching, better not let the judge see we could get on.

Suddenly there was no Joe Jackson. Calderan was quietly seething and said that Jackson had dropped us in favour of a longer, more lucrative case, but subsequent events make me doubt the truth of that. I think that Jackson saw how the case was going and did not fancy being on the defensive. Or perhaps he saw even more, I cannot be sure. To my regret, I had seen the last of Joe Jackson. He had balls; someone with a bit of spunk in him who would get in and fight, instead of the group of collapsed balloons that surrounded me.

And so the second legal superstar orbited into my life. James Comyn QC accepted my brief. One could tell Comyn was a genuine superstar because he never spoke louder than semi-audibly, at least in his own chambers, where I had to crane to hear him. In the High Court, where even the most status-conscious QC has to concede top billing to the judge, his decibel level rose considerably. Comyn soon became a High Court judge himself and I have often wondered whether, in untrammelled control of his own court, anyone heard a word before he eventually retired. Before he became a judge he earned himself a considerable reputation as a fighter for enlightened causes, and his judicial record is, I am told, humane and compassionate. But I can only report that if the law is an ass, he was it. He was one of the most shut-minded, opinionated, self-satisfied, innumerate windbags it has even been my misfortune to meet. However it is not his fat-headedness that leads me to write so unkindly of him, it is his subsequent actions, as will emerge.

His vocal delivery when I met him was quiet and on the breath. 'On the breath, On the breath,' the voice teachers at drama school used to command. Comyn would have been a star pupil. The words came floating out of his podgy face on little puffs, and had to be deftly caught, or they were gone. He was well overweight, but this was not especially apparent, as the best efforts of Savile Row hung from his shoulders. The line of a first-class suit in fine worsted does not draw attention to dimensions that might cause comment on a surfing beach. I often had the feeling that were I to punch him, something I subsequently longed to do with passion, it would have been the same as arguing with him. The fist would sink in, perhaps to the wrist, but when it was withdrawn, the flesh would re-form to its previous shape - or lack of it - leaving no sign.

His first words to me, probably phrased for the benefit of the gathered lawyers, remain engraved in my memory. Perhaps they should be my epitaph. 'You have been a naughty boy, haven't you?' If I hadn't been so demoralised I would have laughed.

I learned, by making enquiries, that in the law as well as in the theatre there is a strange system of type-casting that persists.

Joseph Jackson, QC was, it seemed, a Fighter. James Miskin QC, who had been engaged on behalf of my wife, was, it seemed, a Great Cross-Examiner and James Comyn QC who was engaged for me was the Great Apologiser. Thus it seemed The Show was quite clearly set in the minds of my advisers.

Comyn's chambers were in a spacious room in Queen Elizabeth Building, on the embankment. He presided from an impressive desk, the light behind him, of course. I was on the carpet before it, in both senses, and my advisers dressed the set in the various postures of self effacement that the legal profession assume when in the presence of one of their heavyweights.

Comyn wafted his second goody towards me. 'Well now, Mr Frisby,' my name was used nicely on an upward inflection as punctuation, thrown so lightly that if I hadn't already known who I was I would have remained in ignorance, 'I must tell you I take the gravest view of the situation.' The use of 'gravest' had a most studied air. Doom positively hovered. I tried to explain the way the situation had developed. There was no help from Messrs. Calderan, Taylor and Grafton Green. This trio seemed never to have had the faintest knowledge of my control, *de facto, de jure,* or *de* anything. Comyn brushed me aside, 'I've got a bird's eye view of things, Mr Frisby. You haven't.'

Some discussion with the others led him to talk of 'Rutter's successful voyage of discovery.' In answer to Frank's fears of the possible tax liability bankrupting me, he allowed the sentence, 'Things will probably be all right,' to float out in a way that suggested they would certainly be all right. At a later meeting he said of the tax, looking me squarely in the eye, Polonious bidding his son farewell, 'Take it from me, you'll be all right.' Another overblown Comyn image was, 'I am going to throw Fournier to the wolves.'

I walked out of Queen Elizabeth Building onto the embankment in a daze. Between them, my legal advisers of the last year and a half had utterly sapped my will and energy. Only one lawyer made me want to stand up for myself and that was Rutter. The only person till then that really made me want to fight Christine was him. But my team were like albatrosses round my neck. As I stood on the pavement I knew what I wanted to do, to sack the lot of them, but had no idea what to do after that. In fact, I had earlier suggested to Taylor that I got rid of all lawyers and handled things myself. Taylor had been horrified and gave me dire warnings of what would happen to me. I had had two of the most famous and experienced firms of solicitors in the country, two of the most eminent QCs, and an experienced junior counsel. If I changed again my culpability would be even more evident.

I had no way of doubting their warnings. The law had proved itself for the last year-and-a-bit to be an insane maze, and my idea, to represent myself, was as yet no more than a half-formed wish, without focus or know-how. I also still had a horror of looking inadequate, pathetic, a would-be, know-all, barrack-room lawyer. I still had a journey to make before my fear of what others thought of me in that respect was fully removed.

There was one last sordid development, one that plumbed the depths. It was on the access front

On the eighth June I went for my fortnightly access at Bab's house. It was a shining afternoon and I said to Babs that it would be nice to go into the park. She enthusiastically agreed but declined to come herself. I was glad, as otherwise most of my efforts would have been spent looking after her. The current obese Iranian didn't want to come either. I picked up Dominic and was gone before either could change her mind.

It was a delightful experience being properly alone and free with him for the first time. He was nearly two. I did a lot of grinning down at him as

I walked and he tottered. When he grinned back I picked him up and charged about, holding him in the air, swinging him and then cuddling him and uttering as many rubbishy endearments as have ever been poured into the ear of child or adult. He seemed to think all this a splendid way to pass the afternoon. At the river bank I pointed to boats and said 'boats,' to the ducks and said 'ducks.' Although he didn't break into a stream of coherent English he didn't say anything recognisably Iranian either. Then there was the children's playground and all its wonders, and lastly a man and his child had to endure four eyes staring intently at them as they played with a ball. He soon got the hint and tossed it in our direction. It seemed to me an act of infinite bounty. I made a note to bring a ball, and bread for the ducks, on my next access. Wandsworth Park, after the few square yards of dog-turd-strewn grass in the garden of 16 Bective Road, was like Salisbury Plain.

On twenty-second June I turned up for my next access with Woolworth's ball and a bag of stale bread. Ann, the neighbour, answered the door. She told me that Babs was on holiday and didn't mention the absent Iranian. I took Dominic to the park again. It was lovely.

The next evening Paddy Grafton Green was on the telephone. 'I've just had a meeting with Rutter. They're making an application to have you committed.'

'What does that mean?'

'Committed.'

'Yes, I heard you. What does it mean?'

'Committed for contempt of court. To prison. They contend that you're in contempt of the access order for taking Dominic out of the house.

'Are you tell me that she is trying to have me put in jail for walking Dominic in the park?'

'Precisely.'

When I considered the actions that I have just described above of Babs, Ann and the Iranian girl it is clear the whole thing had been set up.

We all gathered at the Royal Courts of Justice for the committal proceedings. When I say 'we all' I mean my team, Rutter, Good-Old-Harry Law and a gaggle of pressmen and photographers (as this hearing could affect my liberty, it had to be in open court). Christine was absent. The hearing only took a few minutes. I can't remember what Good-Old-Harry did or said, if anything, but Neil Taylor was in fine form, seething with indignation, some of which appeared to be genuine. There was an affidavit from Christine supporting her application. It was another gem of either Sydney's or Good-Old-Harry's composition that gave a contemptible and fictional version of the events I have just described. It was doubly interesting in that Christine had not witnessed anything because she hadn't been there. Hearsay evidence is not admissible, so their application had no validity. I suppose, when the case is as strong as mine, even the Neil Taylors of this world can sound full of juice. He got in a lot of stuff about, 'A proud father walking his child in the park,' and this application was, 'Contemptible,' and, 'Ludicrous.' The judge gratefully got shot of the whole issue by adjourning it to the full hearing. Neil Taylor was still breathing heavily, eyes glinting when he rejoined us in the corridor.

Following Taylor's triumph, Calderan, too, came into his own. As we left the Royal Courts of Justice I was surrounded and questioned by a mob of pressmen and photographers. Rutter tagged on, right behind me. I think he wanted to hear what I might get into the papers. I had been spelling his name out, 'G-U-double-T-E-R' loud enough for him to hear. 'And the barrister representing my wife, who couldn't be bothered to attend, is called Law, spelled L-I-A-R.'

Rutter called to the reporter, 'Just a minute, my friend.' I turned, pretending that I thought he was calling me and said, 'What?' hoping to have a row, at which point Calderan got between us, and he and Rutter had a wonderfully silly argument about Rutter's right to address me directly. This involved a bit of jostling. We left them to it.

When he caught us up, Calderan said, pink with achievement, 'I'm going to write him a letter,' and did just that. Calderan and Rutter then had a petulant postal exchange on whether Rutter would have called me, 'My friend,' and who was ruder to whom. I deemed Rutter the winner of that one, his letter being four times longer than Calderan's.

But, oh, I thought to myself in my private gloom after these grotesque events, how could you let yourself sink to this, Christine? What has happened to you? Whatever is it you imagine I have done to you that you must respond like this, using our child so? And whatever do you think your friends or anyone else think of you? It went round and round. She seemed to have utterly lost touch with common decency. Did she not shrink from this public display as I did? It was all over the newspapers, even the posh ones we all read. I hid behind my answering machine, avoided contact with people, ashamed to be a part of it all.

But in these musings I believe I saw the answer as to how she could excuse herself: Rutter saying to her, 'Oh, don't worry, my dear. They won't put him in jail - or if they do, not for long. It's just tactics, d'you see? Softening him up for the big hearing. It'll show the judge how contemptuous he is of the law. Be good for our image in court ' And with that would come a reassuring pat, perhaps even a heavy wink. And she - yes, I could see this clearly - could use all that to flip her through the moral somersault necessary to deem herself worldly-wise.

Rutter, or someone, then had a sudden rush of generosity to the head. To facilitate my working arrangements, I could (fifteen months after I had asked for them) have my writing desk, chair, lamp, ash tray, cigarette box, some books and posters, all from my study. The previous condition, that in return I sign over the rest of the contents of our house to Christine, was withdrawn. Well, I suppose that would look reasonable to the judge. The last 'without prejudice' demands were spelled out at about the same time. These the judge would not see. Comyn's reaction to them was more depressing than the actual figures.

The demands were for Christine's maintenance to be guaranteed for over four years at nearly £9,000 (my entire income for the previous year was about that), school fees (open-ended), income for Babs for life and I to give her 16 Bective Road. In addition, Christine was to have: the matrimonial home, 1 Genoa Avenue (I to pay off the £7,000 mortgage); nearly all our possessions; all legal costs (over £20,000) plus an extra £500 for Christine to pay Rutter; a substantial insurance on my life; back maintenance for one year (to make up for Rutter's misguided application to Registrar Bayne-Powell); £10,000 lump sum in five annual instalments.

In return I was offered improved access to Dominic.

Comyn looked sagely down the list. He pursed his lips in surprise. 'Oh, they'll accept staggered payments on the lump sum, will they? That's odd.' I pointed out that they understood my predicament, that I didn't have it to pay, better than he. He smiled distantly and gently shook his head as, of course, I refused to sign.

Signing away, on the never-never, capital you don't have, revealed to me a new dimension in divorce as run by Theodore Goddard and Co., Neil Taylor and James Comyn QC

CHAPTER XXXI

July Twelfth - Fourteenth 1971

On Monday morning, twelfth July, we all assembled at the Royal Courts of Justice. The hearing was estimated to last a week. but like all court hearings would be just as long or as short as was necessary to finish it. I was wearing a suit bought specially for the occasion. Calderan had stared at my open necks, pullover, battered suede, whatever happened to be to hand when I went to see him, with considerable distaste. 'Mr Fooisby, I don't want to appear...but I don't want the judge to think, er, you see, we want to make a good um, don't we.'

'OK Suit and tie. I understand.'

'And your hair—'

'Don't worry. I worked behind a tailoring counter for six years. I know.'

'Did you? How inteooesting.'

Now he stared at me with something bordering on approval. My litigation suit was just, by the tips of its fingers, Savile row. The ready-to-wear but trendy tailors where I had bought it being sited on the corner.

In the cool, modern corridor outside the courts of the Family Division, litigants and their advisers were gathered, the advisers with important expressions, the litigants anxious to a man - and woman. My team and Christine's were somewhat apart, my attempt to say good morning to her having been successfully thwarted by the bird's-eye back of Good-Old-Harry. He and Rutter were surrounding Christine in an alcove away from us. She had on a modest tweed jacket, dowdy skirt, sensible shoes, hair scraped back and glasses. She might have just walked Daisy on Putney Common. Her usual accessories were as absent as the hair that normally hung over my collar. James Comyn QC and James Miskin QC were performing the officers-on-watch routine, strolling self-consciously up and down the corridor, scattering the smaller fry and discussing our business inaudibly. There, complete with pauses and shuffles for position at each end of the corridor, is where the real business of litigation goes on.

I got my first look at the third legal superstar to enter my life, James Miskin QC, the Great Cross-Examiner. He was unimpressive: grey suit, greyish hair, greyish face, slim build: a stick. I continued my running challenge to Taylor on the subject of my 'laceration' in the witness box. 'He doesn't look much to me.' Taylor looked as though I had said vipers were cuddly. I tried to work up some anxiety but failed. An usher came out of the court and said the hateful, 'Frisby versus Frisby.'

'We're on,' said Taylor and we all trooped in. Mr Justice Latey entered and bowed to Miskin, then Comyn. We all sat. If I had thought Miskin looked grey that was before I saw Latey. Greyness radiated from him. But he was attractive in a headmasterly way. He looked benevolently down at Miskin. 'Yes?' Thus do all High Court cases start. Miskin got to his feet and after introducing the case started to plough through the first capacious file of Rutter correspondence. Latey soon got bored with this and started flicking. 'What are these?' he asked Miskin, referring to a group of hand-written letters at the front of his file.

Miskin fumbled for a moment, being engaged on something quite different. 'Oh, er, these, my Lord, are letters written by the husband to the wife. I don't think they need concern us now,' and he went on while Latey buried his head in my letters to Christine in New York and the later ones imploring her not to go on with the divorce. He came up from them eventually and looked curiously at me. Our eyes met so he looked quickly away. I was more careful after that.

On the question of marital conduct Miskin said, 'It would be more decent to draw a veil over the past.' Latey primly agreed and so did Comyn. I was outraged; Rutter's reams of documents devoted to calling me every sort of pig just brushed aside; no flicker of an apology offered or sought. I thought, yes, I'll draw a veil if Rutter picks up the bill. Then I heard Miskin adding, 'Sufficient to say that he started behaving badly to her during her pregnancy.' Any previous thoughts I had had that Miskin was a decent stick were cancelled. Some veil. It was to have selective, distorting chinks, was it? I thought of the day and a half of Christine's labour while I sat holding her. Behaving badly?

Rutter's style soon started to work against Christine's case. Miskin saw this but Rutter didn't and sat hunched behind him, pulling at his jacket and pointing out what he had missed or insufficiently stressed. Miskin got rattier, he was not the obsequious Harry Law. 'What is it *now*?' he muttered once, then finally spat in fury, 'Shut up, won't you.' There was an exquisite silence as Miskin and Rutter both went pink. Embarrassment hummed round the court.

'Yes, Mr Miskin,' said Latey mildly, 'it must be very difficult to concentrate with these constant interruptions.' Covert grins appeared on the lowered faces of my team, schoolboys under their desk lids.

The memorable feature of the proceedings after the rancour of solicitors was the courteousness. It seemed a healing balm, but the relief it gave was out of proportion to its importance. It is an irrelevance to the litigant, a convention that allows the case to proceed more smoothly and protects judges. Latey, snug in the insulated atmosphere, sighed as yet another of Rutter's letters was being read. He looked at his copy in distaste. 'This is most unfortunate.' Then, later on, 'All this Frisby versus Frisby stuff. I thought the old-fashioned adversarial system was dead.' God knows what world he lived in, he obviously hadn't heard his usher's announcement.

Miskin played their trump card, the cancellation of the mandatory signature. After the evidence was all before him Latey looked up. 'Of course, this may well have been cancelled for a very different reason to that which you allege, Mr Miskin, may it not?'

I wanted to cheer. Once again that particular gun was shown to be empty.

'Very possibly, my Lord,' said Miskin uncomfortably and Latey stared hard at me. The lawyers could talk till they were black in the face; I am sure he had made up his mind about me after reading my letters and my affidavit of means. He said, 'This man has been very generous. Most generous, indeed.' On that, tears actually started to run down my face. It may sound childish but nothing in my life had hurt like the previous eighteen months of filth. It wasn't that a person like Rutter could ever touch me but I never stopped asking myself how could Christine sign such documents? Now, here we were, apparently returning to civilisation.

After constant pushing from me, Comyn reluctantly applied for and was promptly given a consolidation order. This meant that Latey agreed to hear all the issues raised in the divorce. He would get the full picture. I came out of court for the break brimming. My team, except for Paddy, were unenthusiastic. Calderan arrived from the office and was positively disappointed. This was alarming and incomprehensible to me. Rutter's policy of calling me every sort of villain on any pretext cried out to be presented in full to one judge, to show it up for what it was: just mudslinging. It must then become counter-productive. Once more my own lawyers were my worst allies. Why weren't they as pleased as I? I think a clue lies in a muttered aside I heard Calderan make to Comyn about, 'Next Monday.' Calderan seemed to be referring to another case starting on that day for which he had briefed Comyn. If my case ran over, as it would almost certainly now do in its consolidated state, Comyn would not be available. But, of course, settle mine quickly and he would be. This other case could have been longer, more lucrative, than mine. That seems to me to be the most plausible explanation of what followed.

The consolidation order started working for us at once. Miskin had just asked for £10,000 a year maintenance for Christine and got a dusty response from Latey. 'But this man's income for last year was only £9,000, Mr Miskin. The big years are over. He is not a company director but a writer in a very unstable business. I am going to base the order on his last year's income.' As I nudged Paddy at hearing my own arguments, dismissed by Taylor and Comyn, repeated from the bench, Rutter insisted Miskin claim that Christine needed extra to look after her mother. Latey's eyebrows shot up and the judicial performance slipped for a moment. It was the only time I heard his voice have a hard rasp to it. 'Are you saying that this woman is asking for extra maintenance for her mother at the same time as she is trying to have this man put in jail? That is lunacy, Mr Miskin, lunacy.'

Christine started to cry. We arrived at the moment when she would have to give evidence. I was looking forward to this and was sure she was not. I had already drawn Comyn's attention to several obvious inaccuracies in her affidavits and urged that he expose them. He had refused. He did so again and looked gloomier than ever. We had an argument. Two of her allegations about me directly contradicted each other, because each was designed for a judge who would never hear the other (I have quoted them earlier). Comyn brushed me aside and wanted to raise the offer that he had already - without my consent - made. 'How the hell can I pay that sort of money to the woman?' I asked.

'Well, you'll have to anyway,' was his opaque reply. This line was oft-repeated about many of his assertions. I tried to avoid Comyn and his constant badgering to settle, but he had made up his mind. He never let up and he never listened. Each morning before the proceedings started, each lunchtime and each evening he had tried every argument he could think of. 'They'll go to the Court of Appeal if they don't get what they want.' 'So what?' I had answered. 'It'll cost thousands.' 'Not to me if I win.' He urged me to give Christine our house and £50,000 as a final settlement, 'To get rid of her for good.' That remark alone showed his total lack of comprehension of my finances. I reminded him that even the £10,000 lump sum demanded by Rutter had to be on staggered payments because I didn't have the money. His pressure on me to settle was ceaseless, I am afraid it did not get through. He suggested the same thing an hour later. His pressure on me to settle was ceaseless but it was his behaviour in court that eventually made me crack. He had been throwing points away without regard for their accumulating worth: Christine's shares were undervalued, without challenge from him, by nearly £2,000; Miskin undervalued our house by nearly £10,000 as Comyn said nothing; the Trust was overvalued by about £10,000 with Comyn's agreement; the distortions exceeded £20,000, although Comyn had all the correct figures before him. However his paramount blunder rendered all that obsolete. He rose to his feet and told the judge that the Revenue had been informed about the Trust. I was appalled. It was like a kick in the face. He had confused the Revenue with the Bank of England thus leading Latey to believe that the tax situation was clear. The main prop of my case was thrown away. The risk of the Revenue assessment to the tune of £105,000 was never even suggested. I tried to pass Comyn a note. He crumpled it without looking at it. I tried to whisper that he had got things wrong and was told to shut up. In the end I was physically restrained by Grafton Green as I continued my efforts to get Comyn to understand what he had done. I gave up in despair.

Comyn once more started negotiating in the corridor with Miskin and Rutter. He came to me with some figures. I urged that Rutter's conduct of the case be put under fire. Comyn refused. Instead, he suggested to me, regarding the mandatory signature, that I admit to perjury but plead considerable pressure at the time and was extremely sorry. I refused and repeated that as soon as I got into the witness box I would tell the whole story, accuse Rutter and call on Taylor, Calderan and Grafton Green to confirm the *de facto, de jure* line they had advised. I was told that my conversations with my legal advisers were privileged and would not be allowed as evidence. Nevertheless Calderan and Comyn looked more worried than ever.

So, although the voice from the bench had appeared to be sane and level, the conduct of this case continued on its own mad course.

I see that I used the word 'negotiations' to grace the scene of near-hysterical haggling and squabbles that developed between the lawyers in that corridor. My use of labels was as inflated as Comyn's who always referred to the settlement he was fixed on signing as 'global.' 'I want this settlement to be global,' he said on several occasions to Calderan, making a neat little 'o' of his mouth as he breathed the word, so that I half expected a spherical contract to appear on his lips like legal bubble-gum. And Calderan would nod, eyes earnestly closed. 'Pooecisely.'

The lawyers at last agreed everything except whether the new rate of maintenance should be backdated to the date of Rutter's application the previous September. Rutter was insisting on backdating, probably to save his face, as Christine had lost through his actions. For precisely that reason I said no and sat in the corridor, hoping this piece of intractability on my part would dish everything. The sum involved was not important. Eventually the two QCs decided to put each side to the judge. Comyn took the opportunity, having thrown away so much, to get to his feet and wax quite convincingly emotional on the inappropriateness of concessions from me when she had taken an action for my commitment. Since Latey had already referred to this as lunacy, Comyn's success was predictable though he sat down in considerable puff.

Thus was the last detail settled. I signed, Latey put his stamp on the agreement and it became an official court order known as a consent order. She was given £7,000 p.a. maintenance, £4,000 for her, £3,000 for Dominic; the matrimonial home (I to pay off the £7,000 mortgage); most of our furniture and possessions; an insurance policy on my life; a lump sum of £10,000 (in instalments because I didn't have £10,000); I to pay the legal bills (over £20,000). The settlement left her worth some sixty to seventy thousand pounds-plus with a high, continuing income. I was left with certain bills of £50,000 plus the possible £100,000-plus tax bill, uncertain income and no cash to meet those bills.

My 'gains' were a few possessions from 1 Genoa Avenue. The committal action, which I would have preferred to contest, was dropped, as was the injunction that prevented me from molesting Christine, Dominic, 1 Genoa

Avenue and an unspecified area of paving stones round it. Actually, the fact that I could enter 1 Genoa Avenue to be with Dominic in his home was the sole thing I was glad about.

Latey announced that for procedural reasons he would have to go into open court to dismiss the committal action. So the barristers put wigs and paraphernalia on, the press were allowed in, and Latey returned in full judicial costume.

In his opening remark he said something that was a shock to me, out of all proportion to its importance: 'the husband is considerably older than the wife by nine years.' I had never thought of us as anything but contemporaries. By this 'considerably older' the law seemed to have created some new gap between us. Even this kind-looking man was continuing relentlessly to widen the schism. He uttered some words of sweet reason to the effect that he hoped this unhappy phase in our lives was over and that, without lawyers in such evidence (he made a point of this), perhaps relations between us would improve, especially for the sake of Dominic. He then went on pouring balm to the effect that having observed us in court he had the strong impression that we were two attractive, intelligent people who had somehow gone astray, and now was the time of reconciliation. All this affected me most terribly and as Paddy, who was next to me, averted his eyes, I sat convulsed with suppressed sobs, terrified that this would get into the papers. I must have looked as though I had terminal hiccups.

I tried afterwards to analyse why I was nearly out of control. It was simple. Latey's compassion merely brought to the surface my shame. I had been able to accept everything to date because I had seen it was being on a temporary basis only. I had expected every issue to be aired, that someone in authority would see the whole picture and dispense justice. But now, even when the judge seemed to be just the man I was looking for, despair at my own team had made me sell out. The law is not just an ass, but Comyn and the rest made it a senseless, vicious, humiliating monster. A QC amok and unencumbered by the facts or reason is a sight I never want to see again. To hell with the actual sums of money, in settling I had betrayed everything I believed in about Justice (with the capital), standing up for myself, indeed everything I had done in and with my life. I had betrayed my private dream of discrediting Rutter and thus re-establishing love or at least friendship with Christine (although I still hoped). And I had betrayed Dominic. To settle then was against my every instinct yet I had sat and put my name to that bit of paper. Every time I now read of somebody who has signed a confession and later tried to retract it, I know it could be false. You can do something in such a situation that defies reason. I had lived with guilt all my life, but to find myself under the control of intense self-disgust was a new experience.

We filed out of court and I leaned against a wall hiccoughing. As the press were shooed away there was a minor commotion; the schedule of chattels that I was to take from our house was lost. Rutter had had the sole copy, now nobody could find it. My team couldn't even handle anything as modest as that. He produced the full list of the contents of the matrimonial home and, watched by Grafton Green and Comyn, who both said nothing, made out a new schedule, modified considerably against me. I stared, uncaring, at the trio while this theft was concluded, then ran the gauntlet of photographers on the pavement and went back to my flat.

Bill came with me. We bought a bottle of champagne to drink a toast in celebration of the end of the divorce. Some celebration.

'Now you can get on with your life,' he said after one particularly empty pause. 'I know this is trite but work is the best cure when other things aren't—'

'I know, Bill.'

'How is—?'

'Don't ask me how the writing's coming along. It isn't.' My so-called career sounded like some sickly relative kept discreetly in the back bedroom. 'Don't worry. I'll get restarted now.'

'Good. Good night, Terry.'

'Good night, Bill. Thanks for coming. Thanks for everything. See you soon.' Then I sat catatonically in my expensive pad for the rest of the evening. I had been given a comprehensive hiding on every level of my life, and I hadn't even begun the process of soaking it up.

―――――――

This should, of course, be the end of the story of Christine and me. Unfortunately, we were just getting under way. What was supposed to be (no matter how ill-advised), a document of separation was, in fact, the opposite. We were entangled worse than before it had existed, locked into a closed circle of conflict. How and why would soon become clear. The sell-out of my case by Comyn had already been capped by - of all people - Bill. Bill, the only legal adviser I still felt I could trust, had already committed two cock-ups of monumental proportions and followed them up with something worse: a cover-up designed to save his own skin. And there he was, in my flat, having a comforting drink with me, knowing what was waiting for me just round the next corner.

Chapter XXXII

July - September 1971

I must have been dimly aware of the dimensions of the disaster to which I had been an unwilling party because I telephoned Paddy the next morning. 'Can't we tear up that agreement and have it all out in court?'

'No. It's law now. You've done it.'

My heart continued to sink. I had crossed some sort of watershed, but what? Some answers weren't long in coming, first in minor ways. Comyn and the rest of them had forced me more or less completely into the power of Rutter. I realise that my use of 'forced' and 'into the power of Rutter' sounds melodramatic, but it is both apt and accurate, as I will show, first in small ways.

That same morning Rutter took out the decree absolute without waiting a few more days for me to transfer the house to Christine, thus needlessly incurring for me a capital gains tax bill of about £2,000 for something I was giving away. My team had failed to take the proper legal precaution to prevent this occurring. This caused an expensive squabble about the date of transfer of the house that took them all back in front of Mr Justice Latey without my even knowing. He gave both sides a telling off. Next, I learned from Paddy, in an indiscreet moment, that Derek Clogg, the senior partner of Theodore Goddard and company, had had a row with Calderan about the settlement. Clogg thought it ridiculous. Paddy's indiscretion sprang from the fact that he was clearly most upset about the settlement. His unease came off him in waves at that time, although he was at the heart of Theodore Goddard's calamitous handling of my divorce. Paradoxically, he was a comfort to me, someone who had a fellow-feeling. I believe him to have been a basically honest person who had panicked and now he was ashamed. He was so inexperienced I believe he never realised what disaster his action would lead to - not for him but for his client.

I received my 'chattels', as per the amended schedule to the settlement: my antique ivory chess set had thirty-one pieces ('sorry, Dominic lost one playing with them'); my chess table, nicely inlaid Regency, had deep scratches over its surface ('sorry, Dominic was playing with a knife and before I could stop him...'); a set of six glasses had dwindled to one whole glass, plus one chipped ('sorry, the cleaning lady dropped them'); so the list went on.

But the trivia soon gave way to serious matters.

I had two accesses to Dominic, and walked though the front door of 1 Genoa Avenue for the first time for fifteen months. I longed to make these accesses work. Politeness again ruled between Christine and me. I was a willing handyman. It was very satisfying to sit in the kitchen and mend a fuse or bang a nail in as Dominic sprayed his tea about from the vantage point of his high chair. However, Christine's mother died within the month. I have never found out precisely what killed Babs, perhaps the years of cortisone for her arthritis, perhaps she did it herself she was so unhappy, but I do know that she had already been in hospital, possibly terminally ill, while they were claiming our old house and extra maintenance for her in court. She had been there since I had taken Dominic to the park weeks earlier. Neither we nor Latey had been told of this.

On my next access to 1 Genoa Avenue, as I was leaving, Christine suddenly said in the doorway, 'You killed my mother. Thank you.' That awful semi-hysterical growl was in her voice which had been a moment before relaxed and chatty. I turned in surprise and leaped back as the door was banged. Further entry was forbidden to me. Access became the Berlin Wall hand-over; the doorstep of 1 Genoa Avenue, Checkpoint Charlie. Now that I had given her our house, no injunctions were needed to keep me out, just a simple, 'No.' Nevertheless the inevitable letter from Rutter followed, threatening another injunction if I ever tried to cross the threshold again. Latey's new era of reconciliation had dawned.

A new ingredient surged to the forefront of my feelings: a bitter, boiling, impotent contempt for Christine. She was, after all excuses were made, behind everything. I had, till the hearing before Latey, attempted to canalise my anger onto Rutter - a useful target, as Joe Jackson had pointed out months earlier - believing that he would be, in due course, discredited and removed, prior to Christine and me making some sort of peace. Now, instead, he was vindicated and it seemed that all that was petty and squalid was triumphant. No amount of rationalising could disguise the fact that the buck stopped with her. To have been attacked so vehemently by someone I loved, then let down so comprehensively by those who were paid handsomely to guard my interest, gave a taste to life that I gagged on every hour of every day. Hopelessly I wrote to Paddy Grafton Green regarding Dominic:

> He is extremely fond of me and clings to me a great deal when I
> see him. When I returned him to Genoa Avenue on the access
> after the one mentioned above, he screamed when I left him at
> the front door. There was no way of avoiding this distressing and
> unnecessary scene. On the next access we were about to have a
> repetition of the same business, so I took him from the nanny
> and went into the house with him and told him to go and look
> for his mother, and then slipped out unnoticed. I would suggest

262

that if Christine really gave a monkey's fart about Dominic, she would agree that I bring him in, bath him, read him a story and put him to bed. He's in bed by 6.00 anyway and I would love to do it. If Christine finds it too distressing to see me, then the house is quite large enough for us to avoid each other for half an hour, and the nanny seems to be able to survive my company for one afternoon a week without actually breaking into a cold sweat.

It is Dominic's birthday next Thursday and I hope you will take the opportunity to remind Rutter of that fact and of the Judge's remarks to Christine that access need not be specified hours, but extended to include birthdays, Christmas, etc. I do not expect for one minute that they are going to invite me round for his birthday party, but I would like you to make a formal request that requires from them a formal refusal. Let's try and put them in the wrong for once.

Paddy didn't send that request and, of course, I was not invited, so Dominic's birthday party became the focal point of my resentment. It was my son's birthday, in my house, paid for with my money, was how my logic ran, and if Dominic had had any choice I knew where I would have been on that Sunday afternoon, instead of sitting in my flat burning.

Sian came for lunch. Afterwards she read the papers while I fidgeted. At last I said 'I'm going to Dominic's party.'

She sighed with relief. 'I thought you'd never say it. Have a nice time.'

The front door of 1 Genoa Avenue was open and the house full of people I didn't know. I walked up to Christine and said, 'Hallo,' chummily. She blinked in disbelief, but as I didn't vanish, offered me a glass of champagne. I wandered. There was a newly-acquired baby grand on which stood a silver-framed photograph of her and Rutter outside the Law Courts; she, smiling, taller than he, her arm through his. Robert Peake and a couple of other old friends - theatricals, sparse among the civilians - greeted me with genuine pleasure. I was surprised to see them there. 'Hallo, didn't know you were coming,' said Robert in his affable, half-absent way, and added some weeks later in the same tone, 'Oh, dear, what perfectly frightful people Christine seems to know now.' Hordes of children were in the garden having a game which involved rackets and shuttlecocks and noise. Dominic was participating, grubby and happy. He greeted me with similar affability and abstraction to Robert's, then dragged me to join the game. Rutter was among the guests. I waited for a writ or summons to arrive, tied to the next shuttle, but he kept well away. Nat was matey, and various children pleased. No stranger tried to make my acquaintance. I must have looked like Banquo's ghost. I had a good game with the children, several glasses of champagne (crates of it were consumed, I noticed) and chatted to Christine's Auntie Nancy, who, as I was leaving, suddenly said, 'He's a fine little boy, Terry.

He's well looked after. She brings him up well, don't you worry.' The last three words were not a plea for me to refrain from anxiety, but emphasis.

'I'm sure, Nancy,' I said, neutrally. Then I added, 'Thank you,' to whatever it was in her that had prompted her words and their tone. I kissed Christine and left. She later said to me 'You looked pathetic. Everyone said so. I was ashamed for you' but whether that remark was an accurate observation or a reprisal for gate-crashing I am not sure. Either seems likely. As a result of my action I returned to my flat feeling briefly unpathetic.

The event sparked off a volley of lawyers' letters of standard silliness and length, of which the cherry was Rutter's -

> When our Client saw him he said to her 'Hallo' and being taken
> by complete surprise at his presence, our client said 'Hello.'

There was a protracted argument between Rutter and Paddy as to how many guests were present, then a threat by Rutter:

> It is to be hoped that your client will not make it necessary for
> further lengthy proceedings to be embarked on...

Rutter's underlining of the word 'lengthy' clearly showed his pride in his victory. He thought his legal technique inspired dread and was crowing. Oh, God, how could I have given way to Comyn?

The full financial disaster of the settlement was made clear a week or two later in September. The bungling of my entire team of legal advisers was laid bare on the table for us all to stare at (although the cover-ups of both sets of solicitors, Bill and Paddy, still remained hidden, the ruinous figures were displayed in full view). It was quite an afternoon.

I had already asked Bill how I could use Trust money to resolve the financial problems. This was unsound, of course, before knowing what the Revenue would do, but now necessary. 'We must go to tax counsel,' said Bill. 'He will explain the full position to us.' I was only vaguely aware that a tax counsel was an expert in tax law who, Moses-like, handed down the tablets. The meeting was to have been with Harvey McGregor QC. Suddenly it was changed to a junior tax counsel called Andrew Park. Bill, Frank Young and assistant, Paddy Grafton Green and I trooped into a modern block in Grays Inn and sat on steel-framed chairs round a modern boardroom table with ball-point and pad set for each of us. I fingered a document of some thirty pages that was at my place. It dealt with every detail of the Trust and my actions relating to it to date.

Under the jaw-breaking legalities and quotations of precedents it was a marvellous piece of work. It had clarity, incisiveness and accuracy. It spelled out the law in black and white and made clear down to halfpennies and farthings what my financial position was. It dispelled the doubt and head-shaking of Taylor and his 'tuts', and the vague looks of the others, and the glib assurances of Comyn. It was as neat a bit of work as any scientific paper and could have been produced at any time since my return from France three years earlier, if any one of my army of highly-paid legal advisers had simply thought to suggest it.

What was of paramount importance was that it could and should have been part of my case for all to see. It was clear, hard, irrefutable, legally-binding evidence of my total tax liabilities incurred via the Trust. All the expensive, interminable financial (and therefore access) disputes of the last eighteen months could have been strangled at birth.

Park was early thirties, studious and pleasant-looking. He looked as though he was fast on his feet, an ex-wing-three-quarter who had lived a blameless life. His fair hair kept falling into his eyes which were blue and anxious - the taxman can creep up from any direction. What he had to say was devastating and he knew it. Each missile was fired in a dispassionate, light baritone faintly reminiscent of Alan Bennett.

In essence his Opinion showed that Bill had been talking drivel for years:

1) My action, taken on Bill's advice, in getting the mandatory signature was of no tax consequence whatsoever.

2) My action in sending $2000 from Switzerland to New York for Christine (for the famous mink coat), sanctioned by Bill to be safe as the money never came near this country, rendered me liable to be taxed and surtaxed at the full rate under regulation ICTA 1970 (?) S478 for *every penny that had ever flowed* into the Trust, a total of over £115,000, making a debt of over £100,000 to the Revenue. An expensive fur coat for Christine. (There were additional complexities round that liability but I will keep things simple).

3) Because of the method Bill had selected of bringing Trust money into the UK to buy my flat (i.e. by declaring a dividend between the Trust companies), I was liable to an income and surtax bill of £24,500 on the £27,000 purchase, making the flat cost £51,500 in total. This liability was *due already* and was *in addition* to that in 2) above. Had Bill chosen another method there would have been no tax liability whatsoever.

Thanks to Bill, I owed about £130,000 in tax on the Trust alone, more than the total sum that had ever flowed into it.

Andrew Park suggested that, in all good sense, the Revenue might not seek to gain the double payments that made up the full amount, so my debt might be only £105,000. He paused with a fleeting, nervous smile. 'However, what has good sense got to do with tax law?' I already owed £40,000 to lawyers and Christine, had an outstanding tax liability on any UK earnings and had signed away eighty per cent of my income in maintenance. I was on paper, bankrupt. It was just a question of which bill would deliver the *coup de grace.*

Frank Young told me later that I took it very well. I am not so sure. I think I was studiously blank. Perhaps I was stunned. Anyway, I sat and nodded as Andrew Park explained my financial demise. 'I see. Yes, of course.' 'Ah, yes, so that means...?' 'Hm, and there's no way out of...?' 'Yes, quite. Extraordinary how it works, isn't it?' 'Thank you very much, Mr Park. Good afternoon.'

When the meeting broke up I was conscious that the only pair of eyes I could find to meet mine in the room was Park's, and then only in discreet blue flashes that were intended to be neutral but were not. He, at least, was dying to know what next.

Of course, I still didn't know, as I assimilated Bill's incompetence and negligence, of his far worse action, his cover-up: that he had fixed both this meeting and the paperwork we were looking at. Time to explain.

Early in June (on my prompting, I think), weeks before the divorce hearing, Bill had sent to Harvey McGregor QC a set of questions about Trust matters. Grundy had answered those questions and then added a note, '...however...I am far more perturbed about...' and he had gone on to say exactly what Park said in 3) above. That was why my meeting with the QC, McGregor, had been switched to the junior, Park, and McGregor's Opinion concealed. Bill had then put the same questions to Park but phrased them to pass responsibility for incurring the tax liability on to me. For example, he said:

> At the time of the purchase (of the flat) Mr Frisby was advised by Instructing solicitors (Bill) that liability for UK tax would be a consequence of this purchase,

Well, that was, of course, tosh. I would have slept on the embankment first. But it wasn't his feeble invention that mattered, it was something much shabbier.

Bill had received McGregor's Opinion on June eighteenth, four weeks before the divorce hearing. He could have given me that Opinion at once, for me to make a cornerstone of my case and present to the judge to show him my real financial situation. Instead, to save his skin, as he had sat outside the court for three full days, waiting to give evidence, sometimes chatting amicably with me, he had kept quiet about the written evidence in his briefcase that would have prevented me signing anything. I dare say it might even have stopped Comyn in his tracks. Bill had held the key to it all and concealed it for his own welfare. Then, after coming home with me and having a celebratory glass of champagne, he had gone back to his office, re-phrased his instructions to blame me and sent them to Park, cutting out Grundy.

All this I learned years later.

When I showed Neil Taylor the Andrew Park Opinion his lips were pursed to a vertical straight line. 'Parts of the Consent Order could be varied if there was a change in circumstances,' he said.

'But there is no change in circumstances,' I answered. 'Only in our perception of them. They are the same circumstances as when I signed. Why didn't you tell me to get tax counsel's Opinion for the hearing?'

There was no satisfactory answer from him, or Paddy, or Calderan. The answer was, of course, that not one of them had thought of it. I hadn't even known that such a thing as an Opinion existed.

Calderan trotted me off to see some female partner in his firm, Blanche Lucas 'our tax expert,' who could only suggest that perhaps we could find 'someone more-er-imaginative' than Andrew Park to analyse my tax affairs. The only practical solution Calderan, Grafton ('our trust expert') Green, or Neil Taylor could come up with (and they all arrived at this and suggested it to me separately), was that I should emigrate. In case I took their advice I was promptly presented with their bill for £7,159 outstanding.

Those weeks from the settlement in July into the Autumn of 1971 were the worst I can remember. It was not, of course, the money, it was everything. It seemed that there was no bottom to anything. The choking, blinding frustration engendered by my helplessness gave rise to revenge and action fantasies of lurid colours. Oh, to have gone bankrupt and merely walked away from them all - the knife was infinitely preferable to the rack - but such bracing simplifications were not possible in the closed, vicious circle devised by English divorce law and refined by my legal team.

Something profound happened to me in that time. I had had an excellent memory all my life; now I found myself forgetting everything. That feeling of living in a tunnel with darkened, misty edges became overwhelming. I tried to get a hold on my emotions, but couldn't. I found myself, not only talking to myself - as I had done all my life - but shouting, muttering in public and sometimes just standing in my flat. I seemed to be in a whirlpool that was sucking me out of existence. One day I was sitting at my desk trying to work when Mary, my cleaning lady, arrived (yes, all the trappings of material abundance remained. *Soup* was still running, producing money.

The act of declaring myself bankrupt, something I longed to do, was not possible, I was told). Mary normally stayed over two hours. She said, 'Good morning, would you like some coffee?' I said 'Please.' The next thing I remember was staring at the cup of cold coffee at my elbow. It was afternoon. Mary was long gone. I had sat immobile for hours. If I didn't do something at once I was going to end up in the bin.

I met two people who restored me. The first was a shrink. Our acquaintance was brief but vital. After reviewers, lawyers and priests I view psychiatrists with the most suspicion. However, Philip Akeroyd rejected the term psychiatrist, he called himself a psycho-therapist. He was pleasantly father-like and listened to me with well-paid patience, performing the valuable function of dispelling with casual authority the last vestiges of guilt I felt towards Christine. I suppose the time was ripe. I found myself telling him about my revulsion at Christine's pregnancy; the efforts not to heave when asked by her to feel the foetus kicking, and all the details I have already set down. I cursed my paucity of imagination. Couldn't I see that that bulge and swollen flesh and veins would result in a Dominic? 'I'll never feel the same with a second pregnancy,' I said, 'after seeing and loving the first child.'

But he waved all that away. 'No, no, no, it's very common. And often repeated with the second, third, fourth child. Quite commonplace. About one in four or five fathers-to-be feel like that. If you don't like the mess, stay away from it is the best solution. Plenty do. No point in rubbing your nose in it. You can't do anything anyway, so why worry?'

So the simple flick of a light switch resolved the grotesque shadows and half-shapes of my ignorance into the normal furniture of one household in five. If Christine had been told, by a person with MD after his name, that such feelings were commonplace, instead of my botched attempt at confession, I am sure that she would have given me a metaphorical aspirin and proudly described the symptoms to her girl friends over coffee. And following her lead in all matters domestic, I would have played the inadequate male, laughed and relaxed. How easy life could be.

Philip Akeroyd continued with his offhand bombshells. 'Your present problem, Terry, apart from guilt, is not a psychological one. It is practical.' He then inverted the old joke - you don't have an inferiority complex, you're just inferior - by saying, 'You don't have a persecution complex, you appear to have been well and truly persecuted.' He sat puffing his pipe and staring into the gas-fire. I can't remember if he smoked a pipe or not but he has a pipe in my memory. 'Nobody likes being done, and you seem to have been spectacularly well turned over, so you've reacted accordingly. You must either swallow hard and learn to accept it—'

'I can't. I can't even walk away from it. They won't leave me alone.'

'Well, then, fight.'

'Yes, but how?'

'Well, I don't really know. I'm a psychotherapist. What you need is a lawyer.'

It was one of the worst lines I had ever heard.

Stephen Mitchell was a junior solicitor in the firm of Whitehouse, Vaux and Elborne (later Elborne, Mitchell). Philip Akeroyd's son, Timothy, was his assistant. The firm dealt with Lloyds insurance cases. When yet another oil tanker disappears profitably at sea, Stephen and Timothy were two of those who turn a beady eye on the ship owner who is holding out his hand for the insurance. They became senior partners in the firm.

Stephen and Timothy are two of the goodies in this story, indeed major goodies, but if I had been a casting director, Stephen would never have got the part. He looked like a prototype Mafia lawyer: big, solid rather than fat, black-haired, heavy lids, hooded dark eyes, careful responses. He was in his middle thirties and looked not a little menacing. The only contradiction was a very nice smile, an excellent combination of boyishness and reassurance. His careful responses were explained by an occasional speech hesitation. It was hard to resist the temptation to help him out.

He was sitting in my flat. It is the first picture of him that I can recall. His blue and white candy-striped shirt was squeezing untidily out of his waistband like toothpaste, and his tie was off-centre. He was holding a drink and rumbling quietly in response to my story and the meal we had just eaten, through which he had chomped and listened. I often wonder why Stephen bothered with me. We weren't even acquaintances, let alone friends, and there was little in it for his firm. He merely said later that I obviously needed help and it was interesting. There was once a muttered aside about being ashamed of members of his profession. Neither Stephen nor Timothy had any experience of divorce work.

I finished my story, finally sputtering into silence after the umpteenth afterthought. Stephen had a weighty cogitate then delivered his legal opinion in his pleasant, detached manner.

'Hm. Yes. Hm.' He whirred. I learned that these little noises were to get the vocal motor past the stalling-point of his inhibition. 'It's certainly a terrible fffucking mess, isn't it?'

'Yes. Now. It needn't have been.'

'It sounds like a specimen case compiled to demonstrate all the built-in dangers of our legal system: profusion of decision-making, no proper central management, bad communications...' He trailed off, then gathered himself again. 'Hm. Yes. Hm. and that's *before* we get to your allegations of misconduct.' The motor idled for a few moments, then a smile sidled across his considerable face. 'You reckon that without Rutter there wouldn't have been a divorce in the first place...'

'I'm sure of it.'

'...and that most of the lawyers you've come into contact with for the last eighteen months have been either negligent or dishonest.'

'That's right.'

He looked at me for some while, the grin at the back of his eyes. I resisted any reaction. He went on. 'Hm. Yes. Hm. You know, don't you, that the world is full of divorced men saying that their wives' - sssorry, their ex-wives' lawyers caused it all?'

'I've heard something of the kind.'

'And that the law courts are full of sad little men with writs who claim that they've been done by the legal profession and can't get redress.'

'Yes.'

'They're so common that they have an official legal name. They're called vexatious litigants. They're a pppain in the arse and mostly cracked.'

'I know how I sound,' I said, depressed by his scepticism. My fear of being halfway round the bend was already strong enough.

'Oh, no, no, no,' said Stephen, 'don't misunderstand me. I believe you. But I wouldn't like to have to convince the Law Society.'

I clutched at the straw, indeed almost crushed it in my eagerness. 'You believe me?'

'Oh, yes. It's classic, isn't it. You see, if you allege that these people got together to do you down that's tttripe isn't it? Why the hell should separate respectable legal firms and barristers gang up on one poor little client? You'd be laughed out of any court, and rightly so. But look carefully at what you're really saying. Your case was mishandled, basic mistakes were made early on and then when the whole edifice was seen to be rickety, instead of owning up, everybody ran for cover. It's the oldest one in the business. As for Rutter...' Stephen paused and had a reflective grin into his drink. 'Those little divorce lawyers...it's how they are. I know, I was articled to one. He has spent a lifetime that has conditioned him to contest everything down to the date on the letters. It's very old hat but it's safe. It's taking care of the client. Of course,' he changed gear for emphasis, 'in divorce, it's the worst possible attitude, but that's the system. I don't know whether he has gone over the edge and actually acted improperly in this case, but one thing is interesting...' I had to fight not to say 'What? what?' impatiently '...if he didn't act improperly you seem to have a prima facie case against your mob for alleging that he did'. Stephen had a pause, a drink and a rumble to recover from this speech.

I tried not to feel excited and said with a little more conviction, 'I know it sounds mad, but I'm not just saying he behaved improperly, I'm saying he *caused* our divorce. I've lived through it and I know Christine. He did.'

Stephen cogitated again. 'Well, you're not exactly disinterested, are you? I'm inclined to believe you, but how can you ever prove it? You'll never get her to say it now, and she would be the key witness.' That was a nasty blow to my principal fantasy, the one in which Christine and I were reconciled. I would start casually to get the facts from her. 'Darling, why did you...?' 'When you swore on oath so-and-so, did you really...? 'How could you ever have thought or said that...?' The ravenous curiosity that I had as to why Christine had behaved as she had was always answered in my fantasy by her exposure of Rutter. 'You see, I was mixed up and he said...' 'Everything was so complicated and he made it simple...' 'I didn't know who to turn to and he...' then the tears of relief that the nightmare was over and the peace. Her emotional pattern repeating itself.

Stephen went on with the immediate practical problem. 'You have willingly signed—'

That issue was still too red-hot for me not to react. 'I wasn't willing. It was the way Comyn mishandled my case, coupled with—'

Stephen managed to get going fast enough to override my intervention. 'James Cccomyn QC is one of the most respected and reputable men in the law. You may think he's a ppprick, he may well be one, but that alters nothing. To all intents and pppurposes you have signed a settlement. It is known as a Consent Order and is at the heart of English law. It is the hardest thing in the world to overturn.'

'Who said I wanted to overturn it?'

'Well, wwwhat do you want?'

There was quite a pause. I knew what I wanted to say 'I want this exposed. I want all the lies and deceit publicised. I want people to see what goes on in our divorce system. I want—' Well, it could all have been summed up in one word. I wanted to scream, 'I want justice,' but that was too feeble. In that pause was the shocking realisation that I hadn't said, 'I want my wife and child and home back.' Until that settlement, that was what I had wanted and only that. Now that longing was buried under the bitterness. Was that burial temporary or permanent, I wondered. Perhaps things had gone too far.

I was able to say in a normal voice, because it was acceptable coming from me, 'I want to write a book about the whole story.' Prominent in my mind was the thought that, a long way further down the road, the most important reader of this book would be an adult Dominic. Who knows what he would be told of his father in the years between.

'Hm. Hm. Good. Yes. Admirable. But to get it published you'll have to beat them at their game, too. To defend a libel action you've got to be able to prove that the alleged libel is true. Even when you prove that, you can't defame if there is any malice intended...' he paused and smiled while I pulled a pious face to denote my innocence of such base motives, '...and it must be for the public good.'

'Well, that's open and shut, isn't it,' I said eagerly. 'If ever anything needed shouting from the roof tops, it's the goings-on of our lovely divorce lawyers.'

271

'I think I agree. Right, what we need is to collect our thoughts. You must write down an outline of the whole thing. There's nothing like writing something down to discover what the facts really are and what you think. Then what we will need is evidence. What have you got?'

'Buggerall.'

He started to laugh. 'Tricky, isn't it.'

By now I felt light-hearted enough to join in. 'What d'you need?'

'Dunno. We'll find out when you've written your outline.'

And so I set out, having lost everything to the lawyers at their game, to take them on at mine.

Chapter XXXIII

Winter 1971-72

With an enthusiasm that was entirely lacking from my current attempt at writing a play, I tried to order my thoughts and unravel the facts into the outline that Stephen had suggested. This concentrated the mind wonderfully. Life is not only more complex than fiction, I re-discovered, but a bloody sight untidier. Art was elementary stuff in comparison. Many objectives for this enterprise jostled for precedence in my overheated mind: to sue someone (Rutter? My own advisers?); to get them struck off or whatever; to change the law; just to tell the story for Dominic later; to give myself some peace of mind. All these and more were there, but I had no real idea what I wanted to achieve beyond the generalised aim of 'to put right a wrong.' Mind you, isn't that enough to start from? It seems to have inspired many a quest. So all my creative energies went into this. Talk about misdirection of your talents. People can go wrong in many ways.

Christine suddenly agreed to have lunch with me. Of course it had to be in the best possible place, so I suggested the Mirabelle. I was more excited than I would have admitted. I would be able to ask her some of those questions that had been smouldering in me for over a year and a half. Without litigation pending, and relaxed, I felt sure I would get some answers. I was badly in need of them.

Stephen read my outline, about forty pages. 'Well, if you want to say *that*' he underlined a passage, 'you must have evidence. If you want to say *this*,' more underlining, 'you must be able to prove it.' And so on. The list of things I could, or could not, verify in a supposed libel action grew. The 'could nots' far outnumbered the 'coulds' and my projected book, if it was to include important points, was a non-starter. So came the idea of my tape-recording conversations with my lawyers. I can't remember whether Stephen suggested it or I did, but I grabbed it eagerly. Although little of the evidence we wanted was on paper (lawyers being what they are), when I thought of what my advisers had all privately said to me of each other I guessed I would have little difficulty in getting what we wanted on tape. The tapes would be our last line of defence. If my ex-legal advisers didn't challenge my book, the tapes wouldn't be needed. If they did, we could nail them. The problem was Rutter. It was unlikely that I would be having a heart-to-heart with him. Then I remembered my lunch with Christine. Of course, she was the key. I would tape-record my long-nurtured questions and satisfy both my curiosity and the rules of evidence at the same time. To pre-empt your enquiry, let me say that I had no doubts about the ethics of this tape-recording campaign, nor of starting it with Christine. I was after the truth and merely eager to start.

The best piece of equipment I could find that would do the job (this was 1971, pre-microchip) was a radio microphone. I would have a microphone in my top pocket under a handkerchief, the batteries in my pockets and the aerial wrapped round me. Someone had to be working the tape recorder and receiver within range - say, fifty yards. It was unsatisfactory, but the best I could manage at short notice. I went to Ivor to be my operative.

'I'm all for doing those lawyers, Terry, but Christine...'

'It's not her I want. It's Rutter. Look, if she's been telling the truth in her affidavits she's got no worries. If she hasn't, well, what the hell?'

Ivor became an unwilling conscript. He was going to have to sit in the back of my car outside the Mirabelle with headphones on, change the tapes and keep the machine tuned in, while I ate the expensive lunch. In spite of his discomfort and reluctance, the surprising fact that the operation was fun soon got to him. I was already addicted. Half an hour before Christine was due I parked the car and Ivor on a meter outside the Mirabelle and walked through the front door in Curzon Street talking out loud to myself to test the equipment. I went down the stairs, ignored the head waiter's offer of assistance and walked once round the basement restaurant, still talking, then out again. 'How was it?' I asked Ivor back in the car.

'Oh, wonderful. Loud and clear until you said you were going into the actual restaurant. Then it went dead. Then it came up again as you said you were coming out. It was terrific in the gents. I heard you pee and everything. Perhaps you should give her lunch in there.'

'Bloody Hell. That thing won't transmit from underground.' I could have spat at my ignorance.

'Does that mean it's off? he said, trying not to sound pleased.

'Come on. We've still got fifteen minutes.' I ran to Wheeler's fish restaurant round the corner. They were fully booked. A fiver soon changed that. I tore back to our original parking place and when we got the car round to Wheeler's a convenient meter appeared on cue. I ran back to the Mirabelle and stood panting and dishevelled to greet Christine coming out of the ladies. She was wearing the New York fur coat, (price, under $2,000; potential tax incurred, £105,000). It looked very nice.

'Quick. Come on,' I said, taking her arm and hurrying her out.

'What's up with you?' She did her cool amused stuff in the face of my open panic.

'There's someone in there I don't want to meet,' I said. 'A ghastly shit in films. I've just booked us into Wheelers'. Everywhere else is full. I don't know about trying to prove the truth, I was running up a pretty good score of lies on my own account.

Christine giggled. 'What have you been up to? I bet it was some female in there and you didn't want to be seen with me.' I gave an ambiguous shrug and steered her past the parked car containing Ivor.

The lunch was a weird and painful pleasure. There were enough layers of unreality merely in the set-up, but the content of our conversation was right into never-never land. As long as I didn't touch on the recent past, gaiety prevailed. I positively enjoyed being with her again and she had come determined to impress. But any attempt by me to move onto serious matters was a threat not to be endured. Her old emotional pattern seemed set solid at stage one in the mould of twenty-one months of legal advice. I tried to guess at the internal upheavals that had led to such determined, rosy rationalisations. Pangloss and Barbara Cartland are amateurs in comparison. So that was how she was dealing with the gash across our lives, I thought. It hadn't happened. There had been a messy divorce, yes; her ex had been difficult, but nice Mr Rutter had dealt with that. Her hands were clean and now a veil was drawn. My efforts to draw back the veil and expose the gaping wound were the efforts of a madman. Indeed, I was called that several times. It was tempting to believe her. One typical exchange went roughly thus.

ME:	Darling, why did you do so-and-so?
CHRISTINE:	You're mad.
ME:	But you did do it.
CHRISTINE:	You're mad.
ME:	But you did.
CHRISTINE:	You're mad. You're sick.
ME:	But you did.
CHRISTINE:	I'm not answering your questions.
ME:	But you did. You know you did. We both know it.
CHRISTINE:	Yes. So what?
ME:	So I'm not mad. Madness is in *not* acknowledging it, surely.
CHRISTINE:	You are. You're sick.

And the subject was changed . Here are some verbatim extracts:
After considerable discussion of food, the menu
and the wine list, the waiter left with the order.

ME:	So that's what it all comes down to. I'm taking you out for fish and chips (both laugh). I'm crazy about the lump of rubbish you've got on your hand.
CHRISTINE:	It's not rubbish. They're emeralds.
ME:	You're looking very expensive.

275

CHRISTINE:	I am expensive.
ME:	I know.

Both laugh.

ME:	I get knotted up about Dominic.
CHRISTINE:	You should be happy, like I am.
ME:	You see him, don't you?
CHRISTINE:	You can see him whenever you like.
ME:	That's news to me.
CHRISTINE:	You know jolly well you see him every week.
ME:	Can I take him away with me for the weekend?
CHRISTINE:	Where to?
ME:	My mother's would be best... I've never put him to bed in my life.
CHRISTINE:	No-one asked you to leave.
ME:	What?
CHRISTINE:	No-one asked you to leave.
ME:	No-one asked me to be slung out.
CHRISTINE:	If we are going to have this sort of conversation, I'm going...
ME:	Do you know why I cancel seeing him sometimes, because it hurts too much to see him. It's too painful to see him. Sorry.
CHRISTINE:	That is very, very selfish of you.
ME:	I know. I can't help it. But if it's selfish of me not to see him, why did you stop me for six months?
CHRISTINE:	Oh.
ME:	Then, why? I just want to know why.
CHRISTINE:	You didn't want to anyway.
ME:	What?
CHRISTINE:	You didn't want to... I never, never, never would turn Dominic against you.
ME:	But stopping me seeing him is, sort of.
CHRISTINE:	I have never... I cannot remember one single time when you didn't see Dominic when you wanted to...

I thought of the mountain of documents, the hours of court actions, all created to stop me doing just that. And she was saying these thing to *me*. I began to wonder which of us was mad.

But these extracts don't give the flavour of the whole. Most was a bubbly skate on the thinnest of ice. And if the gaiety was forced initially, the atmosphere became warm and genuine from time to time. The mere fact of the pleasure we took - had always taken - in each other, even in such circumstances, made me doubly sad. To set beside the exchange about Dominic there is one sentence that leaps from the tape all these years later.

CHRISTINE: I used to drive round to your flat in Smith Street and sit
                  in the car and cry.

At first I was moved by this remark - as Christine always moved me -
before I remembered that, like her claim that I could see Dominic whenever
I liked, it did not remotely fit the facts. What it did fit was the myth she had
arranged round herself like an insulating bubble. Facts cannot compete
with myths. In her glossy, glassy myth even to refer to the past as it had
actually happened was - to use her word over that lunch - mad. And now
even her recall of everything was phoney. She had always deceived me, so
my thoughts ran, now she was deceiving herself. There she sat, gay, charming
and apparently utterly sincere, but shut in her never-never land. I wondered
if the door to reality was permanently slammed. It looked it.

We stayed on for hours in Wheelers because we re-discovered some of
our old enjoyment of each other. But we were separated by a chasm; she,
promoting her myth to the one person who knew it to be untrue (and even
then my first reaction had been to believe her and accept it. I never learned),
me, with a wire wrapped round me and a microphone behind the
handkerchief in my breast pocket, there to establish the Truth. I wonder
which of us was the madder. Or sadder.

She had an appointment at three p.m. but she brushed that aside and
we sat talking till nearly four. I walked her round the corner to a shop
where she was picking something up, then raced back to Ivor, excited just
as much by the fact of having been with her as with the taping project. I
practically had to shoehorn him from the car.

'Bloody Hell, you two can't half talk, can't you?' he said, stretching various
bits to get life and warmth back into them. 'I'm frozen, I'm starving, I've
never been so bored in my life and two bobbies knocked on the window to
ask what I was doing.'

'What did you say?'

'That I was listening to a tape recording,' he said, aggrieved. 'What else
could I say, sitting in there like that with headphones on? They went
away.'

The tapes were terrible. Chunks were blotted out by interference, taxi
drivers cut across us, reporting to base that they were going to Hampstead
or Tooting, our voices faded, grew strong, then faded again. But there was
relevant stuff.

I acquired an S N Nagra. This is a miniature recorder, Swiss made, that fits
into an inside pocket and makes stereophonic tapes of a quality good enough
for the sound-track of a wide-screen film. Its tiny weight and size and high
quality had been developed for the American moon-shot. I made a series of
appointments with my legal advisers and turned myself into a walking

bugging device (some might say bugger). I also recorded all telephone conversations with lawyers on my answering machine. One thing to be said to any potential bugger is that, like the other variety, it takes a bit of practice. I was pretty incompetent to start with. There was one telephone call during which I sat back listening to the caller saying just what I wanted, only to have my smugness turn to anger when I afterwards discovered that I had pushed the wrong button. The machine had been wiping the tape clean instead of recording. On another occasion at a meeting with lawyers I was horrified to glance down and see a tangled mass of tape oozing from my inside pocket and over my lapel. The recorder had come open and was relentlessly spewing out tape like a mad mincer. I had to go quickly to the loo to put it all straight. However, during the next month or so, I got what I wanted. Stephen listened to the tapes as they came in, laughing in incredulity at my former team.

To get Paddy Grafton Green to recall events was easy. He was pretty straightforward in his acceptance that the whole thing was a cock-up. John Calderan was more difficult. He used attack as the best means of defence. My complaints were called 'whining,' and so eager was he to say that his firm and the QC he had engaged were above reproach that at one point he used the words, 'And I do ooemember,' about a matter that had taken place when he hadn't even been present.

Neil Taylor behaved wonderfully in character in Comyn's absence. He said that the settlement was 'silly,' that I had a 'real grievance,' that it was a 'bog up.' He advised me to 're-write' the paperwork of the Trust so as to avoid my tax bills. There was one sublime moment at a meeting with Taylor, Calderan and Grafton Green that shows the deep respect the legal profession has for the law. Taylor's double-take when he was put on the spot should have been filmed and used to train comedians in TV sitcom. It was a masterpiece of comic timing. He had been hinting with increasing overtness, and without dissent from the other two, that I should somehow by-pass Andrew Park's written opinion.

TAYLOR: And my accountant would not (bangs desk) be doing what
             this joker says and I will say no more than that. And he is quite
             a reputable accountant but he would go sick (bangs desk) at
             doing that. And there we are. We could just ...you know. All I
             say is that he is a man of the highest standing in the city and if
             you showed him that he would laugh. There. That is that.

                              PAUSE

FRISBY: You are telling me to break the law.
TAYLOR: Yeah...(and here came the double-take) Eh? Hum—I'll
             ex...look here...

FRISBY:	You are telling me to break the law.
TAYLOR:	Look, for heaven's sake, have you ever met any man who…
FRISBY:	I mean, I have heard you all jumping on Fournier, who advised me to keep quiet about something, and here you are, sitting, doing the same thing.

Sheepish murmurs of laughter

Taylor and Grafton Green said repeatedly that they had all known all along that I controlled the Trust, that it was, in effect, common knowledge. Not even Calderan disputed that. This was the crucial admission. My control, remember was at the heart of first Taylor's then Comyn's dire accusations that I was a perjurer. In Stephen's and my view the tapes prove beyond any reasonable doubt that I was the scapegoat, the fall-guy, the patsy. I was wrapped up and presented in that way, because if *I* hadn't been acting shadily then *they* were under suspicion.

But Comyn was the star turn. One day in January, 1972, Calderan, Taylor, Grafton Green, Frank Young and a junior, a bar pupil and I all filed into The Presence in his chamber. He was full of indignant puff that his competence was under attack. His own phraseology paints him exquisitely:-

COMYN:	Well, now look, let's just call a spade a spade, Mr Frisby…
FRISBY:	Yes.
COMYN:	And I told you earlier that my shoulders are broad. They are about as broad as any man's shoulders can be. I have been in this game a long time. I have met an awful lot of people. I have done an awful lot of work. Are you saying, in fact, that I forced you into a settlement which was disastrous for you, lulling you into a sense of security about your tax position with the Cayman Islands?
FRISBY:	No, not on that count, no. But are you saying 'you forced me into a settlement?' Forced is a word—
COMYN:	Well, I accept 'forced.' I—I will. No, fair's fair. I'll accept that I drove you.
FRISBY:	Yes. All right, I'll buy 'drove.' Yes, I am saying that, actually.
COMYN:	I certainly drove you into a settlement. That I won't dissent from at all.

…And later on…

FRISBY:	I think that you were determined to settle that case. You were determined to settle it from the moment you read the papers.
COMYN:	I think that is very fair comment.

…And yet later, Comyn said he would repeat all the above,
'In any court in the world.'

That meeting was the end of my contact with the whole crew of them. I had got on tape all that I could, the extract I have just quoted above between Comyn and me being absolutely crucial. I gladly sacked them.

My tape-recording was not confined to lawyers and Christine. Anyone who knew anything relevant about the behaviour of any of the lawyers involved received a visit or telephone call from me. Their information was recorded and duplicate tapes were made, then stored. There were no exceptions. My life was apparently rich and enviable. *Soup* ran on, coining money (that was pouring, even faster, down the drain, like running water into a bath with no plug in) and many inviting doors were open to me. I was thirty-nine, successful, single, apparently rich. What more could anyone ask? Soup became the longest-running comedy in the history of West End theatre and the press and feature-writers were in attendance at a shindig that Michael threw at the Ritz, full of Very Beautiful People. I was, as author, the most distinguished of guests. Michael said, 'I must give you a new play to direct, Terry.' 'Yes, please, Michael,' I said and heard no more about it.

But all that, the very stuff that should have been at the centre of my life, was a dream when compared to my new obsessions of tapes and evidence and proof. Even Christine would have become peripheral, but divorce, which is supposed to separate, had tied us fast. She was the person to whom I must now pay money I didn't have and to whom I must apply every time I wanted a few hours with my son. These twin humiliations stove a capacious leak in my cup of human kindness. Here is one recorded example of what fatherhood was like under Rutter.

A day or two before Christmas I telephoned to arrange to take Dominic out. 'You can't, said Christine. 'He's not well and can't come out.'

'Well I'd like to see him,' I said. 'I'll pop into the nursery and say, "Hallo," and give him my presents.'

'You know you're not allowed in here,' was the answer. These rules were always quoted impersonally as though some third person, and not she, had created them.

I paused to keep cool. 'Christine, even the Berlin Wall opens at Christmas.'

It was her turn to pause, then permission was given for a brief visit.

Nat Cohen was among those I recorded. Nat was now a regular escort of Christine's, but that wasn't what interested me. He gave me the evidence I needed to make a prima facie case that Rutter had composed an affidavit he knew to be false about the supposed quarter of a million pounds I was about to earn from the film. The doctor who carried out the two abortions on Christine also received a visit.

To sum up: the tapes, together with existing documents, did their job. They enabled me to prove that nearly all I have written so far is true and that small part which I can't prove logically follows.

———

September 1969 - Christine, me and the one - week old Dominic.

Above: **October 1969 - *The Bandwagon*, Mermaid Theatre**. Toni Palmer, Denise Coffey and Peggy Mount, wonderful as the burgeoning Botterills.

Below: **New Year 1971 - Film, *There's A Girl In My Soup.*** Peter Sellers and Goldie Hawn dutifully showing acres of dentistry for the camera.

Right: **October 1969 - During rehearsals for *The Bandwagon*.**

Below: **December 1969 - Mimi, the nanny, with Dominic.**

Overleaf, left: **May 1970 and July 1970 - outside the Royal Courts of Justice;** Christine dressing tactically.
Overleaf, right: **Christine and Rutter;** client holds solicitor's hand, literally.

Below: **Summer 1974 - Bishops Park, Fulham**. Dominic, unaware of what was raging round his head.

Above: **New Year 1977 - *It's All Right If I Do It*, Mermaid Theatre.** John Stride, Prunella Scales, Tony Haygarth and Toni Palmer on the floor, smashed in the final scene.

Below, right: *Seaside Postcard,* **Young Vic production.** Christine Edmonds and Ian Taylor enduring their day on the beach.

Above left: **The Hon Mr Justice James Comyn** at his investiture as a High Court judge some while after he had committed his shoddy little sell-out as my QC.

Above right: **The Hon Mr Justice Trevor (It-may-well-be-that-this-father-is- being-too-possessive-Once-a-fortnight-is-appropriate) Reeve.**

Below, from left to right: **the Rt Hon Lord Justices Phillimore, Davies and Orr**, as I faced them in the Court of Appeal when they covered up for James Comyn, QC soon to join them on the bench.

As I have now sacked all my lawyers it seems like a good moment for an assessment of them.

THE FIRST WAVE

SOLICITORS

NABARRO NATHANSON AND CO (LESLIE TAYLOR AND GUDRUN COLLIS)

In case you have forgotten, this was the firm Bill Fournier originally put me in touch with to handle my divorce. Expensive and useless. I have no idea how good Leslie Taylor might have been, because he did what all those partners do in those firms, they pass you on to a junior while they deal with newer, more lucrative clients. That junior, Miss Collis, although being a warm, sympathetic person, was a hopeless adversarial lawyer who failed again and again to defend my interests when I was attempting reconciliation. In a humane divorce system she could have made an admirable counsellor. In our battlefield Rutter ran rings round her.

BARRISTER

PAUL BEARD

Briefed by Miss Collis. Equally useless. Failed to argue in court the fact that it was my lawyer's illness that made me out-of-time for a particular application and so lost it. Perhaps his brief didn't include the doctor's note.

The following can only be a mid-term assessment because, as I have said, certain of the actions of those below took years to be revealed in their full squalor. The final assessment will, of necessity, be worse.

THE OPPOSITION

SOLICITORS

SYDNEY RUTTER

It is difficult to know what to say about Rutter that won't sound unbalanced. I thought him a monster. Miss Collis condemned him out of hand in a letter to me that she wrote especially to be read in court. Calderan, Neil Taylor and (especially) Grafton Green all accused him of misconduct, but refused to take the proper steps. On other days they said 'he always litigates like this'. If so, that is a damning condemnation of any system that let him. Mr Justice Latey had some hard things to say, but did nothing.

One point worth noting: Latey referred to Rutter's 'successful discovery action,' also described by the ever-inflated Comyn as 'Rutter's voyage of discovery.' These comments would seem to commend his efficiency. But it is pretty easy to discover something that I wasn't hiding and, indeed, that I fought to explain in full to him, for the benefit of everyone involved. The discovery game was the lawyers' red herring. He won that hands down.

There is an old adage that hangs about in legal circles that, in divorce, the husband often blames his wife's lawyer for causing the divorce or, at least, for causing excessive trouble. Well, the facts of his conduct are as I have told you, amply backed up with documents. So judge for yourself. I am convinced he caused the divorce, in the sense that had he, early on, said the right conciliatory words in Christine's ear she would have been only too glad to stop it. I believe that she and our unborn children are victims of Rutter too. Of course, she would never agree with that now.

There remains that suspicious fact of his car parked outside 1 Genoa Avenue at two a.m. on seventh December 1970.

Finally, if I am seeing things with the distorted eyes of a wounded, losing ex-husband and Rutter was behaving reasonably, why did every solicitor and most of the barristers who worked for me say that he wasn't?

BARRISTERS

HARRY LAW

Not worth comment.

JAMES MISKIN QC

Saw too little of him for comment.

MY SOLICITORS

BILL FOURNIER (CAMPBELL HOOPER AND AUSTIN WRIGHT)

Expensive, disastrous and finally dishonest. I first met Bill, representative of this well-known firm of theatrical lawyers, over my first play contract in 1962. Since then he had handled everything legal of mine from house purchase to my will. I thought we had become close friends. It was he who engaged tax counsel (originally Milton Grundy QC, then Harvey McGregor QC) to invent the financial umbrella for all of us, with the Trust at the heart of it. It was Bill who advised me on every step I took regarding the Trust. I never moved without consulting him, for fear of breaking complicated fiscal laws or incurring prohibitive tax bills.

Practically every step I took after the scheme was set up was a wrong one, all on his advice. Acting without reference to tax counsel he made a hash of everything.

Worse was his betrayal of me outside the court at the Latey hearing when he could have stopped the disaster of the consent settlement just by owning up to what a cock-up he knew he had made of everything.

Worst, he forged both the papers and the terms of the meeting with Andrew Park to absolve himself (but I didn't know yet. I carried the blame for Bill's errors for some years).

As with Rutter, though for quite different reasons, I cannot find adequate comment on his conduct.

THEODORE GODDARD AND CO (JOHN CALDERAN AND PATRICK [PADDY] GRAFTON GREEN)

Very expensive and worse than useless. No planning, no overall strategy, no one in charge. Allowed circumstances to blow them this way and that. Calderan, the alleged boss, kept no noticeable checks on Grafton Green who was inexperienced and unstable under pressure. Always happy to pass the big decisions on to the barristers without guiding them properly. Ignored their client's clear unequivocal statement of the realities of his situation and fought their own irrelevant and doomed battle about 'control' of the Trust.

Their biggest omission was failure to advise me to get tax counsel's Opinion to quantify my actual tax situation. It would have been so simple. It was a primary, basic, vital piece of evidence and they didn't think of it. Negligence.

Worse, when events showed their strategy - if you can call it that - to be unsound, they 'mislaid' vital documents to absolve themselves from censure. (I carried the blame for that irrelevant struggle over control for years till the documents finally emerged). I believe them, as I wrote in later legal documents, to be guilty of fraud and contempt of court for their cover-up. They were certainly guilty of something worse than negligence towards their client. It is called 'breach of fiduciary duty.'

As with Rutter and Bill Fournier, what adequate comment I can make about them?

BARRISTERS

NEIL TAYLOR

Then a junior barrister, later a QC. Apparently sensible, in fact expensive and useless. Taylor's major sin of omission was that (like Theodore Goddard) he didn't think of the simple basic idea of getting tax-counsel's Opinion to quantify my tax liability. But worse than that was his habit of sounding authoritative when he was in charge of day-to-day matters, then effacing himself when the QC was present, saying something different, then returning to his own views in the QC's absence. He constantly muddled me.

Joe Jackson QC

Gave a terrific performance at the one hearing for interim relief that he presided over. But, like the others, never thought to advise me to get tax counsel's Opinion, the real rock on which my case should have been based.

And then he disappeared. For a more lucrative case? I don't know, but Calderan muttered some remarks that throw doubt on Jackson's conduct in ditching us. Certainly the remarks showed that Calderan felt let down. Perhaps Jackson didn't like the way my case developed. For whatever reason he wasn't there when he had said he would be. And, oh God, look at his replacement.

James Comyn QC

A disaster. Pigheaded, incompetent and innumerate. Allowed many facts and figures to be presented wrongly in court by the other side without challenge and finally threw away my case when he told the judge that the Revenue (he meant the Bank of England) had been informed of my control and had okayed it (thereby negating my tax liability in the judge's mind). When I urged him, pleaded with him, to correct what he had said, he refused. I was going to have to go into the witness box and, without written evidence to support me, contradict all of my own advisers who had already accused me of committing perjury: an untenable position for me.

Comyn 'forced' me, 'drove' me, was 'determined' I should settle. He 'drove me to sign' I put the words in quotes because they are his, not because I dissent from them. More of them soon.

One of the most pompous, overblown fools I have ever had the misfortune to meet. The only thing I can say for him is that he was falsely briefed by Theodore Goddard. However, before you feel sympathy for him, his worst sell-out is yet to come.

In conclusion, for this mid-term assessment, there is a final fact about lawyers and the law that you should be aware of. It has a beautiful symmetry. If I had sued Theodore Goddard for negligence (not for their still-unseen cover-up, just for their cock-up) they had an exquisite escape clause: they were only following counsel's advice, the advice of the eminent James Comyn QC, top man. Therefore the injured client should blame Comyn, not them. He was responsible. But under English law you cannot sue a barrister who has acted for you in litigation. He is immune. They all have it tied up quite neatly really, don't they?

Now observe how British judges react when faced with evidence of malpractice within their own profession. By 'their own profession' I mean barristers (who become judges), rather than solicitors. Judges don't mind knocking off the odd solicitor, but they are, in their own terminology, 'brother barristers'. They all come from just four Inns of Court. More or less all the top ones know each other well. They go to the same tribal gatherings, wear the same fancy dresses that band them together, swear oaths with each other, belong to the same clubs, and so on. One of the most incestuous relationships in our inbred legal system is that which exists between well-known top barristers and High Court judges. They are indeed brothers. Our divorce system is a positive palace of compassion, light and truth in comparison to the reaction of a British judge when you tell him that a famous member of his Inn of Court is not quite straight.

Chapter XXXIV

Spring 1972

So I became a litigant-in-person. Writing down the story and sacking my lawyers had a most beneficial effect in clearing my mind. My situation was dire but perhaps not hopeless. Time was the key: time to pay, time to make some more money, time to order my affairs. I no longer wanted to declare myself bankrupt. Some months before, that would have been a satisfying way of stopping the war by sinking everyone. Now that I had lost I just wanted to survive and fight back. The first thing I had to do was to plug some of the holes in the leaky boat before it sank completely.

The immediate situation was as follows: the huge potential tax bills were, for the moment, just a shadow on my future. They could wait. I hoped that one day I wouldn't have to face them completely shorn. Theodore Goddard issued a write against me for £7,000. That was unavoidable. Rutter's imminent bill would be at least twice as large because it would cover the entire divorce. That was unavoidable. There were a few other smaller matters of substance that were also unavoidable. The only items I could challenge were the various payments I had to make to Christine under the divorce settlement (doesn't it have an appealing lunacy? The lawyers had got their piece of our cash, leaving us to fight over the dwindling remainder). I could challenge in court: the £7,000 I owed her to pay off the mortgage on 1 Genoa Avenue; the four payments of £2,500 for Christine's capital settlement; the £7,500 maintenance for her and Dominic.

To pay these sums I had no available capital in the UK and the Trust money was untouchable. My income was mostly taken by the maintenance payments. I could not afford to brief another counsel, the case had become too complicated. In any case I didn't want to brief anyone. I was spoiling to fight for myself. Besides the clear survival incentive to take legal action (or rather reaction) was the less-than-clear hope that I could persuade Latey to pass some sort of adverse judgement on my former legal advisers and Rutter. Mostly I wanted a judge to order an investigation into what had gone on (a hopeless cause but I still had some trust in British justice). Perhaps he could in some way, open the way for me to get redress from them, or at the least get them punished.

Stephen and I decided that I should apply to Mr Justice Latey for ancillary relief because of a change in my circumstances. Stephen felt that I had a chance in spite of the fact that it wasn't my circumstances that had changed, only my understanding of them. We would ask him to reduce, remove or defer, as he saw fit, any payment I had to make to Christine. Stephen stayed in the background and guided me; no accusations against lawyers, no rhetoric, nothing except a clear, concise, accurate account of my financial position, combined with Andrew Park's Opinion. It was a pleasure to concentrate on something as impersonal as arithmetic. I had previously said to Taylor that I might apply to Latey, representing myself, as a way of getting out of the mess. I had received bloodcurdling warnings from him and Calderan that I would be in danger of arrest and of the impounding of my property. What tosh they talked to cover their own failings.

I filed my application and affidavit of means, sent the copies to Rutter and waited for Christine's answering affidavit of means that should have come back in fourteen days. It did, but without containing a single fact or figure that told me or the court what she was worth. While I was wondering what to do next, I learned that Christine was going abroad for a fortnight's holiday and Dominic was being sent to Leicestershire with his new nanny (non-Iranian). I realised, while furiously noting that Dominic was loaned to anybody before me, that Christine would be away for the hearing. Not only no facts, but no Christine to give evidence either.

My response caused matters to develop rapidly into some ripe, low comedy. I managed to get a subpoena the day before she was to leave. Get that served and she would have to come to court. She was out for the evening when the server got to Genoa Avenue so he waited. He was an ex-policeman, aged sixty-seven and couldn't have been too quick-witted, because when Christine arrived with two men in a car he let the men obstruct him and the three of them got into the house. He didn't see her again let alone touch her with the subpoena. However, he persevered and rang the doorbell.

'We're going to phone the solicitors. Wait there,' shouted one of the men through the chained door. (I learned later that he had got hold of Rutter fils).

The server waited ten minutes and rang the bell again. 'It must be served on the solicitors,' shouted the man through the chained door. 'You ought to be ashamed of yourself running round to serve a writ on a poor, helpless woman.'

Five minutes later the man appeared at the first floor window above the door and shouted, 'Get out you bastard, you're trespassing. I know a bit about the law, I work for the *Daily Express*,' and he emptied a bucket of water over the server's head.

The server squelched next door to telephone the police. The neighbours must have been delighted to see him, it was by now nearly midnight. When a PC arrived in a Panda Car he couldn't find his warrant card so the *Daily*

Express legal expert wouldn't let him in either. Off he went for his sergeant. The sergeant arrived and, telling the server to keep clear, went in and came out a few minutes later with a brilliant solution. He said he had spoken to the solicitor on the telephone and arranged that the subpoena be served on him the following day after Christine had gone. The server went home to change his wet clothes and Christine disappeared abroad.

Such goings-on were outside my experience but Rutter had obviously had other clients who hadn't wished to appear in court. I wrote him the predictable letter of complaint to be answered with a barrage of counter-complaints including one that I was just doing the whole thing to annoy his client. He demanded that there be an investigation of the matter. When I heartily agreed he dropped that.

So I wrote Christine's affidavit of means for her with facts, figures and evidence to back up my guesses. I answered the mud slung in her affidavit, then stood one morning outside the High Court with a dry mouth and my knees knocking under the trousers of the litigation suit. It was more terrifying than any first night. The usher said, 'Frisby versus Frisby,' the dismal overture, and I shambled in.

I sat on one side of the court with notebook and one small file of papers. On the other, sat James Miskin QC, Good-Old-Harry Law and Sydney Rutter with sheaves of papers and legal paraphernalia. Even the hatchet-faced female usher (they seemed to be picked for their lack of expression and metal-floss hair) looked sympathetic at the ill-matched contest.

Mr Justice Latey came in and we all stood up. He bowed briefly at the trio to his left and sat down. As he hadn't bowed to me I compromised by staring at a point halfway between him and the floor. 'Yes?' he said to me.

'I wonder if I might interrupt, my Lord,' said Miskin, like cream.

'Yes, Mr Miskin?' said Latey, as courteous as an actor in a period play.

'And I hope Mr Frisby doesn't mind. This is his application but I think I might be able to help if I just say a few words.'

'Thank you, Mr Miskin, I'm sure you can. But, as you say, it is Mr Frisby's application, perhaps he won't object if you just...' and here he glanced at me.

'No, no. Carry on,' I said, glad of the respite.

'Thank you,' said Latey and turned his attention to Miskin. I loved it. English court procedure has exquisite style, from the immaculate brevity of that 'Yes?' that starts every trial, to the way the judge has got the first three sentences of final judgement said before you realise he has started. When you are a litigant-in-person you have spent the build-up to this moment running from Room X at the Law Courts with an application, to Room Y to get something stamped, back to Room Z for a form that you should have had at Room X, and so on. You are browbeaten and irritated by the procedures and the wrong directions you are given. Then there is the terrifying Clerk of the Rules Room. The clerk of the rules is a sergeant-major-like figure, perched on a high chair in his basement den with other petty officials who dole out court time. There you are jostled in the queue of solicitors' clerks who know the ropes, and you try to hide your self-consciousness as you mumble, 'Litigant-in-person, Frisby versus Frisby.' 'Oh, another nut,' the looks say as he flicks through his book. 'How long will it take?' 'I don't know. A day or two perhaps.' 'A day or two? Huh.' As though such presumption will be summarily dealt with. 'Well, which is it? One day or two?' 'Dunno. I'll only take a morning, but the other side might go on a bit.' 'Hm. Well, say, two full days then.' And it is never enough. And throughout, a voice says 'What are you doing here? Go home and write a play. Run away from this dung-heap. Or just go and have a game of golf.' But you screw yourself up not to dash from the mock-gothic of that building at the end of the Strand. God, how I hate that place. Just driving past it even now makes my stomach turn over.

But once in court and that is gone. The NCOs may still be present in the form of the ushers and the judge's clerk, but the officer class takes over with that, 'Yes?' and even if you are going to be carved to pieces it will be done politely. There is also a widely-held belief that judges are fair to litigants-in-person. They are not, but they think they are, which is, as far as they are concerned, the same thing.

Miskin's interruption was fascinating. He disavowed himself from part of Christine's affidavit because it was in some way improper. There had obviously been a row between him and Rutter.

I got going. The trial took nearly three full days, but I think it was really all over in the first half hour. I am sure that Latey already knew that something was up and he only needed showing clearly what it was. I gave him my affidavit, talked a bit about the figures, but briefly, briefly ('make your points then shut up,' Stephen had said. 'Don't waffle and don't be clever. And especially don't be funny. There's only one comic in court and that's the judge.'). Then I gave him Andrew Park's Opinion and we adjourned while he read it. Back came Latey after he had finished.

'I propose to accept this as evidence, Mr Miskin. If you've no objection?' Miskin would have needed to have very good reason to have found an objection in the face of the steely glance that went with the mild tone.

So, there it was, the heart of my case won in a few minutes. For more than a year my former legal advisers had all been talking bunk. Nerves gone, I continued until I had finished.

'Thank you, Mr Frisby,' said Latey, stressing the word 'thank' so that he gave the phrase both sincerity and faint surprise. 'The way that you have presented your case was most helpful,' and I had to fight back the grin of pleasure. It really was like being back in school. 'Ten out of ten, Frisby. And A plus for effort.' Latey went on, 'I especially liked these tables showing your and your wife's assets and liabilities. Very clear and helpful. I wish solicitors would take a leaf from your book and present their clients' finances so limpidly.' I had compiled the tables in question because I found the affidavits so confusing. Page after page of writing with the occasional figure buried in them only muddied the issue. In compiling the tables, the clarity to which Latey referred was horrifying. It showed that, when the Revenue got round to me I was easily bankrupt and that Christine was now worth about £60,000 to £70,000 possibly more. The figures themselves were enough, but as I presented my evidence I was able to impugn my former advisers. Without my once calling them names, Latey was getting a clear impression of their incompetence. At one point he said, 'So what you are saying is that you always favoured a high income for your ex-wife so that you should both enjoy the fruits of your success, but that the capital should be conserved until after the Revenue had been cleared?'

I fervently concurred.

'Yes. Hm. Very sensible and generous, I can see. And your former legal advisers have got you into precisely the opposite situation, haven't they?'

'Yes.'

'Hm. It seems to me, Mr Miskin, that the only sensible course in this case would have been to have waited for the tax to be settled before dividing the capital.' And as Miskin, Good-Old-Harry and Rutter sat, silent, I had to refrain from dancing along the desk-lids like Gene Kelly. The judge, with no prompting from me, had come up with the very solution I had been urging for nearly two years.

At one point in my argument I had to refer to the consent order and used Comyn's words that he, 'drove' me, 'forced' me and was 'determined' that I should settle. Miskin interrupted. 'I really find it intolerable to listen to a brother barrister being quoted in a way that suggests, well, something less then honour, when he is not here to defend himself.'

'Perhaps we should get him along, Mr Miskin,' said Latey mildly.

I joined in with ill-considered haste. 'Yes. Please. Yes. Do,' I said. 'He said he'd say what I've just quoted, in front of any court in the world. Those were his words. I am sure he'll be willing and it would be most helpful if I could ask him one or two things.' I'm afraid my eagerness didn't help. Whether Latey would have got Comyn along had I been cooler I don't know, but it is possible that the prospect of me wading into a 'brother barrister' was not appealing. Anyway, he did not 'get him along.'

The great cross-examination from Miskin was next on the agenda. I was about to be 'lacerated.' I stood in the witness box, tense and on my guard for googlies or bouncers. Who knew what was coming from this renowned court assassin? The answer was: nothing. Instead, doors were opened for me. On Stephen's advice I had presented my case without accusation against any of the legal profession, but now, pressed in cross-examination, I could speak without inhibition, and did. The release was therapeutic. I prayed that one or more of my ex-team would be called. They must either help my case or lie under oath, either would do, I had the tapes. But Latey showed no enthusiasm to look into the activities of lawyers, although he seemed to believe me. It was a good example of judges' schizophrenia. If I was telling the truth about them, surely he should have enquired further. If I wasn't, the rest of my story fell down and I was liar. He took a middle course but an illogical one. I was telling the truth in general, but 'mistaken' about my lawyers; a perfect piece of establishment double-think.

Miskin suddenly left; for good. He had to go to 'a longer-standing commitment,' and that was that. I believe he was glad to be shot of it. Good-Old-Harry took over the examination and the proceedings soon descended (or ascended, if you prefer) into farce. If being examined by Miskin was an experience without menace, being examined by Law was a positive entertainment. It went on for nearly two days and I have seldom seen a man get into such a mess. It was a great joy to stand there and correct his questions, amend his dates, show his premises to be false, then sit back with savage satisfaction while Rutter and Law sorted themselves out. Latey, I thought, was enjoying the show, but he looked impassively attentive. If you want to guess what is going on in a judge's mind watch his clerk. Latey's was having a ball.

At one point Law got hopelessly tied up with some stuff about foreign earnings and the Revenue. He blundered through sub-clause after sub-clause of an endless sentence. Eventually he came to a stop and we all stared at one another in bafflement. I was so relaxed by then that I laughed openly. Latey's clerk had a handkerchief in his mouth. I had to ask Law if he had asked a question and, if so, what it was. Latey said, with a completely straight face, 'I must confess, Mr Law; I didn't quite follow it.'

The Electrical Trades Union helped matters along with a series of wildcat strikes; every now and again all the lights went out and we adjourned. Latey commented at one of these interruptions 'Now we are literally in the dark as well as figuratively.' And so, punctuated by blackouts, Law, Rutter and I went round and round in circles that always returned to the conduct of Messrs. Calderan, Taylor, Grafton Green and Comyn.

In one ill-advised line, Law tried to get me to agree that I had settled in order to get improved access to Dominic. The sight of Law and Rutter trying to make financial capital out of that issue was too much. I clung to the witness box trying not to sob and told them in harsh, barely audible gulps what I thought of them. Latey adjourned the proceedings at once. Law didn't return to the subject but that line of questioning shows clearly that access to Dominic was used as a negotiating factor in the settlement. This is common practice and, though improper, is ignored by all judges.

We got to that stage of a hearing when barristers present case history to support arguments. Law submitted three or four cases in support of his. Latey noted them, then asked me if I had any. I had burrowed in the legal books and found two. They were ludicrously irrelevant. Latey told me as much, with carefully arranged features. It was the nearest he came to patronising me in the whole three days, yet I must have given him plenty of opportunity. Law and Rutter were less circumspect and directed half-concealed smiles towards Latey to establish their bond of professionalism. Latey ignored them. 'Mr Frisby, I think I can help you.' Then he produced some case history which he discussed with Law, obliging him, professionally, to agree that it all supported me. Then, 'You see, Mr Frisby, it is my duty to help a litigant-in-person in matters of the law, as well as to be the umpire in the case. It is a path I must tread carefully. Moreover, one of the more civilised aspects of our legal system is that both I and Mr Law are obliged to search for all the relevant case-history. Mr Law must, even if it helps you and not his client. Indeed, as a member of the bar, he has taken vows to that effect.' A flicker of amusement touched Latey's voice as he said to Law 'Is that not so, Mr Law?'

'Indeed, my Lord,' said Law, half-rising. Then he sat weightily, cloaked in the solemnity of his vows. Rutter appeared not to have heard this exchange.

I got to my feet. 'In that case I should like to thank Mr Law for his diligent, though fruitless, search on my behalf.' Latey smiled at Law for his response as Rutter bared his teeth in mirthless servility.

Law again lumbered upright, 'It was a pleasure, My Lord.' As he sat, he took my breath away with a covert wink at me. Latey said he wanted to think things over to give a reserved judgement, so we had to wait till the following Friday.

Stephen came with me to hear the judgement in case there was anything technical that might pass me by. Christine appeared, tanned and chic from her holiday in Africa. Miskin was absent. As Latey entered I put my eyes at half-mast again while the professionals bowed at each other. He gave Stephen a hard glance then dived straight in. The transcript of his judgement is twenty-two foolscap pages long and Latey was no word squanderer.

What it amounted to was that I had won all that I could have expected to, which wasn't much. The payments that Latey deemed he had the power to vary were: Christine's maintenance, (£5,000 p.a.), Dominic's maintenance (£2,500 p.a.) lump sum payments of 4 x £2,500, repayment of mortgage (about £7,000). He was never going to return part-ownership of our house to me or any of its contents. I had given them away. It was also unlikely that he would touch the maintenance payments (they were, after all, tax-deductible) although I hoped he would cut anything that would give me breathing space. He did the simple, sensible thing of giving me time to sort out my finances by deferring the mortgage repayment and lump sum payments while keeping Christine's maintenance untouched. (Note. They were only deferred, not cancelled). He had followed exactly my point about enjoying the high income while conserving the capital.

In its way it was a sensation. Latey had overturned a consent order, an action practically unheard of in English law. But financial relief wasn't all that I was waiting for that morning. What would Latey have to say, or, better still, do, about the lawyers?

He started on Rutter's failure to provide a proper affidavit of means. That was 'unfortunate.' 'More unfortunate' was the tone of the document that he had provided. He noted Miskin's 'proper' disavowal of part of it. The affidavit 'added fuel to the flames of an already deplorably inflammatory situation, and provoked a further affidavit from the husband building up the conflagration.' Excellent. He didn't mention the subpoena-avoiding episode.

Latey went on to say what nice people Christine and I must be and went to some lengths on my character, as it was in question. He threw out all accusations of any sort. If I ever want a reference, either as to character or ability in court, I know where to go. He got on to what a splendid chap Miskin was: 'One of the agreeable features of this case, which has disagreeable ones.' What a splendid chap Law was: how he had 'conducted himself properly (he didn't add hilariously, too) in every way'. When he called the case a 'grim fantasy,' the atmosphere was electric. Surely he was building up to a condemnation of those he hadn't mentioned so far. A judgement delivered in this way is very exciting. The judge keeps you waiting for the big decisions till the end and builds all his little climaxes with a matter-of-factness that is theatrical in its flatness. It is the judge's moment and he enjoys it. Several times he referred to the 'unyielding nature' and 'aggressive and belligerent tone' of Rutter's correspondence and the 'outdated, adversarial' way he had handled things, 'stoking up pain and bitterness unnecessarily.' I was getting more and more keyed up. He got to the 'substantial faulty basis of fact' on which the order was signed and I anticipated the assault on my legal team and Comyn in particular. Instead, there followed a side-step of great deftness. 'As in my opinion this application to vary should be determined on its merits for other reasons, I propose to deal with this particular complaint briefly.' So Latey could give me a favourable judgement without condemning Comyn. Latey said of him, 'It is difficult to believe that the husband did not receive the best possible advice,' and of my complaints that I had been frog-marched into the settlement, 'However, it may well have been a case where the husband did not himself appreciate the balance of factors,' and so on. Then we were on to Rutter. Latey produced two more side-steps. My first accusation, that Rutter had prevented a reconciliation early in the divorce, was met with, 'Well, I haven't been into the details or read the documents so I can't say.' Fair enough. The second, that he had run the costs up deliberately in financial matters, was met with, 'because of the apparent cover-up over the Swiss Bank account Rutter was fully justified in his actions,' which were 'highly efficient.' Latey went on to compliment his 'legal astuteness' while deploring his 'peremptory

293

and aggressive tone' and hoped that would all change now that Rutter could see I was honest.

So there it was. We were all splendid chaps: Comyn and company had given me the 'best possible advice' although the settlement was signed on a 'substantial faulty basis of fact;' Rutter had been 'astute' in uncovering the cover-up that no one had indulged in. And - though peopled with such splendid lawyers and honest litigants - the divorce was a 'a grim fantasy,' a positively baroque phrase in the dry vocabulary of a judge's summing up. No, Latey was indulging in a whitewash all right, possibly with the best of pacifying motives, but a whitewash is a whitewash.

Stephen and I were chewing over the judgement. I felt flat. I had made up my mind that I had won days ago so that was no joy. All I wanted was an investigation. Stephen would have none of it. 'Ha. Hm. Ha. You've overturned a consent order, that's extraordinary, almost unbelievable. You've cleared your name, which was upsetting you a lot and you've proved that you were right all along. What more do you want?'

'I'm still broke and divorced and Comyn, Calderan and Rutter are still practising,' I said ungraciously.

'Ha. Hm. Latey's never going to condemn them. Latey and Comyn are probably mates, worked on cases together, and Theodore Goddard must have employed Latey when he was a barrister. Anyway, there was no real evidence, they weren't called. You never used the tapes, what d'you expect?' Stephen laughed, 'Latey doesn't think much of Rutter, does he?'

'Neither do I, but where does that get us? Latey did nothing about him.' Nevertheless self-respect was returning to me, as welcome as swallows in spring after the eighteen-month winter of humiliations.

Rutter's and Christine's answer was prompt and stony. They appealed against Latey's decision. His clerk delivered Christine's notice of appeal at my flat on the following Friday evening. Thus was Latey's second era of reconciliation ushered in. He had said:-

> "With, one hopes, a calmer and less competitive climate prevailing from now on, would it be possible for them (Christine and her advisers) to wait a while for the results of tax negotiations before embarking on further heavy and expensive litigation?"

Instead, she was applying to the Court of Appeal to overturn Latey's delaying order and to hell with the costs. She wanted her pound of flesh.

The delivery by hand of Christine's notice of appeal well after office hours on the Friday evening was followed by another copy in the post on Saturday morning. At ten p.m. that Saturday evening my doorbell rang and Rutter's clerk delivered a third copy.

I responded to such diligence by having a mini-cab deliver my acknowledgement to his house at one a.m., having given the driver a fiver to se that he put the envelope into Rutter's hand personally. To judge from Rutter's next letter to me I should think that the scene at his front door was all that I hoped. Apparently Rutter and the mini-cab driver had a shouting match through the letter-box. Rutter's postal response was apoplectic and hilarious. The following is his explanation of why he had disturbed me at ten p.m. on a Saturday night.

> The only address at which we can send documents to you or serve them on you is where you are to be found.

I wrote back to him correcting his spelling and grammar and giving his letter marks out of ten for style and tone. Having hit on this idea, I continued it, like an elderly, well-meaning pedant, for all his letters. There was plenty of scope. Correspondence with the dreaded mud-slinger of EC3 became almost a pleasure on this basis. The tone, if not the style, of his correspondence improved overnight. From then on I meticulously stuck to the policy of writing to him in an entirely neutral style until he stepped outside the bounds of courtesy or accuracy. Then I indulged myself. Once he alleged that I had kept Dominic waiting on a 'drafty' station. Before my new policy I would have spent two days prowling my flat, talking to myself, humiliated, furious at my impotence in all things regarding my son. To compose a long, silly, insulting letter to Rutter about his inability to distinguish between 'drafty' and 'draughty' was a great release. I received the following answer:-

Dear Sir,

I am Mr S Rutter's secretary. I am writing this letter to you of my own volition and without the knowledge of anybody in the firm, or Mr S Rutter, but I feel I must do so.

    In your letter to Mr S Rutter of the 23rd instant, you have made offensive remarks about the spelling, for which I am responsible (this is not the first time you have criticised [sic] my spelling.) I may not have had the advantage of the education which you had, but at least I know how to be respectful. I am at all times under extreme pressure of work and errors in spelling can occur. May I suggest that you look at some of your own spelling mistakes before criticising others; for example in your letter of the 23rd instant, you wrongly spelled the words 'access' and 'occurrence' on Pages 1 and 2.

Yours faithfully,

Mrs V L Hart.

Sorry, Mrs Hart, but it is wonderful, isn't it, that it is never a lawyer who is responsible, even for his spelling.

Rutter's next enchantment was to write to Theodore Goddard asking them for details of their advice to me when they were acting for me; privileged information. His letter sought to ingratiate by telling them tales of my rudeness about them in court, then his scruffy enquiry was slipped in. Calderan wrote back to Rutter telling him where to get off and sent copies of the letter to me. I wrote to Rutter telling him to ask me for such information in future, as I would be glad to help. He didn't answer.

But the serious business was what to do in the Court of Appeal. Neither Stephen nor I thought that Christine stood a chance in view of (a) the figures, and (b) Latey's comprehensive, reserved judgement. But how could we press home our advantage, break the whole consent order, publicise the conduct of the professionals concerned, by way of the tapes, and clear up my life ready for a new start? Neither of us had a clue. Latey had gone as far as he could in giving me relief, but it was not really even a sort of half-way house. I was still up to my neck - well, no, now only up to my chest - in financial problems. The Court of Appeal had full power. They could pull me clear. The point was, that any method that I chose to bring my case to them was, as far as we could discover, without precedent. My own deeply-held conviction was that I had only to get the full story and the taped evidence before those judges and their righteous indignation would match my own. Action would be taken. My experience in front of Latey had restored my profound faith in British Justice. Stephen was less sanguine than I.

Our tactic, technically, was that I cross-appeal, seeking leave to appeal out of time, to overturn the whole consent order on the grounds that it was no true consent order because of my former legal advisers' negligence and because I was forced by Comyn to sign. The tape extract that I have already quoted (in which he fulsomely said precisely that) would be a key piece of evidence. There would then have to be a new divorce settlement agreed or ordered, based on the full facts.

I wrote out a forty-page affidavit telling the whole story, including the story of our marriage. I transcribed the relevant parts of the tapes and had everything ready to send to the court and to Rutter. Before that I did one final thing. I gave all the lawyers concerned in the case the chance to speak up, thus rendering the tapes superfluous. I wrote to them asking pertinent questions and telling them their answers would be used as evidence before the Court of Appeal. Only one person would help: nice, jolly, ineffectual Gudrun Collis. After recalling chapter and verse of events, her summing up on Rutter's actions began 'I find it very hard to be rough on fellow-professionals, still I must be honest with you and say…' She then went on to condemn him roundly.

———————

Meanwhile back in what I shall laughingly call my professional life I was acting again, touring with the Ken Campbell Roadshow. Ken and I had known each other since repertory days. He telephoned from Frankfurt. 'Ere, listen, Tel, I've lost me spieler for me roadshow and I need someone over here tomorrow who can go on stage and talk without knowing his lines. I thought of you.'

I thankfully dropped my pen (invention was paralysed anyway) and was on the next plane. Ken has written, compiled or presented all sorts of shows and has become a cult figure, but I must say that particular roadshow of his was his best ever for my money; over two hours of dotty fun that was adapted to fit every setting across Europe from infants' classrooms through youth clubs, fringe theatres, attics and the Young Vic, to large mainstream theatres and - in Dublin - the National Theatre, where we broke the house record and upset numerous clerics. On one occasion we did the show on a double-decker bus riding round London and an emotional member of the audience clasped me afterwards with protestations that it had been the most wonderful night of his life.

Our cast of three (with four others planted in the audience) purported to be a tatty side-show in a fun-fair. Here, the Great Sylvester McCoy (later Dr Who) attempted a series of stunts, either disastrously or with unexpected success. We shoved ferrets down Sylvester's trousers (it became a national fad), fired ourselves into the audience with elastic bands (the Great Elastic Band Pang), tore the clothes off our audience plants, marched our buffeted but happy customers round the block to explode a bomb on Sylvester's chest (too dangerous to do inside), banged six-inch nails up his nose (yes, really), set a mechanical sex-crazed vagina in pursuit of a nervous plasticine penis, commanded Holy Quiet while Sylvester caused cotton-wool to burst into flame by the power of his mind, Oh, the list of idiocies gives me a squirm of pleasure to recall. And all was performed in the conviction of the superstar status of our scrag-end of a hero, Sylvester. As a joint occupation with preparation for the Court of Appeal it threw into sharp focus how wholesome is the theatre - censored, sneered at, shut down, reviled for centuries by moralists - in comparison to the so-called honourable, upper reaches of the law.

We would be gathering in the grottiest of caffs, elbows in the puddles of tea-slops, about to go on our next booking. 'Tel, Tel.' Ken's bulging blue eyes would light up and his mouth hang open in his insanely committed smile. 'Come on, tell us another monopoly-money story,' and after we had piled into the Roadshow dormobile I would recount anecdotes of lawyers, tax counsels and offshore trusts, high life in Cannes, Paris and New York, of people who spent more on dinner than the cast earned in a month. Ken and the others would roll about chortling with glee.

'OK, OK,' Ken would interrupt. 'Here's your week's pay. Forty quid. Never mind about all them thousands. This is real.'

By the time the Court of Appeal hearing was due in June 1972, I had sold the luxury pad in Chelsea and was living in a Victorian semi in Fulham. I was carrying an overdraft on my current bank account of over £25,000 and was earning from the Ken Campbell Roadshow not enough to pay half the interest charges on that, let alone the maintenance order and all the rest of it. But *Soup* ran on in London, keeping the legal money-mincing machine fed with royalties while I moved deeper into debt.

Chapter XXXV

June Fifth, Sixth & Seventh, 1972

The fact that something had gone dreadfully wrong with my life was brought home to me when the uniformed attendant at the main entrance of the Royal Courts of Justice held the door for me, tipped his cap, and said cheerily, 'Morning, Mr Frisby.'

Inside, in that gloomy main hall, I bumped into Latey's clerk. 'Good luck,' he said, clenching his fist in encouragement; judges' clerks don't like their bosses' decisions overturned. Then he looked guiltily round to see if his partiality had been seen and hurried off. On the stairs up to that long row of courtrooms on the first floor Neil Taylor was talking to clients. Our eyes met. 'Fucking up somebody else's life?' I enquired chattily.

Outside the court we had to wait while various brief applications were dealt with. Paul Beard, the barrister who had unsuccessfully argued my attempt to postpone the divorce two years previously in 1970 (a lifetime ago), was there with two clients; the inevitable anxious-looking woman and a boy. The look on her face made me bite back my caustic greeting for Beard. Yet he looked worse, as though he would heave up at any moment. I wasn't the only terror-stricken pleader before the Court of Appeal. I wondered what the woman would lose if he blew it. Money? The boy with her? John Mortimer, the barrister/playwright, was waiting outside the next court in wig and gown. God seemed to have assembled the full company of my acquaintances in the law for this day of days.

'Whatever are you doing here?' asked John.

'Scab labour,' I replied.

I was there for the next step in my struggle for survival. I reflected that for the years since drama school my life had been a matter of achievement. Now, dreary to report, it was reduced to being a matter of survival. But I didn't feel dreary as I arrived for the beginning of Christine's appeal against Latey's judgement. I was frightened, shaking even, but anticipatory. Latey, may I remind you, had merely deferred, not cancelled, my capital payments to Christine and my paying off of the mortgage on 1 Genoa Avenue. Christine had thought that worth going to appeal about. My opponent was Good-Old-Harry Law. I would be using the same arguments and evidence that I had before Latey.

But there was a further, much more exciting development. Christine's action in taking us to a higher court had opened the door for me to do what I wanted most: to get the whole consent order annulled. That could be a prelude to getting a new order based on the true figures and some good sense. It could be the start of my recovery and the prospect of future prosperity. The method I was using to get all this started was to cross-appeal, using my tape-recorded evidence to convince their Lordships of the facts. My principal basic argument was that the existing order was no true consent order because I was forced by Comyn to sign it.

I was not going to try to define 'forced' yet, unless I had to. I was just going to try to establish prima facie that both Comyn and I agreed that 'forced' is what he did. Since there were only two parties to the 'forcing,' him and me, and both agreed (him on tape) that that is what he did, it seemed pretty straightforward. Definition of the word 'forced' and his 'I drove you' could come later. Perhaps, if I got the whole matter re-opened, it would be before another judge in a new hearing, perhaps it would be here and now in the Court of Appeal; it could require cross-examination of us both and others involved; I had no idea. I would not have cross-petitioned with such vague specific objectives but for Christine's appeal. It was now or never. The hearing was really two hearings in one: her appeal on the limited matters (which was simple and we were confident we would win because the figures were so conclusive); then my more general appeal, the biggy. Dealing with my former solicitors would come later. Any question of negligence by Theodore Goddard or Bill Fournier would not be part of this hearing unless (oh, God, yes, please) Their Lordships made it so.

I was beginning to feel sick; the publicness of the event was beginning to get to me. The private hearing before Latey was vested with nostalgic cosiness in my memory beside the awful ceremonial majesty of these courts and the crowds who bustled in, out and around them. Stephen had prayed that I would get Lord Justice Denning. His unorthodox actions on behalf of the individual against authority were just making him famous. But Denning, looking through the lists, had chosen one of his favourite subjects, an appeal about the power of a trade union over one of its members, in preference to what must have looked like a thoroughly boring squabble between husband and wife about money. I had got Lord Justice Davies with Lord Justices Phillimore and Orr. 'Hm. Hm. Davies can't handle litigants-in-person,' said Stephen. 'He doesn't know what to do with 'em. Never mind. Phillimore's a cccunt, I had him when he was a High Court judge. He made an absolutely daft decision. We had to go to appeal to get it put straight. He plays with his wig all the time; picks it up, scratches his head and then puts it on back to front. You'd've thought he'd've learned by now. I've never come across Orr.'

'Aren't you coming with me?' I said.

'No. I can't do anything. You'll get more sympathy on your own, anyway.'

So, armed with that information, I paced outside the court working myself into a fine froth. Law and Rutter sat, heads together, with Christine.

Once more my mind flipped to the past when I had gone to court for the first time, just after the injunctions. I had slid onto the rear bench beside her and greeted her eagerly before our legal advisers had pulled us apart; literally on that occasion. Now I just stared coldly down the corridor and she looked the other way. Miskin was absent. Law must have been miserable too, he was getting the full treatment from Rutter; a stream of hissed instructions. I went and stood pointedly near to them. Law glanced up but Christine remained looking the other way and Rutter merely lowered his voice and head. As I stared at his trendily-long, grey, curly hair and the skin of his neck folding over his collar, I suddenly realised that I had never really looked him in the eyes. Those brown buttons, under heavy brows separated by his thick nose had always avoided mine. His lips, which were considerable, opened and closed in steady rhythm over the vowels and consonants he was pouring into Law's hairy, capsular ear. A year or two later Samuel Beckett's *Not I* played at the Royal Court Theatre. All that could be seen on the blacked-out stage was a writhing twisting object that was a disembodied mouth pouring words into the auditorium. It reminded me of Rutter's mouth and its glutinous emission.

I stared at the pair for a while feeling less awful, then the usher shouted the phrase that I hated most, 'Frisby versus Frisby.'

Law had to open so I had a chance to acclimatise myself. As soon as I had my senses under something like control I had a good look at the Lords of Appeal perched above us. They were a frightening and frightful-looking trio. The legal profession was again performing its old trick of copying bad art. If you had programmed a computer to invent three barnacle-encrusted old buffers for a Gothic comedy-thriller it would have come up with those three. I looked round. Behind me sat a barrister hired by Theodore Goddard on a watching brief (they were taking it seriously, anyway); I took in the reporters scribbling (oh God, it would all be in the papers again); the lawyers, ushers and clerks; at the nearly empty public gallery (it soon filled and stayed full for the three days of the hearing. 'There's fun and games in this one,' cried the usher outside like a fairground barker to the visitors who were wondering in which court to titillate their curiosity about the law in its majesty). I felt so frightened I seemed to be hollow. The three days went by like a dream that alternated the glaringly vivid with foggy half-consciousness. The bits I remember clearly are remembered as feelings rather than events. Even the shapes of the judges are recalled as caricatures. Or were they really so grotesque?

Lord Justice Davies looked as though he had been at the best port too long. His complexion, which changed faster than coastal weather, ranged between mottled and puce. He seemed to grow out of the surrounding furniture like a fly-agaric toadstool with the droop. He was slumped or poured into his place, arms spread territorially; the opposite to a creature in nature that uses protective colouring, he proclaimed danger. His face stood out lividly. I was afraid he would lean over the bench, point his pencil, and bark, 'Off with his head.' In fact he growled 'Yes, Mr Law?' as though we were keeping him from some infinitely more attractive event. Not surprisingly, in view of Davies, Lord Justice Phillimore's appearance is one of the blanks in my memory. However, he was soon at it with the wig and within five minutes had got it on sideways with the pigtail over one ear. I remember he was bald with a pudgy face but that is all. If I have forgotten his appearance I shall always remember his manner. He was the judge with a divorce court background and so we had much to say to each other. Lord Justice Orr I thought of as The Skull and that is what he looked like; a bewigged death's-head. He sat at the far end away from me and only said one sentence in the whole three days. When he spoke, his voice was a shock. It didn't belong to his face and was lovely; excellently balanced and rich, the articulation clear, the whole effect perfect, self-conscious and phoney. It was well placed and had the pitch of the room at once. I was so taken aback I didn't hear the question he asked and just stared at him.

The drama had commenced and was sliding past my unfocused eyes like an endless sausage. Every now and again it would break and I would have a brief view of a cross-section, then it resumed its passage. No, to be more accurate, the scene was like an out-of-focus silent film which broke down spasmodically, leaving the protagonists frozen in front of me for a moment before going quickly on so that I couldn't grasp the essentials of the narrative.

For the whole of the first morning I sat there while Law, after initial stammers and stutters of sheer nerves, lumbered painstakingly over the old ground that I was a perjurious diddler of my wife and child as well as a dangerous, terrorising adulterer. I was getting more and more agitated and on the point of interrupting him when Davies chimed in. 'Mr Justice Latey covers all this, Mr Law. He clears Mr Frisby of that accusation after cross-examination, doesn't he? Look at his judgement.'

'Quite so, my Lord. He does give Mr Frisby the benefit of the doubt there.' Law said this very slowly, rolling with the punch, while he tried to think of a way of re-directing the judge's mind. I was furious at 'benefit of the doubt' and chimed in, 'What doubt?' which got me no marks. Deliverance came to Law in the form of a whisper from Rutter. Law relayed it. 'Mr Justice Latey called Mr Frisby's action a "manoeuvre" my Lords.' It was the most pejorative word they could find in the judgement and was wickedly out of context.

'Quite so. Quite so. I'm sure that is just what it was,' said Davies.

Phillimore looked up from Latey's judgement. 'He called it a lot more than that.' He sounded on my side.

Law stumbled on as I relaxed a bit.

At lunch-time a youngish man in the better-class legal uniform of navy-blue suit, striped shirt and plain tie came up to me. 'Hallo, you won't remember me, we met briefly once at a party. It transpired that he was an unlikely friend of Sylvester McCoy from the Ken Campbell Roadshow. 'I'm a barrister, John Tackaberry, will you have a drink with me?' As we walked to a pub he went on. 'Er—look, excuse my butting in, but may I offer a word.' I was eager. He continued, 'You see I've been watching it all from the back. May I suggest that you...' and there followed a series of tips; dos and don'ts before their terrifying Lordships. He was a marvellous unexpected boon. I told him all that I could in the time, especially about the point that there seemed to be no legal precedents to my cross-appeal out of time. He said he'd look up the books and see what he could find. That evening after the proceedings finished he told me that there was no case history to help me but none to hurt me either. He spent every minute that he could of the next three days in the court, or met me in the breaks to hear the details and advise me. Why he should have bothered I didn't know at the time, but discovered that, like Stephen, he was simply that decent.

Law continued during the afternoon and I sensed, more than consciously realised, that something was going wrong. Law seemed to be getting somewhere but I couldn't put my finger on it. Then I got into an argument with Davies about something trivial in Latey's judgement. My dispute finished with my saying something like 'Well, Mr Justice Latey didn't mean that, he meant the opposite.' Lord Chief Justice Davies glared down at me, changing colours like a faulty television set. 'I can read English just as well as you, young man,' he growled. The urge to cut my tongue out and offer him a slice was hard to resist.

I went home that evening still not knowing whether I would only be answering Law, or whether I would be able to argue my own cross-appeal for leave to appeal out of time. I was in the dark because I had no knowledge of simple rules of procedure and neither Stephen nor John Tackaberry had enlightened me because neither of them was aware of the depth of my ignorance. That evening I wrote an impassioned appeal to the judges to help me out of the difficulties I was in, included some good strong points in support of my case, and managed to get in first with it next morning. Their Lordships listened politely to this detour, then got on with the serious business of hearing Good-Old-Harry.

During that morning, the penny dropped as to where Law's circumlocutions had got us. He was arguing that Latey didn't have the power to upset a consent order. In the hearing before Latey, he and Miskin had agreed at once precisely where the judge's power lay. There was no dispute. Now, behind Miskin's back as it were, Rutter and Law were disputing that. Such was my naiveté that I thought this was cheating; yet another extension of their usual tactic of pointing in whatever direction

303

suited them in front of any particular judge. Of course, what they were doing was perfectly proper, indeed commonplace. It seemed to me that Law had merely tripped over this point about Latey's lack of power as he was trying on any old argument for size, but perhaps he was better than I give him credit for, because gaining it more or less wrapped their case up for them. Davies and Phillimore were saying that some part of Latey's judgement wasn't watertight in its logic. Unctuous agreement with any judicial remark once more oozed from Law's lips and he stared chastely down at his copy of Latey's judgement. 'Yes, my Lords, the language does appear to be somewhat corrupt at this point.' I gave an audible snort of disbelief. That Law, that bender and twister of words and figures, that hack-pleader of any old cause, could use the English language so, without any retribution or ribald laughter, didn't seem possible, and as I sat seething at the semantics, I suddenly realised that the ground had been swept away from all round me. I was marooned on a point of law. Justice was an irrelevance, so was the accuracy of my facts and figures, because the judges agreed that Latey hadn't the necessary power to touch any part of that order. I had now to succeed in my cross-appeal, namely to overturn the whole thing by proving it was no true consent order. To do that I had to make a prima facie case that various members of the legal profession were negligent or dishonourable or go back to square one.

In order to tell the whole story first I asked the judges to read my long affidavit. When they ordered me to read it out loud the bottom seemed to drop out of my stomach. The affidavit contained details of Christine's and my life that were necessary to refute what Rutter had put into documents, but were unbearable to say publicly. With misguided zeal I had even included in my evidence, photos of Christine in bikinis and modelling corsets to show how silly was the accusation in that vile discretionary statement that I had 'taunted her about her fat thighs.' Their Lordships must seldom have had more irrelevant, trivial, and titillating evidence shoved under their noses. The row of poised pencils in the press box look like pointed stakes. I have written earlier, when apologising for what looked like a disloyal indiscretion, of 'the stripping process that enables me to write this.' The Court of Appeal was the climax of that process. After that hearing, embarrassment was for me an extinct emotion. But, as I started reading, it was alive and kicking. I had crawled, emotionally, under a stone.

I was so nervous I read too loudly, then too quickly; once my voice snapped into falsetto. I felt cheap, like a barrack-room barrister in the musty dignity. I had three volumes of legal correspondence and affidavits I had assembled in quintuplicate (one set each for the judges, one for Rutter, one for me) to prove details of the story should Their Lordships ask for supporting evidence. They didn't. However it was a good story, before long I could feel the attentive silence right through the crowded court. At one section Christine had a cry but I can't remember where. Their Lordships, when I glanced up, all had their heads down, riveted to my affidavit. They had long abandoned listening to me and were pages ahead like boys in class who have been given a good yarn as the set book. They industriously underlined and noted points as they read. About three-quarters of the way through the affidavit we adjourned for the day. Things looked all right.

The next morning I finished reading the affidavit which concluded with how I had tape-recorded my former legal advisers. In the following, when I set out a person's words like play dialogue, I am using the shorthand notes of a court reporter who was present:

Frisby: The next evidence I wish to produce to this court are some transcripts of extracts of these conferences and telephone conversations with my former legal advisers. I think they prove without a shadow of doubt all that I have just been telling you.

I looked up and nearly fell over backwards in dismay. If I have ever seen hatred in men's eyes I saw it then, in triplicate. Davies was pulsing like a multicoloured bullfrog; Phillimore had gone indignantly puffy, his wig crooked; Orr stared balefully past me. Any suspicions that they may have harboured about my character were all confirmed at that moment. I was a bad lot and, like the messengers of antiquity who were beheaded for bringing the bad news, I was deemed a scoundrel because of the evidence of dishonesty that I brought. It clung to me in festoons of evil-smelling recording-tape.

After heaving about in his seat for a while and banging his pencil on the bench, Davies spoke.

Davies: To what particular end would this evidence be directed if we permit it to be given?
Frisby: I think I can show without any shadow of doubt sufficient evidence to prove that I was driven and forced to settle by a QC who was determined that I should settle. All the facts are indisputable.

The temperature rose even higher when I singled out Comyn for attack. Their Lordships seethed.

Phillimore: You have a finding by the judge of the other way.
Frisby: No evidence was produced to the judge. I am asking only that you look at these things and decide where we go from there.
Davies: I don't see how you can go behind this order. The judge accepted that you were very unwilling to settle but in the end you did agree. I don't see what evidence you can have to go behind that.

305

The argument that then followed between the three of them and me is a blur. I can extract moments, I believe the important moments, but not the whole. I know that the hands of the clock moved round twenty minutes and that I kept telling myself if I sat down I was a dead duck, so I stayed vertical and just kept talking to try and force them to hear the extracts from the transcripts. There was an argument about the conduct of the various solicitors involved, but my evidence depended first on Comyn's fulsome statements that he had 'forced' me, 'driven' me and was 'determined' I should settle.

'But I'm saying my barristers acted questionably, too, My Lords,' I said. 'And, as you well know, a person cannot sue a barrister who has acted for him in litigation. A barrister is uniquely privileged in this way. I am sure you would not want to send the message out from this court that members of the bar are protected from a client getting just redress.'

This got me minus points. As they would not hear the transcripts, I produced Paddy Grafton Green's note of Rutter's threats that he would destroy me. To my dismay the three judges actually chuckled over this. 'I'll bet there are worse threats than that made in litigation,' said Davies.

'Is that how you think divorce should be conducted?' I asked. 'I hope that is published widely in our press today.' Davies glared even harder. An apt irony was that the court was at that time in the process of being wired so that proceedings could be tape-recorded. I drew their attention to the unconnected wires hanging down and said something about the law limping into the twentieth century. I pointed out that a policeman's notebook and solicitors' notes are accepted as very reliable evidence in courts of law, then why not my electronic one-hundred-per-cent accurate notebook? No answer.

The police had by then got criminal convictions using tape-recordings. They were admissible. 'If the police can get criminal convictions using tapes, why will you not hear tapes from a private person involving members of the bar?' This question got no answer and more minus points for me.

There was some sort of a disturbance in the public gallery and Their Lordships' glares were directed away from me for a moment. I told them that if they wouldn't hear the transcripts I would publish them after the hearing and play the tapes in public. One or all of the above and whatever else came into my head to say in that twenty minutes caused Their Lordships eventually to confer. Their conference produced this.

Davies: Mr Law, what do you say about this suggestion that he should put in transcripts of conversations with his legal advisers to persuade this court, contrary to the finding of Mr Justice Latey in March, that he never agreed or that he was forced to settle against his will?

Well, Law had a wonderful time answering that. He must seldom have stood in court against an opponent who had so much mud clinging.

Law: We don't want to restrict the respondent in any way in adducing any evidence he wishes to put in. But there does come a stage...

Then he went on to say that the recordings all took place before Latey's March hearing (which they didn't), so I should have submitted them to Latey...that I shouldn't be allowed to now...that anyway they may well rebound on my head...that they might be fakes...he was able in sorrow, rather than anger to point simultaneously in more directions than he had dreamed existed.

I stood there repeating myself. I had no further ideas.

Frisby: All that I want to do is to establish beyond reasonable doubt that everything in the affidavit is true. If a QC forced me and drove me to settle, is that not relevant?

Finally their Lordships found a way of shutting me up.

Davies: We are not making any decision yet. Give us an example.
Phillimore: Your best one.
Davies: (He positively snarled this) Your ace of trumps.

At this I froze and caught his eye. He realised he had gone too far. I said, 'I don't understand you. What do you mean "ace of trumps," My Lord?' Davies merely sat and glared; at me, at his papers, at the wall. When it was obvious that he wasn't going to answer I said, 'They are a series of conferences, which is interlocking, containing evidence regarding the negligence or misbehaviour of all or some of my former legal advisers. What does Your Lordship mean, "ace of trumps?" Is that a legal term?'

If Davies has ever been more angry I am glad I wasn't there, but I had long abandoned the lawyers' game of sycophancy to the judge.

Phillimore spat out, 'Get on with it.'

So I read them the extract in which, in spite of my protestations to the contrary, Comyn said, 'No, no, I'll accept forced. Yes, I'll buy that...I certainly drove you...I was determined you would settle.'

There followed an amazing exchange between us. Phillimore practically jeered, his voice sliding upwards in derision.

Phillimore: There's nothing in that.

Davies: Speaking for myself I don't think it takes you anywhere. All
            Comyn is saying is that he takes the view that you ought to
            settle. It is a counsel's duty to do this.

'But that is *not* what he's saying,' I retorted. 'You are saying that is what
he said, but he didn't. He said he forced me. Here.' And I waved the
transcript at them. '"I'll accept forced." Is it a counsel's duty to force his
clients? If so, then say so in your judgement. Let the country know that
barristers may force and are then protected by law.'

Davies ignored that one and changed tack. 'Anyway, I don't believe you
could be forced,' said Davies. 'Look at you now.'

'Now is now,' I said. 'I'm talking about then.' Anyway *I*'m not the only
one saying he forced me, *he* is, too.'

Phillimore: Just think of your tax position if this matter was settled quietly
             and privately before the judge and did not get any publicity.
             Now you see you have brought it all out into the open and I
             should have thought you were more at risk with regard to the
             Inland Revenue. If you publish to the whole world that you
             have engaged in a tax fiddle obviously the Revenue are going
             to follow it up.

That was a Court of Appeal judge saying those words, telling me, like
Taylor, Comyn, Calderan and co, that I should have covered up.

Frisby: I have never believed that I have engaged in a tax fiddle. I
            have engaged in what I understood was a perfectly legitimate
            course of events. If it is a tax fiddle let us go to the Revenue. I
            am bankrupt and following bankruptcy homeless and possibly
            my mother too.

The desperation in my voice must have got through to Davies because
for the first and only time he tried to pacify me.

Davies: We follow the seriousness of it. Don't think we do not follow it.

I tried at about this point to get in some more of the transcripts but the
judges wouldn't allow that so I once more quoted Comyn, 'Yes I forced
you...I drove you. I was determined...you should settle...' and then
produced the following letter from him. I thought it would be conclusive of
Comyn's duplicity.

Queen Elizabeth Building
Temple
EC4Y 9BS

April 16th 1972

Dear Mr Frisby,

I am glad you had success before Mr Justice Latey and I hope it continues in the Court of Appeal.

I am well aware that you have been suggesting that Mr Neil Taylor, Messrs Theodore Goddard and I were all negligent in the handling of our case. You of course are equally aware that we strongly deny it.

Your case was, as you know, a very difficult one for you, for many reasons - particularly in view of the history about Discovery of Documents. I did my best for you as I think you felt at the time.

It is quite correct that I urged you most strongly to settle. I do not recall saying that I 'drove' you into a settlement, but if I did it is rather too strong a phrase. You will accept, I am sure, that you are not the sort of person who can be 'driven' save in the limited sense of feeling the force of circumstances and of the advice you are given.

My view certainly was a 'determined' one but you must not take that word as meaning that I would - or did - use any improper or unfair pressure. I am accustomed to expressing my views forcefully and I felt sure that that was what you wanted of your counsel.

You speak of the question being whether you settled 'willingly or otherwise.' You were undoubtedly *reluctant* to settle but there was full and fervent discussion with you about settlement and you authorised and accepted it. As for 'mistake' I certainly acknowledge no mistake.

I will be very happy if you do in fact achieve something better than the settlement.

Yours sincerely,

JAMES COMYN

When I had finished reading this Phillimore slapped the bench in front of him. 'There you are. He says he didn't force you. There's written evidence.'

There was a noise resembling a corporate hoot from the public gallery. Davies glared and, while I stood wondering what to say next, the judges accepted Comyn's letter as evidence while refusing to accept the transcript. I pointed out again that the police had already used tape-recordings in evidence to get convictions of criminals, and asked why this court wouldn't when I was trying to expose members of the legal profession. Davies came up with 'You have edited these tapes, therefore they are not admissible.'

I answered eagerly. 'I have edited nothing. The tapes are complete. I can bring them along and play them to you. In stereo. Or if you grant an adjournment I'll transcribe the lot.' This was ignored. I noticed in the dialogue above that it reads as though I was standing up for myself rather well. This is misleading. I was crawling. It took all my nerve just to stay on my feet in the face of their combined wrath. The urge to crumple and give in was very strong, but I see in looking at the court reporter's notes that every second sentence I said to them was full of apologies for taping their legal brethren. Lines occur like, 'I view these tapes with a certain amount of distaste as I can see you do,' and, 'I am deeply conscious of Your Lordships' distaste for these tape recordings.'

I had one last go at my key sentence. 'In this matter of my being forced, there are only two participants, Comyn and me. And there are only two witnesses. Us. I say he forced me and he says he forced me. That is all the evidence you have before you. If everybody concerned in the incident says he forced me, surely that is a prima facie case that he forced me.'

Phillimore said, 'He says in his letter, he didn't.

I was dead and knew it. I stared back at him and Davies and tried to muster enough contempt for them in my eyes to match their fury at me. I must say they both had the grace to look embarrassed.

Frisby: It is my understanding of the law that tape recordings have been admitted in certain cases. If you take this decision and don't admit these transcripts and show me the door of this Court, you show me certain bankruptcy. Someone who has acted decently and generously and did his best to settle this divorce.

Davies: What you have shown us as an example does not get you anywhere near where you want to get.

Frisby: I don't think I have any case before you further.

And I sat down.

We adjourned for lunch and I sprinted to lose the reporters and photographers. After lunch Phillimore gave his judgement. They were professionals all right. That judgement was sixteen pages long and watertight. He opened with, 'This is a lamentable piece of litigation,' forgetting that it was not I that who had brought the appeal. They offered me their sympathy for my predicament, then trussed, gagged and wrapped me up so that I would never bother anyone again.

Their judgement rested firmly on two feet of clay.

1) Never mind about the legal niceties, the terms of the
consent order were fair, just and equitable in *FACT*.
2) They had heard my tape transcripts and they were valueless.

Referring to the tapes, as Davies glowered down, Phillimore said something like, 'be warned,' and went on, 'And the long and short of it is that if you talk to Mr Frisby you are liable to find that what you have said is recorded. We asked Mr Frisby to produce the most cogent of all this transcripts so as to satisfy us that there was new evidence to show that he did not agree with the compromise. Having read and listened to the reading of the documents to which he directed our attention, I am bound to say that I do not think they proved anything of the sort.' (Phillimore said 'documents,' in fact they would only hear half of one page of transcript out of sheaves of it.) He then said that they refused to hear more transcripts because I had 'edited' them so they were not 'reliable evidence.' This was simply untrue. Thus were the tapes rendered impotent.

The following exchange took place about the new date they were about to set for me to repay the mortgage.

Phillimore: The only thing is, you have told us about this writ from your
own solicitors.
Frisby: Yes, My Lord.
Phillimore: I would not like them to get in ahead of this mortgage.

Our eyes met and Phillimore stammered, coughed and gave a half giggle as he realised what he had said. Namely, that I was likely to be bankrupted. Since he had just called our divorce settlement 'fair, just and equitable in fact' he was saying that it was 'sound and sensible' to bankrupt a husband in divorce. So I said, 'Would you explain to me how it is a good order when you've just admitted it'll bankrupt me?' They ignored me and I said, 'How's it good for my ex-wife to have me bankrupt?' No answer.

I automatically asked for leave to appeal to the House of Lords (I had no intention of doing so) and Davies snapped back that only they could give leave and they refused it. I could appeal '…only on a question of law and there is no question of law, as I see it, in this case; it is pure fact; that is the trouble.'

And here was the beauty of their craftsmanship: if they had found that Latey had no power to change the consent order (they had said exactly

311

that during the hearing) I could have appealed to the House of Lords on that point of law and, so I have been advised, won. But that legal point was not in their judgement. They found against me in fact, not law, and in findings of fact they are the highest court in the land. So that was the end of that road for me. And when the Court of Appeal says it was 'a fair, just and equitable order in fact,' I no longer had any case for negligence against my former legal advisers. So, that shut off my other route to get recompense. The order not only stood, it was good. Phillimore's slip on my pending bankruptcy, 'Get the wife's claim in first before his former lawyers bust him', was their only stumble.

Sir James Comyn QC was then on the verge of becoming and was subsequently appointed to be a High Court judge. He was a man who belonged to the same crowd as that trio who had just exonerated him, had known them for years, had fought cases against and under them, drank with them, eaten with them, was one of them. He was from the Inner Temple like Davies, and his chambers were in the Queen Elizabeth building with Phillimore's. What could be more incestuous?

Costs were awarded against me.

I had to struggle through the crowd to get out of the court. Press and strangers were talking to me in a babble. A respectable middle-class-looking woman kept tugging my arm, she was crying and repeating 'I always believed in British justice, but I don't now.' Then I gave a silly, emotional press conference in the corridor. When everyone else had cleared off John Tackaberry took me back to his chambers for tea.

As we walked through a lovely sunlit square behind the Royal Courts of Justice he said, apologetically, 'Please don't believe we're all like that.'

Time to sum up again, both on that hearing and the actions of Sir James Comyn QC and Our Lords of Appeal, Davies, Phillimore and Orr.

THE HEARING

Their Lordships boiled the matter down to two simple issues of fact (not law, ordinary facts): 1) Was the original settlement just and fair? 2) Was it a true consent order.

So, 1) Was it just and fair? I have already quoted the figures enough times to show that it was insane, even before Andrew Park's Opinion showed it to be doubly so. I was bankrupted by it. But only on paper so far. The Revenue had not yet assessed me and made their demands. They could claim under law £130,000. Far more than I owned. But would they? Nobody knew. How could any division of such a financial situation be just to both parties? Of course it couldn't. There was only ever one solution to our situation and Latey stated it, it was the one I put in place before Rutter's initial disastrous intervention: pay income fairly to Christine and me from what was still flowing in from *Soup*, then wait and see about the capital division.

But Their Lordships said, against all the evidence, that the consent order was 'just and fair'. Why? My answer is unequivocal: to protect Comyn. I'll return to that.

2) Was it a true consent settlement? If it was, there is an almost overwhelming argument in law to say that whether it was 'just and fair' is not relevant. I consented. If I didn't like it afterwards, tough, I shouldn't have signed.

But Their Lordships had tape-recorded evidence before them which - *prima facie* only - demonstrated that I had been 'forced' to sign, 'was driven' to sign by a QC who 'was determined' I should settle. This evidence was irrefutable. Comyn said these things - indeed, volunteered the words under no pressure whatsoever. The tapes are not faked, the conversations happened.

Therefore, *prima facie*, it was not a true consent order. There is no argument. The matter should have been re-opened, as I was asking the court, even if that re-opening only took us as far as establishing what Comyn meant by his words and why he had said them. But who knows what uncharted tunnels that would have led us down? So Their Lordships refused. Why? Once again my answer is: to protect Comyn. But not only Comyn, their motives are much more subtle and complex than a simple question of look-after-the-boys. What were they? The answer to this I try to give in the following paragraphs. It is, I think, right at the heart of why our legal system is so inadequate when it comes to judging itself.

THE RIGHT HONOURABLE LORD JUSTICES DAVIES, PHILLIMORE AND ORR

These men jointly reached a decision which was obviously unfair, was an affront to good sense and which adversely affected the rest of my life. That doesn't matter, a lawyer would say, if it was right in law. But they based their judgement on facts, not law. Why did they ignore the simple mathematics and the evidence to reach such an unjust verdict? Well, although I say to protect Comyn, it goes much deeper. Let me try two simple hypotheses.

1) Suppose for a moment that I had had a famous QC representing me, who brought all his authority, reputation and weight to bear behind my evidence in that court. He could not have been ignored as I was. That evidence would have been listened to, weighed - possibly fairly - and the meaning of Comyn's words given due consideration.

2) To take it further, suppose those tapes had been obtained by the police, and the person they had recorded was a suspected criminal. Those judges would have gladly accepted those tape-recordings as evidence, and their judgement would have had remarks like, 'We are lucky to have such a fine, intelligent and diligent police force.'

313

Those tape-recordings were, after all, not illegal bugs or invasions of anyone's privacy. They were simply a record of meetings, paid for by me, that took place between me and my hired legal advisers.

But those judges were incapable of looking the facts squarely in the face when those facts upset their lifelong preconceptions. They were protecting Comyn, yes, but not just because they were looking after a chum (which they were) but because to accept my evidence would have taken them down a road that they were not capable of travelling. That road, which would have opened up questions about the status, the rights, the practices of barristers, was an unthinkable route for them. And to have been shown that road by a jumped-up litigant-in-person was an affront to their whole lives. I failed even to consider those things before I looked up from my papers in that courtroom and saw three pairs of eyes looking at me with hatred. Yes, that is what was in them. It would have been unthinkable for them to have James Comyn QC, about to be a High Court judge, cross-examined by a litigant-in-person in their court. They committed the worst of judicial crimes, they were prejudiced.

Some years later Lord Justice Denning, Master of the Rolls, gave a perfect example of what I am arguing. He was giving judgement in an early appeal by the Birmingham Six.

> 'If the case were won it would mean the police were guilty of perjury, violence and threats and that confessions were improperly admitted in evidence...'

Denning simply couldn't contemplate such a breadth and depth of corruption in the police force. So he refused the appeal. He was later proved wrong. Similarly Davies, Phillimore and Orr couldn't accept that Comyn, 'one of us,' was equally guilty of lying, threats and incompetence.

Of course, my case, as I say in the preface to this book, did not involve my being incarcerated for years, or terrorism, or people's death's. It is far less important. But the same forces were at work: those people at the head of our system of justice are simply incapable of looking honestly at themselves. Long-held power has made them too arrogant. And, to cement the myopia into the system, barristers are protected by law from their clients. All judges are ex-barristers.

So, I was some scoundrelly, muck-raking theatrical who was deservedly seen off. And British justice continued on it's unjust way. And still does.

The Hon Mr Justice Latey, later the Rt Hon Lord Justice Latey

Head of the Latey Commission which had lowered the age of suffrage in this country to eighteen, this famous, open-minded, liberal judge did his best to help me out of what he clearly saw as an unfair situation. He also tried to be a peacemaker. He understood the mess I was in and heard my verbal evidence, yet what did he say about all the lawyers involved?

Although the case was 'a grim fantasy' and Rutter was 'aggressive,' 'belligerent,' 'outdated,' 'adversarial,' 'stoking up pain and bitterness unnecessarily' he was also 'astute' and 'highly efficient'. My team had given me 'the best possible advice' although the settlement was signed on a 'substantial faulty basis of fact.' I was 'intelligent', 'generous', 'honest', 'had presented my case to him better than many lawyers,' and 'had a thorough understanding of the issues', but when it came to my opposition to Comyn 'it may well have been a case where the husband did not himself appreciate the balance of factors.'

It's a nonsense, isn't it?

Latey was not prepared to look at what was staring him in the face. Fair-minded or not, he could no more contemplate the incompetence and dishonesty of his legal brethren than could those three judges in the Court of Appeal. So his judgement pointed simultaneously in opposite directions: he overturns a consent order (at the heart of English law), but everything in the legal garden is rosy.

James Comyn QC, later the honourable Mr Justice Comyn

I have already said, in my earlier assessment of him that he was an innumerate, pompous windbag, but after this hearing that judgement is too lenient. He was dishonest too. He was a man at the height of his powers and of his profession who promised to say all those things, 'I forced you,' 'I drove you,' 'I was determined you would settle,' before 'any court in the world.' And then he welshed on his promise. He sat on the sidelines and let his client suffer for years to save his own wretched skin. Comyn should have been struck off, or whatever they do to a dishonest QC. Instead he became a High Court judge.

There was a fitting, I might say sublime, pay-off to all this. Still believing in British justice, I complained about Comyn, with evidence to the Bar Council. My complaint was brushed aside. What I didn't know was that, when I complained, the chairman of the Bar Council was...yes...James Comyn QC.

Chapter XXXVI

1972-3

So, I was left, impotently waiting for bankruptcy. I paid the thousands of capital I was ordered to pay and went deeper into debt. One of the ironies of my situation was that, as income still flowed in from *Soup,* my credit was good. But the flow was too slow to cope with all these demands.

There was one loophole left: the maintenance. Although the capital parts of the consent order had been confirmed for good by Their Lordships, under divorce law every maintenance order is a temporary order, subject to variation when there is a 'change of circumstances' between the parties. There was certainly that now: she was worth at least £80,000; I was bankrupt (still only on paper, that was the complicating factor). My income was running at about £8,000 per annum. I was paying £7,000 of that in maintenance. The law at that time said that you should pay up to a half of your income to your ex-wife and up to one sixth for each child. Orders were generally for less than those maximum figures.

The extraordinary effect, perhaps I should say non-effect, of the judgement was that although it was shattering, it did not dent my belief in the even-handedness of British justice when applied between civilians. Oh, yes, I was convinced that Our Lords had behaved like the three wise monkeys about their own profession but I still thought that the logic of the figures of our financial state must prevail. It was only a question of getting tactics right. I set quickly about the task. Rule one: no more complaints about lawyers; facts and figures only. The next few months were like a brief impressionist dream, so quickly was I disabused.

I made a triple application to Latey on maintenance, improved access to Dominic and joint custody of him. I cancelled Christine's maintenance payments pending the hearing. This was a perfectly proper, even an advisable thing to do in the circumstances. The point being that, whatever order the judge would make at the hearing, he could then date or backdate it to when he considered the change in circumstances to have taken place. Then all payments would be adjusted. It is a practice that ensures that lawyers get on with pre-hearing preliminaries and stops one side or the other benefiting from deliberate delay. As for the application for joint custody, all that meant was that I was asking for an equal say in Dominic's future. Custody is not care and control. That was Christine's and I never disputed it. Then I had to go briefly away with the Ken Campbell Roadshow.

———————

On the morning of my return I looked out of my front window to see bailiff's men taking my car away for sale to pay Christine's maintenance. She had applied for and got a court order in my absence. God knows what Rutter or Law had said about me to some new judge. I put on the litigation suit and went to court to get my car back. Rutter and Law had a field day. The judgement of the Court of Appeal was a magnificent new instrument for them. It was waved, quoted, misquoted, heads were shaken over it, hands were wrung. I had committed crimes I hadn't even heard of. The judge stared at me with curiosity and no little anxiety while the list was poured into his ear. When he learned that my application to Latey had been pending all along he stopped Law at once, gave me my car back and left the maintenance cancelled, as was the proper course in the circumstances. Net result of Rutter's improper action: one hundred and seventy-six pounds down the drain to regain possession of my car and no reprimand for him.

Soup closed. There was no doubt now about my claim to 'a change in circumstances' to Latey. The play had become the longest-running comedy in the history of West End theatre and was second play or musical overall only to *The Mousetrap*. My income from that source was on its terminal dive, having made me well over a third of a million pounds. Meanwhile I was applying to have my ex-wife's maintenance reduced to keep financially afloat. A triumph for British justice.

A legal bombshell followed: Latey refused to hear the case again. He said it would be unfair. I was transferred to Mr Justice Ormrod.

As a preliminary to that hearing I had to get another one for discovery before a registrar to extract the financial facts about Christine because Rutter would supply none. These facts were essential for my case and I had a right to them.

I was nervous but eager for our first face to face confrontation as I waited in that dim, crowded corridor in Somerset House that opened into the registrars' beautifully proportioned, sunny rooms. The hearing was a farce, run quite improperly by a registrar whose name I have unfortunately lost. When you make any application, the form is that you present your case, then your opponent answers it. The registrar wouldn't even let me speak. Rutter started talking as we walked in. Before I could open my mouth he was seated, with documents spread, unctuously rolling out Latey's compliments about him. The registrar, a lowly creature really, was much impressed by such words from a High Court judge. I was reduced to one-line interjections when I could.

'Would you also point out Mr Justice Latey's four condemnations of your handling of this case,' I said. I was ignored. 'Would you also—'

317

'Really, how can I present my application with these constant interruptions?' said Rutter in studied exasperation.

'I thought it was my application' I said and was silenced by the registrar.

'The husband has caused endless trouble in this case, which is why I have asked for extensive discovery,' said Rutter. I gasped involuntarily and was shushed, then had to fume in silence as the accusations against me issued from Rutter's knowing mouth in a malignant, time-consuming queue. It was a marvellous filibuster. I got about seven minutes out of the two hours to put my case. Rutter got a lengthy order for discovery (every item of which had been freely offered by me) and I failed to get some important items I badly wanted.

To be so roundly walloped in head-on contest increased my view of Rutter as a malevolent being. It took Tim Akeroyd, Stephen Mitchell's assistant, to get him into perspective. Tim was late twenties, round-faced and gentle, with large, vague, blue eyes behind glasses. He telephoned me one day. 'I've just had a letter from Rutter.' He sighed, 'He is, as usual, at a loss to understand anything.' I started laughing, it so exactly caught the phraseology. Tim went on, 'I think we'd better call him Splutter from now on, don't you.' This mild joke, far more balanced than Theodore Goddard's 'Gutter,' was appropriate. I always thought of Rutter so in future.

So now we had the prospect of a hearing in front of a new High Court judge without the details of Christine's finances that should have been an important part of my case. It had been demonstrated that, with that Court of Appeal judgement hung round my neck, a registrar wouldn't even listen to me, let alone observe the correct procedures in his own little court. What would a High Court judge do? We reluctantly decided that I must have a barrister represent me. We had enough financial figures to make a go of it.

Douglas Hogg, then a junior counsel (later the Minister of Agriculture who presided over the BSE cock-up), was hired. He did the sums, agreed the situation was dotty and went into court against Good-Old-Harry before Mr Justice Ormrod. As we waited outside, Douglas said 'Ormrod's a fast judge. He hates ditherers.' How right he was. Law shoved the judgement of the Court of Appeal under Ormrod's nose and Douglas's feet never touched the ground. Talking nineteen to the dozen he read Ormrod the figures. Ormrod refused to believe that I couldn't pay all and sundry, heard no verbal evidence, called my financial state 'a Byzantine structure, and a leaky one, too' (how right he was), and threw us all out. Even my application for improved access to Dominic and joint custody was ignored. I was not fit to see my own son more than once a fortnight, nor fit to make decisions about his future. I was just there to be milked.

As we walked back to Douglas's chambers in the Temple I suggested that I play the tape of Comyn, 'forced you…etc.' from a loudspeaker van outside Comyn's chambers until something happened.

Hogg said, 'Comyn'll just get an injunction and have you removed.'

I said 'Well, how about playing it up and down the road outside the Royal Courts of Justice.'

'You'll just make a fool of yourself,' said Douglas. 'And get nowhere, which is worse. Look, Rutter's about sixty. Law's about the same, Comyn's in his fifties. They'll be dead soon. You look healthy, outlive 'em. Outlive your wife. Outlive all of 'em. That's the way to win.'

As legal advice it was an improvement on Taylor's and Theodore Goddard's, 'Emigrate.'

It was obvious that some sort of watershed had arrived in my life - perhaps I should say, yet another watershed. I had to sit down and think again about everything.

To repeat the figures in detail and show how they had worsened would be too tedious, you have the overall picture. Anyway, the figures were never static. What was peculiar, though, to my situation is worth repeating. I was broke but not poor (not yet, anyway). There was all this money in Switzerland which I couldn't touch. It was theoretically earning interest (although not in reality at that time, world stock markets had been bearish since I left France in 1968, when they were at their all-time highs, and the universal inflation that shook the West for a decade or so was just getting under way). Waiting for me at some point down the road was the Revenue with £130,000 bill claimable under law. Yet any bank loaned me money at the drop of a hat as income from *Soup* still came in from tours and other productions. But it went out even quicker without my ever touching it. And, at any moment, there would be coming through my door a very heavy bill from Rutter for the last two-and-a-half years. As he had won everything, I owed for everything. It was a mind-bending situation to be in.

I tried to make sense of my finances: my mother's home was sold to my brother so that she would be secure when I eventually went bust, then I sold everything else that I owned in this country (my house was fully mortgaged) and paid all immediate debts except the overdraft. Rutter was going to have fun trying to get his costs out of me when that day arrived.

I thought long and hard about the Trust. The investments made by the Swiss Bank Corporation, though admirable, could not hope to grow quickly enough to meet the huge demands the Revenue could be about to levy on me. We had to gamble, go for swift capital growth, it was the only way out. There was no point in sitting tight to see if I would eventually go down by £X,000 or £Y,000; down is down.

So, after discussions with the trustees, the Trust sold all its share portfolio and bought paintings, silver, land and - on deferred payments, the biggest gamble of all - a piece of a development scheme in Canada. The point about this purchase was that more land was bought than the Trust could pay for so that we could get the maximum profit when we sold. But it had to grow in value quickly or I had dug an even bigger pit for myself and the Trust. As an investment plan the whole thing was seriously unbalanced but

319

needs must when the devil…etc. It was going to be a race, not a bad strategy in view of everything. The outcomes I faced were: either my next play would make big money again, or the investments would expand quickly enough, or my paper bankruptcy would become reality. I owed Rutter nearly £20,000; a tax demand for £24,500 was imminent and behind that was the big potential tax demand for anything up to another £105,000. I lived my usual comfortable, but not lavish, lifestyle. When the time-bomb went off it wasn't going to be for the price of theatre tickets and a cosy dinner for two afterwards. Indeed, I quite looked forward to the Revenue busting me; an impersonal matter followed by freedom. Confident that I had done the best in the circumstances, I settled down to concentrate on the play I had been scratching at for two and a half years.

There followed thirteen litigation-free months. Besides writing My Play, I resumed acting and had three or four solid leading parts on TV, but the goodie was to be in the new John Osborne play, or rather, anti-play *A Sense of Detachment*. This was a real theatrical event. I was the Interrupter, a boring, middle-class fart who started in the front row, ranged the auditorium and finished on the stage, objecting to whatever was taking place there. It was the sort of thing that I love, ad-libbing in character, arguing with the audience, generally having a wonderful time, with a string of pompous one-liners to fall back on if I got into trouble.

On the first night I was leaning on the circle rail, shouting one of Osborne's self-directed insults at the stage, when I felt a probing finger against my anus. There was a loud audience laugh as I completed the line with a gasp and turned to find myself looking at the grinning face of Jill Bennett the actress, then Mrs Osborne, middle finger triumphantly upraised. I could think of no response that was in character. There were layers of Pirandello-esque unreality; playwright's wife defending husband's work from outraged Interrupter who is really an actor saying husband's lines…etc. There cannot be many actors who have had the playwright's wife's finger up his arse, on the first night (at any rate before the performance was over) in the middle of one of his better lines, in full view of hundreds of people. Jill said afterwards that it seemed like a fun idea. It was, at least, more fun than being screwed in the law courts.

The play was murdered by the reviewers, but the cast came out of it very well. John Standing, Nigel Hawthorne, Denise Coffey, Rachel Kempson, Hugh Hastings and Ralph Michael were those confined to the stage, thus becoming targets for the audience's anger (and there was plenty of it); Dave Hill was a working class reactionary in a box and Jeni Barnett sat with me as my embarrassed, submissive wife. The play had John Osborne's knack of upsetting a wide variety of people and there were nightly rows and scenes of disorder in the theatre; a woman took off a thigh-length boot and threw it from the gallery at the actors (the fools returned it); pennies used to rain down (that is horrid, they are dangerous and they hurt); Rachel Kempson bounded off the stage one night (a wonderful athletic feat for a senior citizen, but by God was she angry) and assaulted two young men who were heckling her; possibly the only occasion in theatrical history when a member of the cast (female) has assaulted two members of the audience (male). One of the males then got set on by another member of the audience (male) and got a front tooth knocked out. It all ended up in Rachel's dressing room the following evening with champagne, forgiveness and headlines. The play's run was extended by public demand. We were packed.

Something took place on the first night which says much of reviewers and gave the cast great satisfaction. Among theatrical professionals the one breed of person you will find universally loathed is the reviewer (I will not flatter with the word, 'critic'). There is at best only wary politeness extended towards them, and at worst, wounded rage.

A Sense of Detachment probably had a unique cast in that more than half were playwrights. The anti-reviewer sentiment was loud and clear backstage. It was generally assumed that we would be slaughtered, but the play was so peculiar nobody was sure.

'I'll guarantee us one good notice,' I said to John Standing, my bombast barely covering my fear. We were queueing for the backstage lavatory, a fully utilised amenity on first nights.

'Who from?' asked John.

'Harold Hobson. You see.'

'Don't do anything silly,' he said, disappearing inside.

Hobson was then on *The Sunday Times*, one of our two or three most influential reviewers. He was sat on the end seat of the front row. When I made my second disgusted exit to the bar I fell over his extended gammy leg, picked myself up, apologising profusely, then gasped in amazement, 'Good God, it's Dobson of the *Telegraph*, isn't it?' He went pink with pleasure at the laughter. 'I can't wait to see what you've got to say about this rubbish.' More laughter, deeper pink. For the rest of the evening I referred and deferred to him drawing his attention to lines that I found especially repellent and chortling at the way he would castigate this tripe. He had a wonderful evening. He was never so important. His review of the play was a purple gurgle of prostrated praise finishing with his famous 'I shall go again and again' (always translated filthily by actors as, 'I shall come again and again'). Sure enough he rolled up three weeks later and, on spotting him, I stopped the play and offered to sue him on the grounds that it was his notice in the *Telegraph* that had gulled me into the theatre. He sat giggling into my face as I thrust my ticket stubs under his nose and demanded my money back. We got a second rave notice and *Soup*, which he hadn't much cared for originally, got a retrospective pat on the head. When it came to arse-crawling, I thought, Rutter and Law in front of a High Court judge weren't in the same class as me in front of one of them.

Christine arrived at the theatre one evening. I was passing through the bar on my way to my front-row seat when I saw her with a well-known theatrical agent. I was still banned from 1 Genoa Avenue, still clocking on and off for Dominic, still forced to perform the weekly Berlin Wall handover at the front door. Now, here she was on my territory. It was a repetition of the first night of the film of *Soup* when she had arrived with Nat. If the occasion was attractive enough, proximity to me could be risked, but if it was a discussion about Dominic's future I was unfit; go and talk to Rutter. I took a couple of deep breaths to keep calm and said to Jeni Barnett, 'Listen to what happens carefully. You may have to give evidence.' I asked an usherette to do the same, then I went up to Christine.

'Hallo, Christine. What are you doing here?' I asked politely.

'Oh, hallo, I've come to see the play.'

'You've got a cheek, haven't you? I thought you had to be protected from me. How is it that you dare to come here?'

'What?' said Christine, dismayed. The well-known agent, shuffled, coughed and said something like, 'Can I help?'

I went on with what I thought was icy calm 'It's a free country, Christine. If you want to go to a theatre where I am, it's your business but I warn you that if you come in there and sit down I'm going to stop the play and tell the audience what you make me go through to see Dominic. I'm going to invite you to stand up and explain to them why you stopped me from seeing him for five months; why you tried to have me put in gaol for walking him in the park; why you won't let me—'

At about this point I was aware of the well-known agent talking at my elbow. 'I don't think I should be hearing this,' he said. 'I don't think you should be involving me in your private...' (aren't agents wonderful?)

I said to him 'You do what you like. But if she comes in she's going to have to answer for her actions. I've no doubt she has very good reasons and will be happy to explain to everybody.'

Christine left, followed by him, poor man. Jeni and I took our places in the auditorium. I glanced at her. Her eyes were full of tears. Jeni has easily stirred emotions, one of those people it is always a bonus to bump into.

'What's up?' I said. 'I behaved perfectly properly, didn't I?'

She started to cry. The play was about to start.

'I didn't shout or rage or threaten or anything, did I?'

'No, no. I've never seen anything so polite. It was horrible.'

'Well, then?'

'That look on your face. It's terrible. Please don't look like that.'

'What d'you mean? I'm quite normal.'

'Your face. It's so bleak. Your eyes. It's the unhappiest face I've ever seen. It's your anti-corpse face. Please, stop it.'

That hit me between the eyes. Corpsing is the actor's word for giggling during a performance. Sitting down in that front row night after night, Jeni and I often had to struggle with giggles. To pull myself together I used to think of Dominic, of Rutter, of injunctions and court. I was always in control at once. I later told Jeni what brought on that face, the one I didn't even know I wore. She said, 'That terrible black expression comes and you look quite different.' It brought home the fact that, no matter what fun the immediate activity, no matter how riveting the work, how delightful the woman, I lived on the edge of a hole into which I could, and did, plunge without warning.

Rutter's letter threatening legal proceedings was predictably inaccurate.

By 1974 I had complained about Rutter and my solicitors to the Law Society: nothing doing. I complained about Comyn and Taylor to the Bar Council: nothing doing. With each of those complaints, Stephen Mitchell, partner in a reputable legal firm, sent a letter saying that there was 'grave cause for concern': nothing doing. I complained to the Lord Chancellor, the Official Solicitor, the Ombudsman, and probably the Metropolitan Water Board: nothing doing. I went to Hugh Jenkins, my former MP in Putney, later Lord Jenkins, who gave me tea in the Houses of Parliament, listened politely, and told me to set down my grievances concisely for Elwyn Jones, the new Lord Chancellor: nothing doing. I went to Sir Michael Stewart my MP in Fulham: couldn't help, but suggested that I contact the Law Society. I tried to get the *Sunday Times* 'Insight Column' and the *Observer* 'Daylight' column to run some of my evidence: not interested. I tried *Private Eye*: too complicated. I gave up.

I used to have dreams that Christine and I were the best of friends and loved one another; then I woke. Frank Young, my accountant, introduced me to a new society he was helping to organise called Families Need Fathers. It was formed by a group of angry divorcees, mostly, but not all, men. I learned that my story was far from unusual; I heard a host of horror stories about how the law and the legal profession had in one of a hundred ways aggravated divorce. FNF is a bit like Alcoholics Anonymous in that the victims try to help each other. I became, for the next ten years, a chairperson for their walk-in/talk-ins. Men and women came in with stories of solicitorial cock-ups, of injustices, of humiliations inflicted by judges (apparently wilfully) through children, that if I hadn't heard week after week I wouldn't have believed possible. Even allowing for bias, distortion, ignorance and the fact that many of these new divorcees were in a state of depression, the stories add up to an overwhelming indictment of our divorce system. My experiences over Dominic were a picnic in comparison to some of what I listened to. The accounts I heard, of how judge after judge had treated parents, made me realise that His Honour Judge Trevor 'Once-a-week-is-too-possessive' Reeve was positively benign.

Families Need Fathers was allocated half an hour of BBC TV time on an *Open Door* programme. As the only professional in the society, I made the programme and took the opportunity to tell the exact truth about my dealings with Theodore Goddard and James Comyn. A BBC lawyer appeared on my doorstep. 'You can't say those things, we'll be sued.' I played him some of my tapes of them. His objections vanished instantly. The programme was transmitted on a Saturday, to be repeated on the following Saturday. On the Monday after the first transmission I heard from a BBC contact that somebody (I think, Comyn) was going to sue. No writ arrived however. Instead, I heard that the Lord Chancellor's office or the Bar Council (not Comyn, he got his friends to do his dirty work) had contacted the Director General of the BBC or the Controller of Programmes and said that no action would be taken against the BBC if the repeat was withdrawn. The BBC, on the advice of their own libel lawyer, gave a raspberry to that and the repeat was transmitted. Nobody sued.

By December 1973 I had also finished the first draft of my new play and before I started my usual re-write I sat down and took a slow, deep breath to see where I was. The answer was: up to my ears in debt and paying Christine maintenance that was more than double my earnings for that year - a bad one.

If it had only been a question of money I might not have bothered to take any action, but things had long gone beyond pounds and pence as far as I was concerned. I burned inside constantly. And the furnace that had been fired in me was regularly re-stoked. On one occasion Rutter made a clatter about my payments of maintenance; I was accused of having underpaid. Accountants had to be hired to check back to the word go. It was found that I had not underpaid but overpaid by quite a bit, so Christine was obliged to refund me some money. I had to use it to pay the accountants.

But the knife that was continuously twisted was aggravation about Dominic; about access, education, holidays; he would be left with a neighbour or au pair rather than me; on one such occasion I took him home to stay with me and received the inevitable letter from Rutter threatening me with gaol; I would be asked to pay for something, anything, once for a garden swing for Christine, while denied additional access or consultation about his school or any sort of real participation in his life. As I flick through the old letters, the old rage is still re-kindled. So, I made out an application for a reduction in maintenance based on 'changes in circumstances.' Stephen and Timothy reckoned that enough time had passed since my last attempt for this one to succeed. I joined that application with twin applications for improved access to Dominic and joint custody of him. Earlier applications on these points had also been refused before, but as he got older, so my case got stronger. He was now four.

Chapter XXXVII

1973-4

Stephen Mitchell, Tim Akeroyd and I agreed that I would represent myself in court again, with Tim Akeroyd as my solicitorial back-up. Once more I started right from scratch with all the preliminaries: the application, my affidavit of means (getting sadder at each re-write), disclosure of bank and income statements, handing over of all relevant information, visits to the Royal Courts of Justice to get the hearing set down, and so on *ad nauseam.* However, this time there was a certain grim pleasure in doing all this for myself with the prospect of once more arguing for myself before a High Court judge. The whole process is addictive, first the chores of preparation then the glittering reward of the court battle, as exciting, intoxicating, as fear-inspiring as any first night.

I watched in disgust, yet again, at how Rutter conducted Christine's affairs and how the registrars and judges condoned his conduct. There should be a motto carved over the entrance to the Family Division of the Royal Courts of Justice. 'Fight. Then fight again. To prosper, be difficult. Make trouble. Escalate the costs. No one will give a damn.' Without Tim Akeroyd I would have exploded before I even got to the door of the High Court. He was everything that my previous lawyers were not: a stabilising wise counsellor who also knew the ropes. His round spectacles over his round blue eyes in his nice round face and a lock of hair over one temple were better than any tranquilliser. My telephone would ring and Tim would be sighing with laughter on the other end. 'I've just heard from your friend, Splutter. He's wonderful, isn't he.'

My financial application was a straightforward effort on my part to get the simple arithmetic before a judge. It met a straightforward effort from Rutter to delay that event as long as possible. Tim and I decided to disclose everything we could think of right at the outset so as to pre-empt all possible accusations. In addition, as I was a litigant-in-person, we kept meticulously to all rules of procedure - to start with. Rutter soon changed all that. As regards the rules, he did just as he liked - to start with. Now note, you aspiring solicitors and litigants-in-person, some splendid dos and don'ts for your pre-hearing campaigns.

My new affidavit of means, containing every detail of my finances, was on his desk by Christmas 1973. I had got the hearing set down for the twenty-fifth of February. Christine's affidavit of means, according to the rules, should have been delivered in fourteen days. It was not. Instead, we got a letter four pages long asking for much back-up evidence to my figures. This I provided while a month passed. I sent reminders. Rutter promised us the affidavit, 'during the course of this week.' But, no. However, we did get a summons from him for discovery by me and for a list of documents with supporting affidavit. We got that list on Rutter's desk some two weeks later, which was pretty good. Still there was no information from him. We agreed to his request for an adjournment, provided I stopped paying maintenance during his delay. Rather than this, he got a sublimely superfluous hearing for discovery before Registrar Bayne Powell one week before the main hearing.

We assembled in that dark, narrow corridor outside Bayne Powell's room in Somerset House with all the other besuited representatives of broken marriages. I, with my secretary, sat shaking (with excitement not fear), such was the unpleasant charge of adrenaline those affairs gave me. In we went to that room, always lovely and sun-filled in my memory, that overlooks the Thames. There was an instant complaint from Rutter. He objected to my secretary's presence at a hearing in chambers. A litigant-in-person has a right to be accompanied by another person, known as a Mackenzie friend, following a decision of the Court of Appeal. That is law. Nevertheless Marie was ordered out by the registrar in spite of my protests and in spite of the fact that Rutter himself had been, on past occasions, accompanied by an assistant.

On the other side of the river what looked like concrete silos were being constructed. It was the National Theatre. I looked across, thinking that I should be over there, rehearsing something by me in their temporary huts and admiring the marble facade of this elegant cesspit, instead of sitting in it. The mudslinging began. The Court of Appeal's judgement was tolled at the registrar like a bell announcing my leprosy. The learned Registrar Bayne-Powell beamed over his glasses, glowing with avuncularity and ineffectualness, seeming quite impressed by one or two of my alleged misdeeds, nodding benignly as he said 'tsch-tsch.' He tightened his mouth primly at the perjury charge. It may have been amusing to see Rutter having no effect, but for the umpteenth time since he had first crossed my path, I wondered why one of these registrars or judges didn't just squash him and shut off the outflow forever. I longed, often, to lean across that table and smash my fist into his face.

'Ah,' said Bayne-Powell, as was his habit each time my mother's house was mentioned, 'Paddock Orchard, I know that. Very nice. I live near there.' And he gave me a warm smile while the acrimony poured on, unchecked.

However, I was learning to channel my anger. Although I wasn't a patch on Rutter at the filibuster I was considerably better at the quick ad-lib and was able to score points by refuting some of the wilder nonsense with documents that were before me. At one point Rutter overplayed his hand and gave me an entertaining five minutes. Bayne-Powell was, in answer to my submission, making out an order for Christine to file an affidavit of means. At last I was going to get it. Rutter interrupted him. 'You don't have the power, sir.'

The registrar's head popped up from his writing. 'What?'

'I'm afraid you don't have the power to order my client to file an affidavit of means, sir.'

The registrar went pink. 'Who says I don't?'

'Rule 75 of the 1973 matrimonial cases rules,' said Rutter and read it out. Regretfully he passed the book across for the registrar to see. The atmosphere was charged. The registrar finished his reading, and glanced up, then down, utterly dumbfounded. Rutter added quietly, but with force, 'So you see, sir, you don't have the power.'

Bayne-Powell kept his head down while he pulled himself together. 'But I've been making out orders for litigants to file affidavits for years. It's what I'm here for.'

Rutter's head gave a tiny shake of sympathy as the registrar riffled through the rule-book. He found something. 'Hm…Yes, well, you appear to be right, Mr Rutter, I don't have the power.' He let the pause hang deliberately. I slumped back into my chair and sighed; there seemed to be a legal loophole for everything. I don't think the registrar even noticed me, I didn't exist in this quiet but bloody little duel that was taking place.

'However,' the registrar returned Rutter's book, open at another page. His finger jabbed down. 'It would seem, would it not, that if your client doesn't file an affidavit of means, then her case falls by default? Mr Frisby's application succeeds.' And he smiled huffily at Rutter. His voice had risen with tension.

Rutter looked at the rule book with a sickly smile. 'Of course, sir, I wasn't suggesting that she wouldn't file an affidavit of means, I was merely drawing your attention to the rules.'

'Thank you, Mr Rutter,' said the registrar. His clerk had done his disappearing act behind his desk, handkerchief to mouth.

'I shall, of course, be advising my client to file an affidavit at once,' said Rutter and started writing as though he were going to post the letter to Christine on the way out.

'Splendid, Mr Rutter,' said the Registrar, turning the pages of the rule book. 'Only I wonder if you should. You see, you client is now out of time. She's over a month late, and you must apply to me…' his voice hung on 'me' for a moment, 'for leave to file an affidavit out of time.' And his finger directed Rutter's attention to yet another rule. An audible smothered noise came from behind the clerk's desk. I sat holding my mirth tight. Did this mean I had won here and now? The registrar still looked as though he would as likely squawk as speak. He was not a man with the capacity to enjoy being challenged and wasn't attractive in reasserting his authority, although I found him positively alluring.

Rutter mumbled his application for leave for his client to file her affidavit of means out of time and the registrar remained silent, looking as though pique might make him refuse. I prayed, but he said, 'Of course, Mr Rutter, I would not penalise your client for any misconception of the rules that her solicitor might have.'

'Thank you, sir,' mumbled Rutter.

'Nevertheless, I'm being penalised', I put in, 'for all that extra time I have to go on paying maintenance at a prohibitive rate.'

The registrar's retribution only extended as far as was necessary to restore his status. It is not the litigant who is important in these machinations but the petty officials. Rutter was given seven more days to file Christine's affidavit of means and got eight after more pleading. I had not got what I applied for, namely a suspension of maintenance payments for the period of delay caused by Rutter's tactics.

So, the High Court hearing was postponed. The registrar started to fix a date in March but Rutter claimed, inaccurately but successfully, that Ormrod, who wasn't free for months, had reserved the case to himself. My case was now in limbo, dragging on indefinitely, just what Christine and Rutter wanted. I continued to be dumbfounded at the way those registrars believed any old lie that a solicitor told them, especially about procedure. They repeatedly ignored my statements, apparently merely because they were the statements of a litigant-in-person, even when they were backed up by the documents. Their attitude is that patronising; they are that protective about their superfluous rituals. Yes, I understand about safeguards and the checks and balances that are necessary in litigation but - especially in the lower echelons of those Royal Courts of Justice - they think that you, the amateur, just cannot understand the intricacies of law and procedure, even though, in divorce, it usually boils down to a simple process of arithmetic, of presenting all the facts (anyway, I was being expertly guided by Tim and Stephen). Yet they imagine that they are falling over backwards to be fair to you. They are not.

I left that hearing steaming, now burdened with months of legal distractions while still paying Christine more than I was earning. So I tried a quick dash at Ormrod to get him to suspend payments for the period of the delay caused by Rutter. I got before him in March. He was on top form, faster than when hearing Douglas Hogg. In overdrive he refused my application, wouldn't listen to my figures of income, showed no interest in Rutter's delaying tactics, reserved the case to himself at Rutter's request, set it down for the twenty-ninth of April and slung us all out.

The legal correspondence and documents multiplied as though spring were causing them to mate and breed. One letter from Rutter appeared, daffodil-like on the first of April, to reveal seven pages of demands for detailed information, every item of which merely confirmed what we all already knew.

On April fourth we were once more before Registrar Bayne Powell, this time for an application by Rutter to have my application knocked out of the lists for want of prosecution by me. The sheer cheek of this was like a tonic to me. I went to the hearing properly fired up. His ploy was thrown out by the registrar but not before Rutter and I had a verbal brawl in front of him that caused him to jump up and down in his seat squeaking with temper. Rutter wouldn't let me make my applications without interruption, so I gave up allowing him the floor to talk us out of time. The hearing lost even its surface of order as he cut in on me and I called the passing time like the speaking clock as he talked. An eerie ingredient to all these exchanges was that he never looked at me whereas I never took my eyes off him, except to turn to the registrar.

As a result of that hearing, Rutter got the order for the list of documents extended yet further. He failed to get an order that I number and list every cheque paid for the last two years (yes, that was the sort of detail we were down to). This hearing created a new mountain of work. Tim Akeroyd said one day, shaking his head at the piles of papers round us, 'Where does he find the time? Is this his only case?'

We were before Registrar Bayne Powell again a week later. Rutter and I burst from the gloom of the corridor into the sun, both of us talking loudly, nineteen to the dozen. He had applied, so I had cross-applied, I think ,or the other way round, for 'further and better particulars' of discovery. Neither of us was going to let the other get in first. The sight that met us made us both stop dead. The registrar's appalled, glaring, crimson face was bobbing up and down behind his little barrier of books. It was doing so because he was beating with rage on his table with both hands.

'Now, listen you two. Shut up. Listen. I've got something to say to you.' He paused to control himself. We stood open-mouthed. He pointed a pencil. 'Last time you were before me, you made me miss my lunch.' He paused again for emphasis then banged his pencil on each word to demonstrate the importance of his statement. 'Well - *it's not going to happen again.*'

We sat down, subdued, and made our applications. I was desolate that I hadn't been wearing the tape-recorder to catch the scene forever. Within ten minutes we were all at it again, the registrar included, squabbling like children.

That hearing was a disaster for Rutter, his own obduracy at last rebounded. Because he had demanded such ridiculous detail I was able to get an order for three items that I wanted very much indeed. The first was any information about how much he had been paid for the case. It was extraordinary, I owed him thousands, and he had never asked for a penny, yet here he was, fighting the case as though his life depended on it. Christine appeared to have paid him nothing, too. The second was information about how Dominic's nanny was paid. We got a written assurance she had always been paid in cash. That was just what I wanted.

The third item was the letter I had written to Christine in March 1970 that had been allowed by Paddy Grafton Green to slip through his discovery net in 1971. This was the letter that referred to her giving me hash to smoke and what I have called my 'rehabilitation letter'. That letter was important and Rutter knew it; his squirms would have made an eel look petrified. We snarled and spat with venom while the registrar huffed impotently.

'The letter doesn't exist,' claimed Rutter.

'Just have your client swear to that,' I answered (that would have served my purpose).

'It has already been discovered.'

'Just have your client swear to that.'

'It is irrelevant.'

'Why protest so if it is irrelevant?'

'He is merely asking for it to upset my client.'

'I thought you said it didn't exist.'

It went on for an hour. The registrar, like Grafton Green before, regarded such a personal letter as of little importance, but at last he gave in to hunger (we had started at midday) and my obviously sincere pleading that it was vital to my application for improved access to Dominic and joint custody. I think, in addition, the sheer ardour of Rutter's resistance roused his suspicions.

It had taken over three months of time-wasting and infuriating litigation to get everything I needed to start the case before a judge. As I was giving myself a pat on the back Rutter simply ignored the order by appealing against it.

————————

The following Friday afternoon Rutter and I were trailing round the Family Division looking for a judge to hear his appeal because Ormrod was busy. I was ignorant of the practice that applicants must look for a judge to be free like a taxi. First thing on the following Monday we were to start the main hearing before Ormrod, so Rutter's evasion of the registrar's order was already successful, no matter what the outcome of this hearing.

An usher said to me out of the side of his mouth, 'Bit tricky finding a judge of a Friday afternoon. Their Lordships like to slope off a bit sharpish.'

There was a minor flurry in the middle distance between Rutter and someone. Then the someone called to me, 'Come on. You're on. In 'ere.' Clearly the body swerve of one judge was inadequate. We were shown down a chill, stone corridor to a gloomy court in the old section of the building.

'Who are we in front of?' I asked someone.

'Mr Justice Trevor Reeve,' he answered. 'In 'ere.'

What can I say? If I had been asked to invent the storyline of a soap opera about the law I might have included such a blatant plot boost on an uninventive morning during a hangover. His Honour, County Court Judge Trevor 'It-may-well-be-that-this-father-is-being-too-possessive-Once-a-fortnight-is-appropriate' Reeve had been promoted to the High Court and was now seating himself in front of me, looking, to my appalled eyes, like the product of coitus between Adolph Hitler and Nicol Williamson in one of his more sadistic roles, always assuming such a union could have been fruitful. I think I was actually sweating with fear and disappointment. I know I was shaking. I thought, well, everything is just hopeless in this place.

'Yes?' said Mr Justice Trevor Reeve to Rutter without warmth, though both of us were on our feet. It was perhaps as well that he ignored me. Before long I was asked to confirm a point and stood up to say, 'That's correct, My Lord.' I heard something like, 'Thast clocket, M'Lord,' come out of my mouth as terror spoonerised the articulatory organs. The brawling that Rutter and I had indulged in before the registrar wasn't on here and Rutter knew that better than I, opening his case with a cool authority that impressed while it infuriated me; you would have thought that I was the one being obliged to appeal. As Rutter produced the judgement of the Court of Appeal and proceeded to smear the mud on, this time with a sort of urbane sorrow, I pulled myself together and tried to see this judge more clearly through my curtain of prejudice.

Mr Justice Trevor Reeve's hair was as aggressively short as ever, darkish and covered in some sort of dressing. The jowl looked as menacing. I cannot for the life of me remember whether the upper lip was free of the toothbrush growth or whether I had imagined it in the first place. His eyes, behind glasses, were quite large and looked clammy. When something displeased him he rolled them up so that the pupils almost disappeared. You could measure his displeasure by the amount of the roll. If he seemed to look straight through the top of his skull you were dead on that point. The sight of him, sitting up there with his eyes searching for heaven like a saint in an El Greco and the bottom half of his face looking as though he had sucked an unripe lemon was one of the grimmest comic sights of my life.

As Rutter's filibuster consumed the afternoon I tried several times to get in. I was most obsequious but to no avail. Rutter had got the judge's full attention and rolled it all out: the injunction, the committal proceedings, things I was surprised to hear and would have been ashamed to mention, were I he, for fear of prejudicing the judge the wrong way.

'He means he tried to have me gaoled for walking my son in the park,' I put in and earned a dirty look from the judge. Rutter added 'The husband made an application about the child that actually came before you, My Lord.'

'Really?' said the judge with interest.

'You rejected it with costs, My Lord,' said Rutter and shuffled his papers, head down, as the corners of Trevor Reeve's mouth descended and his glance passed over my head.

'What has all this to do with a simple discovery order?' I tried and was then afraid that my trying to change the subject looked like an admission of some sort. 'All this is irrelevant. I just want a few bits of paper to help my case,' got me nowhere. 'If he would just hand over the papers or have his client swear they don't exist we could all go home,' just got me a warning frown from the judge's clerk.

Eventually, with a glance at the clock that was about as helpful as a shove in the back to a tight-rope walker, Trevor Reeve allowed me to start. There were five minutes left to the afternoon session. Rutter had used nearly two hours. No judge would have treated a QC like that. The double standard for litigants-in-person remained in place. I got up and gabbled, 'I-don't-know-anything-about-rules-and-procedures-but-I-do-know-a-first-class-smear-campaign-when-I hear-one-and-all-I-want-is-a-few-bits-of-paper-which-if-they-exist-help-my-case-and-if-they-don't-then-the-other-side-could-swear-as-much-quite-easily-but-they-daren't-do-that-and-they-daren't-produce-them-either. He's-dodged-having-Ormrod-hear-this-appeal-because-he-knows-Ormrod-would-order-me-the-papers-because-he-said-he-would-and-Rutter-couldn't-sling-mud-in-front-of-him. In-any-case-Rutter-introduced-my-letters-into-this-case-so-he-should-produce-them-all-not-just-the-the-ones-that-suit-him. That's-only-fair' (It is also a rule of discovery but I didn't know that). I think I was just about wringing my hands. I was certainly leaning forward against the bench trying to drill into Trevor Reeve's eyes my feelings. He seemed to soften a little. 'I-mean-why-not-give-em-to-me? It'll-only-take-em-ten-minutes-to-do-it? This-afternoon-is-so-much-eyewash-to-confuse-the-issue.'

I might just as well have been talking in Urdu. Trevor Reeve said 'I think the fairest thing would be to reserve my decision. We shall adjourn now until Monday morning, Mr Frisby, when you will present your case to me in the full hearing.' And he left. The full hearing? What did he mean?

Once more I was knocked off balance by procedure. So I wouldn't be pleading to Ormrod on Monday. Somehow this man was now in charge. How had we got to the full hearing without my answer to Rutter's appeal against discovery being fully heard? And in reserving his decision, 'the fairest thing,' Trevor Reeve had, in effect, decided against me. Rutter had successfully cocked a snook at the registrar's order without actually succeeding in his appeal. I went home to a wretched weekend full of Trevor Reeve's disapproving stare and the curved line of his jaw that I feared and disliked so.

Chapter XXXVIII

July Eleventh, Twelfth & Thirteenth, 1974

On Monday morning, Tim Akeroyd, Marie my secretary and I took our places. Good-Old-Harry was with Rutter, and Christine put in one of her infrequent appearances. The wide picture hat and make-up for the public Court of Appeal were absent; instead, in chambers, the spectacles were firmly in place, cheeks were pink and shiny, hair scraped back and the demure little tweed jacket was again worn over a simple blouse and row of pearls. The skirt was nondescript. I was polishing the seat of the trousers of the litigation suit as I bobbed up and down trying to stay calm.

Mr Justice Trevor Reeve entered, bowed, crinkled the corners of his eyes and mouth in a token smile of greeting and said courteously, 'Yes, Mr Frisby?'

I was tense, ready for the first fight. 'I hope you don't mind, My Lord, but although I am representing myself I do have my solicitor here to help and guide me and my secretary to take notes and if necessary get any further papers.'

Mr Justice Trevor Reeve glanced at the mountains of papers round us. His eyebrows twitched up. 'More?'

I gave a sycophantic snort of mirth. 'Possibly, My Lord.'

The eyes rolled up towards the top left-hand corner of the Court. 'Hm. No, I haven't the slightest objection to their presence. Mr Law?'

Law lumbered upright, mouth full of butter. 'Neither Mr Rutter, or myself would wish to handicap Mr Frisby in any way, My Lord.' From behind him Rutter's head wagged in pious approval of this sentiment.

'Well, he objected before the registrar,' I blurted.

'Well, there's no objection now, Mr Frisby,' said Trevor Reeve preparing himself for a tedious day. 'And I am not the registrar.'

I had scored minus points and I hadn't even started. I referred to the discovery order and promptly lost more points.

'I have already indicated that I will reserve my judgement on that,' said the judge.

'Yes, I'm sorry, but I didn't understand when you would decide, now or later.'

'Well you do now. Later.'

At least the atmosphere was very different from Friday, I wasn't being given five grudging minutes at the end of the afternoon, the whole day stretched before me to present facts and figures. I knew that I did this competently and got on with it. Under Tim's guidance our preparation had been good; every relevant figure was in one long affidavit with supporting accounts, tax returns, bank statements, valuations; over fifty pages in all, bound together in a book, one copy each for the judge, Law and me. Thus everything was readily available without the shuffling, losing and dropping of papers that characterises court hearings; but, best bonus of all, the convenience of our book meant that the judge worked primarily from our figures, not theirs. Of course, the totals of the finances could have been contained on two sides of a sheet of paper.

I am sure that five minutes after we had started that morning Trevor Reeve thought I was a major pain in the arse and probably dishonest. By lunch time he was neutral, by halfway through the afternoon he could see that Rutter's Friday afternoon allegations bore little relation to reality and that something was very wrong indeed. There came a moment when the penny dropped about the breadth and depth of Theodore Goddard's cock-up over control of the Trust. Up rolled his eyes and a volley of tsch-tsches escaped his lips. 'Why do these lawyers take these narrow legalistic views when the facts are clear to everyone?' He asked a crack in the ceiling. I had enough sense to stand still and keep quiet. He re-focused down onto me. 'It must have been exasperating for you, Mr Frisby.' I shrugged half-wittedly. It was the Latey hearing all over again. Trevor Reeve made some sympathetic noises and had a quick eye-roll. Then, with warmth, 'Yes, Mr Frisby, carry on.' He underwent a transformation that afternoon. The square face and jaw softened, the upward glances of the eyes became almost holy. He looked like a sort of adult Botticelli angel up there, all benign dimples. However, understanding the facts led him to a very awkward position; he could see what tripe Phillimore's judgement was, but it was still a judgement of the Court of Appeal and, if he did anything in my favour, he faced the prospect of his decision being taken back there.

My first witness was Frank Young, my accountant. He was stamping about in the witness box like an unbroken horse. Behind glasses and beard, his mournful eyes were fixed on me with unhealthy fervour. He didn't know it but he was a wonderful witness. When I had hit the jackpot in 1966, Christine and I had visited him for advice, dancing with excitement. He had looked at the figures and shaken his head. '£70,000 in this year. My God, you've got troubles.' When we left an hour later I was depressed and Christine, in tears, refused to go again. You can imagine how he sounded describing the shambles I was in 1974. I finished my questions and sat down not knowing whether to weep at my condition or laugh at Frank's gloom.

Good-Old-Harry rose to his feet and stared at Frank for some time as though he were something pretty nasty. Frank peered anxiously back. His head had sunk into an angled defensive position behind his shoulder. The judge was finding it difficult not to laugh as an attack was launched on Frank's professional good name which just looked silly. According to Law, Frank was some sort of international fiddler cooking the books, and my finances were really very healthy. Frank was horrified at this assertion and every question asked damaged Christine's case further as Frank went from gloom to outright despair on my behalf.

Then Law got onto something solid. He found one, then two, minor discrepancies in my accounts and came down like a flabby sledgehammer to crack these nuts while Frank stood in the witness box, appalled eyes glaring at the offending papers. He looked up to the back of the court where his partner, Harvey, and assistant, Colin, were sitting surrounded by yet more piles of papers. Harvey and Colin, on this look, started burrowing into the papers like demented moles, searching for the errors. Trevor Reeve, in high old good humour, decided that that was enough for the day and adjourned to give Frank time to sort out his problem.

I went to Frank's office on my way home. The floor was covered in my accounts. Harvey, Colin and Frank were going through them. He shook his head earnestly 'I'm sorry, Terry, about the mistakes. We're looking. I can't understand it. I hope we haven't let you down.' Reassurances from me that it couldn't matter less were inadequate.

The next morning Frank had the answers in court. Of course, they were not important, but what was, was that overnight Frank had realised that Law was a paper tiger. A new confident accountant stood there dealing effectively with him and correcting his questions (a constant necessity). At one point Law had to wait while Trevor Reeve and Frank got their heads together and had a good old grumble about some official who had invested and lost millions of pounds of the public's money. The mutual head-shaking was prodigious.

My next witness, subpoenaed, was Christine's boyfriend, the current resident, or semi-resident, at 1 Genoa Avenue. But by the time he was in the witness box I had discovered that, unlike her other chaps since me, he had little money, so, no matter what his residential status, he was irrelevant to the issue of who had been coughing up for her. He denied that he lived with Christine, then owned up to three nights a week plus a lot of weekends, then said he contributed nothing to the household except, 'When we entertained people to dinner.' I picked up the 'we,' and there was a bit of pink-faced stammering. The boyfriend half-owned a boat which he chartered round the Greek islands and Law made a nicely-pitched, but unintentional, contribution to the levity by asking him if he kept his tackle at 1 Genoa Avenue. Tim and I got black looks for giggling.

Next it was my turn in the witness box and the principal supporting comedy turn, Frisby and Law, returned to the High Court after an absence of over two years. We were an anti-climax. Dealing with Law was too simple as he hammered away at point after point that holed, sank and concreted to the bottom his client's case. There was a brief glimpse of potential fun when, to demonstrate my deceitfulness, he got on to my tape-recording activity. I offered to play the tapes to the court to establish once and for all who was telling the truth. Trevor Reeve fervently declined, eyeballs at high roll. As previously when I had faced Law and his inadequate questions, and watched Rutter crouching behind him, hissing, prompting, passing the stream of papers, contempt for them was my only emotion. It was for Comyn and Calderan, unscathed and untouchable, who had put me in the power of such creatures, that my anger was reserved. I felt, in *Boys Own* imagery, like a mammal, or some such creature of higher evolution, delivered, bound, to reptiles.

Law's final sally was to add up the value of everything I had, including my house, and suggest that if I put it all on deposit (and presumably lived in the street) it would produce enough interest to pay Christine's maintenance. This line was backed up by an entire affidavit sworn by Rutter's son, who identified himself as the firm's 'Investment Expert'.

Trevor Reeve let the sorry cross-talk drool on for well over a day, listening to every point, making sure that the conclusions he had already (I think) arrived at were watertight. Then he weighed in with some considerably pithier questions of his own to satisfy himself about my character and actions. The climax of this came when he was taking me through my bank accounts. He had a sheaf of them, not included in our book, and asked about some large payments. They were a mystery to me. I stammered and couldn't answer. Reeve and I came to a halt; tension gripped Rutter and Law; everyone froze as it emerged that I appeared to have bought a house in St. Albans. I started going hot at the atmosphere.

Trevor Reeve peered at the accounts and asked 'Who is Timothy Akeroyd?'

'My solicitor, My Lord,' I answered. He's sitting over there.'

Up rolled Reeve's eyes. 'Do you live in St Albans, Mr Akeroyd?'

'I'm just moving there, My Lord' said Tim, lurching erect.

'Would you come and collect your bank accounts?' said Reeve patiently and stared at Tim with the expression of a weary nanny as, mumbling apologies, Tim approached, stuffed the errant papers into his pocket and hurried, scarlet, back to his place.

———————

At last we came to the real climax of where we had been heading since Rutter had started his campaign of lies four-and-half years earlier: Christine's verbal evidence. You may have wondered why I called, a few paragraphs ago, my cross-examination by Law 'the principal supporting comedy turn.' Well, that is all it was. Now for the main attraction. She had avoided this moment for far too long in my view. Now she was actually going to have to perform. She would have the warm-up with Law before it was my turn.

Christine entered the witness box and took the oath in a hushed, breathy, almost juvenile voice and Law changed his tone to a sort of clumsy reverence, like a peasant lighting a candle at the Madonna's shrine in a Hollywood costume drama. He asked her name and address as though she had suffered a recent bereavement. Christine's answers were barely audible. I wanted to shout, 'Cut,' and walk across the court and say, 'Now look, you lot, this is 1974, let's have a bit of credibility. All this went out donkey's years ago. Come on, try it again. Like real people this time.' But it continued. I looked at Trevor Reeve. He was listening, rapt. I glanced at the court staff to see if any of them were convulsed with suppressed laughter. Not a concealed smirk was in sight. The legal profession was once more parodying itself with utter unconsciousness. Tim passed me a note. 'When you examine, be VERY gentle.'

Reeve threw in a couple of questions of his own in a tone of voice that suggested he thought Christine might need sal volatile if he spoke normally. Then he made a remark which showed that, though his manners were from another age, at least part of his mind was in the present. He looked up from his copy of her alleged living expenses. 'I suppose there are some under-privileged people who are able to exist on less than this. One must cut one's coat according to one's cloth, Mr Law, must one not?'

This remark, thrown mildly into that extraordinary atmosphere, created a quiet sensation. The room seemed to lurch. Law, true to his habit of always agreeing with the judge, said heartily, 'Yes, there is no doubt about that,' as though that were precisely what he had been trying to prove. One of the female ushers gave me a look with raised eyebrows that said clearly if she had a similar amount she would have vanished out of that court never to be seen again. Law recovered himself. 'If you have to run an establishment of this size where you were living before, it does run away with a certain amount of your income.' That earned a forty-five-degree eye-roll from Reeve. So, the oft-repeated argument that I should somehow keep Christine, 'in the style to which I had accustomed her,' cut no ice with Trevor Reeve. He said crisply, 'Look at the figures, Mr Law. The figures. What does he earn?'

And so we came to the melancholy logical conclusion, the *reductio ad absurdum* of the four years of litigation; my cross-examination of Christine. It was a moment to which I had been looking forward eagerly, almost painfully, so anxious was I to put some questions that couldn't be ducked with, 'You're mad', or, 'I won't talk about that.' Of course, most of what I was on fire to ask her was not relevant to the proceedings, but there was enough that was. It could provide a wholesome meal for my curiosity, if not a feast. I could feel my heart pounding ridiculously as I started. If ever I was capable of being obsessed by a subject, an understanding of Christine's mental and emotional processes over the preceding four years was it.

There was some very gentle fencing over her tax returns which were missing (indeed, I had been able to get no information from Rutter as to

337

her true taxable income for the last four years, in spite of all the discovery hearings and orders). Christine reacted as though tax returns were Sanskrit scrolls and I said I couldn't hear her. I could, just, but this was to get her voice up to its normal, perfectly clear level. Trevor Reeve was shuffling about in his place, sending out loud body-language messages to the effect that he didn't approve. I hastily moved on to the value and size of 1 Genoa Avenue. Christine said she hadn't read any of the valuations or papers on the subject. I was cursing under my breath, wondering how to deal with this when Trevor Reeve loudly addressed the ceiling halfway down the court 'I should have thought she had better things to do, looking after Dominic, than reading the appalling proliferation of paper that there has been in this case on both sides. Appalling.' And he banged his pencil down, glared at me, rubbed his eyes and sank his head onto his hand in a very sulky pose.

I found myself saying, à la Law, 'Yes, My Lord, I take your point there,' while I tried to marshal my scattered wits. So I wasn't going to be allowed even a gentle probe.

My next line was to have been on Christine's jewellery. According to her insurance (extracted by discovery), her jewellery was worth £650 when we were divorced. It had grown to over £8,000 now. There had been an increase in value during 1971 alone of over £4,000 (though that had been kept from both Latey and the Court of Appeal). A jewellery income increment of nearly £2,000 a year since our divorce was, I thought, worth inquiry. And if she had been given that much jewellery by admirers, what else had she received? But Trevor Reeve would have a fit at the sexual implications behind such a line of questioning. In the atmosphere of his antimacassared court it would have been suicidal. I stood humming and hawing until Tim pushed my homework on Christine's bank accounts under my nose. I led her through it, adding up her cash withdrawals with her as we went. She said feebly that she wasn't good at sums. This was, remember, pre-credit-card times. You needed cash for daily living.

I said 'So we have £255 for seventeen weeks.'

'Yes.'

'I make that £15 a week exactly.'

'Yes.'

'Do you agree with that?'

'I can't add up that fast.' There was a bit more feminine flutter at the division sum, so I suggested that Christine, her counsel and the judge all do it on paper with me to see that they were correct. We all solemnly divided seventeen into £255 and made the answer £15 per week cash withdrawn.

'You paid your nanny £12 a week in cash?'

'Yes.'

'Every week?'

'Yes.'

'Never failed?'

'No.'

'Always in cash?'

'Always.'

'You paid your cleaning lady weekly?'

'Yes.'

'In cash?'

'Yes.'

'Every week?'

'Yes.'

'How much?'

'Five pounds.'

'You do yourself a disservice. According to your affidavits you paid her £2 in 1971-2.'

'I really can't remember back that far.' More feminine flutter.

'I'll call it £2 for now. You paid a gardener?'

'Yes.'

'Cash?'

'Yes.'

'Every week?'

'Most weeks.'

'How much?

'Two pounds.'

'As it was winter we'll say every other week, making it one pound per week.'

'All right.'

'So, £12 for the nanny, £2 for the cleaning lady, £1 for the gardener makes exactly £15 a week. That accounts for your cash withdrawals for four months. How did you shop?'

There followed what must have been one of the longest pauses in legal history. It was a beautiful, beautiful silence and I savoured it. The fact that it was also shameful didn't occur to me, two people who had loved each other, now positioned so. I looked at Rutter crouching tensely forward in his bench, at Law's expressionless face, at the judge looking attentively down, at the court attendants. The room was utterly still. It was like a silent explosion. Oh, the joy of stuffing some unpalatable facts firmly up the noses of those three over there: Christine, Law and Rutter, who had jointly abused me non-stop for over four years. To pretend mercy or compassion for the small, lost little figure that Christine made in the witness box as she stared down her nose through her glasses at the list of figures before her would be hypocrisy. I wanted to shout with exultation. I watched a fly walk down the window pane near to me. All was quiet. The fly buzzed briefly. A jet wheeled in over London and started its run to Heathrow. Its whine passed out of earshot. The fly's wings buzzed against the glass and were again silent.

I looked again at Christine. Nobody had moved.

'Did you hear the question?'

When she spoke her voice was tiny. Not the girlish affectation that she had opened with but a very different sound. 'What?' she said.

I said in the softest, roundest tones given me, 'How did you shop?'

She shook her head, 'I have no idea.'

'You know that I am alleging that someone else has been supporting you?'

'Yes.'

'You have denied that?'

'Yes.'

'I ask you again, how did you shop for those four months?'

'I see there was one cheque to Harrods, £41. I buy food from Harrods occasionally.'

'You drew out fifteen pounds a week cash. You spent at least that on your nanny, cleaning lady and gardener. You can't live on no pounds a week can you?'

'No, I'm sorry, but I really can't explain it. It seems virtually impossible to me.'

'It seems virtually impossible to me, too.

Law decided the time had come for a rescue operation, or perhaps Rutter had prompted him. He interrupted with 'My Lord, there is no allegation that she was living with anybody at the time—'

'Oh, yes, there is,'

Law ploughed on 'It has only been advanced in this court today—'

'Oh, no it hasn't,' I interrupted. 'It's in my affidavit.'

Law still kept going. 'The allegation against the only gentleman concerned refers to Mr Howard-Johnston and—'

Trevor Reeve had had enough of this. He joined in 'There is a Mr Kennedy, I seem to remember.' And he motioned Law to sit down. He turned to me. 'You may continue with this line of questioning,' and he resumed his attentive pose, all impatience and fidgeting forgotten. His actions not only shut Law up, they demonstrated, of course, the progress I had made. But Trevor Reeve, gentlemanly sap that he was, still had his nineteenth-century protective umbrella round Christine. There was no other line of questioning I could open that would not invite his intervention.

Well, it was easy for me to make hay of Christine's denials that anyone was contributing, so with great politeness and circumspection I did so for a while before Trevor Reeve's fidgeting recommenced. The moment I noticed him, I stopped. 'My Lord, forgive me for saying this but I see you looking at this moment in a way that suggests possibly you want me to terminate this. I do not want to flog any sort of dead horse.'

Mr Justice Trevor Reeve shook himself, the corners of his mouth were mobilised, the eyes rolled, then he stared hard and directly down at me and spoke with some force. 'The look that you see on my face is my realisation of the tragedy of this marriage. The greatest tragedy that befell you two was when you wrote that play. That is why you see that look on my face. I am terribly sorry for both of you.'

I hadn't expected that and it threw me. My first reaction was purely emotional. The tears started to my eyes. I almost wanted to say, 'Thank you,' to him for his compassion, it was so unexpected, as Latey's had been. But that was swept aside by a torrent of indignation. Here was this bloody man, put in a position of authority over my life, who had, four years previously, made The Remark about me and Dominic, without knowing anything about us, now striking a posture of omniscient pity, and wrongly analysing our split-up when he still had no real idea of the facts. He had no idea of the three years of happiness we had had after *Soup* had opened, no clue of what we had been to each other, no concept of how our characters had interlocked and what had pulled them apart and yet here he was...I had an image of him in his club with other judges. 'Had a sad case today...nice couple...couldn't handle sudden wealth.' I stood for some time looking down, fighting to regain my concentration on the matter in hand. When I was able to speak again I said, 'What shall I do about this cross-examination, My Lord?'

'I should continue it,' he said to the angle of the wall and ceiling. I nearly shouted audibly with laughter at the irrelevance of my going on in the face of that.

I got out one more question before he was in again.

'Do not think I am stopping you, Mr Frisby, but I wonder really where this is getting us. Suppose on this line of examination you were able to show that Mrs Frisby was getting cash from some other source for a few months—'

'It's not a few months, My Lord, it's over a considerable period.'

'You are going to say it goes right up to date, are you?'

'The patterns change, I can't be sure and there are many accounts and stubs missing in spite of discovery orders.'

'Well, how is that going to affect what order I make today, except in so far as it effects her credibility. If I vary this order it will be so that she can receive as much as you can afford.'

'If you are telling me this examination will make no difference I will desist at once, My Lord.'

'I cannot see what difference it will make.'

'Then I'll stop right now.'

Trevor Reeve continued. 'I am not stopping you. I am merely saying that I do not think it will help me very much.' And he smiled at me, with great politeness. I stood, baffled, beginning to get a fellow-feeling for barristers. He could not order me to stop. If he stopped me prosecuting my case that could be grounds for an appeal by me. But for me to continue in the face of that polite brick wall would be merely to damage myself.

I said, 'My case rests on the figures of our capital and income and that is all. I am afraid that you will draw a middle line between my figures and those presented by Christine's advisers because that would seem to be fair of you. But if you examine the evidence closely you will discover that mine are always right and theirs often wrong. This is her advisers' customary tactic to always gain a percentage for their client. Also I can prove that, while I have got poorer since our divorce, she has doubled her wealth.'

The judge's answer to this and the following exchange should be noted by all divorcing males. He said 'None of them (her assets) are income-producing unless they are sold, are they?'

'That is the point, My Lord. You can have a vast house, with thousands of pounds' worth of jewellery and thousands of pounds' worth of antiques and say you are broke, or you can behave reasonably. I agree and do not contest that there must be a house, and clearly Dominic must be well cared for, as everyone wants him to be. But what I say is that there are limits that have been surpassed.'

He answered, 'I think that I can probably say this. If Mr Law objects to what I am saying now he will indicate to me. Of course, when I consider whether there should be any variation I will not ignore the fact that Mrs Frisby has got certain assets. But I am not going to attempt to quantify those or to convert them into income-producing assets or anything of that sort. Whether the house is valued at £70,000 or £50,000 makes no difference. Does that answer your question?' Comyn's insistence that I gave her our house, easily our most valuable asset, was revealed in its full stupidity. It is unwise enough to give away your capital, especially as it was doubly hard to acquire in those days from such heavily-taxed income. But to give away your house, the only thing you ever own that is free of capital gains when you sell it, that took you years of work to buy, was the height of folly. It had trebled in value in a few years, yet Christine could sit back in it and live off me till I was broke. My own new home, fully mortgaged, was worth some twenty-odd thousand. To have thrown away capital on the scale that Comyn had was to oblige me to start again from scratch while having a large portion of my income siphoned off before I saw it.

I stood, nearly incoherent with frustration as I saw that all further lines of questioning were useless.

'No difference at all, My Lord?' I asked. He shook his head. 'No. I see. The fact that I live in a house of half the value of hers, with corresponding lower life-style—'

He interrupted me with 'I think I have indicated, have I not, that the value of her capital assets is not going to make any difference.'

'Thank you very much, My Lord. That is all.' How I longed to have a jury there, of people rooted in the daily business of earning a living, so that

I could appeal to their good sense, ignore his outdated attitudes and get to the truth of Christine's lifestyle and considerable worth. The values in that courtroom were unreal on many levels.

Mr Justice Trevor Reeve abruptly set off on his judgement; nineteen pages of it. Early on, he referred to my cross-examination of Christine. 'I was very agreeably surprised to find, when Mrs Frisby was being cross-examined by Mr Frisby (a somewhat embarrassing position for both), the way in which they treated each other. They did so with courtesy. In fact the courtesy between them went rather further than that; I thought there was almost a degree of warmth between them, there was no sign of rancour. As I say I was very agreeably surprised by that.' What a fool he was. I had twice called Christine 'darling' in the course of my examination. Tim said later how shocked he was, that it must have been the first examination in legal history in which the examiner called the examinee 'darling.' But it was not affection, it was simply my ingrained theatrical habit. I had thrown the word around for years and probably said it when I was exasperated with her act: '...oh, come on, darling...' That I am sure is what Trevor Reeve, the amateur psychodabbler, construed as warmth.

Reeve then made his first acknowledgement of the cock-up of our affairs by the lawyers. 'The application with which I am now dealing is another step in a long and unhappy history of proceedings between those two persons, and I very much regret that it is extremely unlikely that it is the last step in proceedings between them. I should like to think that I was able to make an order which would end disputes between them, but I am afraid that the hope is bound to be dashed.' He went on to disagree with Mr Justice Ormrod's comment that I could unscramble the mess I was in if I really tried.

Reeve, the legal technician, wasn't going to have a successful appeal made against his decision as Latey had. He nailed his colours firmly to the mast of 'a substantial change of circumstances' and proceeded to dispose of everything else as irrelevant, not without making a few pointed comments in passing, and making sure that he slammed and bolted any side door. He would have none of my contention that Christine was being supported by someone else, however he couldn't resist, 'I confess that I am somewhat puzzled as to how the wife was able to have sufficient cash in her possession to meet the various commitments which she said she did...for instance...(then examples)...As I say I am rather puzzled...' nevertheless, he had watched her in the witness box and was sure she was splendid and honest.

He came to allegations against me. 'He says that he has throughout been trying - I am using his expression - to knock into the stupid heads of those advising him that of course he had power to direct how those funds should be disposed of...I have seen him pressed on this point and seen him pressed very firmly by Mr Law; and I am quite satisfied that Mr Frisby is telling me the truth about this matter. I accept that he has been exasperated for years at the stupidity of his advisers, who will insist upon relying upon the letter of the law instead of looking at the reality.' He then went on to deal with all the other fiscal allegations. Latey had relied on pious hopes, Reeve meticulously dismantled the whole artifice of accusation. It was a pleasure to listen.

The summing-up of our characters and the litigation so far was a piece of artless prose, delivered with relish. 'In short, I find that both the husband and wife are truthful and honest witnesses. I have no reason to suppose from what I know of her that his wife would not be a reasonable person...but she would inevitably lean upon the advice of others...she has largely allowed herself to be carried along by - and here I am groping for the right word - I will use the word 'zeal' - (he seemed to consider the ceiling for a while) by the zeal (he really hit it this time, giving the z sound a ripe buzz) of those advising her.'

He got down to our changes in circumstances and said there was no change in Christine's, in spite of the arguments of Mr Law 'whose calculations I confess I could not exactly follow...' He went on to ignore tax demands I currently had of over £30,000 and said that my capital circumstances hadn't changed either, thus cutting off the route Rutter had successfully followed to appeal last time.

Trevor Reeve had sown up everything to date without having to say, head on, that the Court of Appeal decision was anything but sensible. He was thus left with merely adding up my income for the last few years (which is all it should ever have been about anyway). This he did, pointing out that, since the play had come off, my income had dropped, after the post-London tour it had dropped again, foreign royalties had dried up, and the film was over the hill. In all, in the first six months I hadn't taken £1,500 gross, (my true net earnings were nil) so there was an obvious substantial change in circumstances for the worse. 'I cannot ignore the possibility that in the foreseeable future the order which I propose to make may be drastically reduced even further... It may be that 1 Genoa Avenue will be very much too large to be occupied just by herself and Dominic and a nanny.'

He cut the maintenance in half to £2,000 for Christine and £1,500 for Dominic. Law was in at once asking for leave to appeal.

Reeve said 'I do not grant leave to appeal - not because I think that the order that I have made is unappealable, but because I do not want any further costs if possible to be spent in litigation. So no further argument; leave to appeal refused.'

He listened briefly to my account of Rutter's pre-hearing tactics and back-dated the new order to the sixth of April. Then he did an odd thing, he upheld Rutter's appeal against Bayne Powell's discovery order but ordered the costs to be charged against Rutter himself; I suppose to stop superfluous argument over the papers while at the same time to tell Rutter what he really thought of the tactic. Reeve made this last order in high good humour, obliging us all, especially the unwilling Rutter, to join in the jovial chuckles. But I never got that letter.

Tim and I walked back to his office arguing. He saw it as a victory, not to say a rout for us. Trevor Reeve had wriggled round the Court of Appeal judgement and wrapped everything up so that Christine couldn't appeal again. I was feeling quite light-hearted, any sort of victory is sweet after a week in court, but was indignant on rational grounds. 'The whole thing is an affront to reason: she is worth over £100,000 clear, I am worth less and am about to go down the drain anyway; I am still ordered to pay her more than I earn although she is fit, young and capable and does no work; she spends months abroad on holidays while that idiot blathers on about her being too busy to read the papers because she's looking after Dominic; Rutter holds up the hearing from February to May and I only get the new order backdated to April, so their reward is two months extra maintenance at the old rate for his time-wasting. And Rutter? No investigation, no report to the Law Society, just one little word 'zeal' and theoretical costs on a minor issue to show what the judge thought of him. No wonder lawyers just laugh at the rules. He'll do it again tomorrow. It's a victory for perversity!'

Tim shrugged 'It's the best he could give you. It's the best you could ever have hoped for. And it beats losing.'

In truth I felt good, though. Although I had been obliged to go in and fight on the figures, most of my complaints were, in reality complaints about my self-respect. And a great deal of that had been returned to me. I could live with the mathematics of my life now and was more than ready and willing to enter the next phase of the hearing, my application for improved access and joint custody. Perhaps I could gain some more self-respect and perhaps even some legal status as a father.

Chapter XXXIX

July Fourteenth & Fifteenth, 1974

The other leg of the case continued the next morning. I was asking the law for three things: to have Dominic to stay the night occasionally at weekends; to take him on holiday once a year; and for a joint say with Christine in his future. He was nearly five. I had not previously contested the custody issue, but pacifism had been rendered untenable after attempts to speak to Christine about him. 'Write to my solicitor,' she answered. I did so and was told by him to mind my own business.

The affidavit in answer to my pleas was in predictable Rutter overkill; fourteen closely-typed pages of invective. However, it wasn't just an exercise in acrimony, the insults had a definite function; if I was not as painted, but was a reasonable father, Christine had no case. To cover this she simply swore she was frightened of me, so joint custody was impracticable. Good stuff, saving all the tiresome business of evidence or proof that so encumbers most legal proceedings.

Two documents had been created to support the 'I am frightened' and 'father is incompetent' allegations; they looked ominously good to me. Rutter's timing in producing these documents was excellent and in contravention of the rules of procedure; they were exhibited to her affidavit which was sent to me just a few days before the hearing, out of time and therefore inadmissible. However, experience had shown me the judge would ignore this. Both documents were written by a Harley Street specialist, a paediatrician.

The first was two years old and used the word 'litigation' five times in several lines; it must have been created for an earlier hearing and not used. It spoke at length of the nervousness, depression and distress suffered by Christine, all brought on by the breakdown of her marriage and the subsequent litigation. It implied that I had started this litigation, which made me wonder what this doctor had been told. Any medical document that uses the word 'litigation' so freely must be suspect, but even so this one still had the power to make me concerned for her. Although it said she was physically healthy, being forced to fight someone for whom you feel concern is a curiously weakening business.

The second effort was up-to-date and concentrated on Dominic. This was a straight-forward hatchet job to block my attempt to have him stay overnight with me by stressing that a night away from his 'devoted mother' and his nanny would distress him. It did not say which of Dominic's many nannies he would miss, nor did it mention the number of nights Christine spent away from him as a matter of course. It laid much emphasis on Dominic's asthma and how a night away from home could bring on an attack. What this highly-paid doctor appeared never to have done was to test Dominic for allergies and learned that his childhood asthma was brought on by his living since birth in close proximity to two fluffy Persian cats to which he was strongly allergic. Every night away from those cats was a tonic for him. So much for Harley Street specialists and their use in litigation.

This second certificate seemed such a blatant assassination job that Tim and I hoped it might be self-defeating. However, I remembered, painfully, that four years previously Rutter had successfully presented to the court a similar-looking report from our GP in Putney to get me barred from my house. She had been horrified when told how her report had been used; perhaps this specialist too, was unaware.

I went to see him, failing to recognise that a highly paid Harley Street paediatrician would be a very different animal from our NHS GP with a practice in Putney. It was a revealing half hour. He was about my age, perhaps younger, very smooth and slight. He had made up his mind about me long before I walked through his surgery door. The amazing, and in my life the recurring, the nearly certifiable, mistake that I made was in thinking that I could change him. Like the judges in the Court of Appeal, this doctor didn't want to see, hear or know, about anything I had to say, and the eagerness with which I tried to press evidence upon him merely increased his resistance. He had no idea of what had passed between Christine and me. As I got more desperate, I offered that he be paid at Harley Street rates while he investigated whether I was telling him the truth or not. No, I was a bad lot and was taking this legal action merely to 'worry and harry' Christine and out of 'revenge.' She was 'frightened' of me, yes physically frightened and had appeared in his surgery 'terrified' and had broken down. If I stopped making trouble about money, my disbelieving ears heard twice, she would about Dominic. I begged him to see my accountant, my lawyer, to act as a conciliator himself, if only the for sake of Dominic, his patient. In answer he lectured me on my duties as a father. The sheer passion of my pleading as my frustration grew at the brick wall he presented must have confirmed in him the idea of my imbalance. I telephoned him again the following morning, fruitlessly, and then wrote an account of our meeting for the judge and sent the doctor a copy. No answer.

And so, with that prologue to the hearing, we stood up in court and bowed at the judge on his entrance. To my surprise Law at once asked for an adjournment so that we could discuss matters. Trevor Reeve readily agreed and we all bowed at each other again and trooped out to the gloomy corridor where Law promptly offered to give way on the matter of access. I could have Dominic to stay and for holidays, for the first time. Tim and I walked away to talk.

'Those bastards know they're going to lose so they're suddenly reasonable,' I snarled, hoping Law was still in earshot. This offer to settle something, the first for four years made more hackles rise than straightforward opposition. Then, with an almost physical shock, something hit me. At every opportunity since this business had started I had said, 'Don't fight, let's talk.' I had suspected that it looked like weakness to such as Rutter and Law, who peered at olive branches through the blinkers of a life-time squabbling over who owned what, but it was only at that moment that I saw just how craven I must have appeared. The system, and these men conditioned by it, simply made peace offers seem either weak or tactical.

I refused to talk to Rutter so that left Tim, Law and me.

'Provided you take the nanny with you,' began Law, 'you can take the kid on holiday '

'You mean Dominic,' I spat.

'You can take Dominic on -'

'Yes, that's his name, Dominic. Try and remember it. You've used it often enough.'

'Perhaps it would be easier if you and I dealt with this,' said Law to Tim.

'I think my client would prefer to be present,' Tim said.

Law turned once more to me with his usual imperturbability. He's an absolute carthorse, I thought; the plodder of the Family Division. 'If you will take the nanny with you on holiday, you can have the holiday access. You can also have the staying access you want without her. In return you drop your application for joint custody.'

'Is that the offer?' I asked.

'Yes.'

'Bollocks,' I said, 'Come on, Tim, let's get on with it,' taking his arm and heading swiftly for the court.

Law called after us. 'Just a minute. Just a minute, don't be so hasty.' And he lumbered up.

'Custody of Dominic is non-negotiable,' I said. 'What else do you want?'

'You can have the access anyway.'

Law told Trevor Reeve that we had settled access 'amicably' and Reeve looked suitably pleased. He asked me if I concurred. I got up and started telling him the details of our discussion outside. He looked most upset. 'I don't think I should be hearing about these discussions should I, Mr Law?'

'Without prejudice discussions are, of course, sacrosanct, My Lord,' said Law, 'but Mr Frisby has been known to ignore these niceties in the past.' I had to swallow so as not to chase that red herring.

'Quite, quite,' said Trevor Reeve. 'A barrister has vows, but perhaps Mr Frisby doesn't quite realise...'

348

'I think he knows, My Lord.'

I got in, 'My Lord, I thought there was no such thing as a without prejudice discussion on any matter pertaining to a child (this was so). Since without prejudice discussions cannot take place about my son, there is no reason for me not to tell you precisely what happened outside. I think you should know.

'I shouldn't be hearing this,' repeated Trevor Reeve. He wasn't in the least authoritative, merely flummoxed.

I ploughed on. 'If they present a doctor's report to the court saying it would be bad for Dominic to have staying access with me, how can they now offer me that access in exchange for me dropping the custody application? That is what they tried on. Surely they are offering me something that they and their doctor believe to be bad for Dominic? They shouldn't do that. Surely Dominic's welfare is a non-negotiable commodity? Or didn't they believe in their own case to start with?' I stood waiting for an answer.

'I think we'd better continue with the hearing for custody,' said Trevor Reeve. 'I really can't listen to this, Mr Frisby.'

'Aren't my questions worthy of answers?' I asked. Reeve ignored me as Law started on his case. I said to an usher, 'I see. Obviously not,' and sat down.

Law's first argument was astounding. Trevor Reeve got the angriest I ever saw him. It was that I was applying to take Dominic away from Christine. And, worse, that I was doing so out of 'revenge' and 'to harry her.' As a result of this she was most distressed and under medical care (this is part of what must have been told to the Harley Street paediatrician).

'But he's not applying for care and control, Mr Law,' said Trevor Reeve. 'He's applying for custody, and joint custody at that.

'We didn't know that, My Lord,' said Law. 'He's a litigant-in-person and it appears from the documents and correspondence that he means 'care and control.'

'Which documents and correspondence?' I butted in, quickly. 'Can we see them?'

Trevor Reeve fished out my application. It said 'custody.' Then he produced my affidavit. 'Mr Law, it says here, "I wish to apply for custody of my son Dominic and for staying access without his nanny." If he were confused and meant care and control, why would he ask for improved access?'

Law waffled. Reeve produced Christine's affidavit, his impatience growing. 'Mr Law, your client's affidavit in answer refers to Mr Frisby's application for 'custody and staying access.' Where is the confusion?'

Law said, 'Nevertheless, the wife is in considerable distress because she believes that he is applying for "care and control" of her son and doing it merely to harass her.'

I thought Trevor Reeve's eyeballs were in danger of disappearing permanently into his skull. His voice cut across the court in exasperation. 'Hasn't she got a lawyer to explain these things to her?'

Law left that and turned elsewhere. I was so full of frustration that I was near tears. I wanted to pursue that. If Law's argument was sincere, he and Rutter deserved the harshest of censure. He was saying that every time I had mentioned 'joint custody' over the last four years he and Rutter had been cruel enough to let Christine believe I was trying to take Dominic away from her. Thus, the nervous crises, visits to the Harley Street doctor, misinforming him of what was going on and all the rest of it. Or, if Law's argument was not sincere, the three of them (Christine included) had hit a new low in this campaign of 'the poor little feminine thing isn't up to understanding legal documents.' My own view was that all three of them understood perfectly well the difference between 'custody' and 'care and control'. But Trevor Reeve did nothing as Law went on to his next point. I had to calm myself down to concentrate.

Tim and I were both sure that I was home and dry. All we had to do was sit tight. Law's efforts seemed to be aiding me. Tim urged that I didn't cross-examine Christine at all. No matter what evidence I wanted the judge to hear, no matter how well my case was prepared to show the contradictions in theirs, now that access was settled just let it all go. I agreed. Sweet reason was the keynote.

Law had his head down in the barrel, scraper working overtime. He came up with a beauty. When I had written the story of our marriage and divorce for the Court of Appeal in 1972 I had told of the ten-minute hearing in which His Honour County Court Judge Trevor Reeve had said, 'It may well be that this father is being too possessive. Once a fortnight is appropriate.' I had added the comment:-

> 'I do not know to what dizzy heights of the legal ladder this judge has since been promoted, but I do know that it is remarks like that that make the judiciary feared and mistrusted by ordinary people for whom the law is supposed to exist.'

God knows what good I had thought that sentence would do. Perhaps I had imagined Our Lords of Appeal falling on my neck sobbing with gratitude that I had exposed this example of judicial inhumanity, or some such fantasy. Now here it was, disinterred by Good-Old-Harry. There was a formal, inevitable beauty about the working of his, or Rutter's, mind.

Mr Justice Trevor Reeve read the sentence about himself and his eyes flicked up to me. My answer had come to me swiftly - and quite well-phrased - from some kind deity. I rolled it out unctuously. 'My Lord, only an amateur like myself would be foolish enough to write such a sentence about a judge for other judges to read.' I paused just long enough. 'And only a professional like Mr Law would draw it irrelevantly to your attention.'

Reeve quite liked that. He gave a couple of hums, his eyes cast down. They swivelled up above Law's head before focusing on him. 'Mr Law, when I made that remark I didn't know what I now know about this case.' And up went the eyebrows and down went the corners of his mouth making him again look like a nanny, this time in the throes of outrage.

It was another one of those court pauses that seem to surge about like surf round your head, but this time I didn't lie back and luxuriate. 'Nevertheless, My Lord,' I said and waited till his eyes were on me. 'You did make the remark. And you did stop me seeing my son. And I don't think you should ever forget it. I shan't.'

And there we all were, frozen now in my memory like an old photo. The silence was more precious than golden. It was heightened by a low noise from Tim behind me as he buried his face in a hand. Reeve and I stared at each other for what I suppose was no time at all, but seemed forever. I looked into those clammy globes and waited for the wrath. Instead he started to go red from the back of his neck. The tops of his ears, his jowls, his temples, then the whole face flushed and suddenly the lovely, lovely moment of melting sweetness was gone and he was listening to Law describing some new-found deficiency in my character.

The question of whether or not I could get joint custody centred round one point only: could Christine and I ever get together and jointly make decisions about Dominic? I didn't believe that she intended to try unless made to, but that could not be said in court, or barely even implied. Her case was that I was impossible.

She was called to give evidence. It knocked me sideways. I had read for four years in legal documents that she was afraid of me and I had heard the Harley Street specialist assuring me so. I didn't merely not believe the allegation, I was certain it was invented for litigation purposes. Earlier in this story I have reported our clinging together and her saying, 'I want to try again but I'm frightened.' That had been converted to, 'I am frightened of him' in an affidavit, then escalated to 'physically frightened.' Now for the first time, there she was in person before me, asserting her fear with apparent conviction. It would be easy to dismiss her performance in the witness box. Certainly she said much that was - I was going to say untrue, but that isn't what I mean - she said much that was not so. For instance, delivered earnestly and without a prompt from Law was, 'I should like to say that, except for my appeal, I have never brought any of this litigation at all.' Now, although this was unreal to the point of dottiness, she meant something by it. Such is the power of the myths that we all create about ourselves.

Law's examination of her was quite short and was punctuated by at least one outbreak of tears. It consisted of him getting her to say that she had told me in 1970 that she had set down Dominic for two schools and had been unable subsequently to discuss anything at all with me because she

351

was 'frightened' of me; because I was 'unbalanced,' had been 'abusive,' had never spoken to her once in four years with any 'kindness or decency;' because I had 'screamed and shouted' at her; because I had written 'abusive' letters to her; because I might go to the school and say the same sort of things about her; because 'he bullied me during most of the years of our marriage' 'and since our divorce;' 'because it is impossible to have a sane conversation with him.'

The official transcript of her evidence is liberally spattered with little series of dots when she became inaudible. These were, as I remember, gulps and sobs. Law sat down and, confused by this new view of myself, I stood up to cross-examine. Tim's advice to ask no questions was pushed aside by the apparent necessity to dispel at least a little of what had been said. There was no question of my trying to get at the truth of anything, I wasn't going to have my persistence on any point labelled 'harrying' or 'bullying.' What is interesting about my questioning is the judge's part in it: Trevor Reeve, the amateur psychologist.

The atmosphere when I started was about as phoney as you could wish. There was a sort of competition between Christine and myself, each to sound more reasonable than the other. To nail the 'bully' allegation I asked some questions about my having pleaded with her in a most unbullying way not to go through with the divorce. Her memory appeared to have failed. The court transcript is full of 'can't remember and 'witness inaudible' (which meant tears). I asked which were the 'abusive ' letters I had written to her. Her answer floored me. 'I think some have been read out.'

I stared. 'They are the ones you call abusive?'

'Yes.'

The letters that she called abusive were the same ones that I had exhibited as evidence of my attempts to behave reasonably.

If the process of that court had borne even a passing relevance to the reality of our lives, this should have been a climactic moment, the moment for the judge, me, Rutter Christine and all to have said corporately, 'Right, let's stop everything and sort this out. What the hell has happened that two people who have lived, loved, thought and acted together for six years in harmony can have got on opposite sides of such a gulf.' I tried to get Reeve to look at one of the letters. The court transcript shows my words but not his reaction. I said, 'I think it is worth a passing look,' the eyes started to roll up and I hurried on, 'But not if you don't want to.'

I switched to the 'frightened' allegations. What followed was a sort to genteel chat about the meaning of frightened. You could practically hear the chink of bone china. I asked why she had come to the Royal Court to see the Osborne play with me in it if she were frightened of me. It caused one of those standard judicial comedy interjections of the, 'What are the Beatles?' type. Reeve said, 'I don't understand this. If you were appearing in the play how could you be sitting in the audience next to her?'

I wondered how to describe Osborne's cultural raspberry, 'It's a very strange play, My Lord.'

Reeve stared. 'I see, well that may be right.'

After we had got that off our chests, the 'physically frightened of you' that the Harley Street specialist believed was quickly abandoned. It was not my beating her up that she was frightened of but my tongue. I learned that instead of being free to do whatever she liked during our marriage she had spent it cowed and bullied. This was beautiful in cross-examination; when decorously cornered the answer was 'You are right and I am wrong, the usual story,' an impenetrable defence, with the ubiquitous 'I don't remember' like a recurring motif. The examination was ridiculous, I should have stopped, it was so divorced from reality, but I hoped some sort of nugget might be extracted. One soon was, but not the one I wanted. It began with another interruption from Reeve. 'I think the questions you are asking are not so important as - at least the facts referred to are not so important, but I am observing the relationship between you - that is what I find so interesting.'

'How to make us both self-conscious and act unnaturally, My Lord,' I said, then backtracked anxiously, 'I am sorry.'

'At the moment I am not observing you, I am observing your wife.'

It was a beautiful cue and it soon got its response. None of us even noticed his omission of the prefix 'ex-'. Christine had been trapped for some time, as a string of 'can't remember' shows. I said to her, 'You never brought any litigation, you said, and I think that remark reflects your feeling, not the facts. You feel you have never brought any litigation. What has happened has coloured the past in your mind.' She let out a deep weary sigh. 'I just want you to leave me alone, that is all I want.' The force of it reverberated round the court; a perfect refuge from answering the unanswerable. I paused, knowing that if I pursued the subject my case would be drowned in tears and interruptions from Reeve. Oh, how I longed for the judge to be a woman. She would soon have let in the twentieth century. I took a nowhere course and said in a hushed voice, 'But there's Dominic, isn't there. You want me to go away and leave Dominic alone, too?'

Christine's eyes opened wide. 'Of course I don't. You are his father.'

Once more I stood stumped and silent. She seemed to mean it. Four years of injunctions and access orders seemed not to exist for her.

Mr Justice Trevor Reeve's judgement covered five pages of foolscap. After some guff about what splendid, caring parents we both were he went on to withdraw his pejorative use of the word 'zeal' about Rutter in his earlier judgement on maintenance. He thought Rutter was doing a good job for Dominic (my God). So Rutter was splendid and caring, too, the judicial answer to my plea to get lawyers out and start a new era.

...To my way of thinking it is in the interests of a boy that the father should, other things being equal, be given an adequate say...

I am an incurable optimist in regard to the goodness of the human nature of parents...I ask myself, however, in this case whether perhaps my optimism may not be misplaced...and with great reluctance I have come to the conclusion quite clearly that in this case my usual optimism would be wholly out of place. It matters not whose fault it is. These two parents are not going to be able to agree...

It might be thought that I had misunderstood the attitude of the mother, and that she was not really trying to co-operate with the father in regard to Dominic's future; that she was quite deliberately being difficult and as awkward as she could in order, I suppose, to score some point against her ex-husband. That is not the position here. I observed her most closely in the witness box, and possibly the most genuine piece of evidence which she gave, which came out from her with startling honesty, was this. She was being cross-examined by the father and she summed up her emotions in these words, which I am abundantly satisfied came straight from the heart: 'I just want you to go away and leave me alone.' That is her attitude to the father. The next question that was asked of her was: 'Does that mean you want me to leave Dominic alone also?' and her next answer also came straight from the heart: 'Of course not, you are his father...'

Mr Frisby suggested that it might be possible for them to discuss the future of Dominic in the presence of some acceptable third party. That was suggested to the mother when she was being cross-examined. She gave a perfectly truthful answer there, and that was: 'That sounds like a lovely idea, but it wouldn't work.' And that, I fear, is the truth of this matter...

...For those reasons I make no Order for variation of the Order for custody.

It was my cross-examination that had sunk my case. Tim, as always, had been right. 'I just want you to go away and leave me alone,' had either done it or contributed greatly. But it was, 'These two parents are not going to be able to agree,' delivered by Reeve, the self-styled optimist, after that brief look at us in those entirely unnatural circumstances, that left me squashed and gurgling with frustration.

While I was still steaming I heard Law arguing costs and quickly joined in. It was an empty exercise. Reeve's mind was already made up. I had 'won' the financial hearing which had incurred most of the costs; Rutter's time-consuming tactics had cost a fortune and consumed months in unnecessary work so that Reeve had even backdated the new maintenance order but he would make no order on costs. I have heard from numerous sources that such is general practice in divorce. If the wife 'wins' the husband pays. If the husband 'wins' he still pays, sometimes for himself, sometimes for both. Of course, in every case, it is only the lawyers who win. All divorce lawyers prefer to represent the wife.

I got to my feet for the last time and said something like, 'My Lord, it would save a lot of everybody's time and money, and my temper, if you reserved this case to yourself so that Mr Rutter and Mr Law won't again be faced with the burden of repeating their allegations to a new judge.

Reeve enjoyed that. 'Yes, Mr Frisby, I think it would be in all interests if I reserved this case to myself. Don't you, Mr Law?'

Law agreed with grim heartiness and it was over.

———

I at once wrote Christine a conciliatory letter. Her answer was prompt: she appealed the new Maintenance Order.

Ten days later - in spite of Reeve having refused leave to appeal - I again faced Rutter and Law in the Court of Appeal. Christine didn't bother to appear. She went on holiday to the tropics instead, leaving Dominic behind, not with me. 'I just want you to leave me alone, that is all I want.'

Whoever was being left alone, it certainly wasn't I.

Chapter XL

1974-75

The reason for the swiftness with which Rutter got us into the Court of Appeal was simple but outrageous: he tried to present his case before Reeve's judgement was available. I learned of the hearing just in time to get there and listen to an hour or more of the usual mud-slinging. In the absence of Reeve's judgement, Law quoted liberally from notes. Whoever had made them appeared to have been listening to a different judgement from the one I had heard. At my request, Their Lordships adjourned matters until Reeve's actual judgement was received from the Official Recording Department.

With that hearing looming, relations between Christine and me sank to a new low. Via Rutter, there was a stream of complaints that I was mistreating Dominic during the new, increased access periods. Fearful of attempts to curtail them, I answered each allegation seriously, but in response to equally noxious letters about money I resorted to a campaign of schoolboy invective, always sent to his home address.

> ...my former solicitors Theodore Goddard & Co., referred to you as Gutter. It has always seemed to me a particularly inappropriate nickname; a gutter is a useful device used by civilised men to drain the filth and muck *out* of our lives. Why not aspire to that at least?...

And among the sillier:

> ...If we chance to meet each other next week in the Court of Appeal I wonder if you would mind ducking down a side corridor somewhere or at least standing still as your walk is so comic I find it difficult to go into Court in the right serious frame of mind having seen you. Your feet have a way of flapping about in a rather uncoordinated fashion at the end of your little legs, which I am surprised has not aroused comment before. If you wish, I should be happy to pass on the address of any good physiotherapist who I am sure will be able to help.

356

In such humour we went into the Court of Appeal. Christine, at least, was left alone, on a different holiday, resting in a first class hotel somewhere in Africa. I don't know who had Dominic. It was not I.

Only two judges entered, Lord Justice Megaw and Mr Justice Cumming-Bruce. We all bowed and I sat, quaking, as I had over two years before in that awful place. It still induced a terror no first night can equal, and the memory of how the previous Lords of Appeal had treated me was still fresh.

Lord Justice Megaw looked down at Law. 'Our brother is not well and because of the pressures on the courts we cannot find a replacement. I trust the opinion of merely two of us will suffice, Mr Law?' Law assured him it would. Megaw didn't bother to ask me.

Law kicked off, ploughing through ancient background. After a while Megaw asked him to be as brief as possible. Law plodded on, giving them Christine's advisers' reasons for the appeal. Lord Justice Megaw said, 'Are we really interested in the wife's advisers' views?' Law got to my character and the mud started to fly again. Megaw said, 'But all this is dealt with in Mr Justice Reeve's judgement. Law tried to argue that some new law that wasn't yet in force should be taken into account. Mr Justice Cumming-Bruce said snottily, 'It is a novel idea that the court should take account prospective bills of the House that haven't had the Queen's assent.' Megaw repeatedly asked Law to get his facts right as Law floundered deeper and deeper into inaccuracy and misquoted Reeve's judgement. Again and again Megaw asked Law to get to his points and brushed aside the attacks on me by quoting from Reeve's judgement. At last Law came to a halt. 'And that's your first point, is it?' said Megaw in disgust. 'If you have any further points, please do not go back again and again. Let us know what they are and come to them. This is an application for an appeal. It requires to be put forward with succinctness and specific points of application.'

Of course, Law's cupboard was bare. He went back over old ground yet again. Megaw was livid. 'Mr Law, we understand that submission. We have understood it for the last forty- five minutes.'

Law said, 'My Lords, I will say no more about that in the circumstances.'

Megaw said, 'Come to your point.'

Law answered, 'I am coming to the point, My Lords.'

'Well, do,' rapped Megaw.

Law again went back over the old stuff. I suppose he deserved points for persistence. I thought Megaw was going to throw something at him. At last he said, 'If these are your only points we have heard them'. And Law sat down.

I rose to my feet, but Megaw waved me down, then he tore Law off a tremendous strip for bringing the appeal when the judge had specifically refused leave in order to save the Frisby family money. He awarded me the costs of the hearing and left, followed by Cumming-Bruce. They didn't bother to bow, I noticed.

I sprawled, too numb to feel relief yet. One of the court reporters leaned over. 'They gave him a rough ride, didn't they.' He was impressed. The judges' clerk looked at me and grinned chummily. 'Does this mean we've seen the last of you, Mr Frisby? Only I seem to have been looking over this bench at you for the last four years.'

I shrugged.

He glanced over his shoulder and lowered his voice. 'I'll tell you something. Every time the case Frisby versus Frisby comes up in the lists, all the judges run and hide in the toilet.'

In the following year I earned virtually nothing; Trust investments, caught in the first post-oil economic crisis earned nothing. I paid Christine £3500 maintenance and £2500 capital; so, with a sinking feeling I applied to Trevor Reeve to give me the next year free of maintenance on the grounds of a further change in my circumstances for the worse, that to be followed by a review of our financial state. My argument was that Christine could work, indeed would have had to had we been married, and that I needed the breathing space. I avoided all the pre-hearing flak that Rutter might have put up by applying straight to Trevor Reeve with the current figures. My application and affidavit received a thirteen-page answer that was out of time. Before we got into court I wrote to Christine hoping we could settle matters between ourselves.

She answered:

4th May 1975

Dear Terry,

I have received from Mr Rutter the news of your application to vary the maintenance payments for Dominic and myself and your supporting affidavit.

It is so tragic that what should have been the success story of a lifetime appears to have turned out badly because of bad investments. It must be a dreadful disappointment to you.

Because of this I think that if possible one should try to come to some reasonable financial arrangement for the sake of Dominic rather than have to go through the ordeal of court proceedings to have the finances sorted out.

Would it be possible therefore, for you to put forward any suggestions or plans you might have regarding Dominic and myself?

Sincerely,

Christine

She avoided the ordeal of court proceedings by taking another foreign holiday while Rutter and I presented ourselves to the judge. Dominic was left with someone or other, again not me. It took a day; I placed the figures before Reeve, after which Rutter cross-examined me. With no other case, he tried to prove that I made a living out of gambling at golf, failed, smartly about-turned and tried to prove that I wasted inordinate sums in the same occupation. That was about it. Trevor Reeve refused my application on the grounds that it was premature and awarded the costs against me. I protested that when I had won he had merely made no order. He said sorry (and seemed to mean it), but he had no choice.

And that was the end of litigation between Christine and me for four years. Rutter senior disappeared from my life without even collecting his fees. Contact between us ended not with the bang of a court action from him for his money, but with a final petty, raspberry from me through the post.

Messrs. S. Rutter & Co

1st August 1975

Sir,

YOUR GOOF

Many thanks for your letter dated 28th July which I received on 28th July first post, so congratters.

Your inaccurate statements about maintenance payments caused me to check with my bank. My enquiries have revealed that far from my being late in maintenance payments your client was in fact paid double for the month of May. The bank are now investigating to see whether she was paid twice for the months of June and July as well. When they have completed their investigations I shall write again and answer your inane letter more fully. In the meantime many thanks, old bean, for drawing my bank's errors to my attention. I would never have discovered the over-payment without your assistance. I am sure your client will be as delighted as I am to learn that your ill-conceived correspondence has saved me at least £195.41 and cost her at least the same amount.

It reminds me of the first time you entered the Frisby family's financial affairs and successfully got your client's weekly payments reduced from over £100 per week voluntary paid by me, to £39.50 on the Registrar's order. Keep it up.

Yours gratefully,

Terence Frisby

I owed Rutter many thousands of pounds that had been awarded to him in costs for the past five years. The total may have been as much as £25,000.

He never sent a bill.

Of all the irregularities in the case that was surely the strangest. I even sent him reminders just to see what response I would get. No answer. Tim and I have often speculated about it. But I think, finally, my speculation ends at that car of his outside 1 Genoa Avenue on the night of sixth December 1970. Why would a lawyer take all that trouble for nothing unless - at least on his side - there was some sort of personal involvement?

The exit of Rutter senior precedes a major change of direction of this story and is the moment for another summing-up, but what can I say about this misuser and abuser of legal processes that will not descend into invective? He was, so I am told, a devoutly religious man. Well. I thought him evil. And still do. But that is subjective. What was it Latey said of him? He spoke of his 'unyielding nature', 'aggressive and belligerent tone', the 'outdated and adversarial' way he had handled things, 'stoking up pain and bitterness unnecessarily' with his 'peremptory and aggressive tone', 'increasing the conflagration' in this 'grim fantasy' of a divorce. Yet Latey, famous and humane High Court judge and later Appeal Court judge, didn't know a tenth of it.

WHAT EFFECT HAD RUTTER HAD ON OUR LIVES?

Well, appalling, of course. He operated in the lower levels of the law, was despised by all who I spoke to about him and should have been seen off without more than a few sighs of irritation and some extra costs. But there was one area where he took up residence early, took hold and was firmly in place before I realised how important he could be. That was in Christine's mind. He brought all the legal dross of detectives, steaming open letters, accusations, deceit, injunctions, grabbing property and grabbing our child into our free-wheeling, easy-going, relaxed lives. The two worlds were incompatible. The presence of legalistic wrangling in almost any form would have been unnecessary and inappropriate between Christine and me, but in the way that Rutter practised, he turned an entirely soluble crisis in our marriage into its agonising, protracted extinction.

Now that it was too late, I had seen Rutter off, as first, Nabarro Nathanson and second, Theodore Goddard and James Comyn should have done years before. If there was one lesson to be learned from contact with him, it was that appeasement to an aggressor is the most disastrous of all courses.

As Rutter moves out of our lives, taking his malign influence with him, and the narrative takes a different course, let me tease out from the mass and mess of detail the important points of the legal part of this story and their effects.

In simple lawyers' terms of winning and losing, it divides quite simply into two parts: I lost - and disastrously so - while I took the advice of first, Nabarro Nathanson, then, Theodore Goddard and James Comyn; I proceeded to win back some ground and (more important) my self-respect after I got rid of them and became a litigant-in-person.

Let me take the first of those two halves: losing. There was a trigger and two main turning-points, all were cock-ups.

The trigger was not a legal cock-up, it was a medical one. The whole, unnecessary juggernaut was set in motion by Dr. Wilfred Lester and his self-opening double doors through which a deeply secret and personal confession by me was overheard by Christine. That subsequent confrontation, unsought by both of us, should never have happened. Without it we would have found our own way through the crisis we were in. Perhaps neither of us would ever have learned of the other's infidelity and we would have joined the vast throng of happy hypocrites who stay married by silence.

The first of the two legal turning-points was allowing that restraining injunction to stand when I was barred from my own house. That was the end of contact between Christine and me and hope of reconciliation. Rutter was in charge. It was the last time I was allowed to see Dominic, except under onerous terms, for many years. It was the last time I ever went freely through my own front door. I was eager to contest that injunction but was persuaded not to by Nabarro Nathanson, who foresaw none of the subsequent restrictions I (not they) would live under.

The second of those two turning points was the consent order into which I was steamrollered by Theodore Goddard and, especially, James Comyn. That settlement, put me financially into the power of Rutter. It was the worst day of my life. I even knew it at the time. By the time I had struggled free from its impossible mathematics, the fortune that I had built up in

361

just a few years from nothing, to take care of all our nearest and dearest for life, was gone.

Thus was Rutter allowed to change the course of our lives. His intervention ended our marriage (and that was the greater disaster), but it was my lawyers who later allowed him to wreck my whole family's finances.

As you read of the blame that I heap on professional people, let me say that I take full responsibility for my own life. If things go wrong, in the end the buck always stops with yourself. No excuses. But, surely - and this is the important public point - when two people are in a crisis and they consult professional advisers, they have the right to expect some sort of help, or understanding, or at least competence, not what we got. The professionals in our lives compounded the existing problems and were the creators of new ones.

The conduct of all the lawyers in this matter demonstrates my overall argument that the legal profession should play no part in divorce. They come from precisely the wrong background: our adversarial legal system. Conciliators, accountants to add up and divide the assets and child experts are all that are needed. Not lawyers.

So to the second part of the legal story: winning. Or, to be more precise, winning a little back.

I started to crawl out of the pit I had got so deeply into when I met Stephen Mitchell, who suggested I write the whole story, collect the evidence to back myself up and become a litigant-in-person.

The first legal action that I took, the one before Mr Justice Latey, went a long way to restore my faith that there still existed such a thing as sweet reason, even in the law. He saw and said that something serious was wrong. As Stephen told me, to have a consent order turned over was a considerable event in English law; to have it turned over by a litigant-in-person was a sensation - even though the actual changes that Latey could make to the order were merely peripheral. Yes, that hearing was a big event for me when I was badly down.

But, Christine, led by Rutter, appealed Latey's modest changes and I was due for more shocks.

The appeal before those three scoundrels, Davies, Phillimore and Orr, was the climax to the first act of my rehabilitation, and a crushing climax it was. I was not only back in the same trap as before, but my only other exit - the remedy of suing Theodore

362

Goddard for negligence - was closed by their monstrous judgement, made to protect Comyn, as I have shown. Losing that hearing didn't make me disgusted with myself again, as the sell-out under Comyn had; instead, I was disgusted with our judiciary, a far healthier emotion.

Some eighteen months later I had to go back into those hateful Royal Courts of Justice, once again as a litigant-in-person. This time, in months of pre-trial skirmishing before the Trevor Reeve hearing, I found myself taking on Rutter in person. Litigation became a positive pleasure. Just to be across a table engaged in combat with that creature, watching him avoid my eyes for hour after hour, gave the fight a flavour it had never had. What a dismal journey this divorce had taken me on: from being forced to oppose Christine at the beginning, to now relishing a fight with her representative. And Rutter was so easy to deal with once I got over the initial error of assuming that anyone obeyed the rules of conduct when before those registrars. I came to realise that Tim Akeroyd's 'Splutter' was the appropriate nickname and the 'Gutter' applied by Calderan and Grafton Green gave Rutter an inflated status of unwholesomeness. So, I got another aspect of my view of the world back into focus by beating him at his own dirty little game.

The final climax, the hearing before Trevor Reeve, had a large plus and a large minus. And both of them lead on to the following chapter of this. The plus was that, after initial antipathy, Trevor Reeve, within one day, understood the financial situation correctly (why shouldn't he, you may well ask; isn't that what judges are for? Well, yes, but look at the list who couldn't or wouldn't). He did the sums, did what he could, got the law right and made his judgement appeal-proof.

But that didn't stop Christine and Rutter appealing and, in the Court of Appeal, their locker was shown to be empty.

So, financially, I could now meet the immediate future. Some pride was restored to me, too. But I was still bankrupt on paper, awaiting those demands from the Revenue that would wipe me out unless the new Trust capital investments grew at a sensational rate, which they were not. I had been living under that sword of Damocles now for over three years.

The minus from the Trevor Reeve hearing was about Dominic and my pleas for joint custody. With no evidence, except Christine saying so in court, Reeve deemed me unfit for joint custody of my son. Trevor Reeve, the self-appointed assessor of human character, said: 'these two parents will never agree'. Those divorce court judges make many similar human judgements without proper investigation and without having suitable qualifications. Trevor Reeve fell for Christine's 'I just want you to go away and leave me alone.' The emptiness of that was shown when she went straight to the Court of Appeal before his judgement was even printed, meanwhile taking a tropical holiday so that she would be 'left alone.' Reeve said 'I am an incurable optimist... but not in this case'. Easily cured, so it seems.

Observe what follows and see whether my assessment of that judgement is accurate or not. I say he was completely fooled. I appealed for a new era of co-operation over Dominic with, if necessary, a third person (not a lawyer) as arbiter in case of need. 'Not possible,' said Reeve. And he even withdrew his mild condemnation of Rutter, saying that he was doing a valuable job for Christine on a personal level. Huh. When Christine decided she would try to co-operate, we didn't need even the arbiter, never mind about Rutter..

Chapter XLI

1970-79

So to Dominic.

From the date of the injunction, May 1970, I was refused permission to see Dominic for five months. From Autumn 1970 until Babs died I saw him at her house, officially once a fortnight, in fact less. After Babs died and until Dominic was nearly five my experience of fatherhood consisted of collecting him and the current nanny or au pair (delivery to me was always refused), to take them on various outings. The constant necessity to make access an event was the most obvious, but still the worst, problem. A parent on access must constantly invent action when probably the thing he/she most wants - the best thing for all - is to do nothing. I couldn't just drop Dominic into my life for one afternoon a week and expect him to get on with it, so I became, like many other fathers I am sure, a jolly figure who appeared and did nice things with him. At the sight of me it was always 'What are we going to *do* today, Daddy?' This gnawed away at me.

After he was three the au pair was dropped from time to time. I was deemed fit to have him without the benefit of Iranian obesity. One indelibly remembered afternoon in drowsy summer an outing became a blissful non-event and he sat on my lap in a swing for hours, both of us drugged by the atmosphere and movement as we went backwards and forwards in the children's playground in Kensington Gardens. We did the Serpentine, the common, the river, the ducks, the zoo, the Science Museum, the Tower, the Palace. I could quickly identify other dads on access, probably as desperate as I about how to be natural with their children in unnatural circumstances. An ordinary relaxed day at home with Dominic doing his thing, and me just being there, then putting him to bed, was the unattainable goal.

However we found one haven: the Danvers' house. Our favourite occupation became an afternoon at Ivor and Henri's, where Dominic grew to worship Tommy, their son. He was four years older than Dominic, the ideal idol-gap. Tommy soon understood his status and filled his role with style and magnanimity. At the Danvers' I could play with the boys or leave them alone in a relaxed atmosphere that reproduced some approximation of my wish to be at home with Dominic. Ivor and Henri's nearness and hospitality were invaluable, but Tommy was from God. If an outing with dull Dad didn't appeal to Dominic, ran my fear, at least he was always eager to see Tommy.

Henri, Ivor, Tommy, Dominic and I were driving back from having watched Tommy act in a school entertainment. Dominic had been enthralled by Tommy's every twitch.

'Oh, oh, dear.' Tommy's wail was the cry of actors throughout the centuries. 'Was I good?' Was I? Was I good?'

'Lovely, dear,' said Henri, with more affection than accuracy. 'You were smashing.'

'Oh,' groaned Tommy.

'I couldn't hear everything you said,' put in Ivor.

'But they made me dance,' protested Tommy.

'What's that got to do with being heard?'

Tommy was indignant about the acoustics in his school hall. Henri said she had heard every word. We arrived at the Danvers'. Tommy and Dominic were in another room as we prepared tea. I went to fetch them and saw them through the half-open door; they were standing facing each other; Tommy was eight years old, Dominic, four. Tommy was running his fingers through his hair in artistic tumult, 'They made me *dance*, Dominic. I can't dance. I felt such a *fool*.' Dominic stared at his hero, baffled and concerned at all this emotion. Tommy had merely been his wonderful self in Dominic's eyes. 'Tell me, Dominic, tell me.' Tommy's hands were spread before him, palms up, fingers bent imploringly, cliché gesture of a whole generation of screen actors who have never learned to use their hands, 'Tell me, *was I good?*'

There was a four-second pause while Dominic scoured his inner self for aid for his wounded idol. Then, 'Would you like one of my soldiers?'

Aside from the Danvers' house my car became our home; we spent more time there than anywhere. Access, though brief enough, is largely taken in going from point A to point B and though, for many, there must be bleak memories of buses and trains, for us it was at least cocooned and plush, with tapes and an ever-changing view sliding past to invent things about. It was, naturally enough, a road sign that provided early evidence to me that Dominic had a brain. We were in a one-way system. 'When the arrow turns you can turn too,' he told me, 'and when it points up you can go straight.'

'Thank you.'

'But you can't go up, only straight. They have to point the arrow up because if they pointed it straight you wouldn't know. You'd only see the back of it.'

'Yes, I see. Did someone tell you that?'

'No, I thought it.'

One day, while journeying to my mother's, Dominic asked me about giants, and Giant Bellybulge was born. He was the last giant on earth, a greedy roly-poly, a cowardly, blubbing, vain boaster who lived on the edge of the woods in a Mini (car, not skirt). His redeeming feature was that he was gentle and ineffectual. He gorged himself on smarties, chips and rhubarb and swelled so much that he couldn't get back into his Mini. Then he got cold and wet, cried, farted and weed his trousers. Dominic would sit on the back seat, strapped in, rapt, frowning, thumb in mouth, as I told how Giant Bellybulge tried to be a skier, pilot, sailor, ballet dancer, all with disastrous results. A shout of laughter would make me jump, then the thumb would be re-inserted and the frown of concentration resumed. Sometimes we invented Giant Bellybulge adventures together. When Dominic went away on holiday I wrote him Giant Bellybulge serial-letters.

Finally there was swimming. Ah, swimming. All dads with access problems take note. Swimming is the answer. Never mind if your children hate or fear the water, lead them to it gently and quickly. Swimming became our saviour. I was a poor swimmer, but no matter, it was something I could teach him. Properly. At last. The fact that I only saw him once a week didn't matter. Once a week, and later twice, was about the right continuity. Dominic and Tommy followed me into Putney baths, at first fearfully, then like eager ducklings. During the first winter of swimming, when Dominic was four, we were sometimes the only people in there. On grey, bitterly cold afternoons, Putney baths was our warm, golden womb. The boys progressed from sitting on my head in the infants' pool (to prove that being underwater was fun) to sitting with me on the bottom at the deep end of the big pool laughing and blowing bubbles at each other. They soon became excellent swimmers, crawling up and down the big pool like tiny Tarzans. I took lessons to keep ahead of them and learned for the first time to embrace the water and not to swim as though I was trying to brush it away.

On swimming days, as I rounded the corner of Genoa Avenue in my car Dominic would be on the pavement running up and down, breathless and shrieking, his towel and bathers under his arm. I was so proud of the one thing I, and I alone, had taught him, that it was difficult to keep a sense of proportion about swimming.

And those few doting pages above contain the whole contribution I was deemed fit by Sidney Rutter to give to my son until he was nearly five. I say Rutter, because the law gave me what Christine allowed, no more. And she allowed what Rutter advised. Our judges permit the likes of him to flourish in it and manipulate it so, without check or rebuke.

During those years I was often bitter, angry, upset or frustrated at the law or lawyers over one matter or another, but all emotions grow faint before the memory of the terrible rage that gripped me because of what was done and allowed to be done 'in Dominic's best interests.' That rage, fired somewhere down in my depths, became damped down, but it never left me. It was like a non-stop growl through which every other sound was distorted. Sometimes the pitch would rise and it would drown all else. On a practical level, acquaintances often had to repeat remarks or I didn't hear them. Books, plays, films, music, even friendships were tossed aside unfinished as they failed to hold my attention through the din that filled my head. The life of relative well-being that I lived was all filtered through the impotent fury of that sound.

Christine and I, together, would have made, I am sure, an excellent home for him. Apart, I could see my faults, unchecked by her influence, at work in the relationships between Dominic and myself. Besides that, I had to watch, mouth clamped shut, as I saw, from a distance, Christine do things of which I disapproved. There was no chance of our being able to talk or to act as correctives to each other. Despite the bounteous material advantages Dominic had, I could only see him as a deprived child. And my view of him as such meant that there was a constant battle with myself not to over-compensate by indulgence, a battle which I must have lost many times. Any question of authority with him during our brief time together was inflated to idiotic proportions in my mind, which would be followed by a week of worry as to whether I had done right and just how I would deal with the next minuscule crisis, which would, of course, arrive in an unexpected way and catch me unprepared. In the early days there was, behind everything, the fear that if I administered a normal parental rebuke near the end of access-time Dominic would return home and say, as any child might in such circumstances, 'I don't like Daddy,' or, 'He told me off, I don't want to see him,' and this would be used to cancel access for good, or until after yet another court battle. This last fear was omnipresent and a dreadful distorter of natural behaviour. Once or twice I found an excuse and cancelled access, such were the cross-currents of emotion its proximity caused.

It was the twenty-seventh November 1972, the eve of my fortieth birthday. Dominic was just over three. I was shunting in the evening rush-hour gloom down the Kings Road. I became aware that the Mini in front of me was Christine's. She was driving, the current obese Iranian beside her, and Dominic standing in the back of the car, jumping about, talking, laughing, pointing out things, filling the car with infant vitality. This scene, I mean the whole scene, them outlined in the street lamps and shop fronts with Dominic's animation making the car glow, and me alone, crawling behind in shadow, became a most potent image in my imagination. It did nothing for the growl in my head.

Dominic was emerging as balanced and unextraordinary. His most positive characteristics were very simple, he was extremely gentle and rather naive. And he wanted to please. True to form I found something to worry about even in that. He related to people rather than to whatever he was doing. If he scored a goal in a game of garden football his pleasure was not in the goal but in my approbation. I, whose pleasure had always been in the achievement itself, turned myself inside-out analysing this perfectly ordinary three-year-old behaviour. One incident, comic in itself, worried me for months. I was sitting in the paddock behind my mother's house. Dominic, about four, was playing with other children. He came up to me under the tree where I was scanning with indifference what Harold Hobson had to say about the latest theatrical offering.

'Daddy, that girl's got my bike.'

'Well, can't she have a ride on it?'

'She has. For hours. Now she won't give it back.'

'Well, ask her for it.'

'I have.'

'OK Go up to her and ask her for it once more, then, if she won't give it to you, take it from her.' The girl was about his size.

He look worried. 'How?'

'Just pull it away from her.'

'What if she won't let go?'

'Push her off it.'

Off he went. I returned to Hobson, smug at not having been over-protective, and at my contribution to male liberation. There was a bawl from the other end of the paddock. Dominic re-appeared, crying.

'What happened?'

Gulps and sobs.

'Stop that noise and tell me what happened.'

'I told her if she wouldn't give it back to me I'd cry and I am.'

You can imagine the overtones that I read into that. Oh, the disastrous effects of an all-female environment on small boys. Months of thought went into the problem of how I could put some backbone into him without being oppressive or over-disciplinary. No answer was forthcoming. I didn't think of saying at the time, 'Now you've learned that crying gets you nowhere.' Perhaps he learned it for himself.

Many of the things that Dominic said were charming and funny, unlike the boring remarks uttered by all other children. I wrote them down after accesses and kept them in a drawer along with the piles of snapshots, but I will not bore you with such unanswerables as 'Where is yesterday?' and 'Is this knife upside down?' The collection has come out of the drawer to see what was relevant to this story and can now go into the wastebasket along with those furious, impotent, bitter, four years.

In the May 1974 hearing before Trevor Reeve, when Dominic was nearly five, I at last won staying access for certain weekends, plus holiday access once a year. These weekends were precious. I put him to bed for the first time. It was the beginning of the realisation of my wish that we could be simply together in the same house without the pressure of clocking on and off for access. Bedtime is surely the best time with a child. He is washed and combed, angelic and happy. A story of Giant Bellybulge is about to come and the delaying tactics of a glass of water, I'm hungry, can I go to the loo, have all been trotted out and done with. The light is about to go out and your are there together, he smiling up from the pillow; the most enchanted of moments.

One still winter's night we sat in his room listening to owls hoot in Bishops Park and then, wonder of wonders, a fox shrieked; a fox in Fulham. For months afterwards Dominic appeared in the sitting room any time up to midnight. 'What are you doing up?' 'I heard a fox.' 'Go back to bed.' 'Honestly.' 'Bed.'

Dominic hated having his hair washed by me and, worst of all, combed. His reaction flipped me straight back to my childhood, to my father's hands doing such things for me, rough and uncomfortable in comparison to my mother's touch. Once more I grappled with the inflated question of should I be abrasive deliberately to give him some roughage, a flavour of maleness, or be more gentle with him. I saw nothing of his life with Christine and the string of au pairs, therefore was infuriatingly in the dark. One evening we fought through a bath, drying and supper. As I brushed his hair he wriggled and sighed in ill-temper.

'This is your favourite, isn't it.' I handled the brush vigorously, testing his powers of self-mockery. He took it badly and tried to hit me. 'Will he ever have a sense of humour?' I wondered.

When he was in bed I read him a story he had brought with him about Jack-The-Giant-Killer, very heroic, very pro-Jack, anti-giant. Dominic told me that Jack had fought and killed a whole variety of giants, he was an absolute paragon.

'We'll have a story tomorrow,' I said, '"Jack-The-Giant-Killer fights Giant Bellybulge."'

There was a moment, then Dominic shouted with laughter. The comic possibilities exploded in his mind. His chortles followed me downstairs, then moments later, so did he. 'Daddy, who d'you think would win?' It was no diversionary tactic to ward off sleep, his imagination was galloping. 'Would Giant Bellybulge be hurt? He'd cry. He'd run away. He'd cheat. He'd wet himself.' I steered him back to bed as storylines abounded, and full-hearted laughs followed me downstairs as Dominic digested the images of Jack setting about Giant Bellybulge. Perhaps I was expecting him to laugh at himself too soon, but there was nothing wrong with his sense of the ridiculous in others.

Our first holiday, when he was nearly five, was in Cornwall with Ivor, Henri, Tommy, Lindsey my God-daughter, and a nanny, insisted on by the access order. The seven of us somehow got into one car for daily trips and we polluted the peace of Cornish lanes and moorland yelling *I Vow To Thee My Country* and *The Sun Has Got His Hat On*, with Lindsey's, Tommy's and Dominic's treble taking the top line. The songs from *Mary Poppins* and *Jungle Book* never sounded better than in that car. When the boys had been put to bed, the noise from their room was staggering. Tommy, for the first few years of his life a shy inhibited child, was benefiting as much from Dominic's worship as was Dominic in having an object to adore. Tommy took upon himself the role of one-man repertory company, acrobat, stuntman, author and director of all Giant Bellybulge stories. Passive Dominic was his natural audience. The combined noise of the entertainer and the entertained was a joy and the farmhouse furniture was mercifully sturdy.

I took the pair of them into the garden one night to look at the carpet of stars. 'I saw God on the moon last night,' Dominic confided to Tommy.

Tommy sighed. 'Ah, Dominic. You're not religious, are you?'

We all had a smashing holiday, but the nanny had the best, I think. She cried when I took her and Dominic back.

An ironic moment of dêja vu occurred when I picked up Dominic from school one day. He was eager to catch me out. 'Do you know what the word is for trees that shed their leaves in winter?' He asked, then told me.

Groucho Marx and his antics in front of the TV camera with newly-wed, perplexed Christine, who to my astonishment didn't know the word 'deciduous', reappeared before my eyes. 'Why don't you ask Mummy that one?'

The questions started about why his parents didn't live together, why I never entered 1 Genoa Avenue, nor Christine come near my house. I didn't know how to cope with them without talking to Christine. What was she saying? Then he said one day, 'Mummy said you don't live at home because you don't like her.'

I thought, then said, 'That's not true, Dominic. If Mummy said that, she's got it wrong and I do like her.'

Weeks later as I was putting him to bed he said, 'Would you tell Mummy that you like her.'

I put myself into neutral, as always when Christine came up. 'Why?'

'Because she doesn't know.'

'Did she tell you to ask me that?'

'No.'

'Who told you to ask me, then.'

'No-one.'

'Why did you?'

'I just thought of it.'

'Hm. Yes, I will tell her.'

———

On Dominic's seventh birthday, Sunday ninth September 1976, the world turned upside down. Or perhaps I mean the right way up. The New Era, that Trevor Reeve had said was not possible, dawned quite simply and easily, as it could have done years earlier had he so ordered.

The day started off normally; I gave Dominic a bicycle and Mao Tse Tung died. Dominic jumped off the top board at Putney baths for the first time, a tiny figure hurtling through the air, hair flying. He wanted to dive off but I vetoed that so he dived off the next board down and flopped alarmingly into the water from over ten feet like a slack-limbed young frog. I was obliged to jump off the top board too. At nearly forty-four it was the first time I had ever been up there. I was nearly sick, and so was Ivor, with laughter, at the expression on my descending face. I returned Dominic and new bicycle to Genoa Avenue. He was leaping about recounting his daring to his mother as I propped the bicycle up against the wall in the hall - if the luggage was of sufficient bulk I was sometimes allowed just inside the front door. Then the sun turned blue and trees sang.

'What would you like to drink?' asked Christine as casually as anything ever uttered.

I think I said, 'Um.'

She must have rehearsed. 'There's some quite nice Macon open or would you prefer coffee?'

'The Macon sounds very nice,' I said. 'I—um—I think I'd better lock the car if I'm coming in.'

'OK. Leave the front door open,' and she went indoors to get the wine and let me recover.

I locked the car, arranged my mind and, almost in a girlish tizzy, entered The Former Matrimonial Home for the first time since the afternoon of Dominic's second birthday party. There followed an eerie half-hour while I stood, then sat, in Christine's drawing-room and drank two glasses of Macon. It is humbug for me to call it Christine's. No matter what the law said, it was ours. I had not relinquished it emotionally. Little had changed. There was an attractive gilt and ormolu clock that I didn't know on the mantelpiece. Some silver-framed photographs of Nat Cohen and Christine being presented to various nobs at film premières had joined the one of Christine and Rutter outside the Royal Courts of Justice. The rest seemed as before.

I sat on the Knole sofa. 'This is nice,' I said, looking at the wine but intending ambiguity.

Christine was at her most formal, her voice almost ceremonial. 'Yes. Dominic loves his swimming. He's very good at it, I hear. I must come and see him. Apparently you're an excellent teacher. Thank you.'

I let that one go with difficulty and the chat continued brightly. I felt like a father of a friend of Dominic's who was being entertained out of politeness. I suppose it was as difficult for her. Dominic came in. 'Can I show Daddy my playroom?'

'Of course, darling,' I had never been there before. It was a moving and extraordinary ten minutes. 'I'm going to have a drink with Mummy, now.' Satisfied, he let me go.

'Well, I must be off,' I said, putting down my glass after a reasonable time.

Christine sounded surprised. 'Oh, all right.' There was just a touch of polite regret in her voice as she went on, 'I'd ask you to lunch, only people are coming.'

Nothing suitable would come to my lips. 'Ah, yes. Well, I'll come for Dom on Thursday after school.'

'Yes, lovely.' Then an afterthought. 'You must stay for tea.' She called up the stairs 'Dominic, come and say goodbye to Daddy.'

And tea it was. The following week, more drinks. Then meals occasionally. All sitting at the butcher's blocks we had made into a vast kitchen table. Plugs were left out for me to connect and other minor jobs were requested. The electric carving knife (her Christmas present to me years before) was produced for me to carve the roast lamb, I nearly said fatted calf, for three. Tommy was dragged in by Dominic after swimming to be shown his treasures. Tommy stood, unnaturally polite, hands behind his back saying, yes, he would like a coke thank you very much, and, thank you he thought Jaffa Cakes were brilliant. And after the mutual, initial stiffness had eased, humanity seeped back into relations between the two principal members of The Frisby family. Even the actual access order itself became redundant. I saw Dominic when we liked. I quickly taught him to ride his new bicycle safely (on pavements only), then showed him a route from Genoa Avenue across Putney Bridge to me in Fulham that involved crossing only two roads by zebra crossings. In the event of any future problems over access he could vote with his wheels. He soon did, though without the problems, and often, when I looked out in answer to a ring on my bell, there he was, grinning furiously at his own initiative. 'Can I come in, please?' Or looking worried, 'I'm not disturbing you am I? I'll just play by myself.' Then, later, 'Could I stay the night, please. Mummy's going out.'

During that autumn, an ITV comedy series I had written was being shot. In the urgent atmosphere of rehearsals and last-minute alterations for weekly deadlines was a new twice-weekly pool of familial pleasure as Christine, Dominic and I went on outings together, for meals, to cinemas, to the studios to join in the over-enthusiastic response of the invited audience. Mutual enjoyment replaced the gritted-teeth Berlin Wall handover. She came with Dominic to my place where I cooked for them. I had become an expert at the sort of food small boys liked. Tommy, whose announced ambition was to be a chip inspector, passed judgement on mine. 'Brilliant,' he said gravely. 'Eight out of ten.' The unreality of the New Era was quickly buried in the ordinariness of cups of tea, meals, friendliness, games and swapped stores of Dominic. There were many of these; so much I didn't know of him. They were recounted to me as though I had been on a long trip. The six previous years might never have been.

Only sometimes did I need to swallow or blink to see if I was awake. On one such occasion we had made some sort of minor cock-up over my taking Dominic out. He was elsewhere when I called for him. 'I'm sorry,' wailed Christine standing in the kitchen, diary in hand, glasses fetchingly on the end of her nose, 'I'd never do a thing like that to you deliberately.' I looked at her sharply, thinking she was mocking me, or herself, or both of us. She seemed absolutely sincere. I don't know what brought about Christine's change of heart (or policy). I suspect that the Harley Street specialist or some such child expert had said something like, 'at seven a child needs his father,' and Christine reverent as always to such voices, acted on the dot. Whatever the explanation, I didn't enquire. That and many other matters were clearly out of court in this new, formal/informal, game. We were two lovely divorcees; civilised friends bringing up our son.

And Dominic? He loved it. His reaction was quiet, but positive; he would come in and out of the room when I was there, apparently just to make sure. He would manoeuvre himself between us in the street, taking our hands. When he did so it was a problem whether to avoid Christine's eye or to meet it. I was afraid that to lift a corner of the veil and show even a glimpse of undefended feeling could only lead to some uncontrollable deluge of emotion. On the rare occasions when I did look at her, my features carefully arranged, I saw, in response, a cool smile that said something trivial and unacceptable like, 'How sweet of him.' I would smile back, inner turbulence covered by impenetrable amicability. Perhaps she was doing the same.

The New Era came to a climax in weeks, before that Christmas. The smart pre-prep school where Christine had sent Dominic had the annual Parents' Association dance coming up. 'Would you take me, please,' said Christine and hurried on before I could say no, which I wasn't going to do. 'For Dominic's sake. I'm secretary of the Association and it would look better if we went together.'

'Willingly,' I said, remembering the Rutter letter threatening legal action if I tried to go to Dominic's nursery school and enquire after him.

While Christine circulated like a good hon.sec. I drank double whiskies with some BBC acquaintances. Christine and I danced, the prehistoric way with my arm round her waist, and when I said, 'You look good,' she said, 'So do you,' and didn't resist as my arm pulled her closer without direct instructions from headquarters. We danced like lovers and I took her home - I mean to her home - and we sat on the Knole sofa and looked at each other awkwardly. Then I was kissing her. She responded and that particular awkwardness was over. We sank silently into the cushions but I couldn't concentrate because of the overtones. I broke it off, 'I'd better be going.'

'All right.'

In the hall I stopped at the foot of the stairs and kissed her again with increased ardour. Again she responded. My hands moved exploratively and were not resisted. The dispute that was proceeding inside me was decided by a majority rather than unanimous vote and I drew her up the stairs. All this was in silence.

She broke away and said in a mock-teenage-Californian accent, 'Not on the first date.'

I thought that was quite good and grinned as, 'Oh, go on, I've paid enough for it' came to my lips, but, 'Goodnight' seemed more prudent, so I said that and left.

The next morning I lay in bed and considered. For six years friends had been telling me I was still in love with my ex-wife. Girl friends and other women were especially fond of this theory. The awful battles of the courts were merely, so the argument ran, perverted love. My protestations that my legal struggles were those of a hooked fish, specifically to get free, were brushed aside. Now I was faced squarely with the issue. What were my feelings about Christine? Suppose we had gone to bed the night before. What then? Our grapple on the sofa had been noticeably silent. What words did we say when each saw the other familiar face on the morning pillow? I couldn't see endearments coming from my lips, or any lowering of defences by either of us.

And what about Dominic? Did I dodge him? He couldn't be allowed to think we were back together if we were not. I couldn't visualise the scene at all.

There was, however, one scene I could see in my imagination, the scene that had been interrupted by my mother on the telephone seven years before to tell me her Aunt Clare was dying. Christine had just said, ' I want to try again but I'm frightened.' I wanted to finish that scene, the last time I had seen her normal, before her emotional pattern had set (at least as far as I was concerned). Why, why, why, why had she done so many things? Who was she? I had never thought the person she had presented as herself for the last seven years was real. The legal documents sworn by her bore no relation to the person I had known.

As I lay there I realised that after last night's skirmish I would have to make a positive move if I were ever going to play that scene. And what when we had played it? When I had my answers and was able to identify the person before me, what then? It was ludicrous to imagine that we just picked up where we had left off, yet I think that had been lurking somewhere, unidentified, in my mind. Did I melt the ice, make her vulnerable and then just walk away? No, I wasn't going to cause any repercussions over Dominic. And if I broke the mould into which she had set, got close again and didn't walk away, what then? What did I want? That was utterly clear and had been all along. I wanted Christine as she had been, Dominic, his unborn brothers and sisters, and our former lost life. But that was all gone and I realised that

I didn't want to start again with her. Or, even if there was some part of me that wanted to, I couldn't. Not at the price.

The thought of wooing her, of exposing my feelings, or lowering any defences, of allowing even the most unintentional of shafts from her to get through to me was repellent; it even made me tense as I lay there, and I realised with certainty that even the playing of that scene, the big, cards-on-the-table, tell-all scene that had been played again and again in my head for years was now a lost dream. I didn't want her, not this her. I could never again be close to this woman who showed such magnanimity towards her own failings and such vindictiveness towards mine. I didn't want to know the answers any longer, I didn't care what they were. Recent observations of her had made me certain they would be banal. The myths, the fantasies, the longings, the wonderings were all gone. On that morning I first realised what had probably been so for years. I had no further feelings of any sort about her. They were extinct. I remembered that just after the injunction of May 1970 I had written to her pleading with her to meet me. The letter was in the divorce papers. I got up and looked out the extract:

> ...as long as we're apart there is the chance that one or other of us will accidentally, or in a rage, strike another terrible blow and widen the gulf that is already there between us. That is what will happen after the lawyers wrangle their way through the next stages. Humanity will be dead and I can see us meeting in the not-too-distant future and eyeing each other with indifference. That is the real horror that I fear. We grow apart, we learn to do without each other, we learn to live with others and our feelings for each other are just a distant memory. It's horrible for us and disastrous for Dominic...

I don't think I even felt sad.

Christine and I continued to play the game of delightful divorcees, perfect parents, for the next three years, while Dominic perhaps nurtured his fantasies of our reunion. A friend who spent some time with us during the New Era hit the nail on the head, I thought. 'I have a sense of regret when I think of her, I feel that somehow she has missed the point of happiness.'

Dominic grew daily to look less like me and more like Christine. On top of the mountain of mistrust created by the years of litigation, my original suspicion, born in an angry moment, that perhaps I wasn't his father, had flourished in secret. In 1970, while inflamed, I had inquired as to how one checked paternity, too diffident to take it further. Years later, clad in the chromium-plated skin automatically awarded to divorcee litigants-in-person, I had no such inhibition, I took him for a paternity test.

Whatever did I hope to gain from such an act? I asked that question of myself even as I took him. The answers were contradictory and unpleasant. The obvious reason, that I sorely needed reassurance covered other, much nastier undercurrents. Oh, the joy of having scientific proof that I was not his father and that every single legal action of the last few years was demonstrably a fake; of turning on that duet of Christine and Rutter and tearing their lies and world into shreds in open court. What a glorious, self-justifying fantasy. Revenge and restitution triumphant. But, oh, the pain of Dominic not being mine. Even if I took him on as mine under my terms, which I would do (thus ran the fantasy). And what of the effects on him, this person with an unknown father, whom I now loved as my own. Considerations of Dominic were low down in the priorities of this particular dream; divorce litigation surely brings out the worst in us.

Anyway, that fantasy was fully dispelled. For good. Dominic is mine, all right, and, once I was sure, a surge of relief and happiness filled me. Being his father beat any revenge scenario. I longed to climb inside that developing head to understand, help and direct what was going on, but he, too, was developing a veneer. His gentle, passivity was asserting itself as a positive characteristic. He and Tommy were discussing their Subbuteo sets of footballers. Dominic said, 'I want the trainers, etcetera.'

'No,' said Tommy. 'You want to get the corner kickers. They do something. The trainers, etcetera, are no good. They don't do anything.'

'I just like to look at them,' said Dominic.

'But they don't *do* anything. They're no good.'

'I just like to look at them.'

Tommy got quite worked up. 'But they don't *do* anything.'

'But I just like to look at them.'

Tommy's vehemence ebbed away. He tried persuasion. 'They're no good. Honest, Dominic.'

Dominic remained imperturbable. 'No. But they look nice.'

They realised that football had started on TV and Tommy leaped for the switch. 'We've only missed the chat,' he said. 'Not the football.'

'That's what I like. I like the chat and the divisions and everything. That's interesting. The football's boring.'

Christine suggested that we go on holiday together with Dominic. It was a moment when I had to fight not to gape. Once more I speculated about us, in spite of everything. I was temporarily flush with ITV money from my series. I could afford it. We went together to Dominic's school sports day. He won the obstacle race, which may or may not have been symbolic, but the day was a disaster: when we returned Daisy was dead. She had been struck by a car while left in the au pair's care. I tried to comfort Dominic. As I did so I realised that there was not a drop of sympathy in me for Christine, although I tried to will some into myself. All that came into my head was Daisy whimpering over me seven years previously, on the day I first saw her after the five-month ban on seeing Dominic and he had to sit in the background until she was calmed.

The next day I arrived for Dominic. He was walking about with Daisy's lead. 'That's all we have left of Daisy. I wish we had some of her fur to touch.'

Christine had just returned from the vet's where she had seen Daisy, she reminisced about the years since I had 'left.' 'I was never lonely with Daisy there. She and Poubelle were always company. I was never alone. People used to say, "All the same, wouldn't it have been easier for you without Dominic?"'

I had to bite back, 'Easier than what?' and went outside to kick a ball about with Dominic. The chasm between Christine and me had widened. Although daily trivia and arrangements about Dominic were pleasant, I couldn't listen to her utter on anything serious without wriggling with embarrassment for her. I declined the holiday trip. Inner speculation died.

In September 1977, the start of year two of the New Era, we took Dominic for his first day at boarding school. He was eight. I didn't care for the idea of his boarding, not that I had any say in the matter, but thought it best in his circumstances. In fact, in the New Spirit, Christine had discussed the matter with me. Dominic appeared to be unmoved about leaving home, staring with dispassionate interest at boys who were crying. He soon loved it there. The school was Colet Court, in Barnes, and Christine and I stopped to have tea there in a cafe opposite the film studios where we had met as extras on the Alka Seltzer commercial fourteen and a half years before. When I realised, I nodded across the road and said with studied neutrality, 'That's where we met. Remember?'

Christine's glance wavered, unfocused across the road. She appeared to make a tiny effort at recalling a previous incarnation, then she gave up and returned to her immediate emotion about Dominic's departure. She shook her head in smiling envy at my good fortune. 'Of course, I suppose you don't feel the loss.'

'Nope. I felt it years ago.'

I only got one good look into Dominic's mind on the subject of his parents being divorced. We were returning from my mother's in the car. He was nearly ten. In vivid contrast to his usual practice he suddenly asked me question after question about where I had lived and what I had done when I was younger. I finished one answer with, 'And that's how Mummy and I met and fell in love and got married.'

The obvious follow-up question didn't come. The silence was brief and electric. Then, I can't quite remember how, we were talking about other boys in the school whose parents were divorced. Dominic's voice went into neutral. 'James's parents are divorced. And Christopher's.' I imagined Dominic, James and Christopher discussing this after lights out in the Boarding House.

'There are lots of divorced people,' I said.

'Yes.' A little colour came into his voice and he shifted in his seat.

I drove on in silence for a while, then said, and it wasn't rhetorical, 'Do you wish Mummy and I were still together?' He had never known that state.

His answer was one definite word followed by an unpunctuated rush. 'Yes. I-don't-know-how-can-I-tell-I-think-so-I'm-not-sure-really-I-don't-know.' But if that was revealing, his body shouted an answer. As my question finished, his hands went up over his head as though to ward off a blow. He wriggled and slid down in his seat. He would had slid off it but the safety strap held him. And there he hung with it caught under his chin.

I made myself calm. 'You don't have to mind what you say, Dominic. I don't like it either.'

Encouraged, he continued. 'I suppose people get divorced because they have rows and that.' He ran out of steam. 'I don't know.' He had said on another occasion that Christine had said we were divorced because we had a big row. That was so inadequate as an explanation that I had never supported it.

'Sometimes,' I said, 'Sometimes it's more complicated than that.'

He went on about some other parents, then said, 'Well, Ben and George's father works in Ghana and their mother is here in London. They live apart.' He stopped, embarrassed.

I tried to keep him going. 'But they're not divorced.'

'I know.' His voice was full of grievance and injury. 'Just because people have rows and that it seems silly getting divorced.' He ran out of conviction again. 'I don't know,' he finished weakly.

Dominic had never seen a cross word between Christine and me.

I drove on in silence. His grievance twanged every nerve in me. I wanted to say something simple and bitchy like, 'It was Kitty Massey's fault,' or, 'We shouldn't have been,' or, 'That stupid doctor and his opening doors caused it,' or, 'Blame Rutter,' but most of all I wanted to ask his forgiveness. The person I loved most was undoubtedly the one I had let down the most.

Chapter XLII

December 1976

At the beginning of the New Era life seemed to be looking up, but I still faced two piles of wreckage, laughingly called my finances and my career. Salvage prospects looked promising. Production of my new play was due early in 1977, and in December 1976 was the survive-or-bust meeting with the Technical Division of the Inland Revenue. I had the highest of hopes for my new play, but no play could have combined the drama and farce of that quiet little meeting with the Revenue.

Settlement with them was vital. If the new play were successful without the financial mess being cleared up, it would be like fitting buoyancy tanks to a half-submerged hulk. I could wallow on, sinking indefinitely. To recap: Andrew Park, my tax counsel, reckoned I owed over £130,000 (the change in money values since then, that makes the figures I have been quoting so archaic, was only just getting under way. But, however you count inflation, I owed well over a million at today's values. Probably two). To pay this, I had nothing. Even my mother's house had been sold, the money going to feed the insatiable beast of the divorce (my mother had remarried and was happily housed, I am glad to say, with her second husband). The smart flat in Chelsea that I had first acquired after divorce had long gone, as had the cheaper house in Fulham where I had lived for the last four years, and all that money I had earned in that time. All down the maw of that beast. I had just moved into a mansion flat in Fulham, bought for £14,750. My mortgage on that, together with my overdraft exceeded £30,000 from time to time. For some mystifying reason my credit was still good. Well, it is obvious that the Revenue were going to have fun getting a penny out of me, although I could end up on the street.

However, the holdings of the Trust were substantial, though I couldn't get at them without incurring further tax liabilities: the old vicious circle. They were worth £80,000 theoretically, but the reality was under half that. The decision, forced on me by the consent settlement, to sell the sound investments and gamble for quick capital growth to meet the £130,000 bill had been precisely the wrong one. We had walked into the first international economic crisis since World War Two - caused by the quadrupling of oil prices - and although various items (some land, silver, some paintings) had done quite well, others had gone badly down - or out. The big risk, the projected land development in Quebec, into which we had gone, deliberately over-extended, had been a disaster. Quebec Libre had put the finishing touch to its demise. After all the legal shenanigans, it was, with apt irony, my very escape plan that had administered the coup de grâce to my financial affairs.

Thus, although almost any demand from the Revenue was going to bust me personally, they couldn't benefit from that and they couldn't get at the Trust assets because the trustees were out of the jurisdiction. To solve this, we were going to offer the Revenue everything from the Trust, including the (worthless) land, if they would accept it in full settlement and let me walk away free to start again. An unlikely outcome.

Meanwhile, correspondence with them had been going on for over five years like an immensely slow game of tennis, full of vicarage lobs and dolly drops. The guiding mind behind this snail-like game was Andrew Park. He had set the initial, torpid rhythm and then decelerated, knowing that what I needed most was time. This meeting would be the deciding set.

Frank Young, my accountant, Andrew Park, and I, crunched on a thin carpet of snow across the car park of the Technical Division of HM Inland Revenue just off the old Kingston by-pass. It was suitably bleak. There were fir trees all round and, because the Nissen-hut-like buildings were shared with the Department of Defence, the area was fenced in by high wire netting with barbed wire on the top. To complete the East European atmosphere was a fur-hatted guard at the gate.

We were shown to a table in an overheated room in one of the low buildings by a Miss Ridley, an extremely nice woman with whom we had been corresponding. She was fascinated by the fact that she had seen me in some episodes of *The Brothers*, a BBC TV serial of that time; during breaks in the proceedings she would ask, *sotto voce*, was so-and-so going to marry so-and-so in the next episode. The principal member of the trio we faced was a Mr Sinfield who was standing-in because his boss, the number one in the department, was in the High Court that day trying to extract millions from another person, under the same S478 regulation that applied to me. Mr Sinfield was left to deal with my mere £130,000 plus.

After a few minutes it transpired that a man at the Revenue who was currently threatening me with legal proceedings if I didn't at once pay £24,500 plus accrued interest, was in another building three miles away. Since I couldn't pay that until the wider issues were clarified there was a pause for half-an-hour while he was fetched. We consumed Revenue coffee and biscuits and I entertained Miss Ridley with anecdotes about her favourites in *The Brothers*. The third member of the opposition team arrived, the Threatener, who turned out to be a pleasant Scot with piercing blue eyes. He then proceeded to bugger everyone up, especially his own team, by refusing a stay of execution over his £24,500 plus accrued (now totalling £27,000). Stalemate.

Eventually Blue Eyes was persuaded to see reason (that is, to fall in with the rest of us) and we got on. The climax came at once. Andrew was going to argue that the Revenue could not claim tax from me on the royalties that had gone into the Trust more than six years earlier because of the Statute of Limitations (the Statute of Limitations is that law which says that any debt or legal claim not made within six years becomes invalid, unless that debt was hidden from you). 'But that argument is no real good,' Andrew had told me in advance. 'Because you only told them of the funds in the Trust four years ago and they will, under section 26, claim to start counting from then.' He removed the ever-errant, now-thinning lock from his eyes and smiled sympathetically. 'But I'll give it a try.'

Andrew's clinical explanations of the jungle of tax laws did not take into account the soul of office-bred, salaried, pensionable man. It soon became apparent that someone, somewhere had dropped a resounding clanger. In our super-slow game of correspondence-tennis the Revenue had left one interval of two years before they had answered one of our letters. God knows which department had passed what buck to where. Mr Sinfield looked as though he knew more than he was saying.

He cleared his throat, looked round at all of us, and said in one of those nasal voices that actors use when they are playing minor civil servants, 'There is, of course, the Statute of Limitations to take into account. We won't be assessing you on income that accrued to the Trust earlier than April 6th 1970.'

There was not a flicker of response from Andrew, Frank or me. Did Sinfield realise what he had said? He gave no sign. We sat, apparently listening attentively for what he had to say next, but I know I received a charge of adrenaline that nearly made me leap up and run screaming round the room. Frank and Andrew admitted subsequently to a similar, though possibly less intense, reaction. The vast majority of my royalties had come in before 1970. Mr Sinfield had opened the proceedings by giving me a present of over £100,000. Frank's foot found mine and pressed on it under the table. I moved mine away, fearful of doing anything that would betray any feeling. I was having great difficulty controlling myself. The unbelievable had happened: I was solvent again after five and a half years. My hand somehow continued to doodle casually without shaking. Then Andrew answered Sinfield's bombshell with one of his own.

'I can't accept that,' he said.

Frank's head jerked round simultaneously with mine and we stared in fear and astonishment at Andrew. He, apparently, didn't notice and went on to explain in his calm academic manner why being given precisely what we had barely dared to hope for was unacceptable. He argued a minor point of tax law that made no real difference to anything and he pursued it pedantically for some while as I sweated. Eventually, he reluctantly conceded, and brushed his forelock from his eyes in a manner that suggested he had given away a fortune. Before we could breathe he went on to win the next point, a more important one. It was a brilliant piece of negotiating. The big, the all-important, concession, was confirmed and incorporated as though nothing had happened.

I had listened to Andrew for five years. He had made intricate tax law simple, after Theodore Goddard and Neil Taylor had made simple divorce law insoluble. He had drafted mild-mannered letters to the Revenue quoting regulation this and sub-section that. Had he been involved earlier he would never have allowed the Gordian knot of the July 1971 consent settlement to have been tied. I had always liked him, but in that moment he showed steel through the anxious look and research-graduate demeanour that commanded more than amicability.

The meeting went on for another two hours. The superiority of private enterprise over the civil service was shown twice more. It was exhilarating to watch my team winning, though the political implications were disturbing; Thatcherism had not then been heard of.

Andrew was arguing, 'But you must agree that if Mr Frisby pays you all that you claim under S478, section 1, you will give him a guarantee that you will not use S478, section II, to assess him on the actual money he pays you, thereby assessing him twice on the same money.'

'Oh, I doubt if we'll do that,' said Mr Sinfield cosily.

'Really, that won't do,' said Andrew. 'We must have written assurances. You could come back at Mr Frisby in two years for thousands, under S478, section II, and he could be in debt for the rest of his life.'

Mr Sinfield laughed. 'Oh, well, I'm not worried about two years from now. I shall be retired by then.'

At twelve-thirty the Revenue team were all shuffling in their seats, anxious to close matters but Andrew wouldn't let go. 'We must settle these final points,' he insisted and kept at it till he got what he wanted. The Revenue gave way on item after item, while glancing at their watches. 'There. That's covered everything,' he announced with satisfaction at one o'clock, checking each item through with Miss Ridley. Mr Sinfield and Blue Eyes looked unhappy.

'That's all very well,' said Blue Eyes plaintively, 'but it's too late now. Our canteen kitchen's already closed. We can only get cold platter now.'

'Shall I ask them to join us for lunch?' I whispered to Frank as we put our coats on. 'It doesn't seem very fair.'

'Shut up,' said Frank into his brief case.

'What a funny idea. A canteen that closes at lunch-time,' I said to Sinfield and Miss Ridley as they walked us down a corridor towards the car park. 'Only the Revenue could dream up that one.'

'No, no, not the canteen, the kitchen,' she said earnestly. 'We can eat, but nothing hot. It's a staff problem. They can't keep the staff.'

Frank, Andrew and I crunched across the snow to my car. I was having difficulty not to jump, shout, sing, slide, make snow-balls.

'Just walk,' hissed Frank. 'Don't give away anything. They're watching from the window.'

I drove decorously past the fur-hatted guard, then I accelerated hard, just to skid madly on the ice. Andrew laughed and Frank went white. We picked up Andrew's wife and went and had a slap-up lunch while the Revenue team, presumably, hunched over their cold platters.

I still owed thousands, but I could pay if my new play, soon to start rehearsal, did just reasonably well. I could stay in my mortgaged flat. The golden years of *Soup* were over. I was a free man again. There remained to clear up only the second of the two piles of wreckage: my so-called career.

Chapter XLIII

Winter 1976-7

So The Play was ready to rehearse - at last. It was seven years since my last play, *The Bandwagon,* had opened at the Mermaid Theatre. Enough creative energy had gone into litigation to have produced several plays. I call the new one The Play, with the capitals, not because of any flippant attitude towards it, but because that is what it had become. All my professional eggs, and indeed many emotional and psychological ones too, had accumulated in this basket. I had - between visits to the Royal Courts of Justice - managed the occasional dabble in my official occupations during those years. Besides many acting jobs, I wrote, in twenty-six weeks, a thirteen-episode ITV sitcom - an occupation I recommend as a short cut to brain damage. That series earned me a substantial sum that immediately disappeared down the legal plug hole along with everything else, thus removing any incentive to write more when asked. The series was called *Lucky Feller* and starred David Jason. I think of *Lucky Feller* as the unknown sitcom, perhaps one day it will be exhumed. It was top of LWT's ratings and viewed by more people each week than would see all my stage plays in my lifetime. But the full-length stage play was the challenge that really engaged me: the gauntlet that always lay there. Since I had picked it up only four times in my life, there were obviously not that many plays struggling to get out of me, never mind the excuses. Each one, possibly, mattered too much.

I finished writing the first draft of The Play at Christmas 1973. My agent urged me to let Michael Codron read it. I wanted no more of Michael after *The Bandwagon,* but Harvey persisted. 'He's the best producer in town, my boy.' I gave way.

Michael telephoned, voice full of concern after the interval of nearly two years. Then he switched. 'I can't wait to get it.' The cool tone carefully balanced the eager phraseology. 'I'll telephone you the minute I've finished.' I loved hearing the old chameleon at work in spite of things and sent a copy at once. Two days later it thudded back through Harvey's letterbox. I have yet to hear from Michael.

Two more producers turned The Play down. Professionals who read it said the structure was muddling. I disagreed but re-wrote it. To determine the question of the structure Bob Chetwyn directed a rehearsed reading of the new version for me. Four actors did it for love, as did Bob: Barbara

Ferris, Nigel Hawthorne, Cheryl Kennedy and Trevor T Smith. I listened to the play in Bob's flat and took them all out to lunch as an inadequate thank you. Actors: irresponsible actors; rogues and vagabonds; that despicable race. In fact the most generous and responsible of people.

The Play sounded right to me, in spite of other people's reservations about the structure. I sent it to the Haymarket Theatre, Leicester. Leicester's new theatre, under Robin Midgeley's direction, had been transferring plays into London. He agreed to present The Play with Bob as director. That was, by then, 1976, legal distractions had not expedited my re-writes.

It's All Right If I Do It was the title, with the 'I' stressed or underlined. It was a comedy about marital infidelity. Not exactly ground-breaking stuff, might be your immediate response. But I wasn't looking for conventional or escapist laughs. I wanted The Play to hurt while it made you laugh. It's purpose, like *Soup*, was subversive. In *Soup* I had tried to present a fresh view of the singles sex-scene, in *It's All Right* I tried to do the same about marital infidelity. I saw The Play as a reflection of the preoccupations and double standards of many divorcing and needlessly unhappy marrieds all round me. Christine and I had been typical; sexual jealousy and insecurity in different guises had been all that had divided us before the lawyers had entered. In The Play I attempted to examine the seeds that had grown into my own, and many other, unnecessary, avoidable divorces.

The premise was simple: marital infidelity is universal; everybody knows it, everybody lies about it, the spouse is always last to know. Put into that situation a catalyst, a husband who prefers to tell the truth, and the action automatically rolls on from there. It is the lying that is unacceptable to him, not the infidelity. Or so he says.

For once casting was swift. Prunella Scales (now CBE) and John Stride promptly accepted the two leads. For the two principal supporting roles Toni Palmer, who had been so good in *The Bandwagon*, and Tony Haygarth were engaged. One actor had previously turned down the Haygarth part: a well-known character actor who returned the script with a letter full of outrage that we had sent him such an offensive piece of filth.

Bob and I decided that if the production at Leicester looked worthy of transfer to the West End we would take it in ourselves. We lacked one vital attribute, the know-how to get the right theatre. I knew just the man for the job, Richard Mills; we played golf together from time to time.

Richard, an amiable and tough competitor on and off the golf course, was the partner of Lord Delfont. Delfont's family, the Grades, between them owned or controlled large chunks of the British entertainment industry. The clout they had was enormous. I put to Richard the proposition that if he would use his considerable influence at the right moment to get a theatre for us, we would pay his company a fee, or percentage, or both. He read The Play. His reaction was immediate and enthusiastic: he didn't want to be on the periphery, he wanted to produce it and back it. Under the banner of 'A Bernard Delfont and Richard Mills production' our theatre-finding problem would be over. Richard left us in artistic control of the production and signed up whoever we asked for.

Rehearsals went smoothly enough, but in a bit of a vacuum. The problem was that none of us had any idea how a provincial audience at Leicester would react. The reason for our uncertainty was twofold. First, we didn't know if the audience would be able to follow the action, it was not chronological, scenes jumped backwards and forwards over thirteen years and, although the clues were all there, there were few explicit signposts. The programme said: 'Act I. Begins two days ago and ends thirteen years ago. Act II. Begins three days after the end of Act I and finishes today,' which must have confused some.

Second, the subject of The Play. Sex is the easiest subject of all to get laughs about. What is not easy is to get the audience reaction we were looking for of painful self-recognition; impossible if they can't follow the story. We wanted only certain laughs.

Something then went wrong with our producer/director-author relationship, but what? I could only guess. Richard kept handing me lists of proposed cuts. These were quite few in number, but each of them involved a direct reference to something sexual. I saw this as censorship and resisted. Richard argued that the writing had gone too far occasionally, The Play would benefit from being more oblique from time to time. He may have had a point, but in my view to cut for Good Taste in that play was, in any case, a futile exercise. It had its own acrid flavour that would give either offence or pleasure. Lord Delfont was away when Richard had read the play and involved their company. He had since returned. I would risk a reasonable sum that the scenario ran roughly as follows: Delfont, Lord Bernie, raised to the peerage for a lifetime's achievements in the production of wholesome family entertainment, had read the play which was about to enter London under his name and was horrified. 'Richard, my friend and partner, what have you let me in for when my back is turned? All this sex. Make sure we don't get egg on our faces.' Richard, lifelong friend and partner of Lord Bernie, was already committed to Terry, author and golfing chum. His position must have been intolerable. As I say, this is guesswork, nevertheless Bob and I felt we no longer had our producer behind us.

———

Prunella Scales and John Stride are two actors for whom my regard is fulsome. I loved watching the way they approached their roles. Prunella walked round the edge, peering in, toe in to test the temperature, drawing back from time to time before tentatively trusting her buoyancy in the unknown liquid. John went straight in at the deep end and learned to swim from there. They were admirable in their rôles; a measure of their achievement was that I thought of the characters (originally Christine and me, in my mind) as them. The rest of the cast were good with the exception of Tony Haygarth who was wonderful.

The opening night was all we could have wished for. The audience followed the supposedly difficult structure easily, and took the content to heart. The blasts of laughter took even such experienced performers as John and Prunella by surprise. Audience reaction extended the running time by an unheard of fourteen minutes (five or six minutes is considered good) and that was extended by a further four minutes on the second night. It meant that the play, already too long, should be cut by about half-an-hour. The box office was besieged. The queue snaked round the spacious foyer of the Haymarket Theatre for two and a half days until every seat for the three-week run was sold. We easily broke the house record.

There is considerable prejudice in the theatre about alleged 'provincial' plays and 'West End' plays. I needn't elaborate about the cultural differences implied. We all felt that *It's All Right* was a West End play. 'If it does this here,' we cautiously muttered, 'What will be the London reaction?' It looked as though, besides popularity, The Play might get the bonus of Cultural Acclaim. Cool though we were about provincial flattery, superlatives were heaped on the cast, director and play. Quotes included, 'a study of the moral and emotional mess we have got ourselves into over our attitudes to sexual liberation and marital infidelity'; 'if any play of our times has treated sex seriously and as a vast joke this is it'; 'that rare thing, an extremely funny look at the problems of staying married which is neither insulting to the intelligence nor depressing to the spirit. The release of laughter is as therapeutic as any surgeon could devise'; 'a very rude, very funny and deeply sad play'. The forecast of a West End smash was universal. Among hardened professionals was an executive from Yorkshire TV who came to see John Stride for a new series. He reported back that John wouldn't be available for a year, the length of his contract with us. John Bedding, of Samuel French, who publish most of the plays written in this country and all of mine, thought it my best to date. The foreign agents appeared, enquiring for world-wide options. Film companies started sniffing and were shooed away by Harvey until after the London opening. If ever a bandwagon was on the roll, this one was. I include all this praise only for the sake of the story. What is said about you on a pre-London tour is irrelevant after you reach your destination.

Bob and I finished work on the play in Leicester, taking out the necessary half hour. The company were all that could be wished for in their approach to changes. Prunella and John were full of suggestions and criticisms that were, besides being pertinent, often painfully abrasive. If the production wasn't right, it wasn't through complacency.

Watching *It's All Right* play in Leicester was one of the special experiences of my creative life. I don't mean just watching the play, but the whole event, play and audience combined. It reminded me what my profession was; what it was I had originally found by accident at drama school twenty-two years previously that had given my adult life meaning; the combination of heart and mind; of gravity and irreverence; the eagerness of going to work for its own sake, never mind about the wonder of being paid for it (let alone make a fortune); compassion, fun, sense, humour. As John and Prunella played out the disputes of love, wives nudged husbands, couples suddenly held hands, men and women laughed, then caught the eye of their spouses and were silent, all the symptoms of personal involvement and self-recognition that are the reactions I want to a play I have written. As I sat in that audience, the seven years of Rutter père et fils, John Calderan and Paddy Grafton Green, James Comyn QC, Lord Justices Davies, Phillimore and Orr, Harry Law, Mr Justice Trevor Reeve, Neil Taylor and the rest of them, were temporarily washed away.

Lord Delfont appeared in Leicester to see his healthy new problem-child. From the moment I saw him I couldn't take him seriously, which was most unimaginative of me. This pleasant, benevolent, showbiz mogul was the most unlikely lord I could have anticipated. With the best will between us we had nothing in common except the current enterprise. Richard, Bob, Bernie and I stood in the foyer of the Haymarket Theatre and had our photographs taken for the local press. The frequent hiatuses between us were friendly but clam-like. I have never in my life subjected anyone to so many silent smiles, and Bob, who is no extrovert, did an imitation of the Cheshire cat, all grin and invisibility.

The totality of Lord Bernie's appearance was uniquely satisfying, almost hypnotic. I had to force myself not to talk to him about his clothes: the most expensive gents' worsted suiting I have ever seen hanging from a man's shoulders, cut and sewn by artists; silk shirt and tie; crocodile shoes; blown-dry tinted hair; he was a credit to the team that had turned him out. The socks were sheer, I noticed later at dinner, I longed for a glimpse of the underpants. Only fear of creasing something inhibited the urge to hug him.

After one of our shuffling silences I managed to get out that I had been writing a sitcom for London Weekend under the patronage of his nephew. Bernie's eyes brightened, common ground at last. 'Ah, yes. London Weekend. My brother Leslie's boy, Michael, is working there. He's head of Light Entertainment.'

As I had just said that, I agreed.

'He's doing very well,' said the proud uncle. He anticipated my thoughts accurately. 'And off his own bat, not because of the family.' He leaned in confidentially. 'We're hoping he'll be promoted soon.' Michael soon justified the family's hopes.

Richard, Bernie, Bob and I assembled in Leicester's most expensive restaurant after the performance. Bernie said that the doubts he had harboured about Bad Taste on reading the play were now banished. It played beautifully without giving offence. He even gently reproved Richard for his list of suggested cuts, when this dog-eared piece of paper reappeared on the spotless, salmon-coloured tablecloth. We broke up in good humour and the waiting Rolls smoothed Lord Bernie away down the M1 and out of my life.

A few days later came the first hammer-blow. Our producers, the most powerful in the business, couldn't get us a theatre in London. No, that is not quite true, they could get us one: a six-week run at the Mermaid while we sought a transfer to the West End. The Mermaid. Again. Just as wrong a house for this play as it had been seven years earlier for *The Bandwagon*. Bob and I felt as though some old film were being re-run before our distressed eyes. I tore back to London and went through my contract in Harvey's office. The wording was clear. The management could keep the play on tour for only so many weeks then could transfer it to an accepted West End theatre, nowhere else. The Mermaid is not an accepted West theatre. I told Richard I wouldn't allow him to take the play there.

We argued for days and covered every conceivable piece of theatrical lore on the subject. However, the issue was really quite simple. We had to take one of two risks. 1) Go to the Mermaid and rely on good reviews - and not just good reviews, *The Bandwagon* had those, but the right sort of good reviews - to generate sufficient business in that concrete desert to get us a transfer. 2) Break up the production to wait for a West End theatre and risk not being able to put the essential components together again.

No theatre was free, I was told, because every producer with a play installed was hanging onto his house for the tourist bonanza that would come with the imminent Royal Silver Jubilee celebrations. There was no real contest. Richard wanted to take the Mermaid. I didn't, but hated to let this production break up. I agreed to the Mermaid although it meant relying, not on the public who I trusted, but on the reviewers who I didn't. The cast was confident, they hadn't Bob's and my prejudices. We left Leicester and did solid business in Leeds and Wimbledon, including a few expected walk-outs. In Norwich we again broke the box-office record.

There were two packed previews at the Mermaid before the press night. The reception of the play at each was terrific. I kept a tight hold on my near-exploding excitement. On our last preview Bernard Levin appeared to review us for *The Sunday Times*. He couldn't come on the official press night. I found myself next to him on the crowded stairs in the interval. He was so small I thought for a moment he was on the step below me. I looked at him warily. Like anyone else I had read him off and on for years and knew that, culturally, we were opposites. He was one of the important half-dozen reviewers we needed. Bob and I had felt sure he would be one who would not like it. He had nothing in common with my Philistine, suburban, average, adulterous characters. His review appeared the following Sunday in prose so convoluted that a few people telephoned me to congratulate me on his approbation. It started with the wonderful quote, 'This is an amazing play', and I had to read a third of it before I realised he was giving us the thumbs down. But he took it seriously, so fair enough.

We all know that an official opening night is an unnatural event. Among the 400-odd patrons and critics at the Mermaid on ours were three small groups of people, all professionals in showbiz, who decided to support us to get the audience going, or perhaps they were just over-demonstrative. Whatever their motives, their enthusiasm was misplaced and insensitive to the point of pachydermatousness. The play was a corpse within two minutes of the lights going up, but a corpse that went on exposing its grisly, dead self for two further hours.

John Stride entered into his well furnished, middle-class sitting-room. There was a smattering of applause to greet him. He called, 'Whoo-oo,' to his offstage wife. This was greeted with laughter from the aforesaid ten or twelve people. 'Whoo-oo, I'm ho-ome,' he went again. Louder laughter. Since what he had done so far was about as funny as a company prospectus, the feeling in the remainder of the audience was of unease. It sounded like a put-up job. Prunella entered, clearly in great emotional pain. Some applause. She walked over to John. 'Hallo, darling,' he said and made a vague kissing noise as he offered his cheek. Louder laughter still at this tiny, unfunny moment. Prunella smashed him hard across the cheek. The three cliques guffawed with glee. She kicked him and he collapsed. Shrieks of delight. She hissed passionately, 'You shit-faced bastard.' This was greeted as though it were a gem of Wildean wit. There were increased guffaws, positive brays filled the theatre, together with a localised burst of applause as she exited. John collapsed, recovered, turned to the audience and said wearily, 'Oh, God, it's going to be one of those evenings.' The brays, guffaws, shrieks and applause were repeated, louder, from these few people.

The remainder of the audience sat frozen in embarrassed silence. Perhaps you have seen the film, *The Producers*, with the famous shot in it of the audience reaction to the opening number, *Springtime For Hitler*, the supposed worst-taste musical ever written. Jaws hang open in disbelief, heads are sunk in shame, eyes are averted or covered. So it was at the Mermaid that evening. One minute after the lights had gone up my head had nearly disappeared into my collar. I could see most of the reviewers; their faces like thunder, heads on chests. They were pink with rage or embarrassment, thoughts clear: this production was aimed to appeal to this offensive, inhuman, infantile reaction. 'We're dead,' I muttered in agonised horror.

'What?' said my companion, surprised at a noise from me.

'We're stone dead. They are going to kill us.'

The nightmare went on till the interval. Each reference to sex was greeted by these noises. No person who had entered the theatre to sit neutrally in the auditorium, open to receive a performance, could respond naturally. To have aligned yourself with that noise was unthinkable. The sounds reminded me of something I couldn't at first place, then I realised what it was. *Today in Parliament* had just gone live on Radio 4 from the House of Commons. *Question Time* was the choicest. We are now all familiar with the public-school-sounding brays that support each leaden sally (I keep saying 'brays', but that is what they were, and are, the mirthless noises of an animal). The BBC now edit-out the more extreme excesses of our elected representatives, perhaps somebody feared for democracy. Nobody seems to have suggested that the MPs themselves desist.

During the interval I asked the most famous member of the loudest group of brayers if they would mind not laughing any more. In response to this unlikely request from an author they all swept out in a flurry of fur coats. Bob had meanwhile seen to it that the other cliques were quietened.

The second half of the play was received in silence, so that, at least, was a mercy. At the party afterwards I couldn't look my various invited friends in the eye. It was a humiliation to be the creator of the event that had just passed. John, Prunella and the cast were confused. To have been on the stage, they said, was weird.

The notices the next morning were not merely appalling, they were, I should guess, the worst for a decade. The Play was not panned, it was executed. My altercation was widely reported. What made our blood boil was that it was not the play that was reviewed but the audience.

Some typical quotes follow:

Daily Telegraph:

I was embarrassed...an able cast work hard to win - as they do - the expected quota of beery guffaws.

The Guardian:

Needless to say such exchanges are greeted with that peculiar braying-noise, like a convention of seaside donkeys, you only hear from a sophisticated first-night audience...what makes me angry is that grant-aided theatres like the Haymarket, Leicester...and the Mermaid can be used as a clearing house for this kind of garbage by a commercial management...it is like being trapped for two-and-a-half hours by a halitosis-ridden saloon-bar bore...one comes out of the Mermaid shrunken in spirit...

Punch:

...the sound in the theatre was not of laughter - it was of people cackling, a mindless reflex action...a uniquely nasty farce...

Sheridan Morley, LBC:

...I beg you not to go to the Mermaid...

Michael Billington, the *Guardian* reviewer, was heard to say, 'I thought it was my duty as a human being to kill that play.'

On the second night Act One was received in attentive but eerie silence, the audience having presumably read their daily papers. After a chance to tell each other in the interval that perhaps it wasn't too awful after all, the play started to be received more naturally, and by the end there was a reasonable reception. Every other night of the run after that it went as it always previously had on tour. That gruesome first night might never have been.

John Bedding of Samuel French and Co wrote to Harvey to say that he still wished to publish.

> ...I am very disheartened by the reviews of this play. I truly think the critics are wrong. This play says a good deal about modern society and its problems and in a manner which is both witty and theatrically imaginative.

> I hope that the London management will reaffirm their faith in the play by fighting on, and that the play will eventually find its way to success in the West End.

Delfont and Richard thought such a campaign would be pointless. They had got the feared odium, West End or not. Richard told me he was putting up the notice at once. Even the six-week run at the Mermaid was to be cancelled. I paid back all the royalties the play had so far earned to help keep it on for that time and give it a chance. The box-office takings curved steadily upwards as the notices were forgotten and word of mouth worked, but the starting point was too low and no West End theatre-owner was interested in being host to such a reviled object.

I had an inarticulate lunch and correspondence with Irving Wardle of *The Times*. I urged him to go again; he wouldn't, not unnaturally. There was a discussion about the relationship between reviewer and playwright between Michael Billington and myself on BBC 2 which, to the producer's chagrin, wasn't a patch on the near-fight we had in the hospitality room afterwards. Then I met the (late) Jack Tinker of the *Daily Mail*. He had given us our one good review from that dreadful night; 'wild and witty', 'explosive', 'put real bite into the floodgates of sexual home truths.'

'How come you saw all that when everyone else hated it?' I asked.

'Well, you see,' he answered. 'I got my training as a critic in Brighton. I sat week after week surrounded by old ladies who tut-tutted or overreacted at perfectly sensible material and, ever since, I haven't noticed the rest of the audience. I just shut them out. Why, was the audience funny or something that night?'

The Play, with its emphasis on much that was biographical to Christine and me, opened at the Mermaid near the beginning of the New Era, so I was seeing Christine regularly. During its short run, its presence was almost tangible between us. She would surely hate it if she saw it, I thought. What of relations between us? Christine dealt with it, as she did all annoyance, by ignoring it - except on one occasion during access. 'Genevieve went to the Mermaid last week,' she said out of the blue.

'Oh, yes?' I said, in neutral, waiting.

'She said it was flawed.'

'Ah.'

The basic point is: would The Play have failed anyway, without that extraordinary - I would say, unique - first night? I think the answer is that it would have - at the Mermaid. My work would never have got the cultural raves necessary to effect a transfer to the West End. But had we had a West End theatre originally, even with only lukewarm reviews, I am sure the word of mouth would have made us a success, just as it did on tour and just as it did with *Soup* for years. And once a play becomes generally known, it establishes its place, wherever that may be. Professionals do that for it: they talk, the play is evaluated, if it appeals to someone it is revived and reviewers fall belatedly into line, revising their opinions, up or down, with hindsight. That basic process not happening to *It's All Right* is what hurt so.

One day I was telling the story of the flop to another professional, 'Oh, yes,' he said. 'I once had a play like that. It, too, was a touring, not a West End play.' That shut me up.

Ted Whitehead, no mean playwright, who was then reviewing for *The Spectator*, came a week late to see The Play. He had been away and missed the brief, showbiz mini-storm. We bumped into each other and he fulminated to me about the ignorance of reviewers. I should like some of his notice to be its obituary.

LET'S DO IT

by Ted Whitehead

A few years ago a sexual comedy with the title, *It's All Right If I Do It*, would almost certainly have been an exposure of male hypocrisy; now of course it's an exposure of the hypocrisy of both sexes. The double standard no longer means one standard for men and another for women, but one standard for *me* and another for you, partner. The author, Terence Frisby, has written three earlier plays, of which the most famous was *There's a Girl in my Soup*, which ran for years in the West End. That was more than just a good boulevard farce; it was also a perceptive study of the clash between male romanticism, represented by the sophisticated old-fashioned seducer, and female realism, represented by the free-living hippie, the nature girl of the sixties. For the commercial theatre of that time, it was very honest. For the commercial theatre of our time, Mr Frisby's new play may be too honest.

The thesis is that monogamy in practice is now extinct (if it ever existed) because infidelity is now the norm, only a thoroughgoing hypocrisy can make the institution work. All that honesty achieves is the most murderous and self-righteous jealousy. So, in the opening scene of the play, Mrs Barnett (Prunella Scales) chases Mr Barnett (John Stride) round the lounge waving a carving knife because she has discovered his latest adultery. She interrogates him about the identity of his mistress, frantic in case it is somebody she knows - or rather, who knows her. Her anguish isn't lessened by the advice of Babs, (Toni Palmer) a neighbour, to 'do what we all do - put the telescope to the blind eye.' Babs thinks that the husband's real failing is that he is a bad liar, as well she might, seeing that she is one of his ex-mistresses.

Mrs Barnett's first thought is to get her own back by finding another man...Now it's the turn of the husband - who had thought of her as 'practically untouched' to mount a humiliating interrogation, punctuated by, 'Who? When? Where? He pretends he is driven not by rage at his 'property' being soiled, but by a passion for truth. Accusations and counter accusations come tumbling out, covering not only infidelity, but also quality of performance, pregnancy, abortion, venereal disease - and mutual disgust...

The contemporary solution to that is divorce: if you can't have your cake and eat it, you can always eat it and have another one. But the problem for these couples is...that over the years they have formed tenacious bonds of affection and need. If nuclear marriage is a hiccup in the history of sexual relations, they are still in mid-spasm...

...Mr Frisby does know his audience and I suspect he knows better than most critics how to get his points across. He has something of Alan Ayckbourn's technical facility, and of his flair for divining what actually is eating away at the soul of suburban man - 'those insatiable little maggots of insecurity' - with the difference that Frisby's characters do what Ayckbourn's dream about...

And that was that. On top of the last seven years it was too much for me. I resolved I would never write another stage play again.

Chapter XLIV

1977

For its conclusion, my story divides into three discrete threads, each leading to a separate climax - or anti-climax. Litigation has still a major part to play, so the unravelling at the end of each of these threads takes place, very properly, in our Royal Courts of Justice - or at their doors. Thus the three ends of my story have unity of place and action, if not of time.

The three threads are, in the order in which they unravelled: my relationship with Bill Fournier of Campbell Hooper and Austin Wright, sacked six years earlier; my relationship with Christine and Rutter and Co; my relationship with Paddy Grafton Green and John Calderan of Theodore Goddard, sacked at the same time as Bill.

At last some chickens come home to roost. You will remember, during the lead up to the consent settlement of 1971, that I told you that certain vital legal documents went missing, though I knew nothing of this at the time. Well, as promised, one by one, like rotten teeth being drawn, they are hauled out into the light.

The first thread: my relationship with Bill Fournier. We are early in 1977, *It's all Right If I Do It* has just failed so I am, of course, as previously, broke; no income or capital, a considerable overdraft. The Revenue (in the shape of the Scottish Threatener, Blue Eyes, from two chapters ago) was demanding £27,000 at once. This derived from the £24,500 tax bill incurred by Bill Fournier in his negligent handling of the Trust money he brought into the UK to buy my post-divorce flat in 1970. The bill had been accruing interest for years. Following my recent overall settlement with the Revenue, I had dealt with all their demands except this one and had nothing left to pay it with. To earn that sort of sum quickly was hopelessly out of my range. The Trust had been wound up as part of that settlement.

There was only one way to get the money: sue Campbell Hooper and Austin Wright, solicitors, the firm in which Bill Fournier was a partner. Bill, who had set up the Trust that was to care for us all for life; friend and adviser; the man who had tried to make peace between Christine and me; sacked by me in 1972. It was with no enthusiasm that I filed the writ against his firm. However, the case against him was unequivocal and his firm's insurance would take the loss if I won, not he personally. I could pretend to myself that it was all impersonally bloodless.

Tim Akeroyd, Andrew Park and I agreed that the case of negligence against Bill Fournier was clear and that I was capable of handling it with Tim's guidance. But Andrew had strong reservations, he said there was a legal loophole through which the opposition would slip even if I proved the negligence. The loophole was that, in tax law, I would have owed the money to the Revenue whether Bill had goofed or not, so I had suffered no legal loss (never mind the actual loss). Tim didn't think much of our chances for other reasons but, with no option, I went ahead anyway.

The firm of solicitors representing the insurers of Campbell Hooper and Austin Wright got it wrong at once. Instead of admitting the negligence and diving through Andrew's loophole they denied the negligence and dived into deep trouble. Bill Fournier claimed that I had been informed of the potential tax liability, but had ordered the purchase of the flat in spite of this. When I read Bill's affidavit saying so, I was astonished. Such an action by me at that time would have been out of the question. We asked for their evidence and received a copy of Bill's Instructions to Andrew Park, dated August 1971 (that date is crucial), just after the divorce settlement. Below is the relevant extract:

> At the time of the purchase Mr Frisby was advised by Instructing Solicitors that liability for UK tax would be a consequence of this purchase...

'I'm positive it's not true,' I said to Tim, beginning to doubt my words.

He answered; 'You told me that you learned of that tax liability in September, 1971, when Andrew produced his written opinion. You were all at a meeting and learned of the liability simultaneously, so you said.'

'Yes. It was a bombshell. We were all staggered.'

'Hm. Yet Bill Fournier wrote this before that date. Either he was clairvoyant or he had warned you as this says—'

'He hadn't. Don't be daft. I would never have bought the flat if I had known it would cost double. And I would never have signed the divorce settlement.' My bluster was covering yet further doubts about my memory, indeed about my rationality. Had I been blaming Bill and others all this time only to have it shown that this blunder at least was certainly my responsibility? Were the three Lords of Appeal right in 1972 when they said I should blame myself, not others, for my troubles.

Tim suggested we saw Andrew Park.

'Oh, yes,' Andrew said casually, 'I remember this. But what about the other instructions?'

'What other instructions?'

'There were some lying about in the chambers in 1971 to Harvey

McGregor, your previous tax counsel. I'm sure he wrote an Opinion at the time. I didn't deal with those instructions and I didn't see his Opinion. I did mine later.'

I had never heard of this earlier Opinion, nor these earlier instructions, so asked Andrew if he would give evidence as to their existence.

'Oh, I couldn't,' he said, as though I had suggested something improper. 'If I went into the witness box I might have to mention their tax loophole. That would destroy your case.'

Tim told me the next step to take. 'You demand Further and Better Particulars of Defence and see what turns up.'

'What are they?'

Tim smiled, anticipating my pleasure. 'Further and Better Particulars in the Queen's Bench Division is roughly the same as Discovery in the Family Division. And we all know about that, don't we.'

I grinned viciously, in happy recollection of the brawls with Rutter before the registrar. 'Not arf.'

There was some prevarication from the other side in answer to our demands; various documents, but not the ones we asked for, were sent. Eventually, on Tim's advice, I told them I would seek a court order, either for the documents or for an affidavit from Bill swearing they did not and never had existed. Shyly, the relevant pages edged into the centre of the stage.

They were a bombshell.

It was an exact repeat of the pressure Rutter had put on Bill seven years earlier over the matter of my 'illegal' signature on the Trust account in Zurich. Now, as then, Bill relinquished the papers in the most damning way. Only this time he damned himself, not me.

On twenty-fifth May 1971, Bill had asked various technical questions. He was answered with a long Opinion. The paragraph that mattered was at the end, an afterthought, a comment on a question that had not even been asked. It said:-

> I must however add that I am far more perturbed by the further statement in Mr W S Walker's letter that Jaco has declared and paid to the Trustees a dividend of as much as $65,000 (£27,000). If this was done at a time subsequent to 1967-68 when Mr Frisby was once again resident in the UK I can see no argument for avoiding a tax liability on Mr Frisby in respect of this sum. It is therefore in my opinion imperative, before anything further is done in relation to the tax returns that the precise date or dates when this dividend was declared, became due, and was paid, should be ascertained.
>
> (signed) Harvey McGregor
> 18th June 1971

This was the first of the missing documents that I have already mentioned. I now saw it for the first time. My qualms about nailing Bill, my former friend and counsellor vanished. His disastrous goof, though forgivable, had been followed by an utterly unforgivable cover-up. The further implications of the documents sank in (perhaps I should say, in legal jargon, the Further and Worse Implications): Bill had learned of my extra liability of £24,500 (due to his negligence) on June eighteenth, 1971. Who knows how dismayed he was, he arrived at his own solution: silence, then fix the papers. Less than a month later he had stood beside me in the corridor outside the High Court and let me sign the consent settlement knowing that I could not meet its terms. A single sentence from him would have stopped the legal madness there and then. Instead, he had kept quiet, replaced McGregor with Andrew, doctored the phrasing of his new instructions accordingly and pretended to learn the news of my debt, along with the rest of us, in Andrew's chambers two months later. In between, on the evening of the divorce settlement, he had come home with me, drunk champagne and said, 'You must be sick of the sight of lawyers. I'll be off. Now you can put all this litigation behind you and write a play.' All the time he knew that I was in a hopeless situation financially, put there by him.

What can one say?

His solicitors offered £20,000 to settle out of court. Tim and I went for tea with them and pushed the offer up to £25,000. We were left alone to discuss the matter.

'If we stick out they'll give me the lot,' I said. 'I've still got to pay the full £27,000 to the Revenue.'

'I know, but give this man a little room to manoeuvre. If he's got nothing to take back to his clients (the insurers) they may fight on.'

'They won't. He's obviously been authorised to settle. They're in deep trouble. Anyway, if they do fight, they'll lose.' The tea could have been jet fuel the way it was going to my head.

Tim was cooler. 'But suppose we don't settle now. Suppose they think it over and tomorrow they accidentally discover Andrew's loophole. They fight on. You win on the negligence, but get nothing. The insurers are laughing. They save their £25,000 and you're bankrupt.'

We took the £25,000 and ran. What has just taken a few pages to describe took nearly two years to run its course.

I spent £1,000 taking Dominic on a glorious Christmas skiing holiday with friends and their children, the first Christmas I had had with him. The Revenue were paid their £27,000 and my overdraft grew by £3,000.

However, the story that one missing document told about Bill Fournier was nothing compared to the beans that were spilled about Theodore Goddard and Co. In the course of our campaign for Further and Better Particulars, a letter came to light that had passed between them and Bill that was sensational. Again, I had never seen it before. Years after the events all sorts of goodies were creeping out of the woodwork. I issued a writ against Theodore Goddard and Co as a holding action. But first, out of the Queen's Bench Division and back to the Family Division for the second of the three final threads.

Chapter XLV

1979-80

The second thread: my relationship with Christine and her legal adviser.

At the end of 1978 Christine and I were beginning the third year of the New Era. Relations between us were satisfactory. She was invited to Barbados for Christmas, so I was allowed to take Dominic on the skiing holiday. Christine had sold 1 Genoa Avenue and moved to a smart flat in South Kensington. She had the excess money from the sale of 1 Genoa cosily invested, but best of all, at last she had a job. Her total income was considerably higher than mine, I had no further legal obligation to her. However, I didn't want to upset our good relations with more litigation so I sent her the details of my finances with the proposal that I continue to pay her the £1,500 for Dominic, but cut her own money from £2,000 a year to £500. As any court would surely award her nothing, wouldn't it be better if we did it by a nice civilised consent order?

No answer. She went off on another holiday. When she returned I tried again and was told to deal with the matter through her lawyer. I decided that a simple application on the grounds of a 'change in circumstances' to Mr Justice Trevor Reeve would do the trick.

I went to the Royal Courts of Justice at the beginning of April to get the hearing set down. There followed one of those grisly afternoons endemic to the system. After hours of bureaucratic shunting I was told that all matters of maintenance must be heard by a registrar, not a judge, and 'Never mind whether Reeve has reserved the case to himself or not, them's the rules.' I ended with the application set down for twenty-fourth April before Registrar Bayne-Powell, who had by then attained the status of the Senior Registrar.

Rutter's answer to my affidavit was a smasher, out of time as usual, posted so that I got it just twenty-nine hours before the hearing. Their affidavit was nineteen pages long with no exhibited supporting evidence about Christine's finances. The first thirteen pages were devoted, in Rutter tradition, to calling me a liar, but the new beauty in this section was a three-page summary of Trevor Reeve's judgement of May 1975. This summary was a fiction. It reported that the judge had said something that he hadn't, namely that I had hidden information from him that would have altered his judgement and the judgement of the Court of Appeal in 1974. The rest consisted of an almost comically conservative estimate of her finances. Tim Akeroyd grinned and adjusted his glasses. 'Hm. I think we can say they take a low profile about her income and assets, don't they.'

In the squalid corridor outside that lovely room in Somerset House where the Senior Registrar presided was surprise number one. Geoffrey - not Sydney - Rutter was waiting. Dad had retired. The sway-backed son with the thin cigar dangling from his lips was now in charge. Their prose-style in affidavit had been indistinguishable. The Senior Registrar's clerk, Mr Cosford, opened the door and smiled with anticipation. 'He's ready now, gentlemen,' and into the spring sunshine we went from the gloom. The stage looked set for another brawl, Cosford certainly thought so, he took root at his desk and made a very poor pretence of doing some work. At least it was p.m. so the SR had got his lunch safely under his waistcoat.

The SR, who seemed to have gained in authority since I had last seen him in 1974, was in determined good humour, beaming at both of us from behind his little barricade of books. As always, he greeted mention of my mother's old house, 20 Paddock Orchard, with affectionate recognition. When I told him that it had been sold, he smiled and nodded that he had heard so on the local grapevine. While Rutter fils argued, I threw in a few one-liners as was my custom with his father. Fils retaliated that he had let me present my case in peace, why shouldn't I let him? I shut up. The new-generation Rutter may write like his father, he didn't plead in his style.

The SR agreed that Christine earned more than me and reduced her maintenance by £1,000 a year, but he raised Dominic's by £250. I was still paying for him at well over the legal maximum (one sixth of my income) and ominously, although I had got a net gain, if Christine married the next day and dropped off the order, I was worse off. I argued, but the SR's message was quite clear: perhaps you are still paying too much, but I've given the other side a face-saver, go away and stop fighting or produce further evidence.

I thought the afternoon relatively uneventful but Sue, my new part-time secretary, who had been present taking notes, had never been into a hearing like that before. 'Is that how they always go on?' she asked, appalled. 'God preserve James and me from divorce.'

Enough was enough. I wrote to Rutter the next day to suggest that we leave it at that. He took a fortnight to answer as Christine was abroad on another holiday:

Frisby v *Frisby*

Our client instructs us that she is not prepared to consider any proposal by you until after you have complied with the Order of Mr Registrar Bayne-Powell dated 24th April 1979 in regard to Discovery of Documents.

We were off again on the mad round of dragging out every piece of paper relating to money for the past five years; world-wide royalty slips about peanuts; all the documents that referred to disposals of houses, assets; property long since sold. Within the twenty-eight days allotted by the Senior Registrar I sent a compliments slip to Rutter with my list of documents.

> Ere's mine. Where's your'n?
> You're late. Again. As usual.

No answer. Rutter merely ignored the order. Furious at having wasted working time while they considered themselves above such drudgery (Christine was away on holiday for the fourth time) I summoned her to fulfil it. No answer. I sent a reminder letter. Rutter answered this by claiming that my list of documents was defective. It was the old Rutter père technique of, 'When you're in breach of an order, don't apologise, attack.'

In July we were before the SR again. He got a bit shirty that his order hadn't been complied with but turned down my request that he order cancellation of all maintenance payments until it was. My point was that if I stopped paying they would soon get their fingers out. He made a new order for discovery, extending its scope into valuations of various items of Christine's property. At last I got her list of documents on August 3rd.

I wrote to Christine spelling out the facts of the hearings to date, in case she had heard a different version, then made a new settlement offer which was refused.

The discovery battle resumed with the maximum of flack from Rutter combined with the minimum of disclosure. Letters with pages of allegations flew. They valued Christine's flat at £65,000 so I made them a formal offer to buy it at £70,000 on the basis that the profit I would make from the resale would abrogate the hearing.

I again applied to the SR to get his orders enforced. We had another hearing in September. It was right back bang on the old form that Rutter père and I had achieved at our best. Angry insults, interruptions, jibes and jeers flew round the room. Since it could be said that both Geoffrey and I had been trained by his father it was a fair match. He had the legal background but I knew more about the case and could think faster for the ad lib.

'This is now the third time we have been before you this year, sir,' I argued, more in simulated sorrow than in anger. 'But we've seen nothing yet. If you will just make an order, cancelling all maintenance payments until the documents are produced, we'll have the lot first post tomorrow. He is saving his client's money and wasting mine with these delays. Punish them, not me.'

But the SR wouldn't do that, so I could only vent my frustration on Rutter fils who hadn't a leg to stand on. I got all the usual orders confirmed and re-confirmed and special mention that her tax returns and assessments be produced. Then things started to get really personal.

There had been a photograph of Christine in the *Daily Express*, William Hickey column, the previous January, in a bikini on the beach in Barbados. Next to her was a picture of Nat Cohen and Sam Spiegel looking unlovely in beach attire. The copy with the photos was suitable.

HOW THE OTHER HALF SHIVERS

...a sunny portfolio from a Barbadian beach...a rest for the ravishing Christine...Tycoon to Marry?...among the guests paying up to £300-a-day was the sprightly 72 year-old film chief Nat Cohen who cavorted on the white sands with a ravishing brunette creature, Christine Frisby...she is evidently inseparable from the diminutive movie-mogul...she calls him 'darling,' coos over him in public and is a frequent visitor to his impressionist-stocked St James's flat. East End butcher's son Cohen has had plenty of popsies to choose from...

There was more in the same vein.

I knew that Christine had been on several holidays since then because of the number of times I had been offered Dominic to stay, but didn't know the details. I presented the Hickey cutting to the SR and asked for discovery of her social diary.

'This is an infringement of my client's privacy,' Rutter exploded.

'I only want to know who's paying for £300-a-day hotels,' I said. 'I'm sure we would all like to be cavorting on the white sands at someone else's expense.'

'Really, Mr Rutter, if your client doesn't mind going to the Bahamas with men,' said the SR, getting ratty (note 'men', not 'a man' - the SR's moral slip was showing), 'why worry about her social diary being revealed? She can't be a prim Victorian maiden.'

I got the necessary discovery order. On the subject of valuations the SR said with unconscious humour. 'Can't one of you suggest a valuer and see if the other will agree?'

Things got sillier: I suggested an estate agent in Gloucester Road, SW7, just round the corner from Christine's flat, but Rutter claimed that Gloucester Road was miles away. It transpired that he meant, or chose to mean, Gloucester Place, W1. The SR, Rutter and I ended this part of the hearing drawing diagrams of central London to establish where Gloucester Road was.

I asked for further orders about anything she owned that might be worth something. In exasperation, the SR made an order for valuation of various things like jewellery and valuable antiques. 'Not every blinking chair but something reasonable,' he snapped.

The last order I sought was the oddest. I had still not received a bill from Rutter and Co for the thousands I owed them. 'No, no, don't do it,' Tim had looked aghast when I told him of my intention. 'Let sleeping dogs lie.' But we were both fascinated; the matter defied explanation. I believed that they had no intention of giving me a bill or they would have done so years previously, so I asked the SR to order that they give me a precise bill or agree there was no liability. Rutter said he would 'consider' the matter and the SR, mystified by the ramifications, said he had no power to make such an order. Sue's note says, 'clerk listening avidly.'

And that concluded another enchanting afternoon of British justice.

I wrote at once making a new offer to settle. Each offer was slightly lower than its predecessor, in contrast to the Theodore Goddard/James Comyn technique of some years earlier, when each offer got higher, thus inviting prolonged resistance. I sent copies of everything to Christine, to make sure she knew what was being done in her name.

Her answer was to go to Florida, then California, on her seventh or eighth holiday of the year. She was out of time again on the new discovery orders. I decided to send no further maintenance payments. Christine returned, tanned and refreshed and one day later, on November first, Rutter wrote.

> ...we have to inform you that unless our client receives a cheque
> for the arrears within the next five days, execution will be levied
> in respect thereof without further notice.

This was too much. I could see their application going before some judge new to the case, followed by the bailiff's men taking away my car as they had years earlier, in 1972, in precisely these circumstances. I got an urgent hearing before the SR and sent the summons to Rutter by hand to prevent any nonsense.

That hearing was the most rancorous of all. It is difficult to say which of us got the angriest, Rutter, the SR or me. I pleaded that the SR cancel all payments by me until they complied with his orders. Rutter argued that the SR had not the power, which upset him dreadfully. 'All right. You can appeal my order and see what good it'll do you.' I half expected him to add yah-boo, such was his tone.

When Rutter offered Christine's absence as an excuse for their lateness, the SR's colour heightened. 'What do you mean she's away in Los Angeles. She should be brought back to comply with my orders.'

Like teacher's pet I pointed out my punctuality on all the orders. I followed up with my bank account showing an overdraft of £23,000 against a limit of £26,000. Rutter said coolly, 'Well, he's got another £3,000 to go before his credit runs out so there is nothing to stop him paying at once.'

I can't remember the next events at all, I was so angry. My notes say that I swore at Rutter and had to walk up and down the room to recover. The SR went puce. He cancelled Christine's maintenance altogether and knocked Dominic's down to £1,000 p.a. He ordered yet again that everything be discovered in fourteen days, yet again that valuations be taken, and that Christine set out on affidavit the duration and accommodation of her holidays in the last twelve months and 'to what extent, if any, in each case, to which she contributed to expenses.'

It was a rout. I wrote to Rutter at once offering to settle, copy to Christine.

The response was twofold. One: they appealed the order. Two: I was banned from Christine's flat. The New Era was over. Henceforth, I must pick up and put down Dominic at the street door of the block.

I wrote her a long, furious letter. It was the first time I told her what I really thought of her actions since she had disappeared under Rutter père's influence years earlier.

Dear Christine,

...That flat, like most other things you possess was bought from the proceeds of <u>our</u> matrimonial home which was given to you as a place to bring up <u>our</u> child. If there were no Dominic you would never have been given them. It is his home too. Perhaps you would care to ask <u>him</u> if he wants his father banned from his home. Our picking up and handing over arrangements have been going on perfectly amicably, conducted agreeably on both sides with good humour and quite often considerable fun - certainly for Dominic, he loves seeing us together and hates our being divorced - for over three years. Now because of the acrimonious handling of your affairs by the Rutters I suppose we go back to the days of the Berlin Wall hand-over. Who do you think suffers when you do this? Only Dominic.

...I offered to settle the financial business at £2,750 - no. I offered again at £1,750 - no. The result is, led on by the unspeakable Rutter fils, you now only get £1,000 (which is still quite high in my view when you compare our financial positions, but again, I accept it). Now to save his face, Rutter fils has to appeal. ...What in God's name do you want, Christine? You are rich. You have lovely furs, jewels, clothes, income, capital, a luxury pad, many holidays, rich boy friends, an incessant social life, all you can wish for. I am nearly broke, yet you come grinding, screwing back for more, more, more. I think it's disgusting of you to let yourself be led by the Rutters. Just think, Christine, what you have started over the last ten years; actions to have me jailed for taking Dominic

406

in the park, the brokers men taking my car away, action after needless action, wrecking our finances, when you and your parents were generously cared for by me. No-one had to tell me my duty. Ever. You should hang your head...Count your lucky stars, Christine, grow up, give it a rest, leave me alone, earn your own living, enjoy your life and use just some of the interest on the many thousands you have from our house towards Dominic's education.

...I think it is disgraceful that your social life is so pressing that you cannot spend two successive nights with Dominic, either when you come back from a lengthy holiday abroad or after he has spent four nights out of seven at boarding school and one night with me. Since last December Dominic has spent over half of his out-of-school nights in my care and not once is he shoved off somewhere else.

...I have put all this down in writing so that there need be no misunderstandings and so that you can read it coldly two or three times. I want you to be quite clear about what I think and of my determination that you behave like a mother to Dominic and not like some social butterfly, flitting off round the world and then gaily alighting for a moment or two with a nice present for him. I think it possible that you live in some world of your own invention where you see yourself as the glam little mum struggling alone against all odds to bring up your only child. If something like that is so then the fantasy doesn't correspond with reality. If I'm wrong, then I'm sorry. In any case, I think it's time you stopped and had a good, long, cold, hard stare at yourself and your life...

Rutter answered for her:

...Our Client's objection to your coming into her flat had nothing to do with the Registrar's Order, as you have suggested.

The originally simple matter of my application had taken a year. The letters and the other documents had grown to a pile over two inches thick. I became more or less continuously seething even though I was 'winning,' as the lawyers say. In this state of mind I had opened at Her Majesty's theatre in a revival of the Aldwych farce of 1926, *Rookery Nook*, by Ben Travers. The production was not a success. I was, at best, adequate in a part I should have done standing on my head. After twenty-two years in the business, to arrive at last in the West End in a leading part and make so little of it did nothing for my humour.

407

I tried a constructive suggestion: as my overdraft and her deposit account were about the same at £20,000, she could lend me her money directly (with my flat as security) and we would make an extra £1,000 a year by cutting out the bank. Wouldn't that be better than squabbling in court about the same amount? No answer.

By chance I heard that in the coming appeal Rutter intended using his notes of the SR's judgement as evidence. I learned this because the SR's clerk was kind enough to let drop a remark about 'current practice directions' when I was telephoning him on another matter. Apparently I had a right to see these notes (it is ignorance of such tactical points that will nearly always sink the litigant-in-person in our courts). With difficulty I extracted them from Rutter. It was no surprise to see that they differed considerably from what SR had actually said. I sent Rutter's notes to the SR together with my comments. He sent me back something that was headed, 'Notes for the Judge.' It began:-

> I have had put before me notes taken by Mr Rutter acting on behalf of the wife and comments on these notes made by Mr Frisby acting in person.
>
> It is evident that Mr Rutter and Mr Frisby do not agree as to the accuracy of the former's notes. I would point out that it must have been very difficult for Mr Rutter to argue the case and make notes. Reading them I am afraid that I cannot accept them as an entirely accurate note. Accordingly I think it best to adopt Mr Frisby's suggestion and to state briefly the reasons for my decision.

The SR then summed up his judgement in a vein that was not helpful to Rutter. Registrars don't like being appealed any more than judges.

The appeal was to be heard in January 1980 by Mr Justice Trevor Reeve (making a decade of litigation between Christine and me). What a relief. I would not have to endure being smeared before a new judge. Rutter and Co., in order to squeeze the case in, had told the judge's clerk that it would only take half a day. This was nonsense and I had the old worry that I would have to listen to my alleged sins for two hours thus leaving five minutes for me to plead my case.

By seventeenth December Rutter had still not fulfilled the discovery orders. My reminders grew ruder. Then he pulled a trick which, even after ten years of the Rutters in my life, revealed anew their attitude to the law, the element which sustained them. At last he sent Christine's tax returns for the years 1977-80. With bated breath I opened them to learn the answer to the big question: what was her real income? In the boxes provided for the figures were written the words 'per accounts.'

No accounts were enclosed.

A few days before the appeal I received a summons to have paragraphs of my original affidavit struck out on the ground that they were 'scandalous, irrelevant or otherwise oppressive.' The paragraphs were the ones in which I was rude about Rutter's fictional version of Trevor Reeve's judgement of 1975.

I answered:-

> 'I acknowledge receipt of your summons dated 4th January, 1980 and will refer to it in future correspondence as The Silly Summons.'

Rookery Nook was about to close. I wrote to Rutter telling him that I would be informing Mr Justice Trevor Reeve that as from the Monday after the appeal I would be signing-on to draw unemployment money for the first time since 1963. Christine would be applying for an increase in maintenance from an unemployed person. No actor ever announced the closing of his show with more savage satisfaction.

Rutter, in answer, produced a final rabbit out of the hat A letter that arrived two days before the appeal began:

> We have been informed by our client that she is contemplating marrying within the next few months...

Useless to pretend that I cheered or broke open the champagne as is traditional; there was Dominic. How would he react? And there was the anxiety about my status when a new family of Christine, X and Dominic was formed. A welcome from them to me seemed, to put it mildly, unlikely. No, maintenance or not, I preferred Christine single, or at least married to someone I knew. Nat Cohen had been mooted in gossip columns, 'will sprightly old King Nat dance up the aisle with...?' and that was fine with me, but I wanted no newcomers.

Rutter's letter went on to say that because of the impending marriage, my imminent unemployment, a salary increase for Christine (she worked for her betrothed), and an increase in the rate of interest on her invested money, she would *not* be applying to have her maintenance restored, but only wanted Dominic's raised. It was beautiful. Christine was now simply a mother pleading to the court for her child. I was the father resisting that appeal.

But first Dominic. He had clearly been happiest during the New Era when Christine, he and I were together. I was sure he still entertained fantasies of our reunion. This was going to be the end of them. It could be a very big moment in his inner life. I thought about leaving the announcement to Christine and had a lurid image: bright smile from her, special voice, 'Dominic, you're going to have a new daddy.' I wasn't having that. A new age was dawning, time to be very wary.

Dominic sat in the kitchen with orange juice and cereal as I fiddled about making coffee. The only sound was of cornflakes being masticated. He had recently (and sadly, I thought) learned diplomacy, and was an excellent fender-off of unwanted questions. I was completely offhand.

'You like Lou, don't you?'

Chomp, chomp. 'He's all right.'

'Only all right?'

'Yes, he's all right.' Chomp.

'Oh,' I let it go a few seconds, 'I thought you liked him.'

Chomp, chomp. 'I do. He's all right.'

None of this was fencing, he was merely not interested in the subject. I had given him every chance to enthuse, nothing doing, so carried on. 'He's nice to you, isn't he?'

'Oh, yes.'

I laughed. 'I see. He's not brilliant and he's not terrible.'

'That's right.'

I felt a bit more secure and left it like that. Suddenly, he was ready to leave, on the landing, in his Parka and jeans, bicycle ready, plastic bag slung over the handlebars looking exactly as a ten-year-boy should look.

'Come inside a minute, Dom.' Damn, I was making it important and hadn't meant to.

'What for?'

'I want to talk to you.'

He stood by my desk. I felt like the form master interviewing the miscreant. 'I'm not sure yet, but I think it's possible that Mummy'll marry Lou.'

There was a grimace, then a nervous, embarrassed laugh. 'Oh.'

I laughed too, equally embarrassed. I longed to know what, if anything, was going on inside him. The pause was unendurable. 'So you may be seeing a lot more of him.'

'He's there every day anyway.' We both laughed at that.

'Has Mummy mentioned it yet?'

'No.'

'Well, I'm not sure whether they will marry or not, but it looks like it, so I thought I'd better prepare you. Then you wouldn't be too surprised.' '*Prepare you*'. Where had that phrase sprung from? Joan, my sister-in-law, on the telephone to tell me that Dad was dying, 'You had better prepare yourself.' Had I no other words?

'Yes.'

'Don't say I mentioned it. Just let Mummy tell you in her own way when she's ready.'

'OK Can I go now?'

'Yes, see you Saturday.'

'Yes.'

What was really there, built-up and dammed-in, was, 'Just remember,

Dominic, no matter what, I'm your father and always will be. Come to me for anything.' But that was too heavy for a small boy to bear. I spent the rest of the morning miserably at my desk, producing nothing.

The following night, the night before the hearing, I got in from the theatre wound up to snapping point and sat in front of the telly. If ever TV reflected the nastiness and pointlessness of the world, it did so then, I thought. After the mid-week football, complete with punch-ups, I flicked channels, bored and nervous. The three-way choice was between: Percy Edwards who had abandoned speech in favour of animal noises; a BBC documentary about girls dying of drugs and rebellion in South America; a topless French cabaret full of girls clearly healthy and unrebellious. BBC 2 changed to the Russians invading Afghanistan followed by the report of sixty-three Saudis being executed for occupying the Holy of Holies; on to white Rhodesians wanting to kill Nkomo and Mugabe and Iranians screaming for death sentences. The French tits, curiously unbouncy in the dance routine, changed to a commercial for *'Peace in the Valley*, twenty-two religious songs by pop-stars for only £4.99.' As that changed into a commercial for army recruitment I went to bed, shaking with tension about the fight on the morrow; the squalid little brawl over a thousand a year. The expectation of losing it (for that is what I thought) after the continuing Rutter-tactics of the preceding year was intolerable. The eighties looked like making the hideous seventies seem rosy.

Chapter XLVI

January - March 1980

Mr Justice Trevor Reeve had advanced from his dreary, intimidating court down the dingy stone corridor in the old Admiralty and Divorce wing to one of the row of dreary, intimidating courts in the functional new Family Division building. The corridor that served them was shrouded in grey January light as Rutter fils and I exchanged last-minute papers. The usual crowd of lawyers and women was there; the lawyers, attentive or pompous in crumpled suits and straggly hair; the women, uniformly anxious. Christine was absent.

In we went and waited for the judge. He entered, the star, and sat. Then came the courteous enquiry that always thrilled me with its sublime economy. 'Yes?'

Rutter kicked off. He went straight into The Silly Summons. As the minute hand on the clock twitched its way round, the adrenaline pumped through me. Reeve read the papers, heard out Rutter and turned to me 'Well, Mr Frisby?'

'This is all a filibuster. He has booked you for one afternoon only, and he's going to take up all that afternoon so that I get a few minutes at the end. I've faced this tactic before from his father -'

'At the moment it is you who is wasting time.' Reeve allowed more edge to creep into his voice.

'There won't be enough this afternoon,' I said, knowing it was daft to upset the judge.

'Mr Rutter, this is your application, will there be time this afternoon?'

'I can manage, all right,' said Rutter comfortably.

I let go a loud 'huh' of derision and held up all the papers of the last year. Reeve's eyebrows rose.

'Well, Mr Frisby, we will go on until it is finished,' he said.

'You mean, tomorrow?'

'If necessary.'

The anxiety dropped away, I would be properly heard. I got on with the job in hand. 'Well, that affidavit was written in outrage at the lies in my former wife's affidavit of—' At the word 'lies' Reeve sucked in his breath and rolled up his eyes. I stopped, on the wrong tack again. 'Well, I don't know what word you use but that affidavit isn't just inaccurate, it's fictional.

Here is the official transcript of your judgement. I was so outraged I ordered it from the Mechanical Recording Department.' As I passed the papers up I chuntered on. 'I am sorry if "lies" is distasteful... that transcript cost me over £35... and all the wasted time...I thought affidavits were supposed to be on oath.'

Reeve read his judgement of five years previously then smiled disarmingly at Rutter. 'Hm, yes, I'm in some difficulty, aren't I, Mr Rutter? You see, your client's affidavit doesn't precisely report what I said, does it?' Oh, that delicious judicial understatement.

'I don't know what that document says, My Lord. I haven't been allowed to see it,' said Rutter. 'This is the first time Mr Frisby has produced it.'

The implication that I had pulled a fast one so riled me that I broke the atmosphere of sweetness and light Reeve had created. It was a mistake, the rancour in my voice, as it cut in harshly, caused the corners of Reeve's mouth to descend abruptly. I said, 'Perhaps you should have got a copy before you invented that affidavit. It's quite simple. It just requires a bit of time and money like I had to waste.'

Rutter remained silent. Reeve let a few moments go then said, 'Perhaps if we delete those parts of Mr Frisby's affidavit that you suggest, Mr Rutter, and those parts of your client's affidavit that refer to my judgement that will be the fairest to all.'

'Possibly, My Lord,' said Rutter.

Reeve looked at me. 'What do you think about that, Mr Frisby?'

I was still wound up. 'I only wrote the affidavit because he—'

'Quite.'

'Could I have a look at that judgement, My Lord?' Said Rutter. 'I wonder if I may take it with me and bring it back tomorrow?'

'Well, I don't know. It is Mr Frisby's,' said Reeve glancing at me. 'But I'm sure he won't mind if you—er—refresh your memory.' And he was already handing it down towards Rutter.

'If he would like to pay me the cost of getting it,' I got in. 'For thirty-five pounds he's welcome to it.'

The look of irritation that Reeve threw at me before the pupils of his eyes rolled out of sight into their sockets made me relinquish my claim, but I hated myself for not pulling the judgement away.

We got onto the main issue. Rutter began, 'I don't think we need concern ourselves with my client's property and income, My Lord. Just Mr Frisby's.'

I had to stop myself from exclaiming out loud at this cheek, but Reeve reacted differently: a look of agreeable surprise occupied his face. 'Why not, Mr Rutter?'

'Recently we wrote to Mr Frisby and told him our client was soon to be married.' Reeve's face recomposed itself to offer some felicitous phrase, but Rutter hadn't finished. 'However that marriage is now off, My Lord.' He paused; justifiably, for the moment was a complete success, Reeve's expression went through further modifications and my jaw dropped open. Rutter resumed comfortably. 'Nevertheless, My Lord, even though my client is not now marrying, she wishes to make no further claims on the respondent. Her only concern now is for Dominic's future. Therefore, although her own future is somewhat—er—uncertain, she is only appealing that part of the registrar's order that applies to Dominic. She is forgoing her own rights.'

'Hm. Yes. Most commendable.' Reeve seemed to think, then, 'Mr Frisby, Mr Rutter is only appealing parts of the order.' He asked nothing, but the silence was interrogative.

I stood up and floundered. 'Yes, I see. They're just appealing the bits they don't like. Funny law that is.' Reeve sighed patiently. I tried, 'What about the Senior Registrar's discovery orders being flouted?'

'But they no longer concern us, Mr Frisby, do they?' said Reeve. 'Now it is only a question of how much you can afford for Dominic.'

I was out-manoeuvred. It was beautiful. I was a man who was fighting a plucky mum, left at the altar rails, fending bravely for herself but no complaints, pleading simply for her child. Boris Karloff would have leapt at the rôle.

'How do we know she was getting married?' I stammered. 'There's no evidence before the court, only Rutter's word. How do we know it's off?' But I sounded nit-picking even to myself. 'This appeal is half-cocked. How can you possibly decide until you know all the financial facts about both of us.' It all seemed deader than the dodo. Rutter got in, in tones of regret that made my ears squeak with anger, how hard it had been to get discovery from me. We adjourned.

The following day a terrible procession crossed our path. It threw into sharp relief the tawdriness of our proceedings. I was in the witness box being questioned about money I no longer had when we were suddenly adjourned. A woman in a wheelchair with a small army of grey-suited men entered the court as we left. The judge's clerk told us in the corridor that it was an urgent interlocutory hearing as to whether the woman was fit to care for her child. She had some dreadful crippling disease; a shrunken, helpless figure, carried into court on a tidal wave of experts. The local authority wanted to take the child into care; she was resisting; a full hearing was due on the matter. Our case, supposed to last for one afternoon only according to Rutter's estimate, had held matters up; so the woman, the welfare officers and the lawyers had been waiting for hours outside while Rutter had been examining me about how much I earned from betting at golf and similar earth-shaking matters.

After perhaps half an hour the army filed out, now with grey faces as well as grey suits. We were ushered back in. The sight was unbearable.

Sitting in his place, raised above the rest of us, literally as well as in power, was Trevor Reeve. He had obviously just ordered that the child be taken from the woman. He was staring down at her with the intensity of a

414

hypnotist. I am sure he was trying to say 'Forgive me, I have to do this. It was in your child's best interests (oh, that legal phrase).' At his feet in her wheelchair was the woman, racked, sobbing till she retched. There was never a more desolate-looking creature. She had nothing; no man, no child, no health. She couldn't even leave this place of her execution until a female companion came in and wheeled her out between the shocked faces of those who had fought for and against her.

But even though she was the emotional centre of the scene, the judge dominated it, he was the one who had taken on our burden and made the intolerable decision. For the first time a feeling of respect glimmered in me for the Family Division and those who work in it, until I remembered, from ten years earlier, Trevor Reeve's 'It may well be that this father is being too possessive. Once a fortnight is appropriate.' And it was gone. It was unthinkable to subscribe to the undeniable truth that in this place it is the judges and lawyers who are the permanent stars, like the doctors and nurses of a TV hospital soap; we, merely the bit players who come, untidily emote, then go.

Reeve addressed us with his customary politeness. 'I am sorry, gentlemen, to have kept you, but it was essential that I heard that matter at once. As it was I had to rebuke counsels for letting that poor woman wait outside for half the morning. It was deplorable.' Oh, the gratitude that woman must have felt for receiving the apology about the procedure before the axe on the issue. Reeve said, 'Yes, Mr Rutter?' And he resumed listening to our trivialities.

Rutter took ages questioning me over some minor sum of money when my patience broke. I said something like, 'You got this appeal fitted in by saying it would only take half a day, perhaps we can organise a queue of crippled women while you count the change in my pocket.' Reeve should, I suppose, have rebuked me but he just stared at the papers before him. Rutter was about to protest, thought better of it and changed the subject. Reeve gave me hope. 'Mr Frisby, you said yesterday that for me to hear this appeal was half-cocked—'

I cursed my loose tongue. 'No, no, My Lord, I didn't mean to imply that—'

Reeve raised his decibel level just enough. 'I was about to say that you seem to be right. We don't know nearly enough, do we?'

I gulped. 'Er, no, My Lord.' But he added nothing to his intriguing comment.

As we were about to adjourn, Reeve commented, 'Dominic is an expensive child, isn't he…I have to ask myself, where is the money to come from, Mr Frisby.'

That night I was sure I had lost, utterly outplayed by the professionals. I didn't give a damn whether I paid Christine £1,000 per annum towards Dominic's school fees, or more, but that Rutter's tactics of the last year should prevail was insupportably galling. In a funny way I felt I was letting down the Senior Registrar who had found for me. I tried to re-think my

415

case and answer Reeve's final, casually delivered remark of the day. Had he been giving me a nudge or not?

The next morning, my final argument was, more or less: 'A veil has been successfully drawn over her income and lifestyle. However, even on what little we know, we can see she was richer in 1974 when you halved the consent order than she was in 1971; she was richer again in January 1979 when the Senior Registrar reduced your order; and she is still richer now. During the same periods the reverse has happened to my income and property. The overall trend is evident; if I go bust tomorrow she will go on getting richer and Dominic will be kept at that boarding school. There is the answer to your question of last night.' I waxed passionate on my last point, that the Senior Registrar's order should be backdated to that first hearing, 'If only as a disciplinary precaution.' I continued, 'She has over £22,000 on deposit from the sale of the Former Matrimonial Home; order that the interest from that pays for Dominic's upbringing, she will still have the capital when he is grown up. That solution will stop any further litigation between us. What greater blessing could you bestow?'

I only have my notes on Reeve's judgement, not the transcript. '…I don't really know the true financial situation…but anyway the issue is simple, if this marriage had gone on this child would have had just such an education…the question is who pays what proportion…the husband is now paying £1,000 and that is right.' Pause for me to take a deep breath and try not to cheer. 'We know it is not enough, but can the mother bear it? We know she has over £20,000 from the Matrimonial Home. If they had acted together, the interest from that is exactly the money they would have used.' And that was that. He refused to backdate the order.

We moved on to costs 'I will make no order as to costs,' said Reeve. I argued hard and believe my case was unanswerable: I had won and that was enough. No dice. I showed that my original offer to Christine, made on paper to avoid litigation, had been twice what Rutter had now got for her so I deserved the costs. No dice.

I tried to show my further attempts to settle the matter. No dice. I tried to show him how I could have saved hundreds of pounds on the flat valuations if Rutter had done it my way. No dice. I pointed out that when I had lost the short hearing in 1975 and he had ordered costs against me, he had said 'I have no choice.' Now I had won, surely he had no choice but to order costs to me. No dice.

As we gathered up our papers Reeve smiled down, the judicial facade dropped. 'Which part are you playing in *Rookery Nook*, the Ralph Lynn part?'

'No, My Lord, the Tom Walls.'

'Ah yes,' Reeve twinkled gently. Everyone in court looked good-humoured at this evidence of informal amiability from on high. Even Rutter was obliged to participate. Reeve continued, 'I was sure it wasn't the Robertson Hare part.' (Robertson Hare, the third member of the original renowned trio from the 1920s, always played the downtrodden little husband).

As so often, I went too far. 'Oh, I don't know, My Lord. There are more ways than one of being henpecked.'

Reeve's smile promptly vanished and with that mouth set once more in a thin downward-pointing crescent he left the court and my life.

The important implication of what Reeve did was that, although I won the hearing, the delaying tactics, the evasions, the empty tax returns, all the behaviour that I have described, were rewarded. If £1,000 was the right maintenance in November when the Senior Registrar made the order, so it was in the preceding April. The implication of the judge's decision to all involved in divorce is clear. 'Fight, fight, fight. Don't compromise. Don't make peace. Don't negotiate. Get in there and fight. You will benefit financially. And if you are a woman or against a litigant-in-person, even when you lose we won't award the costs against you.' In all the times I 'won' in those courts I never got one penny costs and I have never heard of another husband or litigant-in-person who did. Whereas every time I lost, costs were fully and promptly ordered against me.

But then, Rutter and Co. never sent a bill. I must have owed them over £25,000 at early-seventies prices.

Curiouser and curiouser.

So, with the new decade, came the end of litigation between Christine and me, the end of the second of those three final threads, as well as the end of the New Era. The Berlin Wall hand-over remained in operation for good.

I tried to think straight about the rest of my life. The past had a ten-year-wide scar across it. Looking back, the principal image was that of waste. I had set off on my theatrical journey thinking I was the future. I was a spokesman for Us. It was sobering to realise that I had been side-tracked; I was merely another marsupial, not that bad a design, but not in the main evolutionary stream; an aboriginal ripe to have been overrun.

Within days of that last hearing my immediate future was decided. I was offered precisely the acting job I wanted, a six-month tour of *Once A Catholic*, playing the lovely part of the priest, Father Mullarkey. That would take care of the overdraft while I wrote this.

The final scene of the Christine/Terry story came six weeks after the hearing before Reeve. Characteristically, she was absent. *Once A Catholic* was playing Sheffield when I telephoned her about seeing Dominic. 'I'll drive home overnight on Saturday and come for him on Sunday morning.'

'Oh, I won't be here this weekend, I'm going away,' she answered. 'He was going to stay in school. Will you pick him up from there?'

417

I turned up at his school on Sunday morning. Dominic was waiting outside Boarding House. He waved and dived inside to get his stuff. Matron suddenly materialised from somewhere, in a chatty mood. 'Hallo, Mr Frisby, hope you had a good journey. He's all spick and span. Been waiting, quite excited. Gone to get his things. He looked lovely when he went out on Thursday. I saw to that. All sprucé he was.'

'On Thursday?' I was puzzled. Thursday had been Christine's birthday, 6th March, the tenth anniversary of the last night she had - on Rutter's instructions - slept with me. It had not, as far as I knew, been made a school holiday.

'Yes. Thursday. For the wedding.'

Chapter XLVII

1979-83

And so to the unravelling of the last thread: the conclusion of my relationship with Theodore Goddard and Co.

This last chapter is, if you like, an epilogue to the story of Christine and me. But it is the proper conclusion of the story of all the litigation caused by our divorce. During these last few events I ask you to look at a wider scene than our divorce system. Mark how British justice in general is managed, a system which is a failure on every count. It is inaccessible to ordinary people, inefficient in the most trivial of ways and unjust at the highest level of morality. It is expensive, cumbersome and unworkable.

This final episode starts from the actions of Theodore Goddard and Co. First, a few paragraphs to recapitulate, forgive any needless repetition.

I used the word sensational to describe a piece of paper that came to light when I was suing Bill Fournier's firm. It was a letter to him from Paddy Grafton Green dated third December 1970. That date is crucial. The letter mentioned another document, unknown to me: a cable. (I have mentioned this cable earlier, to assist the reader, but it was new to me at this moment.)

> '...In addition, I am a little concerned as I have received a cable from the Cayman Islands which runs as follows -
>
> "RE FRISBY YOURLET 20TH OCTOBER WE CANNOT DIVULGE INFORMATION WITHOUT FULL WRITTEN AUTHORITY FROM FRISBY STOP CAN YOU OBTAIN STOP
> SIGNED
> ROYTRUST"

I was puzzled, then astonished. Then a feeling of serenity stole over me. This piece (perhaps I should say 'peace') of paper utterly disproved the most important of the long-standing fictions that persisted throughout all the litigation, namely: the assertion that I had ever, at any time, misled anyone about my *de facto* control of the Trust, my alleged action that 'justified' all the expensive, acrimonious litigation by Rutter.

Let me remind you of the facts:

Theodore Goddard maintained that I concealed from them, until it came out in March 1971, as a result of Rutter's discovery actions, that I could, *de facto* or *de jure*, control the funds of the trustees of the Trust. That was how they had briefed James Comyn.

I say that I was frank with Theodore Goddard about everything from the word go. My tape recordings show that Theodore Goddard were wrong but our Lords of Appeal, Davies, Phillimore and Orr, ignored those tapes. All written evidence supported Theodore Goddard's lie. Thus was I sunk.

Now, here, at last, written by Paddy Grafton Green himself, and dated 3rd December 1970, *four months too soon,* was flat contradiction of their version of events. The wording of the cable, signed by the Trustees themselves, is unequivocal:

'...WE CANNOT DIVULGE INFORMATION WITHOUT FULL WRITTEN AUTHORITY FROM FRISBY...'

Never mind about the *de jure* question of control, in the light of the words above, only one person was in *de facto* control: me.

I must remind you of Theodore Goddard's (and Neil Taylor's) initial advice to me when I took my case to them. I had said, 'I have £X of property in this country and £Y abroad in the Trust. I control the Trust *de facto*. But the big, the real, the ONLY thing that matters, before any divorce settlement, is FIRST to quantify my four-year, unpaid, unassessed tax bill since I lived abroad. Not till we know what that is, will we know what I am worth.' (If you remember, that took six more years to settle at the Revenue's technical headquarters in December 1976 when I went there with Andrew Park and Frank Young).

In 1970, Theodore Goddard and Neil Taylor, the experts, did not listen to their client. 'No, no, no,' they said. 'This is how you fight this divorce. Your unpaid, unassessed tax bill will be ignored by a judge. (But Mr Justice Latey proved them wrong on that, Andrew Park's written Opinion, sought too late, assessed my bill precisely). Your opinion of what you control *de facto* is not law. You do not control the Trust or the trustees, *de facto* or *de jure.* Thus you keep all that money out of any divorce settlement.'

Of course, that was a policy built on sand, as I learned to my cost (not theirs). And when it collapsed Theodore Goddard was able to produce documents that pointed at me being the liar, the culprit for the cock-up. And they suppressed the vital, single piece of paper that showed that their legal advice had been mistaken and disastrous.

If only they had just come to me at once with the cable and said, 'Look, we were wrong, let's put it right.' (Too many 'if onlys' in this story). But, no, like Bill Fournier, they covered up. So the errors festered and spread underground for years, heath fires creating catastrophe. The oldest crime of the bureaucrat: first the cock-up, then the cover-up.

The cock-up/cover-up scenario was to form the basis of my case against Theodore Goddard. As I have said three chapters ago, I took out a writ at once but did not serve it. This I did to get a start date on the record for subsequent legal action. Time was vital, I was already beyond the six-year Statute of Limitations time-bar to start an action.

I wrote to Grafton Green demanding his brief to James Comyn QC and all other documents that passed between Theodore Goddard and Comyn during the case. I received a large cardboard boxful. The above letter and the cable it referred to were missing. In 1,455 carefully indexed documents relating to my divorce there was no reference to the cable.

It took nearly a year's correspondence, three threats of legal action and threats to report them to the Law Society to get that cable out of Theodore Goddard. What was finally evident was:

1) The cable and everything related to it had not been disclosed by Theodore Goddard for nine years.

2) James Comyn, who was thoughtfully sent the 1,455 other documents mentioned above, never knew of the cable's existence. He was briefed that: I had concealed my control and was therefore 'open to criticism' by the court; I was 'liable to most of the considerable costs'; Theodore Goddard had no knowledge of my control '*de facto* or *de jure*'until March 1971.

3) Neither Rutter nor the court had been allowed to see the cable and surrounding correspondence, yet Theodore Goddard wrote to Fournier on sixteenth November that they had been ordered by the registrar to discover:'

> ...copies of the letters which I had written to the Trustees...accordingly, I have sent (to Rutter) a copy of my letter of the 20th October to the Royal Bank Trust Company (Cayman) Ltd...

So Theodore Goddard 'obeyed' the court order by discovering their letter of enquiry but omitted the bit that mattered: the reply.

4) Theodore Goddard had never tried to get my authority to divulge the information requested in their letter of twentieth October 1970 as the trustees had asked, 'CAN YOU OBTAIN', and as the court required. That is, in spirit at least, evasion of the order.

421

5) There was a discovery order made by Registrar Bayne Powell dated November eleventh 1970. The following is a quote from Grafton Green's notes on the day:

> 'After many heated exchanges, the Registrar made an Order in general terms as to discovery with specific reference to the following points:-

> (i) Full disclosure of all documents relative to the issue of the Discretionary Trust.'

These documents were to be discovered in twenty days with inspection seven days thereafter. The cable had arrived on the nineteenth day and had never been discovered.

I wrote to Theodore Goddard in December 1979: asking all the difficult questions. They refused to answer them.

I sent James Comyn QC, now Mr Justice Comyn, copies of the evidence and asked if he would help. True to form he refused to do anything. He still had my substantial fees in his pocket. As I earlier said, you cannot sue a barrister who has acted for you in litigation.

Theodore Goddard got a hearing before Master Warren (a master in the Queen's Bench is equivalent to a registrar) in July 1981. They were attempting to have my case smothered in a few minutes under the Statute of Limitations, before I could get it under way. Lovely, isn't it? Hide your actions for nine years then claim immunity under the six-year rule.

I got that ten-minute hearing adjourned and re-set down for a full afternoon in December 1981. I thought that would at least give me time to present my evidence and argue my case. I was wrong. The barrister against me presented his case: simply that I was statute-barred. I was sunk before I started. I was, to the master, one of those contentious litigants-in-person who plague the courts trying to sue their ex-lawyers. He refused to let me plead my case my way and he read other documents while I presented the evidence. When I complained to him of his conduct, he said I could do it my way after all and looked at the clock with great frequency as I tried to pull my scattered wits together. When I had finished, he found against me.

The point is, helpful or unhelpful, was Master Warren right in law? Tim Akeroyd and I consulted a barrister about appealing. The barrister started our meeting with, 'Of course, these chambers do a lot of work for Theodore Goddard. My clerk didn't want me to handle this.' He chuckled nervously, 'But I don't mind.' He then advised me not to continue with the action. The power of a firm like Theodore Goddard works in many ways.

I asked, 'Are you telling me that the law says that Theodore Goddard can do me and if they can hide it for six years they get away with it?'

The barrister answered, 'If they hide your cause of action they can't. But you knew you had a cause of action in 1972. You accused them of negligence then. That is well-documented. All they have done is to hide the evidence. You should have taken out a writ within the six years allowed.'

He was making a vital legal distinction that you might like to follow: the difference between a 'cause of action' being hidden and merely 'evidence' being hidden. If the concealment of that telegram could be named as my cause of action we leapt the six-year bar of the Statute of Limitations and went to a full hearing on the merits of the case. I had no doubt we would then kill them in court, a hearing which I intended to handle myself. Of course, if they lost the interlocutory matter they might try to settle out of court like Bill's firm, Campbell Hooper and Austin Wright, had done. Only this action was not going to be for £27,000 to repay the Revenue; two million was the sum for which I intended to sue Theodore Goddard for recompense for my lost fortune (inflation had been raging throughout the seventies) and my years of lost productivity. Since I doubted if they would settle for such a sum I looked forward to facing Calderan and Grafton Green in court and publicly nailing them and Comyn to the wall, fully reported in the press, once and for all.

However, if that cable was merely 'evidence to my cause of action', we would never get past this interlocutory stage; we were statute-barred. My problem was that I seemed to have nothing but 'negligence' to charge them with and I had shouted 'negligence' all over the law courts in 1972, so I could scarcely claim now that my cause of action was hidden. There was another vital - and to me, grossly unjust - point. I had not brought a negligence action against Theodore Goddard in 1972 simply because what happened to me in the Court of Appeal in front of Lords Davies, Phillimore and Orr, when I had called Theodore Goddard and James Comyn negligent, would have stopped any sane person from starting a legal action. And - not being clairvoyant - I didn't know that a single piece of paper existed that would have helped me had I started that hopeless quest. That Court of Appeal judgement would have been waved at any judge (all lower than Court of Appeal judges, remember) - as it was, for years, by Rutter - and I would have been dismissed as a 'vexatious litigant' (legalese for a nutter). So, because I had acted sanely in not bringing an action, I was now statute-barred on negligence.

Indignant at the trap I was caught in I argued passionately with this new barrister, with Tim Akeroyd and, eventually, with John Tackaberry, the barrister who had come up to me and helped me in that very Court of Appeal hearing eight years earlier.

My chief point was that I didn't for one moment believe that the concealment of that telegram was negligence. I felt sure it was deliberate. Therefore my action should be for contempt of court, or fraud, or something appropriate. And if my cause of action was fraud or contempt of court then that had certainly been concealed and we leapt the six-year-statute hurdle. But, I was told, I couldn't bring an action for contempt, only the courts could do that. And, if I could (under certain rare circumstances), I could not claim any damages, even if I succeeded. As for my accusation that my cause of action was fraud: 'Well,' said Tim. 'Look what happened to you before when you originally claimed dishonesty from your legal advisers. You were hammered. You'll have to prove it first and you can't prove it without a full hearing. You were bounced down the Strand by those judges, and would be again.' I took no great persuading that he was right about this; I still nursed those bruises.

So back we came to negligence, a formula judges were used to dealing with; my only, so it seemed, route. But under 'negligence' the cable was relegated to being merely 'evidence'. It was an exquisitely closed circle which once more confirmed my lack of faith in the proper function of the law when you complained about lawyers.

Anyway, John Tackaberry, at least, was never hired by Theodore Goddard, and he agreed to handle my appeal from the master's decision before a High Court judge. There was no point in my even trying to do it myself as a litigant-in-person. We could all see I would never even get started. We needed some weight in court, and John was now a QC.

'But this bloody master has already found against me without even listening,' I said.

'Oh, it doesn't matter what the master said,' said John comfortably. 'He knows that, in any case that matters, his decision will be appealed one way or another. It's a judge we've got to convince.'

It took until nineteenth April 1983 to get before one.

His Honour Judge Lipfriend was a County Court judge sitting in the High Court - common practice when there is a shortage, they serve their apprenticeship like that. He seemed delighted to be where he was, listening to a QC arguing with obsequious understatement to win him over. And understatement was the key to John Tackaberry's approach, no layman's squawks of solicitorial dishonesty for him. The obsequiousness, evident initially, melted away as matters progressed and John saw that he was gaining ground, but he never forgot the lack of law that we had on our side. 'How can I slip this past the judge without his noticing?' He asked me and his junior counsel of one point after another as we prepared the case.

The evidence was tricky. To extract from the morass of documents - over two and a half-thousand in all - the reference and cross-references that showed Theodore Goddard's concealment and its disastrous consequences was to tell a precise, subtle detective story that required diligent attention from both the narrator and audience.

John did it beautifully, sliding each step of the story in. He pointed out that the cable only needed to put Theodore Goddard 'under notice' about my control, a much lower target for him to hit than to claim it was vital. 'Under notice' means that on receipt of that cable my legal advisers should have at least been aware that something was wrong and taken appropriate steps. The judge only need to be satisfied prima facie that the evidence had been concealed, not that the concealment was deliberate. Oral examination in a full trial would establish all the facts eventually. For the dreary truth that I had to keep reminding myself of was that this hearing was merely interlocutory - a hearing to get a full hearing. If we lost here, we were throttled, pre-natally as it were: Theodore Goddard's aim.

The only hiccup in our case was that to do it properly John took nearly two days (the master had not listened to me even for a couple of hours) and he had reserved only half that amount of court time. 'That is inexcusable, Mr Tackaberry. Inexcusable' said the judge at one of the breaks, the form master ticking off a prefect with no great force, token stick-waving.

The opposition's case at this hearing was merely to rely on the Statute of Limitations.

The merits of their case amounted to Calderan denying on affidavit that they had ever advised me to misrepresent the situation over the Trust. He also swore, on affidavit, that the cable was 'not relevant' and that it was 'my belief that it was not concealed' - he daren't even swear it wasn't concealed just *believed* it wasn't. This was so cynical it made my ears pop with rage. Grafton Green - who has admitted on paper that he received the cable, and so was the person who should have disclosed it - said nothing on affidavit. Theodore Goddard wisely kept him out of the firing line, the dog that didn't bark.

The relevant section of the Statute of Limitations of 1939 was that I could have it lifted if there was a 'fraudulent concealment of my Cause (or Right) of Action.' This Act was amended in 1980 to say 'a fraudulent concealment of any fact relevant to my Cause of Action,' a form of words that was distinctly more favourable to me. John got the judge to ignore the 1939 Act and consider the case under the 1980 Act, an excellent move, especially as the concealment had taken place in 1970. What it boiled down to in the end was that both sides agreed that if there had been a fraudulent concealment, I won - but fraudulent concealment of *what* seemed never to quite get defined. Of my Cause of Action? Of a fact relevant to it? Of merely 'evidence'? I didn't know, neither did anyone else apparently, this was part of John's successful approach.

The extremely tall, thin junior barrister, Timothy Barnes, who had been against me before the master (the legal profession seemed to be adhering to its habit of being inhabited by physical oddities) repeated his arguments: my case was frivolous and vexatious; there was no reasonable cause of action; the relationship between solicitor and client was no different from the relationship between other parties; there was no special feature here to justify the judge using his special discretion; there was no fraudulent concealment; the cable was not relevant to my control (how anybody could argue this baffled me and - in spite of subsequent events - still baffles me); that one little document - the cable - didn't stand up against the mountain of opposing evidence in the case; and finally, that with diligence I could and should have uncovered the evidence, if there was any, sooner.

At the end of the submissions the situation, due to John's good work, was that to dismiss my application the judge had to be satisfied that no fact relevant to my Right of Action had been concealed.

Regarding the concealment, the Judge had to decide five matters:

1) Was there a fact?
2) Was that fact relevant?
3) Was it concealed?
4) Was that concealment deliberate?
5) Should I with reasonable diligence have discovered it?

I was pretty hopeful but, as always at the end of these hearings, the tension was high.

In his summary, apart from referring to Grafton Green as Graham Greene, which raised the literary status of my opponents, if not my own, Judge Lipfriend said early on, with reference to my drubbing in the Court of Appeal in 1972 when I complained about each and every one of my legal advisers: 'There seems little doubt that Mr Frisby's view of the negligence of his solicitors or counsel did not commend him to the Court of Appeal - but that may not be relevant.' So that was a good start: understatement combined with a neat side-step. He repeated Trevor Reeve's comment that : 'Frisby must have been exasperated for years at the stupidity of his advisers.' His judgement covered seventeen pages reviewing the case. On the five points he said that:

1) There was a fact - the cable.
2) It was relevant - indeed its very existence meant, *prima facie*, it was relevant.
3) It was concealed - especially, he noted, from James Comyn.
4) As to whether that concealment was deliberate, only a full hearing with oral examination could show and it was only fair to all parties that such a hearing to determine the facts should take place.
5) Regarding my diligence in not uncovering the telegram sooner: 'I do not propose to take a point against Mr Frisby for not spending nine years looking for a piece of paper the he did not know existed.'

He stated that 'I hold there is an arguable case...that the defendant solicitors deliberately concealed...[the cable]'.

We had won. My subsequent yell of triumph echoed down those dreary corridors, hideously embarrassing my team.

Theodore Goddard & Co promptly appealed.

In December 1983 we all met outside the Court of Appeal one morning for the hearing. Our legal system once more showed the grotesque way it functions. First, John Tackaberry was absent as he was still engaged on another case. Second, of the three Lord Justices before whom we were to appear, one was Latey and another was Reeve. It did not seem credible; the two judges in the whole of the British legal system who were most likely to be well-disposed towards me. There were judgements from both Latey and Reeve as part of the evidence, but the other side were going to object only to Reeve's presence, not Latey's. I cannot think how or why they missed that point. However, Reeve was called away anyway and as there was no one to replace him we were to be heard by two judges only: Latey and another. Third, Theodore Goddard, now represented by Mathew Thorpe QC, presented to us outside the court a new affidavit from Calderan with masses more 'new evidence.' After a six-month wait they produced this at a minute's notice. This new evidence was, in fact, selected from the thousands of documents of very old evidence and was supposed to assist their case. I read the affidavit and new evidence and couldn't see that it made any difference to anything - merely more stuff to allege that I was the perjurer not 'them the concealers. Indeed, some of it seemed to help my case.

We were faced with a choice: go in with Rowan Planterose, my junior, against their QC or claim an adjournment to look at the new evidence and wait for John Tackaberry to be free. What I really wanted to do was to fight it myself in front of Latey, who I trusted, but there were various complications, not the least of which was that although I understood the merits - the story - better than anyone, I would be woefully inadequate arguing law, the whole point of this hearing. We decided to get the adjournment, which we did with costs, and to wait for John.

One Friday in April 1984 we again gathered, this time before the Master of the Rolls, Lord John Donaldson and Lord Justices Fox and Stephen Brown. John was in great awe of Donaldson and claimed he was the best legal technician in the country, a title that didn't endear him to me. I would have preferred him to have been called the judge with the most fully developed sense of right and wrong. He was an imposing figure with an ample nose and good voice, but he undermined his majesty by surreptitiously putting sweets in his mouth all day and looking wonderfully furtive at it. Once the goodie was in, he seemed to think he was undetected and sucked openly. Sometimes a hand drifted up to his face, sometimes a handkerchief, to pop in another, under cover. Neither of the other judges was offered one, I noticed. The occasional ill-timed crunch in a pause was mildly diverting.

The opposition opened - it is always best to go first I have been often told - and things seemed to be jogging along for the first morning as expected. At the break John and Rowan both felt the judges were against us but had not yet really plumped for one side or the other. Calderan and Grafton Green appeared for the first time and sat meekly down at the front to show their respect.

The one moment that had disturbed me during the morning had been when the cable was produced and read out. Lord Justice Fox said: 'Of course, it may well be that that document is not relevant, may it not?' I could not believe my ears. Neither apparently could the opposing QC believe his luck. 'No, My Lord, well, that is—er—well—our submission.' He looked as though he had stumbled into the proverbial bed of roses but would jump out if challenged. I wanted John to dive in there and then to ask them to explain how 'CANNOT DIVULGE INFORMATION WITHOUT FULL WRITTEN AUTHORITY FROM FRISBY' was not relevant to control - any interruption to stop that outrageous idea taking root. To force them to talk about the cable must expose the thin ice on which they were skating. But the moment passed.

Halfway through the afternoon John got to his feet. By then it was clear where Donaldson was. He insisted on judging the case under the 1939 Act, not the 1980 Act as Lipfriend had, and he was stuck on what he called a 'fundamental point', namely that I knew they were negligent in 1972 and should have sued within the six years. The possibility that they had concealed evidence was not at all the same as if they had concealed my 'cause (or right) of action'. On the merits of the case Donaldson said, 'You haven't convinced me yet, Mr Tackaberry, that there was a concealment.' And thus we broke for the weekend.

During the weekend, John and Rowan searched the computer for further case history that might help us. I argued that they must first nail the relevance of the telegram and the truth of its concealment or we would never get to first base. They disagreed. Donaldson was stuck on his fundamental point of law, had said as much to John during the proceedings and invited him to find a way round it, which he could not. I expressed the hope that if Donaldson could be convinced on the merits, his 'fundamental point' might become less inflexible.

On Monday morning John got some way on the relevance of the telegram and on its concealment but could do nothing about Donaldson's fundamental stumbling block. I should have taken out the writ years ago and that was that. I knew they had been negligent, had said so in several courts over the years. The Statute of Limitations should not be breached. John had barely sat down, after an hour or so of fruitless arguing, before

428

Donaldson set off on his judgement. He read it. I could see that it was already typed out, had been before the morning session began. So much for hearing the case out before making up his mind. We lost on the very point I have described. Donaldson refused us leave to appeal to the House of Lords. The other two judges agreed.

In John's chambers I urged that we go to the House of Lords in spite of being refused leave. John and Rowan said it would be hopeless. I asked John if he believed in my case.

'Yes,' he answered. 'Perhaps that was the trouble. I didn't at first, but I do now. That telegram was relevant and was concealed. Neither Rowan nor I have any doubts. Once we saw what you were getting at, the evidence grew clearer and clearer the more you looked at the papers. You should have brought your case within the six years. That 1972 Court of Appeal judgement may well have been unfair but you should have taken out your writ in spite of it and that is that. You're too late.' John urged me to get away from the courts, live my life in the theatre and forget them all. He talked of obsession and the futility of continuing to litigate.

I was at that time appearing in a show that I had mounted, a tour of the Young Vic production of two one-act plays, *The Real Inspector Hound* by Tom Stoppard and *Seaside Postcard* by me. We were due to play three weeks in Scotland. While there I thought about little else but what I should do.

That litigation, started in 1980 against Theodore Goddard, had cost over £20,000 as all costs had been awarded against me. It had taken four years without getting off the ground, stifled at the interlocutory stage. My flat was now forfeit. But we had got to first base. The judgement of His Honour Judge Lipfriend said I had a case that they were, prima facie, guilty of the concealment. Donaldson's judgement in the Court of Appeal referred only to the law. It made no mention of the merits of the case. What we had was one judgement against Theodore Goddard on the merits and one against me on the law. For Fox in the Court of Appeal not to see that the telegram was relevant and none of them able to follow the detective story of the concealment confirmed all my beliefs - acquired through my experience in those courts - that while judges and barristers may well be experts on law they are the blindest of men when it comes to simple facts, especially about their own profession. It was, as always, their reading of the law that made it illogical, not the law itself.

The feelings of pent-up frustration, bitterness and anger, the passionate, outraged indignation that I had felt years earlier about Rutter - that he was allowed to flourish unchecked and even admired and respected by some - now centred on Calderan and Grafton Green. That they could get away with it seemed to me a public disgrace. The matter raged round in my head through sleepless nights and absent-minded days, while the beauty of Scotland slid by, barely noticed. I asked a close friend, one of the few I could trust. 'Was I obsessed, a vexatious, possibly half-mad, litigant?' 'Of course you're obsessed,' was the answer. 'But you're right. That's the important point. That's not madness. That's maddening.'

How right my friend was. The smothering of this final attempt at justice nagged and scratched and bit and itched and ached and gnawed. My lifelong inner convictions about Truth and Right and Wrong that had infused everything I had ever written were mocked beyond sufferance by this anti-climactic non-finale to fifteen, litigation-strewn years. Meanwhile, I was still broke. They owed me a lot.

I decided to go to the House of Lords without John and Rowan. Perhaps there was never any doubt that I would. I still did not believe that my case had got a proper or fair hearing. Not that it could now, a litigant-in-person refused leave to appeal, applying to the House of Lords for leave to appeal out of time, would barely be taken seriously. Donaldson had said, 'I have an innate reluctance to strike out and drive a litigant from the seat of judgement.' He had not in the event shown much reluctance. Perhaps there would be one in the House of Lords who would feel a whiff of indignation at the situation and read the law differently.

I wrote out my petition for leave to appeal to the House of Lords. In it I tried to attack Donaldson's 'fundamental point' - which in my belief, was a fundamental point of procedure, not a fundamental point of justice. Law should be based on justice (whatever that is). That is fundamental. The wrongdoer should not benefit from his action. That is fundamental. The Statute of Limitations specifically states that a person should not benefit from his concealment. That is fundamental. I had tried within the allotted six years to bring an action before the Court of Appeal because of Theodore Goddard's negligence. That was fundamental. It failed, probably because of their concealment, and as a result of that I had not taken out a writ against them. That was a fundamental point of injustice. I argued that the Master of the Rolls had got tied up in the letter of the law and forgotten the principles behind it. Reeve had said as much of Theodore Goddard's activities in his judgement of 1974.

> 'I accept that he (Frisby) has been exasperated for years at the stupidity of his advisers, who will insist on looking at the letter of the law instead of at the reality.'

I tried these arguments on John and Rowan and other lawyers. They could not counter them but told me that, nevertheless, I would lose, the Statute of Limitations would prevail. John, after reading my petition to the House of Lords pronounced it a document that they must at least take seriously. For the first time in all this litigation I was going to be arguing law - about which I was ignorant - and not the merits of my case, which I knew backwards.

The procedure is that you must apply for Leave to Appeal Out of Time to the Appellate Committee of the House of Lords. You must get everything you want to argue in to your petition and include with it only other papers relevant to the law. You may not argue the merits of your case (I didn't need to, Lipfriend's judgement did that) only law. You are given about fifteen minutes and if you have got nowhere by then you are out on your ear. The Committee of three Law Lords is supposed to have read your petition before you speak. I would have fifteen minutes to show that the Master of the Rolls was talking through his wig. Not what you would call a safe bet.

I wrote out, for the Appellate Committee to read before I made my fifteen-minute pitch, the history of the case in nine pages and followed that with six pages of argument. As evidence, I submitted the cable, my statement of claim and the five relevant judgements: Latey's in 1972 (for me); the Court of Appeal in 1972 (against me); Reeve's in 1974 (for me and upheld by the Court of Appeal); Lipfriend's in 1983 (for me); the recent Court of Appeal under Lord Donaldson, the Master of the Rolls (against me). That way the Law Lords would see simultaneously all the legal issues with the summaries of the actual events.

I also had to submit reasons as to why my case was of 'general public importance'. This is a vital ingredient of why you are appealing to this lofty legal body. Mine referred to the vital failure by famous solicitors to disclose key documents in litigation, not only to their client, thus ruining him, but also to the client's leading counsel, the High Court and The Court of Appeal.

The principal point of law boiled down to the distinction between the 1939 act and the 1980 act, the old one of: was the cable 'evidence', or 'the cause of action', or ' a fact relevant to the cause of action.' But, anyway, even if I lost on these distinctions, as I thought I would, I had two other main points:

1) That my right of action had been taken away (if not hidden) from me by the various judgements against me, all from mighty courts, all made as a result of Theodore Goddard's concealment, all rendering any legal action I took against Theodore Goddard without that cable and in the faces of those judgements as doomed to failure.
2) The Statute says that nobody should benefit from their 'fraudulent concealment.'

On that second point I argued that: surely to prevent a powerful firm of solicitors to the High Court from benefiting from concealment and thus preventing justice from being done was overridingly in the public interest.

'The British legal system should be, and should be seen to be, open and fair. If I am driven from the seat of justice without a full airing of this matter in open court then I respectfully submit that this working of our legal system will be in disrepute.'

That seemed (and seems) to me to be the most important point of all.

You wait in a better-furnished corridor outside the committee rooms of the House of Lords than at the Royal Courts of Justice. New carpets, antique furniture and imposing oil paintings surround you as you lick your dry lips and wait your turn. Actually, my lips weren't that dry, was I getting hardened? I think not. John Tackaberry had told me I had no chance, so nerves did not enter into it.

There would be three judges on the Appellate Committee. For an interlocutory matter to come before them was even rarer than a litigant-in-person. The three judges were supposed to have read my petition and the papers with it. They would probably have already decided if there was any solid law for me to appeal on. If I succeeded I could then appeal to a full five-judge House of Lords judicial hearing. It was the old one again of having a hearing to get a hearing. Only now I was having a hearing to get a hearing to get a hearing. 'Oh, Kafka,' I wondered, 'Where are you now?' From 10.30 a.m. till lunch-time there were six cases set down. If you lasted longer than fifteen minutes it was unusual, I was told. My case was last. 'That's a good sign.' I suggested eagerly to John. 'They think it might be complicated, that my case has merit.'

'Sorry' was the answer. 'They've just saved the amateur till last. They know they can get rid of the professionals quickly.'

The thin-nosed Mathew Thorpe QC and the lanky junior, Timothy Barnes, turned up with a nondescript solicitor, apparently without any papers. Obviously they did not think them necessary. I went in and listened to another case to get the feel of things. What was immediately clear was that my prepared approach was all wrong. I sat outside and re-wrote my arguments. The first case that morning took nearly an hour and the petition succeeded. I watched the bonhomie exude from the judges and heard Lord Scarman say 'You're lucky, Mr Whatever,' to the relieved, grinning barrister. Two successes in one morning was pushing the bounds of probability.

The next few cases were in and out like yo-yos. I noticed that the barristers, once they got going, tried to keep going, and that, although the three Law Lords made no bones about interrupting them - predictable enough - the barristers made no bones about talking on through the judges' remarks. One barrister, as he exited, flustered and a little humiliated, said to his client, 'That was only a two to one decision against us, I'm sure.' It was satisfying to see self-delusion in operation at all levels.

I had been told I would be lucky if I got Scarman, with his unauthoritarian, liberal reputation. He was the chairman and needs no description from me. Lord Brandon of Oakbrook, a surprisingly young-looking, hard-jawed man was second. 'He's arrogant,' I was told and he looked it as he constantly and affectionately stroked his cheek like a man dissatisfied with his shave. Lord Templeman, who looked the correct, antiquated age was the third. He left no impression on me at all.

Scarman told me at once that I may take it they had all read my petition and that I should address myself to Donaldson's fundamental point. Since that was what I intended that was all right, but first I asked them if they had all read, besides the petition, my statement of claim and the five judgements I had submitted. There was a bit of shilly-shallying and I had to ask two or three times before I extracted the information that Scarman had only read Donaldson's and Lipfriend's judgements; Brandon had read everything; and Templeman, his head down like the boy at the back of the class who hasn't done his homework, had read nothing.

My point, made in the petition, that any reasonable or good cause of action that I may have had early in 1972 was taken from me after the first hearing before the Court of Appeal, was understood by them. Brandon seemed to quite like it, but it didn't get me anywhere. I kept going hopefully on my other points but the three Law Lords weren't having any. Then the proceedings started to take a more interesting turn.

Scarman seemed unhappy about feeling compelled to turn down my petition. He expressed sympathy for the unjust situation in which I found myself. Bitterly I pointed out to him that the Court of Appeal in 1972 also expressed sympathy (albeit crocodile tears) when they castigated me then for accusing my former legal advisers, now the House of Lords was also expressing sympathy while standing in law against me. It wasn't their sympathy I wanted. Scarman shrugged helplessly. Suddenly 'fiduciary' came up. I didn't recognise the word, let alone grasp its meaning in context and, after stumbling over it, said in embarrassment that I couldn't even pronounce it. Scarman said, 'I think you pronounce the word as well as you pronounce the word "soup",' and smiled ingratiatingly at me to notice his little joke. In spite of this obvious attempt to be friendly, to present himself in a certain way, I could only stare coldly back. It was clear I was going to lose, so currying favour was superfluous and I felt no warmth towards these men who had the power to unravel the Gordian knot but were not going to use it. Although the dialogue that follows, except where I say otherwise, is from the official record of the proceedings, taken down in shorthand, it is a woefully incomplete and inaccurate document. Amid its many errors it translates Scarman's 'soup' into 'sue', a natural enough mistake of hearing, but it turns his placatory joke into a waspish remark.

Templeman, who had been belatedly catching up on his prep, looked up from the papers to say that it was all my fault as I had signed a false affidavit in 1970. This red herring exasperated Scarman who tried to shut him up. Brandon joined in with Scarman and at the same time I made a remark to Templeman that does not appear on the record, something like, 'If you had read all the papers supplied by me, you would not just have said—' At which point Scarman got us off that, leaving Templeman huffed with a pink face and ruffled feathers. The three judges were excellent examples of something I continually observed in those courts: the more the judge knew about this grotesquely muddled story, the more he came on my side. Every remark or interjection that Brandon - who had read everything - made seemed helpful, Scarman was warmish, but Templeman solidly against me. I am speaking of their sympathies, they all seemed against me in law. As I tried to present my various reasons for my petition to be allowed, the proceedings got more and more confused. We talked over and through each other. Perhaps it is not surprising the official record missed so much.

It was about two-thirds of the way through the proceedings, which went on for about forty-five minutes, that Lord Brandon dropped a bombshell. He asked, 'Has it ever occurred to you to sue Theodore Goddard, not for their negligence in August 1970 and January 1972 but for their failure to produce to you that document, which is arguably a continuing failure or a continuing breach of fiduciary duty? Has that occurred to you?'

I stared in horror and said something like, 'Are you suggesting that I should start another action?' while the opposing barristers giggled. But that remark does not appear in the official record. Scarman interrupted with, 'That is something for you to consider but it does not arise at the moment.'

Although I was confused, it was obvious something important was being said, so I asked Brandon to repeat himself. He did, but that does not appear in the record either, though I remember the moment with clarity.

Brandon continued, 'It may provide some answer to the injustice that you complain of. Because, if you put your cause of action in the right form there might not be the injustice which you claim. It seems to me it is arguable, Theodore Goddard being under a fiduciary duty to you as their client, that they were under a duty to show you all the documents which were the subject matter of disclosure.'

I answered, mystified by his point, 'But they have now produced all the documents.'

'When did they produce them?'

'1979' I said.

'Well six years haven't passed since then,' Brandon replied and shrugged eloquently.

Brandon's last remark above is also not on the record, I think because Scarman interrupted him at the same time, in an attempt to change the subject. 'You have not taken that action. Whether you do or not is not a matter for us.'

I made my last point; 'It is a fundamental point of the Statute of Limitations that they should not benefit from their concealment. That must be more fundamental than all the others.' Scarman noted it down and I said, 'I am sure you have heard enough of me.'

He thanked me with customary judicial courtesy and said, 'You have certainly put your points clearly and, when not interrupted by us, you have put them very logically.'

I got on with it, 'It has not got me anywhere, has it? It must be a matter of public concern that lawyers of this stature can be allowed to get away with concealment, with evasion of court orders, with contempt of court.'

Scarman wasn't having any of that. 'Mr Frisby, this is not the appropriate place to make that sort of comment.'

'Where the hell is, then?' I wondered to myself.

And once more Brandon stuck to his guns. 'There are other means of redress against solicitors, you know. There is such a thing as the Law Society.

I laughed without a trace of mirth. 'I tried that one in 1972.'

'You have not tried it since you discovered this document?' asked Brandon.

'No, My Lord.'

Once more the eloquent shrug. Lord Brandon's faith in the Law Society showed little awareness of reality and his advice to start a new action did little to endear him to me, though perhaps it should have. I wanted them to find for me on the spot, not to suggest prolonging the business by starting a new action.

The record says at this point 'Their Lordships conferred.' But they didn't, nor did the rest of us leave the room, which had happened after all the other hearings that morning. Scarman simply told me I had lost, he once more apologised as he awarded costs against me.

There was the usual polite bowing from the two barristers who had turned up against me; Scarman thanked me again. I could not bring myself to be even polite, so angry was I at the outrageousness of it all, and turned away pretending to collect up papers. But I was ashamed of that petty action, and that feeling remained my strongest impression of the hearing for some while. On such trivia are our memories of great events formed - not that my failure before the House of Lords Appellate Committee was a great event to anyone but me.

John and Rowan showed considerable interest in Lord Brandon's remark and at last I saw his point. If we had made their concealment the cause of action, under an action for breach of fiduciary duty (instead of negligence), claiming the same damages, Theodore Goddard could not have invoked the Statute of Limitations since it would have been the 'cause of action' that was concealed, not merely 'evidence'. In other words *we were fighting under the wrong law.*

It took days for the full implications of this to sink in on me. I had asked a succession of legal experts, all well disposed to my case, and been told again and again that negligence was my only route to sue Theodore Goddard. I had never for a moment believed that concealment of that telegram was negligence. As I told their Lordships, I believed it was deliberate. I called it fraud, contempt of court, many things, all of which I was advised were legal dead-ends. Yet here was a law I had never heard of, a route, a positive motorway to success that nobody had thought of: that Theodore Goddard were in breach of their fiduciary duty. The whole matter had hinged - and now fallen - on finding the right way through the legal tangle. All those legal experts - close friends - to whom I had spoken on this subject had, without exception, pointed me the wrong way. All the hints and asides that John had been dropping during the High Court hearing about the special relationship between solicitor and client had law to back them up. But he hadn't invoked it. Here was one of the Law Lords, who as a group I viewed as prejudiced upholders of the status quo, handing out free legal advice of a quality that surpassed that which I had paid so much for.

It was a numbing blow, to be knocked out by such a basic error. I wondered if there was anybody in the world who knew how to get justice out of our legal system. But John had worse to deliver. If fighting on the wrong law was not stupid enough, there was a further mistake of such triviality, such banality, that it seemed to be not credible among all these educated, qualified, top-of-the-field barristers and Lords of Justice.

'Did you draw their attention to the last page of your amended statement of claim?'

I did not know what he was talking about. He showed me. There, in black and white, was the very point of law that Brandon had mentioned. John had altered my statement of claim before the Court of Appeal hearing, but had not argued the fiduciary duty point before Donaldson, or mentioned it to me, why, I am not sure. I think he just lost faith in his case or himself. I had stood before the House of Lords Appellate Committee with the very weapon in my armoury that Brandon required and I hadn't used it because I hadn't understood or realised that I had it. It was over the page, on its own, on the back of the papers. Neither the judges nor I had turned the page and seen it. The situation was unbearable.

'I must go back before Brandon and Co with a new petition and say a mistake has been made.' I said.

'You'll be thrown out.'

'But if the very thing he mentioned was before them and we all missed it...?'

'They weren't asked to pass judgement on the fiduciary duty point, only on Donaldson's fundamental point.'

'You mean we start again from scratch?' It seemed inconceivable that the matter could go on perpetuating itself so. The room seemed to be uninhabitable. I had always wanted to attack Theodore Goddard on all fronts, John had shied strongly away from the contempt and the fraud issues. Now that his approach had failed, the gap between his softly-softly line and my wish to take the outraged, indignant attitude was too clear for comfort to either of us.

'But if I merely start a fiduciary action against them, they simply show my old statement of claim to the judge and it's all over.' I said.

'They'll certainly try it,' said John. 'But I'm not sure they'd succeed. No judgement has been handed down on this issue. We are entitled to a judgement.'

'Right, I said.' 'Let's go for them on fiduciary duty. I've lost everything, it's the only chance.'

So I did the necessary work to issue the writ and statement of claim.

Theodore Goddard's answer was prompt: they applied to have the matter knocked out in a hearing before a master. Their grounds were based on some other law that I had never heard of which says that having failed to win a case under one law you cannot bring it up again under another. A fair enough law, actually, to stop pointless litigation, but this wasn't pointless.

So here we were, back before a master again who would throw me out before I started. There was no point in my representing myself. John couldn't manage the hearing, so Rowan Planterose went in against the extremely tall thin junior who had been against me before. He met us in the corridor outside and tried to be friendly, talking about the theatre. The snarled enquiry from me, 'Do you enjoy earning your living in such a shitty way?' soon put a stop to that, and in we went. Rowan did his best, but it was hopeless, even I could see that. And it was obvious to me that it was hopeless to go on, to appeal this master's decision.

I could not ask John or Rowan to go again before a judge and say 'sorry, we didn't think of "fiduciary duty" sooner.' I could not sack them (anyway, I was fond of them both by now) and engage new barristers to plead for me with the excuse that my previous barristers had goofed ('more negligence from the legal profession, Mr Frisby? You seem to be plagued by it'). Apart from anything else, I couldn't even afford it. And I could not go back into court representing myself, it would have been ludicrous.

I wrote to all the partners in Theodore Goddard inviting them to come out from behind the Statute of Limitations and clear the name of their firm in open court on the merits. They declined the invitation. Probably some of them are still there, practising. At the time of publication of this, Patrick Grafton Green is the senior partner of Theodore Goddard and Co. I complained to the Law Society as Brandon had suggested. They appointed a retired solicitor from Essex as investigator. He showed no interest whatever in getting to the bottom of the matter, even with the Lipfriend judgement held under his nose. The Law Society found Theodore Goddard guilty of nothing.

I had appealed to the House of Lords Appellate Committee on the highest and widest grounds of morality and failed on law. But there had been a law to carry my case. John had, as an afterthought, found it, not argued it before the Court of Appeal and not mentioned it to me. I had gone before the Appellate Committee not knowing that the very grounds that Lord Brandon said were arguable were written on the back of my submission. Nobody had turned the page and seen it. Was there ever such a puerile, piffling, footling end to a legal action?

I gave up.

There remained a pleasant postscript. The solicitors representing Theodore Goddard sent me their bill as all costs had been awarded against me. It was nearly £12,000. I contested this. To do so you go before a taxing master and fight it out; for 'taxing' in this context read 'costing.' Both this master, Master Prince, and his clerk clearly knew all about this case and me before we sat down. It was my job to argue that the opposition's costs were: a) too high for each individual item, b) excessive in generalities. Tim Akeroyd had showed me how to go about it and told me that I would save myself two or three thousand pounds if I did it well.

I need not have worried. With considerable and expansive pleasure, Master Prince scrutinised their accounts with much greater expertise than ever I could have shown. 'Oh, no, no, no, this is excessive. Cut it by half.' 'Oh, dear me, you can't ask for this. Remove that.' 'No, no, I cannot possibly allow this in full, let's call it.... Do you not agree, Mr. Frisby?' I just sat there and nodded, trying not to smile. The solicitor against me knew that all that the master knocked off from my bill would be charged to Theodore Goddard, so he joined in the general merriment and a good time was had by all. Their costs ended up as five thousand-odd, about forty per cent of their original bill. One minor master in those Royal Courts of Justice, Master Prince, took the title of the place seriously.

Thirteen years have passed since that last hearing. So what has happened to us all? Well, first of all, far too many of the lawyers are dead, especially the judges. I am sorry; I wanted them to read this. I hope the ones that are still alive hang their heads on behalf of their profession.

What about my work? I soon broke my resolve never to write another play with a one-acter (if that counts) for the Young Vic, *Seaside Postcard*. I directed this and we toured it three times with Tom Stoppard's *The Real Inspector Hound*. I had splendid roles in both plays and it was enjoyable to realise my original, egocentric, student ambition to act in a play written, directed and produced by me.

But it took seventeen years from *It's All Right If I Do It* before I produced another full-length stage play (always my Everest). That play,

438

Rough Justice (nothing to do with divorce, but about a couple who killed their hopelessly brain-damaged baby) more or less flopped in London, was successful in Canada and Australia, where I had a wonderful time adopting it for their legal systems, and could soon be a film. I got a wry laugh when I read some London reviews that told me that what I wrote of what went on in court was inaccurate or could not possibly happen. I have written one more play since, soon to be produced and that will do, I think. Playwriting for me is over, for various reasons not all connected with this story. I am afraid I shall have - with some justification - the label of 'one-hit wonder' although I have, since the litigation, written many TV scripts and one for radio. I have acted, directed, produced, followed my chosen profession and earned my living with great pleasure - even won awards (without tripping half-drunk into the arms of the luckless presenter). So I could say that I have done my thing. But what would have happened without the fifteen-year-wide legal abyss? The obvious guess is that I would have written more plays and probably repeated my success or produced something of note, but that claim could be glib. If I was so good why didn't I do it anyway? On the other hand there are many paths to divert you from the best, the main (if you like) route. If I hadn't found the slip-road of litigation I might have found one of many others. Or I may have kept my head down over the desk and done it again. All idle speculation. Even during the bad years, my life - since that joyous day when Ivor and I got into drama school together - has really been about theatre, creativity, profound satisfaction and enormous fun, never mind the might-have-beens.

And on a personal level? Well, somebody recently asked me if I think my life was hijacked by it all. Yes. That's not a bad way of expressing it. I have sorely missed that core experience having a wife and children and all of us developing together. I couldn't try to start it again, what had happened hurt too much, or I would have betrayed something, perhaps Dominic. Perhaps I felt like that because I already felt I had betrayed him in letting the ghastly juggernaut get under way in the first place. If the litigation was merely a fifteen-year-wide gash across my professional life, it permanently changed the course of my personal life. For the worse, I am sure.

Christine has stayed re-married, happily as far as I know and prosperously. We have no contact. People sometimes say that they are not surprised that I never married again, in view of my experiences, but that angers me. They have misunderstood. 'No,' I invariably protest. 'There is nothing wrong with marriage. Mine was beautiful. It was only the divorce that was so vile.' Although I no longer feel anything for Christine, perhaps I have never fallen out of love with those years we had together.

Sian went her own way quite early on, married and had children.

Dominic is an attractive young man, talented at his chosen profession; one rather like mine. He seems unscarred by events, but, in spite of the money lavished on him and his education, when I compare his childhood to mine it seems to me that he was robbed of so much that it would have been easy to give him.

Though litigation is long finished, too often some connection flips my mind back to those fifteen polluted years and I find myself, when I am alone somewhere, talking savagely to myself, arguing some point, trying retrospectively to re-take a decision - one of the many wrong ones I made - that would have cut short all that filth. The time before then, when my imagination was ruled only by love of my work and of those close to me, before the detritus of the legal professions befouled it, seems like another life.

I have been asked many times why I wrote this story. Who for? What for? Was it merely exorcism? Well, exorcism, yes - but there is no 'merely' about it. It is such a hybrid: part love-story, part confession, part exposé, part David and Goliath - except that David didn't win. Well, I can't help that; that is how it turned out. But, in answer to the first of the questions above, I remember quite clearly why I started it, if not why I kept going. It was for Dominic, to tell him where he came from, why he had no father when he should have, why he had the childhood that he did. Well, he is twenty-eight now, two years younger than I was at the start of this story, and still he knows little of it. So all that remains now is to hand this to him. Perhaps he can forgive us both.

THE END

Letter to Dominic

April 1998

Dear Dominic,

Now you know all of it - well, all that I know, anyway.

The story raises so many questions that are important about life and love, and I don't have the answers. All the ones I have heard offered about your mother and me seem to be superficial, or smug, or spiteful, or naive, or just plain wrong, like that fatuous remark of Mr Justice Trevor Reeve when he grasped the obvious firmly in both hands and then completely missed the ball with his, 'The greatest tragedy that befell you two was when you wrote that play'. I still seethe as I see him pontificating up there, vested with all that power over us.

I have told you the story with as little comment as possible. If I had been writing fiction I would have given more, guiding you through the underlying emotions and motivations of my characters. But how could I presume to sum up actual people with tidy - even if perceptive - insights about them. I have just tried to guess at or remember what made us do what we did. The facts I report are pretty accurate. The motivations? Who knows?

You could make a long list of your parents' 'shouldn't haves'. Oh, God, yes. But it is a pointless exercise. And the most obvious 'shouldn't have' for the moralist or critic to seize on is that none of the horrors would have happened if we had not slept with others after we were married. Well, yes. That's right. But so what? That's how most people in our world lived then, and still do in spite of the claims to the contrary. What people say in public about sex-and-marriage is generally distorted by hypocrisy, or shame, or pain, or fashion, or guilt, or romanticism, or whatever. I long ago said everything I might have to add to the general clamour in *It's All Right If I Do It* and its TV spin-off, *That's Love*, and you have already digested them.

You can dismiss from your mind the picture of the wronged wife, betrayed by her husband. Just as you can dismiss the picture of the outraged husband betrayed by his unfaithful wife. Both pictures have an element of truth in them for people to grab at, but not enough to hold. Truth is not packaged like that. We were both just very normal in our behaviour and we got unlucky. No, our crime, if crime it were, was to ourselves and to you: we had a wonderful life together and we let it go. We were never tested before that

441

crisis, and after Dr Lester's magical opening doors precipitated it, we blew apart like chaff on the wind. So does that mean we were inadequate? Well, yes, of course we were. But who isn't at times? I thought I was playing to some set of rules we had agreed, but Christine changed them without telling me when she felt too hurt to trust me further. She failed to level with me as I failed to make her feel safe when she needed it, so she turned elsewhere. We both asked for it, you could say.

And was our marriage worth saving? Many might say 'no' after reading about us, but I strongly disagree. It had brought me great happiness. And Christine, too, I know. Would we have lasted had we survived that crisis? I think we would. I know I loved her and I believe she did me, no matter how imperfectly each of us did so. We made such fun out of our lives together.

Obviously, what was long overdue was some straight talking. And that brings me to the one overriding irony that glares out of the story like an empty skull, the one thing I willingly hold up my hands and plead guilty to, the one thing that seems to have a general lesson for you and others: there I was, earning a fortune from my powers of communicating with people across the world, in a way that they enjoyed, and I failed to communicate with my wife. She took the road that she did because she did not believe that I loved her any more, or didn't love her enough. And - as I wrestled with my private problems at that time - I, and my actions (not surprisingly), failed to convince her. We both felt betrayed. We should have communicated with each other, to have understood where the other was. Yet even as I write that obvious idea, doubt assails me. How can one lay down any law? I think of the couples I know who get along well *because* they don't understand each other, if they did they couldn't survive. What about them? Heigh ho, the only law, it seems, is that there are no laws. And the only advice to give you about advice is that what people say always applies to their own lives, not yours.

––––––––––

To me, the really interesting moral and personal questions about us are the unanswered hypothetical ones. How would we have behaved if we had mended our marriage? Christine had done as she wished and lied about it. I had done as I wished, having been given permission (always a doubtful concept). But what would we have done? Would we have, could we have, changed our ways for each other? For you? Do people really change? (After we were divorced we both did as we wished, which in my case amounted to most things. Divorcees, emotionally adrift, are notoriously promiscuous, male and female.) How would our marriage have been? It is maddening not to know.

And what difference would it have made to your childhood? There would probably have been brothers and sisters and a family life. But, more importantly, would these things have made any difference to how you have

442

developed? Well, perhaps, but not in any way you should regret. You seem to me to have been precisely who you are since infancy. You are not, and never have been, warped or bitter and twisted (to repeat the clichés); who knows what you might have been, on the other path.

Anyway, Dominic, a similar crisis to ours might well confront you one day. I wonder how you and your partner would deal with it. I hope you would keep your heads, and focus on the real priorities, as we didn't.

Into the delicate, poised situation your mother and I had created stepped Rutter, the destroyer. Before we had time to realise that there were more important things between us than the pain of our infidelities, new, wrong paths were taken.

And once you take the path of a Rutter, with all his training, and your marriage becomes Me versus Him, enemies in a war, all subsequent blows that your deliver are justified. Thus went Christine, I believe. It is easy to condemn her for what followed our split-up, but no. The system encouraged everything. It is awesome to see how one false turning, one day, can lead to an utterly different route for the rest of your life. Ah, well. Outrageous fortune. I didn't complain when it swept me upwards, so...

Remember, above all, that this is a story written by one of the protagonists. I have tried - as hard as I know how - to get things accurate, to portray what happened, to stand in the middle. But you must always suspect the subtle hand of revisionism to favour me in my recall and reporting of events.

So. I wrote the whole thing to you and for myself - and then for one other major reason: to publicise the inadequacies of our legal profession and system. And here I condemn without reservation. Why condemn them, but not your mother and me? Because these people are professionals, trained and paid - and very well paid - to offer services to the public. That - not our follies - is a matter of public concern. And so, grit your teeth, dear Dominic, while I go from the personal to the general.

When I started to write the book I had vague ideas that perhaps it might help to change divorce law. Now I realise that change of law is not the point, it is the complete removal of the legal profession - solicitors, barristers and judges - from divorce that should be the aim.

I have two charges to make, both basic to our legal structure.

My first charge: the legal profession is precisely the least fit, the worst profession to be involved in divorce. They are all taught to fight.

I say there is no point in trying to improve our divorce system, or tinker with it in any way. We should junk it. Completely. In general, reform of existing institutions is better than overturning them, history shows that the replacements are often worse, but in this case, the system; adversarial, based on sin, expensive, rooted in guilt, clumsy, divisive, conducted in - of all places - courts of law, is precisely inappropriate. And the job it has to do is expanding daily. The law is a fighting machine, a tank if you like, based on X versus Y. But in divorce two Xs are involved. Lawyers create Mr X versus Mrs X which is patently wrong. And when there are young Xs involved it is appalling. Divorcing couples are often already distraught. What is wanted is a counsellor/calculator/child-carer. A tank in a cornfield just crushes the stalks; even an adapted, improved tank. For once, let's start again from scratch - without lawyers.

If we start again, let's forget those aspects of marriage and divorce that are rooted in guilt, religion and intolerance, and look freshly at what is needed today.

> First: reconciliation machinery where possible.
> Second: joint custody as routine to defend parents' bonds with their children.
> Third: an accurate financial assessment and adjudication system run by accountants, not lawyers.
> Fourth: various further safeguards, especially for the children, in cases where this is necessary; violence, danger and so on.

To enlarge a little: any civil servant with half his wits could devise a divorce licence, quick and cheap, that cuts out lawyers, magistrates, judges and their impedimenta. At this stage there seems only one safeguard needed: to prevent unnecessary break-ups a pause should be required and a meeting(s) with a divorce counsellor(s), that counsellor(s) to have power to delay matters. Where there are children involved, they should be represented separately and the counsellor(s) should take a higher profile, particularly if reconciliation is possible. Children are the principal sufferers in divorce and are usually unrepresented at present. This new machinery could be a branch of the social services or health service, or perhaps partially privately-run (if our privileged want their plush version, why not?) but with no lawyer near it.

To assess the financial situation, accountants are needed, not lawyers; accountants are up to every financial dodge and are better equipped than any lawyer to get the sums right (anyway when the divorce is affluent, lawyers always have to call in accountants to do the real sums). If the accountants cannot agree, let them present the figures to an accountant-adjudicator, not a legally trained judge, half of those who I was before couldn't even add up properly.

Joint custody should be automatic: the opposite to present practice. Access should be substantial and automatic: the opposite to the present system. Care and control should be joint and automatic except in exceptional circumstances, in contrast to current practice. Every study made has shown

444

that where children have the influence of both parents, even when they are shunted about, they are psychologically, emotionally and intellectually advantaged over the child of the one-parent family.

Women, of course, should be involved as equal partners at all levels in the running of any new divorce machinery, which they are not at present.

The above suggestions could well bring howls of outrage from lawyers. Look at the millions they would lose. And their first line of defence will be that the system has all changed since I was involved with it. Well, yes, there have been some changes, I know of them. But if things are so much better now, why is £390m a year given in legal aid for divorce (and that's without the well-heeled ones)? My basic truth remains, no matter how much lawyers are taught to reconcile, they are basically fighters, hugely expensive and wasteful fighters, when what we need are moderate, affordable harvesters to pacify, save, add and divide what is left of the protagonists lives together.

My second charge: there is no proper policing of the conduct of those who run our legal system; especially the barristers and judges. That branch of the legal profession is so ingrown, so privileged, so incestuous, that it has developed a cemented-in inability even to believe the existence of, let alone identify or evaluate, evidence of the failings of its members, especially its more prominent members.

I have no easy policing system to offer, but, look at what I encountered.

1) the Court of Appeal, April 1984: the Master of the Rolls, Lord John Donaldson, Lord Justices Stephen Brown and Fox

Theodore Goddard and Co had been found by a High Court judge to be prima facie, guilty of concealment of a fact relevant to my cause of action. They kept that document from the eyes of all who mattered, not only their client and the opposition, but his leading counsel, the High Court and the Court of Appeal. There is no doubt.

Yet what did the Court of Appeal do? It let them off at an interlocutory stage without a trial of the issue. The Master of the Rolls, called the legal point on which he let them go 'fundamental.' I do not believe that any intelligent man other than a judge would argue that my procedural error in 1972 in trying to bring Theodore Goddard's negligence before a court by the wrong method is as fundamental a point of law or justice as that which says in the Statute of Limitations that a person should not profit by his concealment, or the fundamental point in common law that a man should not profit by his wrongdoing, and finally - and possibly the most fundamental of all - that, in no circumstances, should people in positions of power and trust in our legal system ever be allowed to flout the rules and cheat their clients.

The three judges named above would, I am sure, regard any accusation about their honesty as ridiculous - certainly they had nothing to gain, there is no doubt of that. No, in their case, my accusation is different. Of course those men believe themselves to be upright, but so built-in have become their prejudices and bias, their attention to the professional technicalities of their trade, that common sense has disappeared; the wood was long since lost sight of in the trees. I think but I am not sure, that Donaldson, Brown and Fox simply could not see the case against Theodore Goddard and so found against me in law. Their fault was merely incompetence at reading evidence. That is the kindest interpretation of their judgement. If I am wrong and they read the truth of the evidence - or were even merely halfway - then their judgement becomes discreditable does it not? Why should Theodore Goddard & Co have been allowed to continue in practice without full investigation?

2) The Court of Appeal 1972: Lord Justices Davies, Phillimore and Orr

Their fault seems worse. One cannot give them the benefit of any doubt on any level. I repeat the nub of my case before them, the spring from which so much could have flowed at that time. I claimed that I was forced by James Comyn QC to sign my divorce settlement, that I was driven into it.

Below is the relevant exchange between James Comyn and me, from the tape. It should be re-read:

COMYN: Well, now look, let's just call a spade a spade, Mr Frisby...

FRISBY: Yes.

COMYN: And I told you earlier that my shoulders are broad. They are about as broad as any man's shoulders can be. I have been in this game a long time. I have met an awful lot of people. I have done an awful of work. Are you saying, in fact, that I forced you into a settlement which was disastrous for you, lulling you into a sense of security about your tax position with the Cayman Islands?

FRISBY: No, not on that count, no. But are you saying 'you forced me into a settlement?' Forced is a word—

COMYN: Well, I accept 'forced.' I—I will. No, fair's fair. I'll accept that I drove you.

FRISBY: Yes. All right, I'll buy 'drove.' Yes, I am saying that, actually.

446

COMYN: I certainly drove you into a settlement that I won't dissent from at all.

Let us put aside the meaning of the word 'forced' for a moment and look at what happened. Two people were involved in the forcing: the forcer and the forced. Both agree the process of forcing took place. The evidence, the only evidence and all the evidence is conclusive one way. What did their Lordships do? They found the opposite without further investigation. If it had not happened to me I would not have believed it. No condemnation can be too strong. The true evidence, in writing and on tape, of the actions and catastrophic errors of several of their fellows was placed clearly in front of them, yet they performed judicial contortions not to see it. Worse, they delivered a judgement designed to ensure that the bearer of the evidence didn't bother anyone again. The case against them is irrefutable and I can think of no worse professional crime for a judge to commit than that of partiality. It negates the reason for his existence.

3) James Comyn QC, later The Honourable Mr Justice James Comyn.

His words are above. They sink him without trace. When I asked him to make them good in public - as he promised he would - he wrote that sordid letter of denial and then hid behind his official robes. He is a key figure, *the* key figure in my view. He let his brother judges cover up for him and ducked behind the law that says a barrister who has acted in litigation cannot be sued by his client. His arrogance, stupidity and, eventually, dishonesty forced me into that awful Gordian knot of a settlement and he kept me tied there for years when a few words could have initiated the unravelling process. He received a large fee.

4) Mr Justice Ormrod merely would not listen: abnegation of his duty.

5) Mr Justice Latey

He didn't have the benefit of the evidence that the Appeal judges had, but he saw the cock-up that had taken place and was told by me of the subsequent cover-up. Instead of peering one inch further into the murk he said, 'I know Mr Comyn and know him to be honourable,' and, 'Theodore Goddard is a firm of the highest repute. I think you have misunderstood the function of your legal advisers.' Nice examples of 'Give a dog a good name...' Latey's efforts to assist me without investigation of my ex-legal advisers led him to his sympathetic but illogical judgement. He revised the consent order in my favour as far as he could, but all the legal gentry who had drawn up the ludicrous document had 'behaved properly,' so he said a 'mistake' had been made. He had the opportunity to sort things out but averted his eyes and relied on pious hopes, a doomed course with Rutter.

6) Mr Justice Trevor Reeve

He too saw the cock-up clearly and was shown enough of the cover-up, but he had to contend with the Court of Appeal judgement. However even had that judgement not existed, it was clear that, like the others, he would not have moved a finger to delve into the deficiencies of his profession. He, too, was well acquainted with all of them. Never mind, let his fitness as a judge, a divorce judge, be assessed in the light of his omniscient words, spoken after a ten-minute access hearing, with no witnesses. 'It may well be that this father is being too possessive. I think once a fortnight is appropriate.'

7) The other QCs, Jackson and Miskin

Miskin, later the Recorder of London, did nothing that was not correct.

I was told by Calderan that Jackson abandoned my hearing for a more lucrative one. No great crime really, but it is not supposed to happen according to the 'high standards' of the Bar.

8) John Tackaberry QC, now a recorder of the Crown Court

Here was a kind man who befriended me and offered advice and sympathy when he didn't even know me. So I later asked him to take up my case against Theodore Goddard and Co. It is sad to report, in such friendly circumstances, that neither he nor his junior, Rowan Planterose, nor other barristers I consulted, could find - in the legal maze - the right law under which to fight my case: breach of fiduciary duty. We fought a case I never believed in: negligence. Thus even the goodies in this story were unable to make the legal system work to bring lawyers to justice. It is a sad commentary, is it not?

9) The junior barristers

What can one say of such minnows? Hacks that ply for trade will surely try to avoid traffic regulations if it will get them to their destination quicker without penalty. There seem to be none for barristers. But for many in serious need, the junior barrister, huffing and puffing, and deferred-to deferentially by his solicitor, is the most authoritative voice they will hear.

Paul Beard was pointless and Good-Old-Harry pedestrian; Neil Taylor (later a QC) was both - and something worse. He knew what was going on, pocketed his fee and kept quiet. It would be Theodore Goddard, not I, who would bring his next brief. The tape-recordings sink him without trace. His religion was a lifetime's reverence for documents: you are all right as long as it is not on paper.

10) The registrars and masters are merely petty officials doing a job which seemed to me to be beyond them.

That leaves the solicitors.

11) Stephen Mitchell and Timothy Akeroyd

Two goodies who were constantly and consistently helpful, kind and wise. I am grateful to them both.

12) John Calderan and/or Paddy Grafton Green of Theodore Goddard

They cooked the books. I report the details in the account of my action against them. John Calderan was in charge of the case; Paddy, his assistant. I believe it to be Paddy who concealed that cable, but when a ship sinks through negligence or worse you don't blame the first mate. Calderan never supervised him properly.

13) Bill Fournier of Campbell Hooper and Austin Wright

He cooked the books. Worse, to save his skin (when it didn't even need saving), he betrayed his client, an old friend, while pretending sympathy.

14) Leslie Taylor of Nabarro Nathanson

Knowing Rutter's reputation, he handed me on to his junior, Gudrun Collis, who, though the nicest and most humane of persons, was not fitted to fight Rutter. The firm's expensive services were worse than useless.

15) Which brings us to Sydney Rutter.

Really, what can one say of him? He fought; he wriggled, he bent or broke every rule he could; he twisted things; he caused anguish; he created hate; yet could argue with force that all that was in his duty to his client. The system required him to fight and he did. When they were properly resisted, his activities were counter-productive; they cost Christine dear as well as me. However, his worst crime, far more serious than his legal wriggling, was that he stood four-square in the way of reconciliation between Christine and me and led her into a divorce she didn't want. Neither did I. And neither, I am sure, did you, Dominic. Sydney Rutter was a self-professed, devoutly religious man, yet he laboured diligently in the trough and no man knew it better.

16) Geoffrey Rutter

He flits in and out of the story, a trainee of his father. His actions, as I have reported them, speak for themselves, but I would like to remind you of what was, in my view, his greatest legal coup. I had obtained a court order demanding his client's tax returns, so that the court could see what she had earned for the preceding years. He obeyed the order and produced the tax returns...minus the figures. It made me furious then, but in retrospect is laughable about our legal processes. It remains a sublime example of a solicitor complying with the letter of the law while ignoring any sort of spirit. The court never saw those figures, but no registrar or judge ever offered even a word of rebuke to Geoffrey for his action. I think that about sums up the lot of them.

———

What about the policing of our legal system? I complained, with evidence, to: The House of Lords, the Court of Appeal, the High Court, the Law Society, the Bar Council, the Lord Chancellor, the Attorney General, personally to two MPs (both ministers) and to other bodies I have forgotten. All to no avail. Some of that evidence is included above.

Any claim that the conduct of our judges, barristers and solicitors is monitored is clearly absurd.

———

Finally, darling Dominic, now that I have dumped all this on you, is truth a curative? Well, yes, I think it is. And more. It's a necessity at times. And this, for me, anyway, is one of those times. For you there is nothing to cure. Now that you know all that I can tell you of the story, having asked for so long, I am sure you can put it behind you, like Satan. That was our life. It's been your turn for some while now. You have made so many important decisions (without any pushing from me) and the creative career you have chosen is about as good a choice as you could have managed. There are such extremes of joy and pressure and anguish in front of you that will make life rich; I couldn't be happier for you.

Just think; you might have chosen to be a lawyer.

Love,

Dad

INDEX OF JUDGES, BARRISTERS AND SOLICITORS

IN ORDER OF APPEARANCE

BERTRAM M (BILL) FOURNIER, SOLICITOR

Partner in Campbell Hooper & Austin Wright, famous theatrical solicitors. Now dead.

Was my family and professional solicitor from 1962 who became a close friend until 1971.

Supervised the set-up of the Cayman Trust and the Swiss Bank Corporation's part in my financial affairs after the success of *There's A Girl In My Soup*. He was a disaster, and eventually a dishonest one.

MILTON GRUNDY QC

HARVEY McGREGOR QC

Renowned QCs who specialised in tax matters and wrote books on the subject. Grundy was later a High Court judge.

Advised Bill Fournier and me on my tax affairs 1967-71.

LESLIE TAYLOR, SOLICITOR

GUDRUN COLLIS, JUNIOR SOLICITOR

Both at Nabarro Nathanson & Co, well-known divorce and general solicitors.

My divorce solicitors from March 1970 to summer 1970.

PAUL BEARD, BARRISTER

Track record unknown.

Engaged by Leslie Taylor to represent me.

Sydney Rutter, Solicitor

Geoffrey Rutter, Solicitor

Father and son firm of solicitors specialising in divorce and criminal. Sydney now dead

Christine's solicitors from March 1970.

Harry Law, Barrister

Run-of-the-mill junior, no known track record; apparently used extensively by Sydney Rutter. Retired. May be still alive.

Represented Christine many times against me, first when Neil Taylor was representing me, then when I represented myself.

His Honour Judge Potter

County Court judge, track record unknown.

I was before him once in 1970 to give the 'molestation' undertaking.

John Calderan, Solicitor

Patrick (Paddy) Grafton Green, Junior Solicitor

Both at Theodore Goddard & Co, very up-market divorce solicitors, renowned for representing King Edward VIII, handling the divorce of Mrs Simpson, Princess Anne and many others. Have since lost some of that prestige. Grafton Green is now the Senior Partner.

My divorce solicitors from July 1970 to Autumn 1971. A disaster: they cocked up, then covered up.

Neil Taylor, Barrister

Junior barrister specialising in divorce and tax. Later a QC.

Engaged by Theodore Goddard to represent me and was my junior barrister under Jackson, then Comyn, 1970-71. Confusing advice and no real help at all.

Joe Jackson QC

*The pre-eminent divorce lawyer of his time. Edited **Rayden on Divorce**, the text book from which they all work, and many other publications. A maverick, disliked by the establishment, which is possibly why he never became a judge (or, perhaps, he was earning so much money he didn't want to).*

Represented me at one hearing before Registrar Bayne-Powell in Autumn 1970. A firecracker.

REGISTRAR BAYNE-POWELL

A divorce registrar (a minor judge), later The Senior Registrar at Somerset House, centre of interlocutory and other divorce hearings.

I appeared before him many times from 1970 to 1979, always representing myself from 1972.

HIS HONOUR JUDGE TREVOR REEVE

A County Court Judge promoted to the High Court during the story, finally sometimes sitting in the Court of Appeal. Lists hobbies as golf, dancing. Alleged by a fellow member of the Bar Golfing Society to have cheated at golf. No reports of his dancing. Now dead.

First heard an application from me for access to Dominic in 1970, then I appeared before him, representing myself, for a week-long hearing in 1974, again in 1975 and finally in 1979-80.

JAMES COMYN QC

*Later a High Court judge, he was a famous Inner Temple, liberal barrister who successfully handled the Thalidomide case for **The Sunday Times**. Described to me as 'a loved figure' in legal circles. Now dead.*

My disastrous QC for the few months leading up to the Gordian divorce settlement of July 14th 1971 that he arranged. A calamity in my life and a dishonest one, too.

JAMES MISKIN QC

Later the Recorder of London. Regarded as a good judge for ten years, he was later affected by Altzheimer's disease while still sitting and made some eccentric decisions. But he could not be sacked. Now dead.

Christine's QC for the divorce settlement of July 14th 1971 and briefly after.

MR JUSTICE LATEY

High Court judge, later the Rt Hon Lord Justice Latey. Liberal figure who chaired the Latey Commission, which recommended the lowering of the age of majority to eighteen in the late sixties, wrote books on divorce. Now dead.

Was the judge for the hearing of the divorce settlement of July fourteenth 1971. I later appeared before him in 1972, representing myself and he briefly reappeared as a Court of Appeal judge in 1982.

ANDREW PARK, BARRISTER

A tax specialist, later a QC, now a High Court judge.

A brilliant and helpful counsellor and negotiator for me from 1971-7.

STEPHEN MITCHELL, SOLICITOR

TIM AKEROYD, JUNIOR SOLICITOR

Both at Whitehouse, Vaux and Elborne, a firm specialising in insurance matters, which became Elborne Mitchell when Stephen became a named partner. After the DC 10 crash in Paris in 1974 (his fiancee was aboard) Stephen made his name fighting the case of the victims, which he took to the USA. Fought many other famous insurance cases. Tim Akeroyd became a partner in Elborne Mitchell, most notably is still fighting the worldwide asbestos claims for compensation.

Stephen helped me from autumn 1971 for about five years. Timothy did likewise from 1972 to 1983.

RT HON LORD JUSTICES ARTHIAN DAVIES, HENRY PHILLIMORE, ALAN ORR

Renowned Lord Justices. Phillimore was a barrister at the Nuremberg War Trials and chaired the committee to reconsider the contempt of court laws. All now dead.

I appeared before them in June 1972, representing myself. They effectively covered up Comyn's dishonesty.

JOHN TACKABERRY QC

A specialist in arbitration who also now sits as a recorder on the Western Circuit.

Befriended me during the first Appeal Court hearing of 1972 and later represented me in the High Court and Court of Appeal 1983 against Theodore Goddard & Co.

DOUGLAS HOGG, BARRISTER

Later a QC. Became the Conservative Minister of Agriculture who presided over the BSE affair, the biggest cock-up in the history of British agriculture.

Represented me briefly before Mr Justice Ormrod in 1972.

Mr Justice Ormrod

Ormrod was also a qualified doctor. As a High Court judge he made the famous decision that a man who had changed his sex was still a man, in law. According to legal gossip was a 'fast judge.'

Douglas Hogg represented me before him in 1972 in a very brief hearing.

Rt Hon Lord Justices Megaw and Cumming-Bruce

Cumming-Bruce was noted for being charged on a drink/drive offence while a judge. He pleaded guilty.

I appeared before them, representing myself in 1974.

Timothy Barnes, Barrister

Later a QC.

Represented Theodore Goddard and Co against me before Master Warren, Judge Lipfriend, The Court of Appeal, The Appellate Committee of the House of Lords and another master, 1980-5

Master Warren, Master of the Queens Bench

A master is a minor judge, like a registrar. Warren became the Senior Queens Bench Master before retirement.

I appeared before him representing myself in 1979.

Rowan Planterose, Barrister

Specialist in arbitration and building matters.

Junior under John Tackaberry for the 1983 action against Theodore Goddard & Co. Later represented me against them before a master in 1984.

His Honour Judge Lipfriend

County Court judge who sometimes sat as a High Court judge.

Heard the interlocutory stage of my case against Theodore Goddard in 1983 in the High Court, when John Tackaberry represented me

Mathew Thorpe QC

Now a High Court judge

Represented Theodore Goddard and Co against me before Lord Donaldson in the Court of Appeal and the Appellate Committee of the House of Lords.

The Master of The Rolls Lord Donaldson, Rt Hon Lord Justices Michael Fox, Stephen Brown

The Master of the Rolls is the third highest judge in the land, Donaldson was famous as 'a brilliant legal technician.' He was the trial judge in the Guildford Four and Maguire Seven cases, all of whom were found not guilty on appeal. He was known to be a conservative judge. He served as President of the Industrial Relations Court set up by Ted Heath. Brown was another conservative, one of the trio of judges who first rejected the appeal of the Birmingham Six. Has been President of the Family Division since 1988.

John Tackaberry represented me before them in 1983.

Lords of Appeal Lord Scarman, Lord Templeman, Lord Brandon of Oakbrook

The Appellate Committee of the House of Lords in 1984. These were some of the top men in the legal hierarchy: Scarman, one of the most famous of liberal judges, headed the Scarman enquiry into the Brixton riots; Templeman was known as 'Sid Vicious' among barristers; Brandon is reputed to be 'intellectually arrogant.'

I appeared before them in 1984, representing myself.

Master Prince, Taxing Master

My last (I hope) appearance at the Royal Courts of Justice was before him in 1985.

A most enjoyable afternoon.